HISTORY

OF THE

CHURCH OF JESUS CHRIST

OF

LATTER-DAY SAINTS

———

PERIOD I.

History of Joseph Smith, the Prophet

BY HIMSELF

———

VOLUME IV

———

AN INTRODUCTION AND NOTES

BY

B. H. ROBERTS

———

PUBLISHED FOR THE CHURCH
Second Edition Revised

———

THE DESERET BOOK COMPANY
Salt Lake City, Utah

1978

TABLE OF CONTENTS.

VOLUME IV.

CHAPTER I.

THE DEPARTURE OF THE TWELVE FOR ENGLAND — MANIFESTATION OF GOD'S POWER IN HEALING THE SICK AT COMMERCE.

PAGE

The Prophet's Literary Methods 1
Farewell to the Twelve 1
The L. D. S. Hymn Book..... 3
Administration to the Sick..... 3
Discourses by the Brothers Pratt....... 4
Prayer Meeting for the Sick 5
Letter to Isaac Russell, reproving him for issuing Pretended Revelations to the Saints....................... 5
Conference in New Jersey 6
Progress of the Work in England............................... 7

PAGE

The Prophet's Letter to Isaac Galland — Nauvoo Affairs.. 8
Brigham Young Starts on his Mission ,........................... 9
Departure of Elders Young and Kimball from Nauvoo..... 9
Items of Doctrine, The Prophet..................................... 11
Minutes of Conference at Commerce, Illinois, October 6th, 7th and 8th, 1839............... 12
Death of John Young, Brigham Young's Father.......... 14
Hardships of the Elders of the British Mission............. 15

CHAPTER II.

THE PROPHET'S JOURNEY TO WASHINGTON—THE PETITION OF THE SAINTS TO THE CONGRESS OF THE UNITED STATES FOR REDRESS OF THE WRONGS INFLICTED UPON THEM IN MISSOURI.

Departure of the Prophet for Washington...................... 19
Progress of the Twelve towards England................. 20
Canadian Saints En Route for Nauvoo 20
Elder Taylor Anointed in the Kirtland Temple....... 21
Excerpt from Parley P. Pratt's

Letter to the Prophet......... 22
First Issue of the *Times and Seasons*. 23
The Elements Obey.............. 23
The Prophet's Adventure En Route to Washington......... 23
The Saints' Petition to Congress................................. 24

CHAPTER III.

THE PROPHET'S EFFORTS AT WASHINGTON TO OBTAIN REDRESS OF GRIEV-
ANCES FOR THE SAINTS—AFFIDAVITS ON MISSOURI AFFAIRS.

PAGE

The Prophet's Letter to Hyrum Smith—Reporting State of Affairs at Washington 39
Letter of the Prophet and Elias Higbee to the High Council at Nauvoo — Preliminary Hearing of Grievances 43
Brigham Young in New York. 44
Letter of Hyrum Smith to Parley P. Pratt—On Printing the Book of Mormon in New York 47
The Prophet in New Jersey 49
Affidavit of Simeon Carter on his Sufferings in Missouri ... 49
Letter of Hyrum Smith to the Prophet and Judge Higbee. 50
Affidavit of William F. Cahoon —Missouri Wrongs 52
Letter of C. Adams to the Prophet — Cause of the Saints before the Illinois Legislature 53
Law Suits to be Abandoned ... 54
Extract from Elder Orson Pratt's Letter to his Wife—Reporting Movements of the Brethren in the Eastern States 54
Letter from John B. Weber to the Prophet — On Supplementing the Latter's Effort to Obtain Redresses from Congress 55
Affidavit of John M. Burke—Missouri Outrages 56
Affidavit of John Lowry—Ditto 56
Affidavit of Jedediah Owen —Ditto 56
Affidavit of T. Alvord—Ditto .. 57
Affidavit of William Hawk—Missouri Affairs 58

PAGE

Affidavit of Timothy B. Clark —Ditto 58
Affidavit of Urban V. Stewart —Ditto 58
Affidavit of John Smith — Ditto 59
Affidavit of Samuel Smith—Ditto 60
Affidavit of Daniel Avery—Ditto 60
Affidavit of James Powell—Ditto. 61
Affidavit of John Smith — Ditto, ... 62
Affidavit of Smith Humphrey —Ditto 62
Affidavit of Henry Root—Ditto 62
Affidavit of Joseph Clark—Ditto. 63
Affidavit of Thomas D. Casper —Ditto. 63
Affidavit of Jesse W. Johnston Ditto. 64
Affidavit of Owen Cole—Ditto. 64
Affidavit of Ezekiel Maginn—Ditto. 64
Affidavit of Addison Green—Ditto. 65
Affidavit of John P. Greene—Ditto. 65
Affidavit of Asahel A. Lathrop—Ditto 65
Affidavit of Burr Riggs 67
Affidavit of Simon P. Curtis ... 67
Affidavit of Elisha H. Groves .. 68
Affidavit of Jacob Foutz, ... 68
Affidavit of Frederick G. Williams 69
Statement of James Sloan 69
Affidavit of David Shumaker .. 69
Affidavit of Levi Richards 70
Affidavit of Gibson Gates 71
Affidavit of David Pettigrew ... 71

CHAPTER IV.

DEPARTURE OF THE PROPHET FROM WASHINGTON—LABORS OF ELIAS
HIGBEE BEFORE THE SENATE JUDICIARY COMMITTEE—REPORT
OF THE COMMITTEE.

PAGE

Ministry of Brigham Young and George A. Smith at Richmond, New York 75

Appointments in the British Mission 76

Matthew S. Davis' Description of the Prophet, and a Report of his Washington Discourse.................. 78

The Prophet's Interview with Van Buren and Calhoun..... 80

Elias Higbee's Letter to the Prophet, Reporting Progress in the Cause of the Saints before the Senate Committee 81

Second Letter of Elias Higbee to the Prophet—Cause of

PAGE

the Saints before the Senate Committee........................ 83

Third Letter of Elias Higbee to the Prophet—Cause of the Saints before the Senate Committee 85

The Fourth Letter of Elias Higbee to the Prophet—Announces that the Senate Committee's Report will be Adverse to the Saints......... 88

The Prophet En Route for Nauvoo............................. 88

Death of James Mulholland ... 89

Report of the Senate Judiciary Committee on the Case of the Saints vs. Missouri....... 90

CHAPTER V.

AFFAIRS OF THE SAINTS BEFORE UNITED STATES SENATE—GENERAL CON-
FERENCE OF THE CHURCH AT NAUVOO—ACTION OF THE CHURCH
WITH REFERENCE TO SENATE COMMITTEE'S REPORT—
MISSION TO PALESTINE.

Extract from the Minutes of the Iowa High Council....... 93

Fifth Letter of Elias Higbee to the Prophet—The Affairs of the Saints at Washington 94

Extract from Elder John Taylor's Letter—Affairs in British Mission....................... 96

Judge Elias Higbee's Course at Washington Approved.... 96

Letter of R. B. Thompson to Elias Higbee, Announcing the Approval of the Church Authorities of the Latter's Course at Washington........ 96

Letter of Horace R. Hotchkiss to Sidney Rigdon and

Joseph Smith, Jun.,—Inquiring Concerning the Progress made before Congress 98

Sixth Letter of Elias Higbee to the Prophet—Affairs of the Saints at Washington — Papers Withdrawn............ 98

Letter of Horace R. Hotchkiss to Joseph Smith, Jun., —Offering Tract of Land for Sale 100

Letter of Sidney Rigdon to the Prophet............................. 102

Arrival of Brigham Young and Associates in England 102

Minutes of the General Conference of the Church........ 105

CHAPTER VI.

DEVELOPMENT OF THE WORK IN ENGLAND—THE PALESTINE MISSION—
POSTOFFICE NAME CHANGED FROM COMMERCE TO NAUVOO.

PAGE

Letter of Hon. Richard M. Young to Elias Higbee 111

Orson Hyde's Credentials as a Missionary to Palestine...... 112

Ordination of Willard Richards to the Apostleship 114

Letter of Heber C. Kimball to the Saints of the United States—Affairs of the British Mission...................... 114

Council Meeting of the Twelve in England — Hymn Book and the *Millennial Star* Projected 118

Letter of Brigham Young to the Prophet 119

Mission opened in Scotland—Orson Pratt 120

Letter of Robert Johnstone to Senator Young—Postoffice Name Changed from Commerce to Nauvoo................. 121

Letter of Senator Young to Judge Elias Higbee—Postoffice Name, etc................. 121

Letter of Wilford Woodruff to Don Carlos Smith—Success of Woodruff's Ministry 122

Letter of Elders Hyde and Page to the Prophet—Plans for the Palestine Mission.... 123

Letter of Brigham Young to the Prophet—Affairs of the British Mission................. 125

Release of Elder Turley from Prison 127

Letter of the Prophet to Elders Hyde and Page—Palestine Mission Considered 128

Letter of Willard Richards to the Editor of the *Millenial Star*—Reporting Labors..... 130

CHAPTER VII.

FIRST FOREIGN PERIODICAL OF THE CHURCH—THE "MILLENNIAL STAR"
—THE PROPHET SEEKS RELEASE FROM SECULAR RESPONSIBILITIES.

The Beacon Hill Conference .. 131

A Letter of Heber C. Kimball, et al., Recommending English Saints to the Bishop of the Church....................... 132

Death of Bishop Partridge..... 132

First Number of the *Millennial Star*....................... 133

The First Company of Saints from England................... 134

Brigham Young's Dream...... 134

Minutes of the Conference Held at Gadfield Elm Chapel, in Worcestershire, England, June 14th, 1840........ 134

Memorial of Joseph Smith, Jun., to the High Council of the Church of Jesus Christ of Latter-day Saints, June 18th, 1840 136

Proceedings of the High Council on the Foregoing Memorial, June 20th, 1840..... 138

Minutes of the Conference Held at Stanley Hill, Castle Froome, Herefordshire, England, June 21st, 1840......... 138

Carpenter's Hall.................. 141

Minutes of the High Council.. 141

Letter of William W. Phelps —Confessing Errors Committed in Missouri............. 141

Letter of Elders Orson Hyde and John E. Page to Presidents Joseph Smith, Hyrum Smith, Sidney Rigdon, Pleading for William W. Phelps.. 142

PAGE   PAGE

Minutes of a Meeting of the
Crooked Creek Branch of
the Church........................ 143
Minutes of High Council at

Nauvoo............................ 144
Reflections of the Prophet on
the Action of Congress....... 145

CHAPTER VIII.

IMPORTANT CONFERENCE OF THE CHURCH IN ENGLAND—KIDNAPPING OF
BROWN AND BOYCE BY MISSOURIANS—ACTION OF THE
CITIZENS OF NAUVOO.

Conference of the Church in
England 146
A Council of Church Officers,
Held at Manchester, Eng-
land.................................. 149
Extract from Elder Woodruff's
Letter to the Editor of the
Millennial Star—Detailing
Incidents of his Ministry.... 150
Special Instruction for High
Councils 154
The First Missionary for Aus-

tralia 154
Kidnapping of Alanson Brown
and Benjamin Boyce—Affi-
davit of Daniel H. Wells.... 154
Statement of James Allred... 156
Action of the Citizens of Nau-
voo in the Matter of the
Kidnapping of Brown and
Boyce by the Missourians... 157
Report of the Committee on
Resolutions....................... 157
Memorial to Governor Carlin . 159

CHAPTER IX.

THE RETURN OF A PRODIGAL—CONDITIONS IN KIRTLAND—PROGRESS OF
THE WORK IN GREAT BRITAIN—THE COMING OF JOHN C.
BENNETT—AUSTRALIAN MISSION.

Extract of a Letter from Elder
William Barratt,................ 161
The Prophet's Letter to Wil-
liam W. Phelps—Welcom-
ing him back into the Church 162
Credentials of Elders Samuel
Bent and George W. Harris 164
The Prophet's Letter to Oliver
Granger — Dealing Chiefly
with affairs at Kirtland...... 164
Letter of John C. Bennett to
Joseph Smith and Sidney
Rigdon — Announcing his
Intention to Join the Saints. 168
Letter of John C. Bennett to
Messrs. Smith and Rigdon
—Making Further Tender
of his Services to the Church 169
Letter of the Prophet to Hor-
ace R. Hotchkiss — Rock
River Lands and the White
Purchase 170

Letter of John C. Bennett to
Messrs. Smith and Rigdon
—Expressing Anxiety to be
with the Saints.................. 172
A Voice from the Holy City—
Rebuilding the Temple of
Solomon—Recall of the Peo-
ple of God to the Land of
Judah 172
Circular 173
Extract of a Letter from Wil-
ford Woodruff to the Editor
of the *Millennial Star*—Re-
porting Labors.................. 176
The Prophet's Letter to John
C. Bennett — Bidding him
Welcome to Nauvoo, to par-
take of—Poverty............... 177
Letter of John C. Bennett to
Messrs. Smith and Rigdon—
Announcing that he will
soon be in Nauvoo 179

CHAPTER X.

A MISSOURI KIDNAPPING—CONTINUED DEVELOPMENT OF THE WORK IN
GREAT BRITAIN—THE DEATH OF JOSEPH SMITH, SEN., FIRST
PATRIARCH OF THE CHURCH.

	PAGE		PAGE
Settlement of a Difficulty	180	The Generosity of John Benbow	188
The Kidnapping of Benjamin Boyce, Mr. Brown, et al	180	Earthquake at Mount Ararat	189
The Beginning of Open-air Meetings	182	The Death of Joseph Smith, Sen	189
The Electric Telegraph	184	Biography of Joseph Smith, Sen., Presiding Patriarch of the Church, by the Prophet, his Son	199
An Address by the First Presidency to the Church	184		
Minutes of the High Council Meeting, at the Office of Joseph Smith, Jun., Nauvoo, September 5th, 1840	187	The Discourse of Elder Thompson at the Funeral of Joseph Smith, Sen	191

CHAPTER XI.

THREATENING PORTENTS IN THE ACTIONS OF MISSOURI—GENERAL CON-
FERENCES IN NAUVOO AND ENGLAND—THE DOCTRINE
OF PRIESTHOOD.

Letter of Samuel Bent and George W. Harris to the Presidency—Reporting Labors	199	Dream	203
		Minutes of the General Conference of the Church of Jesus Christ of Latter-day Saints, held in Nauvoo, October 3d, 1840	204
Letter of John E. Page to the Presidency, Reporting Progress of Palestine Mission	202	Report of the Presidency	212
Extracts from Orson Hyde's Letter—Signs in the Heavens	202	Minutes of a General Conference in England	214
Elder Heber C. Kimball's		Minutes of a Council of the Twelve in England	218

CHAPTER XII.

PROGRESS OF THE WORK IN GREAT BRITAIN—THE SAINTS AT KIRTLAND
REPROVED FOR THEIR COURSE DURING THE MISSOURI PERSECU-
TIONS—THE PROPHET'S ADDRESS TO THE TWELVE AND
SAINTS IN GREAT BRITAIN.

Charge against Oliver Walker	219	Letter of Heber C. Kimball et al. to Messrs. Ebenezer Robin-	
Minutes of the High Council	219		

PAGE

son and Don Carlos Smith—Reporting Affairs in the British Mission.................. 220

"Remarkable Visions" by Orson Pratt....................... 224

Letter of Joseph and Hyrum Smith to the Saints in Kirt-

PAGE

land—Reproving the Saints for Neglect of their Brethren and Sisters During the Missouri Persecutions......... 225

An Epistle of the Prophet to the Twelve....................... 226

CHAPTER XIII.

INTRODUCTION OF THE GOSPEL IN THE ISLE OF MAN—THE NAUVOO CHARTER.

Mormonism in the Isle of Man 234

Opposition to the Work in England 236

Excommunication of Sidney Roberts. 237

Letter of Brigham Young to the Presidency, Detailing Movements of the Mission in England........ 237

Elder Taylor's Defense of the

Work............................... 238

An Act to Incorporate the City of Nauvoo......................... 239

Of the Legislative Powers of the City Council................. 245

Letter of John C. Bennett to the *Times and Seasons*—Announcing the Passage of the Act Incorporating Nauvoo.. 248

CHAPTER XIV.

VALE 1840—ENTER 1841—LIST OF PUBLICATIONS FOR AND AGAINST THE CHURCH—WHEREABOUTS OF THE TWELVE APOSTLES—"ELECTION AND REPROBATION"—PROCLAMATION TO THE SAINTS.

The Acquittal of R.D. Foster.. 250

An Objector Put Down 250

Brigham Young's Letter to the Prophet—Reporting Labors in England....................... 251

Election and Reprobation—by

Brigham Young and Willard Richards..... 256

A Proclamation of the First Presidency of the Church to the Saints Scattered Abroad, Greeting 267

CHAPTER XV.

RECONSTRUCTION OF CHURCH AFFAIRS AT NAUVOO — REVELATION— MUNICIPAL ORGANIZATION OF NAUVOO—INSTALLATION OF CIVIC AND MILITARY OFFICERS.

Reproof of John E. Page and Orson Hyde..................... 274

Revelation given to Joseph Smith at Nauvoo, January 19th, 1841....................... 274

Hyrum Smith Installed as Pa-

triarch................................ 286

First Election of Municipal Officers in Nauvoo............. 287

Joseph Smith made Sole Trustee of the Church....... 287

PAGE

Nauvoo City Council Organized................................. 288
The Mayor's Inaugural Address 288
Minutes of the Meeting which Organized the Nauvoo Legion................................ 295
Nauvoo Council Opened by Prayer................................ 297
The Echo Company............... 297
Minutes of the London Conference................................. 298
Ordinance 299
Missouri's "White-washing".. 299
Legion Resolutions............... 300
Resolution.............................. 300
Ordinance 301
An Act to Incorporate the Nauvoo House Association.. 301
An Act to Incorporate the

PAGE

Nauvoo Agricultural and Manufacturing Association in the County of Hancock... 303
Division of Nauvoo into Municipal Wards.................... 305
Ordinance on Religious Liberty in Nauvoo..................... 306
An Ordinance in Relation to Public Meetings................. 306
Committee Report................ 307
Appointment of City Officers. 308
Letter of Brigham Young to the Editor of the *Star*—On Family Prayer................... 308
Appointment of Joseph Smith Lieutenant-General of the Nauvoo Legion.................. 309
Organization of the Lesser Priesthood at Nauvoo........ 312

CHAPTER XVI.

THE FIRST FOREIGN MISSION OF THE CHURCH, 1837-1841.

History of the British Mission. 313

CHAPTER XVII.

CELEBRATION OF THE TWELFTH ANNIVERSARY OF THE ORGANIZATION OF THE CHURCH—ORDER OF LAYING CORNER-STONES OF TEMPLES —COUNCIL MEETINGS OF THE TWELVE IN ENGLAND.

Staffordshire Conference........ 322
Union of Commerce and Nauvoo Plats.. 322
Letter of Wilford Woodruff to Don C. Smith—Relating to Affairs in England............. 323
Minutes of a Council Meeting of the Twelve.......... 324
Council Meeting of the Twelve —Continued..................... 325
Council Meeting of the Twelve

—Continued 326
Twelfth Anniversary of the Organization of the Church. 326
Sidney Rigdon's Speech........ 327
Conduct of the People........... 331
Order of Laying Corner-stones of Temples 331
Conference at Philadelphia.... 331
Meeting of the Council of the Twelve in Manchester........ 332

CHAPTER XVIII.

GENERAL CONFERENCE AT NAUVOO—EPISTLE OF THE TWELVE TO THE SAINTS IN ENGLAND—DIFFERENCE BETWEEN BAPTISTS AND LATTER-DAY SAINTS.

Minutes of the General Conference of the Church of Jesus Christ of Latter-day Saints, held in Nauvoo, Illi-

nois, on the 7th day of April, One Thousand Eight Hundred and Forty-one........... 336
Report of the First Presidency. 336

PAGE

Letter of George A. Smith to
the *Star*—Report of Labors. 343
Conference in New York City. 344
An Epistle of the Twelve Apostles to the Church of Jesus
Christ of Latter-day Saints
in England, Scotland, Ireland, Wales, and the Isle of

PAGE

Man, Greeting.................. 344
Difference Between the Bap-
tists and Latter-day Saints,
from the *North Staffordshire
Mercury* 348
The Difference Between the
Baptists and the Former-day
Saints......................... 350

CHAPTER XIX.

ORGANIZATION OF THE NAUVOO LEGION—NOTABLE PERSONS AT NAUVOO
—THE PROPHET'S SERMON ON INDIVIDUAL RESPONSIBILITY
FOR SIN AND THE DOCTRINE OF ELECTION.

The Twelve Embark for Home 352
Changes in the Iowa Stake.... 352
Organization of the Legion.... 353
New Burying Gound for Nau-
voo.............................. 353
Nauvoo Legion Affairs........... 354
Letter of the Prophet to the
Times and Seasons—Visit of
Notable Persons to Nauvoo. 356
The Prophet's Discourse....... 358
Minutes of a Conference in
London........................ 360

Arrival of *Rochester* at New
York 360
The Healing of one who was
Deaf........................... 361
Rowdyism in New York Har-
bor............................ 361
Mob Violence in England...... 361
Conference in Kirtland........ 361
Letter of the Presidency to the
Saints — Concentration at
Nauvoo 362
Legion Affairs.................. 362

CHAPTER XX.

ARREST OF THE PROPHET ON DEMAND OF MISSOURI—TRIAL AT MON-
MOUTH—THE ACQUITTAL.

The Prophet's Visit with Gov-
ernor Carlin..................... 364
The Arrest of the Prophet..... 365
Apostles in New Jersey......... 365
News of the Prophet's Arrest
Reaches Nauvoo............... 365
The Prophet at Monmouth..... 366
The Trial. 366

Honorable Conduct of Counsel. 367
Judge Douglas—Ditto........... 368
A Letter from the Editor of the
Times and Seasons to that
Journal, Giving an Account
of the Trial at Monmouth..... 369
The Prophet Set Free............ 371

CHAPTER XXI.

THE MISSION TO JERUSALEM—PROGRESS OF ORSON HYDE IN HIS
JOURNEY.

Elder John E. Page—a Lag-
gard............................. 372
Letter from Elder Orson Hyde
to President Joseph Smith—
Recounting Incidents of his
Journey en route for Jerusa-

lem 372
Elder Hyde's Letter to Rabbi
Hirschell....................... 374
Conclusion of Elder Hyde's
Letter to the Prophet.......... 378

CHAPTER XXII.

SUNDRY EVENTS AT NAUVOO AND THROUGHOUT THE WORLD—THE
MISSION OF THE TWELVE NOTED BY THE PROPHET.

PAGE

Press Misrepresentations....... 380
Imprisonment of Theodore
  Curtis 380
Extract from a Letter in the
  Juliet Courier—Describing
  the Prophet's Trial at Mon-
  mouth, and Affairs at Nau-
  voo 380
Revelation given to Joseph
  Smith, in the House of Brig-
  ham Young, in Nauvoo City,
  July 9th, 1841................. 382
Liquor Selling Licensed in
  Nauvoo............................ 383

PAGE

Manna Rain in Aleppo.......... 383
Press Falsehoods................. 383
Letter of Elder Orson Hyde
  to President Smith—Detail-
  ing Events while en route
  to Jerusalem..................... 384
Death of Senator Little......... 388
General Funeral Sermon....... 389
The Prophet's Account of the
  Mission of the Twelve........ 390
Letter of William Smith to
  President Smith — Land
  Transactions 391

CHAPTER XXIII.

THE DEATH OF DON CARLOS SMITH—HIS LIFE AND LABORS—SPECIAL
CONFERENCE AT NAUVOO.

The Death of Don Carlos
  Smith............................... 393
The Visits of Don Carlos to
  Liberty Prison.................. 398
His Ministrations to the Sick.. 398
Personal Appearance of Don
  Carlos Smith..................... 399
The Iowa Stake of Zion........ 399
New Mission Movement
  Planned 400

General Orders, Nauvoo Le-
  gion................................. 400
Depression of the Times........ 401
Visit of the Sac and Fox In-
  dians to Nauvoo................ 401
Minutes of a Special Confer-
  ence at Nauvoo—Important
  Action in Relation to the
  Twelve.............................. 402

CHAPTER XXIV.

HOTCHKISS LAND PURCHASE TROUBLE—DEATH'S HARVEST, OLIVER
GRANGER, ROBERT B. THOMPSON—IMPORTANT ACTION RELATING
TO THE TWELVE—THE MISSION IN FOX ISLAND.

The Founding of Warren...... 405
Letter of Horace R. Hotchkiss
  to Joseph Smith—Land Af-
  fairs in Nauvoo................. 405
Letter of the Prophet to Hor-
  ace R. Hotchkiss—Nauvoo
  Land Transactions............ 406
Location and Character of the
  Hotchkiss Lands............... 408

Death of Oliver Granger.. 408
An Epistle of the Twelve Apos-
  tles to the Saints Scattered
  Abroad Among the Nations,
  Greeting........................... 409
Death of Robert B. Thompson. 411
Biography of Robert Blashel
  Thompson 411

PAGE

Minutes of a Council Meeting of the Twelve Apostles at the House of Brigham Young, Nauvoo.................. 412

Changes of Officers in the Legion............... 414

Changes Among the Civil Officers of Nauvoo......... 414

The Prophet on Medicine...... 414

A Shower of "Flesh" 415

British-Chinese War............. 415

Extract from Legion Minutes. 415

PAGE

The Coming of Edward Hunter to Nauvoo.................... 416

Bitterness of D. W. Kilbourn. 416

High Council Resolution........ 417

Lumber for the Temple......... 418

The Work on Fox Island....... 418

Sentence Rendered by Pontius Pilate, Acting Governor of Lower Galilee, Stating that Jesus of Nazareth shall Suffer Death on the Cross....... 420

CHAPTER XXV.

THE GENERAL CONFERENCE OF THE CHURCH AT NAUVOO—DOCTRINAL SERMON BY THE PROPHET—BAPTISM FOR THE DEAD—ANGELS AND MINISTERING SPIRITS—EPISTLE OF THE TWELVE REVIEWING STATUS OF THE CHURCH.

Suit against Geo. M. Hinkle 423

Minutes of the General Conference of the Church held at Nauvoo..................... 423

Minutes of a Meeting of the Council of the Twelve........ 429

Copy of a Letter to Smith Tuttle, Esq.,—The Hotchkiss Land Troubles................... 430

An Epistle of the Twelve Apostles, to the Brethren Scattered Abroad on the Continent of America, Greeting..................................... 433

CHAPTER XXVI.

AFFAIRS IN KIRTLAND AND NAUVOO—EPISTLE OF THE TWELVE TO THE SAINTS IN THE BRITISH ISLANDS—ORSON HYDE'S PRAYER ON THE MOUNT OF OLIVES, DEDICATING THE HOLY LAND PREPARATORY TO THE RETURN OF THE TRIBES OF ISRAEL.

Extract from Orson Hyde's Letter............................... 439

Minutes of Conference held at Lima 439

Extract of a Letter from Parley P. Pratt—Emigration of Saints, and Status of the Work in England............... 441

Copy of a Letter of Attorney from Joseph Smith, "Sole Trustee-in-Trust for the Church of Jesus Christ of Latter-day Saints," to Reuben McBride, of Kirtland, Ohio. 441

Excerpt of Hyrum Smith's Letter to the Saints in Kirtland—Disapproving of Certain Plans for Building up Kirtland........................... 443

The Nuisance.................... 444

Reproof of William O. Clark 445

Dedication of the Baptismal Font................................. 446

An Ordinance Concerning Vagrants and Disorderly Persons................................. 447

An Epistle of the Twelve Apostles to the Saints Scattered Abroad in England,

PAGE

Scotland, Ireland, Wales, and the Isle of Man, and the Eastern Continent, Greeting............................ 448

Minutes of a Meeting at Ramus, Illinois — Alanson Brown et al., Disfellow-

PAGE

shiped............................ 453

Baptisms for the Dead.......... 454

Elder Orson Hyde's Letter— His Prayer of Dedication on the Mount of Olives........... 454

Prayer of Orson Hyde on the Mount of Olives............... 456

CHAPTER XXVII.

OFFICIAL DENUNCIATION OF THIEVES AT NAUVOO—THE MORAL LAW OF THE CHURCH—ABANDONMENT OF RAMUS AS A STAKE OF ZION —BAPTISM FOR THE DEAD, AN EPISTLE.

Affidavit of Hyrum Smith— Denouncing Theft............. 460

The Prophet's Estimate of the Book of Mormon............. 461

The Prophet's Denunciation of Thieves...................... 461

Conference in New York....... 462

Warning of the Twelve Apostles against Thieves........... 463

Thieves............................ 466

Revelation 467

Conference at Ramus............ 467

The Prophet Proof Reads Book of Mormon 468

Letter of the Prophet to Esquires Browning and Bushness—Payment of Notes..... 468

The Prophet's Letter to Mr. Hotchkiss—CommerceLands 469

The Prophet's Difficulties in Writing the Annals of the Church........................... 470

Anti-Mormonism at Warsaw.. 471

Further Trouble at Warsaw.... 471

Baptism for the Dead. An Epistle of the Twelve Apostles to the Saints of the Last Days................................ 472

CHAPTER XXVIII.

KIRTLAND VS. NAUVOO—POLITICAL ATTITUDE OF THE PEOPLE OF NAUVOO DECLARED—PUBLICATIONS MORMON AND ANTI-MORMON FOR 1841—CLOSE OF THE YEAR.

Decision in the Case of Almon W. Babbitt and Kirtland..... 476

Affairs at Ramus.................. 477

Expressions of Gratitude to James Gordon Bennett and the New York *Herald*......... 477

Minutes of a Meeting of the Twelve in the House of the Prophet 478

The Prophet on the Attitude of the Saints in Politics...... 479

The Prophet's Letter to Edward Hunter—Business Affairs at Nauvoo 481

Revelation to John Snyder and Amos B. Fuller........... 483

Revelation........................... 483

Work on Proclamation to Kings of the Earth............. 483

Emigration Agency to England................................. 484

Xmas at Nauvoo, 1841......... 484

Conference Minutes — New York and Maine................. 484

Purpose of the Gift of Tongues........................... 485

Instructions to the Twelve..... 486

Warren and Warsaw Affairs.. 486

A Prophecy Respecting Warsaw................................. 487

Mormon Literature (*pro et con*) 1841........................ 487

CHAPTER XXIX

THE OPENING OF THE YEAR 1842—WHEREABOUTS OF THE TWELVE
APOSTLES—CORRESPONDENCE OF ELDER HYDE FROM TRIESTE—
REPORT OF HIGH COUNCIL ON AFFAIRS IN NAUVOO—
EVENTS AND CONDITIONS IN THE BRITISH MISSION.

PAGE

Sundry Labors of the Prophet 490
The Prophet's Letter to Edward Hunter — Reports Opening of the New Store.. 491
Rejoicing of the Prophet....... 492
Tithing and Consecrations for the Temple of the Lord...... 493
Book of Mormon Corrections.. 494
Meeting with the Twelve....... 494
Highly Interesting from Jerusalem.............. 495
Excerpts from Elder Hyde's Letters........................... 496

PAGE

The Prophet's Letter to Isaac Galland—On Settlement of Accounts......................... 499
Isaac Galland Affair............. 500
Seventies' Quorum Affairs..... 501
Revelation............. 503
Report of High Council Committee............................ 504
Letter of G. Walker to Elder Brigham Young et al.—Affairs in England Since Departure of the Apostles...... 505

CHAPTER XXX.

EMIGRATION OF THE SAINTS FROM ENGLAND TO NAUVOO—THE BOOK
OF ABRAHAM.

Emigration 510
Death of Laura Phelps.......... 513
Debates in Nauvoo............... 514
Vindication of Daniel Wood... 514
Letter of Alfred Cordon to Joseph Smith — Reporting Affairs in England............ 515
Confidence in the Nauvoo Charter........................... 516
Announcement of the Trustee-in-Trust for the Church Re-

specting Work on the Temple................................... 517
An Additional Word from the Twelve..... 517
Letter of the Prophet to an Unknown Brother on Tithing.................................... 518
Note of Robert Pierce—Expressing Satisfaction at Financial Settlement............. 519
The Book of Abraham.......... 520

CHAPTER XXXI

THE WENTWORTH LETTER.

CHAPTER XXXII.

THE BENNETT-DYER CORRESPONDENCE—THE PROPHET'S DISCOURSE ON
THE SUBJECT OF THE RESURRECTION, AND THE SALVATION OF
CHILDREN—EPISTLE OF THE TWELVE TO THE SAINTS IN ENG-
LAND CONCERNING THEIR EMIGRATION TO AMERICA.

Tax Controversy................... 542
Attempted Settlement with

Gilbert Granger................. 542
Book of Abraham Fac-similes. 543

PAGE

Letter of the Prophet to John C. Bennett — on Bennett's Correspondence Anent Slavery 544

Correspondence Between Dr. C. V. Dyer and General J. C. Bennett 544

Letter of John C. Bennett to Joseph Smith — Anent the Dyer-Bennett Correspondence 547

Letter of the Prophet to Edward Hunter — Business Transactions 548

Extract from the Legion Minutes......................... 549

Extract from High Council

PAGE

Minutes........................... 550

The Prophet Becomes Editor of the *Times and Seasons*..... 551

Honor Among Thieves.......... 551

Origin of the Female Relief Society. 552

The Prophet's Sermon on Life and Death; the Resurrection and the Salvation of Children........................... 553

An Epistle of the Twelve to the Church of Jesus Christ of Latter-day Saints in its Various Branches and Conferences in Europe, Greeting................................... 558

CHAPTER XXXIII.

A MASON'S ESTIMATE OF NAUVOO AND THE PROPHET—ORGANIZATION OF THE FEMALE RELIEF SOCIETY—"TRY THE SPIRITS"—THE PROPHET'S EDITORIAL.

Nauvoo and the Mormons...... 565

Extract from a Letter from Elder E. P. Maginn, Salem, Massachusetts 566

Organization of the Relief Society........ 567

Character of the Momon Women................................... 568

Mission of John Snyder......... 568

Synopsis of the Prophet's Sermon on Baptism for the

Dead 568

Letter of Lorenzo D. Barnes to Parley P. Pratt—Reporting Labors....................... 569

Synopsis of the Prophet's Remarks to the Female Relief Society.............................. 570

"Try the Spirits"—The Prophet's Editorial in the *Times and Seasons*....................... 571

CHAPTER XXXIV.

SPECIAL CONFERENCE OF THE CHURCH AT NAUVOO—THE PROPHET'S REPROOF OF THE WICKED—EPISTLE OF THE TWELVE TO THE SAINTS IN KIRTLAND—STATUS OF THE CHURCH.

The Thirteenth Anniversary of the Organization of the Church 582

Conference Minutes. Special Conference of the Church of Jesus Christ of Latter-day Saints, City of Nauvoo, April 6th, 1842.................. 582

Remarks of the Prophet at the Funeral of Ephraim Marks. 587

Synopsis of Remarks of the Prophet — Reproof of all Wickedness. 588

A Meteor Fall...................... 588

Council Meeting with the Twelve............................. 589

PAGE

Council Meeting with the
    Twelve............................ 589
An Epistle of the Twelve to

the Saints in America,
    Greeting........................... 590
Military Appointments.......... 593

CHAPTER XXXV.

THE GENERAL BANKRUPT LAW—THE DOCTRINE OF BAPTISM FOR THE
DEAD—THE PROPHET'S ADDRESS TO THE FEMALE RELIEF
SOCIETY—THE KEYS OF THE PRIESTHOOD AND
THE NAUVOO TEMPLE.

The Bankrupt Law...... 594
The Prophet Forced into Bank-
    ruptcy............................. 595
Baptism for the Dead............ 595
Cause of the Prophet's Insolv-
    ency................................. 600
  James   Arlington   Bennett

Honored.. 600
Repast Militaire.................. 601
The Rights and Privileges of
    Women in the Church........ 602
    Remarks of the Prophet to
    the Relief Society.............. 602
The Temple........................ 608

INTRODUCTION TO VOLUME IV.

FIVE subjects may be said to form the outline of the chief events detailed in this volume of the HISTORY OF THE CHURCH *the Founding of Nauvoo; the Appeal of the Church to the National Government for redress of wrongs suffered in Missouri; the Mission of the Twelve Apostles to the British Isles; the Mission of Orson Hyde to Palestine; and the Doctrinal Development of the Church.*

Preliminary Considerations.

Preliminary to a brief consideration of these several subjects, I desire to say a word as to the reception of the Latter-day Saints by the people of Illinois, and the conditions prevailing in that state at the time of their arrival. A knowledge of these conditions is necessary to the understanding of this whole Illinois period of the History of the Church.

Much has been made of the hospitality which the people of Illinois extended to the Latter-day Saints at the time of their expulsion from Missouri. A writer in the *American Historical Magazine* for July, 1906, says: "To the latter state [Illinois] they [the Saints] went in 1839, and were received with such open-armed hospitality as only a very generous and liberty-loving people can extend to those whom they honestly believe to be suffering from a wrongful oppression. The conduct of the Saints in five years turned this feeling of extraordinarily deep-seated sympathy, inducing great practical charities, into a feeling of very bitter hatred, threatening to break into mob violence." Far be it from me me to depreciate the kindness of those who extended a helping hand to the Saints in the hour of their distress. Stripped and sorely wounded they fled from the violence of Missouri militia-mobs, and found for a time a peaceful asylum in Illinois. Many were the acts of disinterested kindness extended to them by the people in the western part of that state; and every such act I am sure was and is remembered, both by those who were the direct recipients of such acts of kindness and by their grateful descendants. But is responding to the calls of humanity so rare a thing in a Christian state, that it must needs be regarded as so exceptional in this case? Such was the condition of the Saints as they fled from Missouri, such the injustice to which they had been subjected in that state, that their situation would have appealed to the generosity of savages, how much more, then, to a civilized and Christian community! And then, speaking of this reception of the Saints *en masse*, by Illinois, and leaving out of consideration

for the moment—since they have already been acknowledged—the
individual acts of kindness bestowed upon the exiles, was this reception
of the Saints by Illinois wholly disinterested? Were there not benefits
which the Saints could bestow upon the state in return for the heartiness of the reception given? Would it not have been, under all the
circumstances, the gravest of blunders for Illinois to have refused asylum to these exiles? Is it to be presumed that the public men of western Illinois were so blind to their own interests as not to see in these
twelve or fifteen thousand people a mighty advantage to the state? It is
true they were poor in this world's goods; but they were rich in labor-
power, and their reputation for habits of sobriety and of industry had
preceded them.   Here were thousands of husbandmen seeking lands.
Illinois had thousands of acres of unoccupied lands awaiting husbandmen. How shortsighted and unstatesman-like it would have been for
the men of Illinois not to have welcomed these settlers into their state?
With half an eye it is easy to see that the benefits of this reception of
the exiled Mormons by Illinois is not by any means a one-sided affair;
and it would be doing an injustice to the intelligence of the people of
that state to suppose they were blind to these advantages.   This will
more fully appear when other conditions are taken into account.
Illinois has an area of 56,650 square miles; and at the time of the
advent of the Saints in that state a white population of less than four
hundred thousand,* as against a present population of five and a half
millions.† It will be seen, then, that in 1839, the year of the advent of
the Saints into that state, Illinois was very sparsely settled, and needed
above all things for her development and prosperity, people to subdue
her wilderness and cultivate her rich lands, especially people desirous of
making homes, and becoming permanent citizens.   Moreover, Illinois
had recently launched an extensive system of internal improvements by
state aid. This system included the construction of 1,300 miles of rail-
roads in the state, besides provisions for the improvement of the navigation of the Kaskaskia, Illinois, Great and Little Wabash, and Rock
rivers. Also the construction of a canal from Lake Michigan to the
navigable waters of the Illinois river, a distance of more than one hundred miles (from Chicago to Peru). To carry out this system of
internal improvements the state legislature of 1836-7 had appropriated
the sum of $12,000,000; and to raise the money state bonds were placed
on the stock markets of the eastern states and in England.   It is not
my province here even to note the wisdom or unwisdom of this policy
of wholesale state aid for these internal improvements; let the wisdom

* The population in 1830 was but 155,061; and in 1840, 472,254.

† The population of Illinois in 1900 was 4,821,550—nearly five millions: the estimated population for 1908 is 5,590,000.

or unwisdom be what it may, these conditions emphasized Illinois' demand for population, and again makes it evident that it would have been the height of folly for the people of that state to do other than give hearty welcome to this body of population so rich in labor-power; so potent in wealth producing energy.

Another thing to be noted is the fact that about the time of the advent of the Saints into Illinois, political parties were just taking form in that state, and it is within the record of facts in the case, as well as of great likelihood, that a desire for obtaining political advantage was at least in the background of motives prompting the heartiness of the reception given to the Saints.

Illinois was admitted into the Union in 1818, but it is a matter of common knowledge that in the early years of her history as a state, her officers were elected not on any well defined political party principles, but chiefly on the strength of the personality of the candidates and the special things for which they individually stood. Indeed, it was not until 1830 that anything like party lines were drawn in the state, and that it became a battle ground for the two great national parties, Whigs and Democrats. It was a committee from a Democratic party organization in Quincy, Illinois, that took the initiative in welcoming the Saints into the state, and strive how one may, it is difficult to think there was not some political advantage sought through this action. On the other hand, the Whigs were not slow to urge upon the incoming exiles that it was a Democratic state and a Democratic administration in that state which had not only permitted, but had really ordered their expulsion from Missouri, and that doubtless the injustice they had suffered was owing to Democratic ideas of the administration of government. Nor were there wanting those among the Saints who were willing to believe that such was the case. Indeed, Joseph Smith, the Prophet, found it necessary to gently reprove some of his people who were rapidly making the question of their expulsion from Missouri a political party question in Illinois. This effort to win the Saints to one political party or the other, continued to be a factor in their affairs so long as they remained at Nauvoo. It was owing to this rivalry for their support that doubtless made it possible for the Saints to obtain larger grants of power for their city government, and greater polical privileges and influence in the State than otherwise could have been obtained by them. It also was this rivalry for their favor, as the events in this, but more especially in the succeeding volume will prove, that made them alternately fulsomely flattered and heartily disliked; fawningly courted, and viciously betrayed.

A knowledge of these circumstances, I say, is essential to the right understanding of the Nauvoo period of the Church's history.

The Founding of Nauvoo.

The founding of the city of Nauvoo was an event, the interest of which extends beyond the people immediately concerned in it. It was a unique movement in its way, and may yet suggest a policy in reference to the government of large cities from which great benefits may arise. Very naturally after the experiences of the Mormon people in Missouri, the Prophet was anxious to environ them with conditions that would insure protection to the community, hence for Nauvoo he secured as large concessions of political power as it was possible to obtain, and an examination of the Nauvoo charter proper with its attendant charters providing as they did for an independent educational system, from common schools to a University; an independent military organization with a lieutenant-general as its commander;* a large grant of commercial as well as municipal power, demonstrates how well he succeeded. Commenting upon the charter immediately after its passage by the state legislature had been formally announced, he said: "The City Charter of Nauvoo is of my own plan and device. I concocted it for the salvation of the Church, and on principles so broad, that every honest man might dwell secure under its protective influence without distinction of sect or party."† On another occasion when defending the right of the city to issue writs of habeas corpus, even against proceesses of the state, he held: "If there is not power in our charter and courts, then there is not power in the State of Illinois nor in the Congress or Constitution of the United States; for the United States gave unto Illinois her Constitution or Charter, and Illinois gave unto Nauvoo her charters conceding unto us our vested rights which she has no right or power to take from us. All the power there was in Illinois she gave to Nauvoo. * * * The municipal court has all the power to issue and determine writs of habeas corpus within the limits of this state that the

---

* Commenting once in a half humorous way upon his "exalted" military rank, the Prophet said to Josiah Quincy, who remarks that the Prophet at the time of his visit to Nauvoo (May, 1843), was at the head of 3,000 men equipped by the state of Illinois, represents him as having said:

"I decided that the commander of my troops ought to be a lieutenant-general, and I was, of course, chosen to that position. I sent my certificate of election to Governor Ford, and received in return a commission of lieutenant-general of the Nauvoo Legion or the militia of the State of Illinois. Now, on examining the constitution of the United States, I find that an officer must be tried by a court martial composed of his equals in rank; and as I am the only lieutenant-general in the country, I think they will find it pretty hard to try me."—*Figures of the Past*, p. 383.

† This volume, p. 249.

Legislature can confer. This city has all the power that the State courts have, and was given by the same authority—the legislature. * * * The charter says that the City Council shall have power and authority to make, ordain, establish, and execute such ordinances not repugnant to the Constitution of the United States, or of this State, as they may deem necessary for the peace, benefit and safety of the inhabitants of said city.* And also that the Municipal Court shall have power to grant writs of habeas corpus in all cases arising under the ordinances of the City Council. The City Council have passed an ordinance 'that no citizen of this city shall be taken out of this city by any writ without the privilege of a writ of habeas corpus.' There is nothing but what we have power over, except where restricted by the Constitution of the United States. 'But,' says the mob, 'what dangerous powers!' Yes—dangerous, because they will protect the innocent and put down mobocrats. There is nothing but what we have power over, except where restricted by the Constitution of the United States. * * * If these powers are dangerous, then the Constitution of the United States, and of this State are dangerous; but they are not dangerous to good men; they are only so to bad men who are breakers of the laws. * * * The lawyers themselves acknowledge that we have all power granted us in our charters, that we could ask for—that we had more power than any other court in the State; for all other courts were restricted while ours was not."

Such views in relation to an ordinary municipal government would unquestionably be stamped as preposterous. No such powers as are here claimed are accorded to ordinary city governments in Illinois or any other of the states of the American Union. What then may be said of the Prophet's claims in respect to the municipal powers of Nauvoo? Nothing in way of defense, except that Nauvoo was *not* an ordinary municipality; that Joseph Smith had sought for extraordinary grants of power for the city of Nauvoo and had obtained them; that his personal experiences and the experiences of his people, both in Ohio and Missouri, had taught him the necessity of having officers charged with the duty of administering government wherein his people were concerned, who were friendly disposed and whose interests were largely identical with those of the Saints; that the things which both the Prophet and his people had suffered justified both him and them in seeking for and obtaining such power as had been conferred by charters upon the city of Nauvoo; that the Prophet was wholly within the lines of right conduct when he invoked the municipal powers in his own protection

---

* Section 11, this volume, p. 241. The Prophet quoted from memory, and is not exact; the exact language is—"As they deem necessary for the peace, benefit, good order, regulation, convenience and cleanliness of said city."

against the aggressions of his old enemies in Missouri and his new betrayers in Illinois. But whether the legislature of Illinois was fully aware of the extraordinary powers they were conferring upon the city of Nauvoo, or being aware of the import of their action the party in control of the legislature was willing to grant the extraordinary powers in the hope of currying political favor with the Saints, may not now be determined; but in any event these extraordinary powers were granted; and wittingly or unwittingly a "city-state" had practically been established within the state of Illinois. Nothing short of this descriptive term can adequately set forth the municipal government of Nauvoo. It seems to be an unconscious reversion, in an incipient way, to the "city-states" or "city-republics" of the old Greek confederations; or the "free-towns" of medieval times, when the cities were more potent than nations in commerce and even in politics. Whether or not the state courts of Illinois and United States courts would have sustained the Nauvoo charters if the matter of their validity had been referred to them for adjudication, may not be determined; but one can scarcely suppress the thought that the likelihood is that they would not have been sustained; on the contrary they would have been most likely declared anomalous to our system of government as it then stood, and now stands. But certainly if the experiment of such a municipal government had not been interrupted in its progress, it might have been an instructive object lesson in the government of cities; and even as it is, the founding of Nauvoo, the "city-state," suggests an important idea which may work out great practical reforms in municipal government in our country.

The founders of our Government dealt with conditions that were very simple in comparison with the complexity of the conditions which government in its various forms, municipal, state and national, is confronted with today. The Municipal problems which now vex the people had not then arisen above the horizon of their experience. The American commonwealths of the early decades of the nineteenth century were practically rural commonwealths. At the time of Washington's inauguration (1789) the population of New York was but thirty-three thousand; Philadelphia forty-two thousand; Boston but eighteen thousand; Baltimore thirteen thousand; Brooklyn one thousand six hundred, and more village than town. Now compare these cities with their present population. New York has a population of over four millions;* Philadelphia a population of one and a half millions;† Boston more than half

---

* The official census of 1905 gives the population of New York at 4,014,304. The estimated population on January 1, 1908, is 4,285,435.

† Official returns for 1900 give Philadelphia a population of 1,293,697. The estimated population for Jan. 1, 1908, is 1,491,161.

a million;* Baltimore over five hundred thousand;† Brooklyn is absorbed in New York, but as a borough of the larger city it has a population of nearly one and a half millions;‡ Chicago, which in 1840 had but four thousand inhabitants, much smaller than Nauvoo, has now a population of more than two millions;§ St. Louis which in 1840 had a population of but 16,469, has now a population of three quarters of a million.‖ Nothing like the growth of urban population within the United States during the last fifty years has been known in the history of the world, and it has brought to the inhabitants of these cities problems undreamed of by the founders of our government. Every year discloses more and more distinctly the fact that between these condensed communities and the town, village, and rural population of the states in which they are located, there are very distinct interests and governmental problems of widely differing character. The differences which justify distinct local governments in the state of New York and the peninsula of Florida are not more insistent than the differences between the great commercial city of New York and the state of the same name. Without entering upon elaborate discussion of these questions (a discussion which is foreign to the character of this writing) I venture the suggestion that separate and complete state governments for our large cities, or the elevation of them into what I have called "city-states," such as Nauvoo was, in an incipient way, will be the solution to most of the problems of municipal government in our very large cities. It would greatly enlarge in them the governmental powers essential to their more perfect peace, security, and prosperity. Also it would separate them from embroilment in those questions of the state governments under which they are now located, and in which they have so little interest—often indeed, there is even sharp conflict of interests, engendering bitterness and strife which hinders progress for both city and state. Besides, granting complete statehood to our larger cities would be but a proper recognition of the right of those great aggregations of citizens with their varied industries, their immense wealth and distinct interests, to that measure of influence in our national affairs which their numbers and intelligence and interests justly demand.

* Official statistics for 1905 give Boston a population of 595,083. The estimated population for Jan. 1, 1908, is 607,340.

† Official returns for 1900 give Baltimore a population of 508,957. The estimated population for Jan. 1, 1908, is 567,000.

‡ The estimated population of Brooklyn as a borough of greater New York is given on Jan. 1, 1908, as 1,448,095.

§ Official statistics for 1900 give Chicago a population of 1,698,575. The estimated population for Jan. 1, 1908, is 2,483,641.

‖ Official statistics for 1900 give St. Louis a population of 575,238. The estimated population on Jan. 1, 1908, is 50,000.

The Appeal of the Church to the National Government for Redress of Wrongs Suffered in Missouri.

The Prophet Joseph Smith, Sidney Rigdon, and Judge Elias Higbee were chosen as the committee to present to the National Congress the petition of the Saints for a redress of their grievances, suffered in Missouri. This journey to the nation's Capital was of importance quite apart from the immediate purpose for which it was undertaken; namely, it brought the Prophet in contact with the leading statesmen of the United States. While in Washington, he was brought in contact with and interviewed such men as Henry Clay, John C. Calhoun, President Martin Van Buren, different members of the Cabinet, Senators, and Representatives. Such contact enabled him to take new measurements, not only of a different class of men from those with whom he had been accustomed to associate, but new measurements of himself by comparison and contrast of himself with those leading spirits of the nation. Comparisons which could not result otherwise than in advantage to him; and I think it must be conceded by all students of the Prophet's character, especially to those who have been at all close observers of its development, that after this trip to Washington, which afforded the above noted opportunities of comparison and contrast, the Prophet's growth was immeasurably greater than at any time before that journey.

In some respects however it was unfortunate that the Prophet was not more cosmopolitan in his training and in his views of life on the occasion of this visit to the nation's capital; for lack of such training and views of life led him to the formation of rather hasty judgments as to the character of our nation's public men at that time. He undoubtedly had sticking to him as yet, some of the prejudices of his New England and New York sectional training; and at the time of his visit the spirit of the public men of the nation at Washington was largely influenced by the Southern character and spirit. Bourbon Democracy was at its height. The gentlemen of the South with their extreme notions of chivalry and polite deportment, predominated. In those days men were held to strict account for their manner of address one to another. An improper word, a slight, magnified into an insult, meant a challenge to mortal combat on "the field of honor," and this sense of personal responsibility for utterances begot, no doubt, an extreme politeness in personal deportment which seemed puerile to those reared in another atmosphere and influenced by other sentiments than those which resulted from education in the South. Joseph Smith's judgment upon manners and customs in Washington, was doubtless New England's judgment upon Southern customs with which it had no patience, much less sympathy. It is only from these considerations that the rather harsh judgment of the Prophet in relation to conditions in Washington can be properly understood.

Relative to the business upon which this committee visited Washington, it should be said that Sidney Rigdon failed to participate in it at all, in consequence of an illness which befell him on his journey, and hindered him from reaching Washington until the business was practically settled. A short stay in Washington convinced the Prophet that nothing was to be expected in the way of obtaining a redress of grievances for his people from the very cautious politicians then in control of the government, all of whom were anxious, apparently, to palliate the actions of Missouri with reference to the Saints, for the sake of retaining her political influence on their side; and also because of a prevailing inclination to a strict construction of the powers of the general government in its relations to the states. The Prophet therefore left Washington to preach the Gospel for a short time in New Jersey and Philadelphia, after which he returned to Nauvoo, leaving Judge Elias Higbee to urge consideration of the petition of the Saints which had been referred to the Senate committee on Judiciary, with what result is made known in detail in the body of this volume of the history. It is sufficient here to say that the net result of the Committee's deliberations was simply to recommend that the Saints appeal for a redress of their wrongs to the United States District Court having jurisdiction in Missouri, or they could, if they saw proper, "apply to the justice and magnanimity of the State of Missouri—an appeal which the committee feel justified in believing will never be made in vain by the injured or oppressed."— (Sic!)

This suggestion to take their case to the United States Courts was never acted upon by the Saints, nor does it appear in what manner it would have been practicable for them to do so. True it is expressly provided in the Constitution that "The Judicial power of the United States shall extend to all cases in law and equity, arising under this Constitution, the laws of the United States, and treaties made, or which shall be made, under their authority; to controversies between two or more states; between a state and citizens of another state; between citizens of different states; between citizens of the same state," etc.* The case of the Saints would fall either under the clauses in the above quotation respecting controversies arising between a state (Missouri) and citizens of another state (the Saints, now citizens, of Illinois); or "between citizens of different states," the Saints, citizens of Illinois, and their former persecutors, citizens of Missouri. In considering the question under the first clause it must be remembered that the eleventh amendment to the Constitution (declared in force 1798) provides that

---

* Art. 111 Const. U. S., Sec. ii.

"The Judicial power of the United States shall not be construed to extend to any suit in law or equity, commenced or prosecuted against one of the United States by citizens of another state, or by citizens or subjects of any foreign state." It is held that "the power as well as the dignity of a state would be gone if it could be dragged into court by a private plaintiff."[*]

The Supreme Court in the case Chisholm *vs.* the State of Georgia, had decided (1793) that an action did lie against the State of Georgia at a suit of a private plaintiff. The state however refused to appear, whereupon the Supreme Court proceeded, a year later, to give judgment against her by default in case she should not appear and plead before a day; whereupon there arose such a storm of protest, not only in Georgia, but in the other states as well, that the eleventh amendment was adopted exempting a state from being sued in the courts of the United States by citizens of another state, or by citizens subjects of any foreign state. Moreover, states are not suable in any event except with their consent;[†] and if a state waive its immunity, it may attach any conditions it pleases to its consent.[‡] Under these circumstances it is not surprising that the Saints never attempted to bring Missouri before the United States courts. They could only have planted suit against the state by its consent, and if she consented, then under such conditions as she might be pleased to attach to that consent. Moreover, the Saints had the best of reasons for believing that Missouri would never consent.

As to suing their persecutors as individuals before the United States courts, as citizens of one state suing citizens of another, it is only necessary to remind the reader of the insuperable difficulties attending upon that procedure to convince him of the futility of such action. The expensiveness of the undertaking, and the extreme poverty of the exiles alone would be sufficient to bar such an undertaking; for every one knows how bitterly hard it is for the poor to set the judicial machinery of organized society in motion in their favor. Then there was the evident conspiracy entered into by the mobs of Missouri to defeat the ends of justice in respect of the Saints: mobs which an unfriendly governor had converted into a state militia; to which that same governor gave an order to expel from the state or exterminate the entire people; under which order said mob-militia did expel from the state some twelve thousand citizens, depriving them of their property and liberty without due process of law; and afterwards the state through its legislature sanctioned and applauded the actions of this mob-militia for the part it had taken in causing said expulsion—though attended by acts of un-

* Am. Commonwealth (Bryce) Vol. I p. 231.
† Railroad Co. v. Tennessee, U. S. Reports 101, 337.
‡ Clark v. Barnard U. S. 108, 436, and Green v. State 73 Cal. 29 et seq.

speakable atrocity—by appropriating 200,000 dollars to meet the expenses of the mob-militia in carrying out the governor's illegal orders. After these crimes against the Constitution and laws of the state, against American institutions and the civilization of the age—after all this, I say, it is not difficult to understand how farcical would be any procedure before either the state or the federal courts in Missouri.   By acts of perjury, in order to still further defeat the ends of justice and protect each other from the penalties due to their crimes, it would have been easy for the people of Missouri to defeat the ends of justice.   And after having committed the crimes of murder and robbery; after having unlawfully expelled a whole people, numbering thousands, from their homes—of which the despoilers were then possessed—it is not to be believed that such characters would hesitate to subborn witnesses, commit perjury, or hesitate to do any other thing, however criminal, in order to escape the just punishment for their crimes.

The offense of the State of Missouri against the Saints was a denial of political as well as of civil rights.   She had in her treatment of the Saints abdicated republican government.   Her officers, including the chief executive of the state had violated the Constitution of the state in that they had entered into a wide-spread conspiracy to deprive the Saints of their liberty and property without due process of law; and in fact had deprived them of those rights by expelling them by force of arms from the state.

These were the wrongs the Saints had endured; this the nature of the crime of the state of Missouri against them, and it seems that for these things which they suffered there could be found no remedy; for, as already explained, a state could not be made party to a suit before the courts, either state or federal, without her consent; and it is a well settled principle of American law that "a suit nominally against an officer but really against a state to enforce performance of its obligation in its political capacity, will not lie." A state, therefore, could not be directly arraigned before the courts or any kind of tribunal for failure to enforce its political obligations; nor could it be indirectly so arraigned through its officers since such an arraignment would undoubtedly have been held to be but "nominally against the officers and really against the state;" hence void.   The only arraignment of the state that could be made was evidently at the bar of public opinion and sentiment, and this sentiment, unfortunately viciated by misrepresentations, was against the Saints. All things considered, then, there was little wisdom behind the recommendation of the Senate Judiciary Committee for the Saints to prosecute their case before the Federal courts having jurisdiction in Missouri; and

* See Cooler's Constitutional Limitations, chapter ii, also Louisiana v. Jumel 107 U. S. Reports, p. 711, 2 sup. ct. rep. 128.

the suggestion that they apply to the justice and magnanimity of the state of the Missouri, borders upon mockery. However, Missouri did not escape the chastisement due to her many acts of predatory injustice upon the Saints; there was measured out to her more than four fold of that sorrow and affliction which she had perpetraded upon the Saints. She sowed to the wind in her conduct towards the Mormon people, she reaped the whirl-wind in the terrible experiences of more then ten years of border warfare, banditti rule, and her enormous sacrifice of blood and treasure in the Civil War; all of which is abundantly set forth in the Introduction to Volume III of this work.

The Mission of the Twelve to England.

The mission of the Twelve to England marks an epoch in the missionary experience of the Church. They undertook this mission in fulfillment of a commandment received of the Lord on the 8th of July, 1838, at Far West, Missouri, which revelation was given in answer to the question of the Prophet: "Show us thy will, O Lord, concerning the Twelve." In answer to that question the Lord directed that the several vacancies then existing in the quorum should be filled by the appointment of John Taylor, John E. Page, Wilford Woodruff, and Willard Richards. "And next spring," said the revelation, "let them [the Twelve] depart to go over the great waters and there promulgate my gospel, the fullness thereof, and bear record of my name. Let them take leave of my Saints in the City Far West on the 26th day of April next, on the building spot of my house saith the Lord."*

Notwithstanding the fact that the Church had been expelled from the state of Missouri before the 26th day of April, 1839, a number of the Twelve accompanied by several of those who had been appointed to fill vacancies in the quorum, returned to Far West, held a meeting on the site of the Lord's house in the public square of that place, on the date appointed, sung some hymns, ordained those present who had been appointed to fill vacancies in the quorum, laid a corner stone of the Lord's house, took leave of a few of the brethren who were there, and thence started for foreign lands, stopping for a time *en route* at Nauvoo. Late in the summer of 1839 the Twelve began their departure, usually in pairs, for foreign lands. The work had already been introduced into England by the labors of Elder Heber C. Kimball and associates, Elder Orson Hyde of the quorum of the Twelve; also Elders Willard Richards, Isaac Russell, John Goodson, John Snyder; and Joseph Fielding, a priest. The mission of the Twelve to England as a quorum, however, established the work in the British Isles on a broader and more permanent basis, and thence forward the body religious was strengthened from this mission; and as much from the character as from the numbers of the British Saints.

The Mission of Orson Hyde to Palestine.

The mission appointed to Elders Orson Hyde and John E. Page, of the quorum of the Twelve, to Jerusalem, was second in importance only to that appointed to the rest of the Twelve to Great Britain. John E. Page utterly failed to fulfill his appointment, notwithstanding the frequent urging and reproofs of the Prophet. He never left the shores of America, and finally returned to Nauvoo to be serverly censured for his lack of faith and energy. Orson Hyde, on the contrary, in the midst of many hardships, persevered in his journey to the Holy Land, until he succeeded in accomplishing that which had been appointed unto him. Elder Hyde it appears, was a descendant of the tribe of Judah;[*] and sometime after the Prophet had become acquainted with him, most probably in the year 1832, in the course of pronouncing a blessing upon him, said: "In due time thou shalt go to Jerusalem, the land of thy fathers, and be a watchman unto the house of Israel; and by thy hand shall the Most High do a great work, which shall prepare the way and greatly facilitate the gathering together of that people."[†] It was in fulfillment of this prediction upon his head that he had been called upon this mission to Jerusalem, to dedicate the land of Palestine by apostolic authority, preparatory to the return of the Jews and other of the tribes of Israel to that land of promise. This mission he fully accomplished. An account of his journey and of his beautiful and powerful prayer of dedication will be found in his letters published in this volume.[‡]

The question will be asked, Has anything resulted from this mission to dedicate the land of Palestine to the return of the Jews and other tribes of Israel? The only answer is an appeal to facts, to events that have taken place since that prayer of consecration was offered up by this Apostle of the new dispensation of the Gospel, on the 24th of October, 1841.

At the time of Elder Hyde's visit and the ceremonies of dedication he performed on the Mount of Olives, there were comparatively but few Jews at Jerusalem. As late as 1876 the British Consul Reports show that there were but from fifteen to twenty thousand Jews in Judea. But twenty years later the same authority declared the number of Jews at sixty to seventy thousand; and, what was of more importance than

* See this Volume, p. 375.
† Ibid.
‡ The prayer of Dedication will be found at pp. 456-459.

the numbers announced, these reports represented that the new Jewish population was turning its attention to the cultivation of the soil, which but requires the blessings of God upon it to restore it to its ancient fruitfulness, and which will make it possible for it to sustain once more a numerous population. The St. Louis *Globe-Democrat* commenting on these Consular Reports of 1896, said:

"Only two decades ago there were not more than fifteen or twenty thousand Jews in Jerusalem. At that time no houses were to be found outside the walls of the city. Since then many changes have taken place and the Hebrew population—mainly on account of the increase of the Jewish immigration from Russia—now stands at between sixty and seventy thousand. Whole streets of houses have been built outside the walls on the site of the ancient suburban districts, which for hundreds of years have remained deserted. It is not, however, only in Jerusalem itself that the Jews abound, but throughout Palestine they are buying farms and establishing themselves in a surprisingly rapid manner. In Jerusalem they form at present a larger community than either the Christian or the Mohammedan."

Also in 1896 that racial movement among the Jews known as "Zionism" took definite form. This movement was really the federation of all the Jewish societies that have cherished the hope of seeing Israel restored to his promised possessions in Palestine. That year the first international conference of Zionists was held in Basel, Switzerland, and since then under the leadership of the late Dr. Herzel of Austria, and since his death under the leadership of Israel Zangwill, and by reason of its annual conferences constantly increasing in interest and attendance, "Zionism" has taken on all the aspects of one of the world's great movements. It is not so much a religious movement as a racial one; for prominent Jews of all shades of both political and religious opinions have participated in it.

After saying through so many centuries at the feast of the Passover, "May we celebrate the next Passover in Jerusalem," the thought seems to have occurred to some Jewish minds that if that hope is ever to be realized some practical steps must be taken looking to the actual achievement of the possibility—hence the "Zionite Movement." The keynotes of that movement are heard in the following utterances of some of the Jewish leaders in explanation of it: "We want to resume the broken thread of our national existence; we want to show to the wor d the moral strength, the intellectual power of the Jewish people. We want a place where the race can be centralized."—(Leon Zoltokoff). "It is for these Jews (of Russia, Roumania and Galicia) that the name of their country (Palestine) spells 'Hope.' I should not be a man if I did not realize that for these persecuted Jews, Jerusalem spells reason,

justice, manhood and liberty."—(Rabbi Emil G. Hirsch).   "Jewish
nationalism on a modern basis in Palestine, the old home of the people."
—(Max Nordau).   Palestine needs a people, Israel needs a country.
Give the country without a people to the people without a country."—
(Israel Zangwill).   In a word it is the purpose of "Zionism" to redeem
Palestine, and give it back to Jewish control, create, in fact, a Jewish
state in the land promised to their fathers.

The age has come when the promises of the Lord to Israel must be
fulfilled; and hence an apostle of the new dispensation of the Gospel is
sent by divine authority to dedicate the land of Palestine preparatory to
the return of Israel to his promised inheritance.   After which follows
this strange and world-wide movement among the Jews looking to the
re-establishment of "Jewish nationalism on a modern basis in Palestine."   What other relationship can exist between the mission of the
Apostle Orson Hyde and this world-wide movement among the Jews for
the re-establishment of Israel in Palestine, but the relationship of cause
to effect—under, of course, the larger fact that the set time for the
restoration of Israel has come?   The apostle's mission to Jerusalem for
the purpose of dedicating that land, preparatory to the return of Israel,
was without doubt part of the general program for the restoration of
Israel to their lands and to the favor and blessing of God.

The Doctrinal Development of the Church.

The doctrinal development in this period of the dispensation of the
fullness of times, namely, between July, 1839, and the month of May,
1842, about three years, was chiefly in relation to salvation for the
dead, and the sacred ritual of the Temple.   The foundation for this
doctrinal development in relation to salvation for the dead, was laid in
the very inception of the work.   On the occasion of the first visit of
the angel Moroni to the Prophet, on the night of the 21st of September,
1823, among other ancient prophecies quoted by him, and which he
declared was soon to be fulfilled, was the prophecy in the fourth chapter of Malachi in relation to the future coming of Elijah the prophet,
"before the coming of the great and dreadful day of the Lord."   As
quoted by the angel there was a slight variation in the language from
King James' version, as follows: "Behold, I will reveal unto you the
Priesthood by the hand of Elijah the prophet, before the coming of the
great and dreadful day of the Lord.   And he shall plant in the hearts of
the children the promises made to the fathers, and the hearts of the children shall turn to their fathers; if it were not so, the whole world
would be wasted at his coming."*

* HISTORY OF THE CHURCH, Vol. I, p. 12.

Here the promise is made, that in consequence of the restoration of a certain Priesthood, or special keys of authority held by Elijah, the promises made to the fathers shall be planted in the hearts of the children, "and the hearts of the children shall turn to their fathers." Why? For a complete answer to that question the Church waited some years. Again, and still early in the history of the work, namely, March, 1830, the Lord in a revelation to Martin Harris through the Prophet Joseph, added another line or two of knowledge to this doctrine; knowledge which pushed out of the horizon of men's conceptions the terrible and unjust doctrine respecting the eternal punishment which God is supposed to inflict upon those who fail to obey the Gospel in this life, and also those who died in ignorance of it. In explanation of the terms, "eternal punishment," and "everlasting punishment," sometimes found in Holy Writ, the Lord said to the Prophet: "Behold, I am endless, and the punishment which is given from my hand is endless, for endless is my name. Wherefore—

"Eternal punishment is God's punishment.

"Endless punishment is God's punishment."

That is to say, the punishment takes the name of Him in whose name it is inflicted; as if it were written, "Eternal's punishment," "Endless's punishment." And also, it must be understood, that the punishment itself is endless. That is, penalties always attend upon law, and follow its violation. That is an eternal principle. Law is inconceivable without accompanying penalties. But it does not follow that those who fall into the transgression of law, and therefore under sentence of Eternal's justice, will have to endure affliction of the penalty eternally. Justice can be satisfied. Mercy must be accorded her claims, and the culprit having been brought to repentance and taught obedience to law through the things which he has suffered, must go free. But only to suffer again the penalties of the law, if he again violates it; for laws and their penalties are eternal. Hence eternal punishment, hence endless punishment administered to the violator of the law, until he learns to live in harmony with law. For, on the one hand, as "that which is governed by law is also preserved by law, and perfected and sanctified by the same;* so "that which breaketh a law and abideth not by the law, but seeketh to become a law unto itself, and willeth to abide in sin and altogether abideth in sin, cannot be sanctified by law, neither by mercy, justice, nor judgment. Therefore they must remain filthy still."† Thus obedience to law becomes a savor of life unto life; while disobedience to law equally becomes a savor of death unto death.

In February, 1832, still further light was shed upon the subject of

---

* Doctrine and Covenants, Sec. lxxxviii, 34.   † *Ibid*, verse 35.

the different states or degrees of glory in which men will live in the future, by the revelation known as "The Vision." This revelation is one of the sublimest ever given to man. It utterly discredits and displaces the dogmas about the future of man held by Christendom, or at least by Protestant Christendom. The orthodox, Protestant view of man's future is that there are two states in one or the other of which man will spend eternity—in heaven or in hell. If one shall gain heaven, even by ever so small a margin, he will enter immediately upon a complete possession of all its unspeakable joys, equally with the angels and the holiest of Saints. Not only in the "Shorter Catechisms," but in nearly all orthodox creeds the accepted doctrine was: "The souls of believers are at their death made perfect in holiness." On the other hand, if one shall miss heaven, even by ever so small a margin, he is doomed to everlasting torment equally with the wickedest of men and vilest of devils, and there is no deliverance for him through all the countless ages of eternity! It will be noted that I have excepted out of participating in the above view of man's future, the Catholic church, by ascribing these views only to orthodox Protestant Christendom. This is because the Catholic church doctrine slightly differs from the doctrine of the Protestants on this subject. That is Catholics do not believe that all Christians at death go immediately into heaven, but on the contrary "believe that a Christian who dies after the guilt and everlasting punishment of mortal sins have been forgiven him, but who, either from want of opportunity, or through his negligence has not discharged the debt of temporal punishment due to his sin, will have to discharge that debt to the justice of God in purgatory." "Purgatory is a state of suffering after this life, in which those souls are for a time detained, which depart this life after their deadly sins have been remitted as to the stain and guilt, and as to the everlasting pain that was due to them, but which souls have on account of those sins still some temporal punishment to pay; as also those souls which leave this world guilty only of venial (that is pardonable) sins. In purgatory these souls are purified and rendered fit to enter into heaven, where nothing defiled enters."[*] As all works of the Catholic church accessible to me have nothing on the different degrees of glory in which men shall subsist in eternity, I conclude that Catholic teaching is that they who finally attain unto heaven are all equal in glory. So that in the last analysis of the matter, Catholic doctrine falls as far below the great truth that God has revealed upon the subject of the future estate of man, as the doctrine of orthodox Protestant Christendom.

Here is not the place for an extended exposition of the doctrine in

---

[*] The quotations in the above are from "Catholic Belief," by Bruno, D.D. of the Catholic church.

relation to the future state of man as revealed to Joseph Smith in the revelation called "The Vision."* It must suffice here to say that its central principle is resident in the justice and the mercy of God, that requires that every man shall be judged according to his works, considered in the light of his intelligence, his consciousness of right and wrong, and the moral law under which he lived. If he lived in the earth when the Gospel of Jesus Christ was not in the world, or if he lived at places or in circumstances where he did not learn of its existence, much less come to a knowledge of its truths, then the plain dictates of justice demand that some means must exist by which its sanctifying powers may be applied to him in the future; so also as to those who have even once rejected the truth (as in the case of the antediluvians who rejected the teaching of righteous Noah, and were disobedient,† when once the long suffering of God waited in vain in those days for their repentance); having paid the just penalty of their disobedience, then justice would demand that some means must exist by which the saving principles of the Gospel of Jesus Christ may be applied to them; for only by the acceptance of the principles of the Gospel, and by the application of its laws and ordinances as the means by which the grace of God is applied to man, can the sons of men hope for salvation. Then as men differ in degree of intelligence; in the intensity of their faith; in the hartiness of their obedience; in the steadiness of their fidelity; and in as much as there is the stern fact of human freedom and responsibility, and the possibility of a short or long resistance to the will of God, even up to eternal resistance to that will, there is an infinitude of states of glory, of so called rewards and punishments, in which man will live in the future. There is one glory of which the sun in heaven is spoken of as being typical; another of which the inferior light of the moon is typical; and another of which the varying light of the stars is typical. And even as one star differs from another star in glory, in light, so differ those states of existence in which men will live in the future, but each assigned to a place, to an environment, that corresponds to the status of his development; which is only the modern way of saying he shall be judged according to his works. These, in brief, are the underlying principles of this remarkable revelation; a revelation which in every way is worthy the encomium that the Prophet Joseph himself bestowed upon it at the time of its inception: "Nothing could be more pleasing to the Saints upon the order of the Kingdom of the Lord, than the light which burst upon the world through the foregoing Vision. Every law, every commandment, every promise, every truth, and every point touching the destiny of man, from Genesis to Revelation, where the purity of the

* Doctrine and Covenants, Sec. lxxvi, and HISTORY OF THE CHURCH Vol. I, 245 et seq.   † I Peter iii, 18-22.

Scriptures remains unsullied by the folly of men, go to show the perfection of the theory [of different degrees of glory in the future life] and witnesses the fact that *that document is a transcript from the records of the eternal world.*"

In June, 1836, while attending to washings and anointings in the Kirtland Temple, previous to its dedication, the Prophet received still further knowledge as to the future state of man. This also was by means of a vision. He says: "The heavens were opened upon us, and I beheld the celestial kingdom of God, and the glory thereof, whether in the body or out, I cannot tell. I saw the transcendent beauty of the gate through which the heirs of that kingdom will enter, which was like unto circling flames of fire; also the blazing throne of God, whereon was seated the Father and the Son. I saw the beautiful streets of that kingdom, which had the appearnce of being paved with gold. I saw Fathers Adam and Abraham, and my father and mother, my brother, Alvin, that has long since slept, and marveled how it was that he had obtained an inheritance in that kingdom, seeing that he had departed this life before the Lord had set His hand to gather Israel the second time, and had not been baptized for the remission of sins. Thus came the voice of the Lord unto me saying—

"*All who have died without a knowledge of this Gospel, who would have received it if they had been permitted to tarry, shall be heirs of the celestial kingdom of God; also all that shall die henceforth without a knowledge of it, who would have received it with all their hearts, shall be heirs of that kingdom, for I, the Lord, will judge all men according to their works, according to the desire of their hearts.*

"And I also beheld that all children who die before they arrive at the years of accountability, are saved in the celestial kingdom of heaven.

The next step in the development of this doctrine of salvation for the dead was the coming of Elijah to "turn the heart of the fathers to the children, and the heart of the children to the fathers," according to Malachi; to restore the priesthood and "plant in the hearts of the children the promises made to the fathers," by which "the hearts of the children shall be turned to the fathers," according to Moroni. And Elijah committed the keys of this dispensation of turning the hearts of the fathers and children towards each other to Joseph Smith and to Oliver Cowdery. This took place in the Kirtland Temple on the 3rd of April, 1836.*

It was not, however, until the Nauvoo period that the doctrine of salvation for the dead was fully developed and active steps taken looking to the actual performance of ordinances in their behalf. In the revelation that was given on the 19th of January, 1841, the Saints

---

* See History of the Church, Vol. II, p. 435-436. Also Doc. and Cov. Sec. cx.

were commanded to build a house unto the Lord, a Holy Temple unto
the Most High. "For," said this revelation, "there is not a place found
on earth that He may come to and restore again that which was lost unto
you, or which He hath taken away, even the fullness of the Priesthood;
for a baptismal font there is not upon the earth, that they, my Saints,
may be baptized for those who are dead; for this ordinance belongeth
to my house, and cannot be acceptable to me, only in the days of your
poverty, wherein ye are not able to build a house unto me. But I command you, all ye my Saints, to build a house unto me; and I grant unto
you a sufficient time to build a house unto me, and during this time your
baptisms shall be acceptable unto me." That is, the baptisms for the
dead should be acceptable unto the Lord in other places than the temple,
until the temple should be prepared for that ordinance, if the Saints
would be dillgent and build it according to the Lord's appointment.
Moreover, the information is imparted in the revelation that, it is "in
Zion, and in her stakes, and in Jerusalem, those places which I [the
Lord] have appointed for refuge, shall be the places for your baptisms
for your dead."

After this revelation was given to the Church baptism for the dead
was a subject frequently expounded in Nauvoo, both by the Prophet
and other leading elders. It was a theme upon which the Twelve Apostles dwelt in their Epistles to the Church both in America and in Great
Britain. Baptisms for the dead were performed for some time in the
Mississippi river, and later, in the latter part of November, 1841, in the
baptismal font erected in the basement of the Temple, and dedicated
for that sacred purpose. For a time some irregularities obtained in relation to this ordinance owing to the fact that the perfect knowledge of
the order of it had not then been obtained, but was developed later in
this Nauvoo period of the History of the Church, as will appear in
Volume V of this work.

It was a mighty stride forward in the doctrinal development of the
Church, this idea of the possibility of salvation for the dead through the
administration of the ordinances of the Gospel for and in their behalf
by their kindred on earth; and greatly enlarged the views of the Saints
in relation to the importance and wide spread effects of their work. The
ends of the earth indeed converged in the labors of the Saints henceforth,
for their activities in the administrations of the holy ordinances of the
Gospel would affect all past generations as well as affect all generations
to come. It was a bringing into view the full half of the work which
up to this time had lain hidden behind the horizon of men's conceptions
of that "great and marvelous work" which God from the beginning
declared was about to be brought forth among the children of men.*

* See Doc. and Cov. the opening paragraph of Sections iv, vi, xi, xii, xiv, all
iven in the year 1829.

Other Doctrines of the Prophet's Teaching.

Other doctrines taught by the Prophet within the period covered by this volume, relate to the Priesthood; to the Status of Translated Persons; to Man's Personal Responsibility for his own conduct, to Election and Reprobation. A word in relation to each of these doctrines must suffice here since they do not reach their full development in the teachings of the Prophet until the last two years of his eventful life, and must therefore receive fuller treatment in the Introduction of Volume V.

Relative to the Priesthood, the most important items advanced by the Prophet in this volume, are, first, the unity of all Priesthood, and second, the place and power assigned to Adam in the order of the dispensations of the Gospel granted to our earth. Treating on the unity of the Priesthood, the Prophet said: "There are two Priesthoods spoken of in the Scriptures, viz., the Melchisedek and the Aaronic or Levitical. Although there are two Priesthoods, yet the Melchisedek Priesthood comprehends the Aaronic or Levitical Priesthood, and is the grand head, and holds the highest authority which pertains to the Priesthood, and the keys of the kingdom of God in all ages of the world to the latest posterity on the earth, and is the channel through which all knowledge, doctrine, the plan of salvation, and every important matter is revealed from heaven. Its institution was prior to 'the foundation of this earth, or the morning stars sang together, or the Sons of God shouted for joy,' and is the highest and holiest Priesthood, and is after the order of the Son of God, and all other Priesthoods are only parts, ramifications, powers and blessings belonging to the same, and are held, controlled, and directed by it. It is the channel through which the Almighty commenced revealing His glory at the beginning of the creation of this earth, and through which He has continued to reveal Himself to the children of men to the present time, and through which He will make known His purposes to the end of time."

Respecting the place of Adam in the Priesthood and his relationship to the dispensations of that Priesthood to our earth, the Prophet said: "Commencing with Adam, who was the first man, who is spoken of in Daniel as being the 'Ancient of Days,' or in other words, the first and oldest of all, the great, grand progenitor of whom it is said in another place he is Michael, because he was the first and father of all, not only by progeny, but the first to hold the spiritual blessings, to whom was made known the plan of ordinances for the salvation of his posterity unto the end, and to whom Christ was first revealed, and through whom Christ has been revealed from heaven, and will continue to be revealed from henceforth. Adam holds the keys of the dispensation of the fullness of times; i. e., the dispensation of all the times have been and will be revealed through him from the beginning to Christ, and from Christ to the end of all the dispensations that are to be revealed. 'Having made known unto us the mystery of His will, according to His good pleasure which He hath purposed in Himself: that in the dispensation of the fullness of times He might gather together in one all things in Christ, both which are in heaven, and which are on earth; even in him· (Ephesians, 1st chap., 9th and 10th verses). Now the purpose in Himself in the winding up scene of the last dispensation is that all things pertaining to that dispensation should be conducted precisely in accordance with the preceding dispensations. And again. God purposed in Himself that there should not be an eternal fullness until every dispensation should be fulfilled and gathered together in one, and that all things whatsoever, that should be gathered together in one in those dispensations unto the same fullness and eternal glory, should be in Christ Jesus; therefore He set the ordinances to be the same forever and ever, and set Adam to watch over them, to reveal them from heaven to man, or to send angels to reveal them.   *   *   *   *   These angels are under the direction of Michael or Adam, who acts under the direction of the Lord.   *   *   *   *   There are many things which belong to the powers of the Priesthood and the keys thereof, that have been kept hid from before the foundation of the world; they are hid from the wise and prudent to be revealed in the last times.''

That it was the design of the Lord in building the Temple at Nauvoo, that there should be other ordinances revealed besides "baptism for the dead," is clearly manifested in the revelation itself, for it says: "And again, verily I say unto you, how shall your washings be acceptable unto me, except ye perform them in a house which you have built to my name.   *   *   *   *   Therefore, verily I say unto you, that your anointings, and your washings, and your baptisms for the dead, and your solemn assemblies, and your memorials for your sacrifices, by the sons of Levi and for your oracles in your most holy places wherein you receive conversations, and your statutes and judgments, for the beginning of the revelations and foundation of Zion, and for the glory, honor, and endowment of all her municipals, are ordained by the ordinance of my holy house which my people are always commanded to build unto my holy name. And verily I say unto you, let this house be built unto my name, that I may reveal mine ordinances therein, unto my people; for I deign to reveal unto my Church things which have been kept hid from before the foundation of the word, things that pertain to the dispensation of the fullness of times.''

The ordinances here mentioned in addition to baptism for the dead are chiefly connected with the Priesthood of the Church, and were fully developed in the teachings of the Prophet before the close of his eventful career.

As to the status of translated personages, he said: "Many have supposed that the doctrine of translation was a doctrine whereby men were taken immediately into the presence of God, and into an eternal fulness, but this is a mistaken idea. Their place of habitation is that of the terrestrial order, and a place prepared for such characters He held in reserve to be ministering angels unto many planets, and who as yet have not entered into as great a fullness as those who are resurrected from the dead."

Of man being personally responsible for his own conduct, he is reported by the Editor of the *Times and Seasons* as saying: "He [the Prophet] then observed that Satan was generally blamed for the evils which we did, but if he was the cause of all our wickedness, men could not be condemned. The devil could not compel mankind to do evil; all was voluntary. Those who resisted the Spirit of God, would be liable to be led into temptation, and then the association of heaven would be withdrawn from those who refused to be made partakers of such great glory. God *would not* exert any compulsory means, and the devil *could not*; and such ideas as were entertained [on these subjects] by many were absurd." What beautiful harmony between the Prophet's doctrine here and that of the Apostle James: "Let no man say when he is tempted, I am tempted of God: for God cannot be tempted with evil, neither tempteth he any man: But every man is tempted, when he is drawn away of his own lusts, and enticed. Then when lust hath conceived, it bringing forth sin: and sin when it is finished, bringeth forth death." *

Of election, a term used generally in connection with reprobation, when commenting on the 9th Chapter of Romans,—wherein Paul is supposed to teach the doctrine of election,—the Prophet is represented as saying: "He then spoke on the subject of election, and read the 9th chapter of Romans, from which it was evident that the election there spoken of was pertaining to the flesh, and had reference to the seed of Abraham, according to the promise God made to Abraham, saying, "In thee, and in thy seed, all the families of the earth shall be blessed. * * * The whole of the chapter had reference to the Priesthood and the house of Israel: and unconditional election of individuals to eternal life was not taught by the Apostles. God did elect or predestinate, that all those who would be saved, should be saved in Christ Jesus, and through obedience to the Gospel, but He passes over no man's sins, but visits them with correction, and if His children will not repent of their sins He will discard them."

These several doctrines mark rapid development in the Prophet's work as an instructor in sacred things, and clearly indicate his increasing capacity and power as Prophet, Seer and Teacher.

* James 1, 13-15.

HISTORY

OF THE

CHURCH OF JESUS CHRIST OF LATTER-DAY SAINTS.

===

VOL. IV.

HISTORY

OF THE

CHURCH OF JESUS CHRIST

OF

LATTER-DAY SAINTS.

***

PERIOD I.
HISTORY OF JOSEPH SMITH, THE PROPHET.

***

CHAPTER I.

THE DEPARTURE OF THE TWELVE FOR ENGLAND—MANIFESTA-
TION OF GOD'S POWER IN HEALING THE
SICK AT COMMERCE.

Friday, July 5, 1839.—I was dictating history, I say dictating, for I seldom use the pen myself. I always dictate all my communications, but employ a scribe to write them.

The Prophet's Literary Methods.

Saturday, 6.—I was at home reviewing the Church records.

Sunday, 7.—I was at the meeting held in the open air, at which a large assemblage was expected to listen to the farewell addresses of the Twelve, who were then about to take their departure on a most important mission, namely to the nations of the earth and the islands of the sea.

Farewell to the Twelve.

Elder John E. Page being the first of the Twelve present, opened the meeting by addressing a few words of an introductory nature; after singing and prayer, Elder Page

delivered a very interesting discourse on the subject of
the Book of Mormon, recapitulating, in short terms, the
principles of a former discourse on the same subject, and
afterwards proceeded to read portions from the Bible and
Book of Mormon concerning the best criterions whereby
to judge of the authenticity of the latter; and then went on
to show in a very satisfactory manner, that no impostor
would ever attempt to make such promises as are contained on pages five hundred forty-one,* and five hundred
and thirty-four.† He then bore testimony.

After noon the meeting was again opened by prayer.
Elder John Taylor spoke on the subject of this dispensation; the other angel which John saw, having the everlasting Gospel to preach, he then bore testimony of the
truth of the Book of Mormon.

Elder Woodruff's address went chiefly to exhortation to
the Saints; after which he also bore his testimony.

Elder Orson Hyde next came forward, and having
alluded to his own late fall,‡ exhorted all to perseverance
in the things of God, expressed himself one with his brethren, and bore testimony to his knowledge of the truth, and
the misery of falling from it.

Elder Brigham Young made some very appropriate
remarks, and also bore testimony to the truth of these
things, and gave an invitation to come forward and be
baptized, when three manifested their determination to
renounce the world and take upon themselves the name
of Jesus Christ.   One brother was then confirmed; after
which President Sidney Rigdon addressed the meeting in
a very feeling manner.   He showed that it must be no
small matter which could induce men to leave their families and their homes to travel over all the earth amidst
persecutions and trials, such as always followed the
preaching of this Gospel.   He then addressed himself to

* See pp. 573-4, current edition.
† See pp. 565-567, current edition.
‡ See History of the Church, Vol. III, pp. 167-8.

the Twelve and gave them some counsel and consolation as far as lay in his power; after which I requested their prayers, and promised to pray for them.

The meeting was large and respectable; a great number were present who did not belong to the Church. The most perfect order prevailed throughout. The meeting was dismissed about half-past five, when we repaired to the water, and the three candidates were baptized and confirmed.

Monday, Tuesday and Wednesday, 8th, 9th and 10th of July.—I was with the Twelve selecting hymns, for the purpose of compiling a hymn book.

The L. D. S. Hymn Book.

About this time much sickness began to manifest itself among the brethren, as well as among the inhabitants of the place, so that this week and the following were generally spent in visiting the sick and administering to them; some had faith enough and were healed; others had not.

Sunday, 21. — There was no meeting on account of much rain and much sickness; however many of the sick were this day raised up by the power of God, through the instrumentality of the Elders of Israel ministering unto them in the name of Jesus Christ.

Administration to the sick.

Monday and Tuesday, 22nd and 23rd.—The sick were administered unto with great success,* but many remain sick, and new cases are occurring daily.

---

* "In consequence of the persecutions of the Saints in Missouri, and the exposures to which they were subjected, many of them were taken sick soon after their arrival at Commerce, afterwards called Nauvoo; and as there was but a small number of dwellings for them to occupy, Joseph had filled his house and tent with them, and through constantly attending to their wants, he soon fell sick himself. After being confined to his house several days, and while meditating upon his situation, he had a great desire to attend to the duties of his office. On the morning of the 22nd of July, 1839, he arose from his bed and commenced to administer to the sick in his own house and door-yard, and he commanded them in the name of the Lord Jesus Christ to arise and be made whole; and the sick were healed upon every side of him.

"Many lay sick along the bank of the river; Joseph walked along up to the lower stone house, occupied by Sidney Rigdon, and he healed all the sick that lay in his

Sunday 28.—Meeting was held as usual. Elder Parley P. Pratt preached on the gathering of Israel. In the afternoon Orson Pratt addressed the Church on the necessity of keeping the commandments of God. I spoke, and admonished the members of the Church individually to set their houses in order, to make clean the inside of the platter, and to

Discourses by the Brothers Pratt.

path. Among the number was Henry G. Sherwood, who was nigh unto death. Joseph stood in the door of his tent and commanded him in the name of Jesus Christ to arise and come out of his tent, and he obeyed him and was healed. Brother Benjamin Brown and his family also lay sick, the former appearing to be in a dying condition. Joseph healed them in the name of the Lord. After healing all that lay sick upon the bank of the river as far as the stone house, he called upon Elder Kimball and some others to accompany him across the river to visit the sick at Montrose. Many of the Saints were living at the old military barracks. Among the number were several of the Twelve. On his arrival the first house he visited was that occupied by Elder Brigham Young, the President of the Quorum of the Twelve, who lay sick. Joseph healed him, then he arose and accompanied the Prophet on his visit to others who were in the same condition. They visited Elder Wilford Woodruff, also Elders Orson Pratt, and John Taylor, all of whom were living in Montrose. They also accompanied him.

"The next place they visited was the home of Elijah Fordham, who was supposed to be about breathing his last. When the company entered the room, the Prophet of God walked up to the dying man and took hold of his right hand and spoke to him; but Brother Fordham was unable to speak, his eyes were set in his head like glass, and he seemed entirely unconscious of all around him. Joseph held his hand and looked into his eyes in silence for a length of time. A change in the countenance of Brother Fordham was soon perceptible to all present. His sight returned, and upon Joseph asking him if he knew him, he, in a low whisper, answered 'Yes.' Joseph asked him if he had faith to be healed. He answered, 'I fear it is too late; if you had come sooner I think I would have been healed.' The Prophet said 'Do you believe in Jesus Christ?' He answered in a feeble voice, 'I do.' Joseph then stood erect, still holding his hand in silence several moments; Then he spoke in a very loud voice, saying, 'Brother Fordham, I command you, in the name of Jesus Christ, to arise from this bed and be made whole.' His voice was like the voice of God, and not of man. It seemed as though the house shook to its very foundations. Brother Fordham arose from his bed, and was immediately made whole. His feet were bound in poultices which he kicked off; then putting on his clothes he ate a bowl of bread and milk and followed the Prophet into the street.

"The company next visited Brother Joseph Bates Noble, who lay very sick. He also was healed by the Prophet. By this time the wicked became alarmed and followed the company into Brother Noble's house. After Noble was healed, all kneeled down to pray. Brother Fordham was mouth, and while praying he fell to the floor. The Prophet arose, and on looking around he saw quite a number of unbelievers in the house, whom he ordered out. When the room was cleared of the wicked, Brother Fordham came to and finished his prayer.

"After healing the sick in Montrose, all the company followed Joseph to the bank of the river, where he was going to take the boat to return home. While waiting meet on the next Sabbath to partake of the Sacrament, in order that by our obedience to the ordinances, we might be enabled to prevail with God against the destroyer, and that the sick might be healed.

All this week chiefly spent among the sick, who in general are gaining strength, and recovering health.

Sunday, August 4.—The Church came together for prayer meeting and Sacrament. I exhorted the Church at length, concerning the necessity of being righteous, and clean at heart before the Lord. Many others also spoke; especially some of the Twelve, who were present, professed their willingness to proceed on their mission to Europe, without either purse or scrip. The Sacrament was administered; a spirit of humility and harmony prevailed, and the Church passed a resolution that the Twelve proceed on their mission as soon as possible, and that the Saints provide for their families during their absence.

Prayer Meeting for the Sick.

Letter to Isaac Russell, reproving him for issuing pretended revelations to the Saints.

COMMERCE, HANCOCK COUNTY, ILLINOIS, 5th August, 1839.

DEAR SIR.—I have been requested to write you on behalf of the Twelve, who are just on the eve of their departure for England, and

for the boat, a man from the West, who had seen that the sick and dying were healed, asked Joseph if he would not go to his house and heal two of his children who were very sick. They were twins and were three months old. Joseph told the man he could not go, but he would send some one to heal them. He told Elder Woodruff to go with the man and heal his children. At the same time he took from his pocket a silk bandanna handkerchief, and gave to Brother Woodruff, telling him to wipe the faces of the children with it, and they should be healed; and remarked at the same time: 'As long as you keep that handkerchief it shall remain a league between you and me.' Elder Woodruff did as he was commanded, and the children were healed, and he keeps the handkerchief to this day.

"There were many sick whom Joseph could not visit, so he counseled the Twelve to go and visit and heal them, and many were healed under their hands. On the day following that upon which the above-described events took place, Joseph sent Elders George A. and Don Carlos Smith up the river to heal the sick. They went up as far as Ebenezer Robinson's—one or two miles—and did as they were commanded, and the sick were healed." *Leaves from my Journal,* (Wilford Woodruff) Ch. XIX.

inform you, that "this thing" which you have thought proper to write as a revelation "to the Church in Alston and the branches round about," to which you yourself administered, has "already come to the knowledge of the Churches" both here and elsewhere, and lest you should have any doubt concerning the fact, we send you a copy of your revelation to that Church.

I am sir, with all respect,

Yours truly,
JAMES MULHOLLAND.

P. S.—Isaiah chap. L, 10th and 11th verses.* In my own behalf I wish to state that I sincerely wish that it may soon come to pass that you, sir, and all our friends at Far West may perceive that you are walking in the light of a fire, and sparks that you have yourselves kindled; and that you may turn around and fear the Lord, obey the voice of His servant, and thereby escape the sentence, "Ye shall lie down in sorrow."

J. M.

To Mr. Isaac Russell, Far West, Missouri.

Friday, 9.—A Conference was held at Brother Caleb Bennett's Monmouth County, New Jersey, Elder John P. Greene presiding. The New York and Brooklyn branches were represented by the President as being in good fellowship. There were represented at this conference the following branches, by Elder Ball, Shrewsbury, New Jersey, numbering twenty members; Montage, three; Minissink, New Hampshire, two; Albany, eight; Holliston, Massachusetts, sixteen; Elder Dunham represented Hamilton, Madison County, forty-six; Samuel James, Leechburg, Pennsylvania, forty.

Conference in New Jersey.

Sunday, 11.—I attended meeting in the forenoon and heard a sermon by Parley P. Pratt. In the afternoon there was one baptized, and four were confirmed, namely,

---

*"Who is among you that feareth the Lord, that obeyeth the voice of His servant, that walketh in darkness, and hath no light? Let him trust in the name of the Lord, and stay upon his God.

"Behold, all ye that kindle a fire, that compass yourselves about with sparks. walk in the light of your fire, and in the sparks that ye have kindled. This shall ye have of mine hand; ye shall lie down in sorrow."

Brother Hibbard, his wife, little son, and daughter. The Sacrament was administered.

This week I spent chiefly in visiting the sick; sickness much decreased.

Sunday, 18.—Rode out in the forenoon. Orson Pratt preached upon the order and plan of creation. Three were baptized.

Afternoon: Three confirmed and one ordained an Elder.

This week I spent chiefly among the sick. The Church made a purchase of eighty acres from William White for four thousand dollars, lying directly north of the Hugh White purchase.

Sunday, 25.—I attended meeting. Sickness decreasing.

Thursday, 29.—Elders Parley P. Pratt and family, Orson Pratt and Hiram Clark, started on their mission to England, in their own two-horse carriage—their route lying through Illinois, Indiana, and to Detroit, the capital of Michigan, situated near the head of Lake Erie, about five hundred and eighty miles distant.

Saturday, 31.—The work is spreading in England. Elder Richards went to the Staffordshire pot- Progress of teries this day, and Presidents Joseph Field- the Work in ing and William Clayton were visiting and set- England. ting in order many of the branches, and ordaining many to the ministry who are diligent in preaching as they have opportunity on the Sabbath in the surrounding villages.

Sunday, September 1.—I attended meeting, and spoke concerning some errors in Parley P. Pratt's writings. This week sickness much decreased.

Monday, 9, and the greater part of the week.—I spent in visiting the sick, and attending to to the settlement of our new town.*

* This has reference to the Hotchkiss purchase which had just recently been laid out as part of the rapidly growing town of Nauvoo. It constituted the north west part of the city, extending some distance along the river front, and back on to the height of land overlooking the river bottom.

The Prophet's Letter to Isaac Galland.—Nauvoo Affairs.

COMMERCE, ILLINOIS, 11th September, 1839.

DEAR BROTHER GALLAND:—We have had the great pleasure of receiving your favor of the 24th July; and learning thereby that you and your family had arrived at Chillicothe in safety and in health. We perceive that you have had a rather narrow escape from a serious accident; and doubtless the hand of the Lord is to be acknowledged in the matter, although unperceived by mortal eye. Time and experience will teach us more and more how easily falsehood gains credence with mankind in general, rather than the truth; but especially in taking into consideration the plan of salvation. The plain simple order of the Gospel of Jesus Christ never has been discerned or acknowledged as the truth, except by a few—among whom were "not many wise men after the flesh, not many mighty, not many noble;" whilst the majority have contented themselves with their own private opinions, or have adopted those of others, according to their address, their philosophy, their formula, their policy, or their fineness may have attracted their attention, or pleased their taste. But, sir, of all the other criterions whereby we may judge of the vanity of these things, one will be always found true, namely, that we will always find such characters glorying in their own wisdom and their own works; whilst the humble Saint gives all the glory to God the Father, and to His Son Jesus Christ, whose yoke is easy and whose burden is light, and who told His disciples that unless they became like little children they could not enter the Kingdom of Heaven.

As to the situation of the Church here, matters go with us as well as can reasonably be expected; we have had considerable sickness amongst us, but very few deaths; and as the greater part are now recovering, we yet hope to have shelters provided before the winter shall set in.

Since you left here, we have purchased out all Mr. Hotchkiss' interest hereabouts. His farm we have laid out as an addition to our town, Nauvoo, and the town of Commerce we also hope to build up.

Some of the Twelve and others have already started for Europe, and the remainder of that mission we expect will go now in a few days. According to intelligence received since you left, the work of the Lord rolls on in a very pleasing manner, both in this and in the old country. In England many hundreds have of late been added to our numbers; but so, even so, it must be, for "Ephraim he hath mixed himself among the people." And the Savior He hath said, "My sheep hear my voice;" and also, "He that heareth you, heareth me;" and, "Behold I will bring them again from the north country, and gather them from the coasts of the earth." And as John heard the voice saying, "Come out of her, my people," even so must all be fulfilled; that the people of the Lord may live when "Babylon the great is fallen, is fallen."

There has quite a number of families gathered up here already; and we anticipate a continuance, especially as upon inquiry we have found that we have not had more than [the usual] ratio of sickness here, notwithstanding the trials we have had, and the hardships to which we have been exposed. Calculating as we do, upon the mercy and power of God in our behalf, we hope to persevere on in every good and useful work, even unto the end, that when we come to be tried in the balance we may not be found wanting.

With all good wishes and prayers for the temporal and eternal salvation of yourself and your family, as well as of all the honest in heart over the face of the earth,

We remain, sir, with sincerity,

Your friend and brother,

JOSEPH SMITH, Jun.

Addressed to Isaac Galland, Esq., Kirtland, Geauga, County, Ohio.

Friday, 13.—I left home for Brother William Smith's place.

Saturday, 14.—President Brigham Young started from his home at Montrose, for England. His health was very poor; he was unable to go thirty rods to the river without assistance. After he had crossed the ferry he got Brother Israel Barlow to carry him on his horse behind him to Heber C. Kimball's where he remained sick until the 18th. He left his wife sick with a babe only ten days old, and all his children sick, unable to wait upon each other. I returned home this evening. *[margin: Brigham Young Starts on his Mission.]*

Sunday, 15.—I was visiting the sick.

Monday and Tuesday, 16 and 17.—Was engaged in arranging the town lots.

Wednesday, 18.—Went to Burlington, Iowa Territory. Elders Young and Kimball left Sister Kimball and all her children sick, except little Heber;* went thirteen miles on their journey towards England, and were left at Brother Osmon M. Duel's, who *[margin: Departure of Elders Young and Kimball from Nauvoo.]*

* The departure of these two Elders upon their mission to England is worthy of a more extended notice. A brother by the name of Charles Hubbard sent a boy

lived in a small cabin near the railway between Commerce and Warsaw. They were so feeble as to be unable to carry their trunks into the house without the assistance of Sister Duel, who received them kindly, prepared a bed for them to lie on, and made them a cup of tea.

Thursday, 19.—I Returned this evening from Burlington.

Brother Duel carried Elders Young and Kimball in his wagon to Lima, sixteen miles, where another brother received them and carried them to Father Mikesell's near Quincy, about twenty miles; the fatigue of this day was too much for their feeble health; they were prostrated, and obliged to tarry a few days to recruit.

Friday and Saturday, 20 and 21.—At home attending to domestic and Church business.

Elders George A. Smith, Reuben Hedlock, and Theodore Turley started for England, and upset their wagon on the bank of the river, before they got out of sight of Commerce. Elders Smith and Turley were so weak they could not get up, and Brother Hedlock had to lift them in again. Soon after, some gentlemen met them and asked who had been robbing the burying ground—so miserable was their appearance through sickness.

Sunday, 22.—I presided at the meeting, and spoke concerning the "other Comforter," as I had previously taught the Twelve.*

---

with a team to take them a day's journey on their way. Elder Kimball left his wife in bed shaking with ague, and all his children sick It was only by the assistance of some of the brethren that Heber himself could climb into the wagon. "It seemed to me," he remarked afterwards in relating the circumstance, "as though my very inmost parts would melt within me at the thought of leaving my family in such a condition, as it were, almost in the arms of death. I felt as though I could scarcely endure it." "Hold up!" said he to the teamster, who had just started, "Brother Brigham, this is pretty tough, but let us rise and give them a cheer." Brigham, with much difficulty, rose to his feet, and joined Elder Kimball in swinging his hat and shouting, "Hurrah, hurrah, hurrah, for Israel!" The two sisters, hearing the cheer came to the door—Sister Kimball with great difficulty—and waved a farewell; and the two apostles continued their journey, without purse, without scrip, for England.

* See Vol. III, pp. 379-381.

This week I spent in transacting various business at home, except when visiting the sick, who are in general recovering, though some of them but slowly.

Wednesday, 25.—President Young went to Charles C. Rich's; 26th, to Brother Wilber's; 27th, Brother Wilber carried Elders Young and Kimball to Pittsfield.

Sunday, 29.—Held meeting at my own house. After others had spoken I spoke and explained concerning the uselessness of preaching to the world about great judgments, but rather to preach the simple Gospel. Explained concerning the coming of the Son of Man; also that it is a false idea that the Saints will escape all the judgments, whilst the wicked suffer; for all flesh is subject to suffer, and "the righteous shall hardly escape;" still many of the Saints will escape, for the just shall live by faith; yet many of the righteous shall fall a prey to disease, to pestilence, etc., by reason of the weakness of the flesh, and yet be saved in the Kingdom of God. So that it is an unhallowed principle to say that such and such have transgressed because they have been preyed upon by disease or death, for all flesh is subject to death; and the Savior has said, "Judge not, lest ye be judged."

Items of Doctrine—the Prophet.

Monday, 30.—The fore part of this week I was at home preparing for Conference. Elders Young and Kimball went to Brother Decker's and Mr. Murray's, Sister Kimball's father.

Tuesday, October 1.—Elders Young and Kimball went to Brother Lorenzo Young's.

Thursday, 3.—I was in counsel with the brethren.

Friday, 4.—Lorenzo Young carried Elders Young and Kimball to Jacksonville.

Saturday, 5.—The friends and brethren conveyed the Elders of the British Mission to Springfield, where they were kindly treated and nursed, for they were yet very feeble.

I attended a general conference of the Church of Jesus

Christ of Latter-day Saints at Commerce, Hancock County, Illinois, of which the following are the minutes:

Minutes of Conference at Commerce, Illinois, October 6th, 7th and 8th, 1839.

The meeting was opened by prayer by President Joseph Smith, Jun., after which he was appointed President, and James Sloan Clerk of the conference, by a unanimous voice of the meeting. The President then spoke at some length upon the situation of the Church; the difficulties they have had to contend with; and the manner in which they had been led to this place; and wanted to know the views of the brethren, whether they wished to appoint this a stake of Zion or not; stating that he believed it to be a good place, and suited for the Saints. It was then unanimously agreed upon that it should be appointed a stake and a place of gathering for the Saints.

The following officers were then appointed—namely, William Marks to be President; Bishop Whitney to be Bishop of middle ward; Bishop Partridge to be Bishop of upper ward; Bishop Knight to be Bishop of lower ward; George W. Harris, Samuel Bent, Henry G. Sherwood, David Fullmer, Alpheus Cutler, William Huntington, Thomas Grover, Newel Knight, Charles C. Rich, David Dort, Seymour Brunson, Lewis D. Wilson, to be the High Council; who being respectfully called upon accepted their appointment.

It was then voted that a stake of the Church be established on the west side of the river, in Iowa Territory; over which Elder John Smith was appointed President; Alanson Ripley, Bishop; and Asahel Smith, John M. Burk, Abraham O. Smoot, Richard Howard, Willard Snow, Erastus Snow, David Pettigrew, Elijah Fordham, Edward Fisher, Elias Smith, John Patten, Stephen Chase, were elected High Council. Don C. Smith was elected to be continued as President of the High Priesthood [High Priest's quorum]. Orson Hyde to stand in his former office, [an Apostle] and William Smith to be continued in his standing, [in the quorum of the Twelve.]

Letters were then read respecting the absence of members on account of ill health. It was voted that Harlow Redfield be suspended until he can have a trial; and in the meantime that he should not act as president of a branch, or preach.

Voted that John Daley, James Daley, and Milo Andrus retain their station in the Church. Voted that Ephraim Owen's confession for disobeying the Word of Wisdom be accepted.

Brothers Edward Johnston, Benjamin Johnston, Samuel Musick, John S. Fullmer, Jabez Lake, Benjamin Jones, Henry Our Bough, Reddin A. Allred, George W. Gee, Jesse McIntyre, James

Brown, Henry Miller, Artemas Johnson, Joseph G. Hovey, Robert D. Foster, Fields B. Jacaway, Zadok Bethers, William Allred, William B. Simmons, William W. Edwards, Sen., William H. Edwards, Jun., Hosea Stout, Thomas Rich, Allen J. Stout, Esaias Edwards, John Adams, Daniel Miller, Simeon J. Comfort, Graham Coltrin, William Hyde, Andrew Henry, Reddick N. Allred, Eli Lee, Hiram W. Mikesell and Thomas S. Edwards were appointed Elders of the Church, who all accepted of their appointment, with the exception of Thomas S. Edwards.

John Gaylord was admitted into the Church upon his confession. Abel Casto was confirmed by the laying on of hands.

The meeting then adjourned until Sunday morning; after which six were baptized by Joseph Smith, Jun. The assembly was very large.

The conference met on Sunday morning, the 6th, pursuant to adjournment at eight o'clock a. m., when Samuel Williams, Reuben Foot, Orlando D. Hovey, Tunis Rappleyee, Sheffield Daniels, Albert Milner, David B. Smith, Ebenezer Richardson, Pleasant Ewell, and William Helm were appointed Elders of the Church, and were ordained under the hands of Reynolds Cahoon, Seymour Brunson, Samuel Bent and Alpheus Cutler.

After some remarks from the President respecting order, and decorum during conference, Elder Lyman Wight spoke concerning the duties of Priests and Teachers. President Joseph Smith, Jun., then addressed the conference, in relation to appointing a Patriarch, and other matters connected with the well being of the Church.

Having now got through the business matters, the President proceeded to give instruction to the Elders respecting preaching the Gospel, and pressed upon them the necessity of getting the Spirit, so that they might preach with the Holy Ghost sent down from heaven; to be careful in speaking on those subjects which are not clearly pointed out in the word of God, which lead to speculation and strife.

Those persons who had been baptized, were then confirmed, and several children received blessings by Elders Cutler, Bent, and Brunson. Elder Lyman Wight then addressed the meeting on the subject of raising funds by contribution, towards paying for the lands which had been contracted for as a settlement for the Church, after which contributions were received for that purpose.

Judge Elias Higbee was appointed to acompany Presidents Joseph Smith, Jun., and Sidney Rigdon to the city of Washington.

The meeting then adjourned until Monday morning.

Conference met on Monday morning, October 7th, pursuant to adjournment.

The President spoke at some length to the Elders, and explained many passages of Scripture. Elder Lyman Wight spoke on the subject of the resurrection, and other important subjects; when he offered the following resolution, which passed unanimously;

Resolved: That a new edition of Hymn Books be printed immediately, and that the one published by D. W. Rogers be utterly discarded by the Church.

Elder Ezra Hayes was then put upon trial for teaching doctrine injurious to the Church, and for falsehoods, which were proven against him; his license was taken from him, and he required to give satisfaction to those whom he had offended.

Charges having been preferred against Brother Rogers, it was agreed that the case be handed over to the High Council.

Asahel Perry made application to be received into fellowship, and was voted into his former standing.

After having referred the business not gone into, to the High Council, the President then returned thanks to the conference for their good attention and liberality, and having blessed them in the name of the Lord, the conference was dismissed.

The next conference was appointed to be held on the sixth day of April next.

Tuesday, 8.—After conference, this week I was mostly engaged in attending to the general affairs of the Church, and principally about home.

Friday, 11.—This evening, Elders Young, Kimball, George A. Smith, Hedlock, and Turley started from Springfield, traveled eight miles on their journey, and stayed with Father Draper.

Saturday, 12.—The Elders of the British Mission left Father Draper's and pursued their journey toward Terre Haute.

This day President Brigham Young's father, John Young, Sen., died at Quincy, Adams County, Illinois. He was in his seventy-seventh year, and a soldier of the Revolution. He was also a firm believer in the everlast-

Death of John Young, Brigham Young's Father.

ing Gospel of Jesus Christ; and fell asleep under the influence of that faith that buoyed up his soul, in the pangs of death, to a glorious hope of immortality; fully testifying to all, that the religion he enjoyed in life was able to sup-

port him in death. He was driven from Missouri with
the Saints in the latter part of last year. He died a martyr to the religion of Jesus, for his death was caused by
his sufferings in the cruel persecution.

Sunday, 13.—I attended meeting in the grove. The
assembly was small on account of the cold weather.

Tuesday, 15.—In the afternoon I went to Quincy in
company with Brother Hyrum Smith, John S. Fullmer,
and Bishop Knight. Quite a number of families moving
into Commerce.

Thursday, 17.—The brethren arrived at Terre Haute.
Brothers Smith, Hedlock, and Turley stopped at Brother
Nahum Milton Stow's.

In the evening Doctor Modisett went down to see the
brethren, and appeared to be very much affected to see
them so sick, and having to lie upon the floor
on a straw bed that had been put into the   Hardships of
wagon at Springfield, by the brethren, for   the British
Elder Young to lie on, as he was not able   Mission.
to sit up when he left there. When the doctor returned
home, he told Elders Young and Kimball, he could not
refrain from shedding tears to see the brethren going
upon such a long mission, and in such suffering circumstances. Elders Young and Kimball said they thought
the doctor might have relieved them from "their suffering and indigent circumstances upon their long mission,"
for he told them in the course of the evening, that his
taxes in that place amounted to over four hundred dollars, besides having other property to a great amount.

Elder Kimball was very sick; he stopped with Brother
Young at Doctor Modisett's. In the evening Doctor Modisett gave Elder Kimball about forty drops of morphine,
saying it would relieve him of his distress, and probably
he would get a nap. In about fifteen minutes Brother
Kimball complained of feeling very strange; he rose
from his seat and would have fallen, but Brother Young
caught him and gently eased him to the floor, where he

lay for some time; and it was by faith and the close attention of Brother Young and the family that his life was preserved through the night.

Friday, 18.—Brothers Smith, Hedlock, and Turley went on their journey.

Saturday, 19.—The High Council appointed for the Stake of the Church in Iowa, met at Asahel Smith's, Nashville, and organized; John Smith, President; Elias Smith, Clerk; Reynolds Cahoon and Lyman Wight were chosen Counselors to President John Smith, and approved by the Council. Council organized according to number.*

Minutes of the Nauvoo High Council, 20th October, 1839.

The members of the High Council elected at the October conference, met and organized at W. D. Huntington's, where Harlow Redfield was restored to fellowship; and voted that this High Council disfellowship any and all persons that shall hereafter carry over or ferry across the river, any people or freight to the injury of said ferry from Commerce to Montrose.

Voted that the Horse Boat be repaired from the moneys received on sale of lots in Nauvoo, and that D. C. Davis be master of said ferry boat for the ensuing year.

Voted that Joseph Smith, Jun., and his family be exempt from receiving in future such crowds of visitors as have formerly thronged his house; and that the same be published in the *Times and Seasons.*

Voted, that this Council disfellowship any and all persons who shall knowingly suffer and allow any animal (subject to their control) to destroy the crops, fruit, or plants of the earth belonging to any other person or persons, and to their injury, and that this resolution be published in the *Times and Seasons.*

Adjourned until tomorrow evening.

High Council met pursuant to adojurnment, and voted that President Joseph Smith, Jun., go as a delegate to Washington; and that if he went he should have a recommend from the Council.

Voted that James Mulholland be Clerk for the land contracts, when needed by President Smith; that Joseph Smith, Jun., be treasurer of said Church, and James Mulholland sub-treasurer.

* That is to say, to quote from the revelation establishing the High Council— "Whenever an High Council of the Church is regularly organized, *   *   * it shall be the duty of the Twelve Counselors to cast lots by numbers and thereby ascertain, who of the Twelve shall speak first, commencing with number one, and so in succession to number twelve."—*Doctrine and Covenants, Section cii.*

Voted that Henry G. Sherwood should set the price upon, exhibit, contract and sell town lots in Nauvoo, when needed, and report his doings to Presidents Joseph Smith and Hyrum Smith, for their approval, and that five hundred dollars be the average price of lots, i. e., none less than two hundred dollars, nor more than eight hundred dollars.

Voted that the High Council meet every Sunday evening at Dimick Huntington's; that D. C. Davis have thirty dollars per month for his services as ferryman; and that these proceedings be published in the *Times and Seasons*.

[Signed]   HENRY G. SHERWOOD, Clerk.

Tuesday, 22.—Brother James Modisett took Elders Young and Kimball in his father's carriage and carried them twenty miles to the house of Brother Addison Pratt; from thence they were carried by Elder Almon W. Babbitt to Pleasant Garden, and put up with Brother Jonathan Crosby. Elder Almon Babbitt was preaching in that region with good success; he had baptized five.

Saturday, 26.—Brother Babbitt took Elders Young and Kimball ten miles on their way to Father Scott's.

King Follett, the last of the brethren in bonds in Missouri, had his trial and was set free some time previous to this day.

Sunday, 27.—John Scott took Elders Young and Kimball on their way fifteen miles, some part of it in the rain; they were yet very feeble, and put up at a tavern in Belville, and when the stage coach came along, took passage, and rode night and day to Willowby, near Kirtland.

The High Council of Nauvoo voted that the Clerk's fees of James Mulholland be thirty dollars per month; that the treasurer pay Vinson Knight one hundred and fifty dollars, for the Iowa side of the ferry at Montrose as per charter.

Voted, that Sister Emma Smith select and publish a hymn-book for the use of the Church, and that Brigham Young be informed of this action and he not publish the hymns taken by him from Commerce; and that the

Council assist in publishing a hymn-book and the *Times and Seasons*.

Monday, 28.—The High Council voted to build a stone house at Upper Commerce, to be used for boarding; that Elder Oliver Granger be requested to assist with funds to print the hymn-book; that Samuel Dent, Davison Hibbard, and David Dort be trustees for building the stone schoolhouse in contemplation; and that Alpheus Cutler and Jabez Durphy be the architects and building committee for said house.

Voted, to finish the office of President Joseph Smith, Jun.

Voted, that the recommends drawn by Elder Sherwood, recommending, constituting, and appointing Joseph Smith, Jun., Sidney Rigdon, and Elias Higbee, delegates for the Church, to importune the President and Congress of the United States for redress of grievances, be signed by this Council.

CHAPTER II.

THE PROPHET'S JOURNEY TO WASHINGTON—THE PETITION
OF THE SANTS TO THE CONGRESS OF THE UNITED STATES
FOR REDRESS OF THE WRONGS INFLICTED UPON THEM IN
MISSOURI.

Tuesday, 29.—I left Nauvoo accompanied by Sidney Rigdon, Elias Higbee, and Orrin P. Rockwell, in a two-horse carriage for the city of Washington, to lay before the Congress of the United States, the grievances of the Saints while in Missouri. We passed through Carthage, and stayed at Judge Higbee's over night, and the next day we arrived at Quincy.

Departure of the Prophet for Washington.

Thursday, 31.—We tarried at Quincy to complete the necessary papers for our mission. Elder Rigdon was sick.

Friday, November 1.—We pursued our journey towards Springfield, Illinois, and put up with Brother Wilber, where we found Doctor Robert D. Foster, who administered to Elder Rigdon.

Saturday, 2.—Continued our journey, and during the day put up with a friend on the bank of the Illinois river, so that Dr. Foster, who had accompanied us so far for that purpose, might administer medicine to Elder Rigdon again.

Sunday, 3.—Continued our journey and staid with a friend over night. Dr. Foster continued to accompany us.

Elders Young and Kimball arrived at Cleveland, Ohio,

about 1 o'clock in the morning; and while waiting for the stage until about noon, Elders Smith, Turley, and Hedlock, who left them at Terre Haute, drove up, having picked up Elder Taylor by the way, he having been left sick by his company in the east part of Indiana. They were in good health, compared with what they had been, and in fine spirits. George A. Smith tarried in Cleveland till the next day, to visit his relatives. Brothers Young, Kimball, Taylor, and Turley rode in the stage, and Brother Hedlock and Mr. Murray in their wagon to Willoughby, and from thence they all rode into Kirtland together.

Progress of the Twelve towards England.

Monday, 4.—We arrived at Springfield, and put up with Brother John Snider. When within one mile of the city, we met William Law* and company with seven wagons from Canada, who returned with us to Springfield, and tarried while we did, until the 8th. I preached several times while here. General James Adams,† judge of probate, heard of me, sought me out, and took me home with him, and treated me like a father.

Canadian Saints En Route for Nauvoo.

President Brigham Young and his brother John visited their sister, Mrs. Kent.

There was some division of sentiment among the Kirtland brethren.

---

* William Law was born September 8th, 1809, and was converted to the gospel through the preaching of Elder John Taylor and Almon W. Babbitt. He lived in Canada some twenty-five miles south of Toronto, and was now leading a company of Saints from Canada to Nauvoo.

† Concerning the antecedent of James Adams nothing can be learned from our Church annals. This is unfortunate, since he was truly a noble character, and remained until his death (1843) a most faithful friend of the Prophet's. In a book of Patriarchal blessings, given by Hyrum Smith, is recorded a blessing upon the head of a James Adams, who in every way would be such a man as the James Adams mentioned in the text—I mean as to age, and character indicated in the blessing. This James Adams of the blessing, and who I am personally convinced was the Prophet's friend of the text, was the son of Parmenio and Chloe Adams, born at Limsbury Township, Hartford county, Connecticut. 24th of January, 1783. He is declared by the Patriarch to be of the tribe of Judah. The blesssing was given the 2nd October, 1841.

Thursday, 7.—The High Council of Iowa completed their organization at Elijah Fordham's, at Montrose.

Friday, 8.—We started from Springfield. Dr. Foster having concluded to continue on the journey on account of Elder Rigdon's health, which was still quite poor. We pursued our journey through Indiana towards Columbus, Ohio. The traveling was bad, and our progress slow.

Sunday, 10.—Elder Taylor preached in the forenoon, and Elder Kimball in the afternoon, in the House of the Lord at Kirtland.

Thursday, 14.—Elder Orson Hyde left Commerce, Illinois, intending to go east as far as Philadelphia. He had just begun to recover from a four months' illness of fever and ague.

Sunday, 17.—President Young preached in the House of the Lord in the forenoon, and John Taylor in the afternoon. In the evening, President Brigham Young anointed Elder John Taylor in the House of the Lord, and Elder Daniel S. Miles anointed Theodore Turley, all of which was sealed with the shout of Hosanna.

Elder Taylor Anointed in the Kirtland Temple.

Monday, 18.—President Young visited Brother R. Potter at Newbury, and returned on Tuesday to Kirtland.

About this time we had arrived near Columbus, where the roads were so bad, Elder Rigdon's health so poor, and the time so fast approaching when it was necessary for the committee to be in Washington, that I started in the stage with Judge Higbee on the most expeditious route to Washington City, leaving Brothers Rockwell, Rigdon, and Foster, to come on at their leisure in the carriage.

Elder Brigham Young and company went to Fairport, where they waited for a steamboat until Tuesday.

Elder Parley P. Pratt and company sold their horses and carriage at Detroit, and went on to New York City by steamboats, the canal and railway.

From New York, Elder Parley P. Pratt wrote me on

the 22nd, directed to Commerce, from which I quote the following:

Excerpt from Parley P. Pratt's Letter to the Prophet.

The churches in these parts are prospering greatly, and are firm in the faith, and increasing in numbers continually. The Church in New York and Brooklyn now numbers from one hundred and fifty to two hundred members, and additions are being made every week. A general conference was held in this city on Tuesday and Wednesday of this week. Elders present: Orson Pratt, Wilford Woodruff, Samuel James, Benjamin Winchester, Elders Foster, Layne, Jenks, Brown, Benedict, and myself. Priests present: Addison Everett, Birge, and Vanvelver. Many branches of the Church in the region round about were represented; several hundred members in all, and the numbers still increasing. Great opportunities are open for preaching, and crowded houses are the order of the day.

I have also received letters from Maine and from Michigan, with joyful accounts of the spread of the work of the Lord. You would now find churches of the Saints in Philadelphia, in Albany, in Brooklyn, in New York, in Jersey, in Pennsylvania, on Long Island, and in various other places all around us. Our New York meetings are now held three times every Sabbath in Columbia Hall, Grand Street, a few doors east of the Bowery; it is very central, and one of the best places in the city; it will hold nearly a thousand people, and is well filled with attentive hearers. Brother Winchester has a good hall well fitted up in Philadelphia, where stated meetings are held—several every week, with crowded audiences.

In short the truth is spreading more rapidly than ever before, in every direction, far and near. There is a great call for our books. I am now reprinting the Voice of Warning, The History of the Missouri Persecution, and my Poems. There is a great call for hymn-books, but none to be had. I wish Sister Smith would add to the old collection such new ones as is best, and republish them immediately. If means and facilities are lacking in the west, send it here, and it shall be nicely done for her; and at least one thousand would immediately sell in these parts wholesale and retail. The Book of Mormon is not to be had in this part of the vineyard for love or money; hundreds are wanting in various parts hereabouts, but there is truly a famine in that respect.

The conference took into consideration the pressing calls for this book, and have appointed a committee to raise means for the publication of the same, and also to publish it if we can obtain leave from you, who hold the copyright. Any hymn-book which Sister Smith or the Church will favor us with, shall also be published on similar conditions.

PARLEY P. PRATT.

Some time this month the first number of the *Times and Seasons*, a monthly religious paper, in pamphlet form, was published at Commerce, Hancock County, Illinois, by my brother Don Carlos Smith and Ebenezer Robinson, under the firm name of Robinson & Smith, Publishers.

First Issue of the "Times and Seasons"

Tuesday, 26.—At one in the afternoon, Elder Brigham Young and company went on board the steamer *Columbus*, at Fairport, and went on towards Buffalo.

Wednesday, 27.—About 1 o'clock this morning the wind arose, when Elder Brigham Young went on deck, prayed to the Father in the name of Jesus, when he felt to command the wind and the waves to cease, and permit them to proceed on their journey in safety. The winds abated, and he gave glory, honor, and praise to the God who rules all things. Arriving in Buffalo in the morning, they took the stage for Batavia.

The Elements Obey.

While on the mountains some distance from Washington, our coachman stepped into a public house to take his grog, when the horses took fright and ran down the hill at full speed. I persuaded my fellow travelers to be quiet and retain their seats, but had to hold one woman to prevent her throwing her infant out of the coach. The passengers were exceedingly agitated, but I used every persuasion to calm their feelings; and opening the door, I secured my hold on the side of the coach the best way I could, and succeeded in placing myself in the coachman's seat, and reining up the horses, after they had run some two or three miles, and neither coach, horses, or passengers received any injury. My course was spoken of in the highest terms of commendation, as being one of the most daring and heroic deeds, and no language could express the gratitude of the passengers, when they found themselves safe, and the horses quiet. There were some members of Congress with us, who proposed naming the incident to that body, believing they would reward such

The Prophet's Adventure En Route to Washington.

conduct by some public act; but on inquiring my name, to mention as the author of their safety, and finding it to be Joseph Smith the "Mormon Prophet," as they called me, I heard no more of their praise, gratitude, or reward.

Thursday, 28.—I arrived in Washington City this morning, and put up at the corner of Missouri and Third streets.

This evening, Elder Brigham Young and company (except Elder Kimball, who stopped at Byron to visit his sister) rode to Rochester in the steam cars, and from thence rode all night in a horse coach, and arrived at ten in the morning on Friday, 29th, at Auburn, New York. Elders Taylor and Turley proceeded on their way to New York.

The following is a copy of our petition to Congress for redress of our Missouri grievances:

THE SAINT'S PETITION TO CONGRESS.

To the Honorable the Senate aud House of Representatives of the United States of America, in Congress assembled:

Your petitioners, Joseph Smith, Sidney Rigdon, and Elias Higbee, would most respectfully represent, that they have been delegated, by their brethren and fellow-citizens, known as "Latter-day Saints" (commonly called Mormons), to prepare and present to you a statement of their wrongs, and a prayer for their relief, which they now have the honor to submit to the consideration of your Honorable Body.

In the summer of 1831, a portion of the society above-named commenced a settlement in the county of Jackson, in the state of Missouri. The individuals making that settlement had emigrated from almost every state in the Union to the lovely spot in the Far West, with the hope of improving their condition, of building houses for themselves and posterity, and of erecting temples, where they and theirs might worship their Creator according to the dictates of their conscience. Though they had wandered far from the homes of their childhood, still they had been taught to believe, that a citizen born in any one state in this great Republic, might remove to another and enjoy all the rights and immunities of citizens of the state of his adoption—that wherever waved the American flag, beneath its stars and stripes an American citizen might look for protection and justice, for liberty in person and in conscience.

They bought farms, built houses, and erected churches. Some tilled the earth, others bought and sold merchandise, and others again toiled as mechanics. They were industrious and moral, and they prospered, and though often persecuted and vilified for their difference in religious opinion from their fellow citizens, they were happy; they saw their society increasing in numbers, their farms teemed with plenty, and they fondly looked forward to a future, big with hope. That there was prejudice against them, they knew; that slanders were propagated against them, they deplored; yet they felt that these were unjust; and hoped that time, and uprightness of life, would enable them to outlive them. While the summer of peace, happiness, and hope shone over the infant settlement of the Saints, the cloud was gathering, unseen by them, that bore in its bosom the thunderbolt of destruction.

On the 20th of July, 1833, around their peaceful village a mob gathered, to the surprise and terror of the quiet "Mormons"—why, they knew not; they had broken no law, they had harmed no man, in deed or thought. Why they were thus threatened, they knew not. Soon a committee from the mob called upon the leading "Mormons" of the place; they announced that the store, the printing office, and the shops must be closed, and that forthwith every "Mormon" must leave the county. The message was so terrible, so unexpected, that the "Mormons" asked time for deliberation and consultation, which being refused, the brethren were severally asked, "Are you willing to abandon your home?" The reply was, "We will not go;" which determination being reported to the committee of the mob, one of them replied that he was sorry, for said he, "The work of destruction must now begin." No sooner said than it was done. The printing office, a two story brick building, was assailed by the mob and torn down, and, with its valuable appurtenances, destroyed. They next proceeded to the store with a like purpose. Its owner in part, Mr. Gilbert, agreed to close it, and they delayed their purpose.

They then proceeded to the dwelling of Mr. Partridge, the beloved Bishop of the Church there, dragged him and his family to the public square, where, surrounded by hundreds, they partly stripped him of his clothing, and tarred and feathered him from head to foot. A man by the name of Allen was at the same time treated in a similar manner. The mob then dispersed with an agreement to meet again on the next Tuesday, the above outrages having been committed on Saturday.

Tuesday came, and with it came the mob, bearing a red flag, in token of *blood*. They proceeded to the houses of Isaac Morley, and others of the leading men, and seized them, telling them to bid their families farewell, that they would never see them again. They were then driven at the point of the bayonet to the jail, and there, amid the jeers and insults of the crowd, they were thrust into prison, to be kept as hostages; in case any of the mob should be killed, they were to die to pay for it. Here some two or three of the "Mormons" offered to surrender up their lives, if that would satisfy the fury of the mob, and purchase peace and security for their unoffending brethren, their helpless wives and children.   The reply of the mob was, that the "Mormons" must leave the county *en masse*, or that every man should be put to death.

The "Mormons," terrified and defenseless, then entered into an agreement to leave the county—one half by the first of January, the other half by the first of April next ensuing.   This treaty being made and ratified, the mob dispersed.   Again, for a time, the persecuted "Mormons" enjoyed a respite from their persecutions; but not long was the repose permitted them.

Some time in the month of October, a meeting was held at Independence, at which it was determined to remove the "Mormons" or die. Inflammatory speeches were made, and one of the speakers swore he would remove the "Mormons" from the county if he had to wade up to his neck in blood.

Be it remarked that up to this time, the "Mormons" had faithfully observed the treaty, and were guilty of no offense against the laws of the land, or of society, but were peaceably following the routine of their daily duties.

Shortly after the meeting above referred to, another persecution commenced; some of the "Mormons" were shot at, others were whipped, their houses were assailed with brickbats, broken open, and thrown down; their women and children were insulted; and thus for many weeks, without offense, without resistance, by night and by day, were they harassed, insulted, and oppressed.

There is a point beyond which endurance ceases to be a virtue.   The worm when trampled upon will turn upon its oppressor.   A company of about thirty "Mormons" fell in with twice that number of the mob engaged in the destruction of "Mormon" property, when a battle ensued, in which one "Mormon" was killed, and two or three of the mob; acting in concert with the officer who commanded the mob, was Lilburn W. Boggs, Lieutenant-Governor of the state of Missouri.   When the noise of the battle was spread abroad, the public mind became much inflamed.   The militia collected in arms from all quarters, and in great numbers, inflamed to fury.   They demanded that the "Mormons" should surrender up all their arms, and immediately quit the county. Compelled by overpowering numbers, the "Mormons" submitted. They surrendered up fifty-one guns, which have never been returned, or paid for.

The next day, parties of the mob went from house to house, threatening women and children with death, if they did not immediately leave their homes. Imagination cannot paint the terror which now pervaded the "Mormon" community. The weather was intensely cold, and women and children abandoned their homes and fled in every direction without sufficient clothing to protect them from the piercing cold. Women gave birth to children in the woods and on the prairies.   One hundred and twenty women and children, for the space of ten days, with only three or four men in the company, concealed themselves in the woods in hourly expectation and fear of massacre, until they finally escaped into Clay county.   The society of "Mormons" after the above disturbances, removed to the county of Clay, where they were kindly received by the inhabitants, and their wants administered to by their charity.

In the meantime the houses of the "Mormons" in the county of Jackson, amounting to about two hundred, were burned down or otherwise destroyed by the mob, as well as much of their crops, furniture, and stock.

The damage done to the property of the "Mormons" by the mob in the county of Jackson as above related, as near as they can ascertain, would amount to the sum of one hundred and seventy-five thousand dollars.   The number of "Mormons" thus driven from the county of Jackson amounted to about twelve hundred souls. For the property thus destroyed they have never been paid.

After the expulsion of the "Mormons" from the county of Jackson as above related, they removed to and settled in the county of Clay. They there purchased out some of the former inhabitants, and entered at the land office wild lands offered for sale by the General Government. The most of them became freeholders, owning each an eighty or more of land.

The "Mormons" lived peaceably in the county of Clay for about three years, and all that time increased rapidly in numbers, by emigration, and also in wealth by their industry.   After they had resided in that county about three years, the citizens not connected with them began to look upon them with jealousy and alarm.   Reports were again put in circulation against them: public meetings were held in the counties of Clay and Jackson, at which violent resolutions were passed against the "Mormons," and rumors of mobs began again to spread alarm among the "Mormons."   At this juncture the "Mormons" desirous of avoiding all conflict with their fellow-citizens, and anxious to preserve the peace and harmony of the society around them, as well as their own, deputized a committee of their leading men to make terms of peace with their fellow-citizens of Clay county.   An interview took place between them and a committee of citizens, at which it was agreed that the "Mormons" should leave the county of Clay, and that the citizens of Clay county should buy their lands.

These terms were complied with. The "Mormons" removed to and settled in the county of Caldwell, and the citizens never paid them value for their lands. Many received nothing at all for their land. The "Mormons," by this removal, sacrificed much both of money and feeling, but the sacrifice was made upon the altar of duty, for the peace of the community.

Your Memorialists would beg here to give what they believe a just explanation of the causes of the prejudice and persecution against the "Mormons" related above, and which will follow. That there might have been some unworthy members among them, cannot be denied; but many aver that as a community they were as moral, as upright, and as observant of the laws of the land as any body of people in the world. Why then this prejudice and persecution? An answer they trust will be found in the fact that they were a body of people distinct from their fellow-citizens, in religious opinions, in their habits, and in their associations. They were numerous enough to make the power of their numerical and moral force a matter of anxiety and dread to the political and religious parties by which they were surrounded; which arose not from what the "Mormons" had done, but from the fear of what they might do.

In addition, the "Mormons" have purchased of the settlers, or of the Government, or obtained by pre-emption, the best lands in all those regions of the state; and at the times of speculation, the cupidity of many was aroused to possess those lands by driving off the "Mormons," and taking forcible possession, or constraining them to sell, through fear and coercion, at a price merely nominal.

After the "Mormons" removed from Clay county, they settled in the county of Caldwell as aforesaid.

Your Memorialists do not deem it necessary for their purpose, to detail the history of the progress, the cares, and anxieties of the "Mormons," from the time they settled in Caldwell in the year 1836 until the fall of the year 1838. They would, however, state, that during all that time they deported themselves as good citizens, obeying the laws of the land, and the moral and religious duties enjoined by their faith. That there might have been some faithless among the faithful is possible. They would not deny that there might have been some who were a scandal to their brethren; and what society, they would ask, has not some unworthy members? Where is the sect, where the community, in which there cannot be found some who trample under foot the laws of God and man? They believe the "Mormon" community to have as few such as any other association, religious or political. Within the above period the "Mormons" continued to increase in wealth and numbers, until in the fall of the year 1838 they numbered about fifteen thousand souls.

They purchased of the Government, or of the citizens, or held by pre-emption, almost all the lands in the county of Caldwell, and a portion of the lands in Daviess and Carroll. The county of Caldwell was set-tled almost entirely by "Mormons," and "Mormons" were rapidly fill-ing up the counties of Daviess and Caldwell. When they first com-menced settling in those counties, there were but few settlements made there; the lands were wild and uncultivated. In the fall of 1838 large farms had been made, well improved and stocked. Lands had risen in value, and sold for from ten dollars to twenty-five dollars [per acre]. The improvement and settlement had been such that it was a common re-mark that the county of Caldwell would soon be the wealthiest in the state.

Thus stood their affairs in the fall of 1838, when the storm of persecu-tion again raged over the heads of the "Mormons," and the fierce demon of the mob drove them forth houseless and homeless, and penni-less, upon the charities of the world, which to them, thank God! have been like angels' visits, but not few, or far between. This last persecu-tion began at an election, which was held in Daviess county on the first Monday of August, 1838. A "Mormon" went to the polls to vote. One of the mob standing by, opposed his voting, contending that a "Mor-mon" had no more right to vote than a negro; one angry word brought on another, and blows followed. They are, however, happy to state that the "Mormon" was not the aggressor, but was on the defensive; others interfered, not one alone, but many assailed the "Mormon." His brethren, seeing him thus assailed by numbers, rushed to the rescue; then came others of the mob, until finally a general row com-menced. The "Mormons" were victorious. The next day, a rumor reached the "Mormons" of Caldwell, that two of their brethren had been killed in this fight, and a refusal had been made to surrender their bodies for burial. Not knowing at the time that this rumor was false, they became much excited, and several of them started for Daviess county, where they arrived next morning, with a view of giving the brethren, whom they supposed to have been killed, a decent interment. Among the citizens this fight produced a great excitement. They held a public meeting and resolved to drive the "Mormons" from the county. Individuals began also to threaten the "Mormons" as a body, and swear that they should leave the county in three days. When the "Mormons" who had gone from Caldwell to Daviess, aforesaid, arrived there, they found this state of excitement to exist. They also heard that a large mob was collecting against them, headed by Adam Black one of the judges of the county court of Daviess county.

Under these circumstances, and with a view to allay the excitement, they called on Mr. Black, and inquired of him whether the reports they had heard in relation to him were true. Upon his denying them to be true, they then requested him to give that denial in writing, which he freely did. This writing they published with a view of calming the public mind, and allaying the excitement. Having done this, they rested in quiet for some time after, hoping that their efforts would produce the desired effect. Their surprise can, under these circumstances, be easily imagined, when a short time after, they learned that said Black had gone before Judge King, and made oath that he was forced to sign the instrument, by armed "Mormons," and procured a warrant for the arrest of Joseph Smith, Jun., and Lyman Wight, which was placed in the hands of the sheriff. It was also reported that the said individuals had refused to surrender themselves, and that an armed force was collecting to come and take them.

Your Memorialists aver that the sheriff had never made any efforts to serve the writ, and that the said Smith and Wight, so far from making any resistance, did not know that such a writ had been issued, until they learned it first by report as above related. In the meantime the rumor had run over the whole country, that the "Mormons" were compelling individuals to sign certain instruments in writing, and that they were resisting the process of the law. The public mind became much inflamed, and the mob began to collect from all quarters and in large numbers, with pretensions of assisting the sheriff to serve the process; and here let it be observed in passing, that Adam Black had sold the improvement and pre-emption claim on which he then resided, to the "Mormons," received his pay for the same, and that through his instrumentality the "Mormons" were driven off, and he now retains both their money and the improvement.

As soon as the above reports reached the ears of the said Smith and Wight, they determined immediately upon the course they ought to pursue, which was to submit to the laws. They both surrendered themselves up to Judge King, underwent a trial, and in the absence of all sufficient testimony they were discharged. They hoped that this voluntary submission of theirs to the law, and their triumphant vindication of the charge, would allay the excitement of the community. But not so; the long-desired opportunity had arrived when the oppression and extermination of the "Mormons" might be made to assume the form of legal proceeding. The mob that had assembled for the pretended purpose of assisting the officers in the execution of process, did not disperse upon the acquittal of Smith and Wight, but continued embodied with the encampments and forms of a military force, and committing depredations upon "Mormon" property. The "Mormons" in this extremity called upon the laws of the land, and the officers of the law, for protection. After much delay, the militia under Generals Atchison, Doniphan, and Parks, were sent to their relief. They arrived on the 13th of September, and encamped between the "Mormons and the mob.

The above officers made no attempt to disperse the mob, excusing themselves by saying, "that their own men had sympathies with the mob." After remaining there for several days, those officers adopted the following expedient of settling the difficulties—they mustered the mob, and enrolled them with their own troops, and then disbanded the whole, with orders to seek their several homes. The officers went home, excepting Parks, who remained for their protection, with his men.

The "Mormons" made an agreement with the citizens of Daviess, to buy out their lands and pre-emption rights, and appointed a committee to make the purchase, and to go on buying till they had purchased to the amount of twenty-five thousand dollars. While these purchases were going on, the citizens were heard to say, that as soon as they had sold out to the "Mormons" and received their pay, they would drive the "Mormons" off, and keep both their lands and the money.

The mob, when disbanded in Daviess by the generals as aforesaid, instead of repairing to their homes as commanded, proceeded in a body to the adjoining county of Carroll, and encamped around Dewitt, a village built and inhabited by "Mormons;" while thus encamped around Dewitt, they sent to the county of Jackson, and procured a cannon. They invested the place so closely, that no person could leave the town in safety; when they did so, they were fired upon by the mob. The horses of the "Mormons" were stolen, and their cattle killed. The citizens of Dewitt, amounting to about seventy families, were in great extremity, and worn out by want and sickness. In their extremity they made application to Governor Boggs for protection and relief; but no protection, no relief was granted them. When reduced to the last extremity, no alternative was left them, but to seek protection by flight, and the abandonment of their homes. Accordingly, on the evening of the 11th of October, 1838, they retreated from Dewitt, and made their way to the counties of Daviess and Caldwell, leaving many of their effects in the possession of the mob.

Your Memorialists will not detail the horrors and sufferings of such a flight, when shared with women and children. They might detail many. One lady, who had given birth to a child just before the flight commenced, died on the road and was buried without a coffin. Many others, sick, worn out, starved, deprived of medical aid, died upon the road. The remnant of "Mormons" from Dewitt arrived in Daviess and Caldwell, and found a short relief and supply of their wants from their friends and brethren there.

After the abandonment of Dewitt, and the flight of the "Mormons" from Carroll, one Sashiel Woods addressed the mob, advising them to take their cannon and march to the county of Daviess, and drive the "Mormons" from that county, and seize upon their lands and other property, saying that the "Mormons" could get no benefit of the law, as they had recently seen. They then commenced their march from Carroll to Daviess, carrying with them the cannon which they had received from Jackson. On their way they captured two 'Mormons," made them ride on the cannon, and taunted them as they went along, telling them that they were going to drive the "Mormons" from Daviess to Caldwell, and from Caldwell to hell; and that they should find no quarters but at the cannon's mouth. The mob at this time was reported to number about four hundred strong.

The "Mormons" in these distresses, in pursuance of the laws of Missouri, made application to Judge King, the circuit judge of that circuit, for protection, and for the aid of the officers of the law to protect them. Judge King, as they have been informed, and believe, gave an order to Major General David R. Atchison to call out the militia to protect the "Mormons" against the fury of the mob. General Atchison thereupon gave orders to Brigadiers Parks and Doniphan. In pursuance of these orders issued as aforesaid, on the 18th of October, 1838, General Doniphan arrived at Far West, a "Mormon" village in the county of Caldwell, with a small company of militia. After he had been at Far West two days, General Doniphan disbanded his company, alleging to the "Mormons," as his reason for so doing, that his company had the same feelings as the mob, and that he could not rely upon them. In a short time General Parks arrived at Far West, and also disbanded his company. At this time the mob was marching from Carroll to Daviess. General Doniphan, while at Far West, directed the "Mormons" to raise a company to protect themselves, telling them that one Cornelius Gilliam was raising a mob to destroy their town, and also advising them to place out guards to watch the motions of the mob. He also directed them to raise a company and send them to Daviess, to aid their brethren there against the mob which was marching down upon them from Carroll. This the "Mormons" did; they mustered a company of about sixty men, who proceeded to Diahman. When General Parks arrived at Far West as aforesaid, and learned that General Doniphan had disbanded his men he expressed great dissatisfaction. The same evening on which General Parks disbanded his company as aforesaid, he proceeded to Diahman, in order to learn what the mob were doing there, and if possible to protect the "Mormons."

When General Parks had arrived in Daviess, he found that the mob had commenced its operations there, which was on the 20th of October, 1838.

They commenced by burning the house of a man [Don Carlos Smith] who had gone to Tennessee on business, and left his wife at home with two small children. When the house was burned down, the wife and two small children were left in the snow, and she had to walk three miles before she could find a shelter, carrying her two children all that distance, and had to wade Grand River, which was three feet deep. The mob on the same evening burned seven other houses, burning and destroying all the property that they thought proper. The next morning, Colonel Lyman Wight, an officer in the militia, inquired of General Parks, what was to be done, as he now saw the course the mob was determined to pursue. General Parks replied that he (Wight) should take a company of men and give the mob battle, and that he would be responsible for the act, saying that they could have no peace with the mob, until they had given them a scourging.

On the next morning, in obedience to this order, David W. Patten was despatched with one hundred men under his command to meet the mob as they were advancing from Carroll, with directions to protect the citizens, and collect and bring into Far West such of the "Mormons" as were scattered through the county, and unprotected, and if the mob interfered, he must fight them. The company under the command of Patten was the same, in part, that had gone from Far West by the order of General Doniphan to protect the citizens of Daviess. As Patten went in the direction of the mob, they fled before him, leaving their cannon, which Patten took possession of. The mob dispered. Patten with his men then returned to Daviess county. Patten in a few days after returned to Far West. It was now supposed that the difficulties were at an end. But contrary to expectation, on the evening of the 23rd of October, messengers arrived at Far West and informed the citizens that a body of armed men had made their appearance in the south part of the county, and that they were burning houses, destroying property, and threatening the "Mormon" citizens with death, unless they left the county the next morning by 10 o'clock, or renounced their religion.

About midnight another messenger arrived with news of the like tenor. Patten collected about sixty men and proceeded to the scene of the disturbance, to protect if possible the lives and property of the "Mormon" citizens. On his arrival at the neighborhood where the first disturbance had commenced, he found that the mob had gone to another neighborhood to prosecute their acts of plunder and outrage. He marched a short distance and unexpectedly came upon the encampment of the mob. The guards of the mob fired upon him and killed one of his men. Patten then charged the mob, and after a few fires, the mob dispersed and fled, but Patten was killed and another of his men.   After the fight and dispersion of the mob, Patten's company returned to Far West.   The report of the proceedings created much excitement.   The community was made to believe that the "Mormons" were in rebellion against the law; whereas the above facts show they were an injured people, standing up in the defense of their persons and their property.

At this time the governor of the state issued an order to General Clark to raise several thousand men and march against the "Mormons," and drive them from the state, or "exterminate them."   Major-General Lucas and Brigadier-General Wilson collected three or four thousand men; and with this formidable force, commenced their march and arrived at Far West.   In their rear marched General Clark with another formidable force.

In the meantime the "Mormons" had not heard of these immense preparations, and so far from expecting an armed force under the orders of the state to war against them, were daily expecting a force from the governor to protect their lives and their property from the mob.

When this formidable array first made its appearance, intent upon peace, the "Mormons sent a white flag several miles to meet them, to ascertain the reason why an armed force was marching against them, and what we might expect at their hands.   They gave us no satisfaction, but continued marching towards Far West.   Immediately on their arrival, a man came bearing a white flag from their camp.   He was interrogated about his business; he answered the interrogations, saying they wanted three persons out of Far West, before they massacred the rest.   Those persons refused to go, and he returned back to the camp. He was closely followed by General Doniphan and his whole brigade marching to the city of Far West in line of battle.   The citizens also of Far West formed a line of battle in full front of Doniphan's army: upon this Doniphan ordered a halt, and then a retreat.   Night closed upon both parties without any collision.

On the next day, towards evening, the "Mormons" were officially informed that the governor of the state had sent this immense force against them to massacre them, or drive them from the state.   As soon as the "Mormons" learned that this order had the sanction of the governor of the state, they determined to make no resistance; to submit themselves to the authorities of the state, how tyrannical and unjust soever the exercise of that authority might be.

The commanders of the Missouri militia before Far West sent a messenger into the town, requesting an interview in their camp with five of the principal citizens among the "Mormons," pledging their faith for their safe return on the following morning at eight o'clock.   Invited, as they supposed, to propose and receive terms of peace, and under the pledge of a safe conduct, Lyman Wight, George W. Robinson, Joseph Smith, Jun., Parley P. Pratt, and Sidney Rigdon, went towards the camp of the militia. Before they arrived at the camp, they were surrounded by the whole army; and by order of General Lucas put under guard, and marched to the camp, and were told that they were prisoners of war. A court martial was held that night, and they, without being heard, and in the absence of all proof, were condemned to be shot next morning.

The execution of this bloody order, was prevented by the manly protest of General Doniphan. He denounced the act as cold blooded murder, and withdrew his brigade. This noble stand taken by General Doniphan, prevented the murder of the prisoners. It is here worthy of note, that seventeen preachers of the gospel were on this court martial, and were in favor of the sentence.

The next morning the prisoners were marched under a strong guard to Independence, in Jackson county, and after being detained there for a week, they were marched to Richmond, where General Clark then was with his troops. Here a court of inquiry was held before Judge King; this continued from the 11th until the 28th of November; while the five prisoners were kept in chains, and about fifty other "Mormons," taken at Far West, were penned up in an open, unfinished court house. In this mock court of inquiry the defendants were prevented from giving any testimony on their part, by an armed force at the court house; they were advised by their lawyers not to bring any [witnesses], as they would be in danger of their lives, or be driven out of the county; so there was no testimony examined only against them.

In this inquiry a great many questions were asked relative to religious opinions.* The conclusion of the court of inquiry was to send the prisoners to jail upon a charge of treason.

They do not deem it necessary to detail their sufferings while in prison, the horrors of a prison for four long months, in darkness, in want, alone, and during the cold of winter, can better be conceived than expressed. In the following April the prisoners were sent to the county of Daviess for trial; they were then indicted for treason, and a change of venue was taken to Boone county. The prisoners were sent to the county of Boone, and while on their way made their escape, and fled to the state of Illinois.

That they were suffered to escape admits of no doubt. The truth is, the state of Missouri had become ashamed of their proceedings against the "Mormons," and as the best means of getting out of the scrape, gave the prisoners an opportunity to escape. In proof of this, the prisoners have ever since been living publicly in the state of Illinois,

* See Vol. III., page 212.

and the executive of Missouri has made no demand upon the executive of Illinois. Can it be supposed that the people of Missouri would thus tamely submit to the commission of treason by a portion of their citizens, and make no effort to punish the guilty, when they were thus publicly living in an adjoining state? Is not this passiveness evidence? They knew the "Mormons" were innocent, and the citizens of Missouri wrong?

But to return to the operations of General Lucas before Far West: We need only say that the exterminating order of Governor Boggs was carried into full effect. After the above-named individuals were taken prisoners, all the "Mormons" in Far West, about five hundred in number, surrendered up their arms to the militia without any resistance. The "Mormons" now fled in every direction—women and children, through the dead of winter, marked their footsteps with blood, as they fled from the state of Missouri.

The orders of the governor were, that they should be driven from the state or destroyed. About fifteen thousand souls, between the sacking of Far West and spring, abandoned their homes, their property, their all, hurried by the terrors of their armed pursuers, in want of every necessary of life, with bleeding hearts sought refuge in the state of Illinois, where they now reside.

We cannot trespass upon your time by the relation of cases of individual suffering; they would fill a volume. We forbear for our regard to humanity, to detail the particulars of the conduct of the Missouri militia. We could relate instances of house-burnings, destruction of property, robbings, rapes, and murder, that would shame humanity. One instance as a sample of many scenes which they enacted: Two hundred of the militia came suddenly upon some "Mormon" families emigrating to the state, and then encamped at Haun's mill in Caldwell county. The "Mormon" men and children took refuge in an old log house which had been used as a blacksmith's shop. On seeing the militia approach, the "Mormons" cried for quarters, but in vain; they were instantly fired upon; eighteen fell dead; and their murderers, putting the muzzle of their guns between the logs, fired indiscriminately upon children, upon the dead and dying. One little boy, whose father (Warren Smith) had just been shot dead, cried piteously to the militia to spare his life. The reply was, "Kill him, kill him (with an oath), he is a son of a damned Mormon." At this they shot his head all open, and left him dead by the side of his father. About the same time an old man by the name of McBride, a soldier of the Revolution, came up to them and begged his life; but they hewed him to pieces with an old corn cutter. They then loaded themselves with plunder and departed.

Your petitioners have thus given a brief outline of the history of the

"Mormon" persecutions in Missouri—all which they can prove to be true, if an opportunity be given them.   It will be seen from this their brief statement, that neither the "Mormons" as a body, nor individuals of that body, have been guilty of any offense against the laws of Missouri, or of the United States; but their only offense has been their religious opinion.

The above statement will also show, that the "Mormons" on all occasions submitted to the law of the land, and yielded to its authority in every extremity, and at every hazard, at the risk of life and property. The above statement will illustrate another truth: that wherever the "Mormons" made any resistance to the mob, it was in self defense; and for these acts of self defense they always had the authority and sanction of the officers of the law for so doing. Yet they, to the number of about fifteen thousand souls, have been driven from their homes in Missouri. Their property, to the amount of two millions of dollars, has been taken from them, or destroyed. Some of them have been murdered, beaten, bruised, or lamed and have all been driven forth, wandering over the world without homes, without property.

But the loss of property does not comprise half their sufferings. They were human beings, possessed of human feelings and human sympathies. Their agony of soul was the bitterest drop in the cup of their sorrows.

For these wrongs, the "Mormons" ought to have some redress; yet how and where shall they seek and obtain it? Your constitution guarantees to every citizen, even the humblest, the enjoyment of life, liberty, and property. It promises to all, religious freedom, the right to all to worship God beneath their own vine and fig tree, according to the dictates of their conscience. It guarantees to all the citizens of the several states the right to become citizens of any one of the states, and to enjoy all the rights and immunities of the citizens of the state of his adoption. Yet of all these rights have the "Mormons" been deprived. They have, without a cause, without a trial, been deprived of life, liberty and property. They have been persecuted for their religious opinions. They have been driven from the state of Missouri, at the point of the bayonet, and prevented from enjoying and exercising the rights of citizens of the state of Missouri. It is the theory of our laws, that for the protection of every legal right, there is provided a legal remedy. What, then, we would respectfully ask, is the remedy of the "Mormons?" Shall they apply to the legislature of the state of Missouri for redress? They have done so. They have petitioned, and these petitions have been treated with silence and contempt. Shall they apply to the federal courts? They were, at the time of the injury, citizens of the state of Missouri. Shall they apply to the court of the state of Missouri? Whom shall they sue? The order for their destruction, then extermination, was granted by the executive of the state of Missouri. Is not this a plea of justification for the loss of individuals, done in pursuance of that order? If not, before whom shall the "Mormons" institute a trial? Shall they summon a jury of the individuals who composed the mob? An appeal to them were in vain. They dare not go to Missouri to institute a suit; their lives would be in danger.

For ourselves we see no redress, unless it is awarded by the Congress of the United States. And here we make our appeal as *American Citizens*, as *Christians*, and as *Men*—believing that the high sense of justice which exists in your honorable body, will not allow such oppression to be practiced upon any portion of the citizens of this vast republic with impunity; but that some measures which your wisdom may dictate, may be taken, so that the great body of people who have been thus abused, may have redress for the wrongs which they have suffered. And to your decision they look with confidence; hoping it may be such as shall tend to dry up the tear of the widow and orphan, and again place in situations of peace, those who have been driven from their homes, and have had to wade through scenes of sorrow and distress.

And your Memoralists, as in duty bound, will ever pray.

CHAPTER III.

THE PROPHET'S EFFORTS AT WASHINGTON TO OBTAIN RE-
DRESS OF GRIEVANCES FOR THE SAINTS—AFFIDAVITS ON
MISSOURI AFFAIRS.

Saturday, November 30, 1839.—Elders Young and George
A. Smith went to Brother Isaac Haight's at Moravia.

Sunday, December 1, 1839.—The High Council at
Nauvoo met at Oliver Granger's, and voted that Hyrum
Smith, George W. Harris, and Oliver Granger, be a committee to send a petition to the legislature to define new
boundary lines of the city of Nauvoo, and also of Commerce, and do all other needful acts relative to those
cities; that Hyrum Smith furnish the maps and plats for
the alteration, and that Seymour Brunson circulate the
petition for signatures.

Voted that Bishop Edward Partridge publish a piece in
the *Times and Seasons,* informing the brethren in the west,
that it is improper to remove from the west for the purpose of locating in Kirtland, Ohio, and that those who do
thus remove, will be disfellowshiped by the council.

*The Prophet's Letter to Hyrum Smith—Reporting State of Affairs at
Washington.*

WASHINGTON CITY, CORNER MISSOURI AND 3RD STS.,
December 5th, 1839.

Dear Brother Hyrum, President, and to the Honorable High Council
of the Church of Jesus Christ of Latter-day Saints—to whom be fellowship, love, and the peace of Almighty God extended, and the prayer of
faith forever and ever. Amen.

Your fellow laborers, Joseph Smith, Jun., Elias Higbee, and agents
as well as the servants that are sent by you, to perform one of the most

arduous and responsible duties, and also to labor in the most honorable cause that ever graced the pages of human existence, respectfully show by these lines, that we have taken up our cross thus far, and that we arrived in this city on the morning of the 28th November, and spent the most of that day in looking up a boarding house, which we succeeded in finding. We found as cheap boarding as can be had in this city.

On Friday morning, 29th, we proceeded to the house of the President. We found a very large and splendid palace, surrounded with a splendid enclosure, decorated with all the fineries and elegancies of this world. We went to the door and requested to see the President, when we were immediately introduced into an upper apartment, where we met the President, and were introduced into his parlor, where we presented him with our letters of introduction. As soon as he had read one of them, he looked upon us with a kind of half frown, and said, "What can I do? I can do nothing for you! If I do anything, I shall come in contact with the whole state of Missouri."

But we were not to be intimidated; and demanded a hearing, and constitutional rights. Before we left him he promised to reconsider what he had said, and observed that he felt to sympathize with us, on account of our sufferings.

We have spent the remainder of our time in hunting up the Representatives in order to get our case brought before the House; in giving them letters of introduction, etc., and in getting acquainted. A meeting of the delegation of the state of Illinois was appointed today, to consult for bringing our case before Congress. The gentlemen from Illinois are worthy men, and have treated us with the greatest kindness, and are ready to do all that is in their power; but you are aware, brethren, that they with us have all the prejudices, superstition, and bigotry of an ignorant generation to contend with; nevertheless we believe our case will be brought before the House, and we will leave the event with God; He is our Judge, and the Avenger of our wrongs.

For a general thing there is but little solidity and honorable deportment among those who are sent here to represent the people; but a great deal of pomposity and show.

We left President Rigdon and others on the road, and received a letter from them this day. They were, at the date of the letter, on the 20th of November, near Washington, in Pennsylvania, expecting to stop a day or two at his brother's on account of his ill health. He has occasionally a chill yet, but his illness is not dangerous. We expect him here soon.

We have already commenced forming some very honorable acquaintances, and have thus far been prospered as much as we had anticipated, if not more. We have had a pleasing interview with Judge Young, who proposed to furnish us with expense money. We can draw on him for funds to publish our book, and we want you to raise some more money for us, and deposit it in the Branch Bank in Quincy, to be drawn to the order of Judge Young. Send us the amount of your deposit, taking a receipt of the same. You need not be afraid to do this. We think from the proceeds of the sale of books, we can make it all straight. Do therefore be punctual, as much depends upon it. We cannot accomplish the things for which we were sent without some funds. You very well know, brethren, we were contented to start, trusting in God, with little or nothing. We have met with but one accident since we started. The lock of our trunk was broken off, and Brother Lyman Wight's petition is missing; but we trust there is a copy of it preserved; if there is, you will please forward it immediately, with the name and affidavit to it.

For God's sake, brethren, be wide awake, and arm us with all the power possible, for now is the time or never. We want you should get all the influential men you can of that section of country, of Iowa, and of every other quarter, to write letters to the members of Congress, using their influence in our behalf, and to keep their minds constantly upon the subject.

Please to forward this to our wives.

Yours in the bonds of the Everlasting Covenant,

JOSEPH SMITH, JUN.,
ELIAS HIGBEE.

P. S.—Congress has been in session for four days, and the House of Representatives is not yet organized, in consequence of some seats being contested in the New Jersey delegation. They have this day succeeded in electing John Q. Adams to the chair *pro tem.*; but whether they will get their Speaker and Clerk chosen is yet unknown, as there is a great deal of wind blown off on the occasion on each day. There is such an itching disposition to display their oratory on the most trivial occasions, and so much etiquette, bowing and scraping, twisting and turning, to make a display of their witticism, that it seems to us rather a display of folly and show, more than substance and gravity, such as becomes a great nation like ours. (However there are some exceptions).

A warm feeling has been manifested in the discussion of the House today, and it seems as much confusion as though the nation had already began to be vexed. We came with one of the Missouri members from Wheeling to this place, who was drunk but once, and that however was most of the time; there was but one day but what he could navigate, and that day he was keeled over, so he could eat no dinner. The horses ran away with the stage; they ran about three miles;

Brother Joseph climbed out of the stage, got the lines, and stopped the horses, and also saved the life of a lady and child. He was highly commended by the whole company for his great exertions and presence of mind through the whole affair. Elias Higbee jumped out of the stage at a favorable moment, just before they stopped, with a view to assist in stopping them, and was but slightly injured. We were not known to the stage company until after our arrival.

In our interview with the President, he interrogated us wherein we differed in our religion from the other religions of the day. Brother Joseph said we differed in mode of baptism, and the gift of the Holy Ghost by the laying on of hands. We considered that all other considerations were contained in the gift of the Holy Ghost, and we deemed it unnecessary to make many words in preaching the Gospel to him. Suffice it to say he has got our testimony. We watch the postoffice, but have received no letters from our sections of the country. Write instantly.

Yours with respect,

J. S. Jun.,
E. H.

Tuesday, 3.—High Council of Iowa met at Elijah Fordham's and voted to come up to the law of tithing, so far as circumstances would permit, for the benefit of the poor, and that Alanson Ripley remove to Iowa; and he was ordained Bishop by the Presidency of the Council.

Affairs in Iowa.

Elder Daniel Avery was instructed to call the Elders together and organize the Elder's Quorum.

Saturday, 7.—The President of the High Council of Iowa proposed the following questions—Have the brethren a right to exact the payment of debts which were due them from others, and were consecrated to the Bishop in the state of Missouri? Six Counselors spoke. The President decided that all such debts ought not to be called for, and that persons making such demands shall be disfellowshiped by the Church; which was approved by the Council. Also that all those who sold goods in Missouri, and were calling for their pay, should be considered as acting in unrighteousness, and ought to be disfellowshiped;

as the property of the Saints had been confiscated by
Missouri.

*Letter of the Prophet and Elias Higbee to the High Council at Nauvoo—
Preliminary Hearing of Grievances.*

WASHINGTON CITY, CORNER OF MISSOURI AND 3RD STS.,
December 7th, 1839.

*To Seymour Brunson and the Honorable High Council of the Church of
Jesus Christ of Latter-day Saints:*

Your humble servants, Joseph Smith, Jun., and Elias Higbee, again
address you for the purpose of informing you of our proceedings here in
relation to our business and prospects of success. We deem it unim-
portant to say anything in relation to our journey, arrival, and interview with his Excellency, the President of these United States; as they
were mentioned in a letter lately addressed to President Hyrum Smith
and the High Council. We mentioned in that letter the appointment of
a meeting to be held by the Illinois delegation, to consult upon the best
measures of getting our business brought before Congress. They met
yesterday in one of the committee rooms of the Capitol. All the delegation were present except ex-Governor Reynolds—who is now one of
the Representatives in Congress—and on account of whose absence, the
meeting was adjourned until today at eleven o'clock; however the subject was partially introduced, and Mr. Robinson took a stand against
us, so far as concerned our presenting claims to be liquidated by the
United States.

We took a stand against him, asserting our constitutional rights.
Brother Joseph maintained the ground in argument against him firmly
and respectfully, setting forth the injuries that we have received, and
the appeals that we have made to the judiciary of Missouri, and also the
governor; their refusals from time to time to do us justice; also the
impracticability of doing anything in the judiciary courts of Missouri—
which tribunal Mr. Robinson thought was the only proper place for our
claims; but he finally said it was his first impression on the subject, not
having considered the matter, but would take it into further consideration.

Judge Young of the Senate made some remarks in our favor, saying
he would get the opinion of some of the prominent members of the Senate, who were also lawyers, and would report to us the next meeting.
We met this day according to appointment, and very friendly feelings
were manifested on the occasion. Our business was taken up, and

Judge Young stated that he had asked the opinion of Judge White of Tennessee, of Mr. Wright, and several other members whose names we do not recollect, but were prominent members of the Senate. They all declined giving an opinion at present, as it was a matter that they had not considered sufficiently to decide upon at this time. The meeting then, after some deliberations, decided in our favor, which decision was that a Memorial and Petition be drawn up in a concise manner, (our Representatives promising so to do), and Judge Young present them to the Senate, that they might thereby refer it to the proper committee, with all the accompanying documents, and order the same to be printed.

We want you to assist us now; and also to forward us your certificates, that you hold for your lands in Missouri: your claims to preemption rights, and affidavits to prove that soldiers were quartered on us and in our houses without our consent, or any special act of law for that purpose; contrary to the Constitution of the United States. We think Brother Ripley and others will recollect the circumstances and facts relative to this matter. You will also recollect the circumstances of Brother Joseph and others being refused the privilege of *habeas corpus* by the authorities of Missouri.

These facts must be authenticated by affidavits. Let any particular ransaction of the outrages in Missouri that can be sworn to by the sufferers, or those who were eye-witnesses to the facts, be sent, specifying the particulars. Have the evidence *bona fide* to the point.

The House of Representatives is not organized. Much feeling and confusion have prevailed in the House for a few days past. The House succeeded in electing John Q. Adams chairman *pro tem.* on the 5th instant. They have not yet elected their Speaker or Clerk. The Senate can do nothing of consequence until the House is organized; neither can the President's message until then be received. We design taking a paper and forwarding it to you.

Your brethren in the bonds of the everlasting covenant,

JOSEPH SMITH, JUN.,
ELIAS HIGBEE.

Brother Isaac Haight took Elders Young and George A.
Smith to Brother Joseph Murdock's, Hamil-
Brigham
Young in   ton, Madison county, New York, where Elder
New York.   Young preached on Sunday, 8th, and spent
the week in preaching, and visiting the brethren. Elder George A. Smith was confined to his room, sick.

This day, the High Council of Nauvoo issued an Epistle

to the Saints west of Kirtland not to return thither. (See *Times and Seasons*, page 29).*

Elders Hiram Clark, Alexander Wright, and Samuel Mulliner arrived in Preston from America. Their licenses were mislaid on their journey, and they had some difficulty in making themselves known.

* This epistle is of interest as showing the spirit of the Church government at that time, (1839) and the recognition of the rights of individuals. For these reasons it is quoted here:

To the Saints scattered abroad, in the region westward from Kirtland, Ohio:

BELOVED BRETHREN:—Feeling that it is our duty, as the servants of God, to instruct the Saints from time to time, in those things which to us appear to be wise and proper—therefore we freely give you a few words of advice at this time.

We have heard it rumored abroad, that some at least, and probably many, are making their calculations to remove back to Kirtland next season.

Now brethren, this being the case, we advise you to abandon such an idea; yea, we warn you, in the name of the Lord, not to remove back there, unless you are counseled so to do by the First Presidency, and the High Council of Nauvoo. We do not wish by this to take your agency from you; but we feel to be plain, and pointed in our advice for we wish to do our duty, that your sins may not be found in our skirts. All persons are entitled to their agency, for God has so ordained it. He has constituted mankind moral agents, and given them power to choose good or evil; to seek after that which is good, by pursuing the pathway of holiness in this life, which brings peace of mind, and joy in the Holy Ghost here, and a fulness of joy and happiness at His right hand hereafter; or to pursue an evil course, going on in sin and rebellion against God, thereby bringing condemnation to their souls in this world, and an eternal loss in the world to come. Since the God of heaven has left these things optional with every individual, we do not wish to deprive them of it. We only wish to act the part of a faithful watchman, agreeably to the word of the Lord to Ezekiel the prophet, (Ezekiel 33 chap , 2, 3, 4, 5, verses,) and leave it for others to do as seemeth them good.

Now for persons to do things, merely because they are advised to do them, and yet murmur all the time they are doing them, is of no use at all; they might as well not do them. There are those who profess to be Saints who are too apt to murmur, and find fault, when any advice is given, which comes in opposition to their feelings, even when they, themselves, ask for counsel; much more so when counsel is given unasked for, which does not agree with their notion of things; but brethren, we hope for better things from the most of you; we trust that you desire counsel, from time to time, and that you will cheerfully conform to it, whenever you receive it from a proper source.

It is very probable, that it may be considered wisdom for some of us, [i. e. at Nauvoo], and perhaps others, to move back to Kirtland, to attend to important business there: but notwithstanding that, after what we have written, should any be so unwise as to move back there, without being first counseled so to do, their conduct will be highly disapprobated.

Done by order and vote of the First Presidency and High Council for the Church of Jesus Christ of Latter-day Saints, at Nauvoo, December 8, 1839.

H. G. SHERWOOD, Clerk.

Times and Seasons, Vol. I, p. 29.

Some time this month, Brother Hyrum Smith wrote a long Epistle "To the Saints scattered abroad, Greeting," setting forth his sufferings, etc., in the State of Missouri, and published the same in the *Times and Seasons*, on page 20 and onward.*

Sunday, 15.—President Young preached at Brother Gifford's, in Waterville.

The High Council at Nauvoo voted that Bishop Knight provide for the families of Joseph Smith, Jun.. Sidney Rigdon, and Orrin Porter Rockwell, during their absence at Washington.

Elder James Mulholland, my scribe, having died, it was voted that debts contracted for building his house be settled. Also approved of Brothers Annis, Bozier, and Edmunds building a water mill adjoining the city.

Monday 16.—President Young returned to Hamilton.

Wednesday, 18.—Elders Woodruff, John Taylor, and Theodore Turley sailed from New York for England.

Friday, 20.—President Young went to Eaton, to see his cousins Fitch, Salmon, and Phinehas Brigham.

---

* This communication of Hyrum Smith's adds nothing to his very elaborate statement of the wrongs suffered by himself and the Saints in Missouri already published in Volume III, pp. 403-424, except his testimony to the truth of the Book of Mormon; and as he was one of the Eight Witnesses to the fact of the existence of the Nephite plates from which the record was translated, the paragraphs relating to that testimony are given here:

"Having given my testimony to the world of the truth of the Book of Mormon, the renewal of the everlasting covenant, and the establishment of the kingdom of heaven, in these last days; and having been brought into great afflictions and distresses for the same, I thought that it might be strengthening to my beloved brethren, to give them a short account of my sufferings, for the truth's sake, and the state of my mind and feelings, while under circumstances of the most trying and afflicting nature.   *   *   *   *   I had been abused and thrust into a dungeon, and confined for months on account of my faith, and the testimony of Jesus Christ. However I thank God that I felt a determination to die, rather than deny the things which my eyes had seen, which my hands had handled, and which I had borne testimony to, [all in plain allusion to his testimony to the existence of the plates from which the Book of Mormon was translated] wherever my lot had been cast; and I can assure my beloved brethren that I was enabled to bear as strong a testimony, when nothing but death presented itself, as ever I did in my life. My confidence in God, was likewise unshaken. I knew that He who suffered me, along with my brethren, to be thus tried, that He could and that He would deliver us out of the hands of our enemies; and in His own due time He did so, for which I desire to bless and praise His holy name."—*Times and Seasons*, Vol. 1, pp. 20 and 23.

For particulars of our proceedings while at Washington, see my letters and Judge Higbee's to friends at Commerce, or Nauvoo, as the place is now frequently called.

Saturday, 21.—I arrived in Philadelphia, direct from Washington City, by the railroad, where I spent several days preaching and visiting from house to house, among the brethren and others.

Letter of Hyrum Smith to Parley P. Pratt—On Printing the Book of Mormon in New York.

NAUVOO, HANCOCK COUNTY, ILLINOIS,
December 22nd, 1839.

DEAR BROTHER PARLEY:—In consequence of the absence of my brother Joseph, your letter has come into my hands, to which I intend to reply, and give such instructions, and advise you respecting the matters and things of which you write, as I feel led by the Spirit of the Lord [to give].

I was truly glad to hear of the prosperity of the churches in and about the vicinity of New York. Truly these things are pleasing to the Saints, and I presume to none more so than yourself, who was the instrument in the hands of God in planting the standard of truth in those regions, around which so many are now rallying.

You express a desire to have the Book of Mormon, etc., printed in New York, etc., etc., and have taken some steps towards accomplishing that object. As respects this matter I would say, that it is one of great importance, and should be properly considered. Not only is the city of New York destitute of this book, but there is truly a famine throughout the Union, and another large edition is certainly required. But at the same time I cannot give any encouragement for the publication of the same, other than at this place, or where it can come out under the immediate inspection of Joseph and his Counselors, so that no one may be chargeable with any mistakes that may occur. I want the books we print here should be a standard to all nations in which they may be printed, and to all tongues into which the same may be translated.

Again, as this place is appointed a Stake and a place of gathering for the Saints, I think that every facility should be rendered it, in order that the Saints may be able to accomplish the great works which have to be performed in this generation. I should therefore strongly advise, yea, urge you and all the Elders of Israel, when they meet with those who have means, and a disposition to forward this work, to send them to this place, where they may receive counsel from time to time.

If when Brothers Joseph and Rigdon return, we should deem it prudent to avail ourselves of the facilities offered in New York for re-printing the Book of Mormon, it is probable that a delegation will be sent to accomplish that object. In the meantime you will be at liberty to go to Europe, for thereunto are you sent.

The above observations will apply to the book of Doctrine and Covenants, Hymn Book, etc., which publications I long to see flowing through the land like a stream, imparting knowledge, intelligence, and joy to all who shall drink at the stream. As to publishing the Book of Mormon in Europe and other nations, I should entirely acquiesce to your proposition. I do not know of any more suitable persons for attending to that business than the Twelve. If it should be deemed wisdom to have the same published in England or elsewhere soon, you will be further advised on the subject, and full powers given you immediately on the return of Joseph, who is at present in the city of Washington, in company with Elder Rigdon and Judge Higbee, endeavoring to get the subject of our late persecutions brought before the councils of the nation.

The families of the Twelve are generally well, but not altogether so comfortably situated as I could wish, owing to the poverty of the Church. I think it would be well for those who have means to spare, to forward the same to their families.

My love to all the brethren. I am your affectionate brother in the bonds of the covenant,   HYRUM SMITH.

Addressed to Elder P. P. Pratt, New York City.

Monday, 23.—President Young went to Waterville with Brother Gifford. About this time Brothers Rockwell and Higbee arrived at Philadelphia with my carriage from Washington, where they had been some time, leaving Elder Rigdon there sick, and Dr. Robert E. Foster to take care of him.

Wednesday, 25.—Elders Wright and Mulliner left Preston for Scotland, and soon commenced preaching and baptising in Paisley and vicinity.

President Young went six miles north of Rome [New York] to see Brother Blakesly; returned on the 27th to Waterville, and on the 28th went to Hamilton.

Saturday, 28.—Heber John, son of Willard and Jennetta Richards, died at Preston, England, aged five months and nine days. He had been sick nine days with the small-pox, and was buried in Elswick Chapel yard.

Sunday, 29.—The High Council of Nauvoo voted to print ten thousand copies of the hymn-books, and an edition of the Book of Mormon, under the inspection of the First Presidency at Nauvoo, so soon as means can be obtained.

Monday, 30.—About this time I left Philadelphia with Brother Orson Pratt, and visited a branch of The Prophet the Church in Monmouth county, New Jersey, in New Jersey where I spent several days, and returned to Philadelphia.

The High Council of Nauvoo voted that a committee be appointed to transact the business relating to the request of the brethren at Washington as follows—Alanson Ripley, in Iowa; Seymour Brunson and Charles C. Rich, at Quincy; Zenas H. Gurley, at Macomb; and that President Hyrum Smith, and Bishops Edward Partridge and Vinson Knight give the committee their instructions.

Wednesday, January 1, 1840.—George A. Smith (who had partially recovered from his illness) and Elder Brigham Young left Hamilton. The brethren helped them on their way, and gave them considerable clothing.

Thursday, 2.—Brother James Gifford brought them to Utica.

As more positive and official testimony was wanted by the authorities at Washington, many of the brethren made affidavits concerning their sufferings in, and expulsion from, Missouri, a few of which I will insert in my history:

Affidavit of Simeon Carter on his Sufferings in Missouri.

I, Simeon Carter, certify that I have been a resident of the state of Missouri for six years and upwards, and that I have suffered many things by a lawless mob; both myself and my family have been driven from place to place, and suffered the loss of much property, and finally were expelled from the state. I further certify, that I belong to the Church of the Latter-day Saints, commonly called "Mormons." And I certify that in the year eighteen hundred and thirty-eight, both I and my people suffered much, by the people of the state of Missouri. And I further certify, that in this same year, in the month of November, between the first and sixth, we were surrounded by a soldiery of the state of

Missouri, in the city of Far West, in Caldwell county, both myself and many of my "Mormon" brethren, and were compelled by the soldiery —which were armed with all the implements of war to shed blood —under a public declaration for our entire extermination, to sign away our all, our property, personal and real estate, and to leave the state of Missouri immediately.

I certify that I had at that time one hundred and sixty-two acres of land, the same which I held the certificate for. I further certify that I was obliged to give up my duplicates to help me to a small sum to carry me out of the state. I further certify not.

SIMEON CARTER.

Territory of Iowa, Lee County.

Sworn to and subscribed before me, a justice of the peace for said county, this 2nd day of January, 1840.

D. W. KILBOURN, J. P.

Letter of Hyrum Smith to the Prophet and Judge Higbee.

NAUVOO. HANCOCK COUNTY, ILLINOIS,
January 3rd, 1840.

To President Joseph Smith, Jun., and Judge Higbee:

DEAR BRETHREN:—It is with feelings of no ordinary kind, that I write you at this time, in answer to the letters with which we were favored. Your letters were truly interesting, and were read with great interest by the brethren here, as well as myself.

We were truly glad to hear of your safe arrival in the city of Washington, your interview with His Excellency the President, and the steps you have since taken for the furtherance of the object you have undertaken to accomplish, and for which you have left the endearments of home, and the society of your friends. The mission on which you are engaged is certainly an important one, and one which every Saint of God, as well as everyone whose breast beats high with those patriotic feelings which purchased our national freedom, must take a deep interest in. And although there may be many who do not value your labors—their sectarian prejudices being greater than their love for truth and the Constitution of our country; yet there are many who will undoubtedly appreciate your services, and will feel it a pleasure to assist you all that they possibly can. Conscious of the righteousness of your cause—having the prayer of the Saints. (amongst whom are many who have shared with you the trials, persecutions, and imprisonments which have been heaped upon the Saints in Missouri), and having the approval of heaven, I would say, go on, dear brethren, in the name of the Lord; and while you are pleading the cause of the widow and the fatherless, may

He who has promised to be a father to the fatherless and a husband to the widow, bless you in your undertakings, and arm you with sufficient strength for the herculean task in which you are engaged. Your exertions will be seconded by the brethren in this region, who are disposed to do all they possibly can.

I had just got ready to start for Springfield when I received your letter. I no sooner read it than I abandoned the idea of going there. I then made exertion to obtain funds for you in this place; but not being able to get any, and hearing that there were brethren in Quincy lately from New York, I started off the following day and succeeded in obtaining from Brother Herringshaw three hundred dollars, which I deposited with Messrs. Holmes & Co., merchants in Quincy, subject to the order of Judge Young. The reason why I deposited it with them was in consequence of the banks not doing any business and refusing to take deposits, etc. I hope that we shall be able to raise you some more soon. Brother William Law has promised to let us have one hundred dollars as soon as he gets a remittance from the east, which he expects daily.

We have not been able to get much on the city lots since you left; not more than enough to pay some wages for surveying, and a few debts. Brother Lyman Wight returned the subscription paper a few days ago, stating that he had not collected anything since you left. In consequence of my health, which has been poor, and the coldness of the weather, I have not been able to attend to it myself. I hardly think we shall be able to raise the one thousand dollars for Mr. William White by the time he will expect it. Elder Granger is yet in Commerce, not being able to move in consequence of the low stage of water in the Ohio river.

I received a letter lately from Parley P. Pratt, stating that he was in the City of New York, and had published another edition of his book, and wanted permission to print an edition of the Book of Mormon and Doctrine and Covenants, with a periodical similar to the *Times and Seasons*, stating that there were men who had means, that would assist in these things. He likewise wanted to get the privilege for the Twelve to print the Book of Mormon in Europe. I wrote in reply, that if there were any of the brethren disposed to aid, and had means to spare for such purposes, to send them to this place, so that not only this place might be benefitted, but that the books might come out under your immediate inspection. I am afraid some have been induced to tarry and assist Parley in these undertakings; and had made arrangements with Elder Granger to assist in liquidating the New York debts.

I want a letter from you, Brother Joseph, as soon as possible, giving me all the instructions you think necessary. I feel the burden in your absence is great. Father expresses a great desire to go to Kirtland, along with Brother Granger, who has promised to pay his and mother's expenses; would you think it advisable for them to go or not?

The High Council met a few days ago, and took your second letter into consideration, and passed some resolutions on the subject; appointed committees to get certificates for land, and to get all other information they could. Some have gone to Quincy, and others to different places. We shall forward from time to time the information you desire.

You will receive enclosed in this a number of duplicates for land from Bishop Partridge and others. The Mississippi is frozen up. The weather is very cold, and a great quantity of snow is on the ground, and has been for some time. Your family is in tolerable good health, excepting one or two having the chills occasionally.

Bishop Knight desires me to inform you, that Brothers Granger and Haws have driven into Commerce a large number of hogs. They are now engaged in slaughtering them. I think there will be a good deal of trade carried on in this line another year.

You may expect to hear from us soon again. I sent you a copy of the deposit I made in Holmes & Co., which I hope you will receive safe.

I am very affectionately,

HYRUM SMITH.

P. S.—We have concluded not to send any duplicates in this letter. The packages of duplicates will be directed to Judge Higbee, thinking they will come more safe to his address.

Friday, 3.—Elders Brigham Young and George A. Smith went from Utica to Albany, on the railway, and put up at the Railroad House.

Affidavit of William F. Cahoon—Missouri Wrongs.

I hereby certify that in the year 1838 I was residing in Daviess county, Missouri, and while from home I was taken prisoner in Far West by the militia, and kept under guard for six or eight days, in which time I was forced to sign a deed of trust, after which I was permitted to return home to my family in Daviess county, and found them surrounded by an armed force, with the rest of my neighbors, who were much frightened. The order from the militia was to leave the county within ten days, in which time my house was broken open, and many goods taken out by the militia. We were not permitted to go from place to place without a pass from the general, and on leaving the county, I received a pass as follows:

"I permit William F. Cahoon to pass from Daviess to Caldwell county, and there remain during the winter, and thence to pass out of the state of Missouri.

"Signed November 10th, 1838.

"REEVES, a Brigadier-General."

During this time both myself and my family suffered much on account of cold and hunger because we were not permitted to go outside of the guard to obtain wood and provision; and according to orders of the militia, in the spring following, I took my family and left the state with the loss of much property.

WILLIAM F. CAHOON.

Territory of Iowa, Lee county, subscribed and sworn before
D. W. KILBOURN, J. P.

Letter of C. Adams to the Prophet—Cause of the Saints before the Illinois Legislature.

SPRINGFIELD, 4th January, 1840.

RESPECTED SIR:—I had the gratification of the receipt of yours of the 16th December, which gave me pleasure to learn that your prospects were, at that early period, in a measure flattering. I also saw yours of the 19th December to Mr. Weber. We are now consulting and feeling the pulsations relative to your case being brought before the legislature, now in session, by a series of resolutions, instructing our senators, and requesting our representatives to urge relief in your case.

What will be done, remains yet uncertain; still it is my strongest impression, it will be found prudent to get the matter before our legislature, for their action thereon. I am happy to learn that all our delegation are friendly to your intended application for relief in some shape; and it strikes me that the views of the President at this period may be the best, and perhaps the only way that relief could at this time be obtained; and in that event, be no injury to a future application to be restored to all your rights, when prejudice shall in a measure have subsided and the true state of the matter be more readily received, even by those whose prejudices may have closed the avenues to reason and justice in a matter identified with the odium so commonly attached to the sound of "Mormons." This odium will naturally wear off when they have-time to learn that "Mormons" are neither anthropophagi or cannibals.

Your friends are generally well.

I am, etc.,

C. ADAMS.

To Joseph Smith, Jun.

Saturday, 4.—The High Council at Montrose voted to utterly discard the practice of suing brethren at the law, and that such as do it, shall be disfellow-shiped by this branch of the Church; that Abraham O. Smoot ordain Daniel Avery President of the Elders' Quorum; and that the sixth instant be devoted to taking affidavits concerning Missouri.

Law Suits to be Abandoned

Elder Young found the brethren in Albany; went to Troy, and Lansingburg, where he heard Elder Phinehas Richards preach.

Sunday, 5.—Elder Young preached at Lansingburg, and returned to Troy and held a meeting with the brethren.

Monday, 6.—Elder Young returned to Albany.

Extract from Elder Orson Pratt's Letter to his wife—Reporting Movements of the Brethren in the Eastern States.

January 6th, 1840.

I am well and hearty. After mailing the last letter to you in Pennsylvania, I went to Philadelphia on Saturday, the 21st of December; there I found President Joseph Smith, Jun.; he had just arrived from Washington City, where he had been about three weeks. Four or five days after, Judge Higbee, with Porter Rockwell, came to Philadelphia; they are well. I wrote to Parley P. Pratt to come and see President Smith; he did so, and probably will go to Washington with him in a few days. I stayed with Brother Smith, in Philadelphia, about eight days; we then took the railroad and went some 35 or 40 miles, to a large branch of the Church in Monmouth county, New Jersey, which numbers ninety members; there I left him [President Smith] on New Year's day, and came to New York, where I am at present.

Elder Benjamin Winchester had, when I left Philadelphia, baptized forty-five in that city, and several more had given in their names for baptism, and scores believing. I preached in Chester county, Pennsylvania, about two weeks, and I think I may safely say there are hundreds believing. The work is prospering throughout all this region.

Elders Taylor, Woodruff, and Turley sailed for Liverpool, December 18th, while I was in Pennsylvania. None of the rest of the Twelve have yet arrived. Parley P. Pratt has another book printed, larger than the Voice of Warning, entitled "The Millennium and other Poems," and a piece on the "Eternal Duration of Matter."[*]

* This treatise on the "Regeneration and Eternal Duration of Matter," was written by Elder Pratt while in Columbia prison, Missouri. He explains that it "was

Letter from John B. Weber to the Prophet—On Supplementing the Latter's Effort to Obtain Redreses from Congress.

SPRINGFIELD, January 6, 1840.

GENTLEMEN:—Your letter of the 19th ult. came to hand ten days after date, immediately after which I called upon many of the prominent members of the Democratic party, with a view to unite them in their influence in your behalf; all of whom expressed a willingness to aid in bringing about justice.   But I regret to inform you that but few have exhibited that energy in the matter which might reasonably be expected from all lovers of liberty and advocates of equal rights.

Your energetic friends were first of the opinion that an effort ought to be made by our legislature to memorialize our representatives in Con-

more calculated to comfort and console myself and friends when death stared me in the face, than as an argumentative or philosophical production." This article has for some time been out of print, yet it has much that is instructive in it. The author states as a basic principle in his treatise the following: "Matter and spirit are the two great principles of all existence. Everything animate and inanimate is composed of one or the other, or both of these eternal principles. I say eternal, because the elements are as durable as the quickening power which exists in them. Matter and spirit are of equal duration; both are self-existent,—they never began to exist, and they never can be annihilated. * * * * Matter as well as spirit is eternal, uncreated, self existing. However infinite the variety of its changes, forms and shapes;—however vast and varying the parts it has to act in the great theater of the universe;—whatever sphere its several parts may be destined to fill in the boundless organization of infinite wisdom, yet it is there, durable as the throne of Jehovah.   And eternity is inscribed in indelible characters on every particle. Revolution may succeed revolution;—vegetation may bloom and flourish, generation upon generation may pass away and others still succeed—empires may fall to ruin, and moulder to the dust and be forgotten—the marble monuments of antiquity may crumble to atoms and mingle in the common ruin—the mightiest works of art, with all their glory, may sink in oblivion and be remembered no more—worlds may startle from their orbits, and hurling from their spheres, run lawless on each other in conceivable confusion—element may war with element in awful majesty, while thunders roll from sky to sky, and arrows of lightning break the mountains asunder—scatter the rocks like hailstones—set worlds on fire, and melt the elements with fervent heat, and yet not one grain can be lost—not one particle can be anihilated. All these revolutions and convulsions of nature will only serve to refine, purify, and finally restore and renew the elements upon which they act. And like the sunshine after a storm, or like gold seven times tried in the fire, they will shine forth with additional luster as they roll in their eternal spheres, in their glory, in the midst of the power of God."   On this theory of the indestructibility of matter the author proceeds to consider the reality of the resurrection from the dead and the future life of man in a sentient, tangible existence.   "The resurrection of the body is a complete restoration and reorganization of the physical system of man; * * * * the elements of which his body is composed are eternal in their duration; * * * * they form the tabernacle—the everlasting habitation of that spirit which animated them in this life; * * * * the spirits and bodies of men are of equal importance and destined to form an eternal and inseparable union with each other."

gress, to use all honorable means to accomplish your desires; but after holding a consultation it was believed that such a course would create a party strife here, and consequently operate against you in Congress. Therefore it was agreed that as many as had friends in Congress should write to them immediately, desiring their aid in your behalf.

If convenient you will please write again. Any information respecting your mission will be thankfully received, and made known to your people here.

Very respectfully yours,

JOHN B. WEBER.

To the Rev. Joseph Smith and his Associates.

Affidavit of John M. Burk—Missouri Outrages.

I hereby certify that General John Clark and his Aid, on their arrival at Far West in Caldwell county, Missouri, came to my tavern stand, and without my leave, pitched their marquees in my yard and did take my wood and hay to furnish the same, and did bring their horses in also, and without my leave, took hay for them, and did take possession of my house, and used it for a council house, and did place a strong guard around it, so as to hinder any person from going in or out, and I myself was not permitted to go in and out; for all this I have received no remuneration, and was not even permitted to pass out of town to water travelers' horses without a permit. The above took place in the first part of November, 1838.

I also certify that Caleb Baldwin, Lyman Wight, Hyrum Smith, Joseph Smith, Jun., and Mr. Alexander McRae, in Clay county, Missouri, did apply for a writ of *habeas corpus* and did not get it.

JOHN M. BURK.

Sworn before D. W. Kilbourn, J. P.

Affidavit of John Lowry—Ditto.

I certify that I saw General John Clark and his Aid, on their arrival at Far West, Caldwell county, Missouri, in the yard of John M. Burk, and gave orders to their waiters to pitch their marquees in his yard, and to take of his wood for fire.

I also saw Captain Samuel Bogart, with his men, come near my dwelling, and did pitch their camp, and took my house logs without my leave, and did burn them. I also saw him with the horse of Joseph Smith, Jun., in his possession.

JOHN LOWRY.

Sworn before D. W. Kilbourn, J. P.

Affidavit of Jedediah Owen—Ditto.

To whom it may concern—This is to certify, that on the day following on which the troops arrived at Far West, that two men of said troops came to my house, broke open my trunk, and took therefrom both money and clothing, and also a number of papers, among which were deeds and notes, and also a number of cooking utensils, and in consequence of the cruel and inhuman treatment which I and others have received from those troops, we are reduced to a state of almost absolute starvation; and Daniel Avery and myself were appointed as a committee to go out and beg corn and meal, or anything we might obtain, that would render assistance or relieve us in our suffering condition.

                                                    JEDEDIAH OWEN.

Sworn before D. W. Kilbourn, J. P.

Affidavit of T. Alvord—Ditto.

I removed my family from the state of Michigan to Clay county, Missouri, in the year 1835, where I lived in peace with the people, on my own land, eighteen months or more, when the people began to be excited in consequence of the emigration of our people to that county. The excitement became so great that I was obliged to sell my place at half price, and removed to the county of Caldwell, where I purchased me a farm, and settled my family, and made a good improvement, and was in a good situation to support my family, and there lived in peace with the people until the summer and fall of 1838, when the mob began to rise, and we were obliged to fly to arms in self defense; but notwithstanding our exertion, they murdered and massacred many of our people. We applied to the governor for assistance, and his reply to us was, "If you have got into a scrape with the mob, you must fight it out yourselves, for I cannot help you." The mob still increased, until I was obliged to remove my family to Far West, and there remained, surrounded with mobs of murderers, until General Clark arrived with his army, with the governor's exterminating order.   Then we were all taken prisoners; our arms taken away; they then treated us with all the cruelty they were masters of, and took possession of whatever they pleased, burnt timber, and laid waste town and country.

I heard General Clark say that he would execute the Governor's order; "but [said he] notwithstanding, I will vary so much as to give some lenity for the removal of this people, and you must leave the state immediately, for you need not expect to raise another crop here."   Those who were not taken to prison, were permitted to return to their homes to make preparations to leave the state. Finding I had no safety for myself and family in Missouri, I fled to Illinois for safety.

                                                    T. ALVORD.

Sworn to before D. W. Kilbourn, J. P.

Tuesday, January 7.—Elder Young took stage for Richmond, Massachusetts.

Affidavit of William Hawk—Missouri Affairs.

MONTROSE, LEE COUNTY, IOWA, January 7, 1840.

I hereby certify, that some time in the month of October, 1838, an armed force collected in the county of Carroll, near De Witt, and in open daylight, drove a man by the name of Humphrey out of his house, and set fire to it, and burnt it to ashes, and then sent an express ordering all the "Mormons" to leave the place as soon as the next day. The next day they sent another express ordering them to leave in six hours, or they would be massacred upon the ground. They also fired their guns at different persons traveling the road near the town. The "Mormons" were at length compelled to leave their possessions, and all removed to Caldwell, consisting of seventy and perhaps one hundred families, many of whom were in want of the sustenance of life, sick, and some died upon the way.

About two weeks after this, another armed force invaded Far West, took my gun, and compelled me to sign away my property, both real and personal, and leave the state forthwith.

WILLIAM HAWK.

Sworn to before D. W. Kilbourn, J. P.

Affidavit of Timothy B. Clark—Ditto.

MONTROSE, LEE COUNTY, IOWA TERRITORY, January 7, 1840.

This is to certify that I was at work on my farm on the last of October, 1838, when an armed company under General Lucas, came and took myself and my three sons prisoners, and threw down my fences, and opened my gates, and left them open, and left my crops to be destroyed, and while I was a prisoner, they declared that they had made clean work in destroying the crops as they passed through the country, and they took from me two yoke of oxen, and three horses and two wagons, and compelled me and my sons to drive them loaded with produce of my own farm, to supply their army.

I had in possession at the time, four hundred and eighty acres of land, and rising of a hundred acres improved, with a small orchard and nursery, the necessary buildings of a farm, etc.; and in consequence of my imprisonment my fences remained down, and most of my crops were destroyed; and further this deponent saith not.

TIMOTHY B. CLARK.

Sworn to before D. W. Kilbourn, J. P.

Affidavit of Urban V. Stewart—Ditto.

MONTROSE, LEE COUNTY, IOWA TERRITORY, January 7, 1840.

This is to certify that about the middle of October, I was driven, by the threats of the Daviess county armed force, to leave my possessions, consisting of preemption right to a quarter section of land with thirty acres under improvement, and a good house. I went to Di-Ahman and remained until about the 1st of November, when I was driven from there by an armed force under General Wilson. I then went to Far West. While at Ondi-Ahman the armed force took from me one cow and calf, and a yoke of oxen, one horse and five sheep; they also took from me fifteen hogs. While at Far West, they took two cows belonging to me, and I saw the soldiery killing the live stock of the inhabitants without leave or remuneration, and burning building timbers, fences, etc.

URBAN V. STEWART.

Sworn to before D. W. Kilbourn, J. P.

Affidavit of John Smith—Ditto.

LEE COUNTY, IOWA TERRITORY.

This day personally appeared before me, D. W. Kilbourn, an acting Justice of the Peace in and for said county, John Smith, and after having been duly sworn, desposeth and saith, "That in the months of October and November, 1838, I resided in the town of Adam-ondi-Ahman. Daviess county, Missouri, and whilst being peaceably engaged in the ordinary vocations of life, that in the early part of November my house was entered by a body of armed men painted after the manner or customs of the Indians of North America, and proceeded to search my house for fire arms, stating that they understood the Mormons knew how to hide their guns, and in their search of a bed in which lay an aged, sick female, they threw [her] to and fro in a very rough manner, without regard to humanity or decency. Finding no arms, they went off without further violence.

"Shortly after this above described outrage, there was a number of armed men, say about twenty, rode into my yard and inquired for horses which they said they had lost, and stated, under confirmation of an oath, that they would have the heads of twenty 'Mormons,' if they did not find their horses. These last were painted in like manner as the first. These transactions took place when the citizens of the village and its vicinity were engaged in a peaceable manner in the ordinary pursuits of life."

This deponent further saith, "That the mob took possession of a store of dry goods belonging to the Church of Latter-day Saints, over which they placed a guard. I went into the store to get some articles to distribute to the suffering poor, and the officer who had the charge of the store ordered me out peremptorily, stating it was too cold to wait on me, that I must come the next morning; and returning the next morning, I found the store almost entirely stripped of its contents.

Thereupon we as a Church were ordered to depart the county and state, under the pains and penalty of death or a total extermination of our society. Having no alternative, (having my wagon stolen), I was compelled to abandon my property, except a few movables which I got off with in the best way that I could, and on receiving a permit or pass which is hereto appended. I then proceeded to depart the state.

"'I permit John Smith to remove from Daviess to Caldwell county, there remain during the winter, or remove out of the state unmolested.

"'Daviess county, November 9th, 1838.

"'R. Wilson, Brigadier-General.   By F.G. Cochnu.'

"I accordingly left the state in the month of February following in a destitute condition."

JOHN SMITH.

Sworn to before D. W. Kilbourn, J. P.

Affidavit of Samuel Smith—Ditto.

MONTROSE, LEE COUNTY, IOWA, January 7, 1840.

I do hereby certify, that I, Samuel Smith, made an improvement and obtained a preemption right upon one hundred and sixty acres of land in Daviess county, Missouri, in 1837. On the first of November, 1838, I was compelled to leave the county, by order of General Wilson, in ten days. They took without my consent, two horses, which have never been returned, nor remunerated for; also destroyed my crop of corn, drove off four head of cattle.

SAMUEL SMITH.

Sworn to before D. W. Kilbourn, J. P.

Affidavit of Daniel Avery—Ditto.

LEE COUNTY, IOWA TERRITORY, March 5th, 1840.*

I, Daniel Avery, do hereby certify that the following scenes transpired in the state of Missouri to my personal knowledge—First, in the year 1838, some time in the fall, I was called on by the martial law of the state of Missouri, to aid and assist to rescue women and children from the hands of a mob, from the waters of Grand river, whose husbands and fathers had been driven off. We found the house invested by the mob, some of whom were in the house threatening the lives of the women and children, if they did not leave their property and effects immediately and follow their husbands and fathers. One family lost a

* This affidavit, it will be observed, was given some time after the others of this group, and appears in the Ms. of the Prophet's History under date of March the 5th, but it is brought forward here, with all those that follow in this chapter, that it may appear in connection with the others of its kind.

child while in this situation, for the want of care; the women being compelled, by these monsters, to provide and cook them food. This company of the mob was commanded by James Weldin.

I also saw about seventy families driven from De Witt by a mob commanded by Sashiel Wood. I helped to bury one woman the first night, who had been confined in childbed a night or two before, and could not endure the sufferings.

The next scene I saw I was peaceably traveling the road; a man by the name of Patrick O'Banion was shot dead at my feet. We advanced a little further, when two men were killed and several wounded. I afterwards learned that this gang of mobbers was commanded by Samuel Bogart.

In consequence of being pursued out of the state, by this lawless mob, I was not an eye witness to the many thousand wicked acts committed by the Governor's exterminating militia.

                                                        DANIEL AVERY.

Sworn to before D. W. Kilbourn, J. P.

Wednesday, March 11.

Affidavit of James Powell—Ditto.

ILLINOIS, ADAMS COUNTY, March 11, 1840.

I, James Powell, do certify, that I was a citizen of the state of Missouri in 1838. I solemnly declare that while I was peaceably traveling to one of my nearest neighbors, I was assaulted by a company of men, to the number of five—Autherston Wrathey, John Gardner, Philomen Ellis, Jesse Clark, and Ariel Sanders. First they threw a stone and hit me between the shoulders, which very much disabled me; they then shot at me, but did not hit me. One of them then struck me with his gun, and broke my skull about six inches—a part of my brain ran out. I have had fourteen pieces of bone taken out of my skull. My system is so reduced that I have not done a day's work since.

I know no reason why they should have done [this act], as I did not belong to the Mormon Church, neither had I ever heard one preach. In this situation I was forced to leave the state forthwith. I was carried three days without having my head dressed. When I arrived at Huntsville, Doctor Head offered me assistance. I refer to him for further testimony.

                                                        JAMES POWELL.

Attest, John Smith.

We certify that the foregoing affidavit of James Powell's is true and correct, as we stood by and saw it with our eyes. We also heard them say they would kill the Mormons, if they did not clear out. We carried the wounded man in our wagon, till he was out of reach of the mob.

PETER WIMMER,
SUSAN WIMMER,
ELLEN WIMMER.

Sworn to before William Oglesby, J. P.

Affidavit of John Smith—Ditto.

ILLINOIS, COLUMBUS, ADAMS COUNTY, March 11, 1840.

I, John Smith, certify that I was a resident in the state of Missouri in 1838, when I was driven from my house, and a pre-emption right, and forbid to stay in the state, [the mob] threatening me if I did not go forthwith. I took my family and pursued my journey one hundred miles. In consequence of cold, snow, water and ice at the inclement season in which I was driven, I fell sick, and for four weeks I was unable to travel; during which time I was threatened daily; yet I was so sick it was considered by many that I could not live, and was compelled to start when I was not able to sit up through the day. I landed in Illinois; the long and fatiguing journey, lying out in the cold, open air, proved too much for my companion; it threw her into a violent fever, with which she died. Many others in the company took sick and died with the same hard fare.

JOHN SMITH.

Sworn to before William Oglesby, J. P.

Affidavit of Smith Humphrey—Ditto.

ILLINOIS, ADAMS COUNTY, March 16, 1840.

I, Smith Humphrey, certify that I was a citizen of Missouri in eighteen hundred and thirty-eight; and some time in the month of October, of the same year, I was fallen upon by a mob commanded by Hyrum Standley. He took my goods out of my house; and said Standley set fire to my house, and burnt it before my eyes, and ordered me to leave the place forthwith. I removed from De Witt to Caldwell county, where I was again assailed by Governor Bogg's exterminating militia. They took me prisoner, and robbed my wagon of four hundred dollars in cash, and one thousand dollars' worth of goods, and drove me out of the state.

SMITH HUMPHREY.

Sworn to before C. M. Woods, Clerk of Circuit Court.

Affidavit of Henry Root—Ditto.

QUINCY, ILLINOIS, 16th March, 1840.

This is to certify that I, Henry Root, am, and was a citizen of De

Witt, Carroll county, Missouri, at the time of the persecutions (known by the name of the "Mormon War") commenced and terminated between the citizens of said state of Missouri and the Mormons; that in the fall of 1838, in the month of September, a mob (under no regular authority) headed by William W. Austin, Sen., consisting of from one hundred to one hundred and fifty men, came into De Witt and ordered the Mormons to leave that place within ten days from that time; that if they did not leave, they would be driven from there by force.

The Mormons did not leave; the appointed time came, and the mob came, armed and equipped for war. The Mormon citizens petitioned to the governor of the state, but no relief came. They sent to the general of the brigade [in that locality], who ordered the militia to repair to De Witt to disperse the mob. On the arrival of the militia, Brigadier-General Parks told me the Mormons had better leave their property and go off, as his men were prejudiced against them, and he could do them no good, nor relieve them. With that the Mormons left.

HENRY ROOT.

Sworn to before C. M. Woods, Clerk of Circuit Court, Adams county, Illinois.

Affidavit of Joseph Clark—Ditto.

QUINCY, ILLINOIS, March 16, 1840.

I, Joseph Clark, certify that I was a citizen of the state of Missouri in 1838; and when peaceably traveling the highway, I was shot at twice by Governor Boggs' exterminating militia, commanded by Major-General John B. Clark.

JOSEPH CLARK.

Sworn to before C. M. Woods, Clerk of Circuit Court, Adams County, Illinois.

Affidavit of Thomas D. Casper—Ditto.

QUINCY, ILLINOIS, March 16th, 1840.

This is to certify that I, Thomas D. Casper, was a resident of the state of Missouri in the year 1838. I was not a member of the Church of Mormons or Latter-day Saints; but witnessed the following acts of distress: As I was on business, I inquired for Perry Moppin, and learned that he, with Samuel Snowden, Esq., had gone after Mr. Wilson, a Mormon, and had threatened and sworn to take his life if he did not tell his name; and they swore they had the tool to take his life if he had not told them his name.

Further they agreed that the Mormons should leave the country of Missouri except they would deny the faith, or their religion. And I heard Anthony McCustian say that he would head a mob in any case, to prevent the lawyers from attending to any case of their (the Mormons') grievances; and he was a postmaster. And I saw two men that said they had been at Haun's mill at the murder; and one by the name of White, and the other Moppin stated that he had slain three Mormons. And I, Thomas D. Casper, witnessed other things too tedious to mention; and solemnly swear, before God and men, that what is here written is a true statement of facts relative to the suffering of the Mormons in the state of Missouri.

THOMAS D. CASPER.

Affidavit of Jesse W. Johnston—Ditto.

QUINCY, ILLINOIS, March 16, 1840.

I, Jesse W. Johnston, certify that the following circumstances took place in the State of Missouri, while I was a resident of that state, viz: I was taken prisoner by Governor Boggs' exterminating militia. I saw one man killed belonging to the Mormon Church, and was forced by them to take corn out of the fields of the Mormon Church without leave. This was in the fall of 1838.

JESSE W. JOHNSTON.

Sworn to before C. M. Woods, Clerk of the Circuit Court, Adams County, Illinois.

Affidavit of Owen Cole—Ditto.

QUINCY, ILLINOIS, March 17, 1840.

This is to certify that I, Owen Cole, was a resident of Caldwell county, state of Missouri, and while residing at my dwelling house, the militia under Governor Boggs, and by his orders, plundered my house, and shot me through my thigh. My damage sustained by the militia, by being driven from the state, besides my wound, was five hundred dollars. The militia men were quartered on the lands of the people called Mormons, contrary to the laws and Constitution of the state. I hereby certify this to be a true statement.

OWEN COLE.

Sworn to before C. M. Woods, Clerk Circuit Court.

Affidavi of Ezekiel Maginn—Ditto.

QUINCY, ILLINOIS, March 17, 1840.

I, Ezekiel Maginn, certify that I was a citizen of the state of Missouri in the year 1838, and was an eye witness to the following facts—First, I saw the militia, called for by Governor Boggs' exterminating order, enter the house of Lyman Wight, and take from it a bed and bedding, pillows, and dishes, personally known to me to be his property.

EZEKIEL MAGINN.

Sworn to before C. M. Woods, Clerk Circuit Court, Adams County.

Affidavit of Addison Green—Ditto.

QUINCY, March 17, 1840.

I, Addison Green, do certify that in the month of October, one thousand eight hundred and thirty-eight, when I was peaceably walking the highroad in Ray county, state of Missouri, I was molested and taken prisoner by ten armed men, who took from me one double-barrel fowling piece and equipage, threatening to blow out my brains and swore that if I was a Mormon they would hang me without further ceremony. They had previously been to my lodging and taken my horse, saddle, and bridle. All was then taken into the woods about one mile to Bogart's camp.

I was kept a prisoner until the next morning, when I was let go; but have not obtained any part of my property, which was worth about one hundred and fifty dollars.

A. GREEN.

Sworn to before John H. Holton, notary public.

Affidavit of John P. Greene—Ditto.

I, John P. Greene, was in company with several of my neighbors walking the road in peace, when one of our company, a young man, by name of O'Banion, was shot down at my side, being shot by a company of mobbers; and soon after this we were fired upon again, and two more were killed and several others wounded. This was about the 25th day of October, one thousand eight hundred and thirty-eight, in the state of Missouri, and I do hereby certify the above to be true according to the best of my knowledge.

JOHN P. GREENE

Sworn to before John H. Holton, notary public.

Affidavit of Asahel A. Lathrop—Ditto.

This is to certify that I, Asahel A. Lathrop, was a citizen of the state of Missouri, at the time the difficulty originated between the people called Mormons and the [other] inhabitants of the aforesaid state, and herein give a statement of the transactions that came under my observation, according to the best of my recollection.

I settled in Missouri in the summer of 1838, in Caldwell county, where I purchased land and erected buildings. The said land I now have a deed of; and in the fall I purchased a claim on what is called the East Fork of Grand River, together with a large stock of cattle and horses, sheep and hogs; it being some sixty miles from the aforesaid county where I first located; and moved on to the latter place, supposing that I was at peace with all men; but I found by sad experience that I was surrounded by enemies; for in the fall of 1838, whilst at home with my family, I was notified by a man by the name of James Welden, that the people of Livingston county, had met at the house of one Doctor William P. Thompson, then living in the attached part of said county, for the purpose of entering into measures respecting the people called Mormons; and the same Welden was a member of the same, and also the aforesaid William P. Thompson was a justice of the peace; and they all jointly agreed to drive every Mormon from the state; and notified me that I must leave immediately, or I would be in danger of losing my life.

All this time some of my family were sick; but after listening to the entreaties of my wife to flee for safety, I committed them into the hands of God and left them, it being on Monday morning; and in a short time after I left, there came some ten or fifteen men to my house, and took possession of the same, and compelled my wife to cook for them, and also made free to take such things as they saw fit; and whilst in this situation, my child died, which I have no reason to doubt was for the want of care; which, owing to the abuse she received, and being deprived of rendering that care she would, had she been otherwise situated.   My boy was buried by the mob, my wife not being able to pay the last respects to her child.

I went from my home into Daviess county and applied to Austin A. King and General Atchison for advice, as they were acting officers in the state of Missouri.   There were men called out to go and liberate my family, which I had been absent from some ten or fifteen days; and on my return I found the remainder of my family confined to their beds, not being able the one to assist the other, and my house guarded by an armed force.

I was compelled to remove my family in this situation, on a bed to a place of safety.   This, together with all the trouble, and for the want of care, was the cause of the death of the residue of my family, as I have no doubt; which consisted of a wife and two more children; as they died a few days after their arrival at my friend's.   Such was my situation, that I was obliged to assist in making their coffins.

I will give the names of some of the men that have driven me from my house and abused my family; those that I found at my house on my return were Samuel Law, Calvin Hatfield, Stanley Hatfield, Andy Hatfield; and those that were leading men were James Welden, Doctor William P. Thompson, a justice of the peace, and William Cochran, and many others, the names I do not recollect.

I have also seen men abused in various ways; and that whilst they were considered prisoners; such as the mob cocking their guns and swearing that they would shoot, with their guns to their face, and the officers of the militia, so called, standing by without uttering a word; and in these councils they have said if a Missourian should kill a Mormon he should draw a pension, same as a soldier of the Revolution.

I was also compelled to give up my gun, and the terms were, I was to leave the aforesaid state of Missouri, or be exterminated. My property is yet remaining in said state, whilst I am deprived of the control of the same.

Written this 17th day of March, 1840.

ASAHEL A. LATHROP.

Sworn to before D. W. Kilburn, J. P., Lee county, Iowa Territory.

Affidavit of Burr Riggs.

I, Burr Riggs, of the town of Quincy, and state of Illinois, do hereby certify that in the year 1836, when moving to the state of Missouri, with my family and others, we were met in Ray county, in said state, by a mob of one hundred and fourteen armed men, who commanded us not to proceed any further, but to return, or they would take our lives; and the leader stepped forward at the same time, and cocked his piece. We turned round with our team; and the mob followed us about six miles and left us.

Some time after this I moved to Caldwell county, in said state, and purchased about two hundred acres of land, and a village lot, on which I erected a dwelling house, staked, and commenced improving my land, and had, at the time I was driven away, about forty acres of corn, vegetables, etc.; and in the year 1838, in the month of November, was compelled to leave my house and possessions in consequence of Governor Boggs' exterminating order, without means sufficient to bear my expense out of the state.

Given under my hand at Quincy, Illinois, 17th March, 1840.

BURR RIGGS.

Sworn to before C. M. Woods, Clerk of the Circuit Court, Adams county, Illinois.

Affidavit of Simons P. Curtis.

I, Simons P. Curtis, a resident of Quincy, Adams county, Illinois, certify that in the year 1838, I was a citizen of Caldwell county, Missouri, residing in the city of Far West. Also that I went in search of a lost steer; and passing by Captain Bogart's camp, while he was guarding the city, I saw the hide and feet of said steer, which I knew to be mine; the flesh of which I suppose they applied to their own use.

I also certify that Wiley E. Williams, one of the Governor's aids, who was gunkeeper, caused me to pay thirty-seven and a half cents to him. I also paid twenty-five cents to a justice of the peace to qualify me to testify that the gun was mine. The said Wiley E. Williams is said to be the one that carried the story to Governor Boggs, which story was the cause of the exterminating order being issued, as stated by the Governor in said order.

SIMONS P. CURTIS.

Sworn to before C. M. Woods, Clerk Circuit Court, Adams County, Illinois.

Affidavit of Elisha H. Groves.

I, Elisha H. Groves, of the town of Quincy, and state of Illinois, upon oath say, that I was a resident of Daviess county, in the state of Missouri, and that on the 16th day of November, in the year of our Lord, 1838, Judge Vinson Smith and others came to my house and ordered myself and family, Levi Taylor, David Osborn and others, to leave our possessions which we had bought of Government and paid our money for the same, saying we must within three days leave the county or they would take our lives, for there was no law to save us after that time. In consequence of those proceedings, together with Governor Boggs' exterminating order, we were compelled to leave the state of Missouri. Furthermore this deponent saith not.

Given under my hand at Quincy, the 17th day of March, A. D. 1840.

ELISHA H. GROVES.

Sworn to before C. M. Woods, Clerk Circuit Court.

Affidavit of Jacob Foutz.

QUINCY, ILLINOIS, March 17, A. D. 1840.

This is to certify that I was a citizen, resident of Caldwell county, Missouri, at the time Governor Boggs' exterminating order was issued; and that I was quartered on by the mob militia, without my leave or consent at different times, and at one time by William Mann, Hiram Cumstock, and brother, who professed to be the captain; also Robert White; and that I was at the murder at Haun's mill, and was wounded; and that I was driven from the state, to my inconvenience, and deprived of my freedom, as well as to my loss of at least four hundred dollars.

JACOB FOUTZ.

Sworn to before C. M. Woods, Clerk Circuit Court.

Affidavit of Frederick G. Williams.

I do certify that I was a resident of Caldwell county, in the State of Missouri, in the year of our Lord 1838, and owned land to a considerable amount, building lots, etc., in the village of Far West; and in consequence of mobocracy, together with Governor Boggs' exterminating order, was compelled to leave the state under great sacrifice of real and personal property, which has reduced and left myself and family in a state of poverty, with a delicate state of health, in an advanced stage of life. Furthermore this deponent saith not.

Given under my hand at Quincy, Illinois, March 17, 1840.

FREDERICK G. WILLIAMS.

Sworn to before C. M. Woods, Clerk Adams county, Illinois.

Statement of James Sloan.

James Sloan made affidavit at Quincy, that the officers of the militia under the exterminating order of Governor Boggs in Missouri in 1838, took possession, carried off and destroyed a store of goods, of several hundred dollars' value, belonging to the people called "Mormons," in Daviess county; that his life was threatened, his property taken, and he was obliged to flee the state with his family, greatly to his disadvantage.

Affidavit of David Shumaker.

QUINCY, ILLINOIS, ADAMS COUNTY, March 18, 1840.

I, Jacob Shumaker, do certify that I went back to the state of Missouri about the first of October last, with the calculation to live with my family, but finding it impossible, as the mob, say to the amount of twenty or thirty of them, surrounded my house, and whilst they were quarreling about me, what they should do, and in what way they should dispose of me, I crept out of the back window and made my escape; and leaving my family to their most scandalous abuses; my wife and oldest daughter barely escaping from their unholy designs.

I was thus a second time obliged to leave the state, or remain at the risk of my life. The former alternative I chose. My loss sustained by the above-mentioned abuses was not less than three hundred dollars. A lot of land containing forty acres, for which I paid four dollars per acre, situated in Caldwell county, was unjustly and unlawfully taken from me, and is still retained by some person or persons to me unknown. I hereby certify that the above is a true statement.

JACOB SHUMAKER.

Sworn to before C. M. Woods.

Affidavit of Levi Richards.

I, Levi Richards, a resident of Quincy, Adams county Illinois, practitioner of medicine, certify that in the year one thousand eight hundred and thirty-eight, I was a citizen of Far West, Caldwell county, Missouri, and that in the fall of said year, I saw the city invaded by a numerous armed soldiery, who compelled its inhabitants to surrender, give up their firearms, and submit to their dictation. They then set a strong guard round the city, thereby preventing egress or ingress, without special permission. Then they collected the citizens together upon the public square, formed around them a strong guard of soldiers, and then at the mouths of their rifles, compelled them to sign what was termed a deed of trust, thereby depriving them of all their property and civil rights.

This occupied several days of most inclement weather, when they were brought to the same order by General Clark, and I judge some forty or fifty were made special prisoners by him. At this time he delivered his speech to the "Mormons," which has been published, and which is substantially correct. I was compelled by a company of men armed with rifles, to leave my house, and go to captain Bogart's camp, (he commanded, as I understood, a part of the guard which surrounded the city,) upon an indirect charge or insinuation; was detained a prisoner two days, examined, and liberated. I then asked the clerk of the company, who had been my keeper, the following questions, which he readily answered:

Were those men who massacred the "Mormons" at Haun's mill, out under the Governor's order, or were they mobbers?

A. Mobbers.

Are Captain Cornelius Gilliam and his company out by legal authority, or are they mobbers?

A. Mobbers.

Where are those mobbers now?

A. They have joined the army.

This company [Gilliam's] at the surrender of Far West were painted like Indians. The army wore a badge of red (blood). I saw a large amount of lumber and timber destroyed, and used for fuel by the soldiers. The destruction of cattle, hogs, etc., seemed to be their sport, as their camp and the fields testified when they withdrew. An excellent gun was taken from me, which I have never seen or heard of since. A gun that was left in my care was taken at the same time, which I afterwards found with Wiley E. Williams of Richmond, (reputed one of the Governor's aids,) to obtain which I had to prove property, affirm before a magistrate and pay said Williams fifty cents.

I was called to extract lead, dress the wounds, etc., for several persons (Saints) who were shot in the above siege, two of whom died. Immediately previous to the above transactions, and for a long time before, the citizens of Caldwell, and particularly Far West, were called upon to watch for mobs by day and guard against them by night, till it became a burden almost intolerable.

LEVI RICHARDS.

Sworn to before C. M. Woods. Clerk Circuit Court, Adams county, Illinois.

Affidavit of Gibson Gates.

I, Gibson Gates, do hereby certify that I was residing in Jackson county, Missouri, in the fall of the year, 1833, and had been for the space of about one year. I was at a meeting one day for worship, when a man by the name of Masters came to us, stating that he was sent by the mob to inform us that if we would forsake our religion, they were willing to be our brethren and fight for us; "but if not," said he, "our young men are ready, and we can scarce constrain them from falling upon you and cutting you to pieces."

Soon after this there came a large company of men, armed, to my place, and with much threatening and profane words, ordered me to be gone by the next day, or they would kill me and my family; in consequence of which threatening, we quit our house in the month of November, leaving most of our effects; suffering very much with cold, fatigue and hunger, we took [set out] on the prairie, and went southward twenty miles or more, where we stayed a few weeks. But still being threatened by the mob, we removed to Clay county, where we lived in peace until the fall of 1838, when a mob arose against the people of the Church of Latter-day Saints, when we were again obliged to leave our home, and seek safety in another place for a few weeks. When we returned our house had been broken open, and the lock of a trunk broken open, and the most valuable contents thereof taken away; the most of our bedding and furniture was either stolen or destroyed; and we were then ordered to leave the state.

GIBSON GATES.

Sworn to before David W. Kilbourn, J P.

Affidavit of David Pettigrew.

This is to certify, that I, David Pettigrew, was a citizen of Jackson county, Missouri, and owned a good farm, lying on the Blue river, six miles west of Independence, and lived in peace with the inhabitants until the summer and fall of 1833, when the inhabitants began to threaten us with destruction.   I was at work in my field, and a man by the name of Allen, and others with him, came along and cried out, "Mr. Pettigrew, you are at work as though you were determined to stay here, but we are determined that you shall leave the county immediately."   I replied that I was a free born citizen of the United States, and had done harm to no man.   "I therefore claim protection by the law of the land," and that the law and the Constitution of the land would not suffer them to commit so horrid a crime.   They then replied that "the old law and Constitution is worn out, and we are about to make a new one."

I was at a meeting where we had met for prayer, and a man by the name of Masters came and desired an interview with us; he then stated that he was sent by the mob to inform us, that if we would forsake our "Mormon" and Prophet religion, and become of their religion, they, the mob, would be our brothers, and would fight for us; "but if you will not, we are ready and will drive you from the county."

A few days after this, a large mob came to my house, commanded by General Moses Wilson, Hugh Braziel and Lewis Franklin, and broke down my door, and burst into my house, armed with guns, clubs and knives; some of them were painted red and black.   This was in the night, and my family was much frightened.   They threatened me with immediate death if I did not leave the place.   After much abuse they left us for the night, but in a few days they returned and drove me and my family into the street, not suffering us to take anything with us.   I saw that we must go or die; we went south to Van Buren county, in company with eighty or ninety others.   In a short time after, I returned to my farm and found my house plundered, my grain and crop, stock, and all my farm and farming tools laid waste and destroyed; and shortly after my house was burned to ashes.

I called on Esquire Western, of Independence, and inquired of him if he could inform me what all this mobbing and riot meant, informing him of the destruction and plundering of my house; to which he gave me no satisfaction, but insulted me and treated me roughly.   Governor Boggs lived in the county, and I have seen him passing through among us in our great distress, and gave no attention to our distresses.   He was then Lieutenant-Governor of the state.   On my return to my family in Van Buren county, I was much abused by a man by the name of Brady; he said he would kill me if I ever attempted to go to my farm, or if he saw me passing that way again.   I returned to my family, and in a few days after, a company of men came where we lived and said they would spill my blood if I did not leave the place immediately.   The leaders of this company were John Cornet, Thomas Langley, and Hezekiah Warden; they lived in Jackson county.

This was in the cold winter, and our sufferings were great. I fled across the Missouri river to Clay county, where I lived three years; in which time I often heard Judge Cameron and others say, that "you Mormons cannot get your rights in any of the courts of the upper country;" and I had not the privilege of voting as a free citizen.

I moved to Caldwell county, bought land and opened a good farm, and lived in peace until the summer and fall of 1838, when mobs arose in the counties round about, and I with the rest was obliged to take up arms in self defense; for the cry was, that mob law should prevail, if we stood against them, until the army came and took us all prisoners of war. I with the rest was obliged to sign a deed of trust at the point of the sword, I with sixty others was selected out and marched to Richmond, in Ray county, by the command of General Clark, where they kept us a number of weeks, pretending to try us as treasoners and murderers. At length I obtained my liberty, and returned to my family in Caldwell county: and I found that there was no safety there, for there was no law, but all a scene of robbing, and plundering, and stealing. They were about to take me again, and I was obliged to leave my family and flee to Illinois. In about two months my family arrived, having suffered much abuse and loss of health and property. Soon after the arrival of my family my son, a young man, died; and I attribute his death to the cruel barbarity of the mob of Missouri, he being a prisoner among them, and having suffered much because of them.

My father was a soldier, and served in the Revolutionary War, under the great Washington, but I have not had protection on my own lands; and I have not been permitted to see my farm in Jackson county, Missouri, in seven years. Soldiers were stationed or quartered in different parts of Far West; and they treated us roughly, threatening to shoot us, and making use of anything they pleased, such as burning house, timber, and rails, and garden fences, and stealing and plundering what they pleased.

When I was at Richmond, a prisoner before Judge King, we sent for many witnesses; and when they came, they were taken and cast into prison with us, and we were not permitted to have any witnesses. The day I came out of prison, they compelled me to sign a writing which was not true or remain in prison.

DAVID PETTIGREW.

Sworn to before D. W. Kilbourn, J. P.

Thus I have given a few of the multitude of affidavits which might be given to substantiate the facts of our persecutions and deaths in Missouri. When the brethren left Missouri,

Comment of
the Prophet
on the Forego-
ing Affidavits.

they were poor, having been plundered of everything valued by mobs. Much of the plundering was done under the eye of the government officers, according to the foregoing affidavits; and all by the sanction of the state of Missouri, as the acts of her legislature testify.* The Saints, being so numerous, were obliged to scatter over the state of Illinois and different states to get bread and clothing—so that but few accounts against Missouri could be collected without unreasonable exertions. About 491 individuals gave in their claims against Missouri, which I presented to Congress—amounting to about $1,381,044.00; leaving a multitude more of similar bills hereafter to be presented, which, if not settled immediately, will ere long amount to a handsome sum, increasing by compound interest.

* That is to say, the legislature had appropriated two hundred thousand dollars to meet the expenses of the mob-militia in unlawfully dispossessing the Saints of their lands and other property, and then expelling them from the state. While on the other hand, it refused to give any consideration worthy of the name to the petition of the Saints for redress of their grievances; and so far was the legislature from giving the Saints any assurance of re-instatement in the rightful possession of their lands and other property and maintaining them in peaceful possession of them, that it finally refused even to investigate the justice of their claims. Under these circumstances the Prophet is undoubtedly justified in using the language of the text. (See Vol. III, chaps. xv, xvi.)

CHAPTER IV.

DEPARTURE OF THE PROPHET FROM WASHINGTON—LABORS OF
ELIAS HIGBEE BEFORE THE SENATE JUDICIARY COMMITTEE
—REPORT OF THE COMMITTEE.

Wednesday, 8.—The High Council at Nauvoo voted to
loan all the moneys possible for the relief of the poor
Saints.

This evening President Young preached at a school
house in the south west part of Richmond,* when the
people present commenced making a noise and   Ministry of
disturbing the meeting, and when President   Brigham
Young was reproving them for their disgrace-   Geo. A. Smith
ful conduct, some of those present fired lucifer   New York.
matches.   President Young rebuked them severely, and
taught them better manners, and proposed to send them
some Indians from the West to civilize them.

Thursday, 9.—About this time I returned to Philadelphia, where I continued to preach and visit for a little
season.

George A. Smith preached at Richmond this evening.
His health is still very poor, and he is almost blind.
President Young also was very feeble.   While they were
opening the meeting, some one threw a quantity of brimstone in the fire, which nearly suffocated them.   As soon
as the fumes of brimstone would pemit, Brother Smith
told them he thought he should be in no danger of catch-
ing the itch in Massachusetts, for the smell of brimstone
indicated that it was thoroughly cured.

Sunday, 12.—Elders Young and Smith held a meeting

* Richmond is in Schoharie county, about seventy miles west of Albany, N. Y.

at William Pierson's, Richmond. After preaching, Elder
Smith had a severe shake of the ague, which lasted some
hours. The weather was extremely cold, but by the kind
attention of Mr. Pierson's family, and William Richards,
he was in some measure relieved of his ague before he
left Richmond. President Young wore a cradle bed quilt
from Far West to Richmond, where Rhoda Richards lined
Doctor Richard's old worn out plaid cloak with President
Young's quilt, with flannel between, which made him very
comfortable.

Monday, 13.—Elders Wilford Woodruff, John Taylor,
and Theodore Turley arrived at Preston, England.

Tuesday, 14.—About this time Elder Rigdon and Doctor
Foster arrived at Philadelphia.

Friday, 17.—A special council was held at the house
of Elder Willard Richards, in Preston, Joseph
Fielding, president, Theodore Turley, scribe.
Present, Wilford Woodruff, John Taylor,
Hiram Clark, and Willard Richards. Council decided
that Elders Woodruff and Turley should go to the Staffordshire potteries; Elders Taylor and Fielding, to Liverpool;
Elder Clark, to Manchester, with Elder William Clayton;
and Elder Willard Richards to go where the Spirit directs;
that the Elders of the council communicate with the presidency at Preston once a month; and Elder Richards
write to Brothers Alexander Wright and Samuel Mulliner
in Scotland, and hold no general conference until more
of the Twelve arrive.

Appointments in the British Mission.

Elders Brigham Young and George A. Smith went to
Canaan, Connecticut, with Edwin D. Pierson, Elder Smith
shaking very severely with the ague in the evening.

Saturday, 18.—Elders Woodruff and Turley started for
the Potteries.

Sunday, 19.—The High Council at Nauvoo voted to
donate a city lot to Brother James Hendrix, who was shot
in Missouri; also voted to build him a house; also donated
a house and lot to Father Joseph Knight.

Elder Brigham Young preached at Sheffield mills, where he stayed till the twenty-sixth.

Wednesday, *22.*—Elders Fielding and Taylor went to Liverpool and commenced their mission.

Saturday, *25.*—About this time I visited the Saints at Brandywine, where I spent some days, and returned to Philadelphia.

Monday, *27.*—Brothers Gibson Smith and Peter French conveyed Elders Brigham Young and George A. Smith to New Haven, where they tarried until the 31st.

About the last of this month, I left Philadelphia for Washington, in company with Brothers Rockwell, Higbee, and Doctor Foster, traveling by railroad, having sold my carriage, and having left Elder Rigdon sick in Philadelphia.

Friday, *31.*—Elders Brigham Young and George A. Smith took steamboat from New Haven for New York City. When within eighteen miles of the city, they took the stage, and arrived at their destination about ten o'clock at night. When they alighted from the carriage they had no funds to pay their fare, and Elder Young asked Captain Stone to pay their bill, fifty cents, which he very readily did; and they found Elder Parley P. Pratt's house in about five minutes, where they stayed Saturday, February 1st.

Sunday, *February 2.*—Elders Brigham Young and George A. Smith preached in the Columbia Hall. Elder Young preached every evening during the week, till Saturday, three times in the Columbia Hall; by which he injured himself so much, that he was not able to dress himself for four or five days.

On Monday George A. Smith went to Philadelphia.

Thursday, *6.*—I had previously preached in Washington, and one of my sermons I find reported in synopsis, by a member of Congress; which I will insert entire.

Mathew S. Davis' Description of the Prophet, and a Report of his
Washington Discourse.

WASHINGTON, 6th February, 1840.

MY DEAR MARY:—I went last evening to hear "Joe Smith," the celebrated Mormon, expound his doctrine. I, with several others, had a desire to understand his tenets as explained by himself. He is not an
educated man; but he is a plain, sensible, strong minded man. Everything he says, is said in a manner to leave an impression that he is sincere. There is no levity, no fanaticism, no want of dignity in his deportment. He is apparently from forty to forty-five years of age, rather
above the middle stature, and what you ladies would call a very good
looking man. In his garb there are no peculiarities; his dress being
that of a plain, unpretending citizen. He is by profession a farmer,
but is evidently well read.

He commenced by saying, that he knew the prejudices which were
abroad in the world against him, but requested us to pay no respect to
the rumors which were in circulation respecting him or his doctrines.
He was accompanied by three or four of his followers. He said, "I
will state to you our belief, so far as time will permit." "I believe,"
said he, "that there is a God, possessing all the attributes ascribed to
Him by all Christians of all denominations; that He reigns over all
things in heaven and on earth, and that all are subject to His power."
He then spoke rationally of the attributes of Divinity, such as foreknowledge, mercy &c., &c. He then took up the Bible. "I believe,"
said he, "in this sacred volume. In it the 'Mormon' faith is to be found.
We teach nothing but what the Bible teaches. We believe nothing, but
what is to be found in this book. I believe in the fall of man, as recorded in the Bible; I believe that God foreknew everything, but did
not foreordain everything; I deny that foreordain and foreknow is the
same thing. He foreordained the fall of man; but all merciful as He is,
He foreordained at the same time, a plan of redemption for all mankind. I believe in the Divinity of Jesus Christ, and that He died for the
sins of all men, who in Adam had fallen." He then entered into some
details, the result of which tended to show his total unbelief of what is
termed *original sin*. He believes that it is washed away by the blood of
Christ, and that it no longer exists. As a necessary consequence, he
believes that we are all born pure and undefiled. That *all* children
dying at an early age (say *eight* years) not knowing good from evil,
were incapable of sinning; and that all such assuredly go to heaven.
"I believe," said he, "that a man is a moral, responsible, free agent;
that although it was foreordained he should fall, and be redeemed, yet
after the redemption it was not foreordained that he should again sin.
In the Bible a rule of conduct is laid down for him; in the Old and New

Testaments the law by which he is to be governed, may be found.   If he violates that law, he is to be punished for the deeds done in the body.

I believe that God is eternal.   That He had no beginning, and can have no end.   Eternity means that which is without beginning or end. I believe that the *soul* is eternal; and had no beginning; it can have no end.   Here he entered into some explanations, which were so brief that I could not perfectly comprehend him.   But the idea seemed to be that the soul of man, the spirit, had existed from eternity in the bosom of Divinity; and so far as he was intelligible to me, must ultimately return from whence it came.   He said very little of rewards and punishments; but one conclusion, from what he did say, was irresistible—he contended throughout, that everything which had a *beginning* must have an *ending;* and consequently if the punishment of man *commenced* in the next world, it must, according to his logic and belief have an *end.*

During the whole of his address, and it occupied more than two hours, there was no opinion or belief that he expressed, that was calculated, in the slightest degree, to impair the morals of society, or in any manner to degrade and brutalize the human species.   There was much in his precepts, if they were followed, that would soften the asperities of man towards man, and that would tend to make him a more rational being than he is generally found to be.   There was no violence, no fury, no denunciation.   His religion appears to be the religion of meekness, lowliness, and mild persuasion.

Towards the close of his address, he remarked that he had been represented as pretending to be a Savior, a worker of miracles, etc.   All this was false.   He made no such pretensions.   He was but a man, he said; a plain, untutored man; seeking what he should do to be saved.   He performed no miracles.   He did not pretend to possess any such power. He closed by referring to the Mormon Bible, which he said, contained nothing inconsistent or conflicting with the Christian Bible, and he again repeated that all who would follow the precepts of the Bible, whether Mormon or not, would assuredly be saved.

Throughout his whole address, he displayed strongly a spirit of charity and forbearance.   The Mormon Bible, he said, was communicated to him, *direct from heaven.*   If there was such a thing on earth, as the author of it, then he (Smith) was the author; but the idea that he wished to impress was, that he had penned it as dictated by God.

I have taken some pains to explain this man's belief, as he himself explained it.   I have done so because it might satisfy your curiosity, and might be interesting to you, and some of your friends.   *I have changed my opinion of the Mormons.*   They are an injured and much-abused people.   Of matters of *faith*, you know I express no opinion.   have only room to add—let William, if you cannot do it, acknwledge the receipt of this, with the enclosure.

Remember me to Sarah and the boys.   Kiss the dear baby for me.

Affectionately your husband,
M. L. DAVIS.

P. S.—I omitted to say, he does not believe in infant baptism, *sprinkling*, but in *immersion*, after *eight* years of age.

To Mrs. Mathew L. Davis, 107 Henry Street, New York.

During my stay I had an interview with Martin Van Buren, the President, who treated me very insolently, and it was with great reluctance he listened to our message, which, when he had heard, he said: *"Gentlemen, your cause is just, but I can do nothing for you;"* and *"If I take up for you I shall lose the vote of Missouri."* His whole course went to show that he was an office-seeker, that self-aggrandizement was his ruling passion, and that justice and righteousness were no part of his composition.   I found him such a man as I could not conscientiously support at the head of our noble Republic.   I also had an interview with Mr. John C. Calhoun, whose conduct towards me very ill became his station.   I became satisfied there was little use for me to tarry, to press the just claims of the Saints on the consideration of the President or Congress, and stayed but a few days, taking passage in company with Porter Rockwell and Dr. Foster on the railroad and stages back to Dayton, Ohio.

The Prophet's Interview with Van Buren and Calhoun.

Friday, 7.—High Council at Montrose voted to disfellowship all brethren who should persist in keeping tippling shops in that branch of the Church.

Sunday, 16.—Elder Brigham Young tarried at Elder Parley P. Pratt's, 58 Mott Street, N. Y., and Elder Heber C. Kimball arrived there this morning.

Thursday, 20.—Judge Higbee I left at Washington, and he wrote me as follows:

*Elias Higbee's Letter to the Prophet, Reporting Progress of the Cause of
the Saints Before the Senate Committee.*

WASHINGTON CITY, Feb. 20th, 1840.

DEAR BROTHER:—I have just returned from the Committee Room,
wherein I spoke about one hour and a half.   There were but three of
the committee present, for which I am very sorry.   I think they will be
obliged to acknowledge the justice of our cause. They paid good attention; and I think my remarks were well received. It was a special
meeting appointed to hear me by my request.   The Missouri Senators
and Representatives were invited to attend.   Dr. Linn, and Mr. Jamieson attended, and God gave me courage, so that I was not intimidated
by them.   Dr. Linn, I thought, felt a little uneasy at times; but manifested a much better spirit afterwards than Mr. Jamieson.

I told them first, that I represented a suffering people, who had been
deprived, together with myself, of their rights in Missouri; who numbered something like fifteen thousand souls; and not only they, but
many others were deprived of the rights guaranteed to them by the
Constitution of the United States.   At least the amount of one hundred and fifty thousand free-born citizens are deprived the enjoyment
of citizenship in each and every state; that we had no ingress in the
state of Missouri; nor could any of us have, only at the expense of our
lives; and this by the order of the executive.

I then took their own declaration of the cause of our expulsion; referred them to Parley P. Pratt's pamphlet, which I held in my hand;
then showed that the first accusation therein contained, was on account
of our religious tenets; furthermore, that the others were utterly
groundless.   I went on to prove that the whole persecution, from beginning to end, was grounded on our religious faith.   For evidence of
this, I referred them to Porter Rockwell's testimony, and P. Powell's.
I stated that there was abundant testimony to prove this to be a fact,
among the documents.

I then gave a brief history of the persecutions, from the first settlement in the state to our final expulsion.   I also stated that the society
were industrious, inoffensive, and innocent of crime; had the *Times and
Seasons*, from which I read Governor Lucas's letter to Alanson Ripley.
I also referred to Judge Young's letter from Pike county, the clerk's and
others, respecting our character in their section of the country.   I gave
them some hints of the Haun's mill massacre, and the murder of the
two little boys, but referred them more particularly to the documents
for information concerning those things; and furthermore that I had
not come here to instruct them in what they were to do in the case, but
to present them with the facts—having all confidence in this honorable
body (the Congress), believing them to be honorable men.

I demanded from them a restitution of all our rights and privileges as citizens of the United States, and damages for all the losses we had sustained in consequence of our persecutions and expulsion from the state; and told them we could have recourse no where else on earth that I knew of; that we could not sue an army of soldiers, neither could we go into the state to sue anyone else. I told them that I knew not how far Congress had jurisdiction in this case, or how far they had not; but as far as they had, we claimed the exercise of it for our relief; for we were an injured people.

These and some others were the principal subjects of my speech; after which Mr. Jamieson said he was once in the "Mormons'" favor; but afterwards learned that it was impossible to live among them, for they stole their neighbors' hogs; and there being so much testimony, he believed it, etc., etc. I replied something like this: making statements was one thing, and proving them was another. Mr Linn then said he wished me to answer one thing, viz.: If the legislature of Missouri did not refuse to investigate the subject of our difficulties solely on account of the trials then pending. In reply I assured him that I knew they had refused us an investigation; but as to that being the cause, I did not know, but told him they might have done it when those trials were discharged. He seemed to think it an injustice for Congress to take it up before the legislature had acted on it.

I occupied all but a few minutes of the time when the Senate was to go into session, so they adjourned until tomorrow at ten o'clock, when the Missourians are to reply. Mr. Linn observed, that there was a gentleman whom he would have before the committee on the morrow, who lived in the upper part of Missouri, that knew everything relative to the affair. I presume *he* is to put in his gab. I suppose I must attend the committee, as I am solicited by the chairman; but I would rather take a flogging; because I must sit still, and hear a volubility of lies concerning myself and brethren. *Lies* I say, for they have nothing but *lies* to tell, that will in the least degree justify their conduct in Missouri. Mr. Linn said he had written to Missouri, to get all the evidence taken before Judge King; so that if the thing must come up, he would be prepared to have a full investigation of the matter, and that the committee should have power to send for persons, papers, &c,. &c.

In my remarks I stated that an article of the Constitution was violated in not granting compulsory process for witnesses in behalf of the prisoners; and that the main evidence adduced, upon which they were committed, (as I understood), was from Dr. Avard, who once belonged to our society, and was compelled to swear as suited them best, in order to save his life; that I knew him to be a man whose character was the worst I ever knew in all my associations or intercourse with mankind; and that I had evidence by affidavits before them, of five or six respectable men, to prove that all he swore to was false.

Brethren and sisters, I want your especial prayers, that God may give me wisdom to manage this case according to His will, and that He will protect me from our foes, both publicly and privately.

Yours in the bonds of love,

ELIAS HIGBEE.

Second letter of Elias Higbee to the Prophet—Cause of the Saints before the Senate Committee.

WASHINGTON CITY, February 21st, 1840.

DEAR BROTHER.—I have just returned again from the Committee Room. Mr. Linn and Mr. Jamieson made some remarks, to which I replied. Mr. Linn is much more mild and reasonable (mostly perhaps from policy) than Mr. Jamieson, who related a long lingo of stuff, which he said was proven before the legislature in Missouri, which amounted to about this: that Joseph Smith gave the "Mormons" liberty to trespass on their neighbors' property; also told them, that it all belonged to them; as they were Israelites. Upon the strength of this they became the agressors. I replied that the Jackson county people in their declaration of causes that induced them to unite in order to drive the "Mormons," the crime of stealing, or trespassing, was not mentioned; and there was no docket, either clerk's or justice's, that could show it, in Jackson, Clay, Caldwell, or in Daviess counties; and that no man ever heard such teaching or doctrine from Joseph Smith, or any other "Mormon;" that we held to no such doctrine, neither believed in any such thing.

I mentioned some things contained in our Book of Doctrine and Covenants; Government and Laws in general. I told them we had published long ago our belief on that subject. Some things I recollected, which were that all persons should obey the laws of the government under which they lived, and that ecclesiastical power should not be exercised to control our civil rights in any way; particularly that ecclesiastical power should only be used in the Church; and then no further than fellowship was concerned. I think they injured their cause to-day. There is another appointment for them on the morrow, at 10 o'clock. Their friend they said was sick, consequently could not attend to-day. Mr. Linn said he thought it would be time enough to take it up in Congress when they [the Saints] could not get justice from the State; and that he was confident there was a disposition in the state of Missouri to do us justice, should we apply; that the reason of their refusing to investigate before was, the trials of the prisoners were pending; and further said, (when speaking of the trials before Judge King,) that he understood from gentlemen that the prisoners commended the Judge for his clemency and fair dealing towards them; and acknowledged they were guilty in part of the charge preferred against them. Mr. Linn said he presumed I was not present, when said men were tried. I replied in the negative, that I was not there, neither any body else that could be a witness in their favor. The lawyers advised them to keep away if they desired the salvation of their lives. I observed that I had read the proceedings of the legislature, but did not now recollect them; but since yesterday I have been reflecting on the subject, and recollect a conversation I had with Mr. Harvey Redfield, who was the bearer of the petition to Jefferson City, and he informed me that the reasons why they refused an investigation, was on account of the Upper Missouri members being so violently opposed to it, that they used their utmost exertions, and finally succeeded in getting a majority against it; and the reason of their taking this course was, in consequence of one of their members being in the massacre at Haun's mill, viz., Mr. Ashley; and Cornelius Gilliam was a leader of the first mob in Daviess county, which the militia were called out to suppress.

Mr. Linn said if it must come out in Congress, it should be fully investigated, and they, the Committee, should have power to send for persons and papers; for if we have a right to claim damages of the United States, so had they, if all were true concerning the acts alleged against the "Mormons;" that they had a right to ask the Government to pay the war against the "Mormons;" but finally seemed to disapprove of the exterminating order, which was admitted to have existed by Mr. Jamieson, or was issued by their legislature, but that no one ever thought of carrying it into effect. He said that General Clark merely advised the "Mormons" to leave the State. To which I replied, General Clark's speech was before them; that I had stated some of its contents yesterday; and if it were necessary, I could prove it by four or five hundred affidavits.

Then Mr. Jamieson stated something about the prisoners making their escape, and that he had no doubt but that they could have a fair trial in Missouri, for the legislature, to his certain knowledge, passed a law whereby they had a right to choose any county in the State to be tried in. To which I replied, that I understood such a law was passed; but notwithstanding, they could not get their trials in the county wherein they desired; for they were forced to go to Boone, whereas they desired to have their trials in Palmyra, where they could get their witnesses, as that was only sixteen miles from the river, and the other was a great distance. He said that Judge King certainly would not go contrary to law. I told him there were some affidavits in those documents that would tell him some things very strange concerning Judge

King. Mr. Linn then wished to know if the affidavits were from any-body else save "Mormons." I replied that there were some others; but how many I knew not. He then wanted to know how they were certified; whether any clerk's name was attached in the business. I told him they were well authenticated by the Courts of Record, with the Clerk's name attached thereto.

After these things and some others were said, the committee refused to consult on the subject. Only the same three attended that were in yesterday. The Chairman observed that they had not expressed any opinion relative to the subject: but observed his mind was made up in ralation to the matter. I think, from all I have discovered, Mr. Smith of Indiana will be on the side of justice; but how the thing will termi-nate I cannot tell. Mr. Crittenden and Mr. Strange are the two absent members of the Committee.

Yours in the bond of love,

ELIAS HIGBEE.

Third Letter of Elias Higbee to the Prophet—Cause of the Saints before the Senate Committee.

WASHINGTON, February 22nd, 1840.

DEAR BROTHER.—I have just returned from the Committee Room. The Committee being present to-day, a Mr. Corwin of St. Louis, former-ly a democratic editor, emptied his budget; which was as great a bundle of nonsense and stuff as could be thought of; I suppose not what he knew, but what gentlemen had told him; for instance, the religious General Clark and others. I confess I had hard work to restrain my feeling some of the time, but I did succeed in keeping silence tolerably well. Himself, Mr. Jamieson, and Mr. Linn summoned all the energies of their minds to impress upon the assembly that "Joe Smith," as he called him, led the people altogether by Revelation, in their temporal, civil, and political matters, and by this means caused all the "Mormons" to vote the "whole-hog" ticket on one side, except two persons. But when I got an opportunity of speaking, I observed that Joseph Smith never led any of the Church in these matters; as we considered him to have no authority, neither did he presume to exercise any of that nature; that Revelations were only concerning spiritual things in the Church; and the Bible being our standard, we received no Revelations contrary to it. I also observed that we were not such ignoramuses, perhaps, as he fain would have people believe us to be; and some other things on this subject. I then told him that every man exercised the right of suffrage according to his better judgment, and without any ecclesiastical restraint being put upon him; that it was all false about a Revelation on voting; and the reason of our voting that ticket was in consequence of the Democratic principles having been taught us from our infancy, and that they ever extended equal rights to all; and further we had been much persecuted previous to that time—many threatenings being made from the counties round about, as well as among us, by those who took the lead in political affairs. It was true we advised our brethren to vote this ticket, telling them we thought that party would protect our rights, and not suffer us to be driven from our lands, as we had hitherto been; believing it to be by far the most liberal party; but in that we were mistaken, because when it came to the test, there were as many Democrats turned against us as Whigs; and indeed less liberality and political freedom were manifested by them; for one Whig paper came out decidedly in our favor.

I made these remarks partly from motives which I may at another time explain to you. He laid great stress on the trials at Richmond, and a constitution, that he said Avard and others (who were in good standing in the "Mormon" Church at this time) swore to; then went on to relate what it contained, and that it was written by Sidney Rigdon.

I flatly denied it, and I could bring all the "Mormons," both men, women, and children, besides myself, that would swear before all the world, that no such thing ever existed, nor was thought of among the "Mormons."

He then related some things which he said John Corril had told him at the legislature, in Missouri; which were to the effect that the "Mormons" had burnt a number of houses in Daviess county, and that for himself, if he could not get to heaven by being an honest man, he would never go there. Then, I, speaking of some of the dissenters, told him Corril was anxious to get into the Church again, and that it was the fact in regard to damages having been done, after we had been driven from Jackson and Clay—relating the De Witt scrape, and calling of the militia, and the mob's marching to Daviess and saying they would drive the "Mormons" from there to Caldwell, and then to hell; their burning our houses; that small parties on both sides were on the alert, and probably did some damages; though I was not personally knowing to [it], as I was not there. I told him Joseph Smith held no office in the country, neither was he a military man, and did not take gun in hand in the affair to my knowledge. I then stated that John Corril's affidavit, which contained some important facts, was before them,—which facts I forgot to mention yesterday,—importing that he (John Corril) was convinced we would get no redress in Missouri (he being a member of the legislature, ought to know). I saw the Chairman of the Committee not long since, who informed me that the Committee had not come to a final conclusion on this matter as yet.

I saw Mr. Jamieson on the walk, who said the first thing the Com-

mittee would do was to decide whether they would take it up and consider it or not; and if they do take it up according to request, the Senate
will grant the Committee power to send for persons and papers. The
Committee made some inquiries respecting our religion, and I answered
them, as a matter of course, as well as I was able.

They inquired very particularly concerning how much land we had
entered there, and how much of it yet remained unsold; when Mr.
Corwin observed that we had never entered much land there, but were
squatters. I then described the size of Caldwell and Daviess counties,
giving an explanation on these matters.

I suppose perhaps on Monday or Tuesday, we shall know something
relative to this matter. Whether power be given them to send for persons and papers, [or not] you may see where they depend to rally their
forces, viz., by endeavoring to make us treasonable characters, by the
constitution, said to govern us, and that everything both civil and political among us is done by revelation. These points I desire to blow to the
four winds, and that you will select a number of firm brethren, possessing good understanding, who will tell the truth, and willingly send me
their names when they know they are wanted. Send plenty of them.
They will get two dollars per day, and ten cents a mile to and from, [as]
expense money. Do not send them until their subpœnas get there, for
they will not draw expense money only for going home.

I will suggest a few names—Alanson Ripley, King Follett, Amasa
Lyman, Francis M. Higbee, as they know concerning the De Witt
scrape; also send Charles C. Rich, Seymour Brunson, and others. You
will know whom to send better than myself.

If the Missourians should send for you, I would say consult God about
going.

ELIAS HIGBEE.

P. S.—Mr. Jamieson stated to me this evening, if the "Mormons"
could make it appear that they had been wronged, they would use their
influence in having them redressed, so the shame should not fall on the
whole state, but on those which had been guilty. I then observed that
there was a minority in the legislature, much in our favor, which seemed
to please him, as they alluded several times to it. The cause of my being so particular, is to show you the whole ground I have taken in this
matter. that there may be no inconsistency. If I have erred in this
matter, it is my head and not my heart.

ELIAS HIGBEE.

Sunday, 23. —Elder Brigham Young had so far recovered as to be able to attend preaching by Parley P.
Pratt, at Columbia Hall, New York.

The High Council of Nauvoo voted, that the notes given into the hands of Bishop Partridge, by certain individuals, as consecrations for building the Lord's House in Far West, be returned to the same by him.

Tuesday, 25.—Elders Brigham Young and Reuben Hedlock went to Hampstead, on Long Island, and preached at Rockaway and the neighborhood till the fourth of March, and baptized nine.

The Fourth Letter of Elias Higbee to the Prophet—Announces that the Senate Committee's Report will be Adverse to the Saints.

WASHINGTON, February 26th, 1840.

DEAR BROTHER.—I am just informed, by General Wall (the Chairman of the Committee), before whom, or to whom, our business is referred, that the decision is against us, or in other words unfavorable, that they believe redress can only be had in Missouri, the courts and legislature. He says, they will report this week. I desire to get a copy of it, and also the papers. I feel a conscience void of offense towards God and man in this matter; that I have discharged my duty here; and as I wish not to be on expense, as soon as I can write to President Rigdon, get my papers, and draw some money to bear my expenses, I shall bid adieu to this city, to return to my family and friends.

I feel now that we have made our last appeal to all earthly tribunals; that we should now put our whole trust in the God of Abraham, Isaac, and Jacob. We have a right now which we could not heretofore so fully claim—that is, of asking God for redress and redemption, as they have been refused us by man.

ELIAS HIGBEE.

To Joseph Smith, Junior.

When I had returned as far as Dayton, Ohio, I found the horses which we left on our journey out, and from thence I pursued my journey through Indiania on horseback, in company with Dr. Foster, leaving Brother Porter Rockwell at Dayton; the traveling being exceedingly bad, my progress was slow and wearisome.

The Prophet en route for Nauvoo.

My clerk, James Mulholland, while I was absent, died

on November 3rd, 1839, aged thirty-five years. He was a man of fine education, and a faithful scribe and Elder in the Church.* Death of James Mulholland.

Wednesday, March 4, 1840. I arrived safely at Nauvoo, after a wearisome journey, through alternate snow and mud, having witnessed many vexatious movements in government officers, whose sole object should be the peace and prosperity and happiness of the whole people; but instead of this, I discovered that popular clamor and personal aggrandizement were the ruling principles of those in authority; and my heart faints within me when I see, by the visions of the Almighty, the end of this nation, if she continues to disregard the cries and petitions of her virtuous citizens, as she has done, and is now doing.

I have also enjoyed many precious moments with the Saints during my journey.

On my way home I did not fail to proclaim the iniquity and insolence of Martin Van Buren, toward myself and an injured people, which will have its effect upon the public mind; and may he never be elected again to any office of trust or power,† by which he may abuse the innocent and let the guilty go free.

I depended on Dr. Foster to keep my daily journal during this journey, but he has failed me.

Elders Brigham Young and Reuben Hedlock returned to New York, and held a conference, when many Elders were ordained.

* Mulholland street in Nauvoo was named in honor of this worthy man. It ran east and west on the south side of the Temple block, and became the principal business street of the city. It was to him that the Prophet dictated a considerable part of his history. See History of the Church, Vol. III, p. 375.

† He never was. In the Presidential election of 1840, Van Buren was renominated by the Democratic Party, but was defeated by William Henry Harrison, the Whig candidate. Harrison received two hundred and thirty-four electoral votes to sixty for Van Buren. In 1848 Van Buren was again a candidate for President being the nominee of the Free Soil Party. Lewis Cass was the nominee of the Democrats, and Zachary Taylor of the Whigs. Taylor was elected, and Van Buren did not receive a single electoral vote.

*Report of the Senate Judiciary Committee on the Case of the Saints vs.
Missouri.*

Twenty-sixth Congress—First Session.—In the Senate of the United
States, March 4th, 1840.   Submitted, laid on the table, and ordered to
be printed, the following Report, made by Mr. Wall—

The Committee on the Judiciary to whom was referred the Memorial
of a Delegation of the Latter-day Saints, report—

The Petition of the Memorialists sets forth, in substance, that a portion of their sect commenced a settlement in the county of Jackson, in
the state of Missouri, in the summer of 1831; that they bought lands,
built houses, erected churches, and established their homes, and engaged in all the various occupations of life; that they were expelled from
that county in 1833 by a mob, under circumstances of great outrage,
cruelty, and oppression, and against all law, and without any offense
committed on their part, and to the destruction of property to the
amount of 120,000 dollars; that the society thus expelled amounted to
about 1,200 souls; that no compensation was ever made for the destruction of their property in Jackson; that after their expulsion from Jackson county, they settled in Clay county, on the opposite side of the Missouri river, where they purchased lands, and entered others at the land
office; where they resided peaceably for three years, engaged in cultivation, and other useful and active employments, when the mob again
threatened their peace, lives, and property; and they became alarmed,
and finally made a treaty with the citizens of Clay county, that they
should purchase their lands, and the Saints should remove; which was
complied with on their part, and the Saints removed to the county of
Caldwell, where they took up their abode and re-established their settlement, not without heavy pecuniary losses and other inconveniences; that
the citizens of Clay county never paid them for their lands, except for a
small part; they remained in Caldwell from 1836 until the fall of 1838,
and during that time had acquired, by purchase from the Government,
the settlers, and pre-emptioners, almost all the lands in the county of
Caldwell, and a portion of the lands in Daviess and Carrol counties—
the former county being almost entirely settled by the Saints, and they
were rapidly filling up the two latter counties.

Those counties, when the Saints first commenced their settlement,
were for the most part wild and uncultivated, and they had converted
them into large and well improved farms, well stocked. Land had risen
in value to ten or even twenty-five dollars per acre, and these counties
were rapidly advancing in cultivation and wealth.

That in August, 1838, a riot commenced, growing out of an attempt
of a Saint to vote, which resulted in creating great excitement, and the

perpetration of many scenes of lawless outrage, which are set forth in the Petition. That they were finally compelled to fly from those counties, and on the 11th October, 1838, they sought safety by that means, with their families, leaving many of their effects behind. That they had previously applied to the constituted authorities of Missouri for protection, but in vain. They allege, that they were pursued by the mob; that conflicts ensued; deaths occurred on each side; and finally a force was organized under the authority of the Governor of the state of Missouri, with orders to drive the Saints from the state, or exterminate them. The Saints thereupon determined to make no further resistance, but to submit themselves to the authorities of the state.

Several of the Saints were arrested and imprisoned on a charge of treason against the state, and the rest, amounting to about 15,000 souls, fled into other states, principally into Illinois, where they now reside.

The petition is drawn up at great length, and sets forth, with feeling and eloquence, the wrongs of which they complain; justifies their own conduct, and aggravates that of those whom they call their persecutors, and concludes by saying they see no redress, unless it be obtained of the Congress of the United States, to whom they make their solemn, last appeal, as American citizens, as Christians, and as men; to which decision they say they will submit.

The committee have examined the case presented by the petition, and heard the views urged by their agent, with care and attention; and after full examination and consideration, unanimously concur in the opinion—

That the case presented for their investigation is not such a one as will justify or authorize any interposition by this government.

The wrongs complained of are not alleged to be committed by any of the officers of the United States, or under the authority of its government in any manner whatever. The allegations in the petition relate to the acts of its citizens, and inhabitants and authorities of the state of Missouri, of which state the petitioners were at the time citizens, or inhabitants.

The grievances complained of in the petition are alleged to have been done within the territory of the state of Missouri. The committee, under these circumstances, have not considered themselves justified in inquiring into the truth or falsehood of the facts charged in the petition. If they are true, the petitioners must seek relief in the courts of judicature of the state of Missouri, or of the United States, which has the appropriate jurisdiction to administer full and adequate redress for the wrongs complained of, and doubless will do so fairly and impartially; *

* The Saints never acted upon the suggestion of the judiciary committee of the Senate, that they take their case before the Federal courts. The reasons why are considered at length in the introduction of this volume which see.

or the petitioners may, if they see proper, apply to the justice and magnanimity of the state of Missouri—an appeal which the committee feel justified in believing will never be made in vain by the injured or oppressed.

It can never be presumed that a state either wants the power or lacks the disposition to redress the wrongs of its own citizens, committed within her own territory, whether they proceed from the lawless acts of her officers or any other persons. The committee therefore report that they recommend the passage of the following resolution:

Resolved, That the committee on the judiciary be discharged from the further consideration of the memorial in this case; and that the memorialists have leave to withdraw the papers which accompany their memorial.

CHAPTER V.

AFFAIRS OF THE SAINTS BEFORE UNITED STATES SENATE—
GENERAL CONFERENCE OF THE CHURCH AT NAUVOO—
ACTION OF THE CHURCH WITH REFERENCE TO SENATE
COMMITTEE'S REPORT—MISSION TO PALESTINE.

Friday, 6.—Attended the meeting of the High Council
of Iowa, at Brother Elijah Fordham's, Montrose.

Extract from the Minutes of the Iowa High Council.

President Joseph Jmith, Jun., addressed the Council on various subjects, and in particular the consecration law; stating that the affairs
now before Congress was the only thing that ought to interest the Saints
at present; and till it was ascertained how it would terminate, no person ought to be brought to account before the constituted authorities of
the Church for any offense whatever; and [he] was determined that no
man should be brought before the Council in Nauvoo till that time,etc.,
etc. The law of consecration could not be kept here, and that it was the
will of the Lord that we should desist from trying to keep it; and if
persisted in, it would produce a perfect defeat of its object, and that he
assumed the whole responsibility of not keeping it until proposed by
himself.*

* This is the record of a very important action. The law of consecration and
stewardship, with which the action deals, was given to the Church by revelation
(Doc. and Cov. sec. xlii). Its fundamental principle is the recognition of God as the
possessor of all things, the earth and the fullness thereof. It is His by right of
proprietorship. He created it and sustains it by His power. This recognized, it
follows that whatsoever man possesses in it, he holds as a stewardship merely.
These principles the Saints were called upon to recognize and act under in the
establishment of Zion in Missouri; and apparently the Saints in Iowa were disposed
to undertake the same order of things in the settlement they were then making,
until stopped by the Prophet. The action of the Prophet in this instance demonstrates the elasticity in Church government, and law. The Lord, who commanded
to move forward, may also command a halt. He who said take neither purse nor
scrip when going to preach the Gospel (Matt. x: 10) may later say, under other circumstances, "He that hath a purse let him take it, and likewise his scrip" (Luke
xxii: 35, 36). So, too, in other matters. The Lord commanded the colony of Lehi
that there should no man among them "have save it be but one wife, and concu-
bines ye shall have none;" yet reserved the right to command His people
otherwise should the accomplishment of His purposes require it. (Book of Mormon,
Jacob ii: 24-30.)

He requested every exertion to be made to forward affidavits to Washington, and also letters to members of Congress.   The following votes were then passed:

First—That this Council will coincide with President Joseph Smith, Jun.'s decision concerning the consecration law, on the principle of its being the will of the Lord, and of President Smith's taking the responsibility on himself.

Second—That a committee of three be appointed, consisting of Wheeler Baldwin, Lyman Wight, and Abraham O. Smoot, to obtain affidavits and other documents to be forwarded to the city of Washington.

Third—That the clerk of this Council be directed to inform Judge Higbee, that it is the wish of this Council that he should not, upon any consideration, consent to accept of anything of Congress short of our just rights and demands for our losses and damages in Missouri.

Sunday, 8.—I attended the Council of Nauvoo, at Brother Granger's.

President Brigham Young preached in Columbia Hall, New York.

Monday, 9.—Elders Brigham Young, Heber C. Kimball, Parley P. Pratt, Orson Pratt, George A. Smith, and Reuben Hedlock, sailed from New York on the *Patrick Henry* for Liverpool.

Fifth Letter of Elias Higbee to the Prophet—the Affairs of the Saints at Washington.

WASHINGTON, March 9th, 1840.

DEAR BROTHER:—I expected, by this time, that we would be through with our business, but the chairman of the committee gave notice last week, he should call it [the committee's Report] up today in the Senate; through Mr. Young's having gone to Philadelphia, it will not be called up until his return, which will be on next Thursday, according to the information that I have obtained relative to this matter. If the resolution is passed, as annexed to the Report, I shall get my papers and leave the city.

I have written some letters to Brother Rigdon, which it seems he did not get. Brother Samuel Bennett writes that Brother Rigdon left Philadelphia for the Jerseys on the 5th instant. He [Rigdon] stated that he expects me to come there to go with him home, and that he would write me soon on the subject. I shall write for him to make the necessary arrangements. He says Dr. Ell's family left about a week ago for Commerce. Also that the Church there numbers about one hundred; and Parley P. Pratt, Orson Pratt, Brother Kimball, Brother Brigham

Young, George A. Smith, and Brother Hedlock were to sail from New York to England on the 7th instant.

As I have lately written several letters to you, I shall bid adieu, not to write again until after the Senate acts upon our business. Mr. Robinson says he has sent you a report; notwithstanding, I shall enclose another for you.

I have changed my place of boarding in consequence of Mrs. Richey's breaking up house-keeping, and going to Baltimore. I am busy here at chimney corner preaching.

Yours as ever in the bonds of everlasting love,

ELIAS HIGBEE.

To President Joseph Smith, Jun., Commerce, Illinois.

P. S.—Lest my previous letters should not come to hand, I merely say that I have been before the committee three days, and done all in my power to effect the object of our mission; have spoken my mind freely on the subject; and feel to have a conscience void of offense towards God in this matter. The subscription of which the report makes mention, was on condition that they could not lawfully do anything for us; after examination we were to submit and wait until the Great Disposer of human events shall adjust these things, in that place where the wicked cease from troubling and the weary are at rest (this I think is nearly the sentiment though perhaps not the very words); and I for one hope and pray the time will soon come when they will not trouble us in the west, as they have hitherto done.

There is a man here on whom I occasionally call, who owns two printing presses and much type, reading our books, I will with the assistance of God, get him to come to the west as soon as possible with his press, that you may set him to printing the truth. He told me, if we had any printing to do, he would do it cheap, and even go to the west if necessary.

Give my respects to Porter Rockwell, Dr. Foster, and also all the household of faith.   E. H.

Friday, 13.—Jacob K. Potts and Levi Stilley made affidavit before William Oglesby, J. P., that they witnessed the massacre at Haun's mill on the 30th of October, 1838, confirming the statements already written in this History. Potts had two balls shot into his right leg.

Sunday, 15.—The High Council of the Church at Nauvoo voted that the First Presidency superintend the affairs of the ferry between Nauvoo and Montrose.

Monday, 16.—Elder John Taylor wrote from Liverpool:

Extract from Elder John Taylor's Letter—Affairs in British Mission.

I told you about our coming to Liverpool. The first time I preached n came forward [for baptism]. We have been baptizing since: last week we baptized nine, we are to baptize tomorrow, but how many I know not. The little stone is rolling forth. One of the brethren dreamed he saw two men come to Liverpool; they cast a net into the sea and pulled it out full of fishes; he was surprised to see them pick the small fish out first and then the large. Well, if we get all the fish I shall be satisfied.

Brother Woodruff has lately left the Potteries and has gone to another neighborhood, and is making Methodist preachers scarce. He baptized 32 persons in one week—13 of them were Methodist preachers. Elder Clark is preaching and baptizing in and about Manchester. The latest account from Elder Turley, he was well, preaching and baptizing in the Potteries. Elder Willard Richards is very busy at this period, in visiting and setting in order the branches of the Church in Preston, Clithero, and all the regions round about, and holding correspondence with the Elders abroad.

The High Council met at my house in Nauvoo, and resolved that Robert B. Thompson write a letter to Judge Higbee at Washington, approving his course, and giving him certain names (for which see Thompson's letter), that he may order subpœnas for them as witnesses in the suit now before Congress, namely, the Latter-day Saints *versus* the State of Missouri, for redress of grievances.

Judge Elias Higbee's Course at Washington Approved.

Letter of R. B. Thompson to Elias Higbee, Announcing the Approval of the Church Authorities of the Latter's Course at Washington.

NAUVOO, HANCOCK COUNTY, ILLINOIS,
March 17th, 1840.

Elias Higbee, Esq.

DEAR AND HONORED SIR:—It is with the greatest pleasure I sit down to write to you at this time, to inform you of the situation and state of the Church as regards the object of your mission.

Since President Joseph Smith returned we have been favored with several communications from you, giving a statement of the proceedings before the committee, etc. On Monday evening last, your letters were read to a large concourse of our brethren, and other persons who were assembled to hear the same; and I must say that the greatest satisfaction was manifested by the assembled multitude, with the noble stand and straightforward and honorable course which you had pursued; and before the assembly separated, a vote of thanks to you was unanimously agreed upon. I can assure you that, from the feelings there, as well as upon other occasions, [expressed] there is not only a disposition, but a fixed determination, to uphold you in your righteous cause and sustain you in your efforts to obtain redress for the injuries which the Saints have borne from their unfeeling oppressors, and in bringing their case before the authorities of the nation.

In the evening the High Council assembled at the house of President Joseph Smith, Jun., and took your letters into consideration, when it was unanimously resolved that a letter should be written to you approving the measures which you were taking. The High Council likewise send you a list of the names of such persons as they think will testify to such facts as you want to substantiate. The names are as follows:

Alanson Ripley,	William Chapplin,
Francis Higbee,	Ira Mills,
Lyman Wight,	Oliver Olney,
Tarlton Lewis,	Hyrum Smith,
Edward Partridge,	Seymour Brunson,
Parley P. Pratt,	Samuel Bent,
Thorit Parsons,	Porter Rockwell,
King Follett,	George A. Smith,
Isaac Laney,	Stephen Markham,
Harvey Redfield,	Thomas Grover,
Ellis Eames,	Amanda Smith,
Chapman Duncan,	Lyman Leonard,
Smith Humphrey,	Alma Smith,
Erastus Snow,	Zebediah Robinson,
John M. Burk,	Orson Hyde,
Rebecca Judd,	Charles C. Rich,
Heber C. Kimball,	Henry G. Sherwood,
William Seyley,	Elias Smith,
Dr. Isaac Galland,	Sidney Rigdon.

There probably may be others, who may occur to your mind, whom you can send for if you think necessary. We should feel glad if you had the assistance of Presidents Smith and Rigdon at this critical time, while you have to contend with Jamieson, Linn [and others]. However I hope you will go forth in the strength of the Lord, and that truth will prevail. And I would say, "Twice is he armed who hath his quarrel just." The principles, sir, for which you contend are true; they are principles of justice, of humanity, of the Constitution, and the eternal principles of righteousness.

Although mankind may depart from those principles and be swayed by popular prejudices, and undue influences; yet at the same time, that man who contends for the same, although he cannot always carry his point, or convince at all times partial and interested judges—the gem or light of truth may be darkened, and its brilliancy for a while hid—yet when the Son of Righteousness shall arise, and disperse the darkness and mist of superstition and bigotry; when the true light shines, then shall it shine with all its glorious splendor and shed forth its luster with a brilliancy upon its advocates as shall altogether surpass the equipage and glories of those who are now in power.

ROBERT B. THOMPSON.

Letter of Horace R. Hotchkiss to Sidney Rigdon and Joseph Smith, Jun. —Inquiring Concerning the Progress Made Before Congress.

FAIR HAVEN, March 17th, 1840,

Reverends Sidney Rigdon and Joseph Smith, Jun.:

GENTLEMEN:—I some time since addressed a letter to Mr. [Joseph] Smith at Philadelphia, to which I have received no reply; and was in that city two or three weeks ago, but not being able to hear anything of Mr. Smith, I suppose he must of course have left; and with the hope of still reaching you, I now send to Washington.   I should have written you long before, and indeed very often this winter, but my health has been miserable; and since my return from Philadelphia, I have been confined to my house.

I beg you to inform me how you are progressing with your petition before Congress, and its probable result; whether you have any friends in the House or in the Senate, who will bring forward your case, and advocate it in sincerity, and persevere in your behalf with skill and ability until something is accomplished. Milk and water friends in Congress are good for nothing.   They must be true, have talents, be zealous, or else they will be detrimental rather than advantageous to you.

Should you, gentlemen, and Judge Higbee, come as far east as this, it will afford [me] much gratification to have you take up your quarters at my house. I did intend to see you at Washington, but my health will not now permit.

With much respect, yours,

HORACE R. HOTCHKISS.

Sixth Letter of Elias Higbee to the Prophet—Affairs of the Saints at Washington—Papers Withdrawn.

WASHINGTON CITY, March 24th, 1840.

DEAR BROTHER:—Our business is at last ended here.   Yesterday a resolution passed the Senate, that the committee should be discharged; and that we might withdraw the accompanying papers, which I have done. I have also taken a copy of the memorial, and want to be off for the west immediately. I have not gotten a letter from President Rigdon, although I have frequently written to him. I have received a letter from Brother Bennett, stating that he was in the Jerseys, and that he was calculating to have me come that way and go home with him; and also that he had business which he wanted me to attend to at the office here. When he last wrote, he stated that as yet he had no money to get home with, and I hardly know what course to take in regard to the matter. If I do not receive a letter in two or three days, I design leaving for Philadelphia or the west.

There is one honest Quaker-looking sort of a man here, by the name of William Green, (instead of John Green, as I stated in a letter to Brother Robinson), who has two iron printing presses, with other things necessary, that would come to Commerce, provided you could find work for him, and inform him of the same. How much work there is to do I know not; therefore merely write that if such a man and establishment are wanted, you could easily obtain them, or would know where they could be obtained. He believes as much in our religion as any other, but not much in any.

Yours in the Lord,

ELIAS HIGBEE.

P. S.—I would just observe, that information has reached this place, through some of the newspapers, that you have come out for Harrison. It is said that the information came by some gentlemen who obtained it from you, whilst in your company in passing through the state of Indiana. Another paper states that 1,000 houses are to be built in Commerce this season, which I hope is the truth.

I would just observe (on the subject of our business) I am sorry Judge Young had not insisted on the motion to print our papers, as it would have been opposed; then a speech from Clay and Mr. Preston would have been brought forth, as I have since learned; but I think it was a trick of the Missouri Senators to slide it along without making a noise, by its going to the committee as it did. Judge Young says he was anxious to have it brought before the committee, but seemed disposed to let it slide along easily, rather than run the risk of its being refused.

If he had let those speeches been made, almost every one would have read them; which would have shamed Missouri, (if there is any shame in her), and waked up the whole country, so that by another year Congress would do something for us. But there is no need of crying for spilt milk. I have done all I could in this matter, depending on the good judgment of Judge Young to legislate for us to the best advantage. I am inclined, however, to think if it was an error, it was one of the head, and not of the heart.

Mr. Hotchkiss, of Fair Haven, Connecticut, has addressed a letter to yourself, Brother Rigdon and myself, which seems to be written with much good feeling. He desires to know concerning our business here, inviting us to make his house our home, should we travel in that region. He writes that his health is very bad. I have been talking with Mr. Steward concerning a memorial, requesting him to bring it before the House; he has promised to do so if he can. He says he will talk with some of the members respecting it. I have answered Mr. Hotchkiss' letter this day, and sent him the report of the committee.

E. H.

At this time the work of the Lord is spreading rapidly in the United States and England—Elders are traveling in almost every direction, and multitudes are being baptized.

Letter of Horace R. Hotchkiss to Joseph Smith, Jun.—Offering Tract of Land for Sale.

FAIR HAVEN, 1st April, 1840.

Reverend Joseph Smith, Jun.:

MY DEAR SIR:—After writing you at, and then going to, Philadelphia, and not finding you, I addressed a letter to Washington City, and received a reply from Judge Higbee, by which I first learned of your return to Illinois; and at the same time I got the committee's report upon your application to Congress for redress of the outrages perpetrated upon your people by the Missourians. I am not, I must confess, much disappointed in the result; as I know the vacillating, fawning character of many in both houses of Congress; and these are not their worst traits either, for they not only lack the moral courage to do right, but will do what they know to be positively wrong, if they can make political capital by it; and will abandon you, me, or any one else, with perfect indifference, and heartless treachery, if by doing it they can obtain governmental favor, or political preferment. If we should not put our faith in princes, it appears most emphatically true that we should repose no confidence in politicians. The idea conveyed in the report, that exact justice will be meted to you by the judicial tribunals of Missouri, is too preposterous to require comment. It is indeed a new doctrine, that we should apply to robbers, or their supporters, to condemn themselves, to restore the valuables they have stolen, and to betray each other for the murders they have committed.

I do not believe (though I am sorry to say it) that you will ever receive a just or honorable remuneration for your losses of property, or any reparation for the personal indignities, privations and sufferings which your people have sustained in Missouri. The greatest reliance you have for regaining your wealth is in the honorable conduct of your people—their pure morals—their correct habits—their indefatigable industry—their untiring perseverance—and their well-directed enterprise. These constitute a capital which can never be shaken by man, and form the basis of all that is great in commercial influence, or in the attainment of pecuniary power.

Judge Higbee informs me that Mr. Rigdon is probably in New Jersey. It would have afforded me much pleasure to have seen you all at my house, and it was my intention to spend some time at Washington while you were there; but my health has been so very infirm, that it has prevented me from executing nearly all the arrangements I had proposed for myself for the last eight months.

Knowing the additions constantly joining your society, it has occurred to me that some of them may be unprovided with farming lands, and I mention at this time, that I am interested in a tract of about 12,000 acres of very choice lands, consisting of timber and prairie, fifteen or twenty miles from Springfield, upon which Mr. Gillett and several other families are settled and cultivating most excellent farms. It is one of the best neighborhoods in the state.

I do not know what my co-partners in this tract would say about disposing of what remains unsold of the tract, (say eight to nine thousand acres,) but I should be disposed to sell upon reasonable terms, provided from twenty to forty families, valuable for their prudence, industry, and good habits, from your society, can be found to form a small colony of practical farmers. I am also interested with the same gentlemen in lands near Rock River, in Henry and Mercer counties, and believe this would, on many accounts, be another extremely desirable place or location for a colony of your people. I have said nothing to those owning with me relative to this subject, but suppose they would be governed materially by two considerations; namely, the characters of the purchasers, and the fact of their being actual settlers or not.

If you think two small colonies of the right sort can be formed from your society, you will oblige by informing me at your earliest opportunity. The price of the balance in the tract near Springfield, including an average proportion of timber, and an average proportion of prairie, I should think $4.50 per acre. None of the prairie alone has been sold for less than three dollars, and some at three and a half; and I am confident that four and a half dollars for timber and prairie is very low, and especially as a credit, except for a small amount, would be extended to purchasers. The other tract is nearly all prairie, but the finest selection of that region. It is probably worth three and a half dollars per acre.

As my paper is out, I have only room to request my respects presented to all friends at Commerce. I beg you to tell the editor of the *Times and Seasons*, that as soon as my health allows me to go to the bank, I shall send him $10.

Your obedient servant,

HORACE R. HOTCHKISS.

Letter of Sidney Rigdon to the Prophet.

AT JAMES IVANS', NEW JERSEY,

April 3rd, 1840.

Brother Joseph Smith, Jun.

DEAR SIR.—I thought I would occupy a portion of this morning in writing to you. By a letter received from Brother Higbee yesterday, I have learned that the Senate has decided that they have no constitutional right to interfere in the case between us and the people of Missouri; and refer us to the courts for redress; either those of Missouri or the United States. Now I am confident, that there is but one person in Missouri that we can sue with safety, and that is Boggs, and he is known to be a bankrupt, and unable to pay his debts; that if we should sue him, we will have the cost to pay, as he has nothing to pay it with. We are therefore left to bear the loss without redress, at present.

Judge Higbee is on the way home, and has been for ten days. He obtained money from Judge Young, to what amount I cannot say, but he will be able to tell you when he gets home. The Judge continues his friendship, and is ready to accommodate with money, whenever called for. Surely he is a friend indeed, and ought never to be forgotten.

I am up to this time without means to get home, but I have no uneasiness about it. I shall doubtless get means as soon as my health will admit of my going. My health is slowly improving, and I think if I have no relapse, I will be able to leave for home some time in the month of May, &c.

SIDNEY RIGDON.

Monday, April 6.—Elders Young, Kimball, Pratt, Smith, and Hedlock landed in Liverpool, on the first day

Arrival of Brigham Young and Associates in England.

of the eleventh year of the Church, after a tedious passage of twenty-eight days, during sixteen of which they encountered head winds, and one severe storm of three or four days; and a great portion of the time the decks were covered with water—all of which tended to increase sea-sickness and suffering.

At the time of sailing President Young's and Elder Kimball's health was very poor. George A. Smith had the ague for six days in succession. When the ship left her moorings the shore resounded with the songs of the Saints, who had come down to bid them farewell; they unitedly sang "The gallant ship is under weigh," * until

---

* The hymn was composed by W. W. Phelps, and is worthy of reproduction in extenso.

> The gallant ship is under weigh
>   To bear me off to sea,
> And yonder floats the streamer gay
>   That says she waits for me.
> The seamen dip the ready oar,
>   As rippled waves oft tell,
> They bear me swiftly from the shore;
>   My native land, farewell!
>
> I go, but not to plough the main,
>   To ease a restless mind,
> Nor yet to toil on battle's plain,
>   The victor's wreath to find.
> 'Tis not for treasures that are hid
>   In mountain or in dell,
> 'Tis not for joys like these I bid
>   My native land, farewell!
>
> I go to break the fowler's snare,
>   To gather Israel home;
> I go the name of Christ to bear
>   In lands and isles unknown.
> And soon my pilgrim feet shall tread
>   On land where errors dwell,
> Whence light and truth have long since fled,
>   My native land, farewell!
>
> I go, an erring child of dust,
>   Ten thousand foes among,
> Yet on His mighty arm I trust,
>   Who makes the feeble strong.
> My sun, my shield, forever nigh.
>   He will my fears dispel,
> This hope supports me when I sigh,
>   My native land, farewell!
>
> I go devoted to His cause,
>   And to His will resigned;
> His presence will supply the loss
>   Of all I leave behind.

out of hearing. The brethren occupied three berths in the forecastle, taking what was called a steerage passage. With the exception of Elder Kimball, not one of them had ever been to sea, and the sailors called them "land lubbers." The ship being loaded with flour and cotton, they were packed in a small compartment with about 100 or 120 passengers, being a motley mixture of English, Welsh, Irish, and Scotch, who were returning home from America to visit their friends, or had got sick of "Yankeedom" and were leaving for "sweet home."

They had scarcely been at sea twelve hours before the whole of them were prostrated by sea-sickness. George A. Smith vomited up his ague.* Brother Brigham Young, although confined to his berth by sea-sickness during the entire journey, was unable to vomit.

On coming into the Mersey the ship cast anchor in order to wait for the tide, when a small boat put off from the shore. Brothers Young, Kimball, and Parley P. Pratt went in it to the landing. On reaching the quay, Brother Young shouted hosannah three times, which he had promised to do whenever he should land on the shores of Old England. The brethren then went to No. 8 Union Street, Liverpool, where they procured bread and wine in order to partake of the Sacrament.

Elders Orson Pratt and George A. Smith, and Reuben Hedlock stayed on board to look after the baggage. About

> His promise cheers the sinking heart
>   And lights the darkest cell,
> To exiled pilgrims grace imparts;
>   My native land, farewell!
>
> I go, it is my Master's call,
>   He's made my duty plain,
> No danger can the heart appall
>   When Jesus stoops to reign.
> And now the vessel's side we've made,
>   The sails their bosoms swell,
> Thy beauties in the distance fade,
>   My native land, farewell!

* It is said that he never had the ague afterwards.

three p. m., Brother Young sent a small boat for them, and the boatmen piloted them to the same place, where they all met together, partook of the Sacrament, and returned thanks for their safe deliverance.

When they landed they were almost penniless. Two or three of them had sufficient to buy hats for those who needed them the worst.

Minutes of the General Conference of the Church.

At a General Conference of the Church of Jesus Christ of Latter-day Saints, held in Nauvoo, Hancock County, Illinois, on the sixth day of April, A.D. 1840, agreeable to previous appointment, Joseph Smith, Jun., was called upon to preside over the meeting, and Robert B. Thompson was chosen clerk.

The Conference was then opened by prayer by Elder John E. Page.

The President rose, made some observations on the business of the Conference, exhorted the brethren who had charges to make against individuals, and made some very appropriate remarks respecting the pulling the beam out of their own eye, that they may see more clearly the mote which was in their brother's eye.

A letter was read from presidents of the Seventies, wishing for an explanation of the steps, which the High Council had taken, in removing Elder F. G. Bishop from the quorum of the Seventies to that of the High Priests, without any other ordination than he had when in the Seventies, and wished to know whether those ordained into the Seventies at the same time F. G. Bishop was, had a right to the High Priesthood,* or not. After observations on the case by different individuals, the president gave a statement of the authority of the Seventies, and stated that they were Elders and not High Priests, and consequently Brother F. G. Bishop had no claim to that office. It was then unanimously resolved that Elder F. G. Bishop be placed back again into the quorum of the Seventies.

On motion, resolved that the Conference adjourn until two o'clock.

Conference met pursuant to adjournment. Prayer by Elder Joseph Young.

Elder Thomas Grover presented charges against Brother D. W. Rogers for compiling a hymn-book, and selling it as the one compiled and published by Sister Emma Smith; secondly, for writing a private letter to New York City, casting reflections on the character of Elder John P. Greene; and thirdly, for administering medicine unskilfully, which had a bad effect.

* To the office of High Priest is what is meant; Seventies, of course, hold the Melchisedek or High Priesthood.

On motion, resolved, that, as Brother Rogers is not present, his case be laid over until tomorrow.

Elder John Lawson then came forward and stated, that in consequence of some difficulty existing in the branch of the Church where he resided, respecting the Word of Wisdom, fellowship had been withdrawn from him, and also from Brother Thomas S. Edwards.   After hearing the particulars, on motion, resolved, that John Lawson and Thomas S. Edwards be restored to fellowship.

Elder Orson Hyde addressed the Conference at some length, and stated that it had been prophesied, some years ago, that he had a great work to perform among the Jews; and that he had recently been moved upon by the Spirit of the Lord to visit that people, and gather up all the information he could respecting their movements, expectations, &c., and communicate the same to this Church, and to the nation at large; stating that he intended to visit the Jews in New York, London, and Amsterdam, and then visit Constantinople and the Holy Land.

On motion, resolved, that Elder Orson Hyde proceed on his mission to the Jews, and that letters of recommendation be given him, signed by the President and Clerk of the Conference.

Elder John E. Page then arose, and spoke with much force on the subject of Elder Hyde's mission, the gathering of the Jews, and the restoration of the house of Israel; proving, in a brief but convincing manner, from the Bible, Book of Mormon, and the Book of Doctrine and Covenants, that these things must take place, and that the time had nearly arrived for their accomplishment.

Adjourned until tomorrow morning, nine o'clock.

Tuesday morning, April 7.

Conference met pursuant to adjournment.   A hymn was sung by the choir, and the throne of grace was addressed by Elder Caleb Baldwin.

Brother D. W. Rogers' case was then called up, and after many observations and explanations, it was on motion resolved, that D. W. Rogers be forgiven, and the hand of fellowship be continued towards him.

Conference adjourned for one hour, and met pursuant to adjournment.   A hymn was sung by the choir, followed by prayer by Elder Reynolds Cahoon.

The President called upon the Clerk to read the report of the First Presidency and High Council, with regard to their proceedings in purchasing lands, and securing a place of gathering for the Saints.   The report having been read, the President made some observations respecting the pecuniary affairs of the Church, and requested the brethren to step forward, and assist in liquidating the debts on the town plot, so that the poor might have an inheritance.

The President then gave an account of their mission to Washington City, the treatment they received, and the action of the Senate on the Memorial which was presented before them. The meeting then called for the reading of the Memorial, and the report of the Committee on Judiciary, to whom the same was referred, which were read.

On motion, resolved that a committee of five be appointed to draft resolutions expressive of the sentiments of this Conference in reference to the report. On motion it was resolved. that Robert D. Foster, Orson Hyde, John E. Page, Joseph Wood, and Robert B. Thompson compose said committee, and report to this Conference.

Resolved, that this meeting adjourn until tomorrow morning.

Wednesday morning, April 8.

Conference met pursuant to adjournment. A number were confirmed who had been baptized the previous evening. Prayer by Elder Marks.

The Committee appointed to draft resolutions on the report of the Senate Committee of the Judiciary were then called upon to make their report. Robert B. Thompson of the Committee then read the

Resolutions:

Whereas, we learn, with deep sorrow, regret, and disappointment, that the Committee on the Judiciary to whom was referred the Memorial of the members of the Church of Jesus Christ of Latter-day Saints (commonly called "Mormons"), complaining of the grievances suffered by them in the state of Missouri, have reported unfavorably to our cause, to justice, and humanity;

Therefore Resolved 1st: That we consider the report of the Committee on Judiciary, unconstitutional, and subversive to the rights of a free people, and justly calls for the disapprobation of all the supporters and lovers of good government and republican principles.

Resolved, 2ndly: That the Committee state, in their report, that our Memorial *aggravates* the case of our oppressors, and at the same time say, that they have not examined into the truth or falsehood of the facts mentioned in said Memorial.

Resolved, 3rdly: That the Memorial does not aggravate the conduct of our oppressors, as every statement set forth in said Memorial was substantiated by indubitable testimony; therefore we consider the statements of the Committee, in regard to that part, as false and ungenerous.

Resolved, 4thly: That that part of the report referring us to the justice and magnanimity of the state of Missouri for redress, we deem it a great insult to our good sense, better judgment, and intelligence, when numerous affidavits, which were laid before the Committee, prove that we could only go into the state of Missouri contrary to the exterminating order of the Governor, and consequently at the risk of our lives.

Resolved, 5thly: That after repeated appeals to the constituted authorities of the state of Missouri for redress, which were in vain, we fondly hoped that in the Congress of the United States, ample justice would have been rendered us; and upon that consideration alone, we pledged ourselves to abide their decision.

Resolved, 6thly: That the exterminating order of Governor Boggs is a direct infraction of the Constitution of the United States, and of the state of Missouri; and the committee in refusing to investigate the proceedings of the Executive and others of the state of Missouri, and turning a deaf ear to the cries of widows, orphans, and innocent blood, we deem no less than seconding the proceeding of that murderous clan, whose deeds are recorded in heaven, and justly call down upon their heads the righteous judgments of an offended God.

Resolved, 7thly: That the thanks of this meeting be tendered to the citizens of the state of Illinois, for their kind, liberal, and generous conduct towards us; and that we call upon them, as well as every patriot in this vast Republic, to aid us in all lawful endeavors to obtain redress for the injuries we have sustained.

Resolved, 8thly: That the thanks of this meeting be tendered to the delegation of Illinois, for the bold, manly, noble, and independent course they have taken in presenting our case before the nation, amid misrepresentation, contumely, and abuse, which were heaped upon us in our suffering condition.

Resolved, 9thly: That the thanks of this meeting be tendered to Governor Carlin of Illinois, Governor Lucas of Iowa Territory, for their sympathy, aid, and protection; and to all other honorable gentlemen who have assisted us in our endeavors to obtain redress.

Resolved, 10thly: That Joseph Smith, Jun., Sidney Rigdon, and Elias Higbee, the Delegates appointed by this Church to visit the City of Washington, to present our sufferings before the authorities of the nation, be tendered the thanks of this meeting for the prompt and efficient manner in which they have discharged their duty; and that they be requested, in behalf of the Church of Jesus Christ of Latter-day Saints throughout the world, to continue to use their endeavors to obtain redress for a suffering people.   And if all hopes of obtaining satisfaction for the injuries done us be entirely blasted, that they then appeal our case to the Court of Heaven, believing that the Great Jehovah, who rules over the destiny of nations, and who notices the falling sparrows, will undoubtedly redress our wrongs, and ere long avenge us of our adversaries.*

On motion, *Resolved,* That the report of the committee on the Judici-

---

* See Introduction to Volume III History of the Church, where retribution on Missouri is considered at length.

ary, as well as the foregoing Preamble and Resolutions, be published in the Quincy papers.

On motion, *Resolved*, That a committee of three be appointed to investigate the recommendations of those persons who wish to obtain an ordination to the ministry, and ordain such as are thought worthy; and that Elders Bent, Wood, and Hyde compose said committee.

Resolved, That this meeting feel satisfied with the proceeding of the Presidency with regard to the sales of town property, &c., and that they are requested to continue in their agency.

Resolved, That this meeting adjourn for one hour.

Conference met pursuant to adjournment.

After singing the President arose and read the 3rd chapter of John's Gospel, after which, prayer was offered by Elder Erastus Snow.

The President commenced making observations on the different subjects embraced in the chapter [previously read] particularly the 3rd, 4th, and 5th verses, illustrating them with a very beautiful and striking figure, and throwing a flood of light on the subjects brought up to review. He then spoke to the Elders respecting their mission, and advised those who went into the world to preach the Gospel, to leave their families provided with the necessaries of life; and to teach the gathering as set forth in the Holy Scripture. That it had been wisdom for the most of the Church to keep on this side of the river, that a foundation might be established in this place; but that now it was the privilege of the Saints to occupy the lands in Iowa, or wherever the Spirit might lead them. That he did not wish to have any political influence, but wished the Saints to use their political franchise to the best of their knowledge.

He then stated that since Elder Hyde had been appointed to visit the Jews, he had felt an impression that it would be well for Elder John E. Page to accompany him on his mission. It was resolved that Elder John E. Page be appointed to accompany Elder Orson Hyde on his mission, and that he have proper credentials given him.

It was then resolved, that as a great part of the time of the Conference had been taken up with charges against individuals, which might have been settled by the different authorities of the Church, that in future no such cases be brought before the Conferences.

The Committee on ordinations reported that they had ordained thirty-one persons to be Elders in the Church, who were ordained under the hands of Alpheus Gifford * and Stephen Perry, which report was accepted.

---

* Alpheus Gifford was born in Adams township, Berkshire County, Massachusetts, August 28, 1793. At the age of eighteen, having scarcely sufficient learning to enable him to read the Bible, he commenced preaching the Gospel, not for hire, but for the salvation of souls. In 1817, he married Anna Nash, who bore him seven sons and three daughters. In the spring of 1831, hearing of the doctrines taught

Fredrick G. Williams presented himself on the stand, and humbly asked forgiveness for his conduct, [while in Missouri], and expressed his determination to do the will of God in the future. His case was presented to the Conference by President Hyrum Smith, when it was unanimously

Resolved,

That Fredrick G. Williams be forgiven, and be received into the fellowship of the Church.

It was reported that seventy-five persons had been baptized during the Conference, and that upwards of fifty had been received into the quorum of Seventies.

President Hyrum Smith dismissed the assembly. After he had made a few observations, the Conference was closed, under the blessings of the Presidency, until the first Friday in October next.

JOSEPH SMITH, JUN.,
President.

by Joseph Smith he made diligent inquiry and found they were scriptural and was baptized and ordained a priest; he brought home five books of Mormon which he distributed among his friends; he was then living in Tioga County, Pennsylvania. Soon after he went to Kirtland, Ohio, to see the Prophet Joseph Smith and the brethren, when he was ordained an elder; he was accompanied by his brother Levi, Elial Strong, Eleazer Miller, Enos Curtis, and Abraham Brown, who were baptized. On returning to Pennsylvania he preached and baptized many, among whom was Heber C. Kimball. The gifts of the Gospel were enjoyed by many, signs followed those who believed; devils were cast out; the sick were healed; many prophesied; some spake with new tongues; while others interpreted the same. Mr. Calvin Gilmour, with whom Brother Gifford had previously been associated in preaching, heard him speak in tongues and interpret. Gilmour declared he undestood the languages and that they were interpreted correctly, and that he knew Gifford had no classical learning; but that he would rather be damned than believe in Mormonism.

In June 1832, Brother Gifford started for Missouri; traveled to Cincinnati and wintered there with a few Saints who had been baptized by Lyman Wight. He arrived in Jackson county, Missouri, in March, 1833, where he preached extensively; he was driven with the Saints from that county in the fall of that year. He removed to Clay county, enduring the persecution incident upon settling in, and final expulsion from, the same. He went to Kirtland, Ohio, and attended the dedication of the Temple and received the ordinances there administered. He returned to Missouri and was driven with the Saints to Far West, Caldwell county. In the winter of 1839, he was driven from Missouri. He located in the Morley settlement near Lima, Illinois, and subsequently five miles above Nauvoo, where he died December 25, 1841.

(*Addenda,* Ms. Church History, Book "C" 2. Also page 404.)

CHAPTER VI.

DEVELOPMENT OF THE WORK IN ENGLAND—THE PALESTINE
MISSION—POST-OFFICE NAME CHANGED FROM COMMERCE
TO NAUVOO.

April 7.—The brethren [President Brigham Young, *et al.*] found Elder John Taylor, who, in company with Joseph Fielding, had recently built up a branch of twenty-eight members in Liverpool.

April 8.—President Brigham Young and company went to Elder Richards', at Preston, by railway; when they arrived there, they had not a single sixpence left. So emaciated was President Young at this time from his long sickness, and journey, that when Elder Richards returned home this day from a mission to Clitheroe, and found him in his room, he did not know him.

Letter of Hon. Richard M. Young to Elias Higbee.

WASHINGTON CITY, April 9, 1840.

Judge Elias Higbee:

DEAR SIR.—Having a private opportunity, by Judge Snow, of Quincy, I have sent you two receipts, one for $50, and the other for $90, making together $140, to Mr. E. I. Philips, cashier of the branch of the State Bank of Illinois, at Quincy. When it is convenient for you to make payment, will you have the goodness to send the money to Mr. Philips, who is instructed to receive it, and apply it towards the payment of a note of mine in that bank.

I received a letter from Mr. Rigdon a few days ago. It was mailed in Philadelphia, but was dated on the inside in New Jersey. His health is gradually but slowly improving, and he thinks he will set out for home some time in May. He wished a small sum of money, $40, deposited in one of the banks here, for a gentleman in Buffalo, New York, which I have attended to according to his direction and request. I also informed him, if he stood in need of more, to call on me and it would give me pleasure to accommodate him; so you need not be uneasy on that score.

Nothing new has transpired since you left us, with the exception of the death of one of the Connecticut Senators, Mr. Thadeus Betts, who died yesterday. His funeral took place today, hence no business was transacted in the Senate. We have also lost the Cumberland Road Bill by a final vote in the Senate, 20 voting for and 22 against it; one single vote from the majority would have saved it, by making a tie. The Vice-President was exceedingly anxious for the opportunity of getting the casting vote in its favor. Mr. Clay, of Kentucky, made a speech against and voted throughout against it. Grundy, of Tennessee, Wright of New York, and Buchanan of Pennsylvania, three of the leading Democrats in the Senate voted for it. There were but seven Whigs who voted for it, and thirteen Democrats. I think we will adjourn about the first or second Monday in June.

I received from Mr. Rigdon the Petition and papers in relation to a change of postmaster at Commerce, with an affidavit from Doctor Galland, all of which have been laid before the proper department. As soon as I get an answer, it shall be communicated to you. Don't forget to have the *Times and Seasons* sent to me. Give my respects to Rev. Joseph Smith, and accept for yourself my best wishes for your happiness.

Yours, etc.,

Richard M. Young.

In the *Times and Seasons* of this month is a prospectus for publishing at Nauvoo, a weekly paper, to be called *The News.**   *The News.*

Orson Hyde's Credentials as a Missionary to Palestine.

To all people unto whom these presents shall come, Greeting—

Be it known that we, the constituted authorities of the Church of Jesus Christ of Latter-day Saints, assembled in Conference at Nauvoo, Hancock county, and state of Illinois, on the sixth day of April, in the year of our Lord, one thousand eight hundred and forty, considering an important event at hand, an event involving the interest and fate of the Gentile nations throughout the world—from the signs of the times and from declarations contained in the oracles of God, we are forced to come to this conclusion. The Jewish nations have been scattered abroad among the Gentiles for a long period; and in our estimation, the

---

* It was announced in the Prospectus that the *News* would "take perfectly neutral ground, in regard to politics, and it is the fixed determination of the publishers to studiously avoid all party strife, and political wranglings which are so prevalent at the present time." The *News*, however, never materialized.

time of the commencement of their return to the Holy Land has already arrived. As this scattered and persecuted people are set among the Gentiles as a sign unto them of the second coming of the Messiah, and also of the overthrow of the present kingdoms and governments of the earth, by the potency of His Almighty arm in scattering famine and pestilence like the frosts and snows of winter, and sending the sword with nation against nation to bathe it in each other's blood; it is highly important, in our opinion, that the present views and movements of the Jewish people be sought after and laid before the American people, for their consideration, their profit and their learning.

And feeling it to be our duty to employ the most efficient means in our power to save the children of men from "the abomination that maketh desolate," we have, by the counsel of the Holy Spirit, appointed Elder Orson Hyde, the bearer of these presents, a faithful and worthy minister of Jesus Christ, to be our Agent and Representative in foreign lands, to visit the cities of London, Amsterdam, Constantinople, and Jerusalem; and also other places that he may deem expedient; and converse with the priests, rulers, and elders of the Jews, and obtain from them all the information possible, and communicate the same to some principal paper for publication, that it may have a general circulation throughout the United States.

As Mr. Hyde has willingly and cheerfully accepted the appointment to become our servant and the servant of the public in distant and foreign countries, for Christ's sake, we do confidently recommend him to all religious and Christian people, and to gentlemen and ladies making no profession, as a worthy member of society, possessing much zeal to promote the happiness of mankind, fully believing that they will be forward to render him all the pecuniary aid he needs to accomplish this laborious and hazardous mission for the general good of the human family.

Ministers of every denomination upon whom Mr. Hyde shall call, are requested to hold up his hands, and aid him by their influence, with an assurance that such as do this shall have the prayers and blessings of a poor and afflicted people, whose blood has flowed to test the depths of their sincerity and to crimson the face of freedom's soil with martyr's blood.

Mr. Hyde is instructed by this Conference to transmit to this country nothing but simple facts for publication, entirely disconnected with any peculiar views of theology, leaving each class to make their own comments and draw their own inferences.

Given under our hands at the time and place before mentioned.

JOSEPH SMITH, Jun., Chairman.
ROBERT B. THOMPSON, Clerk.

Sunday, 12.—Several of the Twelve bore their public testimony to the Gospel in the Cock Pit, Preston.

The High Council of Nauvoo met at my house, when I proposed that Brother Hyrum Smith go east with Oliver Granger to settle some business transactions of the Church which the Council sanctioned; and voted, "that President Joseph Smith, Jun., make the necessary credentials for Oliver Granger and Hyrum Smith."

Monday, 13.—From the second of October, 1839, to this date, there have been one hundred and forty-five shocks of earthquake in Scotland, reported by Mr. Milne

Earthquakes. to the Royal Society of Edinburgh. Some of these shocks were sufficient to alter the natural levels of the ground more than two degrees, and some witnesses thought four degrees, and caused houses to rock like boats on the sea.

Tuesday, 14.—A council of the Twelve, namely, Brigham Young, Heber C. Kimball, Parley P. Pratt, Orson Pratt, Wilford Woodruff, George A. Smith and John

Ordination of
Willard Richards to the
Apostleship.

Taylor, was held at the house of Elder Willard Richards, in Preston, England, when the latter was ordained to the Apostleship,— agreeably to the revelation,—by President Young, under the hands of the quorum present. Other business was transacted, as also on the following days, all of which may be seen by reference to President Young's letter of the 17th instant.

Wednesday, 15.—Elder Orson Hyde left Commerce for Jerusalem.

Thursday, 16.—Elder Orson Hyde met with John E. Page at Lima.

Letter of Brigham Young to the Saints of the United States—Affairs of the British Mission.

Preston, England, April 17, 1840.

To the Saints in the United States of America: For the comfort of the Church in general, in that country, I attempt to address a few lines to you, to let you know where we are, and what we are doing in this country.

The work of the Lord is progressing here, and has been ever since Elders Orson Hyde and H. C. Kimball left this country. According to the account that the Elders give of their labors, there have been about eight or nine hundred persons baptized since they left. The Gospel is spreading, the devils are roaring. As nigh as I can learn, the priests are howling, the tares are binding up, the wheat is gathering, nations are trembling, and kingdoms tottering; "men's hearts failing them for fear, and for looking for those things that are coming on the earth." The poor among men are rejoicing in the Lord, and the meek do increase their joy. The hearts of the wicked do wax worse and worse, deceiving and being deceived.

But I rejoice that I am counted worthy to be one of the number to carry salvation to the poor and meek of the earth. Brethren, I want to say many things, but I shall not have room on this paper, as I design giving the minutes of our conference below.

After a long and tedious voyage of 28 days on the water, we landed in Liverpool, Elders Heber C. Kimball, Parley P. Pratt, Orson Pratt, George A. Smith, Reuben Hedlock and myself, were in the company. We rejoiced in the Lord, and when we cast our minds upon the Saints in that country, [the United States] we could, by faith participate in their joys, realizing they were met in conference, it being the 6th day of April. We soon found a room that we could have to ourselves, which made our solemn assembly glorious. We blest each other and prepared for our labor. The next day we found Elder Taylor in the city. There had been about thirty baptized. On Wednesday went to Preston; met with the church on Sunday, and bore testimony to the things the Lord is doing in these last days. President Joseph Fielding gave out an appointment for a conference for the church on Wednesday, the 15th.

At a council of the Twelve, held in Preston, England, on the 14th of April, 1840, it being the 9th day of the 1st month of the 11th year of the rise of the Church of Jesus Christ, Elders Brigham Young, Heber C. Kimball, Parley P. Pratt, Orson Pratt, Wilford Woodruff, John Taylor, and George A. Smith, being present, Elder Brigham Young was called to preside, and Elder John Taylor chosen secretary.

The council was opened by prayer by Elder Brigham Young. Elder Willard Richards was ordained to the office of an Apostle, and received into the quorum of the Twelve by unanimous vote, according to previous revelation. Elder Brigham Young was unanimously chosen as the President of the Twelve.*

* President Young was also President of the Twelve by virtue of seniority of ordination into the quorum. When the quorum of the Twelve was first organized

Resolved, that he who acts as the secretary of the quorum, shall prepare the minutes of the conference of the quorum, and deposit them in the hands of the president for keeping.

Moved by Elder Kimball, and seconded by Elder Richards, that twenty of the Seventies be sent for, and that it be left discretionary with the President of the Twelve to send for more if he think proper. Conference adjourned. Benediction by Elder Kimball.

At a general conference of the Church of Jesus Christ of Latter-day Saints, held in the Temperance Hall, Preston, Lancashire, England, on the 15th of April, 1840, President Joseph Fielding called upon Elder Kimball to preside, and Elder William Clayton was chosen clerk, it being the 10th day of the 1st month of the 11th year of the rise of the Church

The meeting was opened by singing, and prayer by Elder Kimball. Elder Kimball then called upon the Elders to represent the different branches of the Church. Elder Joseph Fielding represented the church in Preston, consisting of about three hundred members, seven Elders, eight Priests, six Teachers, and two Deacons. Elder Peter Melling represented the church in Penworthan, consisting of seventy-three members, three Elders, one Priest, two Teachers. John Jackson represented the church at Southport, consisting of twenty members, one Priest, and one Teacher. Elder John Moon represented the church at Danbers Lane, and neighborhood—members generally in good standing, consisting of fifty-four members, one Elder, two Priests, three Teachers. Richard Benson, represented the church at Hunter's Hill and neighborhood, consisting of seventeen members, one Elder, one Priest, one Teacher.

Elder Amos Fielding, represented the church at Bolton, consisting of sixty members, one Elder, two Priests, two Teachers. Elder Amos Fielding represented the church at Heskin, consisting of three members, one Elder. Elder Amos Fielding represented the Church at Radcliff, consisting of ten members. Elder Withnal represented the

the members took their place according to age. This arrangement brought Thomas B. Marsh to the head of the quorum, and made him President. After this first arrangement, however, the members of the quorum took their place in it according to seniority of ordination, not of age. (See Volume II this work, pp. 219, 220, and notes). Brigham Young was the second man ordained into the quorum, Lyman E. Johnson being the first. As Lyman E. Johnson was excommunicated from the Church at Far West in 1838, Brigham Young was President of the Twelve by virtue of his seniority of ordination as well as by the choice of his brethren. Indeed the choice of the brethren mentioned in the text can only be regarded as an act recognizing the fact of his presidency by virtue of his seniority of ordination. It may be of interest to remark also, that at the time there was but one man in the quorum President Young's senior by age, namely, John E. Page, born in 1799, and ordained an Apostle in 1838.

church at Whittle, consisting of eighteen members, one Elder, four Priests. Elder Francis Clark represented the church at Ribchester, consisting of twenty-five members, two Elders, one Priest. Elder Thomas Richardson represented the church at Burnley, consisting of twenty four members, generally in good standing, one Priest, one Teacher. Elder Francis Moon represented the church at Blackburn, consisting of fifteen members, one Priest. Elder James Smithies represented the church at Chardgley and Thornley, consisting of twenty-nine members, two Elders, one Priest, one Teacher, one Deacon.

Priest John Ellison represented the church at Waddington, consisting of fifty members, two Priests, two Teachers, one Deacon. Elder Thomas Smith represented the church at Clitheroe, consisting of twenty-seven members, one Elder, three Priests. Elder Thomas Smith represented the church at Catburn, consisting of eighty-four members, one Elder, two Priests, two Teachers, one Deacon. Elder Thomas Smith represented the church at Downham, consisting of twenty members, one Teacher, one Deacon.

Elder Thomas Smith represented the church at Gridleton, consisting of five members. Elder William Clayton represented the church at Manchester, consisting of two hundred and forty member, three Elders, five Priests, four Teachers, one Deacon. Elder William Clayton represented the church at Stockport, consisting of forty members, one Priest, two Teachers, one Deacon. Elder William Clayton represented the church at Peover and Macclesfield, consisting of thirty members, three Priests. Elder William Clayton represented the church at Duckinfield, consisting of thirty members, one Priest. Elder William Clayton represented the church at Altrincham, consisting of eight members, one Priest, one Teacher. Elder William Clayton represented the church at Middlewich, consisting of six members.

Elder David Wilding represented the church at Bury and Elton, consisting of twelve members. Elder Wilford Woodruff represented the church in the Potteries, consisting of one hundred and one members, one Elder, two Priests, four Teachers, one Deacon. Elder Wilford Woodruff represented the church at Herefordshire, consisting of one hundred and sixty members, one Elder, two Priests; about forty of them were Methodist preachers of the United Brethren.

Elder John Taylor represented the church at Liverpool, consisting of twenty-eight members. Elder Joseph Fielding represented the church at Alston, Cumberland, consisting of forty members, two Elders, two Priests, two Teachers. Elder Willard Richards represented the church at Brampton, consisting of thirty members, one Elder, one Priest. Elder Willard Richards represented the church at Bedford, consisting of forty members, one Elder, one Priest. Elder Willard Richards represented the church at Scotland, consisting of twenty-one members, three Elders.

The meeting was then adjourned for one hour. The conference again assembled at half-past one o'clock. Meeting opened by prayer, and business commenced.

Elder John Moon represented the church at Layland Moss, consisting of six members, one Priest.

Elder Willard Richards having been previously ordained into the quorum of the Twelve, according to previous revelation, it was moved by Elder Young, and seconded by Elder Taylor, that Elder Hyrum Clark be appointed as a counselor to Elder Fielding, in the place of Elder Richards; carried unanimously.

Moved by Elder Fielding, seconded by Elder Young, that a hymn-book should be published; carried. Moved and seconded, that the publishing of the hymn-book shall be done by the direction of the Twelve; carried.

Moved and seconded that a monthly periodical shall be published under the direction and superintendence of the Twelve, for the benefit and information of the Church, as soon as a sufficient number of subscribers shall be obtained; carried.

Moved and seconded that Brother John Blazard, of Samsbury, be ordained to the office of a Priest; carried.

Moved and seconded that Brother James Cobridge, of Thornley, be ordained to the office of Priest; carried.

Elder Kimball then laid before the conference the importance and propriety of ordaining a Patriarch to bestow patriarchal blessings on the fatherless, &c.; referred to the Twelve, whose business it is to select one, and ordain him according to the directions of the Spirit.

After various remarks and addresses given by the Elders, President Fielding and his counselors proceeded to ordain Brothers Blazard and Cobridge to their offices, as stated above.

Elder Kimball then called upon the clerk to read over the minutes of the conference, which being done, they were received by the unanimous voice of the conference.

Moved by Elder Young, and seconded by Elder Parley P. Pratt, that this conference be adjourned until the 6th of July next, to be held in Preston, at 10 o'clock a. m.; carried. Meeting then adjourned.

H. C. KIMBALL, President.

WM. CLAYTON, Clerk.

Council Meeting of the Twelve in England—Hymn-Book and the "Millennial Star" Projected.

The Council met pursuant to adjournment, April 16th, 1840. The number of the quorum the same as on the 14th.

Moved by Elder Young, seconded by Elder Taylor, that Elder Parley P. Pratt be chosen as the editor of the monthly periodical for the Church.

Moved by Elder Kimball, seconded by Parley P. Pratt, that a committee of three be appointed to make a selection of hymns.

Moved by Elder Orson Pratt, and seconded by Elder Wilford Woodruff, that Elders Brigham Young, Parley P. Pratt, and John Taylor form the committee for that purpose.

Moved by Elder Willard Richards, seconded by Elder George A. Smith, that the name of the paper or periodical be the *Latter-day Saints Millennial Star.*

Moved by Elder Brigham Young, seconded by Elder Orson Pratt, that the size of the paper, its plan, and price be left at the disposal of the editor.

Moved by Elder Brigham Young, seconded by Elder Heber C. Kimball, that the Saints receive a recommend to the Church in America to move in small or large bodies, inasmuch as they desire to emigrate to that new country.

Moved by Elder Brigham Young, seconded by Parley P. Pratt, that we recommend no one to go to America that has money, without assisting the poor according to our counsel from time to time.

Moved by Elder John Taylor, seconded by Elder Parley P. Pratt, that the copyright of the Book of Doctrine and Covenants and the Book of Mormon be secured as quick as possible.

Moved by Elder Woodruff, seconded by Elder Willard Richards, that Elders Brigham Young, Heber C. Kimball, and Parley P. Pratt be the committee to secure the copyright.

Moved by Elder Heber C. Kimball, and seconded by Elder Willard Richards, that Elder Peter Melling be ordained an evangelical minister [Patriarch] in Preston.

Moved by Elder Heber C. Kimball, that the Twelve meet here on the 6th of July next, seconded by Elder Wilford Woodruff; and carried.

Moved by Elder Willard Richards, and seconded by Elder Wilford Woodruff, that the editor of the periodical keep an account of all the receipts and expenditures connected with the printing, general expense, &c., and the books at all times be open for the inspection of the Council.

The above resolutions were unanimously adopted. The conference closed by prayer.

JOHN TAYLOR, Clerk.

Letter of Brigham Young to the Prophet.

To President Joseph Smith and Counselors:

DEAR BRETHREN:—You no doubt will have the perusal of this letter, and minutes of our conference; this will give you an idea of what we are doing in this country.   If you see anything in or about the whole affair, that is not right, I ask, in the name of the Lord Jesus Christ, that you would make known unto us the mind of the Lord, and His will concerning us.   I believe that I am as willing to do the will of the Lord, and take counsel of my brethren, and be a servant of the Church, as ever I was in my life; but I can tell you, I would like to be with my old friends; I like new friends, but I cannot part with my old ones for them.

Concerning the hymn-book—when we arrived here, we found the brethren had laid by their old hymn-books, and they wanted new ones; for the Bible, religion, and all is new to them.   When I came to learn more about carrying books into the states, or bringing them here, I found the duties were so high that we never should want to bring books from the states.

I request one favor of you, that is, a letter from you, that I may hear from my friends.   I trust that I will remain your friend through life and in eternity.   As ever.   BRIGHAM YOUNG.

April 17.—This day the Twelve blessed and drank a bottle of wine at Penworthan, made by Mother Moon forty years before.   Held a Council at her house in the evening, and ordained Peter Melling, Patriarch.*

The following is the aggregate number of churches, official and private members represented at the above Conferences, held in Preston, England: Elders, 36; Priests, 54; Teachers, 36; Deacons, 11; members, 1,686; all contained in 34 branches.

Saturday, 18.—Elders Young, Woodruff, and George A. Smith went to Burslem, and Elders Kimball and Richards to Chaidgley.

Sunday, 19.—The High Council voted to meet at my office every Saturday at two in the afternoon.

Mission
Opened in
Scotland—
Orson Pratt.
Monday, 20.—Elders Young and Woodruff went to Wolverhampton.   About this time Elder Orson Pratt went to Edinburgh, Scotland.   Elder Taylor returned to Liverpool.

* Peter Melling was the first patriarch ordained in a foreign land, that is, a foreign land from America where the latter-day dispensation of the Gospel was opened.   He was the son of Peter Melling, born in Preston, England, on the 14th day of February, 1787.   He was, therefore, in his 64th year.   He was evidently a man of great force of character, for he proceeded at once with great diligence and ability to fulfill the duties of his high office, all of which is evidenced by the record of the Patriarchial blessings given under his hands, and now in the Historian's office.

Letter of Robert Johnstone to Senator Young — Postoffice Name Changed
from Commerce to Nauvoo.

POSTOFFICE DEPARTMENT, APPOINTMENT OFFICE,
21st April, 1840.

SIR:—I have the honor to inform you, that the Postmaster General has this day changed the name of the postoffice at Commerce, Hancock county, Illinois, to "Nauvoo," and appointed George W. Robinson postmaster thereof.

Very respectfully, your obedient servant,
ROBERT JOHNSTONE,
Second Assistant Postmaster General.

To the Hon. Richard M. Young, U. S. Senate.

Elders Young and Woodruff visited the old cathedral at Worcester on their way to Ledbury, where they arrived this night.

Letter of Senator Young to Judge Elias Higbee—Postoffice Name, etc.

WASHINGTON CITY, April 22, 1840.

DEAR SIR:—After your departure from this city, I received, under cover from the Reverend Sidney Rigdon, the petition mentioned by you, for the appointment of George W. Robinson as postmaster at Commerce. This petition I laid before the Honorable Robert Johstone, second assistant postmaster general, who has appointed Mr. Robinson as requested.

We found, on examination of the papers, and a letter from Dr. Galland, that there was a request that the name of the postoffice should be changed to that of Nauvoo, a Hebrew term, signifying a beautiful place. Mr. Johnstone, at my instance, has changed the name accordingly, in the supposition that it would be agreeable to the citizens concerned. Will you please advise with the Rev. Joseph Smith and others most immediately interested, and if the change of the name to Nauvoo should not be acceptable, it can on application be restored to that of Commerce.

I received a letter from Malcolm McGregor, Esq., postmaster at Carthage, a few days ago, in which he urges the necessity of having the mail carried twice a week, between Carthage and Nauvoo, and expresses the opinion that the additional expenses would not exceed one hundred and fifty dollars, as the mail is carried on horseback. I have brought the subject before the proper department as requested by Mr. McGregor, and hope to be able to succeed; although the Postoffice Department, owing to pecuniary embarrassment, is not in a situation to extend facilities at the present time.

Please present my respects to Mr. Smith, and accept for yourself my kindest regards.

Very respectfully, &c.,

RICHARD M. YOUNG.

To Judge Elias Higbee.

Wednesday, 22.—Elders Young and Woodruff organized a branch of the Church at Frooms Hill, Herefordshire.

Thursday, 23.—Elders Kimball and Richards returned to Preston. Elder Young visited at Moor Ends Cross, and 24th preached at Malvern Hill. Elder Kimball went to Eccleston and continued some days visiting the churches around Preston.

Saturday, 25.—Elder Richards went to Manchester, found the *Prospectus* for the *Millennial Star* ready. Elder Young returned to Frooms Hill, and stayed at Brother John Benbow's till the 30th, preaching, and writing letters to his friends in America.

Wednesday, 29.—Elders Hyde and Page were at Quincy, Illinois.

Elder Woodruff wrote as follows:

Letter of Wilford Woodruff to Don Carlos Smith—Success of Woodruff's Ministry.

LEDBURY, HEREFORDSHIRE, ENGLAND,

April 29, 1840.

Elders Ebenezer Robinson and Don Carlos Smith:

BRETHREN:—As Elder Young is writing, I am privileged with a space of a few lines: knowing that our friends are desirous to hear of the work of the Lord in this land, I make the following remarks concerning the mercy of God and my labors.

Since I last wrote you, (I wrote you a lengthy letter, dated February 27th, in which I gave you an account of my travels, voyage, and labors, from the time I left Montrose unto the date of my letter, which I trust you have received,) I continued laboring in Staffordshire until the first of March, when I felt it to be the will of the Lord that I should go more to the south part of England. I left the care of the Staffordshire church in the hands of Elder Turley, and traveled eighty miles south, in a region where the word had not been preached. I commenced preaching near Ledbury, Herefordshire; this is about forty miles from Bristol, forty from Birmingham, fourteen from Worcester, one hundred and twenty from London. As soon as I began to teach, many received my testimony. I there preached one month and five days, and baptized the superintendent of the church of the United Brethren, a branch of the Methodist church, and with him 45 preachers, mostly of the same order; and about 114 members, making 160 in all. This put into my hands, or under my care, more than forty established places of preaching, licensed according to law, including one or two chapels. This opened a large field for the spread of the work in this country.

Among the number baptized are some of most all churches and classes as well as preachers. There is one constable, and one clerk of the Church of England, with numbers of their members. But in the midst of my labors I received a letter stating that the Twelve had just arrived and wished me to come to Preston, and meet with them in conference. Consequently I traveled 160 miles to Preston, and was once more permitted to strike hands with my brethren from America, and sit in conference with them, the minutes of which you have.

After conference I returned to Herefordshire in company with Elder Brigham Young. We have again commenced our labors here, and there will be many baptized in this region. I have now more than 200 on my list, and scores are now waiting for an opportunity to receive the ordinance of baptism; and the work is progressing in all parts of this country where it is faithfully proclaimed. I understand that Elders Wright and Mulliner are opening some permanent doors in Scotland; and we have many calls through many parts of this country, even more than we are able to fill.

I desire the prayers of the Saints; that I may have wisdom and grace according to my day, and do the work of God in meekness and humility.

WILFORD WOODRUFF.

Thursday, 30.—Elders Young, Woodruff, and Richards met at Elder Kington's, at Dymock.

Letter of Elders Hyde and Page to the Prophet—Plans for the Palestine Mission.

COLUMBUS, May 1, 1840.

President Smith:

SIR:—The mission upon which we are sent swells greater and greater. As there is a great work to be done in Germany, as manifested to us by the Spirit, the following plan has been suggested to us; viz., to write a set of lectures upon the faith and doctrine of our Church, giving a brief history of the coming forth of the Book of Mormon, and an account of its contents in as clear and plain a style as possible; together with the outlines and organization and government of the Church of Latter-day Saints, drawn from the Doctrine and Covenants with all the wisdom and care possible; and get the same translated into German, and publish it when we arrive in Germany, and scatter it through the German empire. Is this correct? Should we consider it necessary to translate the entire Book of Mormon into German, and Doctrine and Covenants too, are we or are we not at liberty to do so? Should we deem it necessary to publish an edition of hymn-books in any country, are we at liberty to do it? The fact is, we need such works, and we cannot get them from the church here; and if we could, we could not well carry them with us, at least in any quantity.

We feel that we are acting under the direction of the Presidency of the Church; and the reason that we make these inquiries, is, that we do not wish to step beyond our limits, or bring ourselves into a snare and dishonor by taking liberties that are not ours. We feel that all our exertions and interests shall become subservient to building up the Kingdom of God. We wish to be co-workers with you and with the Spirit of the Lord. We did not converse so much upon these literary works as we should have done before we left. The fact is, we did not begin to see the greatness of our mission before we left home; our minds were in a nutshell.

It seems to us that we should spread this work among all people, languages and tongues, so far as possible; and gather up all jewels among the Jews besides. Who is sufficient for these things?

As agents for the Church abroad, and as co-workers with yourself, in spreading this kingdom to the remotest corners of the earth, are we at liberty to translate and publish any works that we may think necessary, or that the circumstances in which we are placed seem to require whether original, or works published by the Church? If we are not at liberty to take this wide range, please tell us how far we may go.

We are setting this great work before the people as an inducement to them to help us. If we are setting our standard too high, a word from you will bring it down. We have held a two days' meeting in this place; but in consequence of continual rains, which swelled the creeks so high, the people could not get to us. The meeting was four miles from Columbus; one only baptized.

We have now an opportunity to ride as far east as Indiana, beyond the metropolis, and have the privilege to stop and preach by the way. Will you write to us at Cincinnati, and much oblige

Your brethren in the Kingdom of God,

ORSON HYDE,
JOHN E. PAGE.

P. S.—Will you please send word to Marinda, that I want her to write to me at Cincinnati, Ohio. Please bear it in mind and oblige thy friend.

O. H.

Friday, May 1.—The town of Baji, in the county of Baes, on the river Danube, was almost totally destroyed by fire; about two thousand houses were burnt, with the palace, several churches, and all the great corn magazines; leaving about sixteen thousand inhabitants destitute.   The plague is raging in the East—at Silistria, Broussa, Alexandria, Aleppo, &c.; and wars and rumors of wars in Spain, Mexico and South American governments; French and Arabs in Africa, Russia and Circassia, Egypt, England and the East Indies, and the Canada Revolution; all betoken the fulfillment of prophecy.

Commotions in the World.

Thursday, 7.—The city of Natchez was this day to a great extent destroyed, almost in a moment, by a whirlwind, storm and tempest.   It is reported that sixty boats sunk, houses and churches blown to atoms, more than three hundred persons killed, and $5,000,000 of property destroyed; nearly the whole country on the Mississippi for 1,100 miles from its mouth is under water.

Letter of Brigham Young to the Prophet—Affairs of the British Mission.

LUGWARDINE, HEREFORDSHIRE, ENGLAND,
May 7, 1840.

BROTHER JOSEPH SMITH: — Through the mercy of our heavenly Father, I am alive and in pretty good health; better than I should have been, had I remained in America.   I trust that you and family are well, and I ask my heavenly Father that we may live forever; but not to be chased about by mobs, but live to enjoy each other's society in peace. I long to see the faces of my friends again in that country once more. It is better for me to be here, because the Lord has called me to this great work, but it is hard for me to be parted from my old friends whom I have proved to be willing to lay down their lives for each other. I feel as though the Lord would grant me the privilege of sometime seeing my old friends in America.   Give my best wishes to your wife.   I remember her in my prayers, and also Father and Mother Smith.   I remember the time when I first saw Mother Smith, and the trials she had when the work of the Lord first commenced in her family.   I beg to be remembered to Brother Rigdon and family, also to Brother Hyrum and family, and to all the faithful in Christ.

The brethren that have come from America are all well and doing well.   I want to ask some questions.   Shall we print the Book of of Mormon in this country immediately?   They are calling for it from every quarter.   The duties are so high on books, we need not think of bringing them from America.   Another question, is the Book of Doctrine and Covenants to be printed just as it is now, to go to the nations of the earth; and shall we give it to them as quickly as we can?   Or what shall be do?   Will the Twelve have to be together to do business as a quorum?   Or shall they do business in the name of the Church?   Why I ask this is for my own satisfaction; if the Lord has a word for us, for one I am willing to receive it.

I wish you to write as soon as you receive this, and let me know about the Book of Mormon, whether we shall proceed to publish it immediately or not, or whether we shall do according to our feelings.   If I should act according to my feelings, I should hand the Book of Mormon to this people as quickly as I could.   The people are very different in this country from what the Americans are.   They say it cannot be possible that men should leave their homes and come so far, unless they were truly the servants of the Lord; they do not seem to understand argument; simple testimony is enough for them; they beg and plead for the Book of Mormon, and were it not for the priests, the people would follow after the servants of the Lord and inquire what they should do to be saved.   The priests feel just as they did in the days of the Savior. If they let "this sect alone, all men will believe on them, and the Romans will come and take away our place and nation."

I wish you would tell me how Cousin Lemuel gets along with his business, and all the boys on the half-breed track, and the whole breed.   I think a great deal about our friends, families, and possessions,   I look for the time when the Lord will speak so that the hearts of the rebellious will be pierced.   You will remember the words of the Savior to His disciples; He says, to you is given to know the mysteries of the kingdom of heaven, but to them that are without, all things are in parables.

The brethren here are very anxious to emigrate to that country; some want to come this fall: where shall they go?   Their customs are different from ours, and it would be more pleasant for them to settle by themselves.   Almost without exception it is the poor that receive the Gospel. I think there will be some [who will go] over this fall.   My counsel to such as intend to go is, that they go to the western states, where they can live among the farmers and wait for orders from the authorities of the Church, and all will be well.

You must excuse my bad writing. I have only caught at ideas. I want to know about the brethren's coming over this fall. I think some of us will come. We shall send our papers to you, and to a number of the rest of the brethren. I wish you would have the goodness to give me a pretty general knowledge of the Church, for I feel for them, and pray for them continually. We need help very much in this country. One American can do more here than a number of Elders who are raised up here by the preaching of the Gospel. We have sent for some to come. I wish you would encourage them to come as quickly as they can.

If we could go four ways at a time, we could not fill all the calls we have for preaching. I shall expect such counsel from you about the Elders coming as you shall think necessary for us and them to have. I wish to know what the prospect is about the government's doing anything for us. When we left New York I thought there was but a poor chance for us.

Concerning calling Seventies and sending them to other countries, I should like to know whether it would be proper to ordain them to that office or not while here. Had any of us better come back this fall? I suppose that some that come over with us will return; Brothers Clark and Hedlock, and Brother Turley if the latter gets at liberty. I suppose you have heard that he is in prison. He has been there ever since my arrival in England, and how long he will remain the the Lord only knows. He was put there through the influence of a priest, as nigh as I can learn, for some old pretended claim, but no one can find out what that claim is.

I have just met with Brother Woodruff; he tells me that the Church in this region of country numbers between three and four hundred; it is only about three months since Brother Woodruff commenced to labor here. I have just received a letter from Brother Turley, which states he expects to leave his place the next day. Brother Woodruff sends his respects.

I am as ever,

BRIGHAM YOUNG.

Saturday, 9.—Elder Theodore Turley was released from Stafford jail, where he had been confined since his arrest on the 16th of March last, at the instigation of John Jones, a Methodist preacher, on the pretense of a claim arising under a partnership with another man fifteen years ago, before he left Eng-

Release of Elder Turley from prison.

land; but the real object was to stop his preaching.   He was without provisions for several days, but the poor Saints in the Potteries, on learning his condition, supplied his wants, some of the sisters actually walking upwards of twenty miles to relieve him. He preached several times to the debtors, was visited by Elders Woodruff, Richards, George A. Smith, A. Cordon, and others, and was dismissed from prison on his persecutors ascertaining their conduct was about to be exposed.   This rather encouraged than disheartened the Elders, as I had told them on their leaving Nauvoo, to be of good courage, for some of them would have to look through grates before their return.

Thursday, 14.—The papers of this date report that the island of Ternate* was nearly ruined by earthquakes on the 14th and 15th February, 1840.

*Letter of the Prophet to Elders Hyde and Page—Palestine Mission
Considered.*

NAUVOO, HANCOCK COUNTY, ILLINOIS,
May 14th, 1840.

To Orson Hyde and John E. Page:

DEAR BRETHREN:—I am happy in being informed by your letter that your mission swells "larger and larger."   It is a great and important mission, and one that is worthy those intelligences who surround the throne of Jehovah to be engaged in. Although it appears great at present, yet you have but just begun to realize the greatness, the extent and glory of the same.   If there is anything calculated to interest the mind of the Saints, to awaken in them the finest sensibilities, and arouse them to enterprise and exertion, surely it is the great and precious promises made by our heavenly Father to the children of Abraham; and those engaged in seeking the outcasts of Israel, and the dispersed of Judah, cannot fail to enjoy the Spirit of the Lord and have the choicest blessings of Heaven rest upon them in copious effusions.

Brethren, you are in the pathway to eternal fame, and immortal glory: and inasmuch as you feel interested for the covenant people of the Lord, the God of their fathers shall bless you.   Do not be discouraged on ac-

---

* Ternate is a small island in the Moluccas, west of Jilolo, in the Dutch East Indies.

count of the greatness of the work; only be humble and faithful, and then you can say, "What art thou, O great mountain! before Zerubbabel shalt thou be brought down." He who scattered Israel has promised to gather them; therefore inasmuch as you are to be instrumental in this great work, He will endow you with power, wisdom, might, and intelligence, and every qualification necessary; while your minds will expand wider and wider, until you can circumscribe the earth and the heavens, reach forth into eternity, and contemplate the mighty acts of Jehovah in all their variety and glory.

In answer to your inquiries respecting the translation and publication of the Book of Mormon, hymn-book, history of the Church, &c., &c., I would say that I entirely approve of the same, and give my consent, with the exception of the hymn-book, as a new edition, containing a greater variety of hymns, will be shortly published or printed in this place, which I think will be a standard work. As soon as it is printed, you shall have some sent to you, which you may get translated, and printed into any language you please.

Should we not be able to send some to you, and there should be a great call for hymn books where you may be, then I should have no objection to your publishing the present one. Were you to publish the Book of Mormon, Doctrine and Covenants, or hymn-book, I desire the copyrights of the same to be secured in my name.

With respect to publishing any other work, either original, or those which have been published before, you will be governed by circumstances; if you think necessary to do so, I shall have no objection whatever. It will be well to study plainness and simplicity in whatever you publish, "for my soul delighteth in plainness."

I feel much pleased with the spirit of your letter—and be assured, dear brethren, of my hearty co-operation, and my prayers for your welfare and success. In answer to your inquiry in a former letter, relative to the duty of the Seventies in regulating churches, &c., I say that the duties of the Seventies are more particularly to preach the Gospel, and build up churches, rather than regulate them, that a High Priest may take charge of them. If a High Priest should be remiss in his duty, and should lead, or suffer the church to be led astray, depart from the ordinances of the Lord, then it is the duty of one of the Seventies, acting under the special direction of the Twelve, being duly commissioned by them with their delegated authority, to go to the church, and if agreeable to a majority of the members of said church, to proceed to regulate and put in order the same; otherwise, he can have no authority to act.

JOSEPH SMITH, JUN.

Friday, 15.

Letter of Willard Richards to the Editor of the Millennial Star—Reporting Labors.

LEDBURY, HEREFORDSHIRE, May 15th, 1840.

To the Editor of the Millennial Star:

BELOVED BROTHER:—Two weeks ago this day, I parted with Brothers Young and Woodruff in this place, taking different locations in this part of the vineyard, originally opened by Brother Woodruff, and after visiting various places in Herefordshire, Worcestershire, and Gloucestershire, preaching daily, talking night and day, and administering the ordinances of the Gospel as directed by the Spirit, we have again this day found ourselves together, and Elder Kington in our midst (he is devoted wholly to the ministry). By comparing minutes we find there have been in these two weeks about 112 baptized; 200 confirmed; 2 Elders, about 20 Priests, and 1 Teacher ordained; and the Church in these regions now numbers about 320. The branches are small, the brethren much scattered; consequently the field is so large that the reapers cannot call to each other from side to side, neither can they often see each other without a telescope.

There are many doors open which we cannot fill; calls for preaching on almost every hand, which we cannot answer. Oh! that the Saints would pray to the Lord of the harvest to send forth laborers!

I have this day received a letter from my sister in Massachusetts, giving me the intelligence of the death of my aged father. The work of the Lord is rolling forth in that part of the land, such intelligence as this from our native land makes our hearts rejoice, even in affliction.

Your brother in the everlasting covenant,

WILLARD RICHARDS.

CHAPTER VII.

FIRST FOREIGN PERIODICAL OF THE CHURCH, "THE MILLEN-
NIAL STAR"—THE PROPHET SEEKS RELEASE FROM SECU-
LAR RESPONSIBILITIES.

Sunday, May 17.—Elders Young, Woodruff, and Richards held conference with the Saints at Gadfield Elm
Chapel.

Monday, 18.—The above Elders met the brethren at
Elder Kington's, where they had a tea party, praying,
singing, confirming, ordaining, and about
twenty were baptized; thus they continued   The Beacon
Hill Confer-
their labors from place to place, until Wed-   ence.
nesday 20th, when they found themselves with one accord
on the top of "the Herefordshire Beacon,"* and within
the old fortification, when after prayer they expressed
their feelings concerning the business of the Church,
which were (as they had obtained money from Brother
John Benbow, and other brethren for printing the hymn-
book, and in part sufficient for the Book of Mormon) that
Elder Young repair immediately to Manchester, and join
his brethren previously appointed with him on a committee, for the printing of the hymn-book, and cause 3,000
copies to be issued without delay. Also that the same
committee cause 3,000 copies of the Book of Mormon to be
printed and completed with as little delay as possible,
with an index affixed to the same, the form of the book to
be determined by the committee. Their views were written and signed by Elder Willard Richards and Wilford
Woodruff, when President Young left direct for Manchester. He saw George A. Smith, at the Potteries, who
approved the "Beacon Conference."

* One of the noted heights of the Black Mountains, running through the west
part of Herefordshire.

Sunday, 24.—President Young met with the Church, and on Monday, 25th, visited the printers to inquire their prices, etc.

A Letter of Heber C. Kimball, et al., Recommending English Saints to the Bishop of the Church.

PRESTON, May 25, 1840.

To the Presidency, High Council and Bishop of the Church of Jesus Christ of Latter-day Saints at Commerce. We commend to your notice the brethren and sisters that have commendatory letters from us of this date, that you will do all that you consistently can for them, for I verily believe they have utmost confidence in you, and will receive with gratitude your advice and instruction, and cheerfully submit to the rules and regulations of the Church. They have our blessings, and we trust their subsequent conduct will entitle them to your blessings also, and the Church generally. We rejoice that we can say the work of God here is in a prosperous way. Yea, we rejoice greatly at the aspect of the times, expecting the time to be not far distant when the standard of truth will be conspicuously raised throughout this land. We have witnessed the flowing of the Saints towards Zion; the stream has begun, and we expect to see it continue running until it shall have drained the salt, or the light, from Babylon, when we hope to shout hosanna home.

Dear brethren, accept our love, and present it to the Church.

Your brethren in the new and everlasting covenant,

HEBER C. KIMBALL,
JOSEPH FIELDING,
WILLIAM CLAYTON.

Tuesday, 26.—Elder John Taylor arrived at Manchester, and on the 27th, Elder Kimball arrived. The committee on the hymn-book commenced and continued selecting hymns until the 30th, when Elders Young, Kimball and Taylor went to Liverpool, and preached on Sunday the 31st.

Wednesday, 27.—Bishop Edward Partridge* died at Nauvoo, aged forty-six years. He lost his life in consequence of the Missouri persecutions, and he is one of that number whose blood will be required at their hands. His daughter, Harriet Pamela, died on the 16th of May, aged nineteen years.

Death of Bishop Partridge.

* See Biographical Note, Vol. 1, pp. 128-9.

The first number of *The Latter-day Saints' Millennial Star** was issued at Manchester, in pamphlet form of twenty-four pages. Edited by Parley P. Pratt. Price sixpence. Office 149 Oldham Road.

First Number of the *Millennial Star.*

Monday, June 1, 1840.—The Saints have already erected about two hundred and fifty-houses at Nauvoo, mostly block houses, a few framed, and many more are in course of construction.

The Gospel is spreading through the States, Canada, England, Scotland, and other places, with great rapidity.

* The *Millennial Star* was the first foreign publication of the Church. It was issued as a monthly, but afterwards more frequently, semi-monthly, and finally, and now for many years, a weekly. Its publication has been continuous from the time it was started until the present—1907. Also the *Star* has retained the general character imparted to it by its first publishers. "The *Millennial Star*," said its Prospectus, "will stand aloof from the common political and commercial news of the day. Its columns will be devoted to the spread of the fulness of the Gospel—the restoration of the ancient principles of Christianity—the gathering of Israel—the rolling forth of the kingdom of God among the nations—the signs of the times—the fulfillment of prophecy—recording the judgments of God as they befall the nations whether signs in the heavens or in the earth, blood fire or vapor of smoke—in short, whatever is shown forth indicative of the coming of the 'Son of Man' and ushering in of his universal reign upon the earth. It will also contain letters from our numerous Elders who are abroad, preaching the word both in America and Europe containing news of their success in ministering the blessings of the glorious Gospel."

As an explanation of its title and mission, the editor in its first number also said: "The word *Millennium* signifies a thousand years, and in this sense of the word, may be applied to any [period of a] thousand years, whether under the reign of wickedness or righteousness. But the term *the Millennium*, is generally understood to apply to the particular thousand years which is mentioned in the Scriptures as the reign of peace—the great sabbath of creation, of which all the other sabbaths or jubilees seem to be but types. It is written that a 'thousand years is as one day, and one day as a thousand years with the Lord.' This being the case, then seven thousand years are seven days with the Lord, and the seventh, or last thousand years would, of course, be a sabbath or jubilee; a rest, a grand release from servitude and woe.   *   *   *   The curse will be taken from off the earth, and it will cease to bring forth thorns and thistles, and become fertile as it were a paradise, while sickness, premature death, and all their attendant train of pains and sorrows will scarce be known upon its face; thus peace, and joy, and truth, and love, and knowledge, and plenty, and glory, will cover the face of the earth as the waters do the sea. The tabernacle of God and his sanctuary will be with man, in the midst of the holy cities; and joy and gladness will fill the measure of their cup. Such then, is the *Great Millennium* of which our little '*Star*' would fain announce the dawn."

Elders Young and Kimball were engaged in blessing the brethren who were about to sail for America.

Wednesday, 3.—Elders Young and Taylor visited the printers in Liverpool and Elder Young preached on the Sunday following.

Saturday, 6.—Elder John Moon and a company of forty Saints, to wit., Hugh Moon, his mother and seven others of her family, Henry Moon (uncle of John Moon), Henry Moon, Francis Moon, William Sutton, William Sitgraves, Richard Eaves, Thomas Moss, Henry Moore, Nancy Ashworth, Richard Ainscough, and families, sailed in the ship *Britannia* from Liverpool for New York, being the first Saints that have sailed from England for Zion.

The First Company of Saints from England.

Monday, 8.—Elders Young and Taylor visited Cheshire, and on Tuesday, Manchester, and continued to select hymns.

Elder Young dreamed of his family in health and want, also of the Church and people, and of a contention between two small companies in the west, one north, the other south—the north prevailing from time to time.

Brigham Young's Dreams.

Minutes of the Conference Held at Gadfield Elm Chapel, in Worcestershire, England, June 14th, 1840.

The preachers and members of the Bran Green and Gadfield Elm Branch of the Froomes Hill Circuit, of the United Brethren met at the Gadfield Elm Chapel, Worcestershire, June 14th, 1840, pursuant to previous notice, when the meeting was called to order by Elder Thomas Kington. Elder Willard Richards was chosen president, and Elder Daniel Browett clerk for the meeting. The meeting was opened by prayer by Elder Wilford Woodruff. Remarks were then made by the president respecting the business of the day, and the necessary changes which must take place.

It was then moved by Elder Thomas Kington, seconded by Elder Daniel Browett that this meeting be hereafter known by the name of the "Bran Green and Gadfield Elm Conference of the Church of Jesus Christ of Latter-day Saints," organized and established by the will and commandment of God in the United States of America, on the 6th day of April,

A. D. 1830, this being the eighth day of the third month of the eleventh year of the rise of the Church. Carried unanimously.

[This motion was permitted to accommodate the feelings of the conference, who had all recently been baptized, but there is no such principle in existence, as to transform a church or conference of the world into a church or conference of Christ's fold by vote.]*

Moved by Elder Wilford Woodruff, seconded by Elder T. Kington, that William Jenkins be ordained an Elder; and William Coleman, Joseph Firkins, William Pitt and Robert Harris be ordained to the office of Priest; and that George Burton, James Palmer, and William Loveridge, be ordained Teachers; carried unanimously. Ordained under the hands of Elders Richards and Woodruff.

Moved by Elder Kington, seconded by Elder Woodruff, that Robert Clift, Priest, have the care of the church at Dymock; James Palmer, Priest, have the care of the church at Kilcott; John Hill, Priest, have the care of the church at Twigworth; William Coleman, Priest, have the care of the church at Bran Green; Thomas Brooks, Priest, have the care of the church at Ryton; John Smith, Priest, have the care of the church at Lime Street; Charles Hayes, Priest have the care of the church at Deerhurst; Thomas Smith, Priest, Assistant, have the care of the church at Deerhurst; John Vernon, Priest, have the care of the church at Apperley; William Bayliss, Priest, Assistant, have the care of the church at Apperley; John Arlick, Priest, have the care of the church at Norton; John Spires, Priest, have the care of the church at Leigh; John Davis, Priest, assistant, have the care of the church at Leigh; Thomas Oakley, Priest, have the care of the church at Gadfield Elm.

And that Elder Daniel Browett take charge of the churches on the south, and Elder William Jenkins on the north side, of the river Severn. Carried unanimously.

Moved by Elder Woodruff, and seconded by Elder Richards, that Elder Thomas Kington be the Presiding Elder over the Conference; carried. Meeting adjourned until two o'clock.

Conference met at two o'clock according to adjournment, and administered the sacrament to a large congregation of Saints, accompanied by many observations on many subjects by the President. Ten members were confirmed under the hands of Elders Woodruff and Kington. Remarks were made by the President respecting the "blessing of children." Seven children were then blessed under the hands of Elders Woodruff and Kington.

* The matter in brackets occurs in the Ms. History as also in the History as published in the *Millennial Star*, but it is evidently the comment of the Church Historians.

Moved by Elder Kington, seconded by Elder Woodruff, that Elder Daniel Browett represent this Conference to the general conference, at Manchester, on the 6th day of July next; carried. Moved and carried that the Clerk present to the Presiding Elder, T. Kington, also to the general conference, for safe keeping, a copy of the minutes of this conference.

The above minutes were then read and adopted, article by article, when it was moved by the President, and seconded by Elder Woodruff, that this conference be adjourned to the 13th day of September next at this place; carried unanimously.

Conference closed by prayer; after which the Elders and officers present met in council, and voted unanimously to establish a weekly council of the officers of said conference to be held alternately on the south and north sides of the river Severn, to commence at Leigh on the 25th inst.; and organized the same by appointing Elder Daniel Browett, president and John Hill, Priest, clerk, on the south side of the river; and also on the north side, by appointing Elder William Jenkins, president and John Smith, Priest, clerk; to assemble on the 3rd of July next, at Turkey Hall.

After passing many other votes of minor importance, accompanied by much instruction from Elders Richards and Woodruff, touching the duties of the several officers in their relations to each other, and the Church, the council adjourned. And it is worthy of remark, that no dissenting vote or voice was seen or heard during the day, either in conference or council.

WILLARD RICHARDS, President.
DANIEL BROWETT, Clerk.

Memorial of Joseph Smith, Jun., to the High Council of the Church of Jesus Christ of Latter-day Saints, June 18th, 1840.

The Memorial of Joseph Smith, Jun., respectfully represents—That after the members of the Church of Jesus Christ had been inhumanly as well as unconstitutionally expelled from their homes which they had secured to themselves in the state of Missouri, and although very much scattered and at considerable distance from each other, they found a resting place in the state of Illinois:—That after the escape of your Memorialist from his enemies, he (under the direction of the authorities of the Church) took such steps as has secured to the Church the present locations, viz., the town plot of Nauvoo and lands in the Iowa territory:—That in order to secure said locations, your Memorialist had to become responsible for the payment of the same, and had to use considerable exertion in order to commence a settlement, and a place of gathering for the Saints; and knowing from the genius of the constitution of the Church, and for the well-being of the Saints, that it was necessary that the constituted authorities of the Church might assemble together to act or to legislate for the good of the whole society and that the Saints might enjoy those privileges which they could not enjoy by being scattered so widely apart—your Memorialist was induced to exert himself to the utmost in order to bring about objects so necessary and so desirable to the Saints at large:—Under the then existing circumstances, your Memorialist had necessarily to engage in the temporalities of the Church, which he has had to attend to until the present time:—That your Memorialist feels it a duty which he owes to God, as well as to the Church, to give his attention more particularly to those things connected with the spiritual welfare of the Saints, (which have now become a great people,) so that they may be built up in their most holy faith, and go on to perfection:—That the Church have erected an office where he can attend to the affairs of the Church without distraction, he thinks, and verily believes, that the time has now come, when he should devote himself exclusively to those things which relate to the spiritualities of the Church, and commence the work of translating the Egyptian records, the Bible, and wait upon the Lord for such revelations as may be suited to the conditions and circumstances of the Church. And in order that he may be enabled to attend to those things, he prays your honorable body will relieve him from the anxiety and trouble necessarily attendant on business transactions, by appointing some one to take charge of the city plot, and attend to the business transactions which have heretofore rested upon your Memorialist: That should your Honors deem it proper to do so, your Memorialist would respectfully suggest that he would have no means of support whatever, and therefore would request that some one might be appointed to see that all his necessary wants may be provided for, as well as sufficient means or appropriations for a clerk or clerks, which he may require to aid him in this important work.

Your Memorialist would further represent, that as Elder H. G. Sherwood is conversant with the affairs of the city plot, he would be a suitable person to act as clerk in that business, and attend to the disposing of the remaining lots, &c.

Your Memorialist would take this opportunity of congratulating your honorable body on the peace and harmony which exist in the Church, and for the good feelings which seem to be manifested by all the Saints, and hopes that inasmuch as we devote ourselves for the good of the Church, and the spread of the kingdom, that the choicest blessings of heaven will be poured upon us, and that the glory of the Lord will overshadow the inheritances of the Saints.

JOSEPH SMITH, JUN.

Proceedings of the High Council on the Foregoing Memorial,
June 20th, 1840.

The Council relieved President Joseph Smith, Jun., according to his request in the memorial, and appointed H. G. Sherwood to take charge of the city plot and to act as clerk in that business, and also to attend to the disposing of the remaining lots, and the business transactions which have rested upon him [Joseph Smith]. Alanson Ripley was appointed steward to see that all the necessary wants of the First Presidency be supplied, as well as to provide sufficient means or appropriations for a clerk or clerks to aid President Joseph Smith, Jun., in his important work.

HOSEA STOUT, Clerk.

Minutes of the Conference held at Stanley Hill, Castle Froome, Hereford-
shire, England, June 21st, 1840.

The preachers and members of the Froome's Hill Circuit of the United Brethren met at the house of Elder John Cheese, on Stanley Hill, Herefordshire, England, June 21, A. D. 1840, at ten a. m., according to previous notice; the meeting was called to order by Elder Thomas Kington; Elder Wilford Woodruff was chosen president, and Elder John Benbow, clerk of the meeting.

After prayer by Elder Richards, and remarks by the president concerning the business of the day, it was moved by Elder Thomas Kington, and seconded by Elder John Benbow, that [the several districts represented at] this meeting be hereafter known by the name of the "Froome's Hill Conference of the Church of Jesus Christ of Latter-day Saints," organized and established by the will and commandment of God, in the United States of America, on the 6th day of April, 1830, this being the 15th day of the third month of the eleventh year of the rise of the Church. Carried unanimously.

Moved by Elder Richards, seconded by Elder Kington, that Thomas Clark, Charles Price, James Hill, and Samuel Jones be ordained Elders; also that John James, Joseph Skinn, Henry Jones, James Baldwin, John Morgan, Samuel Badham, and John Dyer, be ordained Priests; also that Robert Hill, George Brooks, James Skinn, and James Watkins be ordained Teachers; carried unanimously; and they were ordained under the hands of Elders Woodruff and Richards.

Moved by Elder Kington, and seconded by Elders Woodruff and Richards, that John James, Priest, have the care of the church at Froome's Hill; John Parry, Priest, have the care of the church at Stanley Hill; James Burns, Priest, have the care of the church at Ridgway Cross; William Possons, Priest, have the care of the church at Moor-end Cross; Jonathan Lucy, Priest, have the care of the church at Caldwell; Thomas Jones, Priest, have the care of the church at Pale House; John Preece,

Priest, have the care of the church at Ledbury; Samuel Warren, Priest, have the care of the church at Keysend Street; James Baldwin, Priest, have the care of the church at Wind Point; George Allen, Priest, have the care of the church at Woferwood Common.

Rough Leasow, Birchwood, Tunbridge, and Dunsclose will all be united in one branch, called Dunsclose.

Samuel Badham, Priest, to have the care of the church at Dunsclose; Edward Phillips, Priest, to have care of the church at Ashfield and Crowcut; John Meeks, Priest, to have care of the church at Old Starridge; John Galley, Priest, to have care of the church at Hope Rough; Benj. Williams, Priest, to have care of the church at Shucknell Hill; John Powell, Priest, to have care of the church at Lugwardine; John Dyer, Priest, to have care of the church at Marden; William Evans, Priest, to have care of the church at Stokes Lane; John Fidoe, Priest, to have care of the church at Bishop Froome.   Carried unanimously.

Moved by Elder Richards, and seconded by Elder Kington, that Elder Thomas Clark have charge of the churches at Dunsclose, Old Starridge, Ashfield, and Crowcut; that Elder Samuel Jones have charge of the churches at Keys-end Street, Wind Point, Colwell, Pale House, and Malvern Hill; that Elder Philip Green have charge of the churches at Shucknall Hill, Lugwardine, and Marden; that Elder John Cheese have charge of the churches at Stokes Lane, Woferwood Common, and Bishop Froome; that Elder Charles Price have charge of the churches at Ledbury, Moor-end Cross, and Ridgway Cross; that Elder James Hill have charge of the churches at Hope Rough and Stanley Hill; that Elder John Benbow have charge of the church at Froome's Hill. Carried unanimously.

Moved by the president, seconded by Elder Richards, that Elder Thomas Kington be the Presiding Elder over this conference.

After remarks by the president, the meeting adjourned till 2 o'clock p. m.   During the recess ten persons were baptized.

Assembled at 2 o'clock according to adjournment, and administered the sacrament to several hundred Saints; after which twenty were confirmed, and twenty children blessed under the hands of Elders Woodruff and Richards, accompanied with instructions by the president, explanatory of the ordinance.

Moved by Elder Richards, seconded by the president, that Elder Thomas Kington represent this Conference to the general conference at Manchester on the 6th of July; carried.   Moved and carried that the clerk of the conference present to the Presiding Elder, T. Lington, a copy of the minutes of this conference for safe keeping; also a copy to present to the general conference at Manchester.   The minutes were then read and accepted.   The president, followed by Elder Richards, then proceeded to give such instruction to the Saints concerning the order of the Church, and the several duties of the members, as the Spirit directed; and bore testimony to the multitude of the truth of the work; followed by Elder Kington; when it was moved by Elder Richards, seconded by the president, that this conference adjourn to the 21st September next, 10 o'clock a. m., at this place; carried.

After prayer and singing, the assembly dispersed, the Elders and officers went into council, when it was moved by Elder Richards, and seconded by Elder Kington, that we proceed to establish and organize monthly councils of the officers of the Froome's Hill Conference, to commence on Friday, the 3rd of July next, at half-past seven o'clock p. m., in the several divisions, respectively assigned to the different Elders, viz.—

Elder Thomas Clark, president, and James Meeks, clerk, Dunsclose; Elder Charles Price, president, Thomas Jenkins, clerk, Moor-end Cross; Samuel Jones, president, William Williams, clerk, Wind Point; James Hill, president, Joseph Pullen, clerk, Stanley Hill; Philip Green, president, Francis Burnett, clerk, Lugwardine; John Benbow, president, John Morgan, clerk, Froome's Hill; John Cheese, president, George Allen, clerk, Stoke's Lane. Carried.

Moved by Elder Richards, and seconded by Elder Kington, that a monthly general council of the officers of this conference be held at Stanley Hill, to commence on Friday, the 17th of July next, at half-past seven o'clock, p. m. Elder Thomas Kington, president, and Elder John Benbow, clerk. Carried unanimously.

The president then proceeded to explain the nature of the Priesthood, and the duties and privileges of the several officers, and gave such instruction as their situation required, followed by Elder Richards, who explained many important principles connected with the building up of the Kingdom.

The minutes of the council were then read and accepted when the council adjourned; and after singing "The Spirit of God," &c., the brethren separated, with feelings of gratitude and thanksgiving, that God had been with His people, and that the spirit of union and love had prevailed in all the deliberations of the day.

WILFORD WOODRUFF, President.
JOHN BENBOW, Clerk.

REMARKS—The different branches in this region are so scattered, that it has not been possible to ascertain the number of members connected with each individual church; but connected with the Bran Green and Gadfield Elm, and the Froome's Hill conferences, together with a small branch of Little Garway of twelve members, one Priest, and one Teacher, are thirty-three churches, five hundred and thirty-four members, seventy-five officers, viz., ten Elders, fifty-two priests, and thirteen teachers. And for the comforting of the Saints, and with heart-felt gratitude to our heavenly Father, we would say that it is less than four months since the fulness of the Gospel was first preached in this region; which is a proof that God is beginning to make a short work in these last days.

WILFORD WOODRUFF.

June 21.—The Saints hired the Carpenters' Hall in Manchester, which is large enough to accommodate ten or fifteen hundred hearers, for five hundred dollars a year, payable by contribution, and Elders Young and Pratt preached therein this day for the first time.

Carpenters' Hall.

Monday, 22.—Elder Young went to Liverpool to see about printing the Book of Mormon, and returned to Manchester on the 26th; and on Sunday, 28th, preached in Carpenters' Hall.

June 27.—High Council met at my office.

Minutes of the High Council.

Alanson Ripley states to the council that he was authorized to inform them that President Joseph Smith, Jun., had vetoed* the proceedings of the Council of the 20th June, in relation to his Memorial. Laid over for hearing until Friday next.

HOSEA STOUT, Clerk.

Letter of William W. Phelps—Confessing Errors committed in Missouri.

DAYTON, OHIO, June 29, 1840.

BROTHER JOSEPH:—I am alive, and with the help of God I mean to live still. I am as the prodigal son, though I never doubt or disbelieve the fulness of the Gospel. I have been greatly abused and humbled, and I blessed the God of Israel when I lately read your prophetic blessing on my head, as follows:

"The Lord will chasten him because he taketh honor to himself, and when his soul is greatly humbled he will forsake the evil. Then shall

---

By reference to the minutes of the High Council which took into consideration the Prophet's "Memorial" it is evident that they failed to grasp the importance of the subjects presented to them, and made such disposition of them as was neither in keeping with the dignity of the Prophet or the weight of the matters on which they acted—hence the "veto," or dissatisfaction with the Council's action—See p. 144 for the conclusion of the matter.

the light of the Lord break upon him as at noonday and in him shall be no darkness," &c.

I have seen the folly of my way, and I tremble at the gulf I have passed. So it is, and why I know not. I prayed and God answered, but what could I do? Says I, "I will repent and live, and ask my old brethren to forgive me, and though they chasten me to death, yet I will die with them, for their God is my God. The least place with them is enough for me, yea, it is bigger and better than all Babylon." Then I dreamed that I was in a large house with many mansions, with you and Hyrum and Sidney, and when it was said, "Supper must be made ready," by one of the cooks, I saw no meat, but you said there was pleanty, and you showed me much, and as good as I ever saw; and while cutting to cook, your heart and mine beat within us, and we took each other's hand and cried for joy, and I awoke and took courage.

I know my situation, you know it, and God knows it, and I want to be saved if my friends will help me. Like the captain that was cast away on a desert island; when he got off he went to sea again, and made his fortune the next time, so let my lot be. I have done wrong and I am sorry. The beam is in my own eye. I have not walked along with my friends according to my holy anointing. I ask forgiveness in the name of Jesus Christ of all the Saints, for I will do right, God helping me. I want your fellowship; if you cannot grant that, grant me your peace and friendship, for we are brethren, and our communion used to be sweet, and whenever the Lord brings us together again, I will make all the satisfaction on every point that Saints or God can require. Amen.*

W. W. PHELPS.

Letter of Elders Orson Hyde and John E. Page to Presidents Joseph Smith, Hyrum Smith, Sidney Rigdon, Pleading for William W. Phelps.

DEAR BROTHER:—We have been in this place a few days, and have preached faithfully, a very great prospect of some able and influential men embracing the faith in this place. We have moved along slowly, but have left a sealing testimony. Baptized a considerable number. We shall write again more particularly as soon as we learn the result of our labors here. We are well and in good spirits through the favor of the Lord.

Brother Phelps requests us to write a few lines in his letter, and we cheerfully embrace the opportunity. Brother Phelps says he wants to

---

* For William W. Phelps' troubles in the Church, which brought him to this great sorrow and repentance, see Vol. III, pp. 3, 7, 56, 358, 359, 360 and notes.

live, but we do not feel ourselves authorized to act upon his case, but have recommended him to you; but he says his poverty will not allow him to visit you in person, at this time, and we think he tells the truth. We therefore advise him to write, which he has done.

He tells us verbally that he is willing to make any sacrifice to procure your fellowship, life not excepted, yet reposing that confidence in your magnanimity that you will take no advantage of this open and frank confession. If he can obtain your fellowship he wants to come to Commerce as soon as he can. But if he cannot be received into the fellowship of the Church, he must do the best he can in banishment and exile.

Brethren, with you are the keys of the Kingdom; to you is power given to "exert your clemency, or display your vengeance." By the former you will save a soul from death, and hide a multitude of sins; by the latter, you will forever discourage a returning prodigal cause sorrow without benefit, pain without pleasure, [and the] ending [of Brother Phelps] in wretchedness and despair. But former experience teaches [us] that you are workmen in the art of saving souls; therefore with greater confidence do we recommend to your clemency and favorable consideration, the author [of the foregoing] and subject of this communication. "Whosoever will, let him take of the waters of life freely." Brother Phelps says he will, and so far as we are concerned we say he may.

In the bonds of the covenant,

ORSON HYDE,

JOHN E. PAGE.

The Committee of the Twelve in England finished the collection of hymns and prepared the index for the press; and on the 30th Elders Kimball and Richards arrived at Manchester.

Wednesday, July 1, 1840.—Elders Wilford Woodruff and George A. Smith arrived at Manchester from the Potteries.

July 2.

Minutes of a meeting of the Crooked Creek Branch of the Church.

At a meeting of the Saints of Crooked Creek Branch, on the 2nd of July, 1840, to take into consideration the propriety of having a Stake of Zion appointed or located somewhere in the bounds of this branch, Brother John Hicks was called to the chair. Meeting was opened by prayer, after which several remarks were made, and the following resolutions were passed:

Resolved: That it be our wishes that a Stake of Zion be appointed or located within the bounds of this Branch, provided it should meet the minds of the First Presidency of this Church.

Resolved: That a committee of three be appointed to ascertain the mind of the First Presidency and report to the Branch.

Resolved: That Joseph Holebrook, Nathaniel Frampton, and John Hicks compose said committee.

It was ascertained that there were about 2,525 acres of land owned by the brethren, and wherever the Stake should be appointed the lands should be donated or purchased for a very small compensation, and that there are one hundred and twelve members belonging to this Branch.

Resolved: That we meet on Thursday next, at one o'clock, p. m., to receive the report of the committee,

Resolved: That the proceedings of this meeting be signed by the president and clerk.

JOHN A. HICKS, President.
WILLIAM WHITEMAN, Clerk.

Friday, 3.—High Council met at my office.

Minutes of High Council at Nauvoo.

The subject of the Memorial of President Joseph Smith, Jun., was brought up for a rehearing, according to the decision of the last Council (June 27) when the following resolutions were entered into:

1st. *Resolved:* That we feel perfectly satisfied with the course taken by Joseph Smith, Jun., and feel a disposition, as far as it is in our power, to assist him, so as to relieve him from the temporalities of the Church, in order that he may devote his time more particularly to the spiritualities of the same, believing by so doing we shall promote the good of the whole Church. But as he (Joseph Smith, Jun.) is held responsible for the payment of the city plot, and knowing no way to relieve him from the responsibility at present, we would request of him to act as treasurer for the city plot and to whom [i.e., President Smith] those persons whom we may appoint to make sales of lots and attend to the business affairs of the Church may at all times be responsible, and make true and correct returns of all their proceedings, as well as to account for all monies, properties, etc., which may come into their hands. Therefore

Resolved: That Elder Henry G. Sherwood act as Clerk for the same. That Bishop Alanson Ripley be appointed to provide for the wants of the Presidency, and make such appropriations to them, and to their clerk or clerks, which they may require.

Resolved: That the funds of the city plot shall not be taken to provide for the Presidency or clerks, but that the Bishops be instructed to raise funds from other sources to meet calls made on them; and monies received for lots shall be deposited in the hands of the Treasurer to liquidate the debts of the city plot.

The resolutions of the Crooked Creek Branch of the 2nd inst., were taken into consideration by President Joseph Smith, Jun., and it was thought proper to establish a Stake on Crooked Creek, agreeably to the request of said Branch, and a letter was written to the brethren to that effect.

ROBERT B. THOMPSON, Scribe.

Since Congress has decided against us, the Lord has begun to vex this nation, and He will continue to do so except they repent; for they now stand guilty of murder, robbery and plunder, as a nation, because they have refused to protect their citizens, and to execute justice according to their own Constitution. A hailstorm has visited South Carolina; some of the stones are said to have measured nine inches in circumference, which swept the crops, killing some cattle. Insects are devouring crops on the high lands, where the floods of the country have not reached, and great commercial distress prevails everywhere.

Reflections of the Prophet on the Action of Congress.

CHAPTER VII.

IMPORTANT CONFERENCE OF THE CHURCH IN ENGLAND—KID-
NAPPING OF BROWN AND BOYCE BY MISSOURIANS—ACTION
OF THE CITIZENS OF NAUVOO.

Monday, July 6, 1840.

Conference of the Church in England.

A General Conference of the Church of Jesus Christ of Latter-day
Saints was held in the Carpenter's Hall, Manchester, on the 6th day of
July, 1840, it being the 1st day of the 4th month of the eleventh year of
the Church, when the following officers of the traveling High Council
were present, viz.: Elders Brigham Young, Parley P. Pratt, Wilford
Woodruff, John Taylor, Willard Richards, Heber C. Kimball, and
George A. Smith; other officers, viz.: High Priests 5, Elders 19, Priests
15, Teachers 11, and Deacons 3.

The meeting being called to order, a little after ten o'clock, by Elder
William Clayton, it was moved by Elder Brigham Young, seconded by
Elder Wilford Woodruff, that Elder Parley P. Pratt be chosen President
of the conference,* which was carried unanimously.   Elder William

---

* At the present time the above arrangement by which Elder Parley P. Pratt was
chosen president of the conference, while Elder Brigham Young was his senior in
the quorum of the Twelve Apostles, will seem somewhat out of order.   Such procedure is recorded a number of times in the minutes of conferences and other
gatherings in the early years of the Church's history; it is therefore proper to say
that in those days the right to presidency by reason of seniority of standing in
quorums and councils was not as well settled as it is now.   Presidency throughout
the councils and quorums of the Church is determined by well settled principles of
seniority of ordination, and as soon as any of these organizations are called to
order for business the president of the council or conference is determined by the
seniority of standing in said organization without any formal action.   In the above
case the brethren may have been influenced by the fact that Elder Pratt was an
older member of the Church than President Young. Also it appears in a subsequent
paragraph that some charges were preferred by President Young against one of the
Elders in the conference. This course may have been decided upon by the Apostles,
who probably thought that it would not be best for the presiding officer over the
conference to make such charges, hence Elder Pratt was chosen to preside and
Elder Young left free to make the charges aforesaid.

Clayton was chosen clerk. The meeting was opened by singing, and prayer by the President.

Elder Brigham Young then proceeded to prefer charges against Elder T. Green, viz., first, for giving way to a false spirit; second, for abusing a young female, by accusing her, in a public meeting, of things which he could not prove; and third, for abuse to the house and congregation at Duckinfield, June 28th, 1840. The president then proceeded to ask Elder Green whether he was guilty of these charges, or not. He immediately pleaded guilty. After Elder Young had made extended remarks to the meeting, touching the conduct of Elder Green, he proposed that Elder Green go to those characters whom he had abused and insulted, and make confession to them as far as the offense extended, and then to be suspended from office for a season. The President then made remarks to the same effect, and put it to the vote of the meeting, viz., that Elder Green shall make confession, as stated above, and be suspended from office for a season. Carried.

The President then asked Elder Green if he was willing to make confession, he immediately agreed to do it the first opportunity. The meeting adjourned a little after twelve o'clock.

At two o'clock business commenced by singing and prayer, when the President called upon the officers to represent the different branches of the Church, which was done in the following order, viz.—

Branches Represented, &c.	Members.	Elders.	Priests.	Teachers.	Deacons.
The branch at Manchester represented by Elder William Clayton	280	3	5	5	1
" Preston " " Joseph Fielding	354	6	8	4	2
Elders Kington and Browett presented the minutes of the conference held in Herefordshire, which were read by Elder Wilford Woodruff, representing 33 branches of the Church . . .	534	10	52	13	—
Elder Alfred Cordon read the minutes of the conference held at Hanley, Staffordshire, representing 7 branches of the Church .	168	4	13	6	2
The branch at Liverpool, represented by Elder John Taylor	78	1	3	2	—
Elder Joseph Fielding read the minutes of the Thornley conference					
The branches at Chaighley and Thornley, represented by Elder William Kay	30	3	2	1	1
The Branch at Ribchester, represented by Elder Francis Clark	22	2	—	1	—
" Waddington " John Ellison	58	—	2	2	1
" Clitheroe " Brother Lofthouse	35	1	3	1	—
" Chatburn " Elder John Bond	91	2	2	2	—
" Downham " John Spencer	25	—	1	—	—
" Grindleton " Elder Joseph Fielding	5	—	1	—	—
" Whitmore " J. Spencer	3	—	—	—	—
" Burnley " Elder H. C. Kimball	27	1	1	1	—
" Blackburn " "	17	—	1	—	—
Elder Reuben Hedlock read the minutes of the conference held at Paisley, Scotland, representing 5 branches of the Church .	106	6	5	3	2

Branches Represented, &c.		Members.	Elders.	Priests.	Teachers.	Deacons.
The Branch at Alston, represented by	Elder John Sanders	36	2	2	2	—
" Brampton "	"	36	1	1	—	—
" Longton "	Elder Bradshaw	54	2	4	2	—
" Penwortham "	Elder P. Melling	77	4	1	1	1
" Whittle "	Elder Richard Withnall	16	1	4	—	—
" Southport "	R. McBride	19	1	—	2	—
" Daubers Lane & Eccleston "	Elder Richard Withnall	42	—	1	3	—
" Hunter's Hill "	Richard Benson	26	1	1	1	—
" Bolton "	Elder David Wilding	61	1	2	2	—
" Bury and Elton "	"	12	—	—	—	—
" Ratcliff "		11	—	—	—	—
" Bedford, &c. "	Elder Amos Fielding	40	1	1	—	—
" Stockport "	Elder Willard Richards	85	2	1	2	1
" Duckinfield "	Elder M. Littlewood	41	1	1	—	—
" Macclesfield "	Elder Henry Royle	14	—	2	—	—
" Middlewich "	Samuel Heath	20	—	1	1	1
" Plover "	"	24	—	1	1	1
" Northwich "	William Berry	14	—	1	—	—
" Altrincham "	"	4	—	—	1	—
" Whitfield "	Walker Johnson	14	—	1	—	—
" Pendlebury "	Elder William Clayton	13	—	1	1	—
" Eccles "	"	5	—	—	—	—
" West Bromwich "	Elder Theodore Turley	16	—	1	1	—

After the officers had got through the representations, the President introduced the new hymn-book; and after suitable remarks had been made by him and Elders Young and Thomas Kington, the President asked the conference if they were satisfied with the labors of those who had made the selection, and if they received the book. The unanimous approbation of the meeting was immediately manifested.

By unanimous vote, Thomas Kington, Alfred Cordon, and Thomas Smith were ordained High Priests; John Albison, John Blezzard, William Berry, John Sanders, John Parkinson, James Worsley, and John Allen were ordained Elders; and Joseph Slinger, George Walker, John Smith, Robert Williams, William Black, John Melling, and John Swindlehurst were ordained Priests.

Elder Brigham Young then called upon those officers, whose circumstances would permit them to devote themselves entirely to the work of the ministry, and would volunteer so to do, to stand up—when the following names were taken, viz.: of the traveling High Council, Brigham Young, Heber C. Kimball, John Taylor, Wilford Woodruff, Willard Richards, and George A. Smith; other officers, namely, William Clayton, Reuben Hedlock, Hiram Clark, Theodore Turley, Joseph Fielding, Thomas Richardson, Amos Fielding, John Parkinson, John Wych, John Needham, Henry Royle, John Blezzard, D. Wilding, Charles Price, Joseph Knowles, Wm. Kay, Samuel Heath, Wm. Parr, R. McBride, and James Morgan.

Moved by Elder Richards, seconded by Elder Kimball, that Elder Peter Melling be appointed to preside over the following branches of the Church, namely—Preston, Longton, Penwortham, North Meols, and Southport: carried.

Moved by Elder Kimball, seconded by Elder Young, that Elder Richard Withnall be appointed to preside over the branches of the Church at Whittle, Daubers Lane, Chorley, Hunter's Hill, and Euxton-burgh: carried.

Moved by Elder Kimball, seconded by Elder Young, that Elder Thomas Smith be appointed to preside over the branches of the Church at Clitheroe, Chatburn, Downham, Chaighley, Grindleton, Whitmore, Burnley, Blackburn, Ribchester, and Thornley: carried.

Moved and seconded, that President Fielding and his counselors be set at liberty from the charge which they have sustained as a presidency, that they may have the privilege of more fully entering into the field of labor; and that their labors be accepted: carried.

Elders Young and Richards then proceeded to ordain those who had been nominated to their respective offices, after which the minutes were read and accepted.

The conference adjourned to the sixth of October next, to be held in the Carpenter's Hall, Manchester, at 10 o'clock, a. m.

Tuesday, 7.

A council of Church Officers, held at Manchester, England.

Pursuant to previous notice, a general council of the Church officers was held in the council room at the *Star* office, Manchester, on the 7th day of July, 1840. The meeting being opened by prayer by Elder Kimball, Elder Young began to speak concerning those officers who had volunteered to devote themselves wholly to the ministry; when it was moved and seconded that Brothers William Kay and Thomas Richardson go to Herefordshire, to labor in that region with Elder Kington: carried.

Moved by Elder Kimball, seconded by Elder Young, that Brothers Hiram Clark and Joseph Knowles go with Elder Hedlock to Scotland: carried.

Moved by Elder Kimball, seconded by Elder Young, that Brother Joseph Fielding go to Bedford: carried.

Moved by Elder Richards, seconded by Elder Kimball, that Brothers Amos Fielding and John Wych go to Newcastle-upon-Tyne: carried.

Moved by Elder Kimball, seconded by Elder Woodruff, that Brother David Wilding go to Garway, Herefordshire: carried.

Moved by Elder Young, seconded by Elder Woodruff, that Brothers William Clayton and John Needham go to Birmingham: carried.

Moved by Elder Richards, seconded by Elder Young, that Brother Henry Royle go to Sheffield: carried.

Moved by Elder Clayton, seconded by Elder Young, that Brother John Albiston take charge of the following Branches of the Church, namely—Duckinfield, Hyde, Woolley Hill, Ashton, and Staley Bridge: carried.

Moved by Elder Pratt, seconded by Elder Woodruff, that Brother William Parr go to Sandbach and Congleton: carried.

Moved by Elder Richards, seconded by Elder Pratt, that Brother Heath continue his labors in Macclesfield: carried.

Moved by Elder Richards, seconded by Elder Woodruff, that Brother John Blezzard go to Cornshaw: carried.

Moved by Elder Kimball, seconded by Elder Richards, that Brother Robert McBride go to Lancaster: carried.

Moved by Elder Richards, seconded by Elder Woodruff, that Brother James Morgan abide in his own neighborhood to labor with Elder David Wilding: carried.

Moved by Elder Pratt, seconded by Elder Woodruff, that Brother Price give up his business, and labor under the advice of Elder Kington as the way opens: carried.

Moved by Elder Richards, seconded by Elder Kimball, that Brother William Black go to Lisburn, Ireland, as the way opens: carried.

Moved by Elder Richards, seconded by Elder Smith, that Brother John Parkinson have a roving commission, so long as he keeps busy, and doing good: carried.

After Elder Young had addressed the meeting upon several important items, the meeting dismissed by blessing from Elder Young.

PARLEY P. PRATT, President.
WILLIAM CLAYTON, Clerk.

At this time Elders Orson Hyde and John E. Page were laboring in Ohio.

Thursday, 9.

Extract from Elder Woodruff's Letter to the Editor of the Millennial Star —Detailing Incidents of his Ministry.

I arrived at Froome's Hill, Castle Froome, Herefordshire, on the 4th of March, and was kindly entertained for the night by Mr. John Benbow, who received my testimony, and opened his door for meeting; and on the evening following, the 5th of March, for the first time I preached the fullness of the Gospel in that place to a small congregation, who manifested much interest in what they heard, and desired to inquire further into those things; and on the evening following I met a large number at Mr. Benbow's, and preached unto them the principles of the Gospel, namely, faith in Christ, repentance, and baptism for the remission of sins and the gift of the Holy Ghost by the laying on of hands; after which I administered the ordinance of baptism unto six persons, Mr. and Mrs. Benbow among the number.   I also preached on Sunday the 8th and baptized seven, confirmed thirteen, and broke bread unto them.   Several of those who were baptized were preachers of the order called the United Brethren.

The United Brethren formerly belonged to the Primitive Methodists, but had separated themselves from the body, and chose the name of the United Brethren.   They had from forty to fifty preachers and about the same number of established places of meeting, including two chapels.

Mr. Thomas Kington was the superintendent of the church of the United Brethren, whose members numbered about four hundred in all, divided into small branches and scattered over an extent of country from fifteen to twenty miles.   This people almost universally appeared willing to give heed to the exhortation of Solomon, to hear a matter before they judged or condemned.   They opened their doors for me to preach, and searched the Scriptures daily to see if the things which I taught were true; and on finding that the word and spirit agreed and bore record of the truth of the fullness of the Everlasting Gospel, they embraced it with all their hearts, which has brought great joy and satisfaction to many souls in that region.

I continued preaching and baptizing daily; the congregations were large and generally attentive.   I was soon privileged with an interview with Mr. Thomas Kington, the superintendent of the United Brethren, before whom I gave an account of the rise and progress of the Church of the Latter-day Saints, and bore testimony of the truth of the great work which God had set His hand to accomplish in these last days.

Mr. Kington received my testimony and sayings with candor; and carried the case before the Lord, made it a subject of prayer, and asked the Father in the name of Jesus Christ, if these things were true; and the Lord manifested the truth of it unto him, and he went forth and was baptized, he and all his household.   I ordained him an Elder, and he went forth and began to preach the fullness of the Gospel.

I also baptized about forty preachers of the same order, and several others belonging unto other churches, and about one hundred and twenty members of the United Brethren, which opened about forty doors or preaching places, where the fullness of the Gospel would meet a welcome reception, and all this during the term of one month and five days.

On the 10th of April I took my departure from the Saints in Herefordshire and adjoining country, numbering about one hundred and sixty;

whom I left rejoicing in the fullness of the Gospel, and hundreds of others who were ready to be baptized as soon as a proper time and opportunity arrived. I arrived in Preston on the 13th, by way of Worcester, Wolverhampton, Burslem, and Manchester, a distance of about one hundred and seventy miles, visiting the churches by the way.

On my arrival in Preston, I was blessed with the happy privilege of once more greeting my brethren of the Traveling High Council and other Elders, and of sitting with them on the 14th, 15th, and 16th of April in the first council and general conference which they had ever held, as a quorum, in a foreign nation. After spending several days together, (during which time much business of importance was transacted for the Church,) it became necessary for us again to separate, in order to labor in different parts of the vineyard which were now open before us. I left Preston on the 17th, accompanied by Elder Brigham Young, and visited the churches by the way, until we arrived among the Saints in Herefordshire, who were anxiously looking for my return. In a few days we were joined in our labors by Elder Willard Richards. We took locations in different parts of this new field of labor, which extended through various places in Herefordshire, Worcestershire, and Gloucestershire.

We continued preaching, and baptizing, and administering in the ordinances of the Gospel daily, unto such as would receive our testimony, and obey the Gospel of Jesus Christ. Truth was mighty and prevailed; the work prospered, and multiplied on every hand, until several hundreds, including more than fifty preachers of various sects, were rejoicing in the fullness of the everlasting Gospel, and felt to praise God that they had lived to behold the day when the Lord had set His hand to prune His vineyard once more with a mighty pruning, and to establish the Gospel in its ancient purity again upon the face of the earth; and in many instances signs followed the believer, according to the promise of the Savior. The Spirit of God accompanied the preaching of the word to the hearts of men. Whole households, on hearing the word, have received it into good and honest hearts, and gone forth and received the ordinances of the Gospel; and frequently we have baptized from eight to twelve the first time of meeting with the people in new places, and preaching the word of God to them.

Elder Young labored with us about one month, during which time many were baptized, confirmed, and numbers ordained to preach the Gospel—and while the Saints were much edified, and their hearts made glad with the teaching and instruction by Elder Young, I also obtained much benefit myself by enjoying his society, sitting under his instruction, and sharing in his counsel.

As it became necessary for Elder Young to return to Manchester, to assist in preparing a collection of hymns, and other matters, he took the parting hand with us on the 20th of May; and Elders Richards and myself continued our labors in the vineyard, in connection with Elder Kington, who had given himself wholly to the work of the ministry.

The Lord still continued to bless our labors, and added daily unto the Church. New doors were opening on every hand; and multiplicity of calls constantly reached our ears, many of which we could not answer for the want of laborers. Notwithstanding there were about fifty ordained Elders and Priests in this part of the vineyard, yet there were equally as many places for preaching to be attended to upon the Sabbath day. Thus we continued our labors in this region until the time drew near for the general conference in Manchester on the 6th of July.

But before leaving the Saints, we considered it wisdom to set in order the church, and organize them into branches and conferences, that they might be properly represented before the general conference. Therefore we held two conferences with the Saints before we took our departure from them. The first was held at the Gadfield Elm Chapel, Worcestershire, on the 14th of June, at which time we organized twelve branches, and transacted such business as the occasion required. The second conference was held at Stanley Hill, Herefordshire, on the 21st of June, twenty branches of the Church were organized. The minutes of the above-named conferences I present you for publication, if you think proper.

On the day following, Elder Richards and myself took our leave of the Saints at Froome's Hill, Herefordshire; but before leaving we repaired to a pool three times to baptize and confirm numbers that came to us and requested these ordinances at our hands.

Elder Richards labored in this part of the vineyard about two months, during which time he traveled extensively, preached night and day, gave much instruction to the Saints generally, and had many souls as seals to his ministry. I received much benefit from the counsel which he gave in the organization of the churches, and it was manifest that he had passed through a profitable school of experience during the three years of his travels in England; and the interesting seasons we have enjoyed together during these two months, will not be easily erased from my memory.

It was with no ordinary fellings that we took our departure from the Saints in Herefordshire on this occasion; for, less than four months since, I proclaimed the fullness of the Gospel in this region for the first time; but now, we were leaving between five and six hundred Saints, who were rejoicing in the new and everlasting covenant, and hundreds of others who were wishing to hear and obey. I parted from Elder Richards at Birmingham, who went direct to Manchester, while I visited

West Bromwich, and preached several times to a small branch of the
Church which had been raised up in that place by Elder Turley, who
baptized several while I was there.   I also attended a conference on
the 29th June, at Hanley, in the Staffordshire Potteries, in company
with Elder George A. Smith and others, after which I arrived in Manchester.
                                                    WILFORD WOODRUFF.
  Manchester, July 9, 1840.

  Saturday, 11.—The High Council met at my office, when
I taught them principles relating to their duty as a Council, and that they might be guided by the same
in future, I ordered it to be recorded as follows: ''That the Council should try no case
without both parties being present, or having had an opportunity to be present; neither should they hear one person's complaint before his case is brought up for trial;
neither should they suffer the character of any one to be
exposed before the High Council without the person being
present and ready to defend him or herself; that the
minds of the councilors be not prejudiced for or against
any one whose case they may possibly have to act upon.''

Special In-
structions for
High Coun-
cils.

  William Barrett, aged 17, was ordained an Elder in
Hanley, Staffordshire, England, by Elders George A.
Smith and Alfred Cordon, and took leave for
South Australia, being the first Elder who
went on a mission to that country.

The First Mis-
sionary for
Australia.

  Sunday, 12—Elias Smith was appointed Bishop by the
High Council of Iowa, in place of Alanson Ripley, removed to Nauvoo.

  Monday, 13.

*Kidnapping of Alanson Brown and Benjamin Boyce—Affidavit of Daniel
                                H. Wells.**

                          STATE OF ILLINOIS, HANCOCK COUNTY.
  This day personally appeared before the undersigned, an acting justice of the peace, in the aforesaid county, Alanson Brown, who, first

  * Daniel Hanmer Wells was the son of Daniel Wells by his second wife Catherine
Chapin. He was born at Trenton, Oneida county, New York, October 27, 1814.

being duly sworn according to law, deposes and says, that on the 7th day of July, A. D. 1840, and in the county of Hancock, in said state, William Allensworth, H. M. Woodyard, William Martin, John H. Owsley, John Bain, Light T. Tait, and Halsay White, in company with several other persons, to this affiant unknown, forcibly arrested this affiant, and one Benjamin Boyce, whilst affiant and said Boyce, were quietly pursuing their own lawful business; and that immediately after said arrest, the said Allensworth, Woodyard, Martin, Owsley, Bain, Tait, and White, did illegally and forcibly take, kidnap, and carry this affiant and said Boyce, bound with cords, from the said county of Hancock, in said state, on the day and year above set forth, in the county of Lewis, in the state of Missouri, without having established a claim for such a procedure, according to the laws of the United States.

Affiant states that in a short time after he was taken into the state of Missouri, he was put into a room with said Boyce, and there kept until about eleven o'clock the following night; when they were taken out of the room where they had been confined, into the woods, near at hand, by said Tait, a man by the name of Huner, and another by the name of Monday, and some others, whose name affiant did not learn; they previously placed a rope about the neck of the affiant; Huner and Monday then proceeded to hang the affiant, and did hang him for some time upon a tree, until affiant was nearly strangled, after which they let him down and loosened the rope. Shortly after this, affiant heard repeated blows, which others—belonging to the same gang of Huner— were inflicting upon Boyce, and he could hear also the cries of Boyce, under the pain arising from the blows; after which affiant and Boyce were taken back to the room where they had been confined, in which they found a man by the name of Rogers, and another by the name of Allred.

Affiant further states that he was kept in imprisonment by the per-

His father was a descendant of Thomas Wells, the fourth governor of Connecticut, while his mother was descended from David Chapin, a veteran of the Revolution, who served under Washington, and was a descendant of one of the oldest and most distinguished families of New England. The father of Daniel H. Wells died when the son was but 12 years old, which threw upon him, at this early age, the care of his mother and younger sister. At the age of 16 he migrated with his mother and sister to Marietta, Ohio, where Daniel H. taught school during the winter, and in the spring moved to Illinois, settling at Commerce, where he made extensive purchases of land. One farm of eighty acres was in the very heart of what became the city of Nauvoo, in fact he platted his farm into city lots which he sold at very reasonable prices to the Saints. The Temple site was selected from the western range of blocks in this addition. In 1835 he married Eliza Robison, and a son was born to them a year later. Mr. Wells served a term as constable in the district in which Commerce was situated, and was now a justice of the peace and familiarly called "Squire Wells." He was a stalwart Whig in politics; a man of high character and great courage.

sons heretofore named, and others to him unknown, until Friday evening next ensuing the Tuesday on which Boyce and himself were kidnapped, when he escaped out of their hands and returned into the state
of Illinois. Affiant had learned that the name of the place in said
county of Lewis, state of Missouri, to which he was taken from the
state of Illinois, is called Tully, to which the said Allensworth, Woodyard, Martin, Owsley, Bain, Tait and White, have fled as fugitives from
justice, and at which they are now to be found.

I hereby certify that the foregoing affidavit was this day subscribed
and duly sworn to before me, by said Alanson Brown.

DANIEL H. WELLS.

Justice of the Peace, July 13, 1840.

Statement of James Allred.

STATE OF ILLINOIS, HANCOCK COUNTY.

This day personally appeared before the undersigned, an acting Justice of the Peace, in and for said county, James Allred, a credible witness, who first being duly sworn according to law, deposes and says that
William Allensworth, John H. Owsley, and William Martin, on the 7th
day of July, 1840, within the limits of said county of Hancock, aided
by several other persons, to this affiant unknown, forcibly arrested this
affiant and one Noah Rogers, whilst the affiant and said Rogers were
peaceably pursuing their own lawful business; and that the said Allensworth, Owsley and Martin, after said arrest, aided by sundry persons, to
affiant unknown, did forcibly take, kidnap and carry this affiant and
said Rogers from the said county of Hancock in the state of Illinois, on
the day and year above mentioned into the state of Missouri, without
having established a claim for such procedure according to the laws of
the United States.

Affiant further states, that in a short time after he had been so taken
into the state of Missouri, he was put into a room with said Rogers, and
there kept until some time during the following night, when they were
taken out of the room where they were confined, into the woods near
by, and this affiant was bound by the persons conducting him, to a tree,
he having been first forcibly stripped by them of every particle of
clothing. Those having him in charge then told affiant that they would
whip him; one of them, by the name of Monday, saying to this affiant,
'G— d—n you, I'll cut you to the hollow.'' They, however, at last
unbound the affiant without whipping him.

Affiant states that said Rogers was taken just beyond the place
where affiant was bound with a rope around his neck, and he heard a
great number of blows, which he then supposed, and has since learned
were inflicted upon said Rogers, and heard him cry out several times as
if in great agony; after which affiant, together with Rogers, was taken

back and placed in the room from which they were taken, together with one Boyce and Brown, and detained until Monday next succeeding the day on which he was kidnapped; at which time he received from one of the company, who had imprisoned him, a passport, of which the following is a copy—

"Tully, Missouri, July 12, 1840. The people of Tully, having taken up Mr. Allred, with some others, and having examined into the offenses committed, find nothing to justify his detention any longer, and have released him. By order of the committe.

"H. M. WOODWARD."

And then this affiant was permitted to return home into the state of Illinois. This place in Missouri, to which affiant and said Rogers were taken, he has learned is called Tully, and is situated in the county of Lewis, and at which place the said Allensworth, Owsley and Martin are now living.

I hereby certify that the forgoing affidavit was this day subscribed, and duly sworn to before me, by the said James Allred.

DANIEL H. WELLS,
Justice of the Peace.

Action of the Citizens of Nauvoo in the Matter of the Kidnapping of Brown and Boyce by the Missourians.

At a meeting of the citizens of Nauvoo, Hancock county, Illinois, 13th July, 1840, Judge Elias Higbee was called to the chair, and Robert B. Thompson was appointed Secretary.

On motion a committee was appointed to report resolutions, expressive of the sense of this meeting, consisting of the following persons, to wit.—Isaac Galland, Robert B. Thompson, Sidney Rigdon, and Daniel H. Wells, who retired, and after a short absence, reported the following preamble and resolutions, which were unanimously adopted—

Report of the Committee on Resolutions.

PREAMBLE—The committee appointed to express the sense of this meeting, in relation to the recent acts of abduction, and other deeds of cruelty and inhumanity committed upon our citizens by [some of] the citizens of the state of Missouri, beg leave respectfully to report:

That having under consideration the principal matters involve in the discharge of their duty, they have been forced to arrive at the following conclusions:

First—That the people of Missouri, not having sufficiently slacked their thirst for blood and plunder, are now disposed to pursue us with a repetition of the scenes of brutality which marked their whole course of conduct towards us during our unhappy residence among them.

Second—That notwithstanding they have already robbed us of our homes, murdered our families, stolen and carried away our property; and to complete the measure of their infamy as a state, their executive caused unoffending thousands to be banished from the state, without even the form of a trial, or the slightest evidence of crime; they are now sending their gangs of murdering banditti, and thieving brigands, to wreak further vengeance, and satisfy their insatiable cupidity in the state of Illinois, and that too before we have even had time to erect shelters for our families.

Third—That for the purpose of giving a semblance of justification to their most unhallowed conduct, the people of Missouri have again commenced concealing goods within the limits of our settlements, as they had done before in the state of Missouri, in order to raise a charge of stealing against our citizens, and under this guise they have within a few days kidnapped, and carried away, several honest and worthy citizens of this county.

Fourth—Under these circumstances the first duty and the only redress which seems to offer itself to our consideration is an appeal to the executive of the state of Illinois, for redress, and protection from further injuries, with a confident assurance that he, unlike the governor of Missouri, will extend the executive arm to protect from lawless outrage, unoffending citizens. Therefore,

Resolved 1st: That we view, with no ordinary feelings, the approaching danger as a necessary consequence following the lawless and outrageous conduct of the citizens of Missouri, in setting at defiance the laws of this, as well as of all other states in this Union, by forcing from their homes, and from the state, civil citizens of Illinois, and taking them into the state of Missouri, without any legal process whatever, and there inflicting upon them base cruelties in order to extort false confessions from them, to give a coloring to their (the Missourians') iniquities, and screen themselves from the just indignation of an incensed public.

Resolved 2ndly: That while we deeply deplore the cause which has brought us together on this occasion, we cannot refrain from expressing our most unqualified disapprobation at the infringement of the laws of this state, as set forth in the above Preamble, and strongest indignation at the manner in which the people of Missouri treated those whom they had thus inhumanly taken from among us.

Resolved 3rdly: That inasmuch as we are conscious of our honest and upright intentions, and are at all times ready and willing to submit to the just requirements of the laws, we claim of the citizens and authorities of this state, protection from such unjust and, before, unheard of oppressions.

Resolved 4thly: That the forcible abduction of our citizens by the citizens of Missouri, is a violation of the laws regulating the federal compact, subversive to the rights of freemen, and contrary to our free institutions, and republican principles.

Resolved, 5thly: That the cruelties practiced upon our citizens, since their abduction, is disgraceful to humanity; the height of injustice and oppression, and would disgrace the annals of the most barbarous nations, in either ancient or modern times; and can only find its parallel in the "*Auto da Fe*"—the inquisitions in Spain.

Resolved, 6thly: That such unconstitutional and unhallowed proceedings on the part of the citizens of Missouri, ought to arouse every patriot to exertion and diligence to put a stop to such procedure, and use all constitutional means to bring the offenders to justice.

Resolved, 7thly: That we memorialize the Executive of this state, of the gross outrage which has been committed on our citizens; and pledge ourselves to aid him in such measures as may be deemed necessary to restore our citizens to freedom, and have satisfaction for the wrongs we have suffered.

ELIAS HIGBEE, Chairman,
R. B. THOMPSON, Secretary.

Memorial to Governor Carlin.

To his Excellency Governor Carlin:—The undersigned being a committee to draft a Memorial to your Excellency relative to the recent outrages, would respectfully represent; that after being driven from our homes, and pleasant places of abode, in the state of Missouri, by the authorities of said state, Illinois seemed to be the first shelter or asylum which presented itself to our view; that having left the state of Missouri, your memorialists found an asylum in the state of Illinois; and notwithstanding the false reports which were circulated to our prejudice, we were received with kindness by the noble hearted citizens of Illinois; who relieved our necessities, and bade us welcome; for which kindness we feel thankful.

That under your Excellency's administration, we have had every encouragement given us, and have every reason, from the kindness and sympathy which you have ever manifested towards us in our sufferings, to feel confident that your aid will ever be offered to us in common with the rest of the citizens of the state. That feeling ourselves so happy and secure, and beginning again to enjoy the comforts of life, we are sorry to say that our quiet has been disturbed, our fears alarmed, and our families annoyed by the citizens of Missouri; who, with malice and hatred, which is characteristic of them, have unconstitutionally sent an armed force and abducted some of our friends, namely, James Allred,

Noah Rogers, Alanson Brown, and one Boyce, and carried them into the state of Missouri, and treated them with the greatest barbarity and cruelty; even now their wives and children, as well as their friends, are alarmed for the safety of their lives.

Therefore we have felt it our duty to place the circumstances of this unheard-of outrage before you, and appeal to your Excellency for protection from such marauders, and take such measures as you may deem proper, that our friends may be again restored to the bosom of their families, and the offenders punished for their crimes.

We have the greatest confidence in your Excellency, that every constitutional means will be resorted to, to restore our friends to the society of their families, &c., that we, in common with other citizens of the state of Illinois, may enjoy all the rights and privileges of freemen.

Your memorialists have under all circumstances paid the greatest respect to the laws of the country, and if any should break the same, they have never felt a disposition to screen such from justice, but when under false pretenses, to gratify and satiate a revengeful disposition—for the citizens of another state, regardless of both the laws of God and man, to come and kidnap our friends, to carry off our citizens to cruelly treat our brethren; such offenders, we think, should be brought to an account, to be dealt with according to their merit or demerit; that we may enjoy the privileges guaranteed to us by the Constitution of the United States.

We therefore humbly pray that your Excellency will satisfy yourself of the gross outrage which has been committed on the citizens of the state, and with that energy which is so characteristic of your Exellency's administration, take such steps as you may deem best calculated to repair the injuries which your memorialists have sustained; that you will vindicate the injured laws of the state.

In conclusion, we beg leave to assure your Excellency, that in the discharge of this, as well as every other constitutional movement, you may rely upon the hearty co-operation of your memorialists, who respectfully submit to your Excellency the accompanying Resolutions, which were passed at a large meeting held in this place on this day, and also the affidavit of one of those persons who was kidnapped, but fortunately has made his escape.

CHAPTER IX.

THE RETURN OF A PRODIGAL—CONDITIONS IN KIRTLAND—
PROGRESS OF THE WORK IN GREAT BRITAIN—THE COM-
ING OF JOHN C. BENNETT.

AUSTRALIAN MISSION.

Extract of a Letter from Elder William Barratt.

DEPTFORD,* July 15, 1840.

DEAR BROTHER IN CHRIST:—I write to inform you of my arrival in
the metropolis this morning, after a tedious journey in the midst of
much profaneness and swearing, such as I never heard in my life before.   I feel, as the Apostle expresses it, like a lamb among wolves,
going into a land of strangers to preach the Gospel; therefore I desire
your prayers in my behalf.   I have witnessed much of the spirit of
revelation since Sunday; in fact, I only thought it a mere thought,
when the Elders testified that they were called by revelation; but now
I know the truth of the assertion, which proves to me who ought to
preach, and that none ought, without they are called by revelation.

Give my love to all the Saints, and tell them that as many as remain faithful I will meet in Zion, bringing my sheaves with me.   Tell
them my faith is fixed, and my resolution is strong to meet you all there,
whom I love in the Lord.   Pray that a door may be opened, and that a
gift of utterance may be given unto me in a foreign land to preach the
Gospel.   Brethren, sorrow not for me, as those that have no hope, for
we have a hope of living and eating together in the kingdom of our God.

Friday, 17.—By my suggestion, High Council voted
that Samuel Bent and George W. Harris go on a mission
to procure money for printing certain books.

Saturday, 18.—Elias Smith was ordained a Bishop.

Sunday, 19.—An answer to Brigham Young's letter of
the 17th of May was sent by Lorenzo Snow,† which gave

---

* Formerly a town in Kent and Surrey, England, on the Thames, noted for its
dock yards, now part of London.

† Lorenzo Snow was born April 30, 1814, in Mantua, Portage county, Ohio.   He

the Twelve permission to publish the Book of Mormon,
Doctrine and Covenants, and hymn-book, but not to ordain any into the quorum of the Seventies; and likewise
some general instructions.

Monday, 20.—Elder John Moon and company arrived
in New York being the first arrival of Saints in America.
Wednesday, 22.

*The Prophet's Letter to William W. Phelps—Welcoming him back into
the Church.**

NAUVOO, HANCOCK COUNTY, ILLINOIS, July 22, 1840.

DEAR BROTHER PHELPS:—I must say that it is with no ordinary
feelings I endeavor to write a few lines to you in answer to yours of
the 29th ultimo; at the same time I am rejoiced at the privilege
granted me.

was the eldest son of Oliver Snow and Rosetta L. Pettibone. The early years of
his life were spent upon his father's farm. Later he entered Oberlin College, a
Presbyterian institution, in the town of Oberlin, in Lorain county, Ohio, about
sixty miles southwest of Kirtland. In June, 1836, he visited Kirtland and attended
the Hebrew classes, then being taught in the Temple. While in Kirtland he became a convert to the faith of the Latter-day Saints and was baptized by Elder
John Boynton, one of the Twelve Apostles. The following year he did some missionary work among his relatives and friends in Ohio, and in 1836, with his parents,
who in the meantime joined the Church, he moved to Missouri, and shortly afterwards went upon a preaching mission through the states of Kentucky and Illinois.
A few days before starting upon this mission mentioned in the text, namely, 17th
of July, 1840, he was ordained a Seventy by President Joseph Young, and the day
following was made a High Priest under the hands of Don Carlos Smith. The testimony which this man received of the truth of the Gospel is very interesting, and
seems to have remained with him throughout his long life, in all the freshness of
its first impression upon him. Having received the usual promise of a testimony
of the truth of the work if he obeyed the Gospel, he sought that testimony most
earnestly in prayer with the following result as stated by himself:

"I had no sooner opened my lips in an effort to pray than I heard a sound just
above my head like the rushing of silken robes; and immediately the Spirit of God
descended upon me, completely enveloping my whole person, filling me from the
crown of my head to the soles of my feet, and oh, the joyful happiness I felt! No
language can describe the almost instantaneous transition from a dense cloud of
spiritual darkness into a refulgence of light and knowledge, as it was at that time
imparted to my understanding. I received a perfect knowledge that God lives,
that Jesus Christ is the Son of God, and of the restoration of the Holy Priesthood,
and the fullness of the Gospel. It was a complete baptism—a tangible immersion
in the heavenly principle or element, the Holy Ghost; and even more physical in
its effects upon every part of my system than the immersion by water."

* When the great offense of Elder William W. Phelps is taken into account—
amounting as it did to a betrayal of the Prophet and the Church in Missouri, dur-

You may in some measure realize what my feelings, as well as Elder Rigdon's and Brother Hyrum's were, when we read your letter—truly our hearts were melted into tenderness and compassion when we ascertained your resolves, &c.　I can assure you I feel a disposition to act on your case in a manner that will meet the approbation of Jehovah, (whose servant I am), and agreeable to the principles of truth and righteousness which have been revealed; and inasmuch as long-suffering, patience, and mercy have ever characterized the dealings of our heavenly Father towards the humble and penitent, I feel disposed to copy the example, cherish the same principles, and by so doing be a savior of my fellow men.

It is true, that we have suffered much in consequence of your behavior —the cup of gall, already full enough for mortals to drink, was indeed filled to overflowing when you turned against us.　One with whom we had oft taken sweet counsel together, and enjoyed many refreshing seasons from the Lord—"had it been an enemy, we could have borne it."　"In the day that thou stoodest on the other side, in the day when strangers carried away captive his forces, and foreigners entered into his gates, and cast lots upon [Far West], even thou wast as one of them; but thou shouldest not have looked on the day of thy brother, in the day that he became a stranger, neither shouldst thou have spoken proudly in the day of distress."

However, the cup has been drunk, the will of our Father has been done, and we are yet alive, for which we thank the Lord.　And having been delivered from the hands of wicked men by the mercy of our God, we say it is your privilege to be delivered from the powers of the adversary, be brought into the liberty of God's dear children, and again take your stand among the Saints of the Most High, and by diligence, humility, and love unfeigned, commend yourself to our God, and your God, and to the Church of Jesus Christ.

Believing your confession to be real, and your repentance genuine, I shall be happy once again to give you the right hand of fellowship, and rejoice over the returning prodigal.

Your letter was read to the Saints last Sunday, and an expression of their feeling was taken, when it was unanimously

ing the troubles of the Saints in that state—this letter is remarkable. The Prophet's frank forgiveness of his erring brother, gently chiding his wrong-doing, but at the same time remembering in a large way that brother's former devotion and labors; the Prophet's willingness to have the prodigal return and occupy his former high standing among the Saints—all this exhibits a broad-mindedness and generosity that can come only from a great soul, influenced by the spirit of charity enjoined upon his disciples by the teachings of the Son of God. One of the surest evidences of Joseph Smith's greatness of mind and of the inspiration of God upon him is to be seen in his treatment of those who had fallen but were willing to and did repent of their sins. His capacity to forgive under these circumstances seemed boundless.

Resolved, That W. W. Phelps should be received into fellowship.

"Come on, dear brother, since the war is past,
For friends at first, are friends again at last."

Yours as ever,
                    JOSEPH SMITH, JUN.

Credentials of Elders Samuel Bent and George W. Harris.

To all whom it may concern:—This is to certify that Elders Samuel Bent and George W. Harris are authorized agents of the Church of Jesus Christ of Latter-day Saints, being appointed by the First Presidency and High Council of said Church to visit the branches of the Church in the east, or wherever they may be led in the providence of God, to obtain donations and subscriptions for the purpose of printing the Book of Mormon, Doctrine and Covenants, hymn-books, the new translation of the Scriptures. They are likewise instructed and authorized to procure loans in behalf of the Church, for carrying into operation the above and other important works necessary to the well being of said Church.

From our long acquaintance with these our beloved brethren, their long, tried friendship under circumstances the most trying and painful, their zeal for the cause of truth, and their strict morality and honesty, we most cheerfully recommend them to the Saints of the Most High. Any statements they may make relative to their mission may be implicitly relied upon, and any loans which they may obtain, will be considered binding on the Church. And we do hope the Saints will do all in their power to effect the object proposed, and lift up the hands of our beloved brethren who have cheerfully come forward to engage in a work so great and important.

Joseph Smith, Jun., President.	Hyrum Smith,
William Marks,	Newel Knight,
Elias Higbee,	Alpheus Cutler.
David Dort,	Henry G. Sherwood,
Charles C. Rich,	David Fullmer,
Seymour Brunson,	Thomas Grover,
William Huntington,	Lewis D. Wilson.

The Prophet's Letter to Oliver Granger—Dealing Chiefly with Affairs at Kirtland.

Brother Granger:

DEAR SIR:—It was with great pleasure I received your and Brother Richards' letter, dated New York, June 23, 1840, and was very happy to be informed of your safe arrival in that place, and your probability of success; and I do hope that your anticipations will be realized, and that you will be enabled to free the Lord's House from all incumbrances, and be prospered in all your undertakings for the benefit of the Church; and pray that while you are exerting your influence to bring about an object so desirable, that the choicest blessings of heaven may rest down upon you, while you are endeavoring to do so, and attending to the duties laid upon you by the authorities of the Church in this place.

I am sorry to be informed not only in your letter, but from other respectable sources, of the strange conduct pursued in Kirtland by Elder Almon W. Babbitt. I am indeed surprised that a man having the experience which Brother Babbitt has had, should take any steps whatever, calculated to destroy the confidence of the brethren in the Presidency or any of the authorities of the Church.

In order to conduct the affairs of the Kingdom in righteousness, it is all important that the most perfect harmony, kind feeling, good understanding, and confidence should exist in the hearts of all the brethren; and that true charity, love one towards another, should characterize all their proceedings. If there are any uncharitable feelings, any lack of confidence, then pride, arrogance and envy will soon be manifested; confusion must inevitably prevail, and the authorities of the Church set at naught; and under such circumstances, Kirtland cannot rise and free herself from the captivity in which she is held, and become a place of safety for the Saints, nor can the blessings of Jehovah rest upon her.

If the Saints in Kirtland deem me unworthy of their prayers when they assemble together, and neglect to bear me up at the throne of heavenly grace, it is a strong and convincing proof to me that they have not the Spirit of God. If the revelations we have received are true, who is to lead the people? If the keys of the Kingdom have been committed to my hands, who shall open out the mysteries thereof?

As long as my brethren stand by me and encourage me, I can combat the prejudices of the world, and can bear the contumely and abuse with joy; but when my brethren stand aloof, when they begin to faint, and endeavor to retard my progress and enterprise, then I feel to mourn, but am no less determined to prosecute my task, being confident that although my earthly friends may fail, and even turn against me, yet my heavenly Father will bear me off triumphant.

However, I hope that even in Kirtland there are some who do not make a man an offender for a word, but are disposed to stand forth in defense of righteousness and truth, and attend to every duty enjoined upon them; and who will have wisdom to direct them against any movement or influence calculated to bring confusion and discord into the camp of Israel, and to discern between the spirit of truth and the spirit of error.

It would be gratifying to my mind to see the Saints in Kirtland flourish, but think the time is not yet come; and I assure you it never will until a different order of things be established and a different spirit manifested. When confidence is restored, when pride shall fall, and every aspiring mind be clothed with humility as with a garment, and selfishness give place to benevolence and charity, and a united determination to live by every word which proceedeth out of the mouth of the Lord is observable, then, and not till then, can peace, order and love prevail.

It is in consequence of aspiring men that Kirtland has been forsaken. How frequently has your humble servant been envied in his office by such characters, who endeavored to raise themselves to power at his expense, and seeing it impossible to do so, resorted to foul slander and abuse, and other means to effect his overthrow. Such characters have ever been the first to cry out against the Presidency, and publish their faults and foibles to the four winds of heaven.

I cannot forget the treatment I received in the house of my friends. These things continually roll across my mind, and cause me much sorrow of heart; and when I think that others who have lately come into the Church should be led to Kirtland instead of to this place, by Elder Babbitt; and having their confidence in the authorities lessened by such observations as he (Elder Babbitt) has thought proper to make, as well as hearing all the false reports and exaggerated accounts of our enemies—I must say that I feel grieved in spirit, and cannot tolerate such proceedings—neither will I; but will endeavor to disabuse the minds of the Saints, and break down all such unhallowed proceedings.

It was something new to me when I heard there had been secret meetings held in the Lord's House, and that some of my friends—faithful brethren—men enjoying the confidence of the Church, should be locked out. Such proceedings are not calculated to promote union, or peace, but to engender strife; and will be a curse instead of a blessing. To those who are young in the work, I know they are calculated to be, and must be, injurious. Those who have had experience, and who should know better than to reflect on their brethren—there is no excuse for them.

If Brother Babbitt and the other brethren wish to reform the Church, and come out and make a stand against sin and speculation, &c., they must use other weapons than lies, or their object can never be effected;

and their labors will be given to the house of the stranger, rather than to the House of the Lord.

The proceedings of Brother Babbitt were taken into consideration at a meeting of the Church at this place, when it was unanimously resolved, that fellowship should be withdrawn from him until he make satisfaction for the course he has pursued: of which circumstance I wish you to apprise him without delay, and demand his license.

Dear sir, I wish you to stand in your lot, and keep the station which was given you by revelation and the authorities of the Church. Attend to the affairs of the Church with diligence, and then rest assured of the blessings of heaven. It is binding on you to act as president of the Church in Kirtland, until you are removed by the same authority which put you in; and I do hope there will be no cause for opposition, but that good feeling will be manifested in future by all the brethren.

Brother Burdick's letter to Brother Hyrum was duly received, for which he has our best thanks; it was indeed an admirable letter, and worthy of its author. The sentiments expressed were in accordance with the spirit of the Gospel, and the principles are correct.

I am glad that Brother Richards has continued with you, and hope he has been of some service to you. Give my love to him.

Our prospects in this place continue good. Considerable numbers have come in this spring. There were some bickerings respecting your conduct soon after your departure, but they have all blown over, and I hope there will never be any occasion for any more; but that you will commend yourself to God and to the Saints by a virtuous walk and holy conversation.

I had a letter from William W. Phelps a few days ago, informing me of his desire to come back to the Church, if we would accept of him. He appears very humble, and is willing to make every satisfaction that Saints or God may require.

We expect to have an edition of the Book of Mormon printed by the first of September; it is now being stereotyped in Cincinnati.

I am, &c., &c.,

JOSEPH SMITH, JUN.

An interesting memorial concerning the Jews, "To the Protestant Powers of Europe and America," signed and sealed in London, the 8th of January, 1839, may be found in the *Millennial Star*, Vol. I, No. 6.* A Jew's Memorial.

* The article which appeared first in a periodical, entitled "Memorial Concerning God's Ancient People of Israel," and then in the *London Times*, seems to have

Sunday, 24.—Elder William Donaldson, member of the British army bound for the East Indies, writes from Chatham, 24th of July, "We go on board tomorrow.   I have had a glorious vision about going into the land of Egypt."
Saturday, 25.

Letter of John C. Bennett to Joseph Smith and Sidney Rigdon—Announcing His Intention to Join the Saints.

FAIRFIELD, ILLINOIS, July 25, 1840.

REVEREND AND DEAR FRIENDS:—The last time I wrote you was during the pendency of your difficulties with the Missourians.   You are aware that at that time I held the office of "Brigadier-General of the Invincible Dragoons" of this state, and proffered you my entire energies for your deliverance from a ruthless and savage, though cowardly foe; but the Lord came to your rescue, and saved you with a powerful arm. I am happy to find that you are now in a civilized land, and in the enjoyment of peace and happiness.

Some months ago I resigned my office with an intention of removing to your town, and joining your people; but hitherto I have been prevented.   I hope, however, to remove to Commerce, and unite with your Church next spring.   I believe I should be much happier with you.   I have many things to communicate which I would prefer doing orally; and I propose to meet you in Springfield on the first Monday in December next, as I shall be there at the time on state and United States business.

If I remove to Commerce, I expect to follow my profession, and to that end I enclose you a slip from the *Louisville Journal*, to give you an idea of my professional standing.

On the first of this month I was appointed to the office of "Quarter-

been written by a Christian Jew.   It deals largely with the promises of God to ancient Israel, especially as to their return as a people to Palestine.   The closing paragraph is an appeal to the Protestant powers of the north of Europe and America to assist in this restoration: "As the spirit of Cyrus, king of Persia, was stirred up to build the Lord a temple, which was in Jerusalem (II Chron., xxxvi: 22, 23), who is there among you, high and mighty ones of all the nations, to fulfill the good pleasure of the holy will of the Lord of heaven, saying to Jerusalem, 'Thou shalt be built,' and to the temple, 'Thy foundation shall be laid?' (Isa. xliv: 28).   The Lord God of Israel be with such.   Great grace, mercy and peace shall descend upon the people who offer themselves willingly; and the free offerings of their hearts and hands shall be those of a sweet smelling savor unto him who hath said, 'I will bless thee (Gen. xii: 3), and contend with him that contendeth with thee.'" (Isa. xlix: 25).

master-General of the State of Illinois," which office I expect to hold some years.

I hope you are all quite well. In haste. Write me immediately.

Yours respectfully,

JOHN C. BENNETT.*

To Messrs. Smith and Rigdon.

Monday, 27.

Letter of John C. Bennett to Messrs. Smith and Rigdon—Making Further Tender of his Services to the Church.

QUARTERMASTER-GENERAL'S OFFICE,
FAIRFIELD, ILLINOIS, July 27, 1840.

To the Reverends Sidney Rigdon and Joseph Smith, Jun.:

RESPECTED FRIENDS:—I wrote you a few days ago from this place, but my great desire to be with you and your people prompts me to write again at this time; and I hope it will not be considered obtrusive by friends whom I have always so highly esteemed as yourselves.

At the last District and Circuit Court of the United States, holden at Springfield, in June last, I had the honor of being on the grand inquest of the United States for the District of Illinois,. and hoped to have seen you there; but was quite disappointed. I attended the meeting of your people opposite Mr. Lowry's hotel, but did not make myself known, as I had no personal acquaintance in the congregation.

It would be my deliberate advice to you to concentrate all of your Church at one point. If Hancock county, with Commerce for its commercial emporium, is to be that point, well; fix upon it, and let us co-operate with a general concerted action. You can rely upon me in any event. I am with you in spirit, and will be in person as soon as circumstances permit, and immediately if it is your desire. Wealth is no material object with me. I desire to be happy, and am fully satisfied that I can enjoy myself better with your people, with my present views and feelings, than with any other. I hope that time will soon come when your people will become my people, and your God my God.

At the time of your peril and bitter persecution in Missouri, you are

---

* "This was a Dr. John C. Bennett, a man who seems to have been without any moral character, but who had filled positions of importance. Born in Massachusetts in 1804, he practiced as a physician in Ohio, and later in Illinois, holding a professorship in Willoughby University, Ohio, and taking with him to Illinois testimonials as to his professional skill In the latter state he showed a taste for military affairs, and after being elected brigadier-general of the Invincible Dragoons, he was appointed quartermaster-general of the state in 1840, and held that position at the state capital when the Mormons applied to the legislature for a charter for Nauvoo." ("The Story of the Mormons," Linn, 1901).

aware I proffered you my utmost energies, and had not the conflict terminated so speedily, I should have been with you then. God be thanked for your rescue from the hand of a savage, but cowardly foe!

I do not expect to resign my office of "Quartermaster-General of the State of Illinois" in the event of my removal to Commerce, unless you advise otherwise. I shall likewise expect to practice my profession; but at the same time your people shall have all the benefit of my speaking powers, and my untiring energies in behalf of the good and holy faith. *Un necessariis unitas, in non necessariis libertas, in omnibus charitas,** shall be my motto with—*Suaviter in modo, fortiter in re.*†

Be so good as to inform me substantially of the population of Commerce and Hancock county, the face of the country, climate, soil, health, &c., &c. How many of your people are concentrated there? Please to write me in full immediately. Louisville paper will accompany this; please inquire for it.

With sentiments of profound respect and esteem, suffer me to subscribe myself,

Yours respectfully,
JOHN C. BENNETT.

Elder John Taylor sailed for Ireland from Liverpool.‡

Tuesday, 28.

Letter of the Prophet to Horace R. Hotchkiss—Rock River Lands and the White Purchase.

NAUVOO, July 28, 1840.

Horace R. Hotchkiss, Esq.:

DEAR SIR:—I acknowledge the receipt of yours of last month, giving me the numbers of the land on Rock River, which you felt disposed to sell. In reply to which I have to say, that we have not yet examined the land, and consequently have not arrived at any conclusion respect-

---

* Translation: In essentials, unity; in non-essentials, liberty; in all things, charity.

† Gently in the manner, firmly in the act.

‡ Elder John Taylor was accompanied on this mission by Brothers McGuffie and William Black. Elder Taylor had baptized Brother McGuffie while laboring in Liverpool; and as the new convert had some acquaintances in Newry, county Down, Ireland, he thought it advisable to take him along. A large company of Saints went with them to see them off. The day after sailing, Elder Taylor and companions arrived in Newry, a beautiful Irish village nestling among rolling hills, characteristic of that part of Ireland. Brother McGuffie obtained the court house to hold a meeting in, and sent around the bell-man to give notice of it. A congregation of six or seven hundred gathered in at seven o'clock in the evening, and Elder Taylor preached to them. This was the introduction of the Gospel into Ireland.

ing it; but it is probable that some of my friends will visit it this fall, and if we should think it wisdom to locate there, or on the other tract, you will be informed of the same, and arrangements entered into.

I am sorry that your health has been so poor, but hope, ere this, you are perfectly recovered. It would afford me great pleasure indeed, could I hold out any prospect of the two notes due next month being met at maturity, or even this fall. Having had considerable difficulty (necessarily consequent on a new settlement) to contend with, as well as poverty and considerable sickness, our first payment will be probably somewhat delayed, until we again get a good start in the world; and I am happy to say, the prospect is indeed favorable. Under these circumstances we shall have to claim your indulgence, which I have no doubt will be extended. However, every exertion on our part shall be made to meet the demands against us, so that if we cannot accomplish all we wish to, it will be our misfortune, and not our fault. Notwithstanding the impoverished condition of our people, and the adverse circumstances under which we have had to labor, I hope we shall eventually rise above them, and again enjoy the blessings of health, peace, and plenty.

You were informed in a former letter that we had paid Mr. William White the one thousand dollars specified in your bond; a few days ago he called at this place and agreed to give us a deed for the ninety acres, (less one-half acre), providing I would give him an indemnifying bond, and pay the interest due from you to him on the one thousand dollars, which I agreed to do. I have therefore got the deed for the land, and paid him the interest. My reasons for so doing were these: there are some who wish to purchase lots, providing they can get a good title deed for the same, and who would be induced to make purchases and make an effort to raise money, for the sake of getting a deed; which effort they would not be so likely to make if we could only give them a bond. This I think will work both to your advantage and ours, and hope that we shall be able by and by to make some cash sales.

I hope this arrangement with Mr. White will meet your approbation, although it is a departure from the common rules of business; but was induced to do so from the advantages which will result from it, which I hope will be mutual. The amount of interest paid to Mr. White, after deducting $61.50, which was coming from him to you for rents, was eighty-four dollars and forty cents. Mr. White told us that you agreed to pay him as much interest for the money as he could get elsewhere. We accordingly (in good faith) allowed him at the rate of ten per cent. Hoping the course pursued will meet your approbation.

I am, respectfully, your obedient servant,

JOSEPH SMITH, JUN.

P. S.—You will recollect the verbal agreement entered into by us, that the notes for the interest would not be exacted for at least five years. Notwithstanding which, we use our endeavors to meet them as fast as possible, and think that when I have the pleasure of seeing you again, you will be fully satisfied with the course we have taken, and our endeavors to meet all our engagements.

J. S., Jun.

Thursday, 30.

Letter of John C. Bennett to Messrs. Smith and Rigdon—Expressing Anxiety to be with the Saints.

Fairfield, Wayne County, Illinois,
July 30th, 1840.

To Reverends Sidney Rigdon, and Joseph Smith, Jun.

Respected Friends:—It is with difficulty that I can forego the felicity of an immediate immersion into the true faith of your beloved people. I have written you several letters, and forwarded you several newspapers to Commerce, which I hope will be duly received, as they contain some matters of importance.

Is Nauvoo, or Commerce, to be the general point of concentration for the Mormon people? For at that point I desire to locate, and ever remain. My anxiety to be with you is daily increasing, and I shall wind up my professional business immediately, and proceed to your blissful abode, if you think it best.

Look at all my letters and papers and write me forthwith. You are aware that at the time of your most bitter persecutions, I was with you in feeling, and proffered you my military knowledge and prowess. My faith is still strong. I believe the God of the whole earth will avenge your wrong in time as well as in eternity.

O my friends, go on and prosper; and may the God of all grace save you with an everlasting salvation.

Yours respectfully,
J. C. Bennett.

Saturday, August 1.—In the *Times and Seasons* of this month I find the following:

A voice from the holy city—rebuilding of the temple of Solomon— Recall of the people of God to the land of Judah.

We have received by the last packet from England, a copy of a very extraordinary "Circular" issued by the Jews, now residing at Jerusaem, and addressed to all the descendants of Abraham to the uttermost ends of the earth.   It is written in the pure Hebrew character, and accompanied with an English translation, which we annex as matter of the deepest curiosity to the people of this country.   Next week, if we possibly can, we shall publish the original Hebrew in a double sheet, but at present we must content ourselves with the translation.—*Morning Herald.*

CIRCULAR.

"*To our Brethren the Israelites of Europe and America:*

"The liberal and benevolent contributors towards every holy and pious purpose—ready to stand in the breach and evince their love for the Land of Promise: to the well-wishers of Jerusalem, and friends of Zion (dearer to us than life) who extend their bounteous aid to this Holy City, and devote their best means, in love and affection, 'to take pity on her stones, and show mercy to her dust.'   To the illustrious and excellent Rabbies—to their worthy and distinguished Assessors—to the noble Chiefs and faithful Leaders of Israel; to all congregations devoted to the Lord, and to every member thereof—health, life, and prosperity.   May the Lord vouchsafe His protection unto them; may they rejoice and be exceedingly glad; and with their own eyes may they behold when the Lord restoreth Zion.   Such be His gracious will.   Amen.

"It is a fact well known throughout Judah and Israel, that 'the glory altogether departed from the daughter of Zion,' since upwards of one hundred years ago, the congregation of German Jews in this Holy City were forcibly deprived of their homes and inheritance.   Dreadful and grievous was the yoke under which the despots of this land oppressed them.   Tyranny and cruel usage ground them to the dust, and forced them to forsake their habitations, to abandon their houses and all their property, and to seek safety in flight.   Thus the large court they inherited from their ancestors remained deserted and uninhabited, until it was seized upon and possessed by aliens.   The sacred edifices it contained, namely, the Synagogue and Medrash, were by them demolished, the whole of the property utterly ruined, and possessions, lawfully ours, devastated before our eyes.   Then did our souls refuse all consolation!   For how could we bear to witness the evil which befell our people!

"As the light gleams forth from a spark, so did our congregation take heart and return again to form their establishments, and to take root on the Holy Mount.   But we could find no rest for our wearied feet—no place consecrated and appointed for our prayer and instruction.   Our aching eyes beheld how every nation and tongue, even from the most distant isles of the ocean, is here possessed of structures defended by walls, gates, and portcullis, whilst the people of the Lord, forcibly ex-

pelled from their inheritances by rapacious barbarians, were covered
with obloquy, scorn, and disgrace.

"The cries of the people ascended unto the Lord who dwelleth in
Zion. He looked down, and in pity beheld their sufferings and oppression. And ever since the ruler of Egypt first assumed the government
of the Holy Land—a ruler who maintains justice throughout his dominions—an edict was issued permitting Jews to do whatsoever they
deemed right and expedient, with respect to the rebuilding of their demolished synagogues and colleges. Us, likewise, the Lord in His
mercy vouchsafed to remember, and caused us to be reinstated into the
heritage of our fathers, even to the aforementioned court, which is
called the Ruin of R. Jehudah the Pious (of blessed memory).

"Blessed be the Lord our God, the God of our fathers, who inspired
the heart of the ruler of Egypt to restore unto us the possessions of our
ancestors. Nor did we delay or lose time in the matter, but exerted
ourselves to rebuild Jerusalem.

"'We fenced it, and gathered up the stones thereof,' and the sacred
undertaking prospered in our hands, so that we have completed the
Medrash, and 'great is the glory of the house;' and also houses for the
teachers of the law, and for the hospitable reception and entertainment
of strangers, which were indispensably necessary to accommodate the
many pious Israelites who visit the Holy City during the festivals. And
on *Rosh Hodesh Shebath* last we joyfully placed a Sepher Torah in the
Medrash, which we consecrated by the name of '*Menahem Zion,*' for the
Lord has vouchsafed to comfort His people.

"But although we have thus, under the blessings of Providence, re-
trieved from devastation a part of the possessions bequeathed unto us
by our pious ancestors, yet our hearts are afflicted and our eyes are
dimmed when we behold the sanctuary of our Lord, the Synagogue,
which still lies in ruins; nor is it in the power of all of us (the German Congregation) to rebuild it; for alas! great is the number of our
poor who stand in need of bread, and the debts we contracted in building the Medrash are large, and weigh heavily upon us.

"The cause of our grief is thus ever present to our eyes—the ruins
of the Synagogue are heaped in the middle of the court, and rank
weeds spread over the consecrated pile. We therefore deem it our
bounden duty to dispatch a messenger unto our brethren, the children of
Israel, who are dispersed and in exile, in order to acquaint them with
'the salvation of the Lord in the land,' so that they may arise and take
pity on Zion, for it is time to show mercy unto her.

"To undertake this laborious duty was the voluntary offer of our
dearly beloved friend, that profound and renowned Rabbi, the zealous
and honorable *Aaron Selig Ashkenazi*. He is a man confirmed in the

fear of the Lord, of a faithful stock; and him we depute as our messenger, worthy of all trust, to make proclamation unto the communities of Israel 'according to the sight which he has seen in the Holy Mount,' and to him we have given letters of authorization, containing full particulars as to his pious mission, and every necessary information relating thereto.

"Now, therefore, let the righteous behold and rejoice. Let the pious exult and triumph in gladness. The day ye have so long hoped for is come, and ye see it. The crown of holiness will again adorn its former abode. Therefore, arise, and take upon yourselves, according to the words of this letter, to devote a portion of your wealth as a sacred tribute towards erecting 'the Temple of the Most Holy King on the mountain of the Lord'—that ye may have a portion and a righteous record in Jerusalem.

"Let no one among you refuse his aid, but let the poor man contribute his mite for himself and his household freely, as the rich dispenses the bounty wherewith the Lord hath blessed him. Let fathers and their offspring, the aged and the youthful, alike arise in mercy to Zion at this propitious season.

"Let each man encourage his neighbor and say, 'We will be zealous and persevering for our people and the City of our God. And for the love of Zion, and the sake of Jerusalem, we will not rest nor be easy until Jerusalem is praised throughout the earth, and foremost in our joys, even as we have vowed:—If I forget thee, Jerusalem, let my right hand forget her cunning; if I prefer not Jerusalem above my chief joy.'

"Such are the words of your brethren who address you for the glory of God, and for the honor of His land, His people and His inheritance—continually praying for our exiled brethren, and offering up our orisons on holy ground and particularly near the *Western Wall*, that it may be well with you everlastingly as you yourself desire, and we most sincerely wish.

"Signed at Jerusalem, the 18th day of year 5597 a. m., by the Wardens of the Medrash, and members of the Building Committee, on behalf of the Congregation of German Jews in this Holy City.

["Signed]　Hirsh Joseph,
　　　　　　"David Reuben,
　　　　　　"Nathan Saddis,
　　　　　　"Abraham S. Salmons,
　　　　　　"Mordecai Avigdor,
　　　　　　"Uriah S. Hyam.

The undersigned Assessors of the Bethdin, by the direction of the

Rev. Chief Rabbi, hereby certify that Rev. Aaron Selig Ashkenazi is actually deputed for the purpose mentioned in the above circular.

"London, the 7th Tebath,

"24 Dec. 5599.

"ISRAEL LEVY,

"AARON LEVY,

"A. L. BARNETT."

Monday, August 3.—Elders Wilford Woodruff and George A. Smith are at Ledbury, Herefordshire.

Tuesday, 4.—Elder Heber C. Kimball left Manchester for Herefordshire, and Joseph Fielding is at Bedford.

Wednesday, 5.

Extract of a Letter from Wilford Woodruff to the Editor of the Millennial Star—Reporting Labors.

BELOVED BRETHREN:—Since Elder George A. Smith and myself left Manchester for the purpose of going to the south of England, we have visited the churches which lay in our route, and found them universally prospering and receiving additions.

We preached in Leek on Sunday, July 10th, and Elder Smith baptized six persons after meeting: and numbers were also baptized in the churches at the Staffordshire Potteries while we were there. We passed through West Bromwich and Birmingham, and found numbers who were anxiously wishing for some of the Elders to visit that region and labor among them. We arrived in Ludbury, Herefordshire, July 22nd, and here spent about two weeks in visiting the churches through this region, and I am happy to inform you, that we have found the Saints universally rejoicing in the truth, and the work progressing upon every hand.

Elder Thomas Richardson has baptized about forty since he came, and Elder William Kay about twenty; they are both much blessed in their labors. Elder Kington is laboring constantly in this wide field, which is under his care; and he with the Elders and Priests generally throughout this region are blessed with many souls as seals of their ministry. We baptized forty on Sunday last in this region, making 250 since the conference. The churches here now number about 800 members and appear [to be] in a very prosperous state. We are expecting Elder Kimball every hour, and soon after his arrival we shall leave the Saints in this region, for the purpose of visiting the city of London and warning the inhabitants thereof.

WILFORD WOODRUFF.

Saturday, 8.—Soon after the July conference at Manchester, Elder Parley P. Pratt started for America for the purpose of getting his family and taking them to England, meantime leaving the *Star* in charge of President Brigham Young, assisted by Elder Willard Richards.

The Prophet's Letter to John C. Bennett—Bidding Him Welcome to Nauvoo, to partake of—its Poverty.

NAUVOO, HANCOCK COUNTY, ILLINOIS,
August 8th, 1840.

DEAR SIR:—Yours of the 25th ultimo, addressed to Elder Rigdon and myself, is received, for which you have our thanks, and to which I shall feel great pleasure in replying.

Although I have not the pleasure of your acquaintance, yet from the kindness manifested towards our people when in bondage and oppression, and from the frank and noble mindedness breathed in your letter, I am brought to the conclusion that you are a friend to suffering humanity and truth.

To those who have suffered so much abuse, and borne the cruelties and insults of wicked men so long, on account of those principles which we have been instructed to teach to the world, a feeling of sympathy and kindness is something like the refreshing breeze and cooling stream at the present season of the year, and are, I assure you, duly appreciated by us.

It would afford me much pleasure to see you at this place, and from the desire you express in your letter to move to this place, I hope I shall soon have that satisfaction.

I have no doubt you would be of great service to this community in practicing your profession, as well as those other abilities of which you are in possession. Since to devote your time and abilities in the cause of truth and a suffering people may not be the means of exalting you in the eyes of this generation, or securing you the riches of the world, yet by so doing you may rely on the approval of Jehovah, "that blessing which maketh rich and addeth no sorrow." Through the tender mercies of our God we have escaped the hands of those who sought our overthrow, and have secure locations in this state, and in the territory of Iowa. Our principal location is at this place, Nauvoo, (formerly Commerce), which is beautifully situated on the banks of the Mississippi, immediately above the lower rapids, and is probably the best and most beautiful site for a city on the river. It has a gradual ascent from the river nearly a mile, then a fine, level, and fertile prairie—a situation in every respect adapted to commercial and agricultural pursuits, but like all other places on the river, is sickly in summer.

The number of inhabitants is nearly three thousand, and is fast increasing. If we are suffered to remain,* there is every prospect of its becoming one of the largest cities on the river, if not in the western world. Numbers have moved in from the seaboard, and a few from the islands of the sea (Great Britain).

It is our intention to commence the erection of some public buildings next spring. We have purchased twenty thousand acres in the Iowa Territory opposite this place, which is fast filling up with our people. I desire all the Saints, as well as all lovers of truth and correct principles, to come to this place as fast as possible, or [as rapidly as] their circumstances will permit, and endeavor, by energy of action and concentration of talent, &c., &c., to effect those objects, that are so dear to us. Therefore my general invitation is, Let all that will, come, and partake of the poverty of Nauvoo freely.

I should be disposed to give you a special invitation to come as early as possible, believing you will be of great service to us; however, you must make arrangements according to your circumstances. Were it possible for you to come here this season to suffer affliction with the people of God, no one will be more pleased to give you a more cordial welcome than myself.

A charter has been obtained from the legislature for a railroad from Warsaw, being immediately below the rapids of the Mississippi, to this place—a distance of about twenty miles, which if carried into operation will be of incalculable advantage to this place, as steamboats can only ascend the rapids at a high stage of water. The soil is good, and I think not inferior to any in the state. Crops are abundant in this section of country—and I think provisions will be reasonable.

I should be very happy could I make arrangements to meet you in Springfield at the time you mention—but cannot promise myself that pleasure. If I should not, probably you can make it convenient to come and pay us a visit here, prior to your removal.

Elder Rigdon is very sick, and has been for nearly twelve months with the fever and ague, which disease is very prevalent here at this time. At present he is not able to leave his room.

Yours, &c.,

JOSEPH SMITH, JUN.

To J. C. Bennett, M. D.

P. S.—Yours of the 30th is just received, in which I am glad to learn that your increasing desire to unite yourself with a people "that are

* "If we are suffered to remain" sounds somewhat prophetic and ominous.

everywhere spoken against," and the anxiety you feel for our welfare—for which you have my best feelings; and I pray that my heavenly Father will pour out His choicest blessings in this world, and enable you by His grace to overcome the evils which are in the world, that you may secure a blissful immortality in the world that is to come.

J. S., JUN.

August 10.—Colonel Seymour Brunson, aged forty years, ten months and twenty-three days, died at Nauvoo. Colonel Brunson was among the first settlers of this place. He has always been a lively stone in the building of God and was much respected by his friends and acquaintances. He died in the triumph of faith, and in his dying moments bore testimony to the Gospel that he had embraced.

Saturday, 15.

Letter of John C. Bennett to Messrs. Smith and Rigdon—Announcing that he will soon be in Nauvoo.

WAYNE COUNTY ILLINOIS, August 15, 1840.

Reverends Joseph Smith, Jun., and Sidney Rigdon.

RESPECTED FRIENDS:—I have written you several communications to Commerce and Nauvoo, supposing they were different places, but a brother to a lady in your community, now in this place, informs me that they are one and the same.

I have received no reply to my letters, and attribute the delay to a press of business or professional absence. I have come to the conclusion to join your people immediately, and take up my abode with you. Let us adopt as our motto—*Licut partribus sit Deus nobius*—(as God was with our fathers, so may He be with us), and adapt the means to the end, and the victory is ours. The winged warrior of the air will not cease to be our proud emblem of liberty, and the dogs of war will be forever chained.

I shall be with you in about two weeks, and shall devote my time and energies to the advancement of the cause of truth and virtue, and the advocacy of the holy religion which you have so nobly defended, and so honorably sustained.

My love to all the brethren.

With sentiments of fraternal regard.

Yours respectfully,

J. C. BENNETT.

CHAPTER X.

A MISSOURI KIDNAPPING—CONTINUED DEVELOPMENT OF THE
WORK IN GREAT BRITAIN—THE DEATH OF JOSEPH SMITH,
SEN., FIRST PATRIARCH OF THE CHURCH.

Monday, 17.—Met with the High Council of Nauvoo at
my office, also the High Council of Iowa. John Batten
Settlement of   preferred many charges against Elijah Ford-
a Difficulty.   ham. After the testimony, and the councillors had spoken, I addressed the Council at some length,
showing the situation of the contending parties, that there
was in reality no cause of difference; that they had better
be reconciled without an action, or vote of the Council,
and henceforth live as brethren, and never more mention
their former difficulties. They settled accordingly.

Tuesday, 18.—Elders Kimball, Woodruff, and George
A. Smith left Cheltenham for London, one hundred and
ten miles, where they arrived in seven and a half hours,
at William Allgood's, No. 19 King Street, Borough, and
were kindly received by Mrs. Allgood, who took them to
the King's Arms Inn.

Great distress is prevailing in Ireland; no work, and
provisions very scarce.

The truth is spreading rapidly in England and Scotland.

Friday, 21—Testimony of Benjamin Boyce:

The Kidnapping of Benjamin Boyce, Mr. Brown, et al.

Ieft my home in Nauvoo to go to Adams county, where I had lived
the summer before, for the purpose of meeting some debts. I fell in
company with a Mr. Brown, who stated to me that he was in search of
some horses that had strayed from him. We had not proceeded far to-

gether, before we were hailed by twelve armed men, who demanded of us where we were going. I stated to them where I was going, and likewise Mr. Brown stated his business. They then asked if we were "Mormons;" we said we were; they then said that we could go no further; they said they were sworn to kill all the damned "Mormons" that they could find, and took us prisoners, tied us with ropes, and took us to a boat, and four of the company (one by the name of Martin, the others not known) took us to Missouri, to a little town called Tully, where we were put under guard, and kept till 11 o'clock in the evening, when three men came to us with a long rope, and tied it round each of our necks. I asked them what they were going to do with us; one said they were going to take us to the river, kill us, and make catfish bait of us, his name was Uno. They then led us to the woods, I should think about three-quarters of a mile distant; they then parted us, took and stripped me naked, and tied me fast to a tree; one of the company cocked a pistol and placed it close to my ear, and swore, if I attempted to get away, that he would blow out my brains. They then commenced to whip me with large gads which they had for the purpose, and literally mangled me from my shoulders to my knees.

There were in the company, as near as I could recollect, twelve or fourteen; they were stripped of their hats and coats, with their sleeves rolled up, and collars open, which made them look like murderers and robbers. The names, as far as I can recollect, Monday, Uno, and Martin; the others I do not recollect. After keeping me tied in this condition I should think an hour and a half, they then brought Mr. Brown to me, and after some consultation, loosed me from the tree where I was tied, and led us back to the town, put us in a room where I saw Noah Rogers and James Allred. They then tied them about the neck, and led them out, and in the course of the night, they brought them back to the room where we were.

Brother Rogers said they stripped him, and whipped him very badly. This was on the seventh of July. The next day Rogers and myself were taken before a magistrate; nothing proven against us, only that we were "Mormons;" and we were ordered to prison. Brown and Allred, by some means, were liberated, but we (Rogers and myself) were put in jail and put in irons until the 21st of August, when through the kindness of God we made our escape and returned to Nauvoo.

BENJAMIN BOYCE.

Sunday, 23.—Ten persons who had been baptized were confirmed at Carpenter's Hall, Manchester.*

* The entry of the text is the only one made in the Prophet's manuscript history for the 23rd of August, but "Uncle" John Smith, brother of the Prophet's father,

Saturday, 29—Elder Kimball writes: "The brethren are beginning to excite attention in some of the public grounds in London." Out-door preaching is common in England.

Sunday, 30.—Twenty were confirmed at the hall in Manchester.*

Elders Kimball, Woodruff, and George A. Smith, after having spent ten days visiting the clergymen and preachers and others of the several denominations, asking the privilege of preaching in their chapels, and being continually refused by them in a contemptuous manner, they determined to preach in the open air, Jonah-like; and accordingly went to Smithfield Market† (to the spot where John Rogers‡ was burnt at the stake), for the purpose of preaching at 10 a. m.,

The Beginning of Open-air Meetings.

and formerly president of Adam-ondi-Ahman Stake of Zion, in Missouri, makes the following entry in his journal:

"Attended meeting at Nashville. Joseph and Hyrum Smith present and a large assembly of Saints, who voted to commence building a city at Nashville and a place of worship." Nashville, by the way, was situated in Lee county, Iowa, on the Mississippi river, at the head of the Des Moines Rapids, about three miles southeast of Montrose, eight miles north of Keokuk. The Church had purchased twenty thousand acres of land in this vicinity and surveyed out of it a townsite on which a number of Saints located.

* Again from the journal of "Uncle" John Smith we learn that on the 30th day of August, the Prophet Joseph was in Nashville and preached on "Eternal Judgment and the Eternal Duration of Matter."

† Smithfield is noted for other historical incidents than being the scene of John Rogers' martyrdom. It is an open space of nearly six acres in London, England. It was formerly used as a market place, but is now partially laid out in gardens. It was the scene of Bartholomew Fair; William Wallace was executed there; it was the place of the meeting of Wat Tyler and King Richard II, in 1380, when the former was stabbed by the Mayor of London, and then dispatched by the King's attendants. It was the scene of many martyrdoms.

‡ John Rogers suffered martyrdom by being burnt at the stake in Smithfield, on he 4th of February, 1555. He was the first victim of what is known in histoy as the "Marian Persecution;" and which conferred on England's Catholic queen the title of "Bloody Mary." Archbishop Gardiner, however, is usually credited with being the prime instigator of that persecution, though he died before it reached its height, and not before he had shown symptoms of relenting. Cardinal Pole though "naturally humane and gentle," shares the guilt of sanctioning it; "but the chief agent was Bonner, bishop of London, in whose diocese the majority of all the executions took place. * * * * The total number of men, women and children who were burnt—for even children were thrown into the flames and some at the very moment of their birth"—is computed as follows:

where they were notified by the police, that the Lord Mayor had issued orders prohibiting street preaching in the city. A Mr. Connor stepped up and said, "I will show you a place outside of his jurisdiction," and guided them to "Tabernacle Square," where they found an assembly of about 400 people listening to a preacher who was standing on a chair. When he got through another preacher arose to speak. Elder Kimball stated to the first clergyman, "There is a man present from America who would like to preach;" which was granted; when Elder George A. Smith delivered a discourse of about twenty minutes, on the first principles of the Gospel, taking for his text, Mark xvi: 16; after which Elder Kimball asked the preacher to give out another appointment at the same place for the American Elder to preach; when he jumped up and said, "I have just learned that the gentleman who has addressed you is a Latter-day Saint; I know them— they are a very bad people; they have split up many churches, and have done a great deal of hurt." He spoke all manner of evil, and gave the Latter-day Saints a very bad character, and commanded the people not to hear the Elders, "as we have got the Gospel, and can save the people, without infidelity, socialism, or Latter-day Saints."

Elder Kimball asked the privilege of standing on the chair to give out an appointment himself. The preacher said, "You shall not do it; you have no right to preach here;" jerked the chair away from him, and ran away with it. Several of the crowd said, "You have as much right to preach here as he has, and give out your appointment;" whereupon Elder Kimball gave out an appoint-

1555, from February—72; 1556—94; 1557,—79; 1558, from February to September—(when the persecution closed), 39; making a total of 284. It was during this persecution that Ridley and Latimer suffered. On the way to the execution the latter, it is said, "with a keen quaintness which adorns his sermons," uttered the words which fortunately became prophetic—addressing himself to his companion— "Be of good comfort, Master Ridley; play the man; we shall this day light such a candle, by God's grace, in England, as I trust shall never be put out." (History of England, by William Smith, p. 156).

ment for 3 o'clock p. m.; at which time a large congregation was gathered.

After opening the meeting by singing and prayer, Elder
Woodruff spoke about thirty minutes, from Gal. i: 8, 9,
upon the first principles of the Gospel. Elder Kimball followed upon the same subjects. The people gave good attention, and seemed much interested in what they had heard.
The inhabitants who lived around the square opened their
windows to four stories high; the most of them were
crowded with anxious listeners, which is an uncommon
occurrence. The meeting was dismissed in the midst of
good feeling.

Mr. Henry Connor invited the Elders to his house. Soon
after they arrived here, Elder Kimball felt impressed to
return to the place of preaching. When he got there he
found a large company talking about the things which they
had heard in the afternoon, and they wished him to speak
to them again. He did so, when several persons invited
him home with them. While Elder Kimball was preaching, several persons came to Brothers Woodruff and Smith
to converse on doctrine, when Mr. Connor offered himself
for baptism.

Monday, 31.—Elder Kimball baptized Henry Connor,
watchmaker, 52 Ironmonger's Row, London, in Peerless
Pool, being the first baptized in that place, and confirmed
him the same evening.

The electric telegraph is beginning to be used on the
The Electric   Great Western Railroad in England, between
Telegraph.   Drayton and Paddington, by which intelligence is communicated at the rate of two hundred thousand miles per second.

An Address by the First Presidency to the Church.

To the Saints Scattered Abroad:

BELOVED BRETHREN:—We address a few lines to the members of the
Church of Jesus Christ, who have obeyed from the heart that form of
doctrine which has been delivered to them by the servants of the Lord,

and who are desirous to go forward in the ways of truth and righteousness, and by obedience to the heavenly command, escape the things which are coming on the earth, and secure to themselves an inheritance among the sanctified in the world to come.

Having been placed in a very responsible station in the Church, we at all times feel interested in the welfare of the Saints, and make mention of them continually in our prayers to our heavenly Father, that they may be kept from the evils which are in the world, and ever be found walking in the path of truth.

The work of the Lord in these last days, is one of vast magnitude and almost beyond the comprehension of mortals. Its glories are past description, and its grandeur unsurpassable. It is the theme which has animated the bosom of prophets and righteous men from the creation of the world down through every succeeding generation to the present time; and it is truly the dispensation of the fullness of times, when all things which are in Christ Jesus, whether in heaven or on the earth, shall be gathered together in Him, and when all things shall be restored, as spoken of by all the holy prophets since the world began; for in it will take place the glorious fulfilment of the promises made to the fathers, while the manifestations of the power of the Most High will be great, glorious, and sublime.

The purposes of our God are great, His love unfathomable, His wisdom infinite, and His power unlimited; therefore, the Saints have cause to rejoice and be glad, knowing that "this God is our God forever and ever, and He will be our Guide until death." Having confidence in the power, wisdom, and love of God, the Saints have been enabled to go forward through the most adverse circumstances, and frequently, when to all human appearances, nothing but death presented itself, and destruction inevitable, has the power of God been manifest, His glory revealed, and deliverance effected; and the Saints, like the children of Israel, who came out of the land of Egypt, and through the Red Sea, have sung an anthem of praise to his holy name. This has not only been the case in former days, but in our days, and within a few months, have we seen this fully verified.

Having through the kindness of our God been delivered from destruction, and having secured a location upon which we have again commenced operations for the good of His people, we feel disposed to go forward and unite our energies for the upbuilding of the Kingdom, and establishing the Priesthood in their fullness and glory. The work which has to be accomplished in the last days is one of vast importance, and will call into action the energy, skill, talent, and ability of the Saints, so that it may roll forth with that glory and majesty described by the prophet; and will consequently require the concentration of the Saints, to accomplish works of such magnitude and grandeur.

The work of the gathering spoken of in the Scriptures will be necessary to bring about the glories of the last dispensation It is probably unnecessary to press this subject on the Saints, as we believe the spirit of it is manifest, and its necessity obvious to every considerate mind; and everyone zealous for the promotion of truth and righteousness, is equally so for the gathering of the Saints.

Dear brethren, feeling desirous to carry out the purposes of God to which work we have been called; and to be co-workers with Him in this last dispensation; we feel the necessity of having the hearty co-operation of the Saints throughout this land, and upon the islands of the sea. It will be necessary for the Saints to hearken to counsel and turn their attention to the Church, the establishment of the Kingdom, and lay aside every selfish principle, everything low and groveling; and stand forward in the cause of truth, and assist to the utmost of their power, those to whom has been given the pattern and design. Like those who held up the hands of Moses, so let us hold up the hands of those who are appointed to direct the affairs of the Kingdom, so that they may be strengthened, and be enabled to prosecute their great designs, and be instrumental in effecting the great work of the last days.

Believing the time has now come, when it is necessary to erect a house of prayer, a house of order, a house for the worship of our God, where the ordinances can be attended to agreeably to His divine will, in this region of country—to accomplish which, considerable exertion must be made, and means will be required—and as the work must be hastened in righteousness, it behooves the Saints to weigh the importance of these things, in their minds, in all their bearings, and then take such steps as are necessary to carry them into operation; and arming themselves with courage, resolve to do all they can, and feel themselves as much interested as though the whole labor depended on themselves alone. By so doing they will emulate the glorious deeds of the fathers, and secure the blessings of heaven upon themselves and their posterity to the latest generation.

To those who feel thus interested, and can assist in this great work, we say, let them come to this place; by so doing they will not only assist in the rolling on of the Kingdom, but be in a situation where they can have the advantages of instruction from the Presidency and other authorities of the Church, and rise higher and higher in the scale of intelligence until they can "comprehend with all Saints what is the breadth and length, and depth and heighth; and to know the love of Christ which passeth knowledge."

Connected with the building up of the Kingdom, is the printing and circulation of the Book of Mormon, Doctrine and Covenants, hymnbook, and the new translation of the Scriptures. It is unnecessary to say anything respecting these works; those who have read them, and who have drunk of the stream of knowledge which they convey, know how to appreciate them; and although fools may have them in derision, yet they are calculated to make men wise unto salvation, and sweep away the cobwebs of superstition of ages, throw a light on the proceedings of Jehovah which have already been accomplished, and mark out the future in all its dreadful and glorious realities. Those who have tasted the benefit derived from a study of those works, will undoubtedly vie with each other in their zeal for sending them abroad throughout the world, that every son of Adam may enjoy the same privileges, and rejoice in the same truths.

Here, then, beloved brethren, is a work to engage in worthy of archangels—a work which will cast into the shade the things which have been heretofore accomplished; a work which kings and prophets and righteous men in former ages have sought, expected, and earnestly desired to see, but died without the sight; and well will it be for those who shall aid in carrying into effect the mighty operations of Jehovah.

By order of the First Presidency,

ROBERT B. THOMPSON, Scribe.

Saturday, September 5.—Elders Young and Richards went from Manchester to Liverpool, and in the evening organized a company of Saints bound for New York, by choosing Elder Theodore Turley to preside, with six counselors.

Minutes of the High Council Meeting, at the Office of Joseph Smith, Jun., Nauvoo, September 5th, 1840.

Joseph Smith, Jun., preferred charges against Elder Almon W. Babbitt, predicated on the authority of two letters, one from Thomas Burdick, the other from Oliver Granger and Levi Richards, accusing Elder Babbitt as follows:

First. For stating that Joseph Smith, Jun., had extravagantly purchased three suits of clothes while he was at Washington City, and that Sidney Rigdon had purchased four suits while at the same place, besides dresses in profusion for their families

Second. For having stated that Joseph Smith, Jun., Sidney Rigdon and Elias Higbee had said that they were worth one hundred thousand dollars each, while they were at Washington, and that Joseph Smith,

Jun., had repeated the same statement while in Philadelphia, and for saying that Oliver Granger had stated that he also was worth as much as they (that is, one hundred thousand dollars).

Third. For holding secret councils in the Lord's House, in Kirtland, and for locking the doors of the house, for the purpose of prohibiting certain brethren in good standing in the Church, from being in the Council, thereby depriving them of the use of the house.

Two were appointed to speak on the case, namely, Thomas Grover, Austin Cowles.

Council adjourned till the 6th September, at 2 o'clock, when Council met according to adjournment, the evidences were all heard on the case pending, and the councilors closed on both sides. The parties spoke at length, after which, Joseph Smith withdrew the charge, and both parties were reconciled to each other, things being adjusted to their satisfacion.

Sunday 6.—Elder Young preached.

Monday 7.—This evening, Elders Kimball, Woodruff and George A. Smith, preached in the south Temperance Hall, London.

On Monday night, Elders Brigham Young and Willard Richards, stayed on board the *North America* with the Saints, and on Tuesday morning, about nine o'clock, the vessel went out with a steamer. The Elders accompanied them fifteen or twenty miles, and left them in good spirits. Elder Richards returned to Manchester the same evening and Elder Young on the 10th.

Elder John Benbow, who had previously furnished two hundred and fifty pounds towards printing the hymn-book, Book of Mormon, etc., relinquished all claim to said money, except such assistance as his friends, who might

The Generosity of John Benbow.

wish to emigrate to America the next season, might need, leaving the remainder to the disposal of Brigham Young, Willard Richards, and Wilford Woodruff, who borrowed said moneys for the benefit of the Church of Jesus Christ of Latter-day Saints, forever, also the avails of the Gadfield Elm Chapel, when sold.

Wednesday, 9.—There was a terrific storm on the North of Scotland.

Friday, 11.—There was a terrible earthquake at Mount Ararat, which destroyed the town of Makitchevan, damaged all the buildings at Erivan, and devastated the two districts of Sharour and Sourmate in Armenia. A considerable mass Earthquake at Mount Ararat. was loosened from Mount Ararat and destroyed everything in its way for nearly five miles. The village of Akhouli was buried, with one thousand inhabitants.

Sunday, 13.—Elder Kimball baptized four in London.

Monday, 14.—My father, Joseph Smith, Sen., Patriarch of the whole Church of Jesus Christ of Latter-day Saints, died at Nauvoo. The Death of Joseph, Sen.

Biography of Joseph Smith, Sen., Presiding Patriarch of the Church, by the Prophet Joseph, his Son.

Joseph Smith, Sen., was born on the 12th day of July, 1771, in Topsfield, Essex county, Massachusetts; he was the second of the seven sons of Asahel and Mary Smith. Asahel was born in Topsfield, March 7th, 1744. He was the youngest son of Samuel and Priscilla Smith. Samuel was born January 26th, 1714, in Topsfield; he was the eldest son of Samuel and Rebecca Smith. Samuel was born in Topsfield, January 20, 1666, and was the son of Robert and Mary Smith, who emigrated from Old England.

My father removed with his father to Tunbridge, Orange county, Vermont, in 1791, and assisted in clearing a large farm of a heavy growth of timber. He married Lucy, daughter of Solomon and Lydia Mack, on the 14th of January, 1796, by whom he had

Alvin Smith, born February 11th, 1798, died November 19th, 1824.

Hyrum, born February 9th, 1800.

Sophronia, born May 16th, 1803.

Joseph, born December 23rd, 1805.

Samuel Harrison, born March 13th, 1808.

Ephraim, born March 13th, 1810, died March 24th, 1810.

William, born March 13th, 1811.

Catherine, born July 28th, 1812.

Don Carlos, born March 25th, 1816.

Lucy, born July 18th, 1824.

At his marriage he owned a handsome farm in Tunbridge. In 1802, he rented it and engaged in mercantile business, and soon after embarked in a venture of [raising] ginseng * to send to China, and was swindled out of the entire proceeds by the shipmaster and agent, he was consequently obliged to sell his farm and all of his effects to pay his debts.

About the year 1816 he removed to Palmyra, Wayne county, New York, bought a farm and cleared two hundred acres, which he lost in consequence of not being able to pay the last installment of the purchase money at the time it was due. This was the case with a great number of farmers in New York, who had cleared land under similar contracts. He afterwards moved to Manchester, Ontario county, New York, procured a comfortable home with sixteen acres of land, where he lived until he removed to Kirtland, Ohio.

He was the first person who received my testimony after I had seen the angel, and exhorted me to be faithful and diligent to the message I had received.† He was baptized April 6th, 1830.

In August, 1830, in company with my brother Don Carlos, he took a mission to St. Lawrence county, New York, touching on his route at several of the Canadian ports, where he distributed a few copies of the Book of Mormon. He also visited his father, brothers and sister residing in St. Lawrence county, bore testimony to the truth which resulted eventually in all the family coming into the Church, excepting his brother Jesse and sister Susan.

He removed with his family to Kirtland in 1831; was ordained Patriarch and President of the High Priesthood [in Kirtland]‡ under the hands of Oliver Cowdery, Sidney Rigdon, Frederick G. Williams and myself, on the 18th of December, 1833; was a member of the First High Council, organized on the 17th of February, 1834, (when he conferred on me and my brother Samuel H., a father's blessing

---

* Ginseng is a plant, the roots of which are highly esteemed as medicine, being quite generally regarded as possessing the most extraordinary virtues, and as a remedy for almost all diseases, but particularly for exhaustion of body or mind. In China ginseng is sometimes sold for its weight in gold. It was once introduced in Europe, but was soon forgotten. It is a native plant of Chinese Tartary, and grows from one to two feet in height. Its leaves are five fingered and almost smooth. It is doubted by many botanists if this species is really distinct from *phanx quinquefolium*, a common North American plant, doubtless the species referred to in the text, the root of which is now an article of export from North America to China, and is used to some extent as a domestic medicine in the states west of the Alleghanies, but which European and American medical practitioners generally regard as almost worthless.

† From that time on the Prophet of the Dispensation of the Fullness of Times had no truer or more constant or faithful friend than his father.

‡ This term, "High Priesthood," is oftenused in these annals—as it is above—for High Priest. The intent of the above statement is to say that "Father Smith,"—for

In 1836 he traveled in company with his brother John two thousand four hundred miles in Ohio, New York, Pennsylvania, Vermont, and New Hampshire, visiting the branches of the Church in those states and bestowing patriarchal blessings on several hundred persons, preaching the Gospel to all who would hear, and baptizing many. They returned to Kirtland on the 2nd of October, 1836.

During the persecutions in Kirtland in 1837, he was made a prisoner, but fortunately obtained his liberty, and after a very tedious journey in the spring and summer of 1838, he arrived at Far West, Missouri. After I and my brother Hyrum were thrown into the Missouri jails by the mob, he fled from under the exterminating order of Governor Lilburn W. Boggs, and made his escape in midwinter to Quincy, Illinois, from whence he removed to Commerce in the spring of 1839.

The exposures he suffered brought on consumption, of which he died on this 14th day or September, 1840, aged sixty-nine years, two months, and two days. He was six feet, two inches high, was very straight, and remarkably well proportioned. His ordinary weight was about two hundred pounds, and he was very strong and active. In his younger days he was famed as a wrestler, and, Jacob like, he never wrestled with but one man whom he could not throw. He was one of the most benevolent of men; opening his house to all who were destitute. While at Quincy, Illinois, he fed hundreds of the poor Saints who were flying from the Missouri persecutions, although he had arrived there penniless himself.

Tuesday, 15.--The funeral of Joseph Smith, Sen., took place this day, when the following address was delivered by Elder Robert B. Thompson:

The Discourse of Elder Thompson at the Funeral of Joseph Smith, Sen.

The occasion which has brought us together this day, is one of no

so he was affectionately called by the Saints—was ordained Patriarch and the President of the High Priests in Kirtland. That he was not made President of the High Priesthood is evident from the fact that the Prophet Joseph himself at that time was President of the High Priesthood of the Church, a position to which he was ordained at a Conference of High Priests in Amherst, Loraine county, Ohio, in 1832 (see Church History, Vol. I, p. 243 and note.) The Presidency of the High Priesthood carries with it the office of President of the Church: "And again, the duty of the President of the office of the High Priesthood is to preside over the whole Church, and to be like unto Moses. Behold, here is wisdom, yea, to be a seer, a revelator, a translator, and a Prophet, having all the gifts of God which He bestows upon the head of the Church." (Doc. and Cov. sec. 107, verses 91-9 ordinary importance: for not only has a single family to mourn and sorrow on account of the death of the individual, whose funeral obsequies we this day celebrate; but a whole society; yes, thousands will this day have to say, *a Father in Israel is gone.*

The man whom we have been accustomed to look up to as a *Patriarch,* a Father, and a Counselor is no more an inhabitant of mortality: he has dropped his clay tenement, bid adieu to terrestial scenes, and his spirit now free and unencumbered, roams and expatiates in that world where the spirits of just men made perfect dwell, and where pain and sick_ ness, tribulation and death cannot come.

The friends we have lost prior to our late venerable and lamented Father, were such as rendered life sweet, and in whose society we took great pleasure, and who shed a lustre in the several walks of life in which they moved, and to whom we feel endeared by friendship's sacred ties. Their virtues and kindnesses will long be remembered by the sorrowing widow, the disconsolate husband, the weeping children, the almost distracted and heart-broken parent, and by a large circle of acquaintances and friends. These, like the stars in yonder firmament, shone in their several spheres, and filled that station to which they had been called by the providence of God, with honor to themselves and to the Church; and we feel to mingle our tears with their surviving relatives.

But on this occasion we realize that we have suffered more than an ordinary bereavement, and consequently we feel the more interested If ever there was a man who had claims on the affections of the community, it was our beloved but now deceased Patriarch. If ever there was an event calculated to raise the feelings of sorrow in the human breast, and cause us to drop the sympathetic tear, it certainly is the present; for truly we can say with the king of Israel, "A prince and a great man has fallen in Israel." A man endeared to us by every feeling calculated to entwine around and adhere to the human heart, by almost indissoluble bonds. A man faithful to his God and to the Church in every situation and under all circumstances through which he was called to pass.

Whether in prosperity, surrounded by the comforts of life, a smiling progeny, and all the enjoyments of a domestic circle; or when called upon, like the Patriarchs of old, to leave the land of his nativity, to journey in strange lands, and become subject to all the trials and persecutions that have been heaped upon the Saints with a liberal hand, by characters destitute of every principle of morality or religion, alike regardless of the tender offspring and the aged sire, whose silvery locks and furrowed cheeks ought to have been a sufficient shield from their cruelty; still, like the Apostle Paul he could exclaim, (and his life and conduct have fully borne out the sentiment) "None of these things move me; neither count I my life dear, so that I may finish my course with joy."

The principles of the Gospel were too well established in that breast, and had got too sure a footing there, ever to be torn down, or prostrated by the fierce winds of persecution, the blasts of poverty, or the swollen waves of distress and tribulation. No; thank God, his house was built upon a *rock*—consequently it stood amid the contending elements, firm and unshaken.

The life of our departed father has indeed been an eventful one, having to take a conspicuous part in the great work of the last days; being designated by the ancient prophets who once dwelt on this continent, as the father of him whom the Lord had promised to raise up in the last days, to lead His people Israel; and by a uniform consistent, and a virtuous course, for a long series of years, he has proved himself worthy of such a son, and such a family by whom he had the happiness of being surrounded in his dying moments; most of whom had the satisfaction of receiving his dying benediction.

He was already in the wane of life, when the light of truth broke in upon the world, and with pleasure he hailed its benign and enlightening rays, and was chosen by the Almighty to be one of the witnesses to the Book of Mormon. From that time, his only aim was the promotion of truth—his soul was taken up with the things of the Kingdom; his bowels yearned over the children of men; and it was more than his meat and his drink to do the will of his Father, who is in heaven.

By unceasing industry of himself and family, he had secured a home in the state of New York, where he no doubt expected, with every honest, industrious citizen, to enjoy the blessings of peace and liberty. But when the principles of truth were introduced and the Gospel of Jesus Christ was promulgated by himself and family, friends forsook, enemies raged, and persecution was resorted to by wicked and ungodly men, insomuch that he was obliged to flee from that place, and seek a home in a more hospitable land.

In Ohio he met with many kind and generous friends, and was kindly welcomed by the Saints; many of whom continue to this day, and can call to mind the various scenes which there transpired; many of which were of such a nature as not to be easily obliterated.

While the House of the Lord was building he took great interest in its erection, and daily watched its progress, and had the pleasure of taking a part at the opening, and seeing it crowded by hundreds of pious worshipers. As the King of Israel longed for and desired to see the completion of the House of the Lord, so did he; and with him he could exclaim, "O Lord, I love the habitation of thine house, and the place where thine honor dwelleth." To dwell in the house of the Lord, and to inquire in his temple, was his daily delight; and in it he enjoyed many blessings, and spent many hours in sweet communion with his heavenly Father. He has trod its sacred aisles, solitary and alone from mankind, long before the king of day has gilded the eastern horizon; and he has uttered his aspirations within its walls, when nature has been asleep. In its holy enclosures have the visions of heaven been opened to his mind, and his soul has feasted on the riches of eternity; and there under his teachings have the meek and humble been instructed, while the widow and the orphan have received his patriarchal blessings.

There he saw the work spreading far and wide; saw the Elders of Israel go forth under his blessing—bore them up by the prayer of faith, and hailed them welcome when they again returned bringing their sheaves with them. There with his aged partner, he spent many happy days in the bosom of his family, whom he loved with all the tenderness of parental affection.

Here I might enlarge, and expatiate on the "scenes of joy and scenes of gladness" which were enjoyed by our beloved Patriarch, but I shall pass on to an event which was truly painful and trying.

The delightful scene soon vanished; the calm was soon succeeded by a storm and the frail bark was driven by the tempest and foaming ocean, for many who had once been proud to acknowledge him a father and a friend, and who sought counsel at his hands, joined with the enemies of truth, and sought his destruction; and would have rejoiced to see his aged and venerable form immured in a dungeon; but, thank God, this they were not suffered to do; he providentially made his escape, and after evading his enemies for some time, he undertook and accomplished a journey of a thousand miles, and bore up under the fatigue and suffering necessarily attendant on such a journey with patient resignation. After a journey of several weeks, he arrived in safety at Far West, in the bosom of the Church, and was cordially welcomed by the Saints, who had found an asylum in the rich and fertile county of Caldwell.

There he, in common with the rest of the Saints, hoped to enjoy the privileges and blessings of peace. There, from the fertile soil and flowery meads, which well repaid the labor of the husbandman, and poured forth abundance for the support of the numerous herds which decked those lovely and wide-spread prairies, he hoped to enjoy uninterrupted, the comforts of domestic life.

But he had not long indulged these pleasing anticipations before the delightful prospect again vanished; the cup of blessing which he began again to enjoy, was dashed from his aged lips; and the cup of sorrow filled to overflowing, was given him instead; and surely he drank it to the very dregs; for not only did he see the Saints in bondage, treated with cruelty, and some of them murdered; but the kind and affectionate parent saw—and ah! how painful was the sight—two of his sons to whom he looked for protection, torn away from their domestic circles, from their weeping and distracted families, by monsters in the shape of men, who swore and threatened to kill them, and who had every disposition to imbrue their hands in their blood.	This circumstance was too much for his agitated and now sinking frame to bear up under; and although his confidence in his God was great, and his conduct was that of a Christian and a Saint, yet he felt like a man and a parent. At that time his constitution received a shock from which it never recovered. Ah! yes, there were feelings agitated in the bosom of our deceased friend at that time of no ordinary kind; feelings of painful anxiety, and emotion too great for his earthly tabernacle to contain without suffering a great and a sensible injury; and which from that time began to manifest itself.

It would be unnecessary to trace him and his aged partner (who shared in all his sorrows and afflictions) from such a scene, as many of the Saints are knowing to the privations and sufferings which they, in common with the Church, endured while moving from that land of oppression; suffice it to say, he arrived in safety in Illinois, broken down in constitution and in health, and since then he has labored under severe afflictions and pain, while disease has been slowly but surely undermining his system.

Whenever he had a short respite from pain, he felt a pleasure in atttending to his patriarchal duties, and with cheerfulness he performed them; and frequently his labors have been more than his strength would admit of; but having great zeal for the cause of truth, he felt willing to be spent in the service of his God.

For some time past he has been confined to his bed, and the time of his departure was near at hand.	On Saturday evening last, a rupture of a blood vessel took place, when he vomited a large quantity of blood. His family were summoned to his bedside, it being now evident that he could not long survive.

On Sunday he called his children and grandchildren around him, and like the ancient patriarchs gave them his final benediction.	Although his strength was far gone, and he was obliged to rest at intervals, yet his mind was clear, perfectly collected, and calm as the gentle zephyrs. The love of God was in his heart, the peace of God rested upon him, and his soul was full of compassion and blessing.

All the circumstances connected with his death, were calculated to lead the mind back to the time when an Abraham, an Isaac and a Jacob bid adieu to mortality, and entered into rest.

His death, like theirs, was sweet, and it certainly was a privilege indeed to witness such a scene; and I was forcibly reminded of the sentiment of the poet:

> The chamber where the good man meets his fate,
> Is privileged beyond the common walk of virtuous life.

There were no reflections of a misspent life—no fearful forebodings of a gloomy nature in relation to the future; the realities of eternity were dawning, the shades of time were lowering; but there was nothing to terrify, to alarm or disturb his mind; no, the principles of the Gospel, which, "bring life and immortality to light," nobly triumphed in nature's final hour. These principles so long taught and cherished by our lamented friend, were honorably maintained to the last; which is not only a consolation to the immediate relatives, but to the Church at large.

The instructions imparted by him will long be remembered by his numerous progeny, who will undoubtedly profit by the same, and strive to render themselves worthy of such a sire; and the whole Church will copy his examples, walk in his footsteps, and emulate his faith and virtuous actions, and commend themselves to his God and to their God.

Notwithstanding his enemies frequently "shot at him, yet his bow abode in strength, and the arms of his hands were made strong by the hands of the mighty God of Jacob," and his courage and resolution never forsook him.

His anxiety for the spread of truth was great, and he lived to see great and important things accomplished. He saw the commencement of the work, small as a mustard seed, and with attention and deep interest he watched its progress; and he had the satisfaction of beholding thousands on this Continent, rejoicing in its truth, and heard the glorious tidings, that other lands were becoming heirs to the richest blessings.

Under these circumstances, he could exclaim, like pious Simeon of old, "Lord, now lettest thou thy servant depart in peace, for mine eyes have seen thy salvation."

Although his spirit has taken its flight and his remains will soon mingle with their mother earth, yet his memory will long be cherished by all who had the pleasure of his acquaintance, and will be fresh and blooming when those of his enemies shall be blotted out from under heaven.

May we, beloved friends, who survive our venerable Patriarch, study to prosecute those things which were so dear to his aged heart, and pray that a double portion of his spirit may be bestowed on us, that we may be the humble instruments in aiding the consummation of the great work which he saw so happily begun; that when we have to stand before the bar of Christ, we may with our departed friend hear the welcome plaudit, "Come up hither, ye blessed of my Father, inherit the kingdom prepared for you from the foundation of the world. Amen.

CHAPTER XI.

THREATENING PORTENTS IN THE ACTIONS OF MISSOURI—
GENERAL CONFERENCES IN NAUVOO AND ENGLAND—THE
DOCTRINE OF PRIESTHOOD.

Tuesday, September 15, 1840.

"The governor of Missouri, after a silence of about two years, has at last made a demand on Governor Carlin of Illinois, for Joseph Smith, Jun., Sidney Rigdon, Lyman Wight, Parley P. Pratt, Caleb Baldwin, and Alanson Brown, as fugitives from justice.

"The demand it seems has been complied with by Governor Carlin, and an order issued for their apprehension; accordingly our place has recently received a visit from the sheriff for these men; but through the tender mercies of a kind Providence, who by His power has sustained, and once delivered them from the hands of the blood-thirsty and savage race of beings in the shape of men that tread Missouri's delightful soil; they were not to be found—as the Lord would have it, they were gone from home, and the sheriff returned, of course without them.

"These men do not feel disposed to again try the solemn realities of mob law in that state; and a free and enlightened republic should respond against it, for Missouri has no claim on them, but they have claim on Missouri.

"What right have they to demand of Governor Carlin, as fugitives from justice, men against whom no process had ever been found in that state—no, not so much as the form of a process?   They were taken by a mob militia, and dragged from everything that was dear and sacred, and tried (without their knowledge) by a court martial, condemned to be shot, but this failing, they were forced into confinement, galled with chains, deprived of the comforts of life, and even that which was necessary to save life, then brought to a pretended trial, without even having a legal process served, and then deprived of the privilege of defense. They were taken by a mob, tried, condemned and imprisoned by the same, and this Missouri cannot deny.

"What a beautiful picture Governor Boggs has presented to the world, after driving twelve or fifteen thousand inhabitants from their homes, forcing them to leave the state under the pain of extermination, and confiscating their property, and murdering innocent men, women and children; then, because that a few made their escape from his murdering hand, and have found protection in a land of equal rights, so that his plans and designs have all been unfruitful, to that extent that he has caused 'Mormonism' to spread with double vigor; he now has the presumption to demand them back, in order that his thirst for innocent blood may yet be satiated.

"He has no business with them; they have not escaped from justice, but from the hands of a cursed, infuriated, inhuman set, or race of beings who are enemies to their country, to their God, to themselves, and to every principle of righteousness and humanity. They loathe Christianity, and despise the people of God; they war against truth, and inherit lies; virtue they tread under their feet; while vice (with her ten thousand offspring) is their welcome associate; therefore, men on whom Missouri has no claim, she cannot, no, she never shall have."*

Sunday, 20.—Elder Willard Richards went to Preston, held a conference, ordained five Elders, eleven Priests, eight Teachers, one Deacon, and returned to Manchester same day.

Letter of Samuel Bent and George W. Harris to the Presidency—Reporting Labors.

CINCINNATI, Sept. 23, 1840.

To the First Presidency and High Council of the Church of Jesus Christ of Latter-day Saints:

We gladly embrace this opportunity of conveying a few lines to you by Ebenezer Robinson, who we expect will leave this place for Nauvoo in a few days.

Brother George W. Harris and myself have visited the several branches of the Church in Adams county, Pike county, Jacksonville, and Springfield. On our way we stopped at Terre Haute, and Pleasant Garden, Indiana. We found the brethren generally very willing and anxious to do all in their power to assist the Church in the great and glorious cause that we have engaged in respecting the printing of the several books in contemplation, but I am sorry to say I found them destitute of the means to relieve our present necessity.

However, we have succeeded in obtaining several notes of hand from

---

* The foregoing is an editorial in the *Times and Seasons* for September, 1840.

different brethren in the state of Illinois, to the amount of about eighty-three dollars, which will come due on the first day of October next, and we have handed them over to Ebenezer Robinson, to be delivered to Joseph Smith, Jun., for collection. We expect Brother Robinson will arrive with them at the time they become due.

We have obtained some money, which we have paid over to Brother Ebenezer Robinson. We have also given our obligations as agents for the Church, to Shepherd and Stearns to the amount of three hundred dollars, two hundred of which becomes due on the twenty-sixth day of November next, and the other one hundred on the twenty sixth day of December next, being the amount due Shepherd and Stearns for the stereotype plates.

We have taken up the bond that Brother Brown gave for the wagon or carriage which he let Joseph Smith, Jun., have, and we have succeeded in procuring a horse and harness to put alongside of the other horse to make it easier for him. We got said horse and harness by contributions from the brethren at Dayton and West Milton, Ohio.

Brother Ebenezer Robinson (we think) has been very economical, diligent, and persevering, and successful in the business whereupon he was sent. He has gained the confidence of the gentlemen with whom he has been transacting business in the city, and has done honor to the cause of Christ and His Church of Latter-day Saints. We can further say to you brethren, we think the course he has taken, and our united exertions with him, have established the credit of the Church of Jesus Christ of Latter-day Saints in this place (I mean as to business transactions), to that extent that we can obtain any amount of paper, type, and other materials requisite to carry on the printing business to a large extent, and upon terms that will warrant our success.

We therefore shall go on with renewed courage and zeal, trusting in the Lord to prepare the way before us, and we feel to ask your prayers that God may peradventure expand the minds of the Saints abroad, that they may be able to comprehend the magnitude of the work we so much desire to accomplish, which in all probability will induce them to donate with alacrity.

Brother John E. Page is preaching with the manifestations of the Spirit and power in this place, and with considerable success. We think when Brother Page leaves the city of Cincinnati, the inhabitants thereof will be left without excuse for not receiving the Gospel of Jesus Christ, and his garments clear from their blood in the day of judgment.

Accept our love and best wishes.

Yours in the bonds of the New and Everlasting Covenant,
                                        SAMUEL BENT,
                                        GEORGE W. HARRIS.

Letter of John E. Page to the Presidency—Reporting Progress of Palestine Mission.

CINCINNATI, September 23, 1840.

To the President and Council of the Church of Jesus Christ of Latter-day Saints, and also to all the Saints Assembled in General Conference:

Your humble servant embraces with pleasure this opportunity to pen for your edification a few lines. I congratulate you upon the steady march and advancement of the cause of Christ, as [it] has fallen under my observation. Elder Hyde and myself have been treated with respect, and had the greatest attention paid us by the brethren and sisters; and by gentlemen and ladies of the first class in society, we have been made welcome very heartily to their dwellings and comforts of life. When we separate from them they grip our hands with tears standing full in their eyes, bidding farewell, and often leave something noble with us to help us on our mission; and a firm promise that they will duly reflect on the great things which we have told them. They ardently request us to send them some competent Elder to preach to them.

Yes, dear brethren, the cause of truth is marching onward with unparalleled rapidity, and victory! Victory! will soon be the shout of all the faithful in Christ; and thank the Lord, thank the Lord, is the language of unworthy me, that I have lived to see 1840, with all its attendant evidences of the truth of the Book of Mormon, and the Book of Doctrine and Covenants.

I must save a place in this communication to make some remarks concerning Brother Ebenezer Robinson. I can say, in truth and soberness, that he merits the esteem and confidence of the Saints and all good men for his diligence and economy while getting the Book of Mormon stereotyped, &c., here. The honest and frank course he has pursued towards the gentlemen with whom he has been concerned in business (viz., Messrs. Shepherd, Stearns, and others), has won their everlasting respect and esteem, judging from their own manifestations to me.

Dear brethren and sisters, your humble servants, Orson Hyde and myself, sincerely solicit your special prayers, sealed with a hearty amen.

Elder Hyde is truly a humble servant of the Lord, and a very agreeable companion in the ministry. Our hearts are one, our faith is one, and the strongholds of Satan quake before us. We desire to have grace to perform our mission, that we may return to our families and brethren with triumph and joy.

I anticipate that Elder Hyde is in New York City. I am waiting to obtain a few copies of the third edition of the Book of Mormon. To raise means is hard, yet we trust in the Lord. I shall go to Philadelphia as soon as possible.

I have baptized thirteen in this city; many are believing, and some halting between two opinions; and have baptized in all since I started, eighty-four.

I have had a vision from the Lord, which manifested the present state of the world respecting the Jews, Jerusalem, the remnant of Israel, and also the Gentile world. As hasty summer fruit, so is this nation; as a vineyard of grapes fully ripe, ready to be gathered for the press, so are all the nations of the earth.

I want the conference to send some faithful and competent Elder to this place, to nurse the seed or word that has been sown here, and shall leave this matter with Ebenezer Robinson to lay before the conference.

Elders Bent and Harris are here, and are using all their energies, both of mind and body, to fill their calling. I deem them amply qualified to discharge the function of their office, provided they keep humble.

Dear brethren, remember me to my family, and pray for them; remember me to Sister Hyde, and also all of the wives of the Elders in particular, whose husbands are in the field. Tell them to pray for us. I hope the authorities of the Church will see that they are provided with food and raiment, that they may enjoy life with you.

Yours in the bonds of the Covenant,

JOHN E. PAGE.

Monday, 28.

Extracts from Orson Hyde's Letter—Signs in the Heavens.

BURLINGTON COUNTY, NEW JERSEY.

I left Elder Page at Cincinnati the latter part of August, and came on up the Ohio river as far as Wellsburgh, Virginia. I stopped with Father James. Here I preached twice, and baptized three persons; came on by stage and steamboats to Pittsburg; from thence took the canal to Leechburgh, where I stopped and preached to a small number of Saints, raised up by the instrumentality of Father Nickerson— in good spirits.

As I left this place about nine o'clock in the morning, the most remarkable phenomenon occurred in the heavens that I ever witnessed. There appeared two bright and luminous bodies, one on the north and the other on the south of the sun; in length about ten yards, inclining to a circle resembling a rainbow, about fifty yards distant from the sun; apparently east about twenty-five yards, was a body of light as brilliant almost as the sun itself; and on the west, a great distance from the sun, appeared a white semi-circle passing half way round the horizon, and another crossing it at right angles, exhibiting a scene of the sublimest kind. It was a great wonder to the passengers on board the boat. Put this with the fact that the Jews are gathering home, and that all Europe is in commotion and on the eve of breaking out in open hostilities; and also that the tree of liberty, which has long flourished in the republican soil of America, has been girdled, and her green foliage, which has shielded and protected the sons of oppression from the scorching rays of despotic power, already begins to wither like the accursed fig tree—and what language do these speak to the Saints! "Lift up your heads, for your redemption draweth near!"   *   *   *   *   *   *

I came on, and met with the Saints in Chester county, Pennsylvania, laboring there about one week with Brother Barnes, where we added six to their number. I preached about one week in Philadelphia, and baptized twelve; came on to this place with Brothers Snow and Barnes, and held a two-days' meeting, at which sixteen were baptized. I shall return to Philadelphia in a few days, where I expect to meet Brother Page, and then, if the Lord will, after holding a few meetings in this country, we shall proceed on to New York, there to take ship and sail over the seas.

Orson Hyde.

On the night of the 28th, Elder Heber C. Kimball had the following dream, as related by himself:

Elder Heber C. Kimball's Dream.

Having great anxiety for the welfare of the small branch which we had raised in London, I retired to rest and had the following dream. I thought that we dug a well on high ground in order to obtain water, and after digging some considerable time, we came to an excellent spring; we then commenced to back it up, but before it was finished, we had occasion to leave for a short time and when we returned to complete it, we found it carefully filled up with sand, and all attempts to remove it proved unavailing, we thought it better to choose another spot on lower ground, where we were successful. When we returned to London, we experienced a perfect fulfillment of my dream—having to open a new preaching place at Barrett's Academy, King Square, Goswell Road, our former place being closed against us.

Tuesday, 29. Elders Heber C. Kimball and George A. Smith left London for the Manchester conference.

Saturday, October 3.

Minutes of the General Conference of the Church of Jesus Christ of Lat-
ter-day Saints, held in Nauvoo, Hancock County, Illinois, Beginning
October 3, 1840.

The conference was opened with prayer by President William Marks.
President Joseph Smith was then unanimously called to the chair, and
Robert B. Thompson appointed clerk.

A letter from Elders Bent and Harris, and one from Elder John E.
Page were then read by the clerk, which gave very satisfactory accounts
of their mission.

On motion, Resolved: That a committee be appointed to ordain such
as have recommends to this conference for ordination, and that Jonathan H. Hale, Elisha H. Groves, Charles C. Rich, John Murdock, and
Simeon Carter, compose said committee, and report their proceedings
before the conference closes.

The President arose and stated that there had been several depredations committed on the citizens of Nauvoo, and thought it expedient
that a committee be appointed to search out the offenders, and bring
them to justice.

Whereupon it was Resolved: That Joseph Smith, Elias Higbee, William Marks, Vinson Knight, William Law, Charles C. Rich, and Dimick
B. Huntington, compose said committee.

On motion, Resolved: That Robert B. Thompson be appointed the
General Church Clerk, in the room of George W. Robinson, who intends to remove to Iowa.

It having been requested by Elder Page, that the conference would appoint an Elder to take charge of the church which he and Elder Hyde
had raised up in Cincinnati, on motion, Resolved: That Elder Samuel
Bennett be appointed to preside there.

The president then arose and stated that it was necessary that something should be done with regard to Kirtland, so that it might be built up;
and gave it as his opinion, that the brethren from the east might gather
there, and also that it was necessary that some one should be appointed
from this conference to preside over that stake. On motion, Resolved:
That Elder Almon W. Babbitt be appointed to preside over the church
in Kirtland, and that he choose his own counselors.

Conference adjourned for one hour.

One o'clock p. m.   Conference met pursuant to adjournment.   An
opportunity was given to the brethren who had any remarks to make
on suitable locations for stakes of Zion.   Elder H. W. Miller stated
that it was the desire of a number of the brethren residing in Adams
county, to have a stake appointed at Mount Ephrain in that county, and
stated the advantages of the place for agricultural purposes.

On motion, Resolved: That a stake be appointed at Mount Ephraim, in Adams county.

There being several applications for the appointment of stakes, it was Resolved: That a committee be appointed to organize stakes between this place and Kirtland, and that Hyrum Smith, Lyman Wight, and Almon W. Babbitt, compose said committee.

The President then spoke of the necessity of building a "House of the Lord" in this place. Whereupon it was Resolved: That the Saints build a house for the worship of God, and that Reynolds Cahoon, Elias Higbee, and Alpheus Cutler be appointed a committee to build the same.

On motion, Resolved: That a commencement be made ten days from this date, and that every tenth day be appropriated for the building of the house.

President Hyrum Smith arose and stated that there were several individuals who, on moving to this place, had not settled with their creditors, and had no recommend from the branches of the churches where they had resided. On motion, Resolved: That those persons moving to this place, who do not bring a recommend, be disfellowshiped.

John C. Bennett, M. D., then spoke at some length, on the oppression to which the Church had been subjected, and remarked that it was necessary for the brethren to stand by each other, and resist every unlawful attempt at persecution.

Elder Lyman Wight then addressed the meeting. Adjourned till tomorrow morning.

Sunday morning, October 4.

Conference met pursuant to adjournment, and was opened with prayer by Elder Almon W. Babbitt.

The clerk was then called upon to read the report of the Presidency in relation to the city plat, after which the President made some observations on the status of the debts on the city plat, which will appear at the close of these conference minutes, and advised that a committee be appointed to raise funds to liquidated the same. On motion, Resolved: That William Marks and Hyrum Smith compose said committee.

On motion, Resolved: That a committee be appointed to draft a bill for the incorporation of the town of Nauvoo, and other purposes.

Resolved: That Joseph Smith, John C. Bennett, and Robert B. Thompson be said committee.

Resolved: That John C. Bennett be appointed delegate, to urge the passage of said bill through the legislature.

President Hyrum Smith then rose and gave some general instructions to the Church. Conference adjourned for one hour.

One o'clock p. m.   Conference met pursuant to adjournment, and was opened with prayer by Elder John P. Greene.

President Joseph Smith then rose and delivered a discourse on the subject of baptism for the dead, which was listened to with considerable interest, by the vast multitude assembled.

Dr. John C. Bennett from the committee to draft a charter for the city, and for other purposes, reported the outlines thereof.   On motion, Resolved: That the same be adopted.

Elder Ebenezer Robinson then rose and gave an account of the printing of another edition of the Book of Mormon, and stated that it was now nearly completed, and that arrangements had been made for the printing of the hymn-book, Book of Doctrine and Covenants, &c.

Conference adjourned to Monday morning.

Monday morning, October 5.

Conference met pursuant to adjournment, and was opened with prayer by Elder Lyman Wight.

Elder Robert B. Thompson, after a few preliminary remarks, read an article on the Priesthood, composed by President Joseph Smith, which will appear at the close of the conference minutes; after which Elder Babbitt delivered an excellent discourse on the same subject, at considerable length.

Conference adjourned for one hour.   During the intermission a large number was baptized.

Two o'clock p. m.   Conference met pursuant to adjournment.   Elder Lyman Wight addressed the congregation on the subject of baptism for the dead, and other subjects of interest to the Church.

The President then made some observations and pronounced his benediction on the assembly.

Dr. John C. Bennett said that many persons had been accused of crime, and been looked upon as guilty, when on investigation it has been ascertained that nothing could be proved against them.   Whereupon, on motion, it was Resolved: That no person be considered guilty of crime, unless proved so by the testimony of two or three witnesses.

He next brought before the conference the treatment the Saints had experienced in Missouri, and wished to know whether the conference would take any further steps in relation to obtaining redress.   On motion, resolved: That Elias Higbee and Robert B. Thompson be appointed a committee to obtain redress for the wrongs sustained in Missouri.

The committee on ordinations reported that they had ordained thirty-nine to the ministry.

On motion, Resolved: That this conference be dismissed, and that
the next conference be held on the 6th day of April next.

　　　　　　　　　　　　JOSEPH SMITH, President.
　　　　　　　　　　　　ROBERT B. THOMPSON, Clerk.

The following is the article on Priesthood referred to in
the conference minutes:

PRIESTHOOD.

In order to investigated the subject of the Priesthood, so important
to this, as well as every succeeding generation, I shall proceed to trace
the subject as far as I possibly can from the Old and New Testaments.
There are two Priesthoods spoken of in the Scriptures, viz., the Melchisedek and the Aaronic or Levitical. Although there are two Priesthoods, yet the Melchisedek Priesthood comprehends the Aaronic or Levitical Priesthood, and is the grand head, and holds the highest authority which pertains to the Priesthood, and the keys of the Kingdom
of God in all ages of the world to the latest posterity on the earth, and
is the channel through which all knowledge, doctrine, the plan of salvation, and every important matter is revealed from heaven.

Its institution was prior to "the foundation of this earth, or the morning stars sang together, or the Sons of God shouted for joy," and is the
highest and holiest Priesthood, and is after the order of the Son of God,
and all other Priesthoods are only parts, ramifications, powers and
blessings belonging to the same, and are held, controlled, and directed
by it. It is the channel through which the Almighty commenced revealing His glory at the beginning of the creation of this earth, and
through which He has continued to reveal Himself to the children
of men to the present time, and through which He will make known
His purposes to the end of time.

Commencing with Adam, who was the first man, who is spoken
of in Daniel as being the "Ancient of Days," or in other words, the
first and oldest of all, the great, grand progenitor of whom it is said in
another place he is Michael, because he was the first and father of all,
not only by progeny, but the first to hold the spiritual blessings, to
whom was made known the plan of ordinances for the salvation of his
posterity unto the end, and to whom Christ was first revealed, and
through whom Christ has been revealed from heaven, and will continue
to be revealed from henceforth. Adam holds the keys of the dispensation of the fullness of times; i. e., the dispensation of all the times
have been and will be revealed through him from the beginning to
Christ, and from Christ to the end of all the dispensations that are to be

revealed. "Having made known unto us the mystery of His will, according to His good pleasure which He hath purposed in Himself: that in the dispensation of the fullness of times He might gather together in one all things in Christ, both which are in heaven, and which are on earth; even in him." (Ephesians, 1st chap., 9th and 10 verses).

Now the purpose in Himself in the winding up scene of the last dispensation is that all things pertaining to that dispensation should be conducted precisely in accordance with the preceding dispensations.

And again. God purposed in Himself that there should not be an eternal fullness until every dispensation should be fulfilled and gathered together in one, and that all things whatsoever, that should be gathered together in one in those dispensations unto the same fullness and eternal glory, should be in Christ Jesus; therefore He set the ordinances to be the same forever and ever, and set Adam to watch over them, to reveal them from heaven to man, or to send angels to reveal them. "Are they not all ministering spirits, sent forth to minister for them who shall be heirs of salvation?" (Hebrews, i, 14).

These angels are under the direction of Michael or Adam, who acts under the direction of the Lord. From the above quotation we learn that Paul perfectly understood the purposes of God in relation to His connection with man, and that glorious and perfect order which He established in Himself, whereby he sent forth power, revelations, and glory.

God will not acknowledge that which He has not called, ordained, and chosen. In the beginning God called Adam by His own voice. "And the Lord called unto Adam and said unto him, Where art thou? And he said, I heard thy voice in the garden, and I was afraid because I was naked, and hid myself." (See Genesis 3rd chap., 9, 10.) Adam received commandments and instructions from God: this was the order from the beginning.

That he received revelations, commandments and ordinances at the beginning is beyond the power of controversy; else how did they begin to offer sacrifices to God in an acceptable manner? And if they offered sacrifices they must be authorized by ordination. We read in Genesis, (4th chap., 4th), that Abel brought of the firstlings of the flock and the fat thereof, and the Lord had respect to Abel and to his offering. And, again, "By faith Abel offered unto God a more excellent sacrifice than Cain, by which he obtained witness that he was righteous, God testifying of his gifts; and by it he being dead, yet speaketh." (Hebrews xi; 4). How doth he yet speak? Why he magnified the Priesthood which was conferred upon him, and died a righteous man, and therefore has become an angel of God by receiving his body from the dead, holding still the keys of his dispensation; and was sent down from heaven unto

Paul to minister consoling words, and to commit unto him a knowledge of the mysteries of godliness.

And if this was not the case, I would ask, how did Paul know so much about Abel, and why should he talk about his speaking after he was dead? Hence, that he spoke after he was dead must be by being sent down out of heaven to administer.

This, then, is the nature of the Priesthood; every man holding the Presidency of his dispensation, and one man holding the Presidency of them all, even Adam; and Adam receiving his Presidency and authority from the Lord, but cannot receive a fullness until Christ shall present the Kingdom to the Father, which shall be at the end of the last dispensation.

The power, glory and blessings of the Priesthood could not continue with those who received ordination only as their righteousness continued; for Cain also being authorized to offer sacrifice, but not offering it in righteousness, was cursed. It signifies, then, that the ordinances must be kept in the very way God has appointed; otherwise their Priesthood will prove a cursing instead of a blessing.

If Cain had fulfilled the law of righteousness as did Enoch, he could have walked with God all the days of his life, and never failed of a blessing. "And Enoch walked with God after he begat Methuselah 300 years, and begat sons and daughters, and all the days of Enoch were 365 years; and Enoch walked with God, and he was not, for God took him." (Gen. 5th chap., 22nd ver.) Now this Enoch God reserved unt Himself, that he should not die at that time, and appointed unto him a ministry unto terrestrial bodies, of whom there has been but little revealed. He is reserved also unto the Presidency of a dispensation, and more shall be said of him and terrestrial bodies in another treatise. He is a ministering angel, to minister to those who shall be heirs of salvation, and appeared unto Jude as Abel did unto Paul; therefore Jude spoke of him (14, 15 verses). And Enoch, the seventh from Adam, revealed these sayings: "Behold, the Lord cometh with ten thousand of His Saints."

Paul was also acquainted with this character, and received instructions from him. "By faith Enoch was translated, that he should not see death, and was not found, because God had translated him; for before his translation he had this testimony, that he pleased God; but without faith, it is impossible to please Him, for he that cometh to God must believe that He is, and that he is a revealer to those who diligently seek him." (Heb. 11, 5).

Now the doctrine of translation is a power which belongs to this Priesthood. There are many things which belong to the powers of the Priesthood and the keys thereof, that have been kept hid from before the foundation of the world; they are hid from the wise and prudent to be revealed in the last times.

Many have supposed that the doctrine of translation was a doctrine whereby men were taken immediately into the presence of God, and into an eternal fullnes, but this is a mistaken idea. Their place of habitation is that of the terrestrial order, and a place prepared for such characters He held in reserve to be ministering angels unto many planets, and who as yet have not entered into so great a fullness as those who are resurrected from the dead. "Others were tortured, not accepting deliverance, that they might obtain a better resurrection." (See Heb. 11th chap., part of the 35th verse.)

Now it was evident that there was a better resurrection, or else God would not have revealed it unto Paul.   Wherein then, can it be said a better resurrection.   This distinction is made between the doctrine of the actual resurrection and translation: translation obtains deliverance from the tortures and sufferings of the body, but their existence will prolong as to the labors and toils of the ministry, before they can enter into so great a rest and glory.

On the other hand, those who were tortured, not accepting deliverance, received an immediate rest from their labors. "And I heard a voice from heaven, saying, Blessed are the dead who die in the Lord, for from henceforth they do rest from their labors and their works do follow them." (See Revelation, 14th chap., 13th verse).

They rest from their labors for a long time, and yet their work is held in reserve for them, that they are permitted to do the same work, after they receive a resurrection for their bodies. But we shall leave this subject and the subject of the terrestrial bodies for another time, in order to treat upon them more fully.

The next great, grand Patriarch [after Enoch] who held the keys of the Priesthood was Lamech. "And Lamech lived one hundred and eighty-two years and begat a son, and he called his name Noah, saying, this same shall comfort us concerning our work and the toil of our hands because of the ground which the Lord has cursed." (See Gen. 5th chap., 28th and 29th verses.) The Priesthood continued from Lamech to Noah: "And God said unto Noah, The end of all flesh is before me, for the earth is filled with violence through them, and behold I will destroy them with the earth." (Gen. 6: 13.)

Thus we behold the keys of this Priesthood consisted in obtaining the voice of Jehovah that He talked with him [Noah] in a familiar and friendly manner, that He continued to him the keys, the covenants, the power and the glory, with which he blessed Adam at the beginning; and the offering of sacrifice, which also shall be continued at the last time; for all the ordinances and duties that ever have been required by the Priesthood, under the directions and commandments of the Almighty in any of the dispensations, shall all be had in the last dispensation, therefore all things had under the authority of the Priesthood at any former period, shall be had again, bringing to pass the restoration spoken of by the mouth of all the Holy Prophets; then shall the sons of Levi offer an acceptable offering to the Lord.   "And he shall sit as a refiner and purifier of silver: and he shall purify the sons of Levi, and purge them as gold and silver, that they may offer unto the Lord. (See Malachi 3: 3).

It will be necessary here to make a few observations on the doctrine set forth in the above quotation, and it is generally supposed that sacrifice was entirely done away when the Great Sacrifice [i. e., the sacrifice of the Lord Jesus] was offered up, and that there will be no necessity for the ordinance of sacrifice in future: but those who assert this are certainly not acquainted with the duties, privileges and authority of the priesthood, or with the Prophets.

The offering of sacrifice has ever been connected and forms a part of the duties of the Priesthood. It began with the Priesthood, and will be continued until after the coming of Christ, from generation to generation. We frequently have mention made of the offering of sacrifice by the servants of the Most High in ancient days, prior to the law of Moses; which ordinances will be continued when the Priesthood is restored with all its authority, power and blessings.

Elijah was the last Prophet that held the keys of the Priesthood, and who will, before the last dispensation, restore the authority and deliver the keys of the Priesthood, in order that all the ordinances may be attended to in righteousness. It is true that the Savior had authority and power to bestow this blessing; but the sons of Levi were too prejudiced. "And I will send Elijah the Prophet before the great and terrible day of the Lord," etc., etc. Why send Elijah? Because he holds the keys of the authority to administer in all the ordinances of the Priesthood; and without the authority is given, the ordinances could not be administered in righteousness.

It is a very prevalent opinion that the sacrifices which were offered were entirely consumed. This was not the case; if you read Leviticus, second chap., second and third verses, you will observe that the priests took a part as a memorial and offered it up before the Lord, while the remainder was kept for the maintenance of the priests; so that the offerings and sacrifices are not all consumed upon the altar—but the blood is sprinkled, and the fat and certain other portions are consumed.

These sacrifices, as well as every ordinance belonging to the Priesthood, will, when the Temple of the Lord shall be built, and the sons of Levi be purified, be fully restored and attended to in all their powers, ramifications, and blessings. This ever did and ever will exist when the powers of the Melchisedic Priesthood are sufficiently manifest; else how can the restitution of all things spoken of by the holy Prophets be brought to pass? It is not to be understood that the law of Moses will be established again with all its rites and variety of ceremonies; this has never been spoken of by the Prophets; but those things which existed prior to Moses' day, namely, sacrifice, will be continued.

It may be asked by some, what necessity for sacrifice, since the Great Sacrifice was offered? In answer to which, if repentance, baptism, and faith existed prior to the days of Christ, what necessity for them since that time? The Priesthood has descended in a regular line from father to son, through their succeeding generations. (See Book of Doctrine and Covenants).*

REPORT OF THE PRESIDENCY.†

The First Presidency of the Church of Jesus Christ of Latter-day Saints would respectfully report—

That they feel rejoiced to meet the Saints at another General Conference, and under circumstances as favorable as the present. Since our settlement in Illinois we have for the most part been treated with courtesy and respect, and a feeling of kindness and of sympathy has generally been manifested by all classes of the community, who, with us, deprecate the conduct of those men whose dark and blackening deeds are stamped with everlasting infamy and disgrace. The contrast between our past and present situation is great. Two years ago mobs were threatening, plundering, driving and murdering the Saints. Our burning houses lighted up the canopy of heaven. Our women and children, houseless and destitute, had to wander from place to place to seek a shelter from the rage of persecuting foes. Now we enjoy peace, and can worship the God of heaven and earth without molestation, and expect to be able to go forward and accomplish the great and glorious work to which we have been called.

Under these circumstances we feel to congratulate the Saints of the Most High, on the happy and pleasing change in their circumstances, condition and prospects, and which those who shared in the perils and distress, undoubtedly appreciate; while prayers and thanksgivings daily ascend to that God who looked upon our distresses and delivered us from danger and death, and whose hand is over us for good.

From the unpropitious nature of the weather, we hardly expected to behold so many of our friends on this occasion; in this, however, we are agreeably disappointed, which gives us strong assurance that the Saints are as zealous, untiring, and energetic as ever, in the great work of the last days; and gives us joy and consolation, and greatly encour-

---

* A discourse on the same subject to the Twelve will be found in vol. iii,p. 385,*et seq.*

† This is the report referred to in the conference minutes.

ages us, while contending with the difficulties which necessarily lie in our way. Let the brethren ever manifest such a spirit, and hold up our hands, and we must, we will go forward; the work of the Lord shall roll forth, the Temple of the Lord be reared, the Elders of Israel be encouraged, Zion be built up, and become the praise, the joy, and the glory of the whole earth, and the song of praise, glory, honor, and majesty to Him that sitteth upon the throne, and to the Lamb for ever and ever, shall reverberate from hill to hill, from mountain to mountain, from island to island, and from continent to continent, and the kingdoms of this world become the kingdom of our God and His Christ.

We are glad indeed to know that there is such a spirit of union existing throughout the churches, at home and abroad, on this continent, as well as on the islands of the sea; for by this principle, and by a concentration of action, shall we be able to carry into effect the purposes of our God.

From the Elders abroad we receive the most cheering accounts. Wherever the faithful laborer has gone forth weeping, sowing the seed of truth, he has returned with joy, bringing his sheaves with him; and the information we receive from all quarters is that the laborers are few and that the harvest is great. Many wealthy and influential people have embraced the Gospel, so that not only will the poor rejoice in that they are exalted, but the rich in that they are made low. The calls to the Southern States are indeed great; many places which a short time ago would think it a disgrace to give shelter to a "Mormon," on account of the many misrepresentations which were abroad, now desire to hear an Elder of the Church of the Latter-day Saints.

On the islands of the sea, namely, Great Britain, there continues to be a steady flow of souls into the Church. Branches have been organized in many large and populous cities, and the whole land appears to be thirsting for the pure streams of knowledge and salvation.

The Twelve have already printed a new edition of the hymn-book, and they issue a monthly periodical in that land. Several families have already arrived here from England, and a number more are on their way to this place, and are expected this fall.

If the work rolls forth with the same rapidity it has heretofore done, we may soon expect to see flocking to this place, people from every land and from every nation; the polished European, the degraded Hottentot, and the shivering Laplander; persons of all languages, and of every tongue, and of every color; who shall with us worship the Lord of Hosts in His holy temple and offer up their orisons in His sanctuary.

It was in consideration of these things, and that a home might be provided for the Saints, that induced us to purchase the present city for a place of gathering for the Saints, and the extensive tract of land on the opposite side of the Mississippi. Although the purchase at the time, and under the peculiar circumstances of the Church, appeared to many to be large and uncalled for; yet from what we now see, it is apparent to all that we shall soon have to say, "This place is too straight, give us room that we may dwell." We therefore hope that the brethren who feel interested in the cause of truth, and desire to see the work of the gathering of Israel roll forth with power, will aid us in liquidating the debts which are now owing, so that the inheritances may be secured to the Church, and which eventually will be of great value.

The good spirit which is manifested on this occasion, the desire to do good, and the zeal for the honor of the Church, inspires us with confidence that we shall not appeal in vain, but that funds will be forthcoming on this occasion, sufficient to meet the necessities of the case.

It is with great pleasure that we have to inform the Church that another edition of the Book of Mormon has been printed, and which is expected on from Cincinnati in a short time; and that arrangements are making for printing the Book of Doctrine and Covenants, hymn-book, &c.; so that the demand which may exist for these works will soon be supplied.

In conclusion we would say, brethren and sisters, be faithful, be diligent, contend earnestly for the faith once delivered to the Saints; let every man, woman and child realize the importance of the work, and act as if success depended on his individual exertion alone; let all feel an interest in it, and then consider they live in a day, the contemplation of which animated the bosoms of kings, Prophets, and righteous men thousands of years ago—the prospect of which inspired their sweetest notes, and most exalted lays, and caused them to break out in such rapturous strains as are recorded in the Scriptures; and by and by we will have to exclaim, in the language of inspiration—

> The Lord has brought again Zion,
> The Lord hath redeemed His people Israel.

Tuesday, October 6.

Minutes of a General Conference in England.

Minutes of a general conference of the Church of Jesus Christ of Latter-day Saints, held at Carpenter's Hall, Manchester, Tuesday, the 6th day of October, 1840, it being the first day of the seventh month of the eleventh year of the Church; when the following officers of the Traveling High Council were present, viz.: Elders Brigham Young, Heber C. Kimball, Orson Pratt, Willard Richards, Wilford Woodruff, and George A. Smith; other officers: High Priests 5, Elders 19, Priests 28, Teachers 4, and Deacons 2.

The meeting being called to order at 10 o'clock by Elder Brigham

Young, it was moved by Elder Young, seconded by Elder Woodruff, that Elder Orson Pratt be president of the conference, which was carried unanimously. Elder George Walker was chosen clerk.

After singing, and prayer by the president, the following statistical report was read:

CONFERENCES AND BRANCHES.	MEMBERS.	ELDERS.	PRIESTS.	TEACHERS.	DEACONS.
Preston Conference (including all the branches in the care of Elders Melling and Withnall) as represented by Elder Melling.	665	18	23	11	2
Potteries were represented by Elder Alfred Cordon	248	9	32	9	9
Birmingham Branch, represented by Elder Alfred Cordon	4	—	—	—	—
West Bromwich, represented by Elder Alfred Cordon	21	—	3	1	—
Clitheroe Conference " Thomas Smith	295	10	11	9	3
Herefordshire, &c., represented by Wilford Woodruff	1007	19	78	15	1
Glasgow, and regions round about, represented by Samuel Mulliner	493	8	7	5	3
Hilsboro Branch, Ireland, represented by Theodore Curtis	5	—	—	—	—
Isle of Man Branch, represented by Hiram Clark	6	—	—	—	—
Liverpool Conference, represented by Priest William Mitchell	100	3	4	2	1
London Branch, represented by Elder Heber C. Kimball	11	—	2	—	—
Macclesfield, represented by Priest I. Brown	71	—	6	2	2
Altrincham Conference, (including Middlewich, Nortwich, and Peover,) represented by Elder William Berry	82	1	3	3	3
Bedford Branch, represented by Elder Brigham Young	36	1	1	—	—
Stockport, represented by Elder Martin Littlewood	140	2	5	2	1
Bolton, represented by Priest Barroes	61	—	2	1	—
Duckinfield, represented by Elder Albiston	76	1	3	1	—
Edinburg Conference, represented by Orson Pratt	43	—	2	—	—
Pendlebury Branch, represented by Henry Royle	36	—	2	—	—
Eccles, represented by Brother E. Leather	13	—	3	—	—
Whitefield, represented by Elder Walker Johnson	39	1	2	3	—
Ratcliffe, represented by John Allen	16	1	2	—	—
Brampton, represented by Thomas Tweddle	40	1	1	1	—
Alston, represented by John Sanders	39	2	1	2	—
Newcastle-upon-Tyne, represented by Amos Fielding	6	—	2	1	—
Manchester, represented by Brigham Young	364	4	27	6	1
Ancrum, represented by Orson Pratt	9	—	—	—	—

The president brought before the conference the subject of ordinations, and after various observations thereon, it was proposed by Elder George A. Smith, that for the future, ordinations be not attended to, except by the Traveling High Council or under such restrictions as they may adopt in reference thereto. Elder Young spoke on the subject of conferences, and also with respect of restricting ordination; and after taking into consideration the great expense attendant upon holding general conferences, and the inconvenience experienced by members attending them, suggested, that for the future, general conferences should in a great measure be done away with, or restricted to the Traveling High Council to hold conferences at such places and times as they may think proper.

The meeting adjourned at 12 o'clock.

At 2 o'clock the meeting opened with prayer, after which Elder Kimball spoke on the subject of Elders taking upon themselves the responsibility of ordaining officers in this Church; after pointing out the evils that might result therefrom, he proceeded to treat upon the duty of members towards those who preside over them in the Lord, and respecting the members administering to the temporal necessities of those whose calling it is to labor amongst them in spiritual things.

Moved by Elder Willard Richards, seconded by Elder Thomas Smith, and carried unanimously, that all ordinations be confined to or under the regulations of the Traveling High Council.

Elder Young called the attention of the conference to the case of Emma Bolton, a sister from the Potteries, who had conducted herself disorderly. Elder Johnson and others spoke of several cases of improper conduct on her part; after which it was moved by Elder Young, seconded by Elder Kimball, and carried unanimously, that Emma Bolton be cut off from the Church.

The president [of the conference, Elder Orson Pratt], then called the attention of the conference to a letter from Isaac Brown and other officers of the Church at Macclesfield, concerning Elder Heath, and also to some half a dozen charges preferred by the said Isaac Brown, James Galley, Edward Horrocks, and John Horrocks, against the said Samuel Heath, for several items of misconduct, and neglecting the duties of his office; to all of which charges Elder Heath pleaded not guilty. The complainants then entered into proof of the several items, to which Elder Heath replied by stating that the charges against him were in consequence of a misunderstanding, &c. The proceedings opened a wide field for instruction from Elder Young, followed by the president, who recommended the parties to become reconciled to each other, stating that he did not consider the charges preferred against Elder Heath sufficiently substantiated to withdraw fellowship from him; when it was moved and seconded, that no further proceeding be taken on this subject; carried unanimously.

The conference then adjourned till 7 o'clock, p. m.

At 7 o'clock the meeting was opened with prayer.

The president having made such preliminary remarks as the importance of the subject called forth, proceeded to call upon those who were willing to volunteer their services to labor in the vineyard of the Lord, when the officers gave their names as follows:

High Priests—Hiram Clark, Thomas Smith, Alfred Cordon, Thomas Kington, Orson Pratt, Brigham Young, Heber C. Kimball, Willard Richards, Wilford Woodruff, George A. Smith.

Elders—George D. Watt, John Parkinson, David Moss, Martin Littlewood, William Parr, Samuel Heath, John Sanders, Theodore Curtis, Henry Royle, Thomas Tweddle, John Leigh, Amos Fielding, Thomas Richardson.

Priests—William Snailam, William Speakman, John Needham, James Mahon, Frederick Cook, Robert Crooks, William Mitchell, William Black, Robert Williams, William Jones, Thomas Pollitt, Richard Steele, John Burns, Joseph Knowles, Richard Benson, John Wyche, William Roylance, Joseph Street, Joseph White.

Moved, seconded, and carried, that Elder George D. Watt go to Edinburgh; Elder Alfred Cordon to Birmingham, and also take charge of the Staffordshire Potteries Conference, and that John Burns, Priest, go with him.

Elder Thomas Kington to take charge of the Herefordshire Conferences as heretofore, also Garway; and William Snailam and Joseph Knowles, Priests, to accompany him.

Robert Crooks, Priest, to go to Bolton; Thomas Richardson, Elder, and John Needham, Priest, to go to Herefordshire; Elder Hiram Clark to go to the Isle of Man; Elder Thomas Tweddle to Glasgow; Elder John Sanders to labor at Alston, and go to Carlisle as soon as practicable.

Elder Amos Fielding to go to Newcastle-upon-Tyne; Elder John Parkinson to Greenock; Elder Henry Royle and Frederick Cook, Priest, to Cly in Flintshire; William Mitchell, Priest, to Leeds; Elder Thomas Smith to remain at Clitheroe; Elder John Leigh, and James Mahon, Priest, to go to Arden, Cheshire, and Joseph White and Richard Steele, Priests, to labor under the direction of Elder Cordon.

Elder John Smith to be ordained High Priest, to take charge of the church in Manchester and the regions round about: Elder Peter Melling to take charge of the church as heretofore, in connection with Elder H. Withnall; and John Wyche, Priest, to go into Staffordshire, and labor under the direction of Alfred Cordon.

Moved and seconded, that the remainder of the officers who have volunteered, be left to the Traveling High Council to dispose of, and appoint to such places as they may judge expedient; carried.

Moved and seconded, that in consequence of there not being time to transact all the business of this conference, the ordination of officers be left to the Traveling High Council to ordain from time to time such members as they may consider requisite; carried.

Elder Young then addressed the meeting on the propriety of establishing a fund for the support and clothing of such members as may from time to time be called out to labor in the vineyard, and whose circumstances may require that their necessities may be administered unto. The president then addressed the meeting on the same subject, and pointed out the difference between preaching for money and the Elders having their necessities ministered unto, while they are called to labor "without taking thought for the morrow." Elder Richards followed upon the same subject; also Elder Kimball; after which Elder Young moved, that wherever a branch of the Church is established, two members be appointed to receive the weekly voluntary contributions of the members, for promoting the spread of the Gospel, and the same to be disposed of by the vote of the church in council with the Twelve Apostles; seconded by Elder George A. Smith, and carried.

The minutes were then read and accepted, and the conference adjourned *sine die*.

ORSON PRATT, President,
GEORGE WALKER, Secretary.

Thursday, 8.

Minutes of Council of the Twelve in England.

Minutes of a Council of the Twelve, viz., Brigham Young, Heber C. Kimball, Orson Pratt, Wilford Woodruff, George A. Smith, and Willard Richards; also Hiram Clark, and Reuben Hedlock, High Priests, at the house of Willard Richards, No. 1, Chapman Street, Manchester; Brigham Young presiding.

Moved by Elder Kimball, that Elder Willard Richards take charge of the *Millennial Star*, seconded and carried. Voted that our publishing office be removed to London as soon as circumstances will permit; and that Elders Hedlock and Curtis go where they please to labor.

WILLARD RICHARDS, Clerk.

CHAPTER XII.

PROGRESS OF THE WORK IN GREAT BRITAIN—THE SAINTS AT
   KIRTLAND REPROVED FOR THEIR COURSE DURING THE
   MISSOURI PERSECUTIONS—THE PROPHET'S ADDRESS TO
   THE TWELVE AND SAINTS IN GREAT BRITAIN.

Saturday, October 10.—Elder George A. Smith returned
to London, and was soon followed by Elder Woodruff.

David Fulmer preferred a charge against Oliver Walker
"for reporting certain slanderous stories of a
fallacious and calumniating nature, calculated
to stigmatize, and raise a persecution against
the Church and individuals in it, in this place, [Nauvoo],
and for other acts of unchristianlike conduct," before the
High Council at Nauvoo. The defendant pleaded that
"he was not prepared to meet the charge, it being too in-
definite." Council adjourned till next day.

Sunday, 11.—High Council met according to adjournment. The charge against Oliver Walker was taken up,
and the following substituted for the first charge:

Minutes of the High Council.

To the High Council of the Church of Jesus Christ at Nauvoo:

For and in behalf of said Church, I prefer a charge against Elder
Oliver Walker, for several different offenses hereinafter set forth, as
said to be by him done, performed, said, and committed, as well as
various duties omitted, all of which was done at different times, periods,
places, and seasons, subsequent to September 1st, A. D. 1838, to-wit.:

For a general course of procedure, of acts, doings, and words, and
suggestions by him, the said Elder Oliver Walker, done, performed,
said, spoken, hinted at, and suggested, both directly and indirectly, and

as calculated to be derogatory to the character of the heads and leaders of the Church, and extremely injurious and hurtful to the upbuilding, welfare, being, and advancement of the same, namely, for fleeing from, quitting, and deserting the society, ranks, and needs of his brethren, in times of difficulty with, and danger from their enemies, "the mob;" restraining from the use of his brethren, his influence, efforts, and needful assistance, at such times of need; as also for joining with, and strengthening the hands, will, evil pursuits, and designs of the mob, and Gentile enemies of the Church, by expressions, hints, and suggestions of wavering and dubious nature, respecting the faith and order of the Church, and of the professed calling, qualifications, proceedings, &c., of Joseph Smith, Jun., as a Seer, Prophet, and one called to bring to light the fullness of the Gospel, &c., in these last days.

Likewise for advancing ideas, notions, or opinions, that the different orders or sects, namely, Methodists and others, could by a pursuit in their faith, order, and pursuits, as readily obtain every celestial attainment and Gospel advantage, as they could by embracing and pursuing the system brought forth by Joseph Smith, Jun., in these last days.

And moreover for suggesting within the last six months, at Alton, Nauvoo, intermediate and adjacent places, that in the Church at Nauvoo there did exist a set of pilferers, who were actually thieving, robbing, plundering, taking and unlawfully carrying away from Missouri, certain goods and chattels, wares and property; and that the act and acts of such supposed thieving, &c., was fostered and conducted by the knowledge and approbation of the heads and leaders of the Church, viz., by the Presidency and High Council; all of which items set forth as aforesaid, together with any and all corroborating acts, doings, hints, expressions, and suggestions in any way belonging to, or connected with, any or all of the aforesaid accusations, he, the said Oliver Walker, is hereby notified to prepare to defend in said trial.

Dated October 11, 1840, Nauvoo.

DAVID FULMER.

Walker pleaded that he was not prepared to defend himself, and the trial was deferred at his request till April conference.

Letter of Heber C. Kimball et al. to Messrs. Ebenezer Robinson and Don Carlos Smith—Reporting Affairs in the British Mission.

MANCHESTER, ENGLAND, October 12, 1840.

Messrs. Ebenezer Robinson, and Don Carlos Smith:

DEAR BRETHREN:—We left Manchester immediately after the July conference, for the purpose of visiting the city of London. We visited the churches which lay on our route through Staffordshire, Herefordshire, Worcestershire, and Gloucestershire; and we had many interesting meetings, baptizing and confirming daily, as we passed along. We baptized forty in one day; many new doors were opening, and all things indicated a short work in England.

The last meeting we held among the Saints while on this journey, was in a field in Leigh, Gloucestershire, on the 16th of August. We had an interesting time; we baptized fifteen, and ordained one Elder and two Priests. Two Methodist priests came twelve miles to hear; we baptized them after the first sermon, and confirmed and ordained them at the same time, and sent them to preach the Gospel. We parted with the Saints there on the 17th, went to Cheltenham, (five miles), and spent the night. There were several Saints in that place.

On the 18th we took coach and rode forty miles, through a level farming country, something like Illinois prairie; we passed through Oxfordshire, leaving the Oxford University a little upon our left. This university consists of twenty colleges endowed, and five halls not endowed; and is considered the largest and most noted university in the world. We then took the railroad and traveled seventy miles, had a splendid view of Windsor Castle as we passed along. We landed at the London terminus of the Great Western Railway at 4 o'clock in the evening. From thence we took coach and rode a few miles into the city; we walked over London Bridge, and called upon Mr. Allgood, 19 King Street, Borough. Mrs. Allgood is sister to Elder Theodore Turley's wife; she treated us kindly, gave us such refreshments as we needed, and directed us to lodgings in the neighborhood, where we spent the night.

After which we immediately commenced our researches through this great metropolis, for the honest in heart and the meek of the earth. We first commenced by visiting the ministers and preachers of the various orders, and requested the privilege of delivering our message unto the people in their churches and chapels; but of course you will not be as tonished when we inform you that they denied us this privilege, and rejected our testimony.

We went to and fro through the city of London, from day to day, endeavoring to get some door open whereby we could warn the people and search out the honest in heart; when on diligent search we found the whole city given to covetousness, (which is idolatry), priestcraft, tradition, superstition, and all manner of abominations, wickedness and uncleanness; and all doors closed against us.

We did not hesitate to stand in the midst of the streets, and, Jonah like, cry repentance unto the inhabitants of that mighty city—the metropolis of England—the pride and glory of Britain—the boast of the Gentiles, and the largest commercial city in the world—containing over one million five hundred thousand souls, who are ripening in iniquity, and preparing for the wrath of God; and like the ox going to the slaughter, know not the day of their visitation.

We shall long remember standing together in the midst of that people, and bearing a message which will prove a savor of life unto life, or of death unto death, not only unto them, but unto all those unto whom the sound of the everlasting Gospel shall come; even unto the whole world; and the judgment of the great day shall manifest the truth of it unto all nations. And it will ever sweeten the memory of that eventful period of our lives, to know that our labors, on that occasion, were not in vain; but we were enabled through toil, labor, diligent search, perseverane, and the great mercy of God, to find some of the blood of Ephraim—a few honest souls who were willing to receive and obey the Gospel; and that we were enabled to lay the foundation of a work in the city of London, which will not be removed until the city is warned, so that they will be left without excuse; and the Saints gathered out to stand in holy places, while judgment works. Until that time, the seed which we have sown there, will bring forth fruit, and the fruit will redound to the honor and glory of God.

We have baptized eleven only, in the city of London, but through the faith and the mercy of God, we ere long expect a harvest of souls in that place; but we are willing to acknowledge, that in our travels, either in America or Europe, we have never before found a people, from whose minds we have had to remove a greater multiplicity of objections, or combination of obstacles, in order to excite an interest in the subject and prepare the heart for the reception of the word of God, than in the city of London.

While conversing with the common people concerning the Gospel, we found their highest attainments to be, "Why, I go to church or chapel and get my children christened, what more is necessary?" When we conversed with the learned, we found them too wise to be taught, and too much established in the traditions of their fathers to expect any change in the last days. While conversing with the ministers of the various orders of the day, upon the principles of the Gospel, they would inform us that the ancient order of things was done away, and no longer needed; and some of them had preached forty years the good old religion, and God was with them, and they needed no more revelation, or healing the sick, or anything as manifest in the days of the Apostles, for we can get along without them in this day of refinement, light and knowledge.

When we arose to preach unto the people repentance, and baptism for the remission of sins, the cry of "Baptist, Baptist," would be rung in our ears. If we spoke of the Church and body of Christ being composed of Prophets, and Apostles; as well as other members, "Irvingites, Irvingites," would immediately dash into the mind. If in the midst of our remarks, we even for once suffered the saying to drop from our lips, "The testimony of Jesus is the spirit of prophecy," "O, you belong to Johanna Southcote," would be heard from several places at once. If we spoke of the second coming of Christ, the cry would be, "Aitkenites." If we made mention of the Priesthood, they would call us "Catholics." If we testified of the ministering of angels, the people would reply, "The Irvingites have their angels, and even the Duke of Normandy is ready to swear that he has the administering of angels every night."

These salutations, in connection with a multitude of others, of a similar nature, continued to salute our ears from day to day, until we were about ready to conclude that London had been such a perfect depot of the systems of the nineteenth century, that it contained six hundred three score and six different gods, gospels, redeemers, plans of salvation, religions, churches, commandments, (essential and non-essential), orders of preaching, roads to heaven and to hell; and that this order of things had so affected the minds of the people, that it almost required a horn to be blown from the highest heavens, in order to awaken the attention of the people, and prepare their minds to candidly hear and receive the doctrine of one Gospel, one faith, one baptism, one Holy Ghost, one God, and one plan of salvation, and that, such as Christ and the Apostles preached.

But notwithstanding this, we do not feel discouraged concerning a work being perfected in London, but firmly believe that many souls will embrace the fullness of the Gospel there, though it will be through faith, diligence, perseverance, and prayer.

Having spent twenty-three days together in this first mission in the metropolis, and the time drawing near for our October conference, Elder Woodruff left the city on the 10th of September for the purpose of attending several conferences. He attended the Bran Green and Gadfield Elm conference, held in Worcester on the 14th of September, and also the Froomes Hill conference, held in Herefordshire on the 21st of September. At these two conferences, he heard represented, 40 branches of the Church, containing 1,007 members, and 113 officers, viz., 19 Elders, 78 Priests, 15 Teachers, and 1 Deacon; the whole of whom had received the fullness of the Everlasting Gospel, and been baptized in less than seven months in that part of the vineyard which he first opened in the month of March; and the work is still progressing very rapidly throughout that region; and among the number baptized there have not been much less than one hundred preachers of various sects.

He also attended the conference in the Staffordshire Potteries, which met at Hanley on the 28th of September; where were represented 231 members, 9 Elders, 32 Priests, 9 Teachers, and 9 Deacons; most of whom received the work since our arrival there last winter and spring. While he was attending these conferences, Elders Kimball and George A. Smith continued their labors in London until the first of October, at which time we met together again in Staffordshire, and enjoyed each other's company while journeying together to Manchester, where the quorum of the Traveling High Council, with many Elders and Saints had the privilege of once more sitting in a general conference together, on the 6th of October in the Carpenter's Hall, where we heard represented 3,636 Saints, and 383 official members.

At the July conference there were 2,513 Saints, and 256 official members, making an increase in three months of 1,113 Saints and 127 official members, besides over 200 Saints, including many Elders, Priests, Teachers and Deacons, who have emigrated to America; which would make over 1,300 additions to the Church in Europe during the last three months, and over two thousand since our conference held in Preston on the 15th of April; which representation at that time was 1,671 Saints, and 132 official members.

Thus you see the Lord hath given us an increase, and blessed the labors of the servants of God universally in this land, for which we feel thankful; and our constant prayer to God is that His kingdom may roll forth, that the messengers bearing the everlasting Gospel may be diligent, meek, and humble, not weary in well doing, but waiting with patience for their reward, which lies at the end of the race, that their joy may be full.   HEBER C. KIMBALL,
                                      WILFORD WOODRUFF,
                                      GEORGE A. SMITH.

Saturday, 17.—A conference was held in Philadelphia, Elder Orson Hyde presiding; 896 members were represented, including 24 Elders, 11 Priests, 6 Teachers, 5 Deacons, in Pennsylvania, New York City, New Jersey, and vicinity.

Parley P. Pratt and family arrived in Manchester, and resumed the editorial labors of the *Star.*

Remarkable Visions by Orson Pratt.

Brother Orson Pratt has recently published a pamphlet, entitled "An interesting account of several Remarkable Visions, and of the late Discovery of Ancient American Records," comprising 31 pages giving a brief sketch of the rise of the Church.

Monday, 19.

Letter of Joseph and Hyrum Smith to the Saints in Kirtland—Reproving the Saints for Neglect of their Brethren and Sisters During the Missouri Persecutions.

NAUVOO, HANCOCK COUNTY, ILLINOIS,
October 19th, 1840.

To the Saints in Kirtland, Ohio:

Dear beloved brethren in the kingdom and patience of Jesus Christ— We take this opportunity of informing you that we yet remember the Saints scattered abroad in the regions of Kirtland, and feel interested in their welfare as well as in that of the Saints at large. We have beheld with feelings peculiar to ourselves the situation of things in Kirtland and the numerous difficulties to which the Saints have been subjected, by false friends as well as open enemies.

All these circumstances have more or less engaged our attention from time to time. We likewise must complain of the brethren who are in office and authority in the stake of Kirtland, for not writing to us, and making known their difficulties and their affairs from time to time, so that they might be advised in matters of importance to the well being of said stake; but above all, for not sending one word of consolation to us while we were in the hands of our enemies, and thrust into dungeons. Some of our friends from various sections sent us letters which breathed a kind and sympathetic spirit, and which made our afflictions and sufferings endurable. All was silent as the grave [from Kirtland]; no feelings of sorrow, sympathy, or affection [was expressed] to cheer the heart under the gloomy shades of affliction and trouble through which we had to pass.

Dear brethren, could you realize that your brethren were thus circumstanced, and were to bear up under the weight of affliction and woe which was heaped upon them by their enemies, and you stand unmoved and unconcerned! Where were the bowels of compassion? Where was the love which ought to characterize the Saints of the Most High? Did those high born and noble feelings lie dormant, or were you insensible to the treatment we received? However, we are disposed to leave these things to God, and to futurity, and feel disposed to forget this coldness on the part of the Saints in Kirtland, and to look to the future with more pleasure than while we contemplated the past; and shall by the assistance of our heavenly Father, take such steps as we think best calculated to promote the interests of the Saints, and for the promotion of truth and righteousness, and the building up of the kingdom in these last days.

The situation of Kirtland was brought before the general conference, held at this place on the 3rd instant, when it was resolved that Elder Almon W. Babbitt should be appointed to preside over the stake of Kirtland, and that he be privileged to choose his own counselors. We therefore hope that the Saints will hold up the hands of our beloved brother, and unite with him in endeavoring to promote the interests of the kingdom.

It has been deemed prudent to advise the eastern brethren who desire to locate in Kirtland, to do so; consequently you may expect an increase of members in your stake, who probably will be but young in the faith, and who will require kind treatment. We therefore hope the brethren will feel interested in the welfare of the Saints, and will use all their endeavors to promote the welfare of the brethren who may think proper to take up their residence in that place.

If you will put away from your midst all evil speaking, backbiting, and ungenerous thoughts and feelings: humble yourselves, and cultivate every principle of virtue and love, then will the blessings of Jehovah rest upon you, and you will yet see good and glorious days; peace will be within your gates, and prosperity in your borders; which may our heavenly Father grant in the name of Jesus Christ, is the prayer of yours in the bonds of the covenant,

JOSEPH SMITH,
HYRUM SMITH.

AN EPISTLE OF THE PROPHET TO THE TWELVE.

To the Traveling High Council and Elders of the Church of Jesus Christ of Latter-day Saints in Great Britain:

BELOVED BRETHREN:—May grace, mercy, and peace rest upon you from God the Father and the Lord Jesus Christ. Having several communications lying before me from my brethren the Twelve, some of which ere this have merited a reply, but from the multiplicity of business which necessarily engages my attention, I have delayed communicating with you to the present time.

Be assured, beloved brethren, that I am no disinterested observer of the things which are transpiring on the face of the whole earth; and amidst the general movements which are in progress, none is of more importance than the glorious work in which you are now engaged; consequently I feel some anxiety on your account, that you may by your virtue, faith, diligence and charity commend yourselves to one another, to the Church of Christ, and to your Father who is in heaven; by whose grace you have been called to so holy a calling; and be enabled to perform the great and responsible duties which rest upon you. And I can assure you, that from the information I have received, I feel satisfied that you have not been remiss in your duty; but that your diligence and faithfulness have been such as must secure you the smiles of that God whose servant you are, and also the good will of the Saints throughout the world.

The spread of the Gospel throughout England is certainly pleasing; the contemplation of which cannot but afford feelings of no ordinary kind, in the bosom of those who have borne the heat and burden of the day; and who were its firm supporters and strenuous advocates in infancy, while surrounded with circumstances the most unpropitious, and its destruction threatened on all hands; like the gallant bark that has braved the storm unhurt, spreads her canvas to the breeze, and nobly cuts her way through the yielding wave, more conscious than ever of the strength of her timbers, and the experience and capability of her captain, pilot, and crew.

It is likewise very satisfactory to my mind, that there has been such a good understanding between you, and that the Saints have so cheerfully hearkened to council, and vied with each other in this labor of love, and in the promotion of truth and righteousness. This is as it should be in the Church of Jesus Christ; unity is strength. "How pleasing it is for brethren to dwell together in unity!" Let the Saints of the Most High ever cultivate this principle, and the most glorious blessings must result, not only to them individually, but to the whole Church —the order of the kingdom will be maintained, its officers respected, and its requirements readily and cheerfully obeyed.

Love is one of the chief characteristics of Deity, and ought to be manifested by those who aspire to be the sons of God. A man filled with the love of God, is not content with blessing his family alone, but ranges through the whole world, anxious to bless the whole human race. This has been your feeling, and caused you to forego the pleasures of home, that you might be a blessing to others, who are candidates for immortality, but strangers to truth; and for so doing, I pray that heaven's choicest blessings may rest upon you.

Being requested to give my advice respecting the propriety of your returning in the spring, I will do so willingly. I have reflected on the subject some time, and am of the opinion that it would be wisdom in you to make preparations to leave the scene of your labors in the spring. Having carried the testimony to that land, and numbers having received it, the leaven can now spread without your being obliged to stay.

Another thing—there have been whisperings of the Spirit that there will be some agitations, excitements, and trouble in the land in which you are now laboring. I would therefore say, in the meantime be diligent: organize the churches, and let everyone stand in his proper place, so that those who cannot come with you in the spring, may not be left as sheep without a shepherd.

I would likewise observe, that inasmuch as this place has been appointed for the gathering of the Saints, it is necessary that it should be attended to in the order that the Lord intends it should. To this end I would say, that as there are great numbers of the Saints in England who are extremely poor, and not accustomed to the farming business, who must have certain preparations made for them before they can support themselves in this country, therefore to prevent confusion and disappointment when they arrive here, let those men who are accustomed to make machinery, and those who can command capital, though it be small, come here as soon as convenient, and put up machinery, and make such other preparations as may be necessary, so that when the poor come on, they may have employment to come to. This place has advantages for manufacturing and commercial purposes, which but very few can boast of; and the establishing of cotton factories, foundries, potteries, &c., would be the means of bringing in wealth, and raising it to a very important elevation.

I need not occupy more space on this subject, as its reasonableness must be obvious to every mind.

In my former epistle I told you my mind respecting the printing of the Book of Mormon, hymn-book, &c. I have been favored by receiving a hymn-book from you, and as far as I have examined it, I highly approve of it, and think it to be a very valuable collection. I am informed that the Book of Mormon is likewise printed, which I am glad to hear, and should be pleased to hear that it was printed in all the different languages of the earth. You can use your own pleasure respecting the printing of the Doctrine and Covenants. If there is a great demand for it, I have no objections, but would rather encourage it.

I can say, that as far as I have been made acquainted with your movements, I am perfectly satisfied that they have been in wisdom; and I have no doubt, but that the Spirit of the Lord has directed you; and this proves to my mind that you have been humble, and your desires have been for the salvation of your fellow man, and not for your own aggrandisement, and selfish interests. As long as the Saints manifest such a disposition, their counsels will be approved of, and their exertions crowned with success.

There are many things of much importance, on which you ask counsel, but which I think you will be perfectly able to decide upon, as you are more conversant with the peculiar circumstances than I am; and I feel great confidence in your united wisdom; therefore you will excuse me for not entering into detail. If I should see anything that is wrong, I would take the privilege of making known my mind to you, and pointing out the evil.

If Elder Parley P. Pratt should wish to remain in England some time longer than the rest of the Twelve, he will feel himself at liberty to do so, as his family are with him, consequently his circumstances are somewhat different from the rest; and likewise it is necessary that someone should remain who is conversant with the rules and regulations of the Church, and continue the paper which is published. Consequently, taking all these things into consideration, I would not press it upon Brother Pratt to return in the spring.

I am happy to inform you that we are prospering in this place, and that the Saints are more healthy than formerly; and from the decrease of sickness this season, when compared with the last, I am led to the conclusion that this must eventually become a healthy place. There are at present about 3,000 inhabitants in Nauvoo, and numbers are flocking in daily. Several stakes have been set off in different parts of the country, which are in prosperous circumstances.

Provisions are much lower than when you left. Flour is about $4 per barrel. Corn and potatoes about 25 cents per bushel; and other things in proportion. There has been a very plentiful harvest throughout the Union.

You will observe, by the *Times and Seasons*, that we are about building a temple for the worship of our God in this place. Preparations are now making; every tenth day is devoted by the brethren for quarrying rock, &c. We have secured one of the most lovely situations for it in this region of country. It is expected to be considerably larger than the one in Kirtland, and on a more magnificent scale, and which will undoubtedly attract the attention of the great men of the earth.

We have a bill before the legislature for the incorporation of the city of Nauvoo, and for the establishment of a seminary of learning, and other purposes—which I expect will pass in a short time.

You will also receive intelligence of the death of my father; which event, although painful to the family and to the Church generally, yet the sealing testimony of the truth of the work of the Lord was indeed satisfactory. Brother Hyrum succeeds him as Patriarch of the Church, according to his last directions and benedictions.*

* The last "directions and benedictions" of the Patriarch Joseph Smith, Sen., here referred to, are stated by "Mother Lucy Smith" in her book, "History of the Prophet Joseph," as follows:

"My son Hyrum, I seal upon your head your patriarchal blessing, which I placed upon your head before, for that shall be verified. In addition to this, I now give you my dying blessing. You shall have a season of peace, so that you shall have

Several persons of eminence and distinction in society have joined the Church and become obedient to the faith; and I am happy to inform you that the work is spreading very fast upon this continent. Some of the brethren are now in New Orleans, and we expect a large gathering from the south. I have had the pleasure of welcoming about one hundred brethren who came with Brother Turley; the remainder I am informed stayed in Kirtland, not having means to get any further. I think that those who came here this fall, did not take the best possible route, or the least expensive. Most of the brethren have obtained employment of one kind or another, and appear tolerably well contented, and seem disposed to hearken to counsel.

Brothers Robinson and Smith lately had a letter from Elders Kimball, Smith and Woodruff, which gave us information of the commencement of the work of the Lord in the city of London, which I was glad to hear. I am likewise informed that Elders have gone to Australia and to the East Indies. I feel desirous that every providential opening of the kind should be filled, and that you should, prior to your leaving England, send the Gospel into as many parts as you possibly can.

Beloved brethren, you must be aware in some measure of my feelings, when I contemplate the great work which is now rolling on, and the relationship which I sustain to it, while it is extending to distant lands, and thousands are embracing it. I realize in some measure my responsibility, and the need I have of support from above, and wisdom from on high, that I may be able to teach this people, which have now become a great people, the principles of righteousness, and lead them agreeably to the will of Heaven; so that they may be perfected, and prepared to meet the Lord Jesus Christ when He shall appear in great glory. Can I rely on your prayers to our heavenly Father on my behalf, and on all the prayers of all my brethren and sisters in England, (whom having not seen, yet I love), that I may be enabled to escape every stratagem of Satan, surmount every difficulty, and bring this people to the enjoyment of those blessings which are reserved for the righteous? I ask this at your hands in the name of the Lord Jesus Christ.

Let the Saints remember that great things depend on their individual exertion, and that they are called to be co-workers with us and the Holy Spirit in accomplishing the great work of the last days; and in consideration of the extent, the blessings and glories of the same, let

sufficient rest to accomplish the work which God has given you to do. You shall be as firm as the pillars of heaven unto the end of your days. I now seal upon your head the patriarchal power, and you shall bless the people. This is my dying blessing upon your head in the name of Jesus. Amen."—*History of the Prophet Joseph Smith*, p. 266.

every selfish feeling be not only buried, but annihilated; and let love to God and man predominate, and reign triumphant in every mind, that their hearts may become like unto Enoch's of old, and comprehend all things, present, past and future, and come behind in no gift, waiting for the coming of the Lord Jesus Christ.

The work in which we are unitedly engaged is one of no ordinary kind. The enemies we have to contend against are subtle and well skilled in manœuvering; it behooves us to be on the alert to concentrate our energies, and that the best feelings should exist in our midst; and then, by the help of the Almight, we shall go on from victory to victory, and from conquest to conquest; our evil passions will be subdued, our prejudices depart; we shall find no room in our bosoms for hatred; vice will hide its deformed head, and we shall stand approved in the sight of heaven, and be acknowledged the sons of God.

Let us realize that we are not to live to ourselves, but to God; by so doing the greatest blessings will rest upon us both in time and in eternity.

I presume the doctrine of "baptism for the dead" has ere this reached your ears, and may have raised some inquiries in your minds respecting the same. I cannot in this letter give you all the information you may desire on the subject; but aside from knowledge independent of the Bible, I would say that it was certainly practiced by the ancient churches; and St. Paul endeavors to prove the doctrine of the resurrection from the same, and says, "Else what shall they do which are baptized for the dead, if the dead rise not at all? Why are they then baptized for the dead?"

I first mentioned the doctrine in public when preaching the funeral sermon of Brother Seymour Brunson; and have since then given general instructions in the Church on the subject. The Saints have the privilege of being baptized for those of their relatives who are dead, whom they believe would have embraced the Gospel, if they had been privileged with hearing it, and who have received the Gospel in the spirt, through the instrumentality of those who have been commissioned to preach to them while in prison.

Without enlarging on the subject, you will undoubtedly see its consistency and reasonableness; and it presents the Gospel of Christ in probably a more enlarged scale than some have imagined it. But as the performance of this rite is more particularly confined to this place, it will not be necessary to enter into particulars; at the same time I always feel glad to give all the information in my power, but my space will not allow me to do it.

We had a letter from Elder Hyde, a few days ago, who is in New Jersey, and is expecting to leave for England as soon as Elder Page reaches him. He requested to know if converted Jews are to go to Jerusalem or to come to Zion. I therefore wish you to inform him that converted Jews must come here.

Give my kind love to all the brethren and sisters, and tell them I should have been pleased to come over to England to see them, but I am afraid that I shall be under the necessity of remaining here for some time; therefore I give them a pressing invitation to come and see me.

I remain, dear brethren, yours affectionately,

JOSEPH SMITH.

CHAPTER XIII.

INTRODUCTION OF THE GOSPEL IN THE ISLE OF MAN—THE
NAUVOO CHARTER.

Wednesday, October 21, 1840.—Elder Lorenzo Snow
arrived in Manchester, England, from Nauvoo.

Thursday, 22.—The committee appointed by the general conference of the Church at Nauvoo on the 3rd inst.,
(my brother Hyrum presiding) organized a Stake at Lima
this evening, by appointing Isaac Morley, president;
John Murdock and Walter Cox, his counselors; also a
Bishop's Court composed of Gardner Snow, Clark Hulet
and Henry Dean, with James C. Snow, clerk.

Friday, 23.—Gardner Snow was ordained Bishop
under the hands of Hyrum Smith.

Sunday, 25.—The committee organized a Stake at
Quincy. The presidency were Daniel Stanton, Stephen
Jones and Ezra T. Benson; the latter was ordained a
High Priest; also bishop and counselors, George W.
Crouse, Azariah Dustin, and Sylvester B. Stoddard.

Tuesday, 27.—The committee organized a Stake called
Mount Hope, at the steam mills, Columbus, Adams
county. President and counselors were Abel Lamb, Sherman Gilbert and John Smith. Bishop and counselors,
were Daniel A. Miller, Isaac Clark, and John Allen; Simeon J. Comfort, clerk.

At Freedom Stake, near Payson, Adams county, Henry
W. Miller, Duncan McArthur, and William Tenney were
appointed to preside. Bishop and counselors, Matthew
Leach, Horra Kimball, and Jacob Foutz.

Wednesday 28.—[On this date a long communication

was sent to the editors of the *Times and Seasons* signed by Heber C. Kimball, Wilford Woodruff and George A. Smith, detailing their visit to various places in London, but as the communication does not in any way bear upon the incidents of the history of the Church, it is thought unnecessary to publish the letter *in extenso*. The following paragraph from the letter, however, it is thought should be preserved, because it refers to the liberty the Elders of the Church incidentally enjoyed while engaged in the ministry; and also because it breathes that spirit of liberty in the pursuit of knowledge characteristic of the work of God in the last days.—EDITORS.]

We consider it perfectly consistent with our calling, with reason and revelation that we should form a knowledge of kingdoms and countries whether at home or abroad, whether ancient or modern, whether of things past or present or to come; whether it be in heaven, earth or hell, air or seas; or whether we obtain this knowledge by being local or traveling, by study or by faith, by dreams or by visions, by revelation or by prophecy, it mattereth not unto us; if we can but obtain a correct [view of] principles, and knowledge of things as they are, in their true light, past, present and to come. It is under such a view of things that we are endeavoring to avail ourselves of every opportunity in our travels among the nations of the earth, to record an account of things as they pass under our observation.

Thursday, 29.—Elder Woodruff preached twice in London, and baptized three.

Friday, 30.—Elder Lorenzo Snow had a discussion with Mr. Barker, a Methodist minister, at Hill Top, near Birmingham, and baptized two.

Sunday, 31.—I copy the following from the *Manx Liberal* of this date:

MORMONISM IN THE ISLE OF MAN.

To the Editor of the Manx Liberal:

SIR—I feel rather surprised and chagrined that the modern delusion, viz., "Mormonism," should have made such rapid strides in this town, hitherto considered exempt from the many systems of irreligious creeds which abound in England, America, and elsewhere. I had thought that the powerful and argumentative addresses of the dissenting ministers would have checked such a gross piece of imposition in its infancy, and thus prevented the great mass of our town's people from becoming dupes of designing knaves, "and being led away by every wind of doctrine." Above all, I imagined the two pamphlets issued by that holy, religious and devout man of God, Mr. Hays, Wesleyan minister, (to which connection I have the happiness and honor to belong) would have been quite sufficient to prove the fallacy of such a system, and prevent its further spread. But, sir, alas! alas! the case is quite the reverse; numbers continually flock to the Wellington room, and listen with eagerness to the principles there advocated. The members of our society (Methodists) seem to be most conspicuous in sanctioning and promoting this vile and abominable doctrine.

Oh, sir, the result to our connection will be dreadful! the havoc tremendous; just think of the majority of our *leading* and intelligent men aiding and abetting a cause of this description! Oh, sir, lament-able and heart-rending to witness the beaming countenances, and smiles of approbation displayed recently at Taylor's meeting! I could enumer-ate a host of our members who regularly attend those anti-Christian meetings; but I will just mention, with your permission, the names of a few who attended one of the last meetings.   (Here followed a list of names.)

O! Mr. Editor! I quake for the consequence; such a wholesale con-version to Mormonism was never before witnessed in any town or coun-try. What will become of our society? What will become of our class meetings? What will become of our brethren in the faith? And above all, what will become of poor Mr. Hays* that nice and humble man, who so nobly stood forward to expose the errors of the Mormon system; God bless him and preserve him from want! But, Mr. Editor, what makes the case worse is, that a rumor is prevalent that all these pious men are to be baptized! That is duly immersed in the salt water of Douglas Bay, by that abominable creature, Taylor! Surely, there must be something enchanting about the vile man. Immersion! (my hand shakes while I write) and in winter, too! Oh, sir! the thought chills my very soul; surely this American dipper intends to drown them; he can have no other object in view, therefore, brethren of the Meth-odist society, beware! Drowning is not to be envied, and that too in your sins. Besides, what would the venerable John Wesley, (if he

* Elder Taylor was also opposed by Rev. Thomas Hamilton, whom he met in a public debate and easily vanquished. "No great honor, however," says Elder Taylor in his account of the affair, "as he was a very ignorant man." Elder Tay-lor secured for his meeting place the Wellington rooms, and from the platform he answered all who opposed him, and succeeded. despite all opposition, in organ-zing a branch of the Church in Douglas.

were alive) say to such conduct? What will the conference say? And what will the world say? I leave these questions to yourselves to answer. In conclusion, brethren, I recommend you to read, mark, learn and inwardly digest the things which belong to your eternal peace, and listen no longer to the follies of men.

A STAUNCH WESLEYAN.

Duke Street, Douglas, 29th Oct.

Sunday, November 1, 1840.—The committee organized a Stake, Geneva, Morgan county, Illinois, and called it Geneva Stake; presidents—William Bosley, Howard S. Smith, and Samuel Fowler. Bishop's Court—Gardner Clark, Moses Clare, and David Orton.

Elder Levi Richards arrived in Manchester.

Tuesday, 3.—The English bombarded St. Jean D'Acre, during which a powder magazine exploded, killing over two thousand men.

Thursday, 5.—The committee organized a Stake of the Church at Springfield; presidents—Edwin P. Merriam, Isaac H. Bishop, and Arnold Stephens. Bishop's Court Abraham Palmer, Henry Stephens, and Jonathan Palmer.

Monday, 9.—Elder George A. Smith received counsel to leave London and go to Staffordshire for his health, as he had injured his lungs by preaching in the streets, so that he discharged considerable blood from them.

Tuesday, 10.—Elder Smith took leave of Elder Woodruff and traveled to Birmingham, met Elder Alfred Cordon, preached and baptized five in the evening.

Thursday, 12.—The *Weekly Dispatch*, England, having published a sarcastic article against the Saints in that country, and blaming the Bishop of Gloucester, and his tithe-fattened clergy for allowing the "Mormons" to delude and baptize five hundred in his Diocese, Elder Wilford Woodruff replied to this, but the *Dispatch* refused to publish his reply.

Opposition to the Work in England.

Saturday, 21.—Elders Young, Kimball and Richards, visited the Church at Bolton.

Thursday, 26.—Elders Brigham Young, Heber C. Kimball, and George A. Smith preached to the Saints in Hanley this day, and on the 27th at Stoke-upon-Trent.

Saturday, 28.—Elders Young and Kimball left for London.

Elders Elias Higbee and Robert B. Thompson, the committee appointed at the October Conference, wrote a petition to Congress for the redress of the grievances of the Latter-day Saints in Missouri, setting forth their wrongs and sufferings, in substance the same as my petition in connection with Elias Higbee and Sidney Rigdon, of the 28th day of November, 1839.

Thursday, December 3.—Elders Young, Kimball and Wooodruff visited the tower of London, the Horse Armory, Jewel Room and the Thames Tunnel.

Friday, 4.—Elders Young and Woodruff visited Buckingham Palace and Westminster Abbey.

There was a conference in New York City, Elder Orson Hyde presiding. The revelations of Elder Sidney Roberts were objected to, which were that a certain brother must give him a suit of clothes, and a gold watch, the best that could be had, also his saluting the sisters with what he calls a holy kiss. Elder Roberts justified himself in these things. Much good counsel was given him, but he said he knew the revelations he had received were from God, and would make no confession; consequently the conference cut him off, and demanded his license, which he refused to give up.

Excommuni-
cation of Sid-
ney Roberts.

Elder John Taylor has been preaching and baptizing for some time in the Isle of Man, where the work is now progressing.

Saturday, 5.—Elder Brigham Young writes as follows:

Letter of Brigham Young to the Presidency, Detailing Movements of the Mission in England.

NO. 40, IRONMONGER ROW, ST. LUKE'S, December 5th, 1840.

BELOVED BRETHREN—I have just returned from a walk with Brothers Kimball and Woodruff. We have only been as far as St. Paul's and

returned by Smithfield Market about three miles. Brother Kimball and
myself had fine weather for our journey here; it was a beautiful day
that we left Macclesfield for Burslem. We found the brethren in Macclesfield in good spirits, and in a good state as to appearance. They
appear to be well suited with Brother James Galley; I think he will be a
useful man in this kingdom. We found Brother George A. Smith in
Burslem, not in the best of health. He is like the rest of us, the climate
does not agree with him; he is affected with a bleeding at the lungs.
We stayed with him at the Potteries. I preached two evenings. The
Church is in a good state; some of the members have a pretty hard time
of it. Brother Smith will stay there for the present.

Saturday, 28th, left for the next stopping place in Grets Green,
where we spent the Sabbath. On Saturday evening we called to see
Sister Roden, Father Patrick's daughter; she was very glad to see us,
and wanted we should stay all night. Her husband was very kind to
us, and bid us or other Elders welcome to his house at any time. We
could not stay; took tea with them, and agreed to send Elder Lorenzo
Snow there if he could come; blessed them, and left them. I preached
in the morning to the Saints in Grets Green, stayed afternoon meeting,
and then walked to Birmingham; was very tired; heard Elder Snow
preach; he is a nice young man, I think. Brother Kimball also spoke
to the people after Brother Snow had got through. We found Brother
Robert Williams here; he opened the meeting; he seems to be full of
the Spirit.

On Monday at 12 o'clock, Brother Kimball and myself took the railway. Brother Williams started on foot for London. We arrived here on
Monday evening about six o'clock; found Brother Woodruff well and in
good spirits. We have been pretty busy since we have been here.

                                                    BRIGHAM YOUNG.

A great part of the city of Messina, Sicily, was this day
destroyed by an earthquake. Such was the force of the
first shock that the inhabitants of the town were buried in
an instant beneath the ruins.

Sunday, 6.—Elders Young and Kimball preached in
Barratt's Academy, London, and administered the sacrament in the evening.

Monday, 7.—Elder John Taylor issued his third
pamphlet in defense of the truth, against the attacks of
the Rev. Robert Hays, Wesleyan Minister,
Douglas, Isle of Man; the three containing
thirty-five pages of closely printed matter,

Elder Tay-
lor's Defense
of the Work.

which are a complete expose of the corruptions of the Wesleyan priesthood, and a clear illustration of the truth of the Latter-day work.

Elders Brigham Young, Heber C. Kimball, and Wilford Woodruff, visited the Anatomical Department of the College of Surgeons, London.

Wednesday, 9.—Elders Young and Kimball visited St. Paul's Cathedral, the Monument, London and Southwark Bridges and also the British Museum.

Thursday, 10.—Elder Levi Richards left Manchester for Herefordshire.

Sunday, 13.—I attended the High Council at my office. Robert D. Foster was on trial for lying, slandering the authorities of the Church, profane swearing, etc. Witness was examined in part and trial adjourned to the 20th.

Monday, 14.—Ebenezer Robinson and Don Carlos Smith dissolved co-partnership. The *Times and Seasons* is to be continued by Don Carlos Smith.

Wednesday, 16.—This day the act chartering the "City of Nauvoo," the "Nauvoo Legion," and the "University of the City of Nauvoo," was signed by the Governor, having previously passed the House and Senate. Following is the act *in extenso*.

AN ACT TO INCORPORATE THE CITY OF NAUVOO.

Section 1. Be it enacted by the people of the State of Illinois, represented in the General Assembly, that all that district of country embraced within the following boundaries, to wit: beginning at the north east corner of section thirty-one in Township seven, north of range eight, west of the fourth principal meridian, in the county of Hancock, and running thence west to the northwest corner of said section, thence north to the Mississippi river, thence west to the middle of the main channel of the said river; thence down the middle of said channel to a point due west of the southeast corner of fractional section number twelve in township six, north of range nine, west of the fourth principal meridian, thence east to the southeast corner of said section twelve, thence north on the range line between township six north, and range eight and nine west, to the southwest corner of section six in township six north of range eight west, thence east to the southeast corner of said section, thence north to the place of beginning, including the town plats of Commerce and Nauvoo, shall hereafter be called and known by the name of the "City of Nauvoo," and the inhabitants thereof are hereby constituted a body corporate and politic by the name aforesaid, and shall have perpetual succession, and may have and use a common seal which they may change and alter at pleasure.

Sec. 2. Whenever any tract of land adjoining the "City of Nauvoo" shall have been laid out into town lots, and duly recorded according to law, the same shall form a part of the "City of Nauvoo."

Sec. 3. The inhabitants of said city, by the name and style aforesaid, shall have power to sue and be sued, to plead and be impleaded, defend and be defended, in all courts of law and equity, and all actions whatsoever; to purchase, receive and hold property, real and personal, in said city, to purchase, receive, and hold real property beyond the city, for burying grounds, or for other public purposes, for the use of the inhabitants of said city, to sell, lease, convey or dispose of property, real or personal, for the benefit of the city, to improve and protect such property, and to do all other things in relation thereto as natural persons.

Sec. 4. There shall be a City Council, to consist of a Mayor, four Aldermen, and nine Councillors, who shall have the qualifications of electors of said city, and shall be chosen by the qualified voters thereof, and shall hold their offices for two years, and until their successors shall be elected and qualified. The City Council shall judge of the qualifications, elections and returns of their own members, and a majority of them shall form a quorum to do business, but a smaller number may adjourn from day to day, and compel the attendance of absent members, under such penalties as may be prescribed by ordinance.

Sec. 5. The Mayor, Aldermen and Councillors, before entering upon the duties of their office, shall take and subscribe an oath or affirmation that they will support the Constitution of the United States, and of this State and that they will well and truly perform the duties of their offices to the best of their skill and abilities.

Sec. 6. On the first Monday of February next, and every two years thereafter, an election shall be held for the election of one Mayor, four Aldermen, and nine Councillors; and at the first election under the Act, three Judges shall be chosen *viva voce* by the electors present. The said Judges shall choose two Clerks, and the Judges and Clerks, before entering upon their duties, shall take and subscribe an oath or affirmation such as is now required by law to be taken by Judges or Clerks of other elections; and at all subsequent elections, the necessary number of Judges and Clerks shall be appointed by the City Council. At the first election thus held, the polls shall be opened at 9 o'clock a. m. and closed at 6 o'clock p. m.,; at the close of the polls the votes shall be counted and a statement thereof proclaimed at the front door of the house at which said election shall be held; and the Clerks shall leave with each person elected, or at his place of residence, within five days after the election, a written notice of his election; and each person so notified shall within ten days after the election take the oath or affirmation hereinbefore mentioned, a certificate of which oath shall be deposited with the Recorder, whose appointment is hereafter provided for, and be by him preserved; and subsequent elections shall be held, conducted and returns thereof made as may be provided for by ordinance of the City Council.

Sec. 7. All free white male inhabitans, who are of the age of twenty one years, who are entitled to vote for State Officers, and who shall have been actual residents of the city sixty days next preceding said election, shall be entitled to vote for City Officers.

Sec. 8. The City Council shall have authority to levy and collect taxes, for city purposes, upon all property, real and personal, within the limits of the city, one-half per cent per annum, upon the assessed value thereof, and may enforce payment of the same in any manner, to be provided by ordinance, not repugnant to the Constitution of the United States or of this State.

Sec. 9. The City Council shall have power to appoint a Recorder, Treasurer, Assessor, Marshal, Supervisor of streets, and all such other officers as may be necessary, and to prescribe their duties and remove them from office at pleasure.

Sec. 10. The City Council shall have power to require, of all officers appointed in pursuance of this Act, bonds, with penalty and security, for the faithful performance of their respective duties, such as may be deemed expedient; and also to require all officers appointed as aforesaid, to take an oath for the faithful performance of the duties of their respective offices.

Sec. 11. The City Council shall have power and authority to make, ordain, establish and execute all such ordinances, not repugnant to the Constitution of the United States or of this State, as they may deem necessary for the peace, benefit, good order, regulation, convenience, and cleanliness of said city: for the protection of property therein from destruction by fire, or otherwise, and for the health and happiness thereof: they shall have power to fill all vacancies that may happen by death, resignation, or removal, in any of the offices herein made elective; to fix and establish all the fees of the office of said corporation not herein established; to impose such fines, not exceeding one hundred dollars, for each offense, as they may deem just, for refusing to accept any office under the corporation, or for misconduct therein; to divide the city into wards; to add to the number of Aldermen and Councillors, and apportion them among the several wards as may be most just and conducive to the interests of the city.

Sec. 12. To license, tax, and regulate auctions, merchants, retailers, grocers, hawkers, peddlers, butchers, pawnbrokers, and money-changers.

Sec. 13. The City Council shall have exclusive power within the city, by ordinance, to license, regulate, and restrain the keeping of ferries; to regulate the police of the city; to impose fines, forfeitures, and penalties for the breach of any ordinance, and provide for the recovery of such fines and forfeitures, and the enforcement of such penalties; and to pass such ordinances, as may be necessary and proper for carrying into execution the powers specified in this Act; provided such ordinances are not repugnant to the Constitution of the United States or of this State, and in fine to exercise such other legislative powers as are conferred on the City Council of the City of Springfield, by an Act entitled an Act to Incorporate the City of Springfield, approved February 3rd, 1840.

Sec. 14. All ordinances passed by the City Council shall, within one month after they shall have been passed, be published in some newspaper printed in the city, or certified copies thereof be posted up in three of the most public places in the city.

Sec. 15. All ordinances of the city may be proven by the seal of the corporation, and when printed or published in book or pamphlet form, purporting to be printed or published by authority of the corporation, the same shall be received in evidence in all courts or places without further proof.

Sec. 16. The Mayor and Aldermen shall be conservators of the peace within the limits of said city, and shall have all the powers of Justices of the Peace therein, both in civil and criminal cases, arising under the laws of the State; they shall, as Justices of the Peace, within the limits of said city, perform the same duties, be governed by the same laws, give the same bonds and security, as other Justices of the Peace, and be commissioned as Justices of the Peace in and for said city by the Governor.

Sec. 17. The Mayor shall have exclusive jurisdiction in all cases arising under the ordinances of the corporation, and shall issue such process as may be necessary to carry such ordinances into execution and effect; appeals may be had from any decision or judgment of said Mayor or Aldermen, arising under the city ordinances, to the Municipal Court, under such regulations as may be presented by ordinance; which court shall be composed of the Mayor as Chief Justice, and the Aldermen as Associate Justices, and from the final judgment of the Municipal Court to the Circuit Court of Hancock county, in the same manner of appeals are taken from judgments of the Justices of the Peace; provided that the parties litigant shall have a right to a trial by a jury of twelve men in all cases before the Municipal Court. The Municipal Court shall have power to grant writs of habeas corpus in all cases arising under the ordinances of the City Council.

Sec. 18. The Municipal Court shall sit on the first Monday of every month, and the City Council at such times and place as may be prescribed by city ordinance; special meetings of which may at any time be called by the Mayor or any two Aldermen.

Sec. 19. All process issued by the Mayor, Aldermen, or Municipal Court, shall be directed to the Marshal, and, in the execution thereof, he shall be governed by the same laws as are or may be prescribed for the direction and compensation of constables in similar cases. The Marshal shall also perform such other duties as may be required of him under the ordinances of said city, and shall be the principal ministerial officer.

Sec. 20. It shall be the duty of the Recorder to make and keep accurate records of all ordinances made by the City Council, and of all their proceedings in their corporate capacity, which record shall at all times be open to the inspection of the electors of said city, and shall perform such other duties as may be required of him by the ordinances of the City Council, and shall serve as Clerk of the Municipal Court.

Sec 21. When it shall be necessary to take private property for the opening, widening, or altering any public street, lane, avenue, or alley, the corporation shall make a just compensation therefor to the person whose property is to be taken, and if the amount of such compensation cannot be agreed upon, the Mayor shall cause the same to be ascertained by a jury of six disinterested freeholders of the city.

Sec. 22. All jurors compelled to inquire into the amount of benefits or damages that shall happen to the owners of property so proposed to be taken, shall first be sworn to that effect, and shall return to the Mayor their inquest in writing, signed by each juror.

Sec. 23. In case the Mayor shall at any time be guilty of a palpable omission of duty, or shall wilfully, and corruptly be guilty of oppression, mal conduct, or partiality, in the discharge of the duties of his office, he shall be liable to be indicted in the Circuit Court of Hancock county, and on conviction he shall be fined not more than two hundred dollars, and the Court shall have power on the recommendation of the jury to add to the judgment of the Court that he be removed from office.

Sec. 24. The City Council may establish and organize an institution of learning within the limits of the city, for the teaching of the Arts, Sciences, and Learned Professions, to be called the "University of the City of Nauvoo," which institution shall be under the control and management of a Board of Trustees, consisting of a Chancellor, Registrar, and twenty-three Regents, which Board shall thereafter be a body corporate and politic, with perpetual succession by the name of the "Chancellor and Regents of the University of the City of Nauvoo," and shall have full power to pass, ordain, establish, and execute, all such laws and ordinances as they may consider necessary for the welfare and prosperity of said University, its officers and students; provided that the said laws and ordinances shall not be repugnant to the Constitution of the United States, or of this State; and provided also, that the Trustees shall at all times be appointed by the City Council, and shall have all the powers and privileges for the advancement of the cause of education which appertain to the Trustees of any other College or University of this State.

Sec. 25. The City Council may organize the inhabitants of said city, subject to military duty, into a body of independent military men, to be called the "Nauvoo Legion," the Court Martial of which shall be composed of the commissioned officers of said Legion, and constitute the law-making department, with full power and authority to make, ordain, establish, and execute all such laws and ordinances as may be considered necessary for the benefit, government, and regulation of said Legion; provided said Court Martial shall pass no law or act, repugnant to, or inconsistent with, the Constitution of the United States, or of this State; and provided also that the officers of the Legion shall be commissioned by the Governor of the State. The said Legion shall perform the same amount of military duty as is now or may be hereafter required of the regular militia of the State, and shall be at the disposal of the Mayor in executing the laws and ordinances of the city corporation, and the laws of the State, and at the disposal of the Governor for the public defense, and the execution of the laws of the State or of the United States, and shall be entitled to their proportion of the public arms; and provided also, that said Legion shall be exempt from all other military duty.

Sec. 26. The inhabitants of the city of Nauvoo are hereby exempted from working on any road beyond the limits of the city, and for the purpose of keeping the streets, lanes, avenues, and alleys in repair, to require of the male inhabitants of said city, over the age of twenty-one, and under fifty years, to labor on said streets, lanes, avenues, and alleys, not exceeding three days in each year; any person failing to perform such labor, when duly notified by the Supervisor, shall forfeit and pay the sum of one dollar per day for each day so neglected or refused.

Sec. 27. The City Council shall have power to provide for the punishment of offenders by imprisonment in the county or city jail, in all cases when such offenders shall fail or refuse to pay the fines and forfeitures, which may be recovered against them.

Sec. 28.   This Act is hereby declared to be a public Act, and shall take effect on the first Monday of February next.

Wm. L. D. Ewing,

Speaker of the House of Representatives.

S. H. Anderson,

Speaker of the Senate.

Approved Dec. 16, 1840.

Thos. Carlin.

State of Illinois, Office of Secretary of State.

I, Stephen A. Douglas, Secretary of State, do hereby certify that the foregoing is a true and perfect copy of the enrolled law now on file in my office.

Witness my hand, and Seal of State, at Springfield, this 18th day of December, 1840.

[L. S.]

S. A. Douglas.

Secretary of State.

The following are the Legislative powers alluded to in the 13th section of the foregoing Act, as pertaining to the City Council of the City of Springfield, and which consequently became a part of the Charter of the City of Nauvoo, to wit:

OF THE LEGISLATIVE POWERS OF THE CITY COUNCIL.

Sec. 1.   The City Council shall have powers and authority to levy and collect taxes upon all property, real and personal, within the city, not exceeding one-half per cent., per annum, upon the assessed valuation thereof, and may enforce the payment of the same in any manner prescribed by ordinance, not repugnant to the Constitution of the United States and of this State.

Sec. 2.   The City Council shall have power to require of all officers appointed in pursuance of the Charters, bonds with penalty and security for the faithful performance of their respective duties as may be deemed expedient, and also to require all officers appointed as aforesaid, to take an oath for the faithful performance of the duties of their respective offices upon entering upon the discharge of the same.

Sec. 3.   To establish, support, and regulate common schools, to borrow money on the credit of the city: provided, that no sum or sums of money shall be borrowed at a greater interest than six per cent per annum, nor shall the interest on the aggregate of all the sums borrowed and outstanding ever exceed one half of the city revenue, arising for taxes assessed on real property within the corporation.

Sec. 4.　To make regulations to prevent the introduction of contagious diseases into the city, to make Quarantine Laws for that purpose, and enforce the same.

Sec. 5.　To appropriate and provide for the payment of the debt and expenses of the city.

Sec. 6.　To establish hospitals, and make regulations for the government of the same.

Sec. 7.　To make regulations to secure the general health of the inhabitants, to declare what shall be a nuisance, and to prevent and remove the same.

Sec. 8.　To provide the city with water, to dig wells and erect pumps in the streets for the extinguishment of fires, and convenience of the inhabitants.

Sec. 9.　To open, alter, widen, extend, establish, grade, pave, or otherwise improve and keep in repair streets, avenues, lanes, and alleys.

Sec. 10.　To establish, erect, and keep in repair bridges.

Sec. 11.　To divide the city into wards, and specify the boundaries thereof, and create additional wards, as the occasion may require.

Sec. 12.　To provide for lighting the streets and erecting lamp posts.

Sec. 13.　To establish, support, and regulate night watches.

Sec. 14.　To erect market houses, establish markets, and market places, and provide for the government and regulation thereof.

Sec. 15.　To provide for erecting all needful buildings for the use of the city.

Sec. 16.　To provide for enclosing, improving, and regulating all public grounds belonging to the city.

Sec. 17.　To license, tax, and regulate auctioneers, merchants, and retailers, grocers, taverns ordinaries, hawkers, peddlers, brokers, pawnbrokers, and money changers.

Sec. 18.　To license, tax, and regulate hackney carriages, wagons, carts and drays, and fix the rates to be charged for the carriage of persons, and for the wagonage, cartage and drayage of property.

Sec. 19.　To license and regulate porters and fix the rates of porterage.

Sec. 20.　To license and regulate theatrical and other exhibitions, shows and amusements.

Sec. 21.　To tax, restrain, prohibit, and suppress, tippling houses, dram shops, gaming houses, bawdy and other disorderly houses.

Sec. 22.　To provide for the prevention and extinguishment of fires, and to organize and establish fire companies.

Sec. 23.　To regulate the fixing of chimneys, and the flues thereof, and stove pipes.

Sec. 24.   To regulate the storage of gunpowder, tar, pitch, rosin, and other combustible materials.

Sec. 25.   To regulate and order parapet walls, and partition fences.

Sec. 26.   To establish standard weights and measures, and regulate the weights and measures to be used in the city in all other cases not provided for by law.

Sec. 27.   To provide for the inspection and measuring of lumber and other building materials, and for the measurement of all kinds of mechanical work.

Sec. 28.   To provide for the inspection and weighing of hay, lime, and stone coal, the measuring of charcoal, firewood, and other fuel, to be sold or used within the city.

Sec. 29.   To provide for and regulate the inspection of tobacco, and of beef, pork, flour, meal, and whiskey in barrels.

Sec. 30.   To regulate the weight, quality, and price of bread, sold, and used in the city.

Sec. 31.   To provide for taking the enumeration of the inhabitants of the city.

Sec. 32.   To regulate the election of city officers, and provide for removing from office any person holding an office created by ordinance.

Sec. 33.   To fix the compensation of all city officers, and regulate the fees of jurors, witnesses, and others, for services rendered under this Act or any ordinance.

Sec. 34.   To regulate the police of the city, to impose fines, and forfeitures, and penalties, for the breach of any ordinance, and provide for the recovery and appropriation of such fines and forfeitures, and the enforcement of such penalties.

Sec. 35.   The City Council shall have exclusive power within the city by ordinance, to license, regulate, and suppress, and restrain, billiard tables, and from one to twenty pin alleys, and every other description of gaming or gambling.

Sec. 36.   The City Council shall have power to make all ordinances which shall be necessary and proper for carrying into execution the powers specified in this Act, so that such ordinances be not repugnant to nor inconsistent with, the constitution of the United States or of this state

Sec. 37.   The style of the ordinances of the city shall be—"Be it ordained by the city council of the city of Springfield—[Nauvoo]."

Sec. 38.   All ordinances passed by the city council shall, within one month after they shall have been passed, be published in some newspaper published in the city, and shall not be in force until they shall have been published as aforesaid.

Sec. 39.   All ordinances of the city may be proven by the seal of the corporation, and when printed and published by authority of the corporation, the same shall be received in evidence in all courts and places without fourther proof.

John C. Bennett who had been delegated to Springfield to carry our petition for a City Charter, announced the passage of the bill, as follows—

Letter of John C. Bennett to the "Times and Seasons"—Announcing the passage of the act incorporating Nauvoo.

CITY OF SPRINGFIELD, December 16, 1840.

Editors of the Times and Seasons:

The act incorporating the city of Nauvoo has just passed the council of revision, and is now a law of the land, to take effect and be in force from and after the first Monday in February next. The aforesaid act contains two additional charters—one incorporating the "Nauvoo Legion," the other the "University of the city of Nauvoo."

All these charters are very broad and liberal, conferring the most plenary powers on the corporators. Illinois has acquitted herself with honor, and her state legislators shall never be forgotten. Every power we asked has been granted, every request gratified, every desire fulfilled. In the senate Mr. Little cancelled every obligation to our people, and faithfully, and honestly, and with untiring diligence, discharged every obligation devolving upon him as our immediate representative in the Upper House. Mark well that man, and do him honor. Snyder, and Ralston, and Moore, and Ross, and Stapp, and numerous others, likewise in that branch of our state government, rendered us very essential services; and the act passed that body without a dissenting voice.

In the House of Representatives, Charles, our immediate Representative in the Lower House, was at his post and discharged his duty as a faithful representative; he is an acting, and not a talking man, and has fulfilled all his obligations to us. Many members in this house, likewise, were warmly in our favor; and with only one or two dissenting voices, every representative appeared inclined to extend to us all such powers as they considered us justly entitled to, and voted for the law; and here I should not forget to mention, that Lincoln,* whose name we erased from the electoral ticket in November (not however on account of any dislike to him as a man, but simply because his was the last name on the ticket, and we desired to show our friendship to the Democratic

* This doubtless refers to Abraham Lincoln who was then a member of the legislature. See Nicolay and Hay's *Abraham Lincoln*, Vol. I, p. 42 *et seq.*

party by substituting the name of Ralston for some one of the Whigs) had the magnanimity to vote for our act, and came forward, after the final vote to the bar of the house, and cordially congratulated me on its passage.

Our worthy governor is certainly disposed to do us ample justice in every respect, and to extend to us every facility for our future happiness and prosperity.

Illinois has certainly done her duty, and her whole duty; and now it becomes us to show ourselves upright, honest, just, worthy of the favors bestowed by noble, generous, and magnanimous statesmen, I have said that we are a law-abiding people, and we must now show it. The state has washed her hands in granting all our petitions, and if we do not now show ourselves approved, the curse must fall upon our own heads. Justice, equal justice, should be our fixed object and purpose, and the Great God will prosper us; length of days will be in our right hand, and in our left, glory and honor.

Yours, &c.,
JOHN C. BENNETT.

The City Charter of Nauvoo is of my own plan and device. I concocted it for the salvation of the Church, and on principles so broad, that every honest man might dwell secure under its protective influence without distinction of sect or party.

CHAPTER XIV.

VALE 1840—ENTER 1841—LIST OF PUBLICATIONS FOR AND
AGAINST THE CHURCH—WHEREABOUTS OF THE TWELVE
APOSTLES—"ELECTION AND REPROBATION"—PROCLAMA-
TION TO THE SAINTS.

Sunday, December 20, 1840.—I was called upon by the
High Council to decide the adjourned case of
Robert D. Foster. Having heard the witnesses, I decided that he be acquitted of the charges
against him, which decision the Council approved.*

The acquittal
of R. D. Fos-
ter.

This is a fair specimen of the wisdom of the nineteenth
century that opposes itself to the work of
the Most High God.

An Objector
Put Down.

"Your preacher preaches false doctrine," exclaimed a sectarian in
Manchester to one of the Saints. "Ah!" inquired the other, "wherein
does he teach false doctrine?" "Why, in telling the people to go to
America, to be sure," said the sectarian; "and" continued he, "there is
nothing in the Bible that commands people to go to America." "Ah!"
replied the other, "and there is nothing in the Bible that commands
people to stop in Manchester; so I wonder how you dare stay in so un-
scriptural a place another night; for certainly no one ought to live in
England unless they can find scripture for it, any more than in
America."

Monday, 21.—The petition of Elias Higbee, and Robert
B. Thompson, under date of 28th November, 1840, was
presented to the House of Representatives of the United

* For the nature of the charges see ch. xiii.

States, referred to the Committee on the Judiciary, and ordered to be printed.

Friday, 25.—Elders Brigham Young and George A. Smith attended a conference at Hanley, Staffordshire Potteries, at which was represented an increase of six Elders, twenty-six Priests, ten Teachers, nine deacons, and three hundred and fifty-six members, since last July Conference; and also ordained six Elders, six Priests, four Teachers, and three Deacons.

Sunday, 27.—Elders Kimball and Woodruff occupied a chapel belonging to the Independents in London.   Elder Woodruff preached.

Monday, 28.—There are ninety-five Saints in Edinburgh, Scotland, raised up by Elder Orson Pratt.   Elder George D. Watt is now laboring in that place.

Wednesday, 30.—Elder Brigham Young writes from Liverpool:

Brigham Young's Letter to the Prophet Reporting Labors in England.

Beloved Brother:—I write to inform you of a few particulars of my journey to London.   I left Manchester November 25th, in company with Elder Kimball; we visited the following places, viz., Macclesfield, Burslem, Hanley, Lane End, West Bromwich, and Birmingham.   We traveled by coach and railway, and arrived in London on Monday 30th: found Elder Woodruff in good health.   He had baptized three or four persons the day before we arrived.   I stayed in London till the 11th December, when I left for Herefordshire.   Brothers Woodruff and Williams came with me to the railway station.   Elder Kimball stayed in London.

The prospect for the spread of the Gospel brightened up while we were there.   Our feelings were very clear and decisive that Elder Kimball had better stay with Elder Woodruff.   I was much interested while there with my brethren.   I pray the Lord to roll on His work in that great city.   I feel much for the people in that place! yea my feelings are exquisite, for why, God knows; but I believe it is for the glory of God, and the good of souls.   May His name be glorified.

I arrived in Cheltenham the same day I left London—only about seven and a half hours going one hundred and one miles, thirty-eight of it by coach.   I stayed over the Sabbath there; preached twice to a very attentive congregation.   In the afternoon the house was full to overflowing. Elder Henry Glover is preaching in this place, and in the region around with much success. I think he is a humble, good man, and will do much good. I attended the Gadfield Elm conference. The minutes of the Garway conference were read, which had been held on the 8th. After this I visited the brethren till the Stanley Hill conference, which was held on the 21st. The church in Garway numbers ninety-five members, one Elder, seven Priests, three Teachers and one Deacon. At Gadfield Elm conference there were seventeen branches represented, three hundred and twenty-seven members, thirteen Elders, thirty-one Priests, nine Teachers. The Stanley Hill conference contains twenty-five branches, which represented eight hundred and thirty-nine members, seventeen Elders, fifty-seven Priests, sixteen Teachers and one Deacon. Including officers there are in these three conferences twelve hundred and sixty-one members, thirty-one Elders, ninety-five Priests, twenty-eight Teachers and two Deacons; making two hundred and fifty-five added since the October conference.

I attended the conference in the Staffordshire Potteries on the 25th; we had a good meeting; but I have not the minutes before me, so I cannot give a particular statement of the church there, yet I can say they are prospering.

In my travels and at the conferences, there were some baptized and many ordained. We can say truly, that the Lord is doing a great work in the land. The Gospel is preached to the poor, and signs follow them that believe. I arrived in Liverpool last evening and expect to tarry here till the Book of Mormon is completed.

I am as ever, your brother in the Kingdom of Patience,

BRIGHAM YOUNG.

About this time, immense quantities of rain fell which produced a flood in the east and south of France, doing immense damage, carrying with it buildings, bridges and everything in its way. Earthquakes have been felt in divers places the past year; and fearful sights and bloody signs have been witnessed in the heavens, fulfilling the words of the ancient Prophets concerning the last days.

I copy the following from a printed sheet:

SIGNS IN THE SKY.

A most wonderful phenomenon was observed last week by the inhabitants of Hull and the neighborhood. A perfectly blood red flag was seen flying in the heavens, which illuminated the horizon for many miles around. At intervals it changed its form, assuming that of a cross, sword and many other shapes.   At one o'clock on Friday morning, the town was nearly as light as noon-day; the inhabitant were parading the streets; fear and dismay pictured in their countenances. This wonder continued until near three o'clock, when it gradually went to the westward, illuminating the Humber as it seemed to sink in her waters.   Then for a few seconds all became total darkness, when from the northwest by north, arose the most beautiful light, which shot away towards the western hemisphere, leaving in its train the most beautiful and varigated colors, and which the eye might readily form into armies drawn up in the order of battle, charging and retreating alternately, and then again all was wrapped in the sable curtain of night.   It appears that many signs were seen on the same night in different parts of the kingdom.

The following is a list of books, pamphlets, and letters published for and against the Latter-day Saints during the past year, so far as such have come under my observation:

List of Books.

Fourteen numbers of the *Times and Seasons* have been issued from the office in Nauvoo, containing two hundred and twenty-four pages, edited by Ebenezer Robinson and Don Carlos Smith, three numbers having been issued during 1839.

Eight numbers of the *Millennial Star* have been published at 149 Oldham Road, Manchester, England, containing two hundred and sixteen pages, edited by Elder Parley P. Pratt.

A selection of hymns was published about the first of July, in England, by Brigham Young, John Taylor, and Parley P. Pratt, for the use of the Saints in Europe.

The Rev. Robert Hays, Wesleyan minister, Douglas, Isle of Man, published three addresses in pamphlet form, against the Latter-day Saints, which were replied to in the following order:

"An Answer to Some False Statements and Misrepresentations," published by the Rev. Robert Hays, Wesleyan minister, in an address to his society in Douglas, and its vicinity on the subject of Mormonism, by John Taylor, October 7th, 1840.

"Calumny Refuted, and the Truth Defended," being a reply to the second address of the Rev. Robert Hays, by John Taylor, Douglas, October 29, 1840.

"Truth Defended and Methodism Weighed in the Balances and Found Wanting," being a reply to the third address of the Rev. Robert Hays against the Latter-day Saints and also an "Exposure of the Principles of Methodism," by John Taylor, Liverpool, December 7, 1840.

"The Latter-day Saints and the Book of Mormon;" being a few words of warning against the Latter-day Saints, from a minister to his flock. W. J. Morrish, Ledbury, Herefordshire, September.

A second warning by the same W. J. Morrish, October 15th.

"A Few More Facts Relating to the Self-styled 'Latter-day Saints,' " by John Simmons, Church of England minister, Dymock, Herefordshire, September 14th.

Several letters written by Mr. Curran, and published in the *Manx Liberal*, Isle of Man, in October, were replied to by John Taylor.

"Mormonism Weighed in the Balances of the Sanctuary and Found Wanting;" the substance of four lectures by Samuel Haining, published in Douglas, Isle of Man; a tract of sixty-six pages.

Interesting account of several remarkable visions, and of the late discovery of ancient American Records giving an account of the commencement of the work of the Lord in this generation, by Elder Orson Pratt, Edinburgh, September.

The Word of the Lord to the Citizens of London, of every sect and denomination; and to every individual into whose hands it may fall; showing forth the plan of salvation as laid down in the New Testament; namely, faith in our Lord Jesus Christ—Repentance—Baptism for the remission of sins—and the Gift of the Holy Ghost, by the laying on of hands, presented by Heber C. Kimball and Wilford Woodruff, Elders of the Church of Jesus Christ of Latter-day Saints.

An exposure of the errors and fallacies of the self-named "Latter-day Saints." By William Hewitt, of Lane End, Staffordshire, Potteries.

An answer to Mr. William Hewitt's tract against the Latter-day Saints. By Elder Parley P. Pratt.

Plain Facts; showing the falsehood and folly of the Rev. C. Bush(the Church of England minister, of the parish of Peover, Cheshire); being a reply to his tract against the Latter-day Saints by Parley P. Pratt.

A few remarks by way of reply to an annonymous scribbler, calling himself "a Philanthropist," disabusing the Church of Jesus Christ of Latter-day Saints, of the slanders and falsehoods which he has attempted to fasten upon it. By Samuel Bennett, Philadelphia.

Mormonism unmasked, and Mr. Bennett's reply answered and refuted. By a Philanthropist of Chester County. Published in Philadelphia.

An Appeal to the American People; being an account of the persecutions of the Church of Jesus Christ of Latter-day Saints, and the barbarities inflicted on them by the inhabitants of the State of Missouri, sixty closely printed pages second edition revised by authority of said Church, Joseph Smith, Jun., Sidney Rigdon, Hyrum Smith, Presidency.

A reply to Mr. Thomas Taylor's Pamphlet, entitled "Complete Failure," etc.; and also to Mr. Richard Livesey's tract, "Mormonism Exposed" by Parley P. Pratt.

The editor of the *London Dispatch*, published an article on November 8th, against the Latter-day Saints, containing some of the false statements of Captain D. L. St. Clair, in his tract against them, which was replied to by Elder Parley P. Pratt, in the November number of the *Millennial Star*.

"The Millennium, and other Poems:" to which is annexed, "A Treatise on the Regeneration and Eternal

Duration of Matter," by Parley P. Pratt, New York.

January 1, 1841.—Elders Brigham Young, Parley P. Pratt, and John Taylor attended a conference in Liverpool.

Elders Heber C. Kimball, and Wilford Woodruff are in London.

Elder Orson Pratt in Edinburgh.

Elder George A. Smith in Burslem.

Elder Willard Richards in Preston.

Elders Orson Hyde and J. E. Page are *en route* for Jerusalem.

Elder William Smith, at Plymouth, Hancock county, Illinois.

The *Millennial Star* [No. 9, Vol. I] contains the following communication, which I have read several times. It is one of the sweetest pieces that has been written in these last days. I therefore insert it entire.

Election and Reprobation—by Brigham Young and Willard Richards.

Do you believe in election and reprobation? To prevent the necessity of repeating a thousand times what may be said at once, we purpose to answer this oft-asked question in writing, so that the Saints may learn doctrine, and all who will may understand that such election and reprobation as is taught in the Old and New Testaments, and other revelations from God, we fully believe, in connection with every other principle of righteousness; and we ask this favor of all into whose hands our answer may come, that they will not condemn until they have read it through, in the spirit of meekness and prayer.

The Lord (Jehovah) hath spoken through Isaiah (xiii: 1), saying, "Behold my servant whom I uphold—mine elect in whom my soul delighteth;" evidently referring to the Lord Jesus Christ, the Son of God, chosen, or elected by the Father. (I Peter i: 20). "Who verily was foreordained before the foundation of the world, but was manifest in these last times for you, who by Him do believe in God to serve Him in the redemption of the world, to be a covenant of the people (Isaiah xlii: 6), for a light to the Gentiles, and the glory of His people Israel, having ordained Him to be the judge of the quick and dead (Acts x: 42), that through Him forgiveness of sins might be preached (Acts xiii: 38), unto all who would be obedient unto His Gospel." (Mark xvi: 16, 17).

Every High Priest must be ordained (Heb. v: 1), and if Christ had not received ordination, He would not have had power to ordain others, as He did when He ordained the Twelve (Mark iii: 14), to take part in the ministry which He had received of His Father; also, (John xv: 16): "Ye have not chosen me, but I have chosen you, and ordained you, that ye should go and bring forth fruit; (Heb. v: 4), for no man taketh this honor unto himself, but he that is called of God, as was Aaron (v: 5), so also Christ glorified not Himself to be made an High Priest; but He that said unto Him, Thou art my Son, today have I begotten Thee." No being can give that which he does not possess; consequently, no man can confer the Priesthood on another, if he has not himself first received it; and the Priesthood is of such a nature that it is impossible to investigate the principles of election, reprobation, &c., without touching upon the Priesthood also; and although some may say that Christ, as God, needed no ordination, having possessed it eternally, yet Christ says, (Matt. xxviii: 18), "All power is *given* unto me in heaven and in earth;" which could not have been if He was in eternal possession; and in the previously quoted verse we discover that He that said unto Him [*i. e.* His Father] glorified Him to be made an High Priest, or ordained Him to the work of creating the world and all things upon it, (Col. i: 16), "For by Him were all things created that are in heaven, and that are in earth," &c., and of redeeming the same from the fall, and to the judging of the quick and dead, for the right of judging rests in the Priesthood, and it is through this medium that the Father hath committed all judgment unto the Son (John v: 22), referring to His administration on earth. It was necessary that Christ should receive the Priesthood to qualify Him to minister before His Father, unto the children of men, so as to redeem and save them. Does it seem reasonable that any man should take it upon him to do a part of the same work, or to assist in the same Priesthood, who has not been called by the spirit of prophecy or revelation as was Aaron, and ordained accordingly? And can it be expected that a man will be called by revelation who does not believe in revelation? Or will any man submit to ordination for the fulfillment of a revelation or call, in which he hath no faith? We think not.

That we may learn still further that God calls or elects particular men to perform particular works, or on whom to confer special blessings, we read, (Isaiah xlv: 4), "For Jacob my servant's sake, and Israel mine elect, I have even called thee [Cyrus] by thy name," to be a deliverer to my people Israel, and help to plant them on my holy mountain, (Isaiah lxv: 9, see connection) "for mine elect shall inherit it, and my servants shall dwell there," even on the mountains of Palestine, the land of Canaan which God had before promised to Abraham and his seed; (Gen. xvii: 8), and the particular reason why Abraham was chosen or elected to be the father of this blessed nation, is clearly told by the Lord, (Gen. xviii: 19), "For I know him, that he will command his children and his household after him, and they shall keep the way of the Lord, to do justice and judgment; that the Lord may bring upon Abraham that which he hath spoken of him;" and this includes the general principle of election, i. e that God chose, elected, or ordained Jesus Christ, His Son, to be the creator, governor, savior, and judge of the world; and Abraham to be the father of the faithful, on account of His foreknowledge of their obedience to His will and commandments, which agrees with the saying in II Tim. ii: 21, "If a man therefore purge himself from these [i. e. iniquities], he shall be a vessel unto honor, sanctified, and meet for the master's use, and prepared unto every good work."

Thus it appears that God has chosen or elected certain individuals to certain blessings, or to the performance of certain works; and that we may more fully understand the movements of the Supreme Governor of the universe, in the order of election, we proceed to quote the sacred writers, (Rom. viii: 29, 30), "For whom He did foreknow, He also did predestinate to be conformed to the image of His Son, that He might be the firstborn among many brethren. Moreover, whom He did predestinate, them He also called: and whom He called, them He also justified: and whom He justified, them He also glorified." And whom did He foreknow? Those that loved Him, as we find in the 28th verse of the same chapter—"And we know that all things work together for good to them that love God, to them who are the called according to His purpose." And "who are the called according to His purpose?" Those whom He foreknew, for He foreknew that those who loved Him would do His will and work righteousness; and it is vain for men to say they love God, if they do not keep His commandments. Cain found it so when he presented an unrighteous offering, for God said unto him, (Gen. iv: 7), "If thou dost well, shalt thou not be accepted?" And yet he was not accepted. "But whoso keepeth his word, in him verily is the love of God perfected; and hereby know we that we are in Him," (I John ii: 5), or, that we "are the called according to his purpose."

The principles of God's kingdom are perfect and harmonious, and the Scriptures of truth must also agree in all their parts, so that one sentiment thereof shall not destroy another, and when we read that, "whom He did foreknow, He also did predestinate;" and that "known unto God are all His works;" so that it might appear from an abstract view thereof, that God foreknew all, and consequently predestinated all "to be conformed to the image of His Son;" we ought also to read, (Mark xvi: 16), "He that believeth not shall be damned;" and (John viii: 14), "If ye believe not that I am he, ye shall die in your sins;" also (Matt. xxv: 41), "Depart from me, ye cursed, * * * for I was an hungered, and ye gave me no meat," &c.

Paul, referring to the Saints, (Rom. 1: 7), calls them beloved of God, called to be Saints; and says, (Rom. viii: 1), "There is no condemnation to them which are in Christ Jesus, who walk not after the flesh, but after the Spirit," and goes on to show in his epistle to the Romans, that the law (the law of carnal commandments given to the children of Israel, the covenant people), could not make the comers thereunto perfect (see also Heb. x: 1), but was given for a schoolmaster to bring us unto Christ (Gal. iii: 24); so that when He had come and offered Himself without spot unto God (Heb. ix: 14), the sacrifice of the law should be done away in him, that the honest in heart all might come unto the perfect law of liberty (James i: 25); or the Gospel of Christ, walking no longer after the flesh but after the spirit, and be of that number who love God and keep His commandments, that they might be called according to His purpose (Rom. viii: 28); and these were the individuals referred to, whom God foreknew; such as Abel, Seth, Enoch, Noah, Melchisedek, Abraham, Lot, Isaac, Jacob, Joseph, Moses, Caleb, Joshua, the harlot Rahab, who wrought righteousness by hiding the servants of God, when their lives were sought by their enemies, Gideon, Barak, Sampson, Jeptha, David, Samuel, and the Prophets; (Heb. xi), "Who through faith, subdued kingdoms, wrought righteousness, obtained promises, stopped the mouths of lions, quenched the violence of fire, escaped the edge of the sword, out of weakness were made strong, waxed valiant in fight, and turned to flight the armies of the aliens." These all died in faith, having kept the commandments of the Most High, having obtained the promise of a glorious inheritance, and are waiting the fulfillment of the promise which they obtained; (Heb. xi: 40), "God having provided some better things for us, that they without us should not be made perfect."

The Prophet Alma bears a similar testimony to the other Prophets concerning election, in his 9th chapter [Book of Mormon] saying, "This is the manner after which they were ordained: being called and prepared from the foundation of the world, according to the foreknowledge of God, on account of their exceeding faith and good works; in the first place being left to choose good or evil; therefore they have chosen good, and exercising exceeding great faith, are called with a holy calling, yea, with that holy calling which was prepared with, and according to, a preparatory redemption for such; and thus they have been called to this holy calling on account of their faith, while others would reject the Spirit of God on account of the hardness of their hearts and blindness of their minds, while, if it had not been for this, they might have had as great privilege as their brethren. Or in fine, in the first place, they were on the same standing with their brethren; thus, this holy calling being prepared from the foundation of the world for such as would not harden their hearts, being in and through the atonement of the only begotten Son, who was prepared; and thus being called by this holy calling, and ordained unto the high priesthood of the holy order of God, to teach His commandments unto the children of men, that they also might enter into His rest: this high priesthood being after the order of His Son, which order was from the foundation of the world: or, in other words, being without beginning of days or end of years, being prepared from eternity to all eternity, according to his foreknowledge of all things." (Rom. ix: 11, 12), "For the children being not yet born, neither having done any good or evil, that the purpose of God according to election might stand, not of works, but of Him that calleth; it was said unto her, The elder shall serve the younger." As we have before shown why God chose Abraham to be the father of the faithful, viz., because He knew Abraham would command his children and his household after him; so now we see, by this, why the purposes of God, according to election, should stand, and that for His oath's sake. (Gen. xxii: 16, 17, 18), "By myself have I sworn, saith the Lord, for because thou hast done this thing, and hast not withheld thy son, thine only son, that in blessing I will bless thee, and in multiplying I will multiply thy seed as the stars of heaven, and as the sand which is upon the sea shore; and thy seed shall possess the gate of his enemies, and in thy seed shall all the nations of the earth be blessed because thou hast obeyed my voice." Here the Lord Jesus, coming through the seed of Abraham, is again referred to, through whose sufferings and death, or in whom all the nations of the earth were to be blessed, or made alive, as they had died in Adam, (1 Cor. xv: 22). In this, election is made manifest, for God elected or chose the children of Israel to be His peculiar people, and to them belong the covenants and promises, and the blessings received by the Gentiles come through the covenants to Abraham and his seed; for through the unbelief of the Jews (Rom. xi: 17) they were broken off, and the Gentiles were grafted in; but they stand by faith (Rom. xi: 20), and not by the oath of election; therefore it becometh them to fear lest they cease quickly to bear fruit and be broken off (verse 21) that the Jews may be grafted in again; for they shall be grafted in again (verse 23), if they abide not in unbelief.

The Gentiles became partakers of the blessings of election and promises, through faith and obedience, as Peter says, writing to the strangers scattered abroad (1 Peter, 1st chap.), who were the Gentiles, the "elect according to the foreknowledge of God the Father, through sanctification of the spirit unto obedience;" (1 Peter, ii: 9) for "ye are a chosen generation, a royal prirsthood, an holy nation, a peculiar people; that ye should show forth the praises of Him who hath called you out of darkness into His marvelous light, (verse 10) which in time past were not a people, but now are the people of God: which had not obtained mercy, but now have obtained mercy."

Why were they a peculiar people? Because God had chosen that generation of Gentiles, and conferred on them the blessings which descended through the Priesthood, and the covenants unto the house of Israel, or grafted them into the good olive tree (Rom. xi: 17); and thus the house of Israel became the ministers of salvation to the Gentiles; and this is what the house of Israel was elected unto, not only their own salvation, but through them salvation unto all others; (John iv: 22) "For salvation is of the Jews," (Rom. xi: 11) and "through their fall salvation is come unto the Gentiles."

Among the promised seed we find Jesus Christ neither last nor least, but the Great High Priest and head of all, who was chosen to lay down His life for the redemption of the world, for without the shedding of blood there could be no remission of sins (Heb. ix: 22). (Deut. vii: 6, 7, 8, 9,) Moses bears a similar testimony with Peter and Paul to the principles of election—"For thou art an holy people unto the Lord thy God: the Lord thy God hath chosen thee to be a special people unto Himself, above all people that are upon the face of the earth. The Lord did not set His love upon you, nor choose you, because ye were more in number than any people; for ye were the fewest of all people: but because the Lord loved you, and because He would keep the oath which He had sworn unto your fathers, hath the Lord brought you out with a mighty hand, and redeemed you out of the house of bondmen, from the hand of Pharoah, king of Egypt. Know therefore that the Lord thy God, He is God, the faithful God, which keepeth covenant and mercy with them that love Him and keep His commandments to a thousand generations;" which proves the long continuance of the blessings of this highly favored people.

And the Lord said unto her, (Rebecca, Gen. xxv: 23) "The elder shall serve the younger." And why? Because that Isaac, the father of Esau and Jacob, the husband of Rebecca, and the son of promise to Abraham, was the heir; and as Esau was the elder son of his father Isaac, he had a legal claim to the heirship; but through unbelief, hardness of heart, and hunger, he sold his birthright to his younger brother Jacob (Gen. xxv: 33); and God knowing beforehand that he would do this of his own free will and choice, or acting upon that agency which God has delegated to all men, said to his mother, "The elder shall serve the younger;" for as the elder son Esau, has sold his birthright, and by that means lost all claim to the blessings promised to Abraham; those blessings and promises must have failed, if they had not descended with the purchased birthright unto the younger son, Jacob, for there was no other heir in Abraham's family; and if those blessings had failed, the purposes of God according to election must have failed in relation to the posterity of Israel, and the oath of Jehovah would have been broken, which could not be though heaven and earth were to pass away. (Rom. ix: 13) "As it is written, Jacob have I loved, but Esau have I hated." Where is it written? (Mal. i: 1, 2). When was it written? About 397 years before Christ, and Esau and Jacob were born about 1,773 years before Christ, (according to the computation of time in Scripture margin), so Esau and Jacob lived about 1,376 years before the Lord spoke by Malachi, saying, "Jacob have I loved, but Esau have I hated," as quoted by Paul. This text is often brought forward to prove that God loved Jacob and hated Esau before they were born, or before they had done good or evil; but if God did love one and hate the other before they had done good or evil, He has not seen fit to tell us of it, either in the Old or New Testament, or any other revelation: but this only we learn that 1,376 years after Esau and Jacob were born, God said by Malachi—"Jacob have I loved, and Esau have I hated;" and surely that was time sufficient to prove their works, and ascertain whether they were worthy to be loved or hated.

And why did He love the one and hate the other? For the same reason that He accepted the offering of Abel and rejected Cain's offering. Because Jacob's works had been righteous, and Esau's wicked, and where is there a righteous father who would not do the same thing? Who would not love an affectionate and obedient son more than one who was disobedient, and sought to injure Him and overthrow the order of His house? (Objection). But God seeth not as man seeth, and He is no respecter of persons. (Acts x: 34). True, but what saith the next verse, "He that feareth God and worketh righteousness is accepted of Him;" but it does not say that he that worketh wickedness is accepted, and this is a proof that God has respect to the actions of persons; and if He did not, why should He commend obedience to His law? For if he had no respect to the actions of men, He would be just as well pleased with a wicked man for breaking His law as a righteous man for keeping it; and if Cain had done well, he would have been accepted as well as Abel (Gen. iv: 7), and Esau as well as Jacob, which proves that God does not respect persons, only in relation to their acts, (see Matt. xxv: 34 to the end) "Come, ye blessed of my Father, inherit the kingdom prepared for you from the foundation of the world: for I was an hungered, and ye gave me meat," &c.; and because that God blessed Abel and Jacob, this would not have hindered His blessing Cain and Esau. if their works had been righteous like unto their brethren; so God's choosing one nation to blessing does not doom another to cursing or make them reprobate, according to the reprobation of God, as some suppose; "But by resisting the truth they became reprobate concerning the faith" (II Tim. iii: 8); and are "abominable, and disobedient, and unto every good work reprobate" (Titus i: 16); consequently, are not fit subjects for the blessings of election.

Rom. ix: 15, "For He saith to Moses, I will have mercy on whom I will have mercy, and I will have compassion on whom I will have compassion." (See Exod. xxxiii: 13 to the 19) "My presence shall go with thee, and I will give thee rest, * * * for thou hast found grace in my sight, and I know thee by name, and I will make all my goodness to pass before thee, * * * and I will proclaim the name of the Lord before thee; and I will be gracious to whom I will be gracious, and will show mercy on whom I will show mercy." (Rom. ix: 16) "So then it is not of him that willeth, nor of him that runneth, but of God that showeth mercy;" having His eye at the same time directed towards His covenant people in Egyptian bondage. For the Scripture saith unto Pharoah (Exod. ix: 16, 17), "And in very deed for this cause have I raised thee up, for to show in thee my power; and that my name may be declared throughout all the earth. As yet exaltest thou thyself, against my people, that thou wilt not let them go?"

God has promised to bring the house of Israel up out of the land of Egypt at his own appointed time; and with a mighty hand and an outstretched arm, and great terribleness (Deut. xxvi, 8.) He chose to do this thing that His power might be known and his name declared throughout all the earth, so that all nations might have the God of heaven in remembrance, and reverence his holy name; and to accomplish this it was needful that He should meet with opposition to give Him an opportunity to manifest His power; therefore He raised up a man, even Pharaoh, who, He foreknew, would harden his heart against God of his own free will and choice, and would withstand the Almighty in His attempt to deliver His chosen people, and that to the utmost of his ability; and he proved himself worthy of the choice, for he left no means unimproved which his wicked heart could devise to vex the sons of Abraham, and defeat the purposes of the Most High, which gave the God of Abraham an opportunity to magnify his name in the ears

of the nations, and in sight of this wicked king, by many mighty
signs and wonders, sometimes even to the convincing of the wicked king
of his wickedness, and of the power of God, (Exod. viii: 28, etc.) and
yet he would continue to rebel and hold the Israelites in bondage; and
this is what it meant by God's hardening Pharaoh's heart. He manifested Himself in so many glorious and mighty ways, that Pharaoh
could not resist the truth without becoming harder; so that at last, in
his madness, to stay the people of God, he rushed his hosts into the Red
Sea and they were covered with the floods.

Had not the power of God been exerted in a remarkable manner, it
would seem as though the house of Israel must have become extinct,
for Pharaoh commanded the midwives to destroy the sons of the Israel-
itish women as soon as they were born (Exod. i: 15, 16), and called them
to account for saving the men children alive (verse 18), and charged all
his people saying, "Every son that is born, ye shall cast into the river"
(verse 22), and yet God would have mercy on whom He would have
mercy (Rom. ix: 18); for he would have mercy on the goodly child,
Moses, when he was hid and laid in the flags (Exod. xi: 3) by his
mother to save him from Pharaoh's cruel order, and caused that he
should be preserved as a Prophet and deliverer to lead His people up to
their own country; and whom He would He hardened, for He hardened
Pharaoh by passing before him in mighty power and withdrawing His
Spirit, and leaving him to his own inclination, for he had set task-
masters over the Israelites to afflict them with their burdens, and caused
them to build treasure cities for Pharaoh, and made them to serve with
rigor; and made their lives bitter with hard bondage, in mortar and
brick and all manner of service in the field (Exod. 1st chap.); besides
destroying the men children, thus proving to the God of heaven and all
men that he had hardened his own hard heart, until he became a vessel
of wrath fitted for destruction (Rom, ix: 22); all this long before God
said unto Moses, "I will harden his (Pharaoh's) heart" (Exod.
iv: 21).

Are men, then, to be saved by works? Nay, verily, "By grace are
ye saved through faith, and that not of yourselves, it is the gift of
God" (Eph. ii: 8); "Not of works, lest any man should boast" (v. 9);
"Not by works of righteousness which we have done, but according to
His mercy He saved us" (Titus iii: 5); and yet faith without works is
dead, being alone (James ii: 17). Was not Abraham, our father, justified by works (v. 21)? Shall we then be saved by faith? Nay, neither
by faith nor works, but by works is faith made perfect (v. 22); but "by
grace are ye saved" (Eph. ii: 8); "And if by grace, then it is no more
of works, otherwise grace is no more grace; and if it be of works, then
it is no more grace; otherwise works is no works" (Rom. xi: 6); "Ye

see then how that a man is justified by works, and not by faith only"
(James ii: 24).

Rom. x: 3,4, "For they (Israel) being ignorant of God's righteousness
and going about to establish their own righteousness, have not submitted themselves unto the righteousness of God; for Christ is the end of
the law for righteousness to every one that believeth." Thus the
righteousness of God is made manifest in the plan of salvation by His
crucified son; for there is none other name under heaven given among
men whereby we must be saved," but the name of Jesus Christ of Nazareth (Acts iv: 10, 12); but of this the Jews were ignorant, although
they themselves crucified Him; and they have been going about wandering among all the nations of the earth ever since, for the space of
eighteen hundred years, trying to establish their own righteousness,
which is of the law of Moses, which law can never make the comers
thereto perfect (Heb. x: i.); yet notwithstanding their darkness and
long dispersion, there is a remnant, according to the election of
grace (Rom. xi: 5); whom God will gather from among all people
whither they are scattered and will be sanctified in them in the sight of
the heathen; then shall they dwell in their land which God gave to His
servant Jacob, and they shall dwell safely therein, and shall build
houses and plant vineyards; "Yea, they shall dwell with confidence
when I have executed judgments upon all those that despise them round
about; and they shall know that I am the Lord their God" (Ezek.
xxviii: 25, 26; Is. xi: 11 to 16); and when this gathering shall be completed, "It shall no more be said, The Lord liveth, that brought up the
children of Israel out of the land of Egypt, but the Lord liveth that
brought up the children of Israel from the land of the north, and from
all the lands whither he had driven them: and I will bring them again into
their land that I gave unto their fathers" (Jer. xvi: 14 to the
end).

Rom. xi: 7. "What then? Israel hath not obtained that which he
seeketh for; but the election hath obtained it." And why have they
not obtained it? Because they sought it not by faith, but as it were by
the works of the law, for they stumbled at the stumbling stone; as it is
written, "Behold, I lay in Zion a stumbling stone and rock of offense"
(Rom. ix: 32, 33); "to both the houses of Israel, for a gin and
for a snare to the inhabitants of Jerusalem. And many among them
shall stumble" (Isaiah viii: 14, 15); but "have they stumbled that they
should fall? God forbid; but rather through their fall. salvation is
come unto the Gentiles" (Rom. xi: 11). "And Jerusalem shall be
trodden down by the Gentiles, until the times of the Gentiles be
fulfilled (Luke xxi: 24); and when the house of Israel shall be restored
to their possessions in Canaan, it may truly be said, the election hath

obtained it; for the fulfillment of God's oath of election to Abraham as the father of the faithful, and the promises to His children will obtain that for Israel, which he has sought for in vain by the law of Moses.

This is the election that we believe in, viz., such as we find in the Prophets and Apostles, and the word of the Lord Himself, and as we have not room to give all the quotations in full, in relation to election in this epistle, we would invite the Saints to examine the Scriptures, in connection with these quoted; and whenever they find election, or any other principle or blesssing, given or applied to the house of Israel, let those principles continue with the house of Israel, and not apply that to Esau which belongs to Jacob; or to the churches of modern times which belong to the ancient covenant people; and always ascertain how the Lord, the Apostles and Prophets have applied their words, and ever continue the same application, and knowledge and wisdom will be added unto you; and in the words of the beloved Peter and Paul, we would exhort you to "work out your own salvation with fear and trembling, for it is God which worketh in you both to will and to do of His good pleasure" (Phil. ii: 12, 13); "Giving all diligence to make your calling and election sure" (2 Peter i: 10); for this is that sealing power spoken of in Ephesians (i: 13, 14)—"in whom ye also trusted, after that ye heard the word of truth; the gospel of your salvation, in whom also, after that ye believed ye were sealed with that Holy Spirit of promise, which is the earnest of our inheritance, until the redemption of the purchased possession, until the praise of His glory" (2 Peter i: 11); "For so an entrance shall be ministered unto you abundantly into the everlasting kingdom of our Lord and Savior Jesus Christ." Amen.

Friday, January 8.—Elder Parley P. Pratt wrote President Sidney Rigdon, from Manchester, England, in part as follows:

*　　*　　*　　*　　*　　As to the progress of the work of God in this county, it is increasing at every step. It is now prospering in Ireland and in Wales, as well as in Scotland and England. It is spreading into various new places in England. We have several hundred faithful preachers, and the spirit of inquiry seems to be more generally awakened. The clergy of the Church of England, the Methodist priests, the Baptist ministers, and Unitarians, are all in arms, as it were, against the Saints.

The country is flooded with pamphlets, tracts, papers, &c., published against us.　　*　　*　　*　　*　　*　　I must now inform you of the

fact that we have reaped the first fruits of Campbellism in England, at
a place called Nottingham.

A Proclamation of the First Presidency of the Church to the Saints Scattered Abroad, Greeting:

BELOVED BRETHREN:—The relationship which we sustain to the
Church of Jesus Christ of Latter-day Saints, renders it necessary that
we should make known from time to time, the circumstances, situation, and prospects of the Church, and give such instructions as may
be necessary for the well being of the Saints, and for the promotion of
those objects calculated to further their present and everlasting happiness.

We have to congratulate the Saints on the progress of the great work
of the "last days," for not only has it spread through the length and
breadth of this vast continent, but on the continent of Europe, and on
the islands of the sea, it is spreading in a manner entirely unprecedented in the annals of time. This appears the more pleasing when we
consider, that but a short time has elapsed since we were unmercifully
driven from the state of Missouri, after suffering cruelties and persecutions in various and horrid forms. Then our overthrow, to many,
seemed inevitable, while the enemies of truth triumphed over us, and
by their cruel reproaches endeavored to aggravate our sufferings. But
the Lord of Hosts was with us, the God of Jacob was our refuge, and
we were delivered from the hands of bloody and deceitful men; and in
the state of Illinois we found an asylum, and were kindly welcomed by
persons worthy the character of freemen.

It would be inpossible to enumerate all those who, in our time of deep
distress, nobly came forward to our relief, and, like the good Samari-
tan, poured oil into our wounds, and contributed liberally to our necessities, and the citizens of Quincy *en masse*, and the people of Illinois,
generally, seemed to emulate each other in this labor of love. We
would, however, make honorable mention of Governor Carlin, Judge
Young, General Leech, Judge Ralston, Rev. Mr. Young, Col. Henry,
N. Bushnell, John Wood, J. N. Morris, S. M. Bartlett, Samuel Holmes,
and J. T. Holmes, Esquires, who will long be remembered, by a grateful community, for their philanthropy to a suffering people, and whose
kindness, on that occasion, is indelibly engraved on the tablets of our
hearts in golden letters of love.

We would likewise make mention of the legislators of this state, who,
without respect to parties, without reluctance, freely, openly, boldly,
and nobly, have come forth to our assistance, owned us as citizens and
friends, and took us by the hand, and extended to us all the blessings

of civil, political, and religious liberty, by granting us, under date of December 16, 1840, one of the most liberal charters, with the most plenary powers ever conferred by a legislative assembly on free citizens, "The City of Nauvoo," the "Nauvoo Legion," and the "University of the City of Nauvoo."

The first of these charters (that for the "City of Nauvoo") secures to us, in all time to come, irrevocably, all those great blessings of civil liberty which of right appertain to all the free citizens of a great civilized republic; it is all we ever claimed. What a contrast does the proceedings of the legislators of this state present when compared with those of Missouri, whose bigotry, jealousy, and superstition, prevailed to such an extent as to deny us our liberty and our sacred rights. Illinois has set a glorious example to the whole United States, and to the world at large, and has nobly carried out the principles of her Constitution, and the Constitution of these United States, and while she requires of us implicit obedience to the laws, (which we hope ever to see observed) she affords us the protection of law, the security of life, liberty, and the peaceable pursuit of happiness.

The name of our city (Nauvoo) is of Hebrew origin, and signifies a beautiful situation, or place, carrying with it, also, the idea of rest; and is truly descriptive of the most delightful location. It is situated on the east bank of the Mississippi river, at the head of the Des Moines Rapids, in Hancock county, bounded on the east by an extensive prairie of surpassing beauty, and on the north, west, and south, by the Mississippi. This place has been objected to by some on account of the sickness which has prevailed in the summer months, but it is the opinion of Doctor Bennett, that Hancock county, and all the eastern and southern portions of the City of Nauvoo, are as healthful as any other portions of the western country, to acclimatized citizens; whilst the northwestern portion of the city has experienced much affliction from fever and ague, which, however, Doctor Bennett thinks can be easily remedied by draining the sloughs on the adjacent islands in the Mississippi.

The population of our city is increasing with unparalleled rapidity, numbering more than 3,000 inhabitants. Every facility is afforded, in the city and adjacent country, in Hancock county, for the successful prosecution of the mechanical arts and the pleasing pursuits of agriculture. The waters of the Mississippi can be successfully used for manufacturing purposes to almost an unlimited extent.

Having been instrumental, in the hands of our heavenly Father, in laying a foundation for the gathering of Zion, we would say, let all those who appreciate the blessings of the Gospel, and realize the importance of obeying the commandments of heaven, who have been blessed of heaven with the possession of this world's goods, first prepare for the general gathering; let them dispose of their effects as fast as circumstances will possibly admit, without making too great sacrifices, and remove to our city and county; establish and build up manufactures in the city, purchase and cultivate farms in the county. This will secure our permanent inheritance, and prepare the way for the gathering of the poor. This is agreeable to the order of heaven, and the only principle on which the gathering can be effected. Let the rich, then, and all who can assist in establishing this place, make every preparation to come on without delay, and strengthen our hands, and assist in promoting the happiness of the Saints. This cannot be too forcibly impressed on the minds of all, and the Elders are hereby instructed to proclaim this word in all places where the Saints reside, in their public administrations, for this is according to the instructions we have received from the Lord.

The Temple of the Lord is in process of erection here, where the Saints will come to worship the God of their fathers, according to the order of His house and the powers of the Holy Priesthood, and will be so constructed as to enable all the functions of the Priesthood to be duly exercised, and where instructions from the Most High will be received, and from this place go forth to distant lands. Let us then concentrate all our powers, under the provisions of our *magna charta* granted by the Illinois legislature, at the "City of Nauvoo" and surrounding country, and strive to emulate the action of the ancient covenant fathers and patriarchs, in those things which are of such vast importance to this and every succeeding generation.

The "Nauvoo Legion" embraces all our military power, and will enable us to perform our military duty by ourselves, and thus afford us the power and privilege of avoiding one of the most fruitful sources of strife, oppression, and collision with the world. It will enable us to show our attachment to the state and nation, as a people, whenever the public service requires our aid, thus proving ourselves obedient to the paramount laws of the land, and ready at all times to sustain and execute them.

The "University of the City of Nauvoo" will enable us to teach our children wisdom, to instruct them in all the knowledge and learning, in the arts, sciences, and learned professions. We hope to make this institution one of the great lights of the world, and by and through it to diffuse that kind of knowledge which will be of practicable utility, and for the public good, and also for private and individual happiness. The Regents of the University will take the general supervision of all matters appertaining to education, from common schools up to the highest branches of a most liberal collegiate course. They will establish a regular system of education, and hand over the pupil from teacher to professor, until the regular gradation is consummated and the education finished.

This corporation contains all the powers and prerogatives of any other college or university in this state. The charters for the University and Legion are *addenda* to the city charter, making the whole perfect and complete.

Not only has the Lord given us favor in the eyes of the community, who are happy to see us in the enjoyment of all the rights and privileges of freemen, but we are happy to state that several of the principal men in Illinois, who have listened to the doctrines we promulgate, have become obedient to the faith, and are rejoicing in the same; among whom is John C. Bennett, M. D., Quartermaster-General of Illinois. We mention this gentleman first, because, that during our persecutions in Missouri, he became acquainted with the violence we were suffering while in that state, on account of our religion; his sympathy for us was aroused, and his indignation kindled against our persecutors, for the cruelties practiced upon us, and their flagrant violation of both the law and the Constitution. Amidst their heated zeal to put down the truth, he addressed us a letter, tendering to us his assistance in delivering us out of the hands of our enemies, and restoring us again to our privileges, and only required at our hands to point out the way and he would be forthcoming, with all the forces he could raise for the purpose. He has been one of the instruments in effecting or safety and deliverance, from the unjust persecutions and demands of the authorities of Missouri, and also in procuring the city charter. He is a man of enterprise, extensive acquirements, and of independent mind, and is calculated to be a great blessing to our community.

Dr. Isaac Galland also, who is one of our benefactors, having under his control a large quantity of land, in the immediate vicinity of our city, and a considerable portion of the city plat, opened both his heart and his hands, and "when we were strangers, took us in," and bade us welcome to share with him in his abundance, leaving his dwelling house, the most splendid edifice in the vicinity, for our accommodation, and partook himself to a small, uncomfortable dwelling. He sold us his large estates on very reasonable terms, and on long credit, so that we might have an opportunity of paying for them without being distressed, and has since taken our lands in Missouri in payment for the whole amount, and has given us a clear and indisputable title for the same. And in addition to the first purchase, we have exchanged lands with him in Missouri to the amount of eighty thousand dollars. He is the honored instrument the Lord used to prepare a home for us, when we were driven from our inheritances, having given him control of vast bodies of land, and prepared his heart to make the use of it the Lord intended he should. Being a man of extensive information, great talents, and high literary fame, he devoted all his powers and influence to give us a standing.

After having thus exerted himself for our salvation and comfort, and formed an intimate acquaintance with many of our people, his mind became wrought up to the greatest feelings, being convinced that our persecutions were like those of the ancient Saints, and, after investigating the doctrines we proclaimed, he became convinced of the truth and of the necessity of obedience thereto, and, to the great joy and satisfaction of the Church, he yielded himself to the waters of baptism, and became a partaker with us in our sufferings, "Choosing rather to suffer afflictions with the people of God than enjoy the pleasures of sin for a season."

In connection with these, we would mention the names of General James Adams, judge of probate, of Sangamon county; Dr. Green of Shelby county, R. D. Foster, and Sidney Knowlton, of Hancock county; Dr. Knight, of Putnam county, Indiana; many others of respectability and high standing in society, and nearly all the old settlers in our immediate neighborhood. We make mention of this that the Saints may be encouraged, and also that they may see that the persecutions we suffered in Missouri were but the prelude to a far more glorious display of the power of truth, and of the religion we have espoused.

From the kind, uniform, and consistent course pursued by the citizens of Illinois, and the great success which has attended us while here, the natural advantages of this place for every purpose we require, and the necessity of the gathering of the Saints of the Most High, we would say—let the brethren who love the prosperity of Zion, who are anxious that her stakes should be strengthened and her cords lengthened, and who prefer her prosperity to their chief joy, come and cast in their lots with us, and cheerfully engage in a work so glorious and sublime, and say with Nehemiah, "We, His servants, will arise and build." It probably would hardly be necessary to enforce this important subject on the attention of the Saints, as its necessity is obvious, and is a subject of paramount importance; but as watchmen to the house of Israel—as shepherds over the flock which is now scattered over a vast extent of country, and the anxiety we feel for their prosperity and everlasting welfare, and for the carrying out the great and glorious purposes of our God, to which we have been called, we feel to urge its necessity, and say—Let the Saints come here; this is the word of the Lord, and in accordance with the great work of the last days. It is true, the idea of a general gathering has heretofore been associated with the most cruel and oppressing scenes, owing to our unrelenting persecutions at the hands of wicked and unjust men; but we hope that those days of darkness and gloom have gone by, and, from the liberal policy of our state government, we may expect a scene of peace and prosperity we have never before witnessed since the rise of our Church, and the happiness and prosperity which now await us, is, in all human probability, incalculably great. By a concentration of action, and a unity of effort, we can only accomplish the great work of the last days which we could not do in our remote and scattered condition, while our interests, both temporal and spiritual, will be greatly enhanced, and the blessings of heaven must flow unto us in an uninterrupted stream; of this, we think there can be no question.

The greatest temporal and spiritual blessings which always flow from faithfulness and concerted effort, never attended individual exertion or enterprise. The history of all past ages abundantly attests this fact. In addition to all temporal blessings, there is no other way for the Saints to be saved in these last days, [than by the gathering] as the concurrent testimony of all the holy Prophets clearly proves, for it is written—"They shall come from the east, and be gathered from the west; the north shall give up, and the south shall keep not back." "The sons of God shall be gathered from far, and His daughters from the ends of the earth."

It is also the concurrent testimony of all the Prophets, that this gathering together of all the Saints, must take place before the Lord comes to "take vengeance upon the ungodly," and "to be glorified and admired by all those who obey the Gospel." The fiftieth Psalm, from the first to the fifth verse inclusive, describes the glory and majesty of that event.

"The mighty God, and even the Lord hath spoken, and called the earth from the rising of the sun unto the going down thereof. Out of Zion, the perfection of beauty, God hath shined. Our God shall come, and shall not keep silence; a fire shall devour before Him, and it shall be very tempestuous round about Him. He shall call to the heavens from above, and to the earth (that He may judge the people). Gather my Saints together unto me; those that have made covenant with me by sacrifice."

We might offer many other quotations from the Scriptures, but believing them to be familiar to the Saints, we forbear.

We would wish the Saints to understand that, when they come here, they must not expect perfection, or that all will be harmony, peace, and love; if they indulge these ideas, they will undoubtedly be deceived, for here there are persons, not only from different states, but from different nations, who, although they feel a great attachment to the cause of truth, have their prejudices of education, and, consequently, it requires some time before these things can be overcome. Again, there are many that creep in unawares, and endeavor to sow discord, strife, and animosity in our midst, and by so doing, bring evil upon the Saints. These things we have to bear with, and these things will prevail either to a greater or less extent until "the floor be thoroughly purged," and "the chaff be burnt up." Therefore, let those who come up to this place be determined to keep the commandments of God, and not be discouraged by those things we have enumerated, and then they will be prospered—the intelligence of heaven will be communicated to them, and they will, eventually, see eye to eye, and rejoice in the full fruition of that glory which is reserved for the righteous.

In order to erect the Temple of the Lord, great exertions will be required on the part of the Saints, so that they may build a house which shall be accepted by the Almighty, and in which His power and glory shall be manifested. Therefore let those who can freely make a sacrifice of their time, their talents, and their property, for the prosperity of the kingdom, and for the love they have to the cause of truth, bid adieu to their homes and pleasant places of abode, and unite with us in the great work of the last days, and share in the tribulation, that they may ultimately share in the glory and triumph.

We wish it likewise to be distinctly understood, that we claim no privilege but what we feel cheerfully disposed to share with our fellow citizens of every denomination, and every sentiment of religion; and therefore say, that so far from being restricted to our own faith, let all those who desire to locate themselves in this place, or the vicinity, come, and we will hail them as citizens and friends, and shall feel it not only a duty, but a privilege, to reciprocate the kindness we have received from the benevolent and kind-hearted citizens of the state of Illinois.

JOSEPH SMITH,
SIDNEY RIGDON,
HYRUM SMITH,
Presidents of the Church.

Nauvoo, January 15th, 1841.

CHAPTER XV.

RECONSTRUCTION OF CHURCH AFFAIRS AT NAUVOO—REVELA-
TION—MUNICIPAL ORGANIZATION OF NAUVOO—INSTALLA-
TION OF CIVIC AND MILITARY OFFICERS.

Friday, January 15, 1841.—I published the following in
the *Times and Seasons*—

Reproof of John E. Page and Orson Hyde.

Elders Orson Hyde and John E. Page are informed that the Lord is
not well pleased with them, in consequence of delaying their mission,
(John E. Page in particular) and they are requested, by the First
Presidency, to hasten their journey towards their destination.

Sunday, 17.—Elder Brigham Young preached twice in
the Music Hall, Liverpool.

Monday, 18.—Elders Brigham Young and Willard Richards commenced reading the Book of Mormon, and writing an index to the English edition.

Tuesday, 19.—Elder Amos Fielding has baptized twenty-nine at Newcastle-upon-Tyne, England.

I received the following revelation:*

Revelation Given to Joseph Smith at Nauvoo, January 19th, 1841.

Verily, thus saith the Lord unto you, my servant Joseph Smith, I am
well pleased with your offering and acknowledgments, which you have
made, for unto this end have I raised you up, that I might show forth
my wisdom through the weak things of the earth.

Your prayers are acceptable before me, and in answer to them I say
unto you, that you are now called immediately to make a solemn proclamation of my Gospel, and of this Stake which I have planted to be a

* See Doctrine and Covenants, section cxxiv.

corner-stone of Zion, which shall be polished with the refinement which is after the similitude of a palace.

This proclamation shall be made to all the kings of the world, to the four corners thereof; to the honorable President elect, and the high-minded Governors of the nation in which you live, and to all the nations of the earth, scattered abroad.

Let it be written in the spirit of meekness and by the power of the Holy Ghost, which shall be in you at the time of the writing of the same;

For it shall be given you by the Holy Ghost to know my will concerning those kings and authorities, even what shall befall them in a time to come.

For, behold! I am about to call upon them to give heed to the light and glory of Zion, for the set time has come to favor her.

Call ye, therefore, upon them with loud proclamation, and with your testimony, fearing them not, for they are as grass, and all their glory as the flower thereof which soon falleth, that they may be left also without excuse,

And that I may visit them in the day of visitation, when I shall unveil the face of my covering, to appoint the portion of the oppressor among hypocrites, where there is gnashing of teeth, if they reject my servants and my testimony which I have revealed unto them.

And again, I will visit and soften their hearts, many of them for your good, that ye may find grace in their eyes, that they may come to the light of truth, and the Gentiles to the exaltation or lifting up of Zion.

For the day of my visitation cometh speedily, in an hour when ye think not of, and where shall be the safety of my people, and refuge for those who shall be left of them?

Awake, O kings of the earth! Come ye, O, come ye, with your gold and your silver, to the help of my people, to the house of the daughters of Zion.

And again, verily I say unto you, let my servant Robert B. Thompson help you to write this proclamation, for I am well pleased with him, and that he should be with you;

Let him, therefore, hearken to your counsel, and I will bless him with a multiplicity of blessings; let him be faithful and true in all things from henceforth, and he shall be great in mine eyes;

But let him remember that his stewardship will I require at his hands.

And again, verily I say unto you, blessed is my servant Hyrum Smith, for I, the Lord, love him because of the integrity of his heart, and because he loveth that which is right before me, saith the Lord.

Again, let my servant John C. Bennett, help you in your labor in sending my word to the kings and people of the earth, and stand by you, even you my servant Joseph Smith, in the hour of affliction, and his reward shall not fail, if he receive counsel;

And for his love he shall be great, for he shall be mine if he do this, saith the Lord. I have seen the work which he hath done, which I accept, if he continue, and will crown him with blessings and great glory.

And again, I say unto you, that it is my will that my servant Lyman Wight should continue in preaching for Zion, in the spirit of meekness, confessing me before the world, and I will bear him up as on eagle's wings, and he shall beget glory and honor to himself, and unto my name.

That when he shall finish his work, that I may receive him unto myself, even as I did my servant David Patten, who is with me at this time, and also my servant Edward Partridge, and also my aged servant Joseph Smith, Sen., who sitteth with Abraham at his right hand, and blessed and holy is he, for he is mine.

And again, verily I say unto you, my servant George Miller is without guile: he may be trusted because of the integrity of his heart; and for the love which he has to my testimony I, the Lord, love him;

I therefore say unto you, I seal upon his head the office of a bishopric, like unto my servant Edward Partridge, that he may receive the consecrations of mine house, that he may administer blessing upon the heads of the poor of my people, saith the Lord. Let no man despise my servant George, for he shall honor me.

Let my servant George, and my servant Lyman, and my servant John Snider, and others, build a house unto my name, such an one as my servant Joseph shall show unto them; upon the place which he shall show unto them also.

And it shall be for a house for boarding, a house that strangers may come from afar to lodge therein; therefore let it be a good house, worthy of all acceptation, that the weary traveler may find health and safety while he shall contemplate the word of the Lord; and the cornerstone I have appointed for Zion.

This house shall be a healthy habitation if it be built unto my name, and if the governor which shall be appointed unto it shall not suffer any pollution to come upon it. It shall be holy, or the Lord your God will not dwell therein.

And again, verily I say unto you, let all my Saints come from afar;

And send ye swift messengers, yea, chosen messengers, and say unto them: Come ye, with all your gold, and your silver, and your precious stones, and with all your antiquities; and with all who have knowledge of antiquities, that will come, may come, and bring the box-tree, and the fir-tree, and the pine-tree, together with all the precious trees of the earth;

And with iron, with copper, and with brass, and with zinc, and with all your precious things of the earth, and build a house to my name for the Most High to dwell therein;

For there is not a place found on earth that He may come and restore again that which was lost unto you, or which He hath taken away, even the fullness of the Priesthood;

For a baptismal font there is not upon the earth, that they, my Saints, may be baptized for those who are dead;

For this ordinance belongeth to my house, and cannot be acceptable to me, only in the days of your poverty, wherein ye are not able to build a house unto me.

But I command you, all ye my Saints, to build a house unto me; and I grant unto you a sufficient time to build a house unto me, and during this time your baptisms shall be acceptable unto me.

But behold, at the end of this appointment, your baptisms for your dead shall not be acceptable unto me; and if you do not these things at the end of the appointment, ye shall be rejected as a church, with your dead, saith the Lord your God.

For verily I say unto you, that after you have had sufficient time to build a house to me, wherein the ordinance of baptizing for the dead belongeth, and for which the same was instituted from before the foundation of the world, your baptisms for your dead cannot be acceptable unto me,

For therein are the keys of the holy Priesthood, ordained that you may receive honor and glory.

And after this time, your baptisms for the dead, by those who are scattered abroad, are not acceptable unto me, saith the Lord;

For it is ordained that in Zion, and in her stakes, and in Jerusalem, those places which I have appointed for refuge, shall be the places for your baptisms for your dead.

And again, verily I say unto you, how shall your washings be acceptable unto me, except ye perform them in a house which you have built to my name? For, for this cause I commanded Moses that he should build a tabernacle, that they should bear it with them in the wilderness, and to build a house in the land of promise, that those ordinances might be revealed which had been hid from before the world was;

Therefore, verily I say unto you, that your anointings, and your washings, and your baptisms for the dead, and your solemn assemblies, and your memorials for your sacrifices, by the sons of Levi, and for your oracles in your most holy places, wherein you receive conversations, and your statutes and judgments, for the beginning of the revelations and foundation of Zion, and for the glory, honor, and endowment of all her municipals, are ordained by the ordinance of my holy house which my people are always commanded to build unto my holy name.

And verily I say unto you, let this house be built unto my name, that I may reveal mine ordinances therein, unto my people;

For I deign to reveal unto my Church things which have been kept hid from before the foundation of the world, things that pertain to the dispensation of the fullness of times;

And I will show unto my servant Joseph all things pertaining to this house, and the Priesthood thereof; and the place whereon it shall be built;

And ye shall build it on the place where you have contemplated building it, for that is the spot which I have chosen for you to build it;

If ye labor with all your might, I will consecrate that spot that it shall be made holy;

And if my people will hearken unto my voice, and unto the voice of my servants whom I have appointed to lead my people, behold, verily I say unto you, they shall not be moved out of their place.

But if they will not hearken to my voice, nor unto the voice of these men whom I have appointed, they shall not be blest, because they pollute mine holy grounds, and mine holy ordinances, and charters, and my holy words which I give unto them.

And it shall come to pass, that if you build a house unto my name, and do not do the things that I say, I will not perform the oath which I make unto you, neither fulfill the promises which ye expect at my hands, saith the Lord;

For instead of blessings, ye, by your own works, bring cursings, wrath, indignation, and judgments upon your own heads, by your follies, and by all your abominations, which you practice before me, saith the Lord.

Verily, verily I say unto you, that when I give a commandment to any of the sons of men, to do a work unto my name, and those sons of men go with all their might, and with all they have, to perform that work, and cease not their diligence, and their enemies come upon them, and hinder them from performing that work; behold, it behooveth me to require that work no more at the hands of those sons of men, but to accept of their offerings;

And the iniquity and transgression of my holy laws and commandments, I will visit upon the heads of those who hindered my work, unto the third and fourth generation, so long as they repent not, and hate me, saith the Lord God.

Therefore for this cause have I accepted the offerings of those whom I commanded to build up a city and a house unto my name, in Jackson county, Missouri, and were hindered by their enemies, saith the Lord your God.

And I will answer judgment, wrath, and indignation, wailing, and anguish, and gnashing of teeth upon their heads, unto the third and fourth generation, so long as they repent not and hate me, saith the Lord your God.

And this I make an example unto you, for your consolation concerning all those who have been commanded to do a work, and have been hindered by the hands of their enemies, and by oppression, saith the Lord your God;

For I am the Lord your God, and will save all those of your brethren who have been pure in heart, and have been slain in the land of Missouri, saith the Lord.

And again, verily I say unto you, I command you again to build a house to my name, even in this place that you may prove yourselves unto me that ye are faithful in all things whatsoever I command you, that I may bless you, and crown you with honor, immortality, and eternal life.

And now I say unto you, as pertaining to my boarding house which I have commanded you to build for the boarding of strangers, let it be built unto my name, and let my name be named upon it, and let my servant Joseph, and his house have place therein, from generation to generation;

For this anointing have I put upon his head, that his blessing shall also be put upon the head of his posterity after him,

And as I said unto Abraham concerning the kindreds of the earth, even so I say unto my servant Joseph, in thee and in thy seed, shall the kindred of the earth be blessed.

Therefore, let my servant Joseph and his seed after him have place in that house, from generation to generation, for ever and ever, saith the Lord.

And let the name of that house be called Nauvoo House, and let it be a delightful habitation for man, and a resting place for the weary traveler, that he may contemplate the glory of Zion, and the glory of this, the corner stone thereof;

That he may receive also the counsel from those whom I have set to be as plants of renown, and as watchmen upon her walls.

Behold, verily I say unto you, let my servant George Miller, and my servant Lyman Wight, and my servant John Snider, and my servant Peter Haws, organize themselves, and appoint one of them to be a president over their quorum for the purpose of building that house.

And they shall form a constitution whereby they may receive stock for the building of that house.

And they shall not receive less than fifty dollars for a share of stock in that house, and they shall be permitted to receive fifteen thousand dollars from any one man for stock in that house;

But they shall not be permitted to receive over fifteen thousand dollars stock from any one man;

And they shall not be permitted to receive under fifty dollars for a share of stock from any one man in that house;

And they shall not be permitted to receive any man as a stockholder in this house, except the same shall pay his stock into their hands at the time he receives stock;

And in proportion to the amount of stock he pays into their hands, he shall receive stock in that house; but if he pays nothing into their hands, he shall not receive any stock in that house.

And if any pay stock into their hands, it shall be for stock in that house, for himself, and for his generation after him, from generation to generation, so long as he and his heirs shall hold that stock, and do not sell or convey the stock away out of their hands by their own free will and act, if you will do my will, saith the Lord your God.

And again, verily I say unto you, if my servant George Miller, and my servant Lyman Wight, and my servant John Snider, and my servant Peter Haws, receive any stock into their hands, in moneys or in properties, wherein they receive the real value of moneys, they shall not appropriate any portion of that stock to any other purpose, only in that house;

And if they do appropriate any portion of that stock anywhere else, only in that house, without the consent of the stockholder, and do not repay fourfold for the stock which they appropriate anywhere else, only in that house, they shall be accursed, and shall be moved out of their place, saith the Lord God, for I, the Lord, am God, and cannot be mocked in any of these things.

Verily I say unto you, let my servant Joseph pay stock into their hands for the building of that house, as seemeth him good; but my servant Joseph cannot pay over fifteen thousand dollars stock in that house, nor under fifty dollars; neither can any other man, saith the Lord.

And there are others also who wish to know my will concerning them, for they have asked it at my hands.

Therefore I say unto you concerning my servant Vinson Knight, if he will do my will, let him put stock into that house for himself, and for his generation after him, from generation to generation,

And let him lift up his voice long and loud, in the midst of the people, to plead the cause of the poor and the needy, and let him not fail, neither let his heart faint, and I will accept of his offerings, for they shall not be unto me as the offerings of Cain, for he shall be mine, saith the Lord.

Let his family rejoice, and turn away their hearts from affliction, for I have chosen him and anointed him, and he shall be honored in the midst of his house, for I will forgive all his sins, saith the Lord. Amen.

Verily I say unto you, let my servant Hyrum put stock into that house as seemeth him good, for himself and his generation after him, from generation to generation.

Let my servant Isaac Galland put stock into that house, for I, the Lord, love him for the work he hath done, and will forgive all his sins; therefore, let him be remembered for an interest in that house from generation to generation.

Let my servant Isaac Galland be appointed among you, and be ordained by my servant William Marks, and be blessed of him, to go with my servant Hyrum, to accomplish the work that my servant Joseph shall point out to them, and they shall be greatly blessed.

Let my servant William Marks pay stock into that house, as seemeth him good, for himself and his generation, from generation to generation.

Let my servant Henry G. Sherwood pay stock into that house, as seemeth him good, for himself and his seed after him from generation to generation.

Let my servant William Law pay stock into that house, for himself and his seed after him, from generation to generation.

If he will do my will, let him not take his family unto the eastern lands, even unto Kirtland; nevertheless, I, the Lord, will build up Kirtland, but I. the Lord, have a scourge prepared for the inhabitants thereof.

And with my servant Almon Babbitt, there are many things with which I am not pleased; behold, he aspireth to establish his council instead of the council which I have ordained, even the Presidency of my Church, and he setteth up a golden calf for the worship of my people.

Let no man go from this place who has come here essaying to keep my commandments.

If they live here let them live unto me; and if they die, let them die unto me; for they shall rest from all their labors here, and shall continue their works.

Therefore let my servant William put his trust in me, and cease to fear concerning his family, because of the sickness of the land. If ye love me, keep my commandments, and the sickness of the land shall redound to your glory.

Let my servant William go and proclaim my everlasting Gospel with a loud voice, and with great joy, as he shall be moved upon by

my Spirit, unto the inhabitants of Warsaw, and also unto the inhabitants of Carthage, and also unto the inhabitants of Burlington, and also
unto the inhabitants of Madison, and await patiently and diligently for
further instructions at my general conference, saith the Lord.

If he will do my will, let him from henceforth hearken to the counsel
of my servant Joseph, and with his interest support the cause of the
poor, and publish the new translation of my holy word unto the inhabitants of the earth;

And if he will do this, I will bless him with a multiplicity of blessings, that he shall not be forsaken, nor his seed be found begging
bread.

And again, verily I say unto you, let my servant William be appointed, ordained, and anointed as a counselor unto my servant Joseph,
in the room of my servant Hyrum; that my servant Hyrum may take
the office of Priesthood and Patriarch which was appointed unto him
by his father, by blessing and also by right,

That from henceforth he shall hold the keys of the Patriarchal
blessings upon the heads of all my people,

That whomsoever he blesses shall be blessed, and whomsoever he
curses shall be cursed; that whatsoever he shall bind on earth shall be
bound in heaven; and whatsoever he shall loose on earth shall be
loosed in heaven;

And from this time forth I appoint unto him that he may be a
prophet, and a seer and a revelator unto my Church, as well as my
servant Joseph.

That he may act in concert also with my servant Joseph, and that he
shall receive counsel from my servant Joseph, who shall show unto
him the keys whereby he may ask and receive, and be crowned with the
same blessing, and glory, and honor, and Priesthood, and gifts of the
Priesthood, that once were put upon him that was my servant Oliver
Cowdery;

That my servant Hyrum may bear record of the things which I shall
show unto him, that his name may be had in honorable remembrance
from generation to generation forever and ever.

Let my servant William Law also receive the keys by which he may
ask and receive blessings; let him be humble before me, and be without guile, and he shall receive of my Spirit, even the Comforter, which
shall manifest unto him the truth of all things, and shall give him in
the very hour what he shall say.

And these signs shall follow him; he shall heal the sick, he shall cast
out devils, and shall be delivered from those who would administer
unto him deadly poison;

And he shall be led in paths where the poisonous serpent cannot lay hold upon his heel, and he shall mount up in the imagination of his thoughts as upon eagle's wings;

And what if I will that he should raise the dead, let him not withhold his voice.

Therefore, let my servant William cry aloud and spare not, with joy and rejoicing, and with hosannas to Him that sitteth upon the throne forever and ever, saith the Lord your God.

Behold I say unto you, I have a mission in store for my servant William and my servant Hyrum, and for them alone; and let my servant Joseph tarry at home, for he is needed; the remainder I will show unto you hereafter. Even so. Amen.

And again, verily I say unto you, if my servant Sidney will serve me and be counselor unto my servant Joseph, let him arise and come up and stand in the office of his calling, and humble himself before me;

And if he will offer unto me an acceptable offering, and acknowledgments, and remain with my people, behold, I, the Lord your God, will heal him that he shall be healed; and he shall lift up his voice again on the mountains, and be a spokesman before my face.

Let him come and locate his family in the neighborhood in which my servant Joseph resides,

And in all his journeyings let him lift up his voice as with the sound of a trump, and warn the inhabitants of the earth to flee the wrath to come;

Let him assist my servant Joseph; and also let my servant William Law assist my servant Joseph, in making a solem proclamation unto the kings of the earth, even as I have before said unto you;

If my servant Sidney will do my will, let him not remove his family unto the eastern lands, but let him change their habitation even as I have said.

Behold, it is not my will that he shall seek to find safety and refuge out of the city which I have appointed unto you, even the city of Nauvoo.

Verily I say unto you, even now, if he will hearken unto my voice, it shall be well with him. Even so. Amen.

And again, verily I say unto you, let my servant Amos Davis pay stock into the hands of those whom I have appointed to build a house for boarding, even the Nauvoo House;

This let him do if he will have an interest, and let him hearken unto the counsel of my servant Joseph, and labor with his own hands that he may obtain the confidence of men;

And when he shall prove himself faithful in all things that shall be entrusted unto his care, yea, even a few things, he shall be made ruler over many;

Let him therefore abase himself that he may be exalted. Even so. Amen.

And again, verily I say unto you, if my servant Robert D. Foster will obey my voice, let him build a house for my servant Joseph, according to the contract which he has made with him, as the door shall be open to him from time to time.

And let him repent of all his folly, and clothe himself with charity, and cease to do evil, and lay aside all his hard speeches,

And pay stock also into the hands of the quorum of the Nauvoo House for himself and for his generation after him, from generation to generation,

And hearken unto the counsel of my servants Joseph and Hyrum and William Law, and unto the authorities which I have called to lay the foundation of Zion, and it shall be well with him for ever and ever, Even so. Amen.

And again, verily I say unto you, let no man pay stock to the quorum of the Nauvoo House, unless he shall be a believer in the Book of Mormon, and the revelations I have given unto you, saith the Lord your God;

For that which is more or less than this cometh of evil, and shall be attended with cursings and not blessings, saith the Lord your God. Even so. Amen

And again, verily I say unto you, let the the quorum of the Nauvoo House have a just recompense of wages for all their labors which they do in building the Nauvoo House, and let their wages be as shall be agreed among themselves, as pertaining to the price thereof;

And let every man who pays stock bear his proportion of their wages, if it must needs be, for their support, saith the Lord; otherwise, their labors shall be accounted unto them for stock in that house. Even so. Amen.

Verily I say unto you, I now give unto you the officers belonging to my Priesthood, that ye may hold the keys thereof, even the Priesthood which is after the order of Melchisedek, which is after the order of my Only Begotten Son.

First, I give unto you Hyrum Smith, to be a Patriarch unto you, to hold the sealing blessings of my church, even the Holy Spirit of promise, whereby ye are sealed up unto the day of redemption, that ye may not fall, notwithstanding the hour of temptation that may come upon you.

I give unto you my servant Joseph, to be a presiding elder over all my church, to be a translator, a revelator, a seer, and prophet.

I give unto him for counselors my servant Sidney Rigdon, and my servant William Law, that these may constitute a quorum and First Presidency, to receive the oracles for the whole church.

I give unto you my servant Brigham Young, to be a President over Twelve traveling Council;

Which Twelve hold the keys to open up the authority of my kingdom upon the four corners of the earth, and after that to send my word to every creature.

They are Heber C. Kimball, Parley P. Pratt, Orson Pratt, Orson Hyde, William Smith, John Taylor, John E. Page, Wilford Woodruff, Willard Richards, George A. Smith;

David Patten I have taken unto myself; behold, his Priesthood no man taketh from him; but verily I say unto you, another may be appointed unto the same calling.

And again, I say unto you, I give unto you a High Council, for the corner stone of Zion;

Viz., Samuel Bent, Henry G. Sherwood, George W. Harris, Charles C. Rich, Thomas Grover, Newel Knight, David Dort, Dunbar Wilson; (Seymour Brunson I have taken unto myself, no man taketh his Priesthood, but another may be appointed unto the same Priesthood in his stead; and verily I say unto you, let my servant Aaron Johnson be ordained unto this calling in his stead); David Fullmer, Alpheus Cutler, William Huntington.

And again, I give unto you Don C. Smith, to be a president over a quorum of High Priests;

Which ordinance is instituted for the purpose of qualifying those who shall be appointed standing presidents or servants over different Stakes scattered abroad,

And they may travel also if they choose, but rather be ordained for standing presidents, this is the office of their calling, saith the Lord your God.

I give unto him Amasa Lyman, and Noah Packard, for Counselors, that they may preside over the quorum of High Priests of my Church, saith the Lord.

And again, I say unto you, I give unto you John A. Hicks, Samuel Williams, and Jesse Baker, which Priesthood is to preside over the quorum of elders, which quorum is instituted for standing ministers, nevertheless they may travel, yet they are ordained to be standing ministers to my Church, saith the Lord.

And again, I give unto you, Joseph Young, Josiah Butterfield, Daniel Miles, Henry Harriman, Zera Pulsipher, Levi Hancock, James Foster, to preside over the quorum of seventies,

Which quorum is instituted for traveling elders to bear record of my name in all the world, wherever the traveling High Council, my apostles, shall send them to prepare a way before my face.

The difference between this quorum and the quorum of elders is.

that one is to travel continually, and the other is to preside over the churches from time to time; the one has the responsibility of presiding from time to time, and the other has no responsibility of presiding, saith the Lord your God.

And again, I say unto you, I give unto you Vinson Knight, Samuel H. Smith and Shadrach Roundy, if he will receive it, to preside over the bishopric; a knowledge of said bishopric is given unto you in the book of Doctrine and Covenants.

And again, I say unto you, Samuel Rolfe and his counselors for priests, and the president of the teachers and his counselors, and also the president of the deacons and his counselors, and also the president of the stake and his counselors;

The above offices I have given unto you, and the keys thereof, for helps and for governments, for the work of the ministry, and the perfecting of my Saints;

And a commandment I give unto you that you should fill all these offices and approve of those names which I have mentioned, or else disapprove of them at my general conference;

And that ye should prepare rooms for all these offices in my house when you build it unto my name, saith the Lord your God. Even so. Amen.

Thursday, 21.—Elders Brigham Young and Willard Richards completed the index to the Book of Mormon, and it was immediately put in type, which closed the printing of the first English edition.

Sunday, 24.—Elder Brigham Young preached twice at Liverpool on election and reprobation.

Hyrum Smith, who received the office of Patriarch in the Church, in place of Joseph Smith, Sen., deceased, has by revelation been appointed a Prophet and Revelator. William Law has by revelation been appointed one of the First Presidency, in place of Hyrum Smith, appointed Patriarch. George Miller has been appointed, by revelation, Bishop in place of Edward Partridge, deceased.

Hyrum Smith Installed as Patriarch.

Saturday, 30.—At a special conference of the Church of Jesus Christ of Latter-day Saints, held at Nauvoo pursuant to public notice, I was unanimously elected sole Trustee-in-Trust for the Church of Jesus Christ of Latter-day Saints.

Also Saturday the 30th and Sunday 31st, a Conference was held at Walnut Grove, Knox county, Illinois; Elder William Smith presiding; 113 members, 14 Elders were present; several branches were represented, and several persons baptized.

Monday, 1.—The first election in Nauvoo, for members of the City Council took place, and the following persons were elected by majorities varying from 330 to 337 votes; to wit, for Mayor, John C. Bennett; Aldermen, William Marks, Samuel H. Smith, Daniel H. Wells, Newel K. Whitney; Councilors, Joseph Smith Hyrum Smith, Sidney Rigdon, Charles C. Rich, John T. Barnett, Wilson Law, Don Carlos Smith, John P. Greene, Vinson Knight.

First Election of Municipal Officers in Nauvoo.

CITY OF NAUVOO, HANCOCK COUNTY, ILLINOIS, Feb. 1, A. D. 1841.

To the County Recorder of the County of Hancock:

DEAR SIR:—At a meeting of the Church of Jesus Christ of Latter-day Saints, at this place on Saturday, the 30th day of January, A. D. 1841, I was elected sole Trustee for said Church, to hold my office during life (my successors to be the First Presidency of said Church) and vested with plenary powers, as sole Trustee in Trust for the Church of Jesus Christ of Latter-day Saints, to receive, acquire, manage or convey property, real, personal, or mixed, for the sole use and benefit of said Church, agreeably to the provisions of an act entitled, "An Act Concerning Religious Societies," approved February 6, 1835.

JOSEPH SMITH, (L. S.)

STATE OF ILLINOIS HANCOCK CO., ss.

This day personally appeared before me, Daniel H. Wells, a justice of the peace, within and for the county of Hancock, County aforesaid, Isaac Galland, Robert B. Thompson, and John C. Bennett, who being duly sworn, depose and say that the foregoing certificate of Joseph Smith is true.

ISAAC GALLAND,
ROBERT B. THOMPSON
JOHN C. BENNETT.

Sworn to and subscribed this third day of February in the year of our Lord one thousand eight hundred and forty-one before me,

DANIEL H. WELLS,
Justice of the Peace.

The above is recorded in the county records at Carthage, in book No. 1, of Bonds and Mortgages, page 95, No. 87.

Wednesday 3.—Elder Taylor reports 160 baptized in Liverpool, England; in Ireland about 25; in the Isle of Man, 70; Hawarden, 30.   Elder Lorenzo Snow is laboring in London.

The City Council of Nauvoo was organized; the open-
Nauvoo City Council Organized.
ing prayer was offered by myself, after which the Mayor-elect delivered his inaugural address as published in the *Times and Seasons*, page 316, as follows:

INAUGURAL ADDRESS.

CITY OF NAUVOO, ILLINOIS, Feb. 3rd, 1841.

Gentlemen of the City Council, Aldermen and Councillors:

Having been elected to the Mayoralty of this city by the unanimous suffrage of all parties and interests, I now enter upon the duties devolving upon me as your Chief Magistrate under a deep sense of the responsibilities of the station.   I trust that the confidence reposed in me, by my fellow citizens, has not been misplaced, and for the honor conferred they will accept my warmest sentiments of gratitude.   By the munificence and wise legislation of noble, high-minded, and patriotic statesmen, and the grace of God, we have been blessed with one of the most liberal corporate acts ever granted by a legislative assembly.   As the presiding officer of the law-making department of the municipal government, it will be expected that I communicate to you, from time to time, by oral or written messages, for your deliberative consideration and action, such matters as may suggest themselves to me in relation to the public weal; and upon this occasion I beg leave to present the following as matters of paramount importance:

The 21st section of the addenda to the 13th section of the City Charter, concedes to you plenary power "to tax, restrain, prohibit and suppress, tippling houses, dram shops," etc., etc., and I now recommend, in the strongest possible terms, that you take prompt, strong, and decisive measures to "prohibit and suppress" all such establishments.   It is true you have the power "to tax," or license and tolerate, them, and thus add to the city finances; but I consider it much better to raise revenue by an advalorem tax on the property of sober men, than by licensing dram shops, or taxing the signs of the inebriated worshipers at the shrine of Bacchus.   The revels of bacchanalians in the houses of blasphemy and noise will always prove a disgrace to a moral people. Public sentiment will do much to suppress the vice of intemperance, and its concomitant evil results; but ample experience has incontrovertibly proven that it cannot do all—the law must be brought to the rescue, and an effective prohibitory ordinance enacted. This cannot be done at a better time than at the present. Let us commence correctly, and the great work of reform, at least so far as our peaceful city is concerned, can be summarily consummated. It would be difficult to calculate the vast amount of evil and crime that would be prevented, and the great good that would accrue to the public at large by fostering the cause of temperance; but suffice it to say that the one would be commensurate to the other. No sales of spirituous liquors whatever, in a less quantity than a quart, except in cases of sickness on the recommendation of a physician or surgeon duly accredited by the Chancellor and Regents of the University, should be tolerated. The liberty of selling the intoxicating cup is a false liberty—it enslaves, degrades, destroys; and wretchedness and want are attendant on every step,—its touch, like that of the poison upas, is death. Liberty to do good should be cheerfully and freely accorded to every man; but liberty to do evil, which is licentiousness, should be peremptorily prohibited. The public good imperiously demands it—and the cause of humanity pleads for help. The protecting ægis of the corporation should be thrown around every moral and religious institution of the day, which is in any way calculated to ennoble, or ameliorate the condition of the human family.

The immediate organization of the University, as contemplated in the 24th section of the act incorporating our city, cannot be too forcibly impressed upon you at this time. As all matters in relation to mental culture, and public instruction, from common schools up to the highest branches of a full collegiate course in the arts, sciences, and learned professions, will devolve upon the Chancellor and Regents of the University, they should be speedily elected, and instructed to perfect their plan, and enter upon its execution with as little delay as possible. The wheels of education should never be clogged, or retrograde, but roll progressively from the Alpha to the Omega of a most perfect, liberal, and thorough course of university attainments. The following observations in relation to false education, from Alexander's Messenger, so perfectly accords with my feelings and views on this highly important subject, that I cannot do better than incorporate them in this message.

"Among the changes for the worse, which the world has witnessed within the last century, we include that specious, superficial, incomplete way of doing certain things, which were formerly thought to be deserving of care, labor and attention. It would seem that appearance is now considered of more moment than reality. The modern mode of educa-

tion is an example in point.   Children are so instructed as to acquire
a smattering of everything, and as a matter of consequence, they know
nothing properly.   Seminaries and academies deal out their moral and
natural philosophy, their geometry, trigonometry, and astronomy, their
chemistry, botany, and mineralogy, until the mind of the pupil becomes a
chaos; and, like the stomach when it is overloaded with a variety
of food, it digests nothing, but converts the superabundant nutriment
to poison.   This mode of education answers one purpose—it enables
people to seem learned; and seemingly, by a great many, is thought all
sufficient.   Thus we are schooled in quackery, and are early taught to
regard showy and superficial attainments as most desirable.   Every
boarding school Miss is a Plato in petticoats, without an ounce of that
genuine knowledge, that true philosophy, which would enable her to be
useful in the world, and to escape those perils with which she must
necessarily be encompassed.   Young people are taught to use a variety
of hard terms, which they understand but imperfectly—to repeat lessons
which they are unable to apply—to astonish their grandmothers with a
display of their parrot-like acquisitions; but their mental energies are
clogged and torpified with a variety of learned lumber, most of which
is discarded from the brain long before its possessor knows how to use
it.   This is the quackery of education.

"The effects of the erring system are not easily obliterated. The habit of
using words without thought, sticks to the unfortunate student through
life, and should he ever learn to think, he cannot express his ideas without the most tedious and perplexing verbosity.   This is, more or less,
the fault of every writer in the nineteenth century.   The sense is encumbered with sound.   The scribbler appears to imagine that if he puts
a sufficient number of words together he has done his part; and, alas!
how many books are written on this principle.   Thus literature, and
even science itself, is overloaded with froth and flummery.   Verbaliz-
ing has become fashionable and indispensable, and one line from an
ancient author will furnish the materials for a modern treatise."

Our University should be a "utilitarian" institution—and competent,
industrious teachers and professors should be immediately elected for
the several departments.   "Knowledge is power,"—foster education
and we are forever free!   Nothing can be done which is more certainly
calculated to perpetuate the free institutions of our common country,
for which our progenitors "fought and bled, and died," than the general diffusion of useful knowledge amongst the people.   Education
should always be of a purely practical character, for such, and such
alone, is calculated to perfect the happiness and prosperity of our fellow-citizens—ignorance, impudence, and false knowledge, are equally
detestible,—shame and confusion follow in their train.   As you now

possess the power, afford the most ample facilities to the Regents to make their plans complete; and thus enable them to set a glorious example to the world at large. The most liberal policy should attend the organization of the University, and equal honors and privileges should be extended to all classes of the community.

In order to carry out the provisions of the 25th section of the act incorporating our city, I would recommend the immediate organization of the Legion. Comprising, as it does, the entire military power of our city, with a provision allowing any citizen of Hancock county to unite by voluntary enrollment, early facilities should be afforded the court martial for perfecting their plans of drill, rules, and regulations. Nothing is more necessary to the preservation of order and the supremacy of the laws, than the perfect organization of our military forces, under a uniform and rigid discpline and approved judicious drill; and to this end I desire to see all the departments and cohorts of the Legion put in immediate requisition. The Legion should be all powerful, panoplied with justice and equity, to consummate the designs of its projectors— at all times ready, as minute men, to serve the state in such way and manner as may, from time to time, be pointed out by the Governor. You have long sought an opportunity of showing your attachment to the state government of Illinois—it is now afforded; the Legion should maintain the constitution and the laws, and be ready at all times for the public defense. The winged warrior of the air perches upon the pole of American liberty, and the beast that has the temerity to ruffle her feathers should be made to feel the power of her talons; and until she ceases to be our proud national emblem we should not cease to show our attachment to Illinois. Should the tocsin of alarm ever be sounded, and the Legion called to the tented field by our Executive, I hope to see it able, under one of the proudest mottoes that ever blazed upon a warrior's shield—*Sicut patribus sit Deus nobis;* "as God was with our fathers, so may He be with us"—to fight the battles of our country, as victors, and as freemen; the juice of the uva, or the spirit of insubordination should never enter our camp,—but we should stand, ever stand, as a united people—one and indivisible.

I would earnestly recommend the construction of a wing-dam in the Mississippi, at the mouth of the ravine at or near the head of Main street, and the excavation of a ship canal from that point to a point terminating in a grand reservoir on the bank of said river, east of the foot of said street, a distance of about two miles. This would afford, at the various outlets, the most ample water power for propelling any amount of machinery for mill and manufacturing purposes, so essentially necessary to the building up of a great commercial city in the heart of one of the most productive and delightful countries on earth. I would advise that an agent be immediately appointed on behalf of the city corporation, to negotiate with eastern capitalists for the completion of this great work, on the most advantageous terms, even to the conveyance of the privilege for a term of years. This work finished, and the future greatness of this city is placed upon an imperishable basis. In addition to the great advantages that will otherwise accrue to the city and country by the construction of this noble work, it would afford the best harbor for steamboats, for winter quarters, on this magnificent stream.

The public health requires that the low lands, bordering on the Mississippi, should be immediately drained, and the entire timber removed. This can and will be one of the most healthful cities in the west, provided you take prompt and decisive action in the premises. A board of health should be appointed and vested with the usual powers and prerogatives.

The Governor, council of revision, and legislature of Illinois, should be held in everlasting remembrance by our people—they burst the chains of slavery and proclaimed us forever free! A vote of thanks, couched in the strongest language possible, should be tendered them in our corporate capacity; and, when this is done, Quincy, our first noble city of refuge, when we came from the slaughter in Missouri with our garments stained with blood, should not be forgotten.

As the Chief Magistrate of your city I am determined to execute all state laws and city ordinances passed in pursuance to law, to the very letter, should it require the strong arm of military power to enable me to do so. As an officer I know no man; the peaceful, unoffending citizen shall be protected in the full exercise of all his civil, political, and religious rights, and the guilty violator of law shall be punished, without respect to persons.

All of which is respectfully submitted.* JOHN C. BENNETT.

The following persons were elected by the council to their offices, to-wit—Henry G. Sherwood, marshal; James Sloan, recorder; Robert B. Thompson, treasurer; James Robinson, assessor; Austin Cowles, supervisor of streets. I presented to the city council the following resolution, which was unanimously adopted:

* The foregoing speech is not printed in the "History of Joseph Smith" as published in the *Deseret News* and *Millennial Star*, but such is the prominence of John C. Bennett in the period of the history now reached, and such the dispicable part he later plays, that, as affording an insight into his character, the speech becomes important, hence given here *in extenso*, as it was published in the *Times and Seasons*, Vol. II, No. 8.

Resolved by the City Council of the City of Nauvoo, that the un-feigned thanks of this community be respectfully tendered to the Gov-ernor, Council of Revision, and Legislature of the state of Illinois, as a feeble testimonial of their respect and esteem for noble, high-minded, and patriotic statesmen; and as an evidence of gratitude for the signal powers recently conferred; also that the citizens of Quincy be held in everlasting remembrance, for their unparalleled liberality and marked kindness to our people, when in their greatest state of suffering and want.

I presented a bill for an ordinance concerning the Uni-versity of Nauvoo, which passed as follows:

Sec. 1. Be it ordained by the City Council of the City of Nauvoo, that the "University of the City of Nauvoo," be, and the same is here-by organized by the appointment of the following Board of Trustees, to-wit—John C. Bennett, chancellor; William Law, registrar; and Joseph Smith, Sidney Rigdon, Hyrum Smith, William Marks, Samuel H. Smith, Daniel H. Wells, Newel K. Whitney, Charles C. Rich, John T. Barnett, Wilson Law, Don Carlos Smith, John P. Greene, Vinson Knight, Isaac Galland, Elias Higbee, Robert D. Foster, James Adams, Robert B. Thompson, Samuel Bennett, Ebenezer Robinson, John Snider, George Miller, and Lenos M. Knight, Regents of the "Uni-versity of the City of Nauvoo;" as contemplated in the 24th section of "An Act to incorporate the City of Nauvoo," approved December 16, 1840.

Sec. 2. The board named in the first section of this ordinance, shall hold its first meeting at the office of Joseph Smith, on Tuesday, the 9th day of February, 1841, at 2 o'clock p. m.

Passed February 3, 1841.　　　　　　JOHN C. BENNETT, Mayor.
　　　　　　　　　　　　　　　　　　JAMES SLOAN, Recorder.

I also presented a bill for an ordinance organizing the Nauvoo Legion, which passed the same day, as follows:

Sec. 1. Be it ordained by the City Council of the City of Nauvoo, that the inhabitants of the City of Nauvoo, and such citizens of Hancock county as may unite by voluntary enrollment, be, and they are hereby organized into a body of independent military men, to be called the "Nauvoo Legion," as contemplated in the 25th section of "An Act to incorporate the City of Nauvoo," approved December 16, 1840.

Sec. 2. The Legion shall be, and is hereby divided into two cohorts; the horse troops to constitute the first cohort, and the foot troops to constitute the second cohort.

Sec. 3.   The general officers of the Legion shall consist of a lieuten-ant-general, as the chief commanding and reviewing officer, and presi-dent of the court martial and Legion; a major-general, as the second in command in the Legion, the secretary of the court martial and Legion, and adjutant and inspector-general; a brigadier-general, as the commander of the first cohort; and brigadier-general, as commander of the second cohort.

Sec. 4.   The staff of the lieutenant-general shall consist of two prin-cipal aids-de-camp, with the rank of colonels of cavalry; and a guard of twelve aids-de-camp, with the rank of captain of infantry; and a drill officer, with the rank of colonel of dragoons, who shall likewise be the chief officer of the guard.

Sec. 5.   The staff of the major-general shall consist of an adjutant, a surgeon-in-chief, a cornet, a quarter-master, a paymaster, a commis-sary, and a chaplain, with the rank of colonels of infantry; a surgeon for each cohort, a quarter-master-sergeant, sergeant-major, and chief musician, with the rank of captains of light infantry, and two musicians, with the rank of captains of infantry.

Sec. 6.   The staff of each brigadier-general shall consist of one aid-de-camp, with the rank of lieutenant-colonel of infantry, provided that the said brigadiers shall have access to the staff of the major-general, when not otherwise in service.

Sec. 7.   No officer shall hereafter be elected by the various companies of the Legion, except upon the nomination of the court-martial; and it is hereby made the duty of the court-martial to nominate at least two candidates for each vacant office, whenever such vacancies occur.

Sec. 8.   The court-martial shall fill and supply all offices ranking be-tween captains and brigadier-generals by granting brevet commissions to the most worthy company officers of the line, who shall thereafter take rank, and command according to the date of their brevets, pro-vided that their original place in the line shall not thereby be vacated.

Sec. 9.   The court-martial, consisting of all the military officers, com-missioned or entitled to commissions, within the limits of the city cor-poration, shall meet at the office of Joseph Smith, on Thursday, the 4th day of February, 1841, at 10 o'clock a.m.; and then and there proceed to elect the general officers of the Legion, as contemplated in the 3rd section of this ordinance.

Sec. 10.   The court-martial shall adopt for the Legion, as nearly as may be, and so far as applicable, the discipline, drill, uniform, rules, and regulations of the United States army.

Passed February 8, 1841.

JOHN C. BENNETT, Mayor.
JAMES SLOAN, Recorder.

Joseph Smith, Hyrum Smith, Don C. Smith, and Charles C. Rich were duly sworn as members of the City Council.*

The following addition has been made to the Charter of the Nauvoo Legion by the legislature—

Any citizen of Hancock county may, by voluntary enrollment, attach himself to the Nauvoo Legion, with all the privileges, which appertain to that independent military body.

I gave a general invitation to my friends to enroll themselves, so as to have a perfect organization by the fourth of July. I was appointed chairman of several committees, viz: "On the Canal," "For Vacating the Town of Commerce," "Vending Spirituous Liquors," "Code of City Ordinances," "Board of Health," &c. Council adjourned to the 8th.

Thursday, 4.

Minutes of the Meeting which Organized the Nauvoo Legion.

Pursuant to an ordinance of the City Council of the City of Nauvoo, entitled, "An ordinance organizing the Nauvoo Legion," passed February 3, 1841, a court-martial, composed of the commissioned officers of the militia of the state of Illinois, within the city of Nauvoo, assembled at the office of Joseph Smith, on Thursday at 10 o'clock a. m., the 4th day of February, 1841: present—John C. Bennett, quarter-master-general of the state of Illinois; Lieutenant-Colonel Don Carlos Smith; Captains Charles C. Rich, Wilson Law, Albert P. Rockwood, William Law, Titus Billings, Stephen Markham; first lieutenants, Francis M. Higbee, John T. Barnett, John D. Parker, Benjamin S. Wilber, Amos Davis; second lieutenants, Chancy L. Higbee, Nelson Higgins, David H. Redfield, Hosea Stout, Stephen Winchester, Thomas Rich; third lieutenants, John C. Annis, and Alexander Badlam. The court was

* Following is the form of oath taken:

We, Joseph Smith, Hyrum Smith, Don C. Smith, and Charles C. Rich, do solemnly swear in the presence of Almighty God that we will support the Constitution of the United States, and of the State of Illinois, and that we will well and truly perform the duties of councilors of the City of Nauvoo, according to law, and the best of our abilities.

JOSEPH SMITH,
HYRUM SMITH,
DON C. SMITH,
CHARLES C. RICH.

December 3, 1841.

called to order by General Bennett. On motion, Joseph Smith and Hugh McFall were requested to sit in the court. The court-martial then proceeded to the election of the general officers of the Legion; whereupon Joseph Smith was duly elected lieutenant-general of the Nauvoo Legion, and John C. Bennett, major-general. Colonel Wilson Law was elected brigadier-general of the first cohort, and Lieutenant-Colonel Don Carlos Smith brigadier-general of the second cohort, by unanimous vote of the court-martial. Lieutenant-general Joseph Smith, after being duly sworn into office, appointed the following named persons for his staff, to-wit—Captain A. P. Rockwood to be drill officer; Captains William Law and Robert B. Thompson, aids-de-camp; and James Allred, Thomas Grover, C. M. Kreymeyer, John L. Butler, John Snider, Alpheus Cutler, Reynolds Cahoon, Elias Higbee, Henry G. Sherwood, Shadrack Roundy, Samuel H. Smith, and Vinson Knight, guards, and assistant aids-de-camp. The Legion, at its organization, was composed of six companies.

Friday, 5.—Elder Reuben Hedlock is laboring in Glasgow, Scotland. The Church in that place numbers 55, and the spirit of enquiry increases.

Saturday, 6.

Minutes of a Council at Brother Richard Harrison's, 72 Burlington Street, Liverpool, for organizing a company of Saints going to New Orleans on the ship "Sheffield," Captain Porter.

Elders Brigham Young, Willard Richards, John Tayor, and other officers, present. Elder Hyrum Clark was chosen president, and Thomas Walmsley, Miles Romney, Edward Martin, John Taylor, Francis Clark, and John Riley, counselors to President Clark. Edward Martin, clerk and historian. Peter Maughan and John Taylor were ordained Elders. President Clark and his counselors were blessed and set apart for their mission.

Sunday, 7.—Ship *Sheffield* sailed from Liverpool with 235 Saints.

Monday, 8.—Levi Richards writes from Lugwardine—

To the Editor of the Star:

Since Stanley Hill conference, I have attended about thirty council meetings of Church officers, in eleven different places in Herefordshire, Gloucestershire, and Worcestershire, making a circuit of nearly one hundred miles. Union and harmony prevail among them, and a disposition to add to their faith. New places are frequently opened for preaching, which is generally supplied. Many are baptized every week, although the ice has to yield its natural claims, and be put aside. The gift of healing is manifested to quite an extent in this region. The gift of tongues is received in most of the branches where I am acquainted. The spirit of persecution is not yet wholly cast out of the world: for recently preaching was held for the first time in Pendock parish, eight miles from Ledbury, when a congregation, respectable in numbers and appearance, were compelled to retire prematurely, in consequence of the quantity of gravel thrown upon the roof and against the windows. The mob were numerous, and pelted the Saints on their way home with mud. The meeting was held at the shop of a tradesman, who had been clerk of the parish, but was so fortunate as to obey the Gospel, and be turned out of his stewardship; and his wife was dismissed from her school, for the same reason, by the parson of the parish. More or less of the Saints are turned out of employ, and out of their houses, for obeying the Gospel.

City Council met according to adjournment and opened by prayer, which was made a standing rule of the council. I reported a bill for the survey of a canal through the city, which was accepted; and I was appointed to contract for its survey. I also reported a bill for an ordinance on temperance, which was read and laid over.

Nauvoo Council Opened by Prayer.

Wednesday, 10.—Elder James Burnham writes from Overton, Flintshire, North Wales—

I have organized two branches, with about 150 members; and we are continually baptizing, whether it be cold or hot. There is great opposition.

Thursday, 11.—Elders Young, Richards, and Taylor, in council at 72 Burlington Street, Liverpool, set apart, by the laying on of hands, Elder Daniel Browett, to take charge of a company of Saints, about to sail for New Orleans on ship *Echo*, Captain Wood; and John Cheese, David Wilding, James Lavender, William Jenkins, Robert Harris, and John Ellison, to be his counselors. Robert Harris was ordained an Elder, and Elder Browett was appointed clerk and historian of the company.

The *Echo* Company.

Saturday, 13.—Elder Orson Hyde sailed from New York for Liverpool, on his way to Jerusalem, accompanied by Elder George J. Adams.

Sunday, 14.

Minutes of the London Conference.

A conference of the Church of Jesus Christ of Latter-day Saints was held at Barrett's Academy, 57 King Square, Goswell Road, London, on Sunday, the 14th of February, 1841, there being present—Elders Heber C. Kimball, Wilford Woodruff, Lorenzo Snow, William Pitt, and four Priests. The meeting was called to order by Elder Kimball at 2 o'clock p. m. Moved by Elder Kimball, seconded by Elder Pitt, that Elder Woodruff be president of this conference; carried unanimously. Moved by Elder Kimball, seconded by Elder Woodruff, that Dr. W. Copeland be clerk; carried unanimously. The meeting opened by Elder Kimball with prayer and singing. The president then called upon the official members to represent their respective branches. The church at Ipswich was represented by Elder Pitt, as consisting of twelve members, one Elder, one Priest, and one Teacher. The church at Bedford was represented by Robert Williams, Priest, as consisting of forty-two members, one Priest, seven moved, two died. The church at Woolwich was represented by John Griffith, Priest, as consisting of six members, one Priest. The church in London was represented by Elder Kimball as consisting of forty-six members, one Elder, two Priests: excellent prospects of a continued increase. James Allen was ordained an Elder, and Thomas Barnes a Priest. Robert Williams was ordained an Elder, to preside over the branch at Bedford; and William Smith and John Sheffield were ordained Priests. Richard Bates was ordained a Priest, in the branch of Woolwich, and A. Painter a Teacher—all under the hands of Elders Kimball, Woodruff and Snow. It was then moved by Elder Kimball, seconded by Elder Woodruff, that Elder Snow be appointed president of this [the Woolwich] conference, also to take the superintendency of the branch in London. Much valuable instruction was given by Elders Kimball and Woodruff in relation to the duties of the official members. It was then moved by Elder Kimball, and seconded by Elder Snow, that this conference be adjourned to Sunday, 16th of May, 1841. The conference was then closed at half-past five, by singing and prayer.

DR. W. COPELAND, Clerk.

Monday, 15.—As chairman of the committee [on the vending of spirituous liquors] I reported a bill to the City

Council, which, after a long discussion, passed into "An ordinance in relation to temperance."

ORDINANCE.

Sec. 1.   Be it ordained by the City Council of the City of Nauvoo, that all persons and establishments whatever, in this city, are prohibited from vending whisky in a less quantity than a gallon, or other spirituous liquors in a less quantity than a quart, to any person whatever, excepting on the recommendation of a physician, duly accredited in writing, by the Chancellor and Regents of the University of the City of Nauvoo; and any person guilty of any act contrary to the prohibition contained in this ordinance, shall, on conviction thereof before the Mayor or municipal court, be fined in any sum not exceeding twenty-five dollars, at the discretion of said Mayor or municipal court; and any person or persons who shall attempt to evade this ordinance by giving away liquor, or by any other means, shall be considered alike amenable, and fined as aforesaid.

Passed February 15, 1841.

JOHN C. BENNETT, Mayor.
JAMES SLOAN, Recorder.

In the discussion of the foregoing bill, I spoke at great length on the use of liquors, and showed that they were unnecessary, and operate as a poison in the stomach, and that roots and herbs can be found to effect all necessary purposes.

Tuesday, 16.

Missouri's "White-washing."

Resolved by the Senate [of the state of Missouri], the House of Representatives concurring, that two thousand copies of the evidence taken before the examining court in relation to "Mormon" difficulties, and such of the letters, orders, and correspondence on that subject, on file in the office of the secretary of state, as may be selected by a joint committee of the two houses, shall be published in pamphlet form, under the direction of the secretary of state; that one copy, in lieu of the manuscript copies, heretofore ordered, be sent to our delegation in Congress, to be laid before the House to which they respectively belong, one to each member of Congress, and the residue be distributed among the Mormons of the general assembly.

Approved February 16, 1841.*

* For a proper characterization of this document see Vol. III, this History, p. 256

Is this Missouri's last struggle to retrieve her lost character to publish to the world a one-sided statement of her robberies, murders, and extermination which she had committed without provocation, at a time when not one Saint was left in Missouri to tell the truth about them?

The ship *Echo* sailed from Liverpool for New Orleans, with 109 Saints, led by Daniel Browett.

Saturday, 20.—Elder Brigham Young went to Harwarden and preached twice on Sunday.

Elders William Kay and Thomas Richardson introduced the Gospel into the City of Hereford.

The court-martial of the Nauvoo Legion, by a unanimous vote, adopted the following resolutions, to-wit —

Legion Resolutions.

That no person whatever, residing within the limits of the City of Nauvoo, betweent the ages of 18 and 45 years, excepting such as are exempted by the laws of the United States, shall be exempt from military duty, unless exempted by a special act of this court; and the fines for neglecting or refusing to appear on the days of general parade were fixed at the following rates: for generals, $25; colonels, $20; captains, $15; lieutenants, $10; and musicians and privates, $5; and for company parade at the following rates—for commissioned officers, $5; noncommissioned officers, $3; musicians and privates, $2. The 1st and 6th of April, and the 3rd of July, were fixed upon as days for general parade for this year.

Ordered that Edward P. Duzette enlist and organize a band of music, not exceeding twenty men. It was also reported that John Scott had been elected captain in the place of William Law, and Lieutenant Hosea Stout in the place of Albert P. Rockwood, who has been promoted.

Monday, 22.—I laid before the City Council the following—

RESOLUTION.

Resolved by the City Council of the City of Nauvoo, that the freedom of the city be, and the same hereby is, conferred on the present Governor, lieutenant-governor, council of revision, and members of both houses of the general assembly, of the state of Illinois, as an evidence of our gratitude for their great liberality and kindness to this community, during the present winter, which was adopted unanimously.

I also presented the following bill for "An ordinance in relation to the University."

ORDINANCE.

Sec. 1.　Be it ordained by the City Council of the City of Nauvoo, that all matters and powers whatever in relation to common schools, and all other institutions of learning within the City of Nauvoo be, and the same hereby are transferred from the City Council of the City of Nauvoo, to the chancellor and regents of the University of the City of Nauvoo.

Passed February 22, 1841.

John C. Bennett, Mayor.
James Sloan, Recorder.

Tuesday, 23.—Elder Kington writes from Bristol, England, that eight have been baptized in that place.

AN ACT TO INCORPORATE THE NAUVOO HOUSE ASSOCIATION.

Sec. 1.　Be it enacted by the people of the state of Illinois, represented in the general assembly, that George Miller, Lyman Wight, John Snider, and Peter Haws, and their associates, are hereby declared a body corporate, under the name and style of the "Nauvoo House Association;" and they are hereby authorized to erect and furnish a public house of entertainment, to be called the "Nauvoo House."

Sec. 2.　The above-named George Miller, Lyman Wight, John Snider, and Peter Haws, and their associates, are hereby declared to be the trustees of the association, with full power and authority to hold in joint tenancy, by themselves and their successors in office, a certain lot in the City of Nauvoo, in the county of Hancock, and state of Illinois, known and designated on the plat of said city, as the south half of lot numbered fifty-six, for the purpose of erecting thereon the house contemplated in the first section of this act.

Sec. 3.　The said trustees are further authorized and empowered to obtain by stock subscription, by themselves or their duly authorized agents, the sum of one hundred and fifty thousand dollars, which shall be divided into shares of fifty dollars each.

Sec. 4.　No individual shall be permitted to hold more than three hundred, nor less than one share of stock, and certificates of stock shall be delivered to subscribers, so soon as their subscriptions are paid in and not before.

Sec. 5.　As soon as the contemplated house shall have been completed and furnished, the stockholders shall appoint such agents as the trustees may deem necessary in the management of the affairs of said association.

Sec. 6.　The trustees shall have power to sue and be sued, plead and be impleaded in any court in this state, in the name and style of the "Trustees of the Nauvoo House Association."

Sec. 7.　They shall also take the general care and supervision in procuring materials for said house, and constructing and erecting the same, and further to superintend its general management, and to do and perform all matters and things which may be necessary to be done, in order to secure the interest and promote the objects of this association.

Sec. 8.　This association shall continue twenty years from the passage of this act, and the house herein provided for shall be kept for the accommodation of strangers, travelers, and all other persons who may resort therein for rest and refreshment.

Sec. 9.　It is moreover established as a perpetual rule of said house, to be observed by all persons who may keep or occupy the same, that spirituous liquors of every description are prohibited, and that such liquor shall never be vended as a beverage, or introduced into common use, in said house.

Sec. 10.　And whereas Joseph Smith has furnished the said association with the ground whereon to erect said house, it is further declared that the said Smith and his heirs shall hold, by perpetual succession, a suite of rooms in the said house, to be set apart and conveyed in due form of law to him and his heirs by the said trustees, as soon as the same are completed.

Sec. 11.　The Board of Trustees shall appoint one of their number as president thereof.

Approved February 23, 1841.

THOMAS CARLIN,

Governor.

W. L. D. EWING,

Speaker of the House of Representatives.

S. H. ANDERSON,

Speaker of the Senate.

State of Illinois,　　　　　} s.s.
　　Office of Secretary of State,

I, Stephen A. Douglas, Secretary of State, do hereby certify the foregoing to be a true and perfect copy of the enrolled law on file in my office.

Witness my hand and the seal of State.

Springfield, February 24, A. D. 1841.

[SEAL.]   S. A. DOUGLAS,
                                    Secretary of State.

AN ACT TO INCORPORATE THE NAUVOO AGRICULTURAL AND MANUFAC-
    TURING ASSOCIATION IN THE COUNTY OF HANCOCK.

Sec. 1. Be it enacted by the people of the state of Illinois, repre-
sented in the general assembly, that Sidney Rigdon, George W. Robin-
son, Samuel James, Wilson Law, Daniel H. Wells, Hyrum Smith,
George Miller, William Marks, Peter Haws, Vinson Knight, John Scott,
Don Carlos Smith, William Huntington, Sen., Ebenezer Robinson,
Robert B. Thompson, William Law, James Allred, John T. Barnett,
Theodore Turley, John C. Bennett, Elias Higbee, Isaac Higbee, Joseph
Smith, Alpheus Cutler, Israel Barlow, R. D. Foster, John F. Olney, John
Snider, Leonard Soby, Orson Pratt, James Kelley, Sidney A. Knowlton, John P. Greene, John F. Weld, and their associates and successors,
are hereby constituted a body corporate and politic, by the name of
"The Nauvoo Agricultural and Manufacturing Association," and by
that name shall be capable of suing and being sued, pleading and
being impleaded, answering and being answered, in all courts and
places, and may have a common seal, and may alter the same at
pleasure.

Sec. 2. The sole object and purpose of said association shall be for
the promotion of agriculture and husbandry in all its branches, and for
the manufacture of flour, lumber, and such other useful articles as are
necessary for the ordinary purposes of life.

Sec. 3. The capital stock of said association shall be one hundred
thousand dollars, with the privilege of increasing it to the sum of three
hundred thousand dollars, to be divided into shares of fifty dollars,
which shall be considered personal property, and be assignable in such
manner as the said corporation may, by its by-laws, provide; which
capital stock shall be exclusively devoted to the object and purposes set
forth in the second section of this act, and to no other object and purposes, and to the same end the said corporation shall have power to purchase, hold, and convey real estate, and other property, to the amount
of its capital.

Sec. 4. Said corporation shall have power, by the trustees, or a majority of them present at any regularly called meeting, to make by-
laws for its own government, for the purpose of carrying out the objects

of this association, provided the same are not repugnant to the laws and constitution of this state, or of the United States.

Sec. 5. Joseph Smith, Sidney Rigdon, and William Law shall be commissioners to receive subscriptions for, and distribute said capital stock for said corporation; said commissioners, or a majority of them, shall, within six months after the passage of this act, either by themselves or their duly appointed agents, open a subscription book for said stock at such times and places as they shall appoint, and at the time of subscription for such stock, at least ten per cent upon each share subscribed for, shall be paid to said commissioners, or their duly appointed agents; and the remainder of said stock, so subscribed for, shall be paid in such sums, and at such times, as shall be provided for by the by-laws of said corporation.

Sec. 6. In case the stock of said corporation shall not all be taken up within one year from the passage of this act, the duties of said commissioners shall cease, and the trustees of said corporation, or a quorum thereof, may thereafter receive subscriptions to said stock, from time to time, until the whole shall be subscribed.

Sec. 7. The stock, property, and concerns of said corporation shall be managed by twenty trustees, who shall be stockholders of said corporation, any five of whom, to be designated by a majority of the trustees, shall form a quorum for the transaction of all ordinary business of said corporation, the election of which trustees shall be annual. The first mentioned twenty persons, whose names are recited in the first section of this act, shall be the first trustees of said corporation, and shall hold their offices until the first Monday in September, A. D. 1841, and until others shall be elected in their places.

Sec. 8. The trustees of said corporation for every subsequent year shall be elected on the first Monday in September, in each and every year, at such place as the trustees for the time being shall appoint, and of which election they shall give at least fifteen days previous notice by advertisement in some newspaper, in or near the City of Nauvoo. At every election of trustees, each stockholder shall be entitled to one vote on each share of stock owned by him: provided that no stockholder shall be entitled to more than twenty votes, and said stockholders, may vote either in person or by proxy. The election for trustees shall be conducted in such manner as shall be pointed out by the by-laws of said corporation, and whenever a vacancy shall happen by death, resignation, or otherwise, among the trustees, the remaining trustees shall have power to fill such vacancy, until the next general election for trustees.

Sec. 9. The trustees of said corporation, as soon as may be, after their appointment or election under this act, shall proceed to elect, out of their number, a president, treasurer, and secretary, who shall respectively hold their offices during one year, and until others shall be elected to fill their places, and whose duties shall be defined and prescribed by the by-laws of the corporation; and said trustees shall also appoint such agents and other persons as may be necessary to conduct the proper business, and accomplish the declared objects of said corporation, and shall likewise have power to fill any vacancy occasioned by the death, resignation, or removal of any officer of said corporation.

Sec. 10.   This act shall be construed as a public act, and continue in force for the period of twenty years.   And the trustees appointed under the provisions of this act, shall hold their first meeting at the City of Nauvoo, on the first Monday of April, A. D. 1841.

Approved February 27, 1841.

THOMAS CARLIN,

Governor.

W. L. D. EWING,

Speaker of the House of Representatives.

S. H. ANDERSON,

Speaker of the Senate.

State of Illinois, Office of Secretary of State.

I, Lyman Trumbull, Secretary of State, do hereby certify the foregoing to be a true and perfect copy of the enrolled law on the file in my office.

Given under my hand and seal of State, Springfield, March 10, 1841.

LYMAN TRUMBULL,

Secretary of State.

Wednesday, 24.—Elder Brigham Young returned to Liverpool, and on the 25th attended a patriarchal blessing meeting at Brother Dumville's. Father Melling officiated; Elder James Whitehead, scribe.

Saturday, 27.—President Brigham Young went to Manchester, and preached in Lombard Street room on Sunday, the 28th.

Monday, March 1.—The City Council divided the city into four wards, at my suggestion, to-wit: all the district of country within the city limits, north of the center of Knight street, and west of the center of Wells street, shall constitute the first ward.   North of the center of Knight street and east of the center of Wells street, the second ward.   South

Division of Nauvoo into Municipal Wards.

of the center of Knight street, and east of the center of Wells street, the third ward. South of the center of Knight street, and west of the center of Wells street, the fourth ward.

I attended the City Council, and presented a bill for "An ordinance in relation to Religious Societies."

Ordinance on Religious Liberty in Nauvoo.

Sec. 1. Be it ordained by the City Council of the City of Nauvoo, that the Catholics, Presbyterians, Methodists, Baptists, Latter-day Saints, Quakers, Episcopals, Universalists, Unitarians, Mohammedans, and all other religious sects and denominations whatever, shall have free toleration, and equal privileges, in this city; and should any person be guilty of ridiculing, and abusing or otherwise depreciating another in consequence of his religion, or of disturbing or interrupting any religious meeting within the limits of this city, he shall, on conviction thereof before the Mayor or Municipal Court, be considered a disturber of the public peace, and fined in any sum not exceeding five hundred dollars, or imprisoned not exceeding six months, or both, at the discretion of said Mayor or Court.

Sec. 2. It is hereby made the duty of all Municipal officers to notice and report to the Mayor any breach or violation of this, or any other ordinance of this city, that may come within their knowledge, or of which they may be advised; and any officer aforesaid, is hereby fully authorized to arrest all such violators of rule, law and order, either with or without process.

Passed March 1, 1841.

JOHN C. BENNETT, Mayor.
JAMES SLOAN, Recorder.

I also presented a bill as follows:

An Ordinance in Relation to Public Meetings.

Sec. 1. Be it ordained by the City Council of the City of Nauvoo, that in order to guarantee the constitutional right of free discussion upon all subjects, the citizens of this city, may from time to time peaceably assemble themselves together for all peaceable or lawful purposes whatever; and should any person be guilty of disturbing or interrupting any such meeting or assemblage, he shall on conviction thereof before the Mayor or Municipal Court, be considered a disturber of the public peace, and fined in any sum not exceeding five hundred dollars, or imprisoned not exceeding six months, or both, at the discretion of said mayor or court.

Sec. 2.   Should any person be guilty of exciting the people to riot or rebellion, or of participating in a mob, or any other unlawful riotous or tumultuous assemblage of the people, or of refusing to obey any civil officer, executing the ordinances of the city, or the general laws of the state or United States, or of neglecting or refusing to obey promptly, any military order for the due execution of said law or ordinances, he shall, on conviction thereof as aforesaid, be fined or imprisoned, or both, as aforesaid.

Passed March 1, 1841.

JOHN C. BENNETT, Mayor.
JAMES SLOAN, Recorder.

I also offered a bill for "An ordinance, creating certain additional City Officers."

ORDINANCE.

Sec. 1.   Be it ordained by the City Council of the City of Nauvoo, that in addition to the city officers heretofore elected, there shall be elected by the City Council, one high constable for each ward; one surveyor and engineer, one market master, one weigher and sealer, and one collector for the city, whose duties shall hereafter be defined by ordinance.

Passed March 1, 1841.   JOHN C. BENNETT, Mayor.
JAMES SLOAN, Recorder.

I presented the following report:

COMMITTE'S REPORT.

Your committee, to whom was referred that portion of the address of his honor, the Mayor, which recommended the propriety of vacating the town plats, Commerce, and the City of Commerce, and incorporating them with the city plat of Nauvoo, would respectfully report—That they consider the recommendation contained in the address as one of great importance to the future welfare and prosperity of this city, and if carried into effect would make the streets regular and uniform, and materially tend to beautify this city.   We would therefore respectfully recommend that the survey of the City of Nauvoo be carried through the town plats of Commerce and the City of Commerce, as soon as it may be practicable.

We would therefore recommend to the council the passage of the following resolution—That the town plats of Commerce, and Commerce City be vacated, and that the same stand vacated from this time forth, and forever; and that the same be incorporated with the City of Nauvoo, from this time henceforth and forever.

All of which is respectfully submitted.

JOSEPH SMITH, Chairman.

The report was received and adopted, and an ordinance passed accordingly.

A vote of thanks, and the freedom of the city were conferred on the Honorable Richard M. Young, United States Senator for Illinois.

Tuesday, 2.—Elder Brigham Young visited Oldham, and returned on Wednesday, 3rd, to Manchester. Elders Orson Hyde and George J. Adams arrived in Liverpool.

Thursday, 4.—Elder Willard Richards left Liverpool for Preston, and was followed by Elders Hyde, Adams, and Fielding on the 5th.

General William Henry Harrison was inaugurated President of the United States.

Friday, 5.—Elder Parley P. Pratt removed the *Star* office to 47 Oxford Road, Manchester.

Sunday, 7.—Elders Young and Kimball preached at the Carpenter's Hall, Manchester.

Monday, 8.—I attended the City Council. The follow-

Appointment of City Officers.

ing appointments were made, viz: Alanson Ripley, city surveyor; Theodore Turley, weigher and sealer; James Robinson, assessor; Stephen Markham, market master; James Allred was sworn supervisor of streets, and James Allred, Dimick B. Huntington, and George Morey, high constables.

I gave my views on several local measures proposed by the council.

Wednesday, 10.

Letter of Brigham Young to the Editor of the Star—On Family Prayer.

LIVERPOOL, March 10, 1841.

To the Editor of the Star:

DEAR BROTHER:—I feel anxious to address a few lines to you, on the subject of family prayer (and shall feel obliged by your inserting the same in your next *Star*), for the purpose of imparting instruction to the brethren in general. Having traveled through many branches of the Church in England, I have found it to be a general custom among the brethren I visited, that when any of the Traveling Elders are present, they wait for the Elder to go forward in family prayer, instead of attending to that duty themselves. That is not right; and I would say to them that it would be better for them to understand their duty on this subject. My dear brethren, remember that the Lord holds all of us responsible for our conduct here. He held our father Adam responsible for his conduct, but no more than He does us, in proportion to the station we hold. The kings of the earth will have to give an account to God, for their conduct in a kingly capacity. Kings are heads of nations, governors are heads of provinces; so are fathers or husbands governors of their own houses, and should act accordingly. Heads of families should always take the charge of family worship, and call their family together at a seasonable hour, and not wait for every person to get through with all they may have to say or do. If it were my prerogative to adopt a plan for family prayer, it would be the following: Call your family or household together every morning and evening, previous to coming to the table, and bow before the Lord to offer up your thanksgiving for His mercies and providential care of you. Let the head of the family dictate; I mean the man, not the woman. If an Elder should happen to be present, the head of the house can call upon him, if he choses so to do, and not wait for a stranger to take the lead at such times; by so doing we shall obtain the favor of our Heavenly Father, and it will have a tendency to teach our children to walk in the way they should go, which may God grant for Christ's sake. Amen.

BRIGHAM YOUNG.

Governor Carlin issued the following Commission—

APPOINTMENT OF JOSEPH SMITH LIEUTENANT-GENERAL OF THE NAUVOO LEGION.

Thomas Carlin, Governor of the State of Illinois, to all to whom these presents shall come: Greeting—

Know ye that Joseph Smith, having been duly elected to the office of lieutenant-general, Nauvoo Legion, of the militia of the State of Illinois, I, Thomas Carlin, governor of said state, do commission him lieutenant-general of the Nauvoo Legion, to take rank from the fifth day of February, 1841. He is, therefore, carefully and diligently to discharge the duties of said office, by doing and performing all manner of things thereunto belonging; and I do strictly require all officers and soldiers under his command to be obedient to his orders: and he is to obey such orders and directions as he shall receive, from time to time, from the commander-in-chief or his superior officer.

In testimony whereof, I have hereunto set my hand, and caused the great seal of state to be hereunto affixed. Done at Springfield, this tenth day of March, in the year of our Lord one thousand eight hundred and forty-one, and of the independence of the United States the sixty-fifth.

By the Governor,

[SEAL]   THOMAS CARLIN.

LYMAN TRUMBALL,
Secretary of State.

The commission was endorsed on the back as follows—

Headquarters, Nauvoo Legion, City of Nauvoo, Illinois, March 15, 1841—Oath of office administered by me, the day and year above written.

JOHN C. BENNETT,
Major-General of the Nauvoo Legion.

Thursday, 11.—Elders Young, Kimball, Richards, and Taylor met in Liverpool.

Monday, 15.—I attended the City Council, and took part in the discussion concerning Mr. Annis' mill, in the southwest part of the city.

Elder Wilford Woodruff attended a conference at Gadfield Elm; 408 members in eighteen branches represented.

Thursday, 16.—Elder George A. Smith attended a conference at Macclesfield, which branch contains ninety-one members, one Elder, six Priests, five Teachers, and three Deacons. In consequence of incessant preaching, his lungs are much affected.

Wednesday, 17.—Ship *Alesto* sailed from Liverpool for New Orleans, with 54 Saints, led by Elders Thomas Smith and William Moss.

Elders Heber C. Kimball, Willard Richards, and Father Melling went to Preston; Elders Young and Hedlock to Hawarden, and George A. Smith to Leek.

Thursday, 18.—Elder George A. Smith attended a council of the officers and members of the Church at Leek, numbering sixty-three members, one Elder, six Priests, two Teachers, and two Deacons. Stephen Nixon was ordained an Elder; and John Hudson, Jacob Gibson, and Joseph Knight, Priests; and Frederick Rushton and Edwin Rushton, Teachers.

Saturday, 20.

An Inquiry.

CITY OF NAUVOO, March 20, 1841.

Brother William Allred, Bishop of the stake at Pleasant Vale, and also Brother Henry W. Miller, president of the stake at Freedom, desire President Joseph Smith to inquire of the Lord His will concerning them.

I inquired of the Lord concerning the foregoing question, and received the following answer—

Revelation.

Let my servants, William Allred and Henry W. Miller, have an agency for the selling of stock for the Nauvoo House, and assist my servants Lyman Wight, Peter Haws, George Miller, and John Snider, in building said house; and let my servants William Allred and Henry W. Miller take stock in the house, that the poor of my people may have employment, and that accommodations may be made for the strangers who shall come to visit this place, and for this purpose let them devote all their properties, saith the Lord.

About this time I received a revelation, given in the City of Nauvoo, in answer to the following interrogatory— "What is the will of the Lord, concerning the Saints in the Territory of Iowa?"*

Revelation.

"Verily, thus saith the Lord, I say unto you, if those who call themselves by my name, and are essaying to be my Saints, if they will do my will and keep my commandments concerning them; let them gather themselves together, unto the place which I shall appoint unto them by my servant Joseph, and build up cities unto my name, that they may be prepared for that which is in store for a time to come. Let them build up a city unto my name upon the land opposite to the City of

* See Doctrine and Covenants, section cxxv.

Nauvoo, and let the name of Zarahemla be named upon it. And let all those who come from the east, and the west, and the north, and the south, that have desires to dwell therein, take up their inheritances in the same, as well as in the City of Nashville, or in the City of Nauvoo, and in all the stakes which I have appointed, saith the Lord.

Sunday, 21.—Elder George A. Smith preached at Leek, and confirmed one.

The Lesser Priesthood was organized in the City of Nauvoo, March 21, 1841, by Bishops Whitney, Miller, Higbee, and Knight. Samuel Rolf was chosen president of the Priests' quorum, and Stephen Markham and Hezekiah Peck, his counselors. Elisha Everett was chosen president of Teachers, and James W. Huntsman and James Hendricks, counselors. Phinehas R. Bird was chosen president of Deacons, and David Wood and William W. Lane counselors.

Organization of the Lesser Priesthood at Nauvoo.

CHAPTER XVI.

THE FIRST FOREIGN MISSION OF THE CHURCH 1837-1841

Tuesday, March 23, 1841.—Elder Young returned to Liverpool, and Elder Richards wrote the following history of the "Mission to England, or the first foreign mission of the Latter-day Saints."

History of the British Mission.

About the first of June, 1837, Elder Heber C. Kimball was called by the Spirit of Revelation, and set apart by the First Presidency of the Church of Jesus Christ of Latter-day Saints, then at Kirtland, Ohio, North America, to preside over a mission to England, accompanied by Elder Orson Hyde, who was set apart for the same work at the same time. In a few days Brother Joseph Fielding, Priest, was set apart; and on the eve of the 12th, Elder Willard Richards, (having been absent several months on a long journey, and having returned the day previous) was called and set apart for the same mission.

The following morning, Tuesday, 13th, these brethren gave the parting hand, bid farewell to home, and, without purse or scrip, started for England. They were accompanied twelve miles to Fairport on Lake Erie by Elders Brigham Young, John P. Greene and Brother Levi Richards, and Sisters Kimball, Greene and Fielding (Brother R. B. Thompson and wife accompanied the mission to Buffalo, and Brother Fitch Brigham to Utica) and others with whom they parted in the afternoon, and went on board a steamer for Buffalo; where they arrived next day.

At this place the brethren expected to receive some means from Canada, to assist them on their journey, but they were disappointed. In the evening they took passage on a canal boat, and arrived in Albany on the 19th (Elder Hyde having gone forward to New York from Rochester.) Brother Fielding proceeded to New York, and on the 20th Elder Kimball accompanied Elder Richards to his father's house in Richmond, Massachusetts, thirty miles east, where they spent one day, and having received some assistance from his friends, bade them farewell for the last time (his father and mother having since died, also a sister whom he had left in Kirtland) and on the 21st returned to Albany, and arrived in New York on the 22nd, where they found Brothers Orson Hyde and Fielding, also Elders John Goodson and Isaac Russell, John Snider, Priest, (who had come from Canada to join the mission) anxiously awaiting their arrival, so that they might take passage on the *United States*, which was to sail next day, but they arrived too late.

In New York Elder Richards received some further means, quite providentially, and on the 23rd the brethren engaged passage to Liverpool, on board the *Garrick*, which was to sail on the 1st of July.

In the meantime the brethren received every possible assistance from Elder Elijah Fordham. At that time he was the only member of the Church residing in the city [New York], and having no house of his own, he procured his father's storehouse for the use of the brethren, where they lodged on the floor, amid straw and blankets, one week, eating their cold morsel, and conversing with the people as they had opportunity; for no place could be procured to preach in, and there was no one to receive them into their houses.

Sunday, the 25th, the brethren held a council at their lodgings (Mr. Fordham's store), and organized ready for taking their departure.

On the 29th the brethren sealed, superscribed, and forwarded one hundred and eighty of Elder Orson Hyde's "Timely Warnings" to the ministers of the different denominations in the city, and went on board the *Garrick*, which hauled out into the river and cast anchor.

July 1st, the ship weighed anchor and was towed to Sandy Hook by a steamer, where she spread sail, and in four hours and a half was out of sight of land. With the exception of a strong wind on the 12th, there was generally a gentle breeze from the northwest during the voyage. On the 16th, Elder Orson Hyde preached on the aft quarter deck. On the 18th Cape Clear was visible (eighteen days out of sight of land;) and on the morning of the 20th, the brethren landed in Liverpool twenty days from New York. Here Elders Kimball, Hyde, and Richards found themselves on a foreign shore, surrounded by strangers, without the first farthing in their possession; but the brethren unitedly took lodgings in a private house in Union Street, till after the inspection of the ship; and on Saturday, the 22nd, took coach for Preston. When they had alighted from the coach, and were standing by their trunks in front of the hotel in Preston, a large flag was unfurled over their heads on which was printed in golden letters, "*Truth will prevail;*" at the sight of which their hearts rejoiced, and they cried aloud, "Amen, thanks be unto God, TRUTH WILL PREVAIL."

Brother Joseph Fielding lodged with his brother, Rev. James Fielding, then a preacher in Vauxhall-road Chapel, and the remainder of the brethren took lodgings in St. Wilford Street, Fox Street. The same evening the Elders visited the Rev. Mr. Fielding, by his request at his lodgings. He had previously been apprized of the coming forth of this work in America, through the medium of letters from his relatives and others and had requested his church to pray that God would send them His servants, and exhorted his people to receive their message when they should come.

Sunday the 28th. As they had no place in which to preach, the seven brethren went to Vauxhall Chapel to hear the Rev. Mr. Fielding; and at the close of the morning service, Mr. Fielding gave public notice that an Elder of the Latter-day Saints would preach in the afternoon in his pulpit. This was voluntary with Mr. Fielding as no one had requested the privilege; and in the afternoon, according to the notice, Elder Kimball gave a brief history of the rise of the Church and the first principles of the Gospel, and Elder Hyde bore testimony; after which the Rev. Mr. Fielding requested the brethren to give out an appointment for the evening, when Elder Goodson preached, and Elder Joseph Fielding bore testimony.

At the close Mr. Fielding again gave leave for preaching at the same place on Wednesday evening, when Elder Hyde preached and Elder Richards bore testimony; and from that time the Rev. Mr. Fielding closed his doors against the Elders and began to oppose the work, and stated that the Elders promised to say nothing about baptism in their preaching before he ever consented to let them preach in his pulpit; whereas the subject of the Elders preaching in his chapel had not been named between the parties, before Mr. Fielding gave out the public appointment before referred to: much less (if possible) that they would "say nothing about baptism."

Nine of Mr. Fielding's members offered themselves for baptism; and Mr. Fielding presented himself before the Elders, and forbade their baptizing them, but he received for answer, that "they were of age and could act for themselves." On Sunday, the 30th, they were baptized under the hands of Elder Kimball; Brother George D. Watt being the first who offered himself for baptism in England, and is now an Elder laboring in Edinburgh, Scotland.

Elder Russell preached in the market place in the afternoon, and from that day the doors of private houses were opened on almost every hand for the Elders.

July 31st, a council of the Elders decided that Elders Goodson and Richards should go on a mission to Bedford, and Elder Russell and Priest Snider on a mission to Alston, Cumberland; and after a night of prayer, praise and thanksgiving, the brethren took their departure on the morning of the first of August for their several stations.

The Rev. Mr. Fielding continued to oppose the doctrine of baptism for a season; but finding that he was likely to lose all his "best members," he offered to baptize them himself; but they being aware that he had no authority, declined his friendly offer, whereupon he engaged the Rev. Mr. Giles, a Baptist minister in Preston, of as little authority as himself, to do the baptizing for his flock; but this iniquitous scheme succeeded little better than the other—only one coming forward to his baptism, so far as we have heard. Mr. Fielding's people also stated that he acted the part of a hypocrite and deceived them, when he read the letters to them in public, which he received from America, by keeping back that part which treated on baptism, which, since the foregoing failure he has opposed.

Elders Kimball and Hyde, and Priest Fielding continued to preach daily in different parts of Preston, and on Wednesday and Thursday (August 2nd and 3rd), the meetings were attended by Miss Jeanetta Richards who was visiting her friends in Preston, and on Friday she requested baptism, which was attended to by Elder Kimball, after which she was confirmed at the water side by Elders Kimball and Hyde, it being the first confirmation in a foreign land in these last days.

The day following Sister Richards returned home to her friends, and informed her father, the Rev. Joseph Richards, an Independent minister at Walker-fold, Chaidgely, whom she had found at Preston, what she had done, and requested him to send for Elder Kimball to preach in his chapel. Mr. Richards complied with his daughter's request. Elder Kimball arrived at Walker-fold Saturday eve, August 12, and the day following preached three times in Mr. Richards' pulpit, to crowded assemblies; also twice during the week, and twice the Sunday following, being most kindly and cordially entertained by Mr. and Mrs. Richards for nine days, during which time Elder Kimball baptized several in the neighborhood.

After a short visit to Preston, where Elder Hyde continued to preach and baptize, Elder Kimball returned to Walker-fold, and continued to receive the hospitality of Mr. Richards' house for some days, while the work spread in the neighborhood; and from thence the work went forth to Clitheroe, Waddington, Downham, Cathburn, Thornley, and Ribchester, through the labors of Brothers Kimball and Fielding.

Elders Goodson and Richards arrived in Bedford on the 2nd of August, and having letters of introduction to the Rev. Timothy R. Matthews from Brother Joseph Fielding (Mrs. Matthew's brother), they immediately waited on Mr. Matthews, who expressed great joy at their arrival, and manifested his sincerity by walking arm in arm with the

Elders through the streets of Bedford, calling on the members of his church, and inviting them to attend the lectures of the Elders at his chapel vestry that evening. Mr. Matthews had previously been apprized of the Saints in America through the medium of the Rev. James Fielding of Preston and the letters from America, before referred to. In the evening, his church assembled in the vestry, and Elders Goodson and Richards continued to lecture and testify of the work of God, on that and the three following evenings in the same place, with the entire approbation of Mr. Matthews, who, at the close of the lectures, publicly bore testimony to the truths advanced, and called upon his people to know why they did not come forward for baptism; while they in return wished to know why he did not set them the example.

After this Mr. Matthews engaged another house in the neighborhood for the Elders to preach in, under the pretense that some of the proprietors of the chapel might not be pleased with the Elders occupying the vestry, and Mr. Matthews continued to attend the preaching of the Elders, and also spent a great share of his time, from day to day, in conversation with them.

Mr. Matthews told the Elders that he had received two ordinations, one from Bishop West, whom he had proved to be an impostor, and another from the Church of England, which he acknowledged to be descended from the Church of Rome, and he further acknowledged that he had no authority from God for administering in the ordinances of God's house.

On the 10th Mrs. Braddock and four others were baptized by Elder Goodson. Soon after this, Mr. Joseph Saville, member of Mr. Matthews' church, being very desirous of receiving baptism at the same time with Mr. Matthews, waited on him at his house, in company with Elders Goodson and Richards and Mr. Matthews, and Mr. Saville mutually agreed to meet the Elders on the bank of the river Ouse at a specified hour in the afternoon, and attend to the ordinance of baptism. At the hour appointed Mr. Saville met the Elders at the place previously designated by Mr. Matthews; but as he (the latter) did not make his appearance according to promise, after waiting for him an hour, Mr. Saville was baptized, when the Elders repaired to Mr. Matthews' to learn the cause of his not fulfilling his engagement, and were informed by Mr. Matthews' family that he had gone out into the country to preach.

In a day or two it was currently rumored that Mr. Matthews had baptized himself, and this rumor was afterwards confirmed by Mrs. Matthews, who stated to Elder Kimball at Preston, that Mr. Matthews had baptized himself, reasoning upon this principle within himself: "If I have authority to administer the sacrament to my people, why not have authority to baptize myself," &c.—and all this after Mr. Matthews had acknowledged to Elders Goodson and Richards that he had no authority to administer in the ordinances of God's house; and altogether regardless of the words of the Apostles (Heb. v: 4), "No man taketh this honor unto himself but he that is called of God as was Aaron."

By the foregoing it is plainly to be seen, that Mr. Matthews has attempted to take that upon himself which was never conferred upon him by the spirit of revelation, either by God, His angels, or His servants; viz., the holy Priesthood; and from that period, Mr. Matthews began to preach baptism, and baptized those who felt it their duty to be baptized, and then invited them to the penitent form to get remission of their sins; but finding that would not answer all the design which he intended, he afterwards began to baptize for the remission of sins.

Mr. Matthews appears to have well understood that counterfeit coin is more current the nearer it approximates to the true, and governed himself accordingly; for he continued to preach faith, repentance, baptism for the remission of sins, the second coming of Christ, &c., &c., adding one thing to another in imitation of truth, as fast as it answered his purpose, from those doctrines which he had heard from the Latter-day Saints; but it was some time before he arrived at that heaven-daring conscience-seared hardihood, to lay hands on those whom he had baptized for the reception of the Holy Ghost, and at the same time he acknowledged that he had not got the Holy Ghost himself, by praying that he might receive it—(Query. How can a man communicate that which he is not in possession of?) and he now calls his church "The Church of Latter-day Saints."

Thus has Mr. Matthews been running about from Bedford to Liverpool, from Liverpool to Northampton, from Northampton to Bedford, and other places, crying aloud in public and private, that the Latter-day Saints and their doctrines came from hell; at the same time he has been preaching the same doctrines, calls his church by the same name, is administering in the same ordinances, just as though he fully believed that the doctrines and sacraments of hell would be sanctified and made holy and heavenly, when administered by the tongue and hands of an impostor.

About the time that Mr. Matthews rejected the truth in Bedford, his son (as Mr. Matthews called him), the Rev. Robert Aitkin, commenced his attack on the principles of righteousness in Preston; and while furiously pounding his pulpit with the Book of Mormon, and warning his people to beware of the Latter-day Saints and their doctrines, saying, that they and their record came from hell; called upon his people to use all their efforts to put down the work of God, or stop the progress of the

Latter-day Saints; and, if it could not be put down without, prayed that God would smite the leaders; and from that time to the present, his prayer has been answered on his own head.

After Mr. Aitkin had preached against the corruptions of the Church of England for years, and established many flourishing chapels in Liverpool, Preston, Manchester, Burslem, London, &c.; after he had been visited by the Elders of the Church of Latter-day Saints, and acknowledged to them at one time that baptism was right, but he could find no man who had authority to baptize; and at another time, that he was afraid of them, and rejected their testimony; and last of all would not receive the Elders into his house; after all this, and deserted by a part of his flock, he has fled from the remainder because he was an hireling, and cared not for the sheep; yes, he has deserted his "Christian Society"—ceased to be an Aitkenite, and dissolved his co-partnership with Father Matthews, as may well be supposed, returned, and taken "holy order" in "Mother Church," against the corruptions of which he testified so diligently from year to year, and is now about to enter on his parochial duties in St. John the Evangelist's Church, Hope street, Liverpool, for no other reason, that the writer knows of, only that he could find no one who had authority to baptize for the remission of sins, and not possessing the faith of his father, Matthews, to believe that the doctrines of the pit would become holy and gospel doctrines when taught by the tongue of wickedness and imposture, he has concluded thus publicly to acknowledge himself a servant of those very errors he has so long contended against, for the sake of filthy lucre.

About the 12th of September, Elder Goodson and Priest Snider returned to Preston, and soon after sailed for America.

Some years previously, the principles of the Temperance Society (originally established in America), were introduced into England, and Preston was the first town to receive them. Among the many interesting and valuable items held forth by the Temperance people, it was often remarked by them that Temperance was the fore-runner of the Gospel, which prophecy proved true; for when the fullness of the Gospel came from America to England, it was first preached in Preston, and through the influence of the Temperance Society, the Latter-day Saints procured the use of the Temperance Hall in Preston (a commodious building, originally erected for cock fighting) for their chapel, and commenced meeting therein on the 3rd of September, 1837, and continued until they were ejected through the influence of others, the Temperance Society not having it entirely at their control. Similar favors have been received from several other Temperance Societies in England, for which the Lord reward them.

Elder Richards continued to labor against much opposition in Bedford, and the region round about, until the 7th of March, 1838, when he returned to Preston, leaving about forty members in charge of Elder James Lavender.   Elder Russell continued to labor in Alston, Brampton, &c , and returned to Preston near the same time, leaving about sixty member in the care of Elder Jacob Peart.

At Christmas, 1837, Priest Joseph Fielding was ordained Elder, and several were ordained Teachers, &c., at Preston; and in March, 1838, the Church had extended from Preston to Penwortham, Longton, Southport, Eccleston Whittle, Hunter's Hill, Chorley, and the intermediate region, through the labors of Elders Hyde, Kimball, and Fielding, and the members amounted to several hundreds in the regions of Preston and Clitheroe.   During this month, Elders Kimball and Hyde were diligently engaged in organizing the different branches; and on the first of April a general conference was called at Preston, when the organization of the churches was completed, and many were ordained, among whom were Elders Joseph Fielding, Willard Richards, and William Clayton to the High Priesthood, [i. e. they were ordained High Priests], and set apart by Elders Kimball and Hyde to preside over all the churches in Elgland.

On the 9th, Elders Kimball, Hyde and Russell took leave of the Saints in Preston, and went to Liverpool, where they were visited by Elders Fielding, Richards, Clayton, and others, and on the 20th of April, sailed for New York, on board the *Garrick*, the same ship they came out on to England.

When Elders Fielding and Richards had returned to Longton, they found a pamphlet, purporting to be written by the Rev. Richard Livesey, a Methodist minister, who had spent some time on a mission to the United States, as he says, and having nothing more important to attend to during his mission, it appears that he spent his time in gathering up a heap of lies and filth from the American papers, and imported them to England on his return; and finding that the work of God had commenced in his native land, and was likely to destroy his craft, set himself at work to condense his heterogeneous mass of trans-Atlantic lies, and form the wonderful production of the Rev. Richard Livesey's tract against the Latter-day Saints; it being the first thing of the kind that the enemy of all righteousness had found means to export from America, and circulate in England; but since which he has found servants in abundance, to assist in this nefarious merchandise of his heart's delight.

The Church at this time was in its infancy, and needed much instruction, which necessarily occupied the attention of the presiding Elders to a great extent; and as there were few laborers in the field, the spread of the work was not very rapid for some time.

Sister Alice Hodgin died at Preston on the 2nd of September, 1838; and it was such a wonderful thing for a Latter-day Saint to die in England, that Elder Richards was arraigned before the Mayor's Court at Preston, on the 3rd of October, charged with "killing and slaying" the said Alice with a "black stick," &c., but was discharged without being permitted to make his defense, as soon as it was discoved that the iniquity of his accusers was about to be made manifest.

October 19, 1838, Elder Clayton gave himself wholly to the work, and soon after commenced preaching and baptizing in Manchester, and from thence the work spread into Stockport, and other places in the neighborhood, through the labors of Elders Clayton, Fielding, John Moon, and David Wilding. A small church had previously sprung up in Bolton, through the labors of Elder David Wilding, and was continued by Elder Amos Fielding.

In the summer of 1839 Elders Clayton Richards, and John Moon, labored in Burslem, with some success, and a small church was planted in Burnley by Elder Thomas Richardson, besides many who were added in the older branches, through the instrumentality of the local Elders and Priests, who were generally very faithful.

December 8, 1839, Elders Hiram Clark, Alexander Wright, and Samuel Mulliner arrived in Preston from America; and on the 25th, Brothers Wright and Mulliner started for Scotland and soon commenced preaching and baptizing in Paisley and vicinity.

January 13, 1840, Elders Wilford Woodruff, John Taylor, and Theodore Turley arrived in Preston, from America; and on the 18th Brothers Woodruff and Turley started for the Potteries in Staffordshire, passing through Manchester; and on the 22nd, Elder Taylor left for Liverpool.

April 6, 1840, just ten years from the organization of the Church, Elders Brigham Young, Heber C. Kimball, Parley P. Pratt, Orson Pratt, George A. Smith, and Reuben Hedlock, landed in Liverpool from New York; and on the 9th Elder Kimball arrived in Preston, just two years from the day he left for America.

The arrival of the Elders caused the Saints to rejoice exceedingly, for it had been prophesied by many (not of the Church), that they would never come, and that Elders Kimball and Hyde would never return, but they are both now in England, Elder Orson Hyde having arrived in Liverpool on the 3rd instant from New York.

HEBER C. KIMBALL,
ORSON HYDE,
WILLARD RICHARDS.

Preston, March 24, 1841.

CHAPTER XVII.

CELEBRATION OF THE TWELFTH ANNIVERSARY OF THE
ORGANIZATION OF THE CHURCH—ORDER OF LAYING COR-
NER-STONES OF TEMPLES—COUNCIL MEETINGS OF THE
TWELVE IN ENGLAND.

March, 25, 26 and 27, 1841.—Elders Young and Richards were detained at the Liverpool post office, as witnesses
in the case of "The Queen vs. Joseph Holloway," for
detaining letters.

Saturday, 27.—Elders Wilford Woodruff, and Geo. A.
Smith attended a council of the official members of the
Staffordshire Conference, at Hanley.

Sunday, 28.—Elders Wilford Woodruff and George
A. Smith attended a general meeting of the Staffordshire Conference at Hanley, when 13 branches were represented, containing 1 High Priest, 17 Elders,
55 Priests, 25 Teachers, 14 Deacons, and 663
members. Thomas J. Filcher, J. Taylor,
Osmond Shaw, W. Ridge, and H. Ridge were ordained
Elders, also 8 Priests, 7 Teachers, and 2 Deacons,
under the hands of Wilford Woodruff, Geo. A. Smith, and
Alfred Cordon. There have been 141 baptized during the
past three months.

Staffordshire
Conference.

Monday, 29.—I attended city council, and moved
that the city surveyor be ordered to survey Commerce,
and plat the same so as to correspond with the
city plat of Nauvoo, and make out a map to
be recorded, which was carried by the Council. Much was said in council about fining the owners of
dogs, and I contended that it was right to fine individuals

Union of Com-
merce and
Nauvoo Plats.

who would keep unruly dogs, to worry cattle, sheep, or the citizens, and an ordinance was passed to that effect.

William Marks, president of the stake at Nauvoo, made choice of Charles C. Rich and Austin Cowles as his counselors.

Elders Young and Richards were at Liverpool packing Books of Mormon, to pay off those who had loaned them money in order to carry forward the printing and binding.

The following are extracts from Elder Woodruff's letter.

Letter of Wilford Woodruff to Don C. Smith—Relating to Affairs in England.

BURSLEM, March 29, 1841.

BROTHER DON CARLOS SMITH:—The following is a brief sketch of my journey from London to this place.   Elder Kimball left London on the 19th February.   I left on the 26th, and arrived at Bristol on the same day, where I found Elder Kington, who was busily engaged in the work of the Lord in that city, and had established a small branch of fourteen members.   I tarried there a short time and preached three times in a theatre, had large congregations, good attention, and baptized one, and there appears a good prospect of a work being done in that city.   Population of Bristol, 200,000.   While there I visited the suspension bridge, now erecting across the river Avon, at St. Vincent's Rocks, Clifton; which bridge is one hundred feet in height above the river, and seven hundred in length.   I spent one evening in Monmouth, on the borders of Wales; preached to a large congregation; several applied for baptism after meeting.   On the 8th of March I attended a conference in Garway; Elder Levi Richards was chosen president, and James Morgan, clerk; heard four branches represented, containing one hundred and thirty-four members; three were ordained to the ministry.   I also preached at Lugwardine, Shucknall Hill, Ledbury, Dymock, and Turkey Hall to large congregations, and find the work of the Lord still progressing throughout that region, The excitement upon the subject in the city of Hereford has been so great, that it has assembled together in the market place three thousand persons at a time to hear something upon the cause of the Latter-day Saints.   On the 15th of March I attended the Gadfield Elm conference, which met at the Gadfield Elm Chapel.   Elder Wilford Woodruff was chosen president; John Hill, clerk; 18 branches represented, containing 408 members, 8 Elders, 32 Priests, 11 Teacher

and 1 Deacon; when such business was transacted as was deemed nec-
essary. I also met large congregations at Keysend street, Coldville,
Browcut; Dunclose, Froom's Hill, and Stanley Hill, and left many
churches on the right and left, which time would not permit me to visit.
I also met with the Froom's Hill conference, on the 22nd March, at
Stanley Hill, Herefordshire, there being present one of the traveling
High Council, 2 High Priests, 20 Elders, 30 Priests, 9 Teachers, two
Deacons. Elder Levi Richards was chosen president, and Elder Woodruff, clerk. On this occasion I heard represented 30 branches, containing 997 members, 24 Elders, 66 Priests, 27 Teachers, 7 Deacons, and 6
were ordained to the ministry. The sum total represented at these conferences was 1,539 members, 36 Elders, 103 Priests, 41 Teachers, 7
Deacons; all of whom have embraced the work in that part of the vineyard in one year, besides many members and officers who have
emigrated to America; and I am happy to say that the officers and
members, have universally been ready to hearken to counsel, and
give heed to our instructions, and it was with no ordinary feelings that
I took my farewell of those churches who have been so ready to receive
and embrace the truth. I called upon the Saints in Birmingham and
Gret's Green, but had not time to hold any meetings among them.
I arrived in Hanley on the 25th, where I had the privilege of again
meeting with Elder Geo. A. Smith, and was rejoiced to find the
churches universally prospering in Staffordshire. I spent one evening
with the church at Longton, and baptized seven.

Tuesday, 30.—Elders Woodruff and Geo. A. Smith
arrived in Manchester, after a ride of forty miles.

Wednesday, 31.—Elders Young and Richards attended
conference in Liverpool.

Thursday, April 1, 1841.—Elders Young and Richards
went to Manchester, where they found Elders Kimball,
Hyde , Woodruff and Smith, and had a happy meeting.

Friday, 2.—Elders Orson Pratt and John Taylor
arrived at Manchester and went into council.

Minutes of a Council Meeting of the Twelve.

MANCHESTER, ENGLAND, April 2, 1841.

This day Elders Brigham Young, Heber C. Kimball, Orson Hyde,
Parley P. Pratt, Orson Pratt, Willard Richards, Wilford Woodruff,
John Taylor and Geo. A. Smith, of the quorum of the Twelve, met
together at the house of Brother James Bushaw, coachman No. 4, Gray
Street, near Oxford road, in this city, in council, after having been sep-

arated and sent into various counties. To meet once more in council after a long separation, and having passed through many sore and grievous trials, exposing our lives and our characters to the slanders and violence of wicked and murderous men, caused our hearts to swell with gratitude to God for His providential care over us. Elder Young opened the council by prayer. Elders Brigham Young, Heber C. Kimball, and Parley P. Pratt, the committee appointed about a year ago to secure a copyright for the Book of Mormon, in the name of Joseph Smith, Jun., presented the following certificate:

"Feb. 8, 1841. Then entered for his copy—the property of Joseph Smith, Jun.,—'The Book of Mormon; an account written by the hand of Mormon, upon plates taken from the plates of Nephi; translated by Joseph Smith, Jun. First European, from the second American edition. Received five copies.

"GEORGE GREENHILL."

"'The above is a true copy of an entry in the register book of the Company of Stationers kept, at the hall of the said company. Witness my hand, this 17th day of February, 1841.

"GEORGE GREENHILL,
Warehouse-keeper of the Company of Stationers."

The quorum voted that they accepted the labors of said Committee.

Resolved: That as the quorum of the Twelve have had nothing to do with the printing of the Book of Mormon, they will not now interfere with it, but that the said Committee settle the financial or business matters thereof with Joseph Smith, Jun., to whom the profits rightly belong.

Resolved: That Elder Amos Fielding be appointed to superintend fiting out the Saints from Liverpool to America, under the instruction of Parley P. Pratt.

Resolved: That Brother Geo. J. Adams go to Bedford and Northampton and labor in that region.

Adjourned till tomorrow at 10 o'clock, a. m.; Elder Kimball closed by prayer.

ORSON HYDE, Clerk.

Council Meeting of the Twelve—Continued.

MANCHESTER, April 3, 1841.

This day the quorum of the Twelve met pursuant to adjournment. The president called upon Elder Hyde to open by prayer. The quorum then signed a letter of commendation to the churches in England for Elder Hyde.

The business of publishing the *Star* and hymn-book was then taken into consideration. Brother John Taylor moved that those who have had the care and superintendence of publishing the *Star* and hymn-book, should dispose of them according to their own wishes, and dispose of the proceeds in the same way; seconded by Elder Orson Pratt, and carried by unanimous vote. Moved by Elder Young, and seconded by Elder Kimball, that Elder Parley P. Pratt conduct the publication of the *Millennial Star* as editor of the same, after the close of the present volume. *Resolved*, that Elder Parley P. Pratt reprint the hymn-book if he deem it expedient. The hymn-book is not to be altered, except the typographical errors. The above resolution was moved by Elder Geo. A. Smith, and seconded by Elder Wilford Woodruff; carried unanimously. Conference adjourned.

Orson Hyde, Clerk.

Sunday, 4.—The President of the United States, William Henry Harrison died at Washington of the pleurisy.

Nine of the Twelve at Manchester attended meeting at Carpenter's hall, and individually bore testimony of the fulness of the everlasting Gospel.

Council Meeting of the Twelve—Continued.

Manchester, April 5, 1841.

Met pursuant to adjournment. Elder Orson Pratt opened the council by prayer. It was resolved that the 17th day of April be the day appointed for the Twelve who are going to America, to set sail from Liverpool. Moved by Elder Kimball and seconded by Elder Woodruff that the Twelve do business at the conference as a quorum, and call upon the Church or conference to sanction it. Adjourned till the 6th instant, to meet in general conference at Carpenter's Hall, at 10 o'clock a. m.

O. Hyde, Clerk.

April 6, 1841.—The first day of the twelfth year of the Church of Jesus Christ of Latter-day Saints! At an early hour the several companies comprising the "Nauvoo Legion," with two volunteer companies from Iowa Territory, making sixteen companies in all, assembled at their several places of rendezvous, and were conducted in due order to the ground assigned for general review. The appearance, order and movements of the Legion, were chaste, grand and imposing, and reflected great credit upon the taste, skill and tact of the men comprising said Legion. We doubt whether the like can be presented in

Twelfth Anniversary of the Organization of the Church.

any other city in the western country. At half-past seven
o'clock a. m., the fire of artillery announced the arrival
of Brigadier-Generals Law and Don Carlos Smith, at the
front of their respective cohorts; and at 8 o'clock Major-
General Bennett was conducted to his post, under the discharge of cannon, and took command of the Legion.

At half-past nine o'clock a. m., Lieutenant-General
Smith, with his guard, staff and field officers arrived at
the ground, and were presented with a beautiful silk
national flag by the ladies of Nauvoo, which was respectfully received and hailed by the firing of cannon, and
borne off by Colonel Robinson, the cornet, to the appropriate position in the line; after which the Lieutenant-
General with his suite passed the lines in review.

At twelve m., the procession arrived upon the Temple
ground, enclosing the same in a hollow square, with
Lieutenant-General Smith, Major-General Bennett, Brigadier-Generals Wilson Law and Don Carlos Smith, their
respective staffs, guard, field officers, distinguished visitors, choir, band, &c., in the centre, and the ladies and
gentlemen, citizens, surrounding in the interior. The
superior officers, together with the banner, architects,
principal speaker, &c., were duly conducted to the stand
at the principal corner stone, and the religious services
were commenced by singing from page 65 of the new
hymn book.

President Sidney Rigdon then addressed the assembly,
and remarked the circumstances under which   Sidney Rig-
he addressed the people were of no ordinary   don's Speech..
character, but of peculiar and indescribable interest, that
it was the third occasion of a similar nature, wherein he
had been called upon to address the people, and to assist
in laying the corner stones of houses to be erected in
honor of the God of the Saints. Various scenes had transpired since the first was laid—he with some who were
with him on that occasion, had waded through scenes
that no other people had ever seen—not cursed, but blessed

with. They had seen the blood of the innocent flow, and
heard the groans of those dying for the witness of Jesus; in
all those scenes of tribulation, his confidence, his courage
and his joy had been increasing instead of diminishing.
Now the scene had changed; persecution had in a measure
subsided; peace and safety, friendship and joy crowned
their assembling; and their endeavors to serve God were
respected and viewed with interest.   The Saints had
assembled, not to violate law and trample upon equity
and good social order; not to devaste and destroy; but to
lift up the standard of liberty and law, to stand in defense
of civil and religious, rights, to protect the innocent, to
save mankind, and to obey the will and mandate of the
Lord of glory; to call up to remembrance the once crucified, but now exalted and glorified Savior; to say that He
is again revealed, that He speaks from the heavens, that
He reigns; in honor of Him to tell the world that He lives,
and speaks, and reigns and dictates—that not every people can build a house to Him, but that people whom He
Himself directs—that the present military display is not
to usurp authority, but to obey as they are commanded
and directed; to honor, not the world, but Him that is
alive and reigns, the all in all, the invisible, but beholding, and guiding and directing—that the Saints boast of
their King; of His wisdom, His understanding, His
power and His goodness—that they honor a God of
unbounded power and glory—that He is the chief corner
stone in Zion, also the top stone—that He cannot be con-
quered—that He is working in the world to guide, to conquer, and to subdue—that as formerly, so now He works
by revelation—that this is the reason why we are here,
and why we are thus—that the Saints have sacrificed all
things for the testimony of Jesus Christ—that some from
different parts of Europe and from Canada, as well as the
different parts of the United States, are present, and
among all, a unanimity of purpose and feeling prevails—
and why?   Because the same God over all had spoken

from the heavens and again revealed Himself. He remarked that he defied the devil to collect such an assembly; none but Jesus would or could accomplish such things as we are about to behold; the devil will not build up, but tear down and destroy; the work of Jesus is like Himself in all ages—that as light shines from the east, and spreads itself to the west, so is the progress of spiritual light and truth—that Jesus is a God of order, regularity and uniformity—that he works now by revelation and by messengers as anciently—shows Himself—lifts the veil; that such things are marvelous, but nevertheless true— that the order of laying the corner stones was expressive of the order of the kingdom—that the minutiæ were subject matter of revelation, and all the scenery, acts of obedience are understood by the Saints—that the ancient Prophets beheld and rejoiced at this scene, and are near to witness the fulfillment of their predictions—that we are highly favored of God, and brought near to the spirits of just men made perfect. He then closed by exhortation, first to the multitude, and lastly to the Church. The speaker then gave out a hymn, page 205, and closed by prayer.

The architects then, by the direction of the First Presidency, lowered the first (the south-east corner) stone to its place, and President Joseph Smith pronounced the benediction as follows:

This principal corner stone in representation of the First Presidency, is now duly laid in honor of the Great God; and may it there remain until the whole fabric is completed; and may the same be accomplished speedily; that the Saints may have a place to worship God, and the Son of Man have where to lay His head.

President Sidney Rigdon then pronounced the following:

May the persons employed in the erection of this house be preserved from all harm while engaged in its construction, till the whole is completed, in the name of the Father, and of the Son, and of the Holy Ghost. Even so. Amen.

Adjourned for one hour.

Assembled according to adjournment, and proceeded to lay the remaining corner stones, according to previous order.

The second (south-west corner) stone, by the direction of the president of the High Priesthood, with his council and President Marks, was lowered to its place, when the president of the High Priesthood pronounced the followng:

The second corner stone of the Temple now building by the Church of Jesus Christ of Latter-day Saints, in honor of the Great God, is duly laid, and may the same unanimity, that has been manifested on this occasion continue till the whole is completed; that peace may rest upon it to the laying of the top stone thereof, and the turning of the key thereof; that the Saints may participate in the blessings of Israel's God, within its walls, and the glory of God rest upon the same. Amen.

The third (the north-west corner) stone, superintended by the High Council, was then lowered to its place, with the benediction of Elias Higbee, as follows:

The third corner stone is now duly laid; may this stone be a firm support to the building that the whole may be completed as before proposed.

The fourth (the north-east corner) stone, superintended by the Bishops, was then lowered to its place, and Bishop Whitney pronounced the following:

The fourth and last corner stone, expressive of the Lesser Priesthood, is now duly laid, and may the blessings before pronounced, with all others desirable, rest upon the same forever. Amen.

The services were then declared closed, and the military retired to the parade ground and were dismissed with the approbation and thanks of the commanding officer. The military band, under the command of Captain Duzette, made a conspicuous and dignified appearance, and performed their part honorably. Their soul-stirring strains met harmoniously the rising emotions that swelled each bosom, and stimulated us onward to the arduous but pleasing and honorable duties of the day. The choir also, under the direction of B. S. Wilber, deserve commendation.

What added greatly to the happiness we experienced on this interesting occasion, is the fact that we heard no bscene or profane language; neither saw we any one intoxicated. Can the same be said of a similar assemblage in any other city in the Union? Thank God that the intoxicating beverage, the bane of humanity in these last days, is becoming a stranger in Nauvoo.

Conduct of the People.

In conclusion, we will say we never witnessed a more imposing spectacle than was presented on this occasion, and during the sessions of the conference. Such a multitude of people moving in harmony, in friendship, in dignity, told in a voice not easily misunderstood, that they were a people of intelligence, and virtue and order; in short, that they were *Saints;* and that the God of love, purity and light, was their God, their Examplar, and Director; and that they were blessed and happy.

If the strict order of the Priesthood were carried out in the building of Temples, the first stone would be laid at the south-east corner, by the First Presidency of the Church. The south-west corner should be laid next. The third, or north-west corner next; and the fourth, or north-east corner last. The first Presidency should lay the south-east corner stone and dictate who are the proper persons to lay the other corner stones.

Order of Laying Corner Stones of Temples.

If a Temple is built at a distance, and the First Presidency are not present, then the Quorum of the Twelve Apostles are the persons to dictate the order for that Temple; and in the absence of the Twelve Apostles, then the Presidency of the Stake will lay the south-east corner stone; the Melchisedec Priesthood laying the corner stones on the east side of the Temple, and the Lesser Priesthood those on the west side.

A Conference was held at Philadelphia; President Hyrum Smith presiding; many branches were represented and the branch at Philadelphia was organized by electing Benjamin Winchester, President, and Edson Whipple, and William Wharnot, his Counselors. Jacob Syphret was elected Bishop, and Jesse Prince and James Nicholson his Counselors.

Conference at Philadelphia.

Meeting of the Council of the Twelve in Manchester.

The Council of the Twelve assembled at Manchester, in Carpenter's Hall, on the 6th day of April, 1841, for the first time to transact business as a quorum in the presence of the Church, in a foreign land; being the first day of the 12th year of the rise of the Church of Jesus Christ of Latter-day Saints.   Nine of the quorum were present; viz., Brigham Young, Heber C. Kimball, Orson Hyde, Parley P. Pratt, Orson Pratt, Wilford Woodruff, Willard Richards, John Taylor and Geo. A. Smith, President Young having called the meeting to order, and organized, the conference then opened by prayer.   Elder Thomas Ward was chosen Clerk.   The President then made some introductory remarks relative to the organization of the Church in the House of the Lord in America, in reference to the different quorums in their respecttive orders and authorities in the Church.

The representation of the churches and conferences throughout the kingdom was then called for.

LOCATION.	BY WHOM REPRE-SENTED.	MEMBERS.	ELDERS.	PRIESTS.	TEACHERS.	DEACONS.
Manchester	Parley P. Pratt.	443	7	15	9	0
Clitheroe Conference.................	Heber C. Kimball.	318	6	12	13	3
Preston Conference	Peter Melling.	675	11	15	13	3
Liverpool.	John Taylor.	190	9	8	4	3
Isle of Man	John Taylor.	90	2	4	2	0
London Conference	Lorenzo Snow.	137	3	8	4	2
Birmingham Conference	Alfred Cordon.	110	4	13	4	1
Staffordshire Conference	Alfred Cordon.	574	19	49	28	16
Garway Conference.	Wilford Woodruff.	134	5	6	4	1
Gadfield Elm Conference.	Wilford Woodruff.	408	8	33	11	1
Froom's Hill Conference............	Wilford Woodruff.	1008	27	67	27	8
Edingburgh	Orson Pratt	203	6	9	6	2
Glasgow, Paisley, Johnstone, Bridge of Weir. and Thorney Bank........	Reuben Hedlock.	368	12	15	13	11
Ireland	Theodore Curtis.	35	2	0	1	0
Wales	James Burnham.	170	2	5	3	3
Newcastle-upon-Tyne	Amos Fielding.	23	1	3	1	0
Alston.	John Sanders.	26	1	0	1	0
Brampton.	John Sanders.	46	0	1	0	0
Carlisle	John Sanders.	43	1	0	0	0
Bolton	Robert Crooks.	189	1	11	8	1
Dukinfield	John Albertson.	120	2	4	3	2
Northwich, Middlewich, &c....	Samuel Heath.	112	2	6	6	6
Oldham..............................	William Black.	86	1	4	1	2
Stockport...........................	Elder Magan.	161	1	5	2	2
Eccles	Elder Magan.	24	1	3	1	0
Pendlebury	Elder Magan.	62	0	2	1	1
Whitefield...........................	Elder Magan.	41	1	2	3	0
Radcliffe Bridge	Elder Magan.	18	1	3	0	0
Total...		5814	136	304	169	68

Nearly eight hundred Saints have emigrated to America during the past season. These are not included in this representation.

Conference adjourned till 2 p. m.

Conference met pursuant to adjournment; opened by prayer.

Scattering members were then represented, consisting of nearly fifty, not included in any of the above branches.

President Young then proceeded to make some remarks on the office of Patriarch, and concluded by moving that Elder John Albertson * be ordained to that office. Seconded by Elder Kimball, and carried unanimously.

Resolved: That George D. Watt, George J. Adams, Amos Fielding, William Kay, John Sanders, Thomas Richardson, James Whitehead, Thomas Domville, James Galley and George Simpson be ordained High Priests.

Resolved: That the following persons be ordained Elders—William Miller, William Leach, John Sands, William Moon, William Hardman, William Black, John Goodfellow, Joseph Brotherton, Richard Benson, Theophilus Brotherton, John McIlwick, and William Green.

Resolved: That Manchester, Stockport, Dukinfield, Oldham, Bolton, and all the neighboring branches be organized into one conference, to be called the Manchester Conference.

That the Church in Brampton, Alston, and Carlisle be included in one conference.

That the churches of Liverpool, Isles of Man, Wales, viz., Overton, Harding and Ellsmere, be organized into one conference, to be called the Liverpool conference.

Resolved: That the Macclesfield Conference include Macclesfield, Northwich, Middlewich, and Lostock.

That Edinburgh Conference include Glasgow, Paisley, Bridge of Weir, Johnstone and Thorney Bank.

That George D. Watt preside over the Edinburgh Conference.

That John Greenhow preside over the Liverpool Conference.

That Thomas Ward preside over the Clitheroe Conference.

That Lorenzo Snow preside over the London Conference.

That James Galley preside over the Macclesfield Conference.

That Alfred Cordon preside over the Staffordshire Conference.

That James Riley be ordained a High Priest, and preside over the Birmingham Conference.

That James McAnley preside over the Glasgow Conference.

That Thomas Richardson preside over the Gadfield Elm Conference.

That William Kay preside over the Froom's Hill Conference.

That Levi Richards have the superintendence of the Garway Conference.

* John Albertson was the second Patriarch ordained in England, Peter Melling being the first, he was ordained the 17th of April, 1840.

That Peter Melling preside over the Preston Conference.

That John Sanders preside over the Brampton Conference.

Adjourned till seven o'clock, p. m.

Met pursuant to adjournment; commenced by singing, "When shall we all meet again," and prayer.

The Patriarch Peter Melling, was then called upon to pronounce a patriarchal blessing upon the head of John Albertson, previous to his being ordained to the office of Patriarch. Laying his hands upon him he blessed him in the following words:

"John, I lay my hands upon thy head, in the name of Jesus Christ; and by the authority of the Holy Priesthood committed unto me, I pronounce upon thy head the blessings of Abraham, Isaac and Jacob; and I say unto thee, that, inasmuch as it is in thy heart to do the will of the Lord, thou shalt be blessed, and the desires of thy heart shall be granted thee; and the Lord God will enlarge thy heart; and, inasmuch as thou wilt be humble and faithful before the Lord in thy calling, even that of a Patriarch, thou shalt be blessed, strengthened, and have great wisdom and understanding; thy bowels shall be filled with compassion for the widow and fatherless; and I pray that our Father in Heaven will take thee into His own care, and as He feels for thy welfare, thou shalt be made strong in faith, and the Lord shall bless thee and open thy understanding. Thou shalt know the doctrine of Jesus Christ, and the mysteries of heaven shall be opened to thy mind. Thou shalt also have the gift of prophecy and revelation, and thou shalt predict those things that shall take place to the latest generation. I pray that our Father in heaven may confer these blessings upon thy head; yea, thou shalt be a mighty man, if thou wilt be a faithful man, and a humble man, so that thou mayst be an ornament to thy calling, and a blessing to thy posterity; yea, thy posterity shall be blessed, and they shall become mighty upon the earth, and become blessed inasmuch as thou wilt be faithful in all things, and watch unto prayer. Thou shalt finally overcome, and be lifted up on high, and inherit the mansions prepared for thee in the kingdom of our God. Thou art of the blood of Ephraim; and I seal these blessings upon thy head in the name of Jesus Christ. Amen, and amen."

The Apostles then laid hands on John Albertson, and ordained him to the office of Patriarch.

The ordinations of the High Priests then took place; but, from the pressure of business, it was directed that the High Priests who were present should retire to the vestry, with those who were to be ordained Elders, and there ordain them at the same time that the ordinations of the High Priests were proceeding.

Several appropriate discourses were delivered by different members of the Twelve Apostles in relation to the duties of the officers in their respective callings, and the duties and privileges of the members; also on the prosperity of the work in general.

A very richly ornamented cake, a present from New York, from Elder George J. Adams' wife to the Twelve, was then exhibited to the meeting. This was blessed by them and distributed to all the officers and members, and the whole congregation, consisting, perhaps, of seven hundred people; a large fragment was still preserved for some who were not present. During the distribution several appropriate hymns were sung, and a powerful and general feeling of delight universally pervaded the meeting.

While this was proceeding, Elder Parley P. Pratt composed, and handed over to the clerk, the following lines, which the clerk then read to the meeting:

> When in far distant regions,
>   As strangers we roam,
> Far away from our country,
>   Our friends and our home:
>
> When sinking in sorrow,
>   Fresh courage we'll take,
> As we think of our friends,
>   And remember the *cake*.

Elder Orson Hyde appealed powerfully to the meeting, and covenanted with the Saints present, in a bond of mutual prayer, during his mission to Jerusalem and the East, which was sustained on the part of the hearers with a hearty amen.

Elder Fielding remarked respecting the rich cake of which they had been partaking, that he considered it a type of the good things of that land from whence it came, and from which they had received the fullness of the Gospel.

The number of official members present at this conference was then taken, viz., quorum of the Twelve Apostles, 9; Patriarchs, 2; High Priests, 16; quorum of the Seventies, 2; Elders, 31; Priests, 28; Teachers, 17; Deacons, 2.

Elders Brigham Young and William Miller then sang the hymn "Adieu, my dear brethren," &c., and President Young blessed the congregation and dismissed them.

BRIGHAM YOUNG, Chairman.
THOMAS WARD, Clerk.

CHAPTER XVIII.

GENERAL CONFERENCE AT NAUVOO—EPISTLE OF THE TWELVE
TO THE SAINTS IN ENGLAND—DIFFERENCE BETWEEN BAP-
TISTS AND LATTER-DAY SAINTS.

*Minutes of the General Conference of the Church of Jesus Christ of Latter-
day Saints, held in Nauvoo, Illinois, on the 7th day of April, one
thousand eight hundred and forty-one.*

The names of the presidents of the several quorums were called, and
they took their seats on the stand, with their counselors in front. The
meeting was called to order. Choir sang a hymn; prayer by William
Law.

The clerk then read the report of the First Presidency, as follows—

REPORT OF THE FIRST PRESIDENCY.

The Presidency of the Church of Jesus Christ of Latter-day Saints,
feel great pleasure in assembling with the Saints at another general
conference, under circumstances so auspicious and cheering; and with
greatful hearts to Almighty God for His providential regard, they cordially unite with the Saints, on this occasion, in ascribing honor,
glory, and blessing to His Holy name.

It is with unfeigned pleasure that they have to make known the steady
and rapid increase of the Church in this state, the United States, and
Europe. The anxiety to become acquainted with the principles of the
Gospel, on every hand is intense, and the cry of "come over and help
us," is reaching the Elders on the wings of every wind; while thousands who have heard the Gospel have become obedient thereto, and are
rejoicing in its gifts and blessings. Prejudice, with its attendant train
of evil, is giving way before the force of truth, whose benign rays are
penetrating the nations afar off.

The reports from the Twelve Apostles in Europe are very satisfactory,
and state that the work continues to progress with unparalleled rapidity,
and that the harvest is truly great. In the Eastern States the faithful
laborers are successful, and many are flocking to the standard of truth

Nor is the South keeping back. Churches have been raised up in the Southern and Western States, and a very pressing invitation has been received from New Orleans, for some of the Elders to visit that city; which has been complied with. In our own state and immediate neighborhood, many are avowing their attachment to the principles of our holy religion, and have become obedient to the faith.

Peace and prosperity attend us; and we have favor in the sight of God and virtuous men. The time was, when we were looked upon as deceivers, and that "Mormonism" would soon pass away, come to nought, and be forgotten. But the time has gone by when it is looked upon as a transient matter, or a bubble on the wave, and it is now taking a deep hold in the hearts and affections of all those who are noble-minded enough to lay aside the prejudice of education, and investigate the subject with candor and honesty. The truth, like the sturdy oak, has stood unhurt amid the contending elements, which have beat upon it with tremendous force. The floods have rolled, wave after wave, in quick succession, and have not swallowed it up. "They have lifted up their voice, O Lord; the floods have lifted up their voice; but the Lord of Hosts is mightier than the mighty waves of the sea;" nor have the flames of persecution, with all the influence of mobs, been able to destroy it; but like Moses' bush, it has stood unconsumed, and now at this moment presents an important spectacle both to men and angels. Where can we turn our eyes to behold such another? We contemplate a people who have embraced a system of religion, unpopular, and the adherence to which has brought upon them repeated persecutions. A people who, for their love to God, and attachment to His cause, have suffered hunger, nakedness, perils, and almost every privation. A people who, for the sake of their religion, have had to mourn the premature death of parents, husbands, wives, and children. A people, who have preferred death to slavery and hypocrisy, and have honorably maintained their characters, and stood firm and immovable, in times that have tried men's souls. Stand fast, ye Saints of God, hold on a little while longer, and the storm of life will be past, and you will be rewarded by that God whose servants you are, and who will duly appreciate all your toils and afflictions for Christ's sake and the Gospel's. Your names will be handed down to posterity as Saints of God and virtuous men.

But we hope that those scenes of blood will never more occur, but that many, very many, such scenes as the present will be witnessed by the Saints, and that in the Temple, the foundation of which has been so happily laid, will the Saints of the Most High continue to congregate from year to year in peace and safety.

From the kind and generous feelings, manifested by the citizens of this state, since our sojourn among them, we may continue to expect the enjoyment of all the blessings of civil and religious liberty, guaranteed by the Constitution. The citizens of Illinois have done themselves honor, in throwing the mantle of the Constitution over a persecuted and afflicted people: and have given evident proof that they are not only in the enjoyment of the privileges of freemen themselves, but also that they willingly and cheerfully extend that invaluable blessing to others, and that they freely award to faithfuless and virtue their due.

The proceedings of the legislature, in regard to the citizens of this place, have been marked with philanthropy and benevolence; and they have laid us under great and lasting obligations, in granting us the several liberal charters we now enjoy, and by which we hope to prosper until our city becomes the most splendid, our University the most learned, and our Legion the most effective of any in the Union. In the language of one of our own poets, we would say—

> In Illinois we've found a safe retreat,
> A home, a shelter from oppression dire;
> Where we can worship God as we think right,
> And mobbers come not to disturb our peace;
> Where we can live and hope for better days,
> Enjoy again our liberty, our rights:
> That social intercourse which freedom grants,
> And charity requires of man to man.
> And long may charity pervade each breast,
> And long may Illinois remain the scene
> Of rich prosperity, by *peace secured*.

In consequence of the impoverished condition of the Saints, the buildings which are in course of erection do not progress as fast as could be desired; but from the interest which is generally manifested by the Saints at large, we hope to accomplish much by a combination of effort, and a concentration of action, and erect the Temple and other public buildings, which we so much need for our mutual instruction and the education of our children.

From the reports which have been received. we may expect a large emigration this season. The proclamation which was sent, some time ago, to the churches abroad, has been responded to, and great numbers are making preparations to come and locate themselves in this city and vicinity.

From what we now witness, we are led to look forward with pleasing anticipation to the future, and soon expect to see the thousands of Israel flocking to this region in obedience to the heavenly command; numerous inhabitants—Saints—thickly studding the flowery and wide-spread prairies of Illinois; temples for the worship of our God erecting in various parts, and great peace resting upon Israel.

We would call the attention of the Saints more particularly to the building of the Temple, for on its speedy erection great blessings depend. The zeal which is manifested by the Saints in this city is, indeed, praiseworthy, and, we hope will be imitated by the Saints in the various stakes and branches of the Church, and that those who cannot contribute labor will bring their gold and their silver, their brass and their iron, with the pine tree, and box tree, to beautify the same.

We are glad to hear of the organization of the different quorums in this city, and hope that their organization will be attended to in every stake and branch of the Church, for the Almighty is a lover of order and good government.

From the faith and enterprise of the Saints generally, we feel greatly encouraged and cheerfully attend to the important duties devolving upon us, knowing that we not only have the approval of heaven, but also that our efforts for the establishment of Zion and the spread of truth, are cheerfully seconded by the thousands of Israel.

In conclusion we would say, brethren, be faithful, let your love and moderation be known unto all men; be patient, be mindful to observe all the commandments of your Heavenly Father, and the God of all grace shall bless you. Even so, Amen.

JOSEPH SMITH, President,
ROBERT B. THOMPSON, Clerk.

On motion, Resolved that the report be printed in the *Times and Seasons*.

President Rigdon arose and stated that, in consequence of weakness from his labors of yesterday, he would call upon General John C. Bennett to officiate in his place.

General Bennett then read the revelations from "The Book of the Law of the Lord," which had been received since the last general conference, in relation to writing a proclamation to the kings of the earth, building a temple in Nauvoo, the organization of the Church, &c.*

President Joseph Smith rose, and made some observations in explanation of the same; and likewise of the necessity which existed of building the Temple, that the Saints might have a suitable place for worshiping the Almighty; and also the building of the Nauvoo Boarding House, that suitable accommodations may be afforded for the strangers who visit this city.

The choir sung a hymn, and the meeting adjourned for one hour.

* This is the revelation of 19th January, 1841, now section cxxi, Doctrine and Covenants.

Conference met pursuant to adjournment, and was called to order by William Law.

Choir sung a hymn, and President William Marks addressed the throne of grace.

General Bennett read the charters granted by the legislature of this state, for incorporating "the City of Nauvoo," "the Nauvoo Legion," "the University of the City of Nauvoo," "the Agricultural and Manufacturing Association," and "the Nauvoo House Association."

On motion, Resolved that the charters now read be received by the Church.

President Don Carlos Smith arose, and gave an exhortation to the assembly.

General John C. Bennett then spoke at some length on the present situation, prospects, and condition of the Church, and remarked that the hand of God must indeed be visible, in accomplishing the great blessings and prosperity of the Church, and called upon the Saints to be faithful and obedient in all things, and likewise forcibly and eloquently urged the necessity of being united in all their movements; and before he sat down, he wished to know how many of the Saints who were present felt disposed to continue to act in concert and follow the instructions of the First Presidency; and called upon all those who did so, to arise on their feet—when immediately the Saints, almost without exception, arose.

The choir sung a hymn, and the meeting, after prayer, adjourned until tomorrow morning.

Thursday, 8th.

Thursday morning, April 8. At an early hour this morning the different quorums, who had previously been organized, came to the ground and took their seats as follows: The First Presidency, with the presidents of the quorums on the stand, the High Council on the front of the stand, the High Priests on the front to the right of the stand, the Seventies immediately behind the High Priests, the Elders in the front to the left, the Lesser Priesthood on the right.

On motion, Resolved, that this conference continue until Sunday evening.

President Joseph Smith declared the rule of voting to be, a majority in each quorum; exhorted them to deliberation, faith, and prayer; and that they should be strict and impartial in their examinations. He then old them that the presidents of the different quorums would be presented before them for their acceptance or rejection.

Bishop Whitney then presented the First Presidency to the Lesser

Priesthood.   President John A. Hicks presented them to the Elders' quorum.   President Joseph Young presented them to the quorums of the Seventies. President Don Carlos Smith presented them to the High Priests' quorum.   Counselor Elias Higbee presented them to the High Council; and the clerk then presented them to the presidents of all the quorums on the stand, and they were unanimously accepted. John C. Bennett was presented, with the First Presidency, as Assistant President until President Rigdon's health should be restored.

The presidents and counselors belonging to the several quorums were then presented to each quorum separately, for approval or rejection, when the following persons were objected to, viz., John A. Hicks, president of the Elders' quorum; Alanson Ripley, Bishop; Elder John E. Page, one of the Twelve Apostles; and Noah Packard, High Priest. Bishop Newel K. Whitney moved their cases be laid over, to be tried before the several quorums.

President Joseph Smith presented the building committee of the "House of the Lord," viz., Alpheus Cutler, Reynolds Cahoon, and Elias Higbee, to the several quorums collectively, and they were unanimously received.

President Smith observed that it was necessary that someone should be appointed to fill the Quorum of the Twelve Apostles, in the room of the late Elder David W. Patten; whereupon President Rigdon nominated Elder Lyman Wight to that office; and he was unanimously accepted. Elder Wight stated that it was an office of great honor and responsibility, and he felt inadequate to the task; but, inasmuch as it was the wish of the authorities of the Church that he should take that office, he would endeavor to magnify it.

Resolved: That James Allred be appointed to the office of High Councilor, in the place of Charles C. Rich, who had been chosen a counselor to the president of this stake, and that Leonard Soby be appointed one of the High Council, in the room of David Dort, deceased.

The choir sung a hymn, and after prayer by President Rigdon, the meeting adjourned for two hours.

Conference met pursuant to adjournment.   A hymn was sung by the choir.

President Rigdon delivered an interesting discourse on the subject of "Baptism for the dead."

President Joseph Smith followed on the same subject; and threw considerable light on the doctrine which had been presented.

The choir then sung a hymn; and after prayer by Elder William Smith, conference adjourned until tomorrow morning at 10 o'clock.

Friday morning, the 9th, conference met pursuant to adjournment.

The quorums reported that they had investigated the conduct of the persons who had been objected to, and that they had rejected Alanson Ripley and James Foster. Leave was given to James Foster to make a few remarks respecting the charges preferred against him: after which it was resolved that Elder James Foster continue his standing in the Church. *Resolved:* That, as Alanson Ripley has not appeared to answer the charges preferred against him, that his Bishopric be taken from him.

President Joseph Smith made some observations respecting the duty of the several quorums, in sending their members into the vineyard, and also stated that labor on the Temple would be as acceptable to the Lord, as preaching in the world, and that it was necessary that some agents should be appointed to collect funds for building the Temple.

Resolved: That John Murdoch, Lyman Wight, William Smith, Henry William Miller, Amasa Lyman, Leonard Soby, Gehiel Savage, and Zenos H. Gurley be appointed to travel and collect funds for the same.

A hymn was then sung by the choir. Prayer by President Don Carlos Smith.

President Joseph Smith then stated that he should resign the meeting to the presidency of the stake, and the president of the High Priests' quorum.

The building committee were called upon to address the assembly. Elder Cahoon spoke at length on the importance of building the Temple, and called upon the Saints to assist them in their great undertaking. Elder Alpheus Cutler made some very appropriate remarks.

Conference adjourned one hour.

Conference met pursuant to adjournment.

Elias Higbee spoke on the same subject [*i. e.* importance of building the Temple]. Elder Lyman Wight then came forward and addressed the meeting at considerable length.

The clerk read a letter from Elder John Taylor in England, to President Joseph Smith, which gave an account of the prosperity of the work of the Lord in that land.

On motion, adjourned until tomorrow morning at 10 o'clock.

Saturday, 10th The weather was unfavorable, consequently no business was transacted.

Sunday, 11th. The conference again met.

Elder Zenos H. Gurley preached on the literal fulfillment of prophecy.

President Rigdon made some observations on baptism for the remission of sins.

Conference adjourned for one hour.

Conference met, and was addressed by the Bishops of the stake, who stated the situation of the poor who had to be supported, and called upon the Saints to assist in relieving the necessities of the widows and fatherless.

Elder Lyman Wight made some observations on the subject.

President Joseph Smith then addressed the assembly, and stated that in consequence of the severity of the weather the Saints had not received as much instruction as he desired, and that some things would have to be laid over until the next conference. As there were many who wished to be baptized, they would now go to the water, and give them opportunity.

The procession was then organized, and proceeded to the Mississippi.

After the baptisms were over, the conference adjourned to the first of October next.

JOSEPH SMITH, President.
R. B. THOMPSON, Clerk.

On the 7th of April, 1841, the Twelve Apostles were in England and were busy in council, visiting the Saints in Manchester, and in the evening supped at "Mother Miller's." On the 9th, they visited the Zoological Gardens, Manchester, England. Elder W. J. Barratt writes from Australia, "he had arrived safe at Adelaide after a rough passage, but had not baptized any persons. Obstacles to the introduction of the work of the Lord are very great."

Letter of George A. Smith to the Star—Report of Labors.

BOLTON, April 11, 1841.

Elder P. P. Pratt:

I thought good to give your readers (through the medium of the *Star*) a short account of my labors in England. I landed in Liverpool on the 6th of April, 1840; and, after attending the Preston conference, I went to the Staffordshire Potteries, where there were about 100 Saints; I remained there three months. The work continued to prosper, and 80 were added to the church in that time. I then left the church there to the care of Elder Alfred Cordon, and, in company with Elders Kimball and Woodruff, visited the churches in Herefordshire and vicinity. Hundreds received our testimony, and were baptized. From thence we proceeded to London, where we met with much difficulty in introducing the fullness of the Gospel; the hearts of the people were barred against the truth, but the Lord blessed our labors, and we succeeded in establishing a branch of the Church there. My health being poor, I was counseled by my brethren of the Twelve Apostles to return to the field of my former labors in Staffordshire; which I did, leaving in London but eleven members. Since that time, my labors have been chiefly confined to the limits of the Staffordshire conference, which has, until lately, included Birmingham and Macclesfield, containing eighteen branches of the Church, 580 members having been added since the time I commenced laboring there. Many have been called to the ministry, who are faithful men, and willing to receive counsel. Although I have suffered much bodily affliction during the past year, the Lord has blessed my labors abundantly, and I can say I never enjoyed myself better in the discharge of my duty, than I have on this mission. Among the greatest blessings I have enjoyed, has been the privilege of attending four general conferences, and meeting in council with the Twelve Apostles. I can assure you that a meeting with those in whose company I have suffered so much tribulation for the Gospel's sake, both at home and abroad, by land and sea, is to me a privilege indeed. I am now preparing to return home with my brethren, according to the instructions of the First Presidency of the Church; and, as I take my leave of the Saints in this land, my prayer to God is that He will preserve His people from the hand of Satan, and prepare them for the coming Redeemer, who is near at hand.

I remain your servant for the Gospel's sake,

GEORGE A. SMITH.

Tuesday, 13.—Elder Heber C. Kimball left Manchester for Preston.

Thursday 15.

Conference in New York City.

A conference of the Church was held in New York City. Elder George W. Harris, of Nauvoo, chairman. Lucien R. Foster was elected president of the branch, and Addison Everett and George Holmes, his counselors. John M. Bernhisel was elected Bishop, and Richard Burge and William Acker his counselors. These six, having been chosen, were ordained and set apart to the several offices under the direction of Elder Harris, he having been specially appointed and authorized by President Hyrum Smith, at the Philadelphia conference, to organize more perfectly the branch in New York.

LUCIEN R. FOSTER, Secretary.

An Epistle of the Twelve Apostles to the Church of Jesus Christ of Latter-day Saints in England, Scotland, Ireland, Wales, and the Isle of Man, Greeting:

BELOVED BRETHREN:—Inasmuch as we have been laboring for some time in this country, and most of us are about to depart for the land of our nativity; and, feeling anxious for your welfare and happiness in time and in eternity, we cheerfully offer you our counsel in the closing number of the first volume of the *Star*, hoping you will peruse it when we are far away, and profit by the same.

First of all, we would express our joy and thanksgiving to Him who rules, and knows the hearts of men, for the heed and diligence with which the Saints in this county have hearkened to the counsel of those whom God has seen fit to send among them, and who hold the keys of this ministry.   By this means a spirit of union, and, consequently, of power, has been generally cultivated among you.   And now let the Saints remember that which we have ever taught them, both by precept and example, viz., to beware of an aspiring spirit, which would lift you up, one above another, to seek to be the greatest in the kingdom of God. This is that spirit which hurled down the angels. It is that spirit which actuates all the churches of the sectarian world, and most of the civil and military movements of the men of the world.   It is that spirit which introduces rebellion, confusion, misrule, and disunion, and would, if suffered to exist among us, destroy our union, and, consequently, our power, which flows from the Spirit, through the Priesthood; which Spirit, and power, and Priesthood, can only exist with the humble and meek of the earth.   Therefore, beware, O ye Priests of the Most High! lest ye are overcome by that spirit which would exalt you above your fellow-laborers, and thus hurl you down to perdition, or do much injury to the cause of God.

Be careful to respect, not the eloquence, not the smooth speeches, not the multitude of words, not the talents of men, but the offices which God has placed in the Church.   Let the members hearken to their officers, let the Priests, Teachers, and Deacons hearken to the Elders, and let the Elders hearken to the presiding officers of each church or conference, and let all the churches and conferences hearken to the counsel of those who are still left in this country to superintend the affairs of the Church; and, by so doing, a spirit of union will be preserved, and peace and prosperity will attend the people of God.

We have seen fit to appoint our beloved brethren and fellow-laborers, Levi Richards and Lorenzo Snow to travel from conference to conference, and to assist Brother Pratt in the general superintendency of the Church in this country.   These are men of experience and soundness of principle, in whose counsel the Church may place entire confidence, as long as they uphold them by the prayer of faith.

The spirit of emigration has actuated the children of men, from the time our first parents were expelled from the garden until now.   It was this spirit that first peopled the plains of Shinar, and all other places; yes, it was emigration that first broke upon the death-like silence and loneliness of an empty earth, and caused the desolate land to teem with life, and the desert to smile with joy. It was emigration that first peopled England, once a desolate island, on which the foot of man had never trod, but now abounding in towns and cities. It was emigration that turned the wilds of America into a fruitful field, and besprinkled the wilderness with flourishing towns and cities, where a few years since the war hoop of the savage, or the howl of the wild beasts was heard in the distance. In short, it is emigration that is the only effectual remedy for the evils which now afflict the over-peopled countries of Europe. With this view of the subject, the Saints, as well as thousands of others, seem to be actuated with the spirit of enterprise and emigration, and as some of them are calculating to emigrate to America, and settle in the colonies of our brethren, we would here impart a few words of counsel on the subject of emigration.

It will be necessary, in the first place, for men of capital to go on first and make large purchases of land, and erect mills, machinery, manufactories, &c., so that the poor who go from this country can find employment. Therefore, it is not wisdom for the poor to flock to that place extensively, until the necessary preparations are made. Neither is it wisdom for those who feel a spirit of benevolence to expend all their means in helping others to emigrate, and thus all arrive in a new country empty-handed. In all settlements there must be capital and labor united, in order to flourish. The brethren will recollect that they are not going to enter upon cities already built up, but are going to "build cities and inhabit them." Building cities cannot be done without means and labor. On this subject we would call the particular attention of the Saints to the Epistle, and also to the proclamation signed by the First Presidency of the Church, published in the eleventh number of this work (the *Star*), and would earnestly exhort them to observe the order and instructions there given.

We would also exhort the Saints not to go in haste, nor by flight, but to prepare all things in a proper manner before they emigrate; and especially in regard to their dealings with the world, let them be careful to settle everything honestly, as becometh Saints, as far as lies in their power, and not go away in debt, so far as they have the means to pay. And if any go away in debt, because they have not the means to pay, let it be with the design of paying as industry shall put it in their power, so that the cause of truth be not evil spoken of.

We have found that there are so many "pick-pockets," and so many that will take every possible advantage of strangers in Liverpool, that we have appointed Elder Amos Fielding as the agent of the Church, to superintend the fitting out of the Saints from Liverpool to America.

Whatever information the Saints may want about the preparation for a voyage, they are advised to call on Elder Fielding at Liverpool, as their first movement when they arrive there as emigrants. There are some brethren who have felt themselves competent to do their own business in these matters and, rather despising the counsel of their friends, have been robbed and cheated out of nearly all they had. A word of caution to the wise is sufficient. It is also a great saving to go in companies, instead of going individually.

First, a company can charter a vessel, so as to make the passage much cheaper than otherwise.

Secondly, provisions can be purchased at wholesale, for a company, much cheaper than otherwise.

Thirdly, this will avoid bad company on the passage.

Fourthly, when a company arrives at New Orleans they can charter a steamboat, so as to reduce the passage near one-half. This measure will save some hundreds of pounds on each ship load.

Fifthly, a man of experience can go as leader of each company, who will know how to avoid rogues and knaves.

Sovereigns are more profitable than silver or any other money, in emigrating to America; and the brethren are also cautioned against the American money, when they arrive in that country. Let them not venture to take paper money of that country, until they become well informed in regard to the different banks, for very few of them will pass current very far from the place where they are issued, and banks are breaking almost daily.

It is much cheaper going by New Orleans than by New York; but it will never do for emigrants to go by New Orleans in the summer, on account of the heat and sickness of the climate. It is, therefore, advisable for the Saints to emigrate in autumn, winter, or spring.

Let the Saints be careful also to obtain a letter of recommendation, from the Elders where they are acquainted, to the brethren where they are going, certifying their membership; and let the Elders be careful not to recommend any who do not conduct themselves as Saints; and especially those who would go with a design to defraud their creditors.

In regard to ordaining and licensing officers, each conference is now organized under the care of their respective presidents, who, with the voice of the Church, may ordain, according to the gifts and callings of God, by the Holy Spirit, and under the general superintendence of Elders Pratt, Richards, and Snow. Licenses should be signed by the presiding officers.

There are many other items of importance, which we would gladly mention, had we time and space sufficient; but this must suffice for the present; and may the God of our fathers bless you all with wisdom and grace to act each your part in the great work which lies before you, that the world may be warned, and thousands brought to the knowledge of the truth; and may He bless and preserve you blameless until the day of His coming. Brethren and sisters, pray for us.

We remain, your brethren in the new and everlasting covenant,

BRIGHAM YOUNG,
HEBER C. KIMBALL,
ORSON HYDE,
PARLEY P. PRATT,
ORSON PRATT,
WILLARD RICHARDS,
WILFORD WOODRUFF,
JOHN TAYLOR,
GEO. A. SMITH.

Manchester, April 15, 1841.

Elders Brigham Young, Orson Pratt, Wilford Woodruff, George A. Smith, and Levi Richards went from Manchester to Liverpool to attend a tea-party at the Music Hall.

DIFFERENCE BETWEEN THE BAPTIST AND LATTER-DAY SAINTS, FROM THE "NORTH STAFFORDSHIRE MERCURY."

SIR:—In a late publication, you reported the case of some persons who were taken before T. B. Ross, Esq., for disturbing a congregation of Latter-day Saints, or believers in the "Book of Mormon." A teacher of that sect, on being asked by the magistrate wherein they differed from the Baptists, replied, "In the laying on of hands;" but declined making an honest confession of those peculiarities which separate them as widely from the Baptists, as from every other denomination of the Christian church. This was certainly prudent; but as the Baptists feel themselves dishonored by such an alliance, they would be unjust to themselves were they to leave unanswered such a libel upon their denomination. the following very prominent marks of difference will enable your readers to judge for themselves.

1. The Saints admit all persons indiscriminately to baptism, encouraging them to pass through that rite, with the promise that great spiritual improvement will follow. They baptize for remission of sins, without waiting for creditable evidence of repentance for sin. But the Baptists admit none to that ordinance who do not exhibit this qualification in the most satisfactory manner; and if they found a candidate looking to the water of baptism as having virtue to cleanse him from sin, he would be put back until better instructed.

2. After baptism the Saints kneel down, and their Priest, laying on his hands, professes to give them the Holy Ghost. If effects similar to those produced by the laying on of the Apostles' hands were seen to follow, scepticism must yield to the force of such evidence; but in their case no such effects are produced; the baptized sinner is a sinner still, though flattered and deluded with the epithet "Latter-day Saint." The Baptists regard such mummery with as much disgust as all Christians do.

3. Having, as they suppose, the extraordinary gifts of the Spirit, the Saints consistently pretend to have the power of working wonders, and profess to heal the sick with holy oil; also to the power of prophecy. As most moral evils bring with them their own remedy, these lofty pretensions will ruin them in due time, by opening the eyes of the most deluded, as in the case of the countless sects of impostors who have appeared upon the stage before them. It need not be added, that the Baptists stand far removed from such conceits, and have no part in them.

4. Not satisfied with the Bible as a complete revelation from God, the "Latter-day Saints" have adopted a romance, written in America, as a fresh revelation, and have added a trashy volume of 600 pages to that book, which we are forbidden to add to, or take from, under the most awful penalties! But even this is not enough for their impious presumption. They have published a monthly magazine, in which "new revelations" are served up fresh, as they arrive, for the use of all who can swallow them. The disgust with which the Baptists regard such a melancholy exhibition of human folly and wickedness, separates them to an impassable distance from such people.

5. In order to carry on this order of things, the Latter-day Saints have appointed two Priesthoods. "The Lesser, or Aaronic Priesthood, is to hold the keys of the ministering of angels, and to administer in outward ordinances. The power and authority of the higher, or Melchisedek Priesthood, is to hold the keys of all the spiritual blessings of the Church—to have the privilege of receiving the mysteries of the kingdom of heaven—to have the heavens opened to them—to commune with the general assembly and Church of the First-born; and to enjoy the communion and presence of God the Father, and of Jesus the Mediator of the new covenant," (see page 13). So that, in this wonderful Priesthood, they have provided for an ample supply of new things, in endless variety, and without end, from the hands of wretched men, who blasphemously aspire to a dignity which belongs alone to Him who is the only "Priest forever after the order of Melchisedek."

The fear of trespassing upon your valuable columns, Mr. Editor, prevents my enlarging upon these and very many other points of difference; but enough has been done to show your readers, that no two sects can differ more widely from each other, than the Baptists and the Latter day Saints; and that to confound them in any way together is not only unjust to the former, but involves them in the disgrace of being partakers in a bold imposition, or a pitiable delusion, which they regard with equal abhorrence and disgust.

A BAPTIST.

Hanley, Feb. 16, 1841.

The foregoing article attempts to show the difference between the Baptists and Latter-day Saints. We will now attempt to show the difference between the Baptists and Former-day Saints.

THE DIFFERENCE BETWEEN THE BAPTISTS AND THE FORMER-DAY SAINTS.

1st. The Former-day Saints baptized *for remission of sins*, Acts ii: 38. The Baptists baptize those only who are supposed to have their sins forgiven before they are baptized.

2nd. The Former-day Saints admitted all persons indiscriminately to baptism, as soon as they professed faith and repentance, encouraging them to pass through that rite, with the promise that great spiritual improvement would follow, Acts ii: 38-41 inclusive. But if the Baptists found the penitent believer looking for remission of sins through that rite, they would be put back to "get religion" where they could find it.

3rd. After baptism, the Former-day Saints prayed for, and laid hands on the disciples in the name of Jesus, and professed to give them the Holy Ghost, Acts viii: 17, also Acts xix: 6. The Baptists say, "They regard such mummery with as much disgust as all Christians do."

4th. Having, as they supposed, the extraordinary gifts of the Spirit, the Former-day Saints consistently pretended to have the power of working wonders, and professed to heal the sick with holy oil; James v: 14, 15. Also to the power of prophecy; First Corinthians from 12th to 14th chapter. It need not be added that the Baptists stand far removed from "such conceits," and have no part in them; nor in anything partaining to the gifts and power of God: or, to use the Apostle's own words, "they have a form of godliness, denying the power."

5th. Not satisfied with the Bible as a complete revelation from God, the Former-day Saints have added a volume of several hundred pages (the New Testament), to that book, which (according to Baptist logic)

Moses forbid them to add to, or take from; but new revelations were served up almost daily, fresh as they arrived, for all those who could swallow them. "The disgust with which the Baptists regard such things, considering them but a melancholy exhibition of human folly and wickedness," separates them to an impassable distance from the Former-day Saints; and how, with all these differences, the Baptists should ever have been thought, by themselves, or anybody else, to be the Church of Christ, is difficult to imagine!

6th. In order to carry on their strange work, or order of things, the Former-day Saints had two Priesthoods. The Aaronic Priesthood administered in outward ordinances, as in the case of John the Baptist. The power and authority of the higher, or Melchisedek Priesthood, was to hold the keys of all the spiritual blessing of the Church, as Jesus said, "I give unto thee the keys of the kingdom of heaven—whatsoever thou shalt bind on earth shall be bound in heaven," &c. They were to have the privilege of knowing the mysteries of the kingdom of heaven. "To you it is given to know the mysteries of the kingdom"—to have the heavens opened unto them—to commune with the general assembly and Church of the First born; and to enjoy the communion and presence of God the Father, and of Jesus the Mediator of the new covenant: Heb. xii: 22, 23, 24. So that in this wonderful Priesthood, they have provided for an ample supply of new things, in endless variety, and without end, from those who are and were counted the off-scouring of all things; and who, as the Baptists would insinuate, "did aspire to a dignity," which they say, "Belongs alone to Him who is the only Priest forever after the order of Melchisedek."

The fear of trespassing upon the time and patience of our readers, prevents our enlarging upon these and many other points of difference; but enough has been said to show, that no two sects can possibly differ more widely from each other than do the Baptists and Former-day Saints, and to amalgamate the two systems in any way is not only an act of injustice—but would involve the Baptists, who by the way are an honorable body, in the disgrace of that sect which was "everywhere spoken against." See Acts 28:23.

CHAPTER XIX.

ORGANIZATION OF THE NAUVOO LEGION—NOTABLE PERSONS
AT NAUVOO—THE PROPHET'S SERMON ON INDIVIDUAL RE-
SPONSIBILITY FOR SIN AND THE DOCTRINE OF ELECTION.

Tuesday, 20.—Elders Brigham Young, Heber C. Kim-
ball, Orson Pratt, Wilford Woodruff, John Taylor, George
A. Smith and Willard Richards and family,
The Twelve
Embark for   went on board of the ship *Rochester*, at Liver-
Home.
pool, Captain Woodhouse (who delayed his
sailing two days, to accommodate the Elders), bound for
New York with a company of 130 Saints.

Elder Parley P. Pratt tarried in England to preside
over the Church, and continue the publication of the
Millennial Star, and Elder Hyde to pursue his mission to
Jerusalem.

Mr. James Robinson, Assessor for the City of Nauvoo,
died, aged 30. He had resided in this county many years,
and for his business habits and kind disposition, he was
highly respected.

Wednesday, 21.—The *Rochester* sailed.

Saturday, 24.—The High Council of Iowa selected
David Pettigrew and Moses Nickerson Counselors to President John Smith, in place of Reynolds
Changes in
the Iowa   Cahoon and Lyman Wight, removed by
Stake.
appointment; James Emmett in the place of
David Pettigrew in the High Council, Joseph C. Kings-
bury in place of George W. Pitkin, removed to Nauvoo,
and William Clayton in place of Erastus Snow, absent.

Monday, 26.—I attended the City Council. Several
members being absent, I moved that the Marshall be
ordered to enforce the attendance of Aldermen and Coun-

cillors, at one o'clock on Saturday next, and Council adjourned.

Wednesday, 28.—The ship *Rochester* encountered a tempest, shipped a heavy sea, Wilford Woodruff got thoroughly drenched; Willard Richards escaped under the bulwarks.

Saturday, May 1.—Elder Robert B. Thompson became associate editor of the *Times and Seasons*.

The first Regiment, first cohort of the Nauvoo Legion, consisting of four companies, was organized, and Captain George Miller was elected colonel; Captain Stephen Markham, lieutenant-colonel, and Captain William Wightman, major. Organization of the Legion.

The first regiment, second cohort, consisting of four companies, was also organized, and Captain Charles C. Rich was elected colonel, Captain Titus Billings, lieutenant-colonel, and Captain John Scott, major.

Also the second regiment, second cohort, consisting of four companies, was organized, and Captain Francis M. Higbee was elected colonel; Captain Nelson Higgins, lieutenant-colonel, and Aaron H. Golden, major.

I attended the City Council, and moved that the sympathies of the Council be tendered to the relatives of James Robinson, deceased, the late assessor and collector for the city, which was carried.

I also moved that a new burying ground be procured, outside the city limits, and purchased at the expense of the corporation; which was carried; and Alderman Daniel H. Wells, and New Burying Ground for Nauvoo. Councillors Wilson Law and John T. Barnett were appointed a committee, and ten acres were ordered to be purchased.

I spoke at length on the rights and privileges of the owners of the ferry, showing that the City Council has no right to take away ferry privileges, once granted, without damages being paid to the proprietor; and also moved that an ordinance be passed to protect citizens killing dogs running at large, which were set upon cattle or hogs, or molest individuals. And also spoke on other subjects before the council.

Sunday, 2.—The Teachers' quorum was organized in Nauvoo, Elisha Averett, President, James Hendricks and James W. Huntsman, Counselors.

Tuesday, 4.—

Nauvoo Legion Affairs.

HEADQUARTERS, NAUVOO LEGION, CITY OF
NAUVOO, ILLINOIS, May 4, 1841.

General Orders. Pursuant to an act of the Court Martial, the troops attached or belonging to the Legion will parade at the place of general rendezvous, in the City of Nauvoo, for drill, review and inspection, on Saturday, the 3rd day of July, at half-past nine o'clock a. m., armed and equipped according to law. At ten o'clock the line will be formed and the general officers conducted to their posts, under a fire of artillery. The commandants of the 1st and 2nd companies, 2nd battalion, 1st regiment, 2nd cohort, are directed to enroll every man residing within the bounds of their respective commands, and not attached to any other company of the Legion, between the ages of eighteen and forty-five years, and notify them of their attachment to the service, and their legal liabilities.

As will be seen by the following legal opinion of Judge Douglas, of the Supreme Court of the State of Illinois, than whom no man stands more deservedly high in the public estimation, as an able and profound jurist, politician and statesman; the officers and privates, belonging to the Legion, are exempt from all military duty, not required by the legally constituted authorities thereof. They are, therefore, expressly inhibited from performing any military services, not ordered by the general officers, or directed by the court martial:

CITY OF NAUVOO, ILLINOIS, May 3, 1841.

General Bennett:

DEAR SIR.—In reply to your request, I have examined so much of the Nauvoo City Charter, and Legislative Acts, as relate to the "Nauvoo Legion," and am clearly of opinion, that any citizen of Hancock county, who may attach himself to the Nauvoo Legion, has all the privileges that appertain to which independent military body, and is exempt from all other military duty, as provided in the 25th section of the City Charter; and cannot, therefore, be fined by any military or civil court, for neglecting or refusing to parade with any other military body, or under the command of any officers who are not attached to said Legion. The language of the laws upon this subject, is so plain and specific as to admit of no doubt as to its true meaning and intent. I do not consider it necessary, therefore, to enter into an argument to prove a position which is evident from an inspection of the laws themselves.

I am very respectfully, your friend,
S. A. DOUGLAS.

The Legion is not, as has been falsely represented by its enemies, exclusively a "Mormon" military association, but a body of citizen soldiers, organized (without regard to political preferences or religious sentiments) for the public defense, the general good, and the preservation of law and order—to save the innocent, unoffending citizens from the iron grasp of the oppressor and perpetuate and sustain our free institutions against misrule, anarchy, and mob violence; no other views are entertained or tolerated. The general parades of the Legion will be in the City of Nauvoo, but all other musters will be within the bounds of the respective companies, battalions, regiments and cohorts.

The 8th section of "An Act for the Organization and Government of the Militia of this State," in force July 2, 1833, provides that "when any person shall enroll himself in a volunteer company, he shall forthwith give notice in writing to the commanding officer of the company in which he was enrolled," &c., and that the commanding officer of a regiment or battalion, may, in a certain contingency, "dissolve such company;" and some of the petty, ignorant, and imprudent militia officers maintain that such is still the law; but those blind leaders of the blind are informed that the 11th section of "An Act Encouraging Volunteer Companies," approved March 2, 1837, reads as follows: "So much of the 8th section of an Act entitled, "An Act for the Organization and Government of the Militia of this State," in force July 2, 1833, as requires a volunteer to give notice in writing to the commanding officer of the company in which he was enrolled, and authorizes commandants of regiments to disband independent companies, be and the same is hereby repealed."

If officers act upon the obsolete laws of the "little book" which have been repealed, years since, it will be sweet to the taste, but "make the belly bitter;" and should any civil or military officer attempt to enforce the collection of any military fines upon the members of the Legion, excepting when such fines are assessed by the court martial of the Legion, such persons are directed to apply to the master in chancery, for Hancock county, for an injunction to stay the illegal proceedings.

The militia companies of Hancock county, and citizens generally, are respectfully invited to unite with the Legion, and partake of its privileges.

All officers are required to enforce the most rigid discipline on all days of public parade.

Persons holding enrolling orders are directed to act with energy; consummate their trust, and make prompt returns to the office of the Major-General.

The Lieutenant-General desires that all his friends should attach themselves to some company, either in the first or second cohort. This will enable them to receive correct military instruction, under the teachings of experienced officers, according to the drill and discipline of the United States army—and qualify them for efficient service in the cause of their beloved country and state, in the hour of peril.

The eleven companies of minute men will, at all times, hold themselves in readiness to execute the laws, as originally instructed by the general officers.

The officers and troops of the Legion are directed to treat with proper respect and decorum, all other officers and troops in the service of this state, or of the United States.

Officers are ordered to treat their troops with marked respect; and, while they discharge their duties with promptitude and boldness as officers, they must not forget or neglect to observe the requisites of gentlemen.

The second company (light infantry), 1st battalion, 1st regiment, 2nd cohort; and the 1st company (lancers), 1st battalion, 3rd regiment, 2nd cohort of the Legion, will act as an escort for the reception of such visiting companies from Illinois and Iowa, as may be present. Should the Governor be present, it will be announced by a fire of artillery, by the 1st and 2nd companies, 1st battalion, 1st regiment, 1st cohort, and the 1st company, 1st battalion, 1st regiment, 2nd cohort, when he will be received by the entire Legion, with the honors due so conspicuous a personage as the Commander-in-Chief of the forces of the state.

Officers, receiving copies of these orders, will promulgate the same without delay, throughout the bounds of their respective commands.

JOSEPH SMITH, Lieutenant-General.

Letter of the Prophet to the "Times and Seasons"—Visit of Notable Persons to Nauvoo.

CITY OF NAUVOO, May 6, 1841.

To the Editors of the "Times and Seasons:"

GENTLEMEN:—I wish, through the medium of your paper, to make known that, on Sunday last, I had the honor of receiving a visit from the Hon. Stephen A. Douglas, Justice of the Supreme Court, and Judge of the Fifth Judicial Circuit of the state of Illinois, and Cyrus Walker,

Esq., of Macomb, who expressed great pleasure in visiting our city, and were astonished at the improvements which were made. They were officially introduced to the congregation who had assembled on the meeting ground, by the mayor; and they severally addressed the assembly.

Judge Douglas expressed his satisfaction of what he had seen and heard respecting our people, and took that opportunity of returning thanks to the citizens of Nauvoo, for conferring upon him the freedom of the city; stating that he was not aware of rendering us any service sufficiently important to deserve such marked honor; and likewise spoke in high terms of our location and the improvements we had made, and that our enterprise and industry were highly creditable to us, indeed.

Mr. Walker spoke much in favor of the place, the industry of the citizens, &c.,and hoped they would continue to enjoy all the blessings and privileges of our free and glorious Constitution, and, as a patriot and a freeman, he was willing, at all times, to stand boldly in defense of liberty and law.

It must indeed be satisfactory to this community to know that kind and generous feelings exist in the hearts of men of such high reputation and moral and intellectual worth.

Judge Douglas has ever proved himself friendly to this people, and interested himself to obtain for us our several chartes, holding at that time the office of Secretary of State.

Mr. Walker also ranks high, and has long held a standing at the bar, which few attain, and is considered one of the most able and profound jurists in the state.

The sentiments they expressed on the occasion were highly honorable to them as American citizens, and as gentlemen. How different their conduct from that of the official characters in the state of Missouri, whose minds were prejudiced to such an extent that, instead of mingling in our midst and ascertaining for themselves our character, kept entirely aloof, but were ready, at all times, to listen to those who had the "poison of adders under their tongues," and who sought our overthrow.

Let every person who may have imbibed sentiments prejudicial to us, imitate the honorable example of our distinguished visitors (Douglas and Walker), and I believe they will find much less to condemn than they anticipated, and probably a great deal to commend.

What makes the late visit more pleasing, is the fact that Messrs. Douglas and Walker have long been held in high estimation as politicians, being champions of the two great parties that exist in the state; but laying aside all party strife, like brothers, citizens, and friends, they mingle with us, mutually disposed to extend to us that courtesy, respect, and friendship, which I hope we shall ever be proud to reciprocate.

I am, very respectfully, yours, &c.,

JOSEPH SMITH.

Saturday, 8.—Brother William Smith is preaching in Pennsylvania.

Accounts of the progress of the Gospel from the Elders abroad are very encouraging.

A magazine of 300 barrels of gunpowder, at Fort Moultrie, South Carolina, exploded, blowing the fort, seven other buildings, and forty persons to atoms.

Wednesday, 12.—The *Rochester*, with the Elders, came in sight of Cape Sable, Nova Scotia.

Saturday, 15.—Good news has recently reached us from Tennessee, New York, Upper Canada, and New Orleans. The Elders are baptizing in all directions.

Sunday, 16.—I addressed the Saints. The following is a sketch of my sermon by the editor of the *Times and Seasons:*

THE PROPHET'S DISCOURSE.

At 10 o'clock a. m., a large concourse of the Saints assembled on the meeting ground, and were addressed by President Joseph Smith, who spoke at considerable length.

He commenced his observations by remarking that the kindness of our Heavenly Father called for our heartfelt gratitude. He then observed that Satan was generally blamed for the evils which we did, but if he was the cause of all our wickedness, men could not be condemned. The devil could not compel mankind to do evil; all was voluntary. Those who resisted the Spirit of God, would be liable to be led into temptation, and then the association of heaven would be withdrawn from those who refused to be made partakers of such great glory. God would not exert any compulsory means, and the devil could not; and such ideas as were entertained [on these subjects] by many were absurd. The creature was made subject to vanity, not willingly, but Christ subjected the same in hope—all are subjected to vanity while they travel through the crooked paths and difficulties which surround them. Where is the man that is free from vanity? None ever were perfect but Jesus; and why was He perfect? Because He was the Son of God, and had the fullness of the Spirit, and greater power than any man. But notwithstanding their vanity, men look forward with hope (because they are "subjected in hope") to the time of their deliverance.

The speaker then made some observations on the first principles of the Gospel, observing, that many of the Saints who had come from different states and nations had only a very superficial knowledge of these principles, not having heard them fully investigated.

He then briefly stated the principles of faith, repentance, and baptism for the remission of sins, these were believed by some of the righteous societies of the day, but the doctrine of laying on of hands for the gift of the Holy Ghost was discarded by them.

The speaker then referred to the 6th capter of Hebrews, 1st and 2nd verses. "Not laying again the foundation of repentance from dead works," &c., but of the doctrines of baptisms, laying on of hands, the resurrection, and eternal judgment, &c. That the doctrine of eternal judgment was perfectly understood by the Apostles, is evident from several passages of Scripture. Peter preached repentance and baptism for the remission of sins to the Jews who had been led to acts of violence and blood by their leaders; but to the rulers he said, "I would that through ignorance ye did it, as did also those ye ruled." "Repent, therefore, and be converted, that your sins may be blotted out, when the times of refreshing (redemption) shall come from the presence of the Lord, for He shall send Jesus Christ, who before was preached unto you," &c. The time of redemption here had reference to the time when Christ should come; then, and not till then, would their sins be blotted out. Why? Because they were murderers, and no murderer hath eternal life. Even David must wait for those times of refreshing, before he can come forth and his sins be blotted out. For Peter, speaking of him says, "David hath not yet ascended into heaven, for his sepulchre is with us to this day." His remains were then in the tomb. Now, we read that many bodies of the Saints arose at Christ's resurrection, probably all the Saints, but it seems that David did not. Why? Because he had been a murderer. If the ministers of religion had a proper understanding of the doctrine of eternal judgment, they would not be found attending the man who forfeited his life to the injured laws of his country, by shedding innocent blood; for such characters cannot be forgiven, until they have paid the last farthing. The prayers of all the ministers in the world can never close the gates of hell against a murderer.

He then spoke on the subject of election, and read the 9th chapter of Romans, from which it was evident that the election there spoken of was pertaining to the flesh, and had reference to the seed of Abraham, according to the promise God made to Abraham, saying, "In thee, and in thy seed, all the families of the earth shall be blessed." To them belonged the adoption and the covenants, &c. Paul said, when he saw their unbelief, "I wish myself accursed"—according to the flesh—not according to the spirit. Why did God say to Pharaoh, "For this cause have I raised thee up"? Because Pharaoh was a fit instrument—a wicked man, and had committed acts of cruelty of the most atrocious nature. The election of the promised seed still continues, and in the last day, they shall have the Priesthood restored unto them, and they shall be the "saviors on Mount Zion," the ministers of our God; if it were not for the remnant which was left, then might men now be as Sodom and Gomorrah. The whole of the chapter had reference to the Priesthood and the house of Israel; and unconditional election of individuals to eternal life was not taught by the Apostles. God did elect or predestinate, that all those who would be saved, should be saved in Christ Jesus, and through obedience to the Gospel; but He passes over no man's sins, but visits them with correction, and if His children will not repent of their sins He will discard them.

This is an imperfect sketch of a very interesting discourse, which occupied more than two hours in delivery, and was listened to with marked attention, by the vast assembly present.

In the afternoon the assembly was addressed by President Hyrum Smith.

Minutes of a Conference in London.

Conference met in London pursuant to adjournment.

Elder Orson Hyde (of the Twelve Apostles) Lorenzo Snow, George J. Adams (High Priest), two Elders, several Priests, Teachers, and Deacons, with a respectable company of members present.

Elder Snow represented the London branch, consisting of 74 members, and good prospect for increase. The branch at Bedford, represented by George J. Adams, consisted of 68 member, 8 Priests, 1 Teacher. John Griffith, Priest, represented the branch at Woolwich, consisted of 6 members. Elder John Bourne, who was sent to labor at Ipswich, was obliged to leave, there being no prospect of success, and the brethren refusing to entertain him, so that he had to sleep on the ground. In consequence of this the conference passed a resolution condemnatory of their conduct.

Wednesday, 19.—The *Rochester* arrived at quarantine ground, New York, after a toilsome passage. At one

Arrival of
Rochester at
New York.

time they were beset with head winds and a tedious storm, when the Twelve Apostles united in prayer, the storm abated, the sea became calm, and they went on their way rejoicing.

The following is copied from the *Times and Seasons:*

THE HEALING OF ONE WHO WAS DEAF.

BATAVIA, N. Y., May 19, 1841.

To the Saints scattered abroad, and to all whom it may concern, greeting:

Be it known that on or about the first of December last, we, J. Shamp and Margaret Shamp, of the town of Batavia, Gennesee county, N. Y., had a daughter that had been deaf and dumb four and a half years, and was restored to her hearing, the time aforesaid, by the laying on of the hands of the Elders (Nathan R. Knight and Charles Thompson) of the Church of Jesus Christ of Latter-day Saints, commonly called Mormons, through the power of Almighty God, and faith in the Lord Jesus Christ, as believed and practiced by them in these last days.

[Signed]   J. SHAMP,
                      M. SHAMP.

Several other instances of healing are mentioned by Brother Shamp; and such things are common in the Church at this day, according to the faith of the Saints.

Thursday, 20.—The Twelve Apostles arrived at the dock in New York about four o'clock p. m., but were prevented from landing by the carters and rowdies, until late in the evening. Rowdyism in New York Harbor. Such is the confusion in New York on the arrival of a ship, steamboat, or coach, that strangers may well suppose the city is without mayor, marshal, police, or any other officer, to keep the peace.

Elder A. Cordon attempted to speak several times at Swan Village, near Birmingham, England, but was interrupted by a mob. Several of the Saints were struck with stones, but none of them seriously hurt. Mob Violence in England.

Friday, 21.—I attended City Council, and moved that Parley Street be opened and improved to the state road.

Saturday, 22.—A conference was held at Kirtland, Ohio, Elder Almon W. Babbitt presiding. Elder Babbitt was elected president of that stake, and Lester Brooks and Zebedee Coltrin his coun- Conference in Kirtland.

selors.   Thomas Burdick was elected Bishop of Kirtland,
and Hiram Winters and Reuben McBride his counselors.
Hiram Kellogg was elected president of the High Priests'
quorum, and Amos Babcock, president of the Elders'
quorum.   By-laws were adopted for the preservation of
the Lord's House.

Sunday, 23.—The Twelve addressed the Saints at the
Columbian Hall, Grand Street, New York.

Monday, 24.

LETTER OF THE PRESIDENCY TO THE SAINTS—CONCENTRATION AT NAUVOO.

To the Saints abroad—

The First Presidency of the Church of Jesus Christ of Latter-day
Saints, anxious to promote the prosperity of said Church, feel it their
duty to call upon the Saints who reside out of this county [Hancock],
to make preparations to come in without delay.   This is important, and
should be attended to by all who feel an interest in the prosperity of
this corner-stone of Zion.   Here the Temple must be raised, the University built, and other edifices erected which are necessary for the
great work of the last days, and which can only be done by a concentration of energy and enterprise.   Let it, therefore, be understood, that
all the stakes, excepting those in this county, and in Lee county, Iowa,
are discontinued, and the Saints instructed to settle in this county as
soon as circumstances will permit.

JOSEPH SMITH, President.

City of Nauvoo, Hancock county,
    Illinois, May 24, 1841.

Tuesday, 25.

Legion Affairs.

HEADQUARTERS NAUVOO LEGION,
    CITY OF NAUVOO, ILLINOIS, May 25, 1841.

General Orders—The 1st company (riflemen) 1st battalion, 2nd regiment, 2nd cohort, will be attached to the escort, contemplated in the
general orders of the 4th inst., for the 3rd of July next.   See p. 354.

In forming the Legion, the adjutant will observe the rank of companies in the order they are named, to-wit—1st cohort; flying artillery
lancers, visiting companies of dragoons, cavalry, lancers, riflemen. Second

cohort: artillery, lancers, riflemen, light infantry, infantry.   Visiting companies in their appropriate places on the right of the troops of their own grade.

The ranking company of the 1st cohort will be formed on the right of said cohort; and the ranking company of the 2nd cohort will be formed on the left of said cohort; the next on the left of the right, the next on the right of the left, and so on to the center.

The escort will be formed on the right of the forces.

                              JOSEPH SMITH, Lieutenant-General.

Wednesday, 26.—Elder Lorenzo Snow writes from London, that the Church there numbers 74 members, having baptized 18 since his return from Manchester conference, and that Elder Orson Hyde was at the London conference on the 16th instant.

Elder Joseph Fielding was at the Isle of Man.

Thursday, 27.—Elders Willard Richards, Wilford Woodruff, George A. Smith, and John M. Bernhisel visited the shipping and principal buildings in New York.

Sir Hugh Gough being about to storm Canton with the British forces, the Chinese agreed to pay a ransom of $6,000,000.

Monday, 31.—Elder Brigham Young visited the Saints on Long Island.

CHAPTER XX.

ARREST OF THE PROPHET ON DEMAND OF MISSOURI—TRIAL
    AT MONMOUTH   THE ACQUITTAL.

Tuesday, June 1, 1841.—I accompanied my brother
Hyrum and William Law, as far as Quincy, on their mission to the East.

Elder Sidney Rigdon has been ordained a Prophet,
Seer, and Revelator.

Elder Brigham Young returned from Long Island to
New York, Elder Willard Richards started to Richmond,
Massachusetts with his family and Elder Wilford Wood-
ruff to Portland, Maine.

Friday, 4.—Elders Young, Kimball and Taylor left
New York for Nauvoo, by way of Philadelphia, Pittsburgh, and St. Louis. Geo. A. Smith, and Reuben Hedlock started at the same time, and went to New Egypt,
New Jersey.

I called on Governor Carlin, at his residence in Quincy.

The Prophet's
Visit with
Governor Car-
lin.
During my visit with the Governor, I was
treated with the greatest kindness and
respect; nothing was said about any requisition having come from the Governor of Mis
souri for my arrest.   In a very few hours after I had left
the Governor's residence he sent Thomas King, Sheriff of
Adams county, Thomas Jasper, a constable of Quincy,
and some others as a posse, with an officer from Missouri, to arrest me and deliver me up to the authorities of
Missouri.

Saturday, 5.—While I was staying at Heberlin's Hotel,

Bear Creek, about twenty-eight miles south of Nauvoo,
Sheriff King and posse arrested me.   Some of the posse
on learning the spirit of the officer from Mis-   The Arrest
souri, left the company in disgust and returned   of the
to their own homes.   I accordingly returned   Prophet
to Quincy and obtained a writ of *habeas corpus* from
Charles A. Warren, Esq., Master in Chancery; and
Judge Stephen A. Douglas happening to come to Quincy
that evening, he appointed to give a hearing on the writ
on the Tuesday following, in Monmouth, Warren county,
where the court would then commence a regular term.

Elders William Smith, and George A. Smith attended
a meeting in the woods near New Egypt, New
Jersey, and preached to a large assembly;   Apostles in
also preached on Sunday 6th, and three were   New Jersey.
baptized; and after preaching on the 7th four   more were
baptized.

Sunday, 6.—News of my arrest having   arrived in
Nauvoo last night, and being circulated   News of the
through the city, Hosea Stout, Tarleton Lewis,   Prophet's Ar-
William A. Hickman, John S. Higbee,   rest Reaches
                                                  Nauvoo.
Elijah Able, Uriel C. Nickerson, and George W. Clyde
started from the Nauvoo landing, in a skiff in order to
overtake me and rescue me, if necessary.   They had a
heavy head wind, but arrived in Quincy at dusk; went up
to Benjamin Jones's house, and found that I had gone to
Nauvoo in charge of two officers.

I returned to Nauvoo in charge of the officers (Sheriff
King had been suddenly seized with sickness; I nursed
and waited upon him in my own house, so that he might
be able to go to Monmouth), and notified several of my
friends to get ready and accompany me the next morning.

Monday, 7.—I started very early for Monmouth,
seventy-five miles distant (taking Mr. King along with me
and attending him during his sickness), accompanied by
Charles C. Rich, Amasa Lyman, Shadrack Roundy, Reynolds Cahoon, Charles Hopkins, Alfred Randall, Elias Hig-

bee, Morris Phelps, John P. Greene, Henry G. Sherwood, Joseph Younger, Darwin Chase, Ira Miles, Joel S. Miles, Lucien Woodworth, Vinson Knight, Robert B. Thompson, George Miller and others. We traveled very late, camping about midnight in the road.

Tuesday, 8.—Arrived at Monmouth and procured

The Prophet at Monmouth.

breakfast at the tavern; found great excitement prevailing in the public mind, and great curiosity was manifested by the citizens who were extremely anxious to obtain a sight of the Prophet, expecting to see me in chains. Mr. King, (whose health was now partly restored) had considerable difficulty in protecting me from the mob that had gathered there. Mr. Sidney A. Little, for the defense, moved "That the case of Mr. Smith should be taken up," but was objected to by the States' Attorney, *pro tem.*, on account of his not being prepared, not having had sufficient notice of the trial. By mutual consent it was accordingly postponed until Wednesday morning.

In the evening, great excitement prevailed, and the citizens employed several attorneys to plead against me.

I was requested to preach to the citizens of Monmouth; but as I was a prisoner, I kept closeted in my room, for I could not even come down stairs to my meals, but the people would be crowding the windows to get a peep at me, and therefore appointed Elder Amasa Lyman to preach in the Court House on Wednesday evening.

Wednesday, 9.—At an early hour the Court House was

The Trial.

filled with spectators desirous to hear the proceedings.

Mr. Morrison, on behalf of the people, wished for time to send to Springfield for the indictment, it not being found with the rest of the papers. This course would have delayed the proceedings, and, as it was not important to the issue, the attorneys for the defense admitted that there was an indictment, so that the investigation might proceed.

Mr. Warren, for the defense, then read the petition, which stated that I was unlawfully held in custody, and that the indictment, in Missouri, was obtained by fraud, bribery and duress, all of which I was prepared to prove.

Mr. Little then called upon the following witnesses, viz.,—Morris Phelps, Elias Higbee, Reynolds Cahoon and George W. Robinson, who were sworn. The counsel on the opposite side objected to hearing evidence on the merits of the case, as they could not go beyond the indictment. Upon this a warm and long discussion occurred, which occupied the attention of the court during the entire day.

All the lawyers on the opposite side, excepting two, viz. Messrs. Knowlton and Jennings, confined themselves to the merits of the case, and conducted themselves as gentlemen; but it was plainly evident that the design of Messrs. Knowlton and Jennings was to excite the public mind still more on the subject and inflame the passions of the people against me and my religion.

The counsel on behalf of the defense, Messrs. Charles A. Warren, Sidney H. Little, O. H. Brown- Honorable ing, James H. Ralston, Cyrus Walker, and Conduct of
Counsel. Archibald Williams, acted nobly and honorably, and stood up in the defense of the persecuted, in a manner worthy of high-minded and honorable gentlemen.

Some had even been told that if they engaged on the side of the defense, they need never look to the citizens of that county for any political favors. But they were not to be overawed by the popular clamor or deterred from an act of public duty by any insinuations or threats whatever, and stated, that if they had not before determined to take a part in the defense, they, after hearing the threats of the community, were now fully determined to discharge their duty. The counsel for the defense spoke well without exception; and strongly urged the legality of the court examining the testimony to prove that the whole proceedings on the part of Missouri, were base and illegal, and that the indictment was obtained through fraud, bribery and corruption.

The court, after hearing the counsel, adjourned about half past six p. m.

When I was at dinner, a man rushed in and said, "Which is Jo Smith? I have got a five dollar Kirtland bill, and I'll be damned if he don't take it back I'll sue him, for his name is to it." I replied, "I am the man;" took the bill and paid him the specie, which he took very reluctantly, being anxious to kick up a fuss.

The crowd in the court was so intense that Judge Douglas ordered the sheriff of Warren county to keep the spectators back; but he neglected doing so, when the judge fined him ten dollars. In a few minutes he again ordered the sheriff to keep the men back from crowding the prisoner and witnesses. He replied, "I have told a constable to do it," when the judge immediately said, "Clerk, add ten dollars more to that fine." The sheriff, finding neglect rather expensive, then attended to his duty.

A young lawyer from Missouri volunteered to plead against me; he tried his utmost to convict me, but was so high with liquor, and chewed so much tobacco, that he often called for cold water. Before he had spoken many minutes, he turned sick, requested to be excused by the court and went out of the court house, puking all the way down stairs. As the Illinoians call the Missouri people "pukes," this circumstance caused considerable amusement to the members of the bar. During his plea, his language was so outrageous that the judge was twice under the necessity of ordering him to be silent.

Mr. O. H. Browning then commenced his plea, and in a short time the puking lawyer returned, and requested the privilege of finishing his plea, which was allowed.

Afterwards Mr. Browning resumed his pleadings which were powerful; and when he gave a recitation of what he himself had seen at Quincy, and on the banks of the Mississippi river' when the Saints were "exterminated from Missouri," where he tracked the persecuted women and children by their bloody footmarks in the snow, they were so affecting that the spectators were often dissolved in tears. Judge Douglas himself and most of the officers also wept.

Elder Amasa Lyman during the evening, preached a brilliant discourse in the Court House, on the first principles of the Gospel, which changed the feelings of the people very materially.

A Letter from the Editor * of the Times and Seasons to that Journal Giving an Account of the Trial at Monmouth.

AMERICAN HOTEL, MONMOUTH, WARREN COUNTY, ILLINOIS,
June 9, 1841. Wednesday Evening.

We have just returned from the Court House, where we have listened to one of the most eloquent speeches ever uttered by mortal man, in favor of justice and liberty, by O. H. Browning, Esq., who has done himself immortal honor in the sight of all patriotic citizens who listened to the same. He occupied the attention of the court for more than two hours, and showed the falsity of the arguments of the opposite counsel, and laid down principles in a lucid and able manner which ought to guide the court in admitting testimony for the defendant, Joseph Smith. We have heard Browning on former occasions, when he has frequently delighted his audience by his eloquence; but on this occasion he exceeded our most sanguine expectations. The sentiments he advanced were just, generous and exalted; he soared above the petty quibbles which the opposite counsel urged, and triumphantly, in a manner and eloquence peculiar to himself, avowed himself the friend of humanity, and boldly, nobly and independently stood up for the rights of those who had waded through seas of oppression and floods of injustice, and had sought a shelter in the State of Illinois. It was an effort worthy of a high-minded and honorable gentleman, such as we ever considered him to be, since we have had the pleasure of his acquaintance. Soon after we came out of Missouri, he sympathized with us in our afflictions, and we are indeed rejoiced to know that he

---

* Don Carlos Smith and Robert B. Thompson were at this time editors and publishers of the *Times and Seasons*, and the above letter was doubtless written by Thompson as he is named as among those who accompanied the Prophet to Monmouth, while Don Carlos Smith is not named as being in the company.

yet maintains the same principles of benevolence. His was not an effort of a lawyer anxious to earn his fee, but the pure and patriotic feelings of Christian benevolence, and a sense of justice and of right. While he was answering the monstrous and ridiculous arguments urged by the opposing counsel, that Joseph Smith might go to Missouri and have his trial; he stated the circumstances of our being driven from that State, and feelingly and emphatically pointed out the impossibility of our obtaining justice there. There we were forbidden to enter in consequence of the order of the Executive, and that injustice and cruelties of the most barbarous and atrocious character had been practiced upon us, until the streams of Missouri had run with blood, and that he had seen women and children, barefoot and houseless crossing the Mississippi to seek refuge from ruthless mobs. He concluded his remarks by saying that to tell us to go to Missouri for a trial was adding insult to injury; and then he said: "*Great God! have I not seen it? Yes, my eyes have beheld the blood-stained traces of innocent women and children, in the drear winter, who had traveled hundreds of miles barefoot, through frost and snow, to seek a refuge from their savage pursuers. 'Twas a scene of horror sufficient to enlist sympathy from an adamantine heart. And shall this unfortunate man, whom their fury has seen proper to select for sacrifice, be driven into such a savage land and none dare to enlist in the cause of Justice? If there was no other voice under heaven ever to be heard in this cause, gladly would I stand alone, and proudly spend my latest breath in defense of an oppressed American citizen.*"

Thursday, 10.—The court was opened about 8 o'clock a. m. when Judge Douglas delivered his opinion on the case. He said:

That the writ being once returned to the Executive by the sheriff of Hancock county was dead, and stood in the same relationship as any other writ which might issue from the Circuit Court, and consequently the defendant could not be held in custody on that writ. The other point, whether evidence in the case was admissible or not, he would not at that time decide, as it involved great and important considerations relative to the future conduct of the different states. There being no precedent, as far as they had access to authorities to guide them, but he would endeavor to examine the subject, and avail himself of all the authorities which could be obtained on the subject, before he would decide that point. But on the other, the defendant must be liberated.

This decision was received with satisfaction by myself and the brethren, and all those whose minds were free from prejudice. It is now decided that before another writ can issue, a new demand must be made by the Governor of Missouri. Thus have I been once more delivered from the fangs of my cruel persecutors, for which I thank God, my Heavenly Father.

The Prophet Set Free.

I was discharged about 11 a. m., when I ordered dinner for my company now increased to about sixty men; and when I called for the bill, the unconscionable fellow replied, "Only one hundred and sixty dollars."

About 2 p. m., the company commenced their return, traveled about twenty miles, and camped by the wayside.

Friday, 11.—Started very early, arrived at La Harpe for dinner and returned safely to Nauvoo by 4 p. m., where I was met by the acclamation of the Saints.

CHAPTER XXI.

ELDER GEORGE A. SMITH met Elder John E. Page at
Philadelphia, and advised him to take up contributions to
Elder John E.   enable him to sail within three days in the
Page—a Lag-   *Garrick* for England, and overtake Elder
gard.   Orson Hyde and accompany him to Jerusalem, promising to use all the influence and exertion in
his power to assist him. Elder Page rejected the
proposition. Elder Smith subsequently learned that
Elder Page had sufficient money, without collections to
have taken him through to England.

Tuesday, 15.

*Letter from Elder Orson Hyde to President Joseph Smith—Recounting
Incidents of his Journey en Route for Jerusalem.*

LONDON, June 15, 1841.

President Smith:

SIR—With pleasure I take my pen to write you at this time, and
through you to the *Times and Seasons*, and through it to the Saints at
large, and to all whom it may concern. May grace, mercy, and peace
from God our Father, and from the Lord Jesus Christ, rest upon you
abundantly, and enable you to serve Him acceptably, secure to yourself
that honor which cometh from above, guide the counsels of the Saints in
wisdom, that peace and good will may reign predominant in Zion, and
joy and gladness swell every grateful heart. Most gladly would I embrace an opportunity of a personal interview with you, did one offer,
but such a favor is beyond my reach at this time. I have just seen the
12th number of the *Times and Seasons*, containing the minutes of your
conference, the report of the Presidency, the celebration of the anniver-

sary of the Church and the laying of the foundation of the Temple. This, to me was a precious gem; it brought tidings from my own country, and from the place rendered doubly endearing from the fact that there is the home of my wife and children.

I was sorry that Elder Page had been so tardy in his movements that objections were made to him. Most gladly would I have hailed him as a companion to the oriental continent; but my hopes of that are fled. I shall go alone or find some other person, in all probability, to go with me.

I have written a book to publish in the German language, setting forth our doctrine and principles in as clear and concise a manner as I possibly could. After giving a history of the rise of the Church, in something the manner that Brother Orson Pratt did, I have written a snug little article on every point of doctrine believed by the Saints; I began with the Priesthood and showed that the Saints were not under the necessity of tracing back the dark and bloody stream of papal superstition to find their authority; neither were they compelled to seek for it among the floating and transient notions of Protestant reformers; but God has sent His holy angel directly from heaven with this seal and authority, and conferred it upon men with His own hands— quoting the letter and testimony of Oliver Cowdery; next was on the use and validity of the holy scriptures in the Church; next on faith, set forth from the scriptures and the Book of Covenants; then on repentance, baptism; laying on of hands; then the different offices of the Church; next the power and authority of each one; and, in fine, the whole order, doctrine and government of the Church. I have not written it as a law binding on the *German Saints;* but have taken this course to illustrate and set forth the true principles of our doctrine to them, fully believing that it would meet with the cordial approbation of those whom I have the distinguished honor to represent, could they but see it. I have written a lengthy preface and introduction to it. I here copy an extract from the introduction: "When in the course of divine Providence it becomes our duty to record one of those remarkable events which gives birth to a new era, and lays the foundation for the renovation of the moral world, it fills the mind with wonder, astonishment and admiration. How welcome are the rays of the morning light, after the shades of darkness have clothed the earth in gloom! So after a long and tedious night of moral darkness under which the earth has rolled, and her inhabitants groaned for the last fourteen hundred years, an angel commissioned from the Almighty, descended and rolled back the curtains of night from the minds of some and caused the sunbeams of truth to enlighten, cheer, and warm the hearts of many. Welcome, welcome to our earth, thou messenger of the Most High! and thrice welcome the tidings which thou hast borne! O Gracious Father! I ask Thee, in the name of Thy holy child, Jesus, to bless with Thy royal favor, the weak exertions of Thy humble servant, and make this production a blessing to all people who may be favored with a perusal of its pages. Wherever it shall go let it be a messenger of conviction to the wicked, and a harbinger of peace to the righteous. Let its contents be borne upon every breeze, and wafted to the remotest climes. Let the angel of the covenant go before it, and prepare its way. Let its heavenly influence be distilled upon the rich and fertile soil of humble and honest hearts. Go forth, therefore, little volume to other nations and tongues, and may the Almighty speed your way, and like a sharp, two-edged sword cut the way through the prejudices of this generation; encamp with all thy virtues in the hearts of the people, and there let thy principles be enthroned.''

One thing I was pleased with, which I noticed in the *Times and Seasons*—the remarks made on the use of intoxicating spirits. In my heart they found a corresponding echo. I should not be willing to indulge the thought for a moment that the Saints in Nauvoo would quietly stand by and see a brother gorge himself with that strong drink which makes a hell of his home, and rolls the fiery flood of ruin over the affections of his once happy family. No! they will dash from his lips the cup of wretchedness, and sharply rebuke the homicide that sells to him the wine of wrath, and measures to him his wife's tears. * * * May the lightnings of heaven forever blast (I had almost said) those brewers of strong drink which send forth their corrupt and poisonous streams to sweep down in their filthy current men of sterling talents to an untimely grave. May the Saints of God stand as far from them as Lot stood from Sodom in its evil day. This dizzy flood has sometimes entered the house of worship, invaded the sacred desk, and hushed in death forever the voice that could plead like an angel, the cause of God and man.

I havs just received a note from Dr. S. Hirschell, President Rabbi of the Hebrew community of this country, in reply to a very polite note which I sent him, requesting the indulgence of a personal interview with him. But in consequence of a very severe accident which befell him he is confined to his room, and unable at this time to grant the asked indulgence. (His leg is broken.)

I have addressed to him a communication upon the subject of my mission, a copy of which I transmit to you. It may not be altogether uninteresting to the Saints and friends in America.

Elder Hyde's Letter to Rabbi Hirschell.

REV. SIR:—I cannot but express my sorrow and regret at the misfortune under which you labor, in consequence of the severe accident which befell you, and by which you are confined to your room. Please accept, sir, the sincere wishes of a stranger, that you may speedily recover from the injury you sustained in consequence of the accident, and resume the labors which your high and responsible station calls you to perform.

Feeling that I may not enjoy the privilege and happiness of a personal interview with you, I hope you will indulge the liberty which I now presume to take, in addressing a written communication to you, embracing some of those things which I had fondly hoped would have been the foundation of a mutual interchange of thought between us. But as Providence has laid an embargo upon that distinguished privilege, I must forego, at this time, the pleasure of a verbal relation of those things pertaining to your nation, with which my mind is deeply affected.

Since I have arrived to years of more mature reflection, and become religiously inclined, the writings of the Jewish Prophets have won my affections; and the scattered and oppressed condition of that people has enlisted the finest sympathies of my heart. Believing, therefore, that the words of Hosea, the Prophet, ii; 23, connected with your magnanimity, will prohibit the indulgence of any prejudices in your feelings against the author of this production, in consequence of his not being able by any existing document or record, to identify himself with your nation.

"About nine years ago, a young man with whom I had had a short acquaintance, and one, too, in whom dwelt much wisdom and knowledge—in whose bosom the Almighty had deposited many secrets, laid his hand upon my head and pronounced these remarkable words—'in due time thou shalt go to Jerusalem, the land of thy fathers, and be a watchman unto the house of Israel; and by thy hands shall the Most High do a great work, which shall prepare the way and greatly facilitate the gathering together of that people.' Many other particulars were told me by him at that time, which I do not write in this letter. But sufficient is written to show that divine appointment is claimed as the mainspring that has sent me forth from the embraces of an affectionate family and kind friends, as well as from the land that gave me birth.

My labors since that period have been bestowed upon the Gentiles in various countries, and on both sides of the Atlantic, until in the early part of March, 1840, I retired to my bed one night as usual; and while meditating and contemplating the field of my future labors, the vision of the Lord, like clouds of light, burst into my view (see Joel ii: 28).

The cities of London, Amsterdam, Constantinople and Jerusalem, all appeared in succession before me, and the Spirit said unto me, "Here are many of the children of Abraham whom I will gather to the land that I gave to their fathers; and here also is the field of your labors. Take, therefore, proper credentials from my people, your brethren, and also from the Governor of your state, with the seal of authority thereon, and go ye forth to the cities which have been shown you, and declare these words unto Judah, and say, "blow ye the trumpet in the land; cry, gather together, and say, assemble yourselves, and let us go into the defensed cities. Set up the standard towards Zion—retire, stay not, for I will bring evil from the north and a great destruction. The lion is come up from his thicket, and the destroyer of the Gentiles is on his way—he is gone forth from his place to make thy land desolate, and thy cities shall be laid waste, without an inhabitant. Speak ye comfortably to Jerusalem, and cry unto her, that her warfare is accomplished—that her iniquity is pardoned, for she hath received of the Lord's hand doubly for all her sins. Let your warning voice be heard among the Gentiles as you pass; and call yet upon them in my name for aid and for assistance. With you it mattereth not whether it be little or much; but to me it belongeth to show favor unto them who show favor unto you." The vision continued open about six hours, that I did not close my eyes in sleep. In this time many things were shown unto me which I have never written; neither shall I write them until they are fulfilled in Jerusalem.

It appears from the Prophets, that Jerusalem has none to guide—none to take her by the hand among all the sons whom she hath brought forth and reared. But these two sons are come unto thee! the sons of strangers shall build up thy walls.

Permit me now, Rev. Sir, to trouble you with the reflections of a mind that feels completely untrammelled from every party interest, and from every sectarian influence.

When I look at the condition of your fathers in the days of David and Solomon, and contrast that with the present condition of their descendants, I am led to exclaim, "How are the mighty fallen." Then they possessed a kingdom—a land flowing with milk and honey—then the strong arm of Jehovah taught the surrounding nations to pay tribute and homage to them -- then their standard was raised high, their banner floated on every breeze; and under its shade the sons and daughters of Israel reposed in perfect safety; and the golden letters of light and knowledge were inscribed on its folds. But now, no kingdom—no country—no tribute of gain or honor—no standard—no security: Their sceptre has departed! and instead of that light and knowledge which once gave them a transient elevation above other nations, the height of their ambition is now (with some honorable exceptions) the accumulation of sordid gain, by buying and selling the stale refuse with which their fathers would never have defiled their hands.

Why this wonderful change? Is the God of Abraham, Isaac and Jacob a just God? Most certaily He is. If, then, He is a just God, of course He will mete out and apportion the chastisement or penalty to the magnitude of the offense or crime committed. Allowing, then, the law of Moses to be the standard by which actions are weighed: were not idolatry and the shedding of innocent blood the greatest sins which your fathers committed? And was not the penalty inflicted upon them for that transgression, captivity in Babylon seventy years? Have they ever been guilty of idolatry at all since their return from Babylon? No! Have they been guilty of shedding innocent blood, to that extent since their return, that they were before they were taken captive by Nebuchadnezzar? The Jew says, No! Very well; there will none deny, with any claim upon your credulity, but that the disaster and overthrow that befell the Jewish nation in the days of Vespasian, very far exceeded in severity, in almost every particular, the disaster and overthrow that befell them in the days of Nebuchadnezzar.

Now, then, if God be just and mete out and apportion the chastisement or penalty to the magnitude of the offense or crime committed, it follows, of course, that your fathers committed some far greater crime subsequent to their return to Babylon, than ever they before committed. Be that crime whatever it may; know ye that for it, or because of it, the Roman armies were permitted to crowd their conquests to the heart of your city—burn your temple—kill your men, women and children, and disperse your remnant to the four quarters of the earth. The fiery storm that burst upon your nation at that time, and the traces of blood which they have ever since left behind them in their flight and dispersion, together with the recent cursed cruelties inflicted upon them in Damascus and Rhodes, but too plainly declare that the strong imprecation which they uttered on a certain occasion has been fulfilled upon them to the letter. "Let his blood be on us and on our children." If condemning and crucifying Jesus of Nazareth was not the cause of this great evil, what was the cause of it?

Aware that I have written very plainly upon these points, that have come within my notice, you believe me, sir, when I assure you, that my pen is pointed with friendship, and dipped in the fountain of love and good will toward your nation. The thoughts which it records have proceeded from a heart grateful to the Almighty, that the time has arrived when the day-star of your freedom already begins to dispel the dark and gloomy clouds which have separated you from the favor of your God. Ere long it will be said to you, "Arise, shine, for thy light has

has come, and the glory of the Lord has risen upon thee.''

> The morning breaks, the shadows flee,
>   Lo! Zion's standard is unfurled;
> The dawning of a brighter day
>   Majestic rises on the world.
>
> The Gentile fulness now comes in,
>   And Israel's blessings are at hand:
> Lo! Judah's remnant, cleansed from sin,
>   Shall in their promised Canaan stand.

Now, therefore, O ye children of the covenant, repent of all your backslidings, and begin, as in days of old, to turn to the Lord your God. Arise! arise! and go out from among the Gentiles; for destruction is coming from the north to lay their cities waste. Jerusalem is thy home. There the God of Abraham will deliver thee (Joel ii: 32.) There the bending heavens shall reveal thy long looked-for Messiah in fleecy clouds of light and glory, to execute vengeance upon thine enemies; and lead thee and thy brethren of the ten tribes to sure conquest and certain victory. Then shall thrones be cast down, and the kingdoms of this world become the kingdoms of our God. Then will they come from the east, west, north, south, and sit down in the kingdom of God with Abraham, Isaac and Jacob. But the children of the kingdom (Gentiles) shall be cast out, and the kingdom restored to Israel.

With sentiments of distinguished consideration, I have the honor, sir, to subscribe myself,

Your most obedient servant,
ORSON HYDE.

Rev. Dr. Solomon Hirschell, President Rabbi of the Hebrew Society in England.

Conclusion of Elder Hyde's Letter to the Prophet.

It is very hard times in England. Thousands have nothing to do, and are literally starving. Trade of all sorts is at the lowest ebb. Very cold and dry. No harvest unless rain come soon. You will discover that the greater part of the English brethren have always worked under masters; and they have not so much notion of planning and shifting for themselves, particularly in a a strange country, as the Americans. They want some one to be a kind of father to them, to give them plenty of work, and plenty to eat; and they will be content. They are a very industrious people whenever they can get employment: and by a little fatherly care, they will soon get way-wised to the country, and be enabled to shift for themselves. I trust that exertions are made to give

employment to as many as possible.   You know the reasons there better than I do, and you have received a specimen of the English Saints.
Now if you have any counsel to give concerning the gathering, in
addition to that already given, I shall be happy to receive and execute
it, as far as opportunity offers.

I shall not remain here long, it is true; but Brother Pratt is here, and
I shall return here some time if the Lord will.

I must now close by saying for one and all, God bless Zion for ever
and ever.

Your brother in Christ,
ORSON HYDE.

CHAPTER XXII.

SUNDRY EVENTS AT NAUVOO AND THROUGHOUT THE WORLD—
THE MISSION OF THE TWELVE NOTED BY THE PROPHET.

THE newspapers of the United States are teeming with all
Press Misrepresentations. manner of lies, abusing the Saints of the Most
High, and striving to call down the wrath of
the people upon His servants.

Wednesday, 16.—Elder Brigham Young and company
arrived at Wheeling at 4 p. m., and Sunday, 29th, visited
the brethren at Cincinnati.

Monday, 21.—Hyrum Smith and William Law visited
the Saints in Chester county, Pennsylvania, on their mission
east; and there met Elder George A. Smith on his
return home.

Tuesday, 22.—Elder Theodore Curtis, having previously
been arraigned before a magistrate, and bound over in
Imprisonment of Theodore Curtis. the sum of forty pounds, for "blasphemy,"
i. e., preaching the Gospel, appeared at the
Court of Sessions, at Gloucester, England,
and after remaining five days [in prison], was informed
on inquiry, that no bill was found against him, and he was
suffered to go at large again after paying one pound and
one shilling cost. Thus we see that the same opposition to
truth prevails in other countries, as well as in this.

*Extract from a Letter in the "Juliet Courier"—Describing the Prophet's
Trial at Monmouth, and Affairs at Nauvoo.*

MONMOUTH, June, 1841.

MY DEAR SIR.—Before this reaches you, I have no doubt you will
have heard of the trial of Joseph Smith, familiarly known as the Mor-

mon Prophet. As some misrepresentations have already gone abroad, in relation to Judge Douglas' decision, and the merits of the question decided by the judge; permit me to say, the only question decided, though many were debated, was the validity of the executive writ which had once been sent out, I think in September, 1840, and a return on it that Mr. Smith could not be found. The same writ was issued in June, 1841. There can really be no great difficulty about this matter, under this state of facts.

The judge acquitted himself handsomely, and silenced clamors that had been raised against the defendant.

Since the trial I have been at Nauvoo, on the Mississippi, in Hancock county, Illinois; and have seen the manner in which things are conducted among the Mormons. In the first place, I cannot help noticing the plain hospitality of the Prophet, Smith, to all strangers visiting the town, aided as he is, in making the stranger comfortable by his excellent wife, a woman of superior ability. The people of the town appear to be honest and industrious, engaged in their usual vocations of building up a town, and making all things around them comfortable. On Sunday I attended one of their meetings, in front of the Temple now building, and one of the largest buildings in the state. There could not have been less than 2,500 people present, and as well appearing as any number that could be found in this or any state. Mr. Smith preached in the morning, and one could have readily learned, then, the magic by which he has built up this society, because, as we say in Illinois, "they believe in him," and in his honesty. It has been a matter of astonishment to me, after seeing the Prophet, as he is called, Elder Rigdon, and many other gentlemanly men anyone may see at Nauvoo, who will visit there—why it is, that so many professing Christianity, and so many professing to reverence the sacred principles of our Constitution (which gives free religious toleration to all), have slandered, and persecuted this sect of Christians.

Saturday, 26.—Elder Young and company arrived on the steamer *Mermaid*, at the mouth of the Ohio river.

Thursday, July 1.—Elders Young, Kimball, and Taylor arrived at Nauvoo, after an interesting mission to England. The accounts of their missions are highly satisfactory.

During a heavy thunderstorm at Derby, England, hundreds of small fish and frogs descended, and were picked up alive by the people.

Saturday, 3.—The following is an extract from the

Legion Minutes:

The second regiment, first cohort, consisting of four companies, was organized, and Captain George Coulson was elected colonel, Josiah Ells lieutenant-colonel, and Hyrum Kimball major.   On the same day, the third regiment, second cohort, consisting of four companies, was organized; Samuel Bent was elected colonel, George Morey, lieutenant-colonel, and William Niswanger, major; and the Legion was called out to celebrate our National Independence (the 4th being Sunday), and was reviewed by Lieutenant-General Joseph Smith, who made an eloquent and patriotic speech to the troops, and strongly testified of his regard for our national welfare, and his willingness to lay down his life in defense of his country, and closed with these remarkable words, "I would ask no greater boon, than to lay down my life for my country."

An elaborate dinner was got up in the grove, of which I partook, in company with the officers of the Legion, President Rigdon and many others, with their ladies.

Elder Willard Richards left his family with his sisters at Richmond, Massachusetts, and started for Nauvoo.

Elder Orson Pratt has published in New York an edition of his History of the Coming Forth of the Book of Mormon, first printed in Edinburgh.

*Revelation given to Joseph Smith, in the house of Brigham Young, in Nauvoo City, July 9, 1841.**

Dear and well beloved Brother Brigham Young, verily thus saith the Lord unto you, my servant Brigham, it is no more required at your hands to leave your family as in times past, for your offering is acceptable to me; I have seen your labor and toil in journeyings for my name. I therefore command you to send my word abroad, and take special care of your family from this time, henceforth and forever. Amen.

Monday, 12.—Elder William Clayton was appointed clerk of the High Council of Iowa, and John Patton recorder of baptisms for the dead in Iowa.

At the urgent solicitations of the brethren at Zarahemla,

* Doctrine and Covenants, sec. cxxvi.

I had consented, at a previous date, that they might baptize for the dead on the Iowa side of the river.

I was in the City Council, and moved that any person in the City of Nauvoo be at liberty to sell vinous liquors in any quantity, subject to the city ordinances.

Liquor Selling Licensed in Nauvoo.

Tuesday, 13.—Elder George A. Smith returned from his mission in England.

A treaty was signed between Turkey, Russia, England, France, Austria, and Prussia, whereby the Dardanelles are closed to all foreign ships of war, as long as the Ottoman Porte enjoys peace.

Wednesday, 14.—The following is translated from the Arabic, in the *Malta Times*—"Aleppo, 3rd May. A great famine has happened in Aleppo, Malitia, and Karbat, insomuch that many people died with hunger, and others sold their sons and daughters to get bread to eat. But the Almighty God rained upon them seed (manna), and fed them withal." "Of the veracity of these words," adds the *Malta Times*, "extracted from an Arabic letter, we are perfectly satisfied. The seed alluded to is known in Malta, being nearly like 'hab' or 'dazz,' and which being kept a little while becomes white, like 'semola' (very fine wheaten flour)."

Manna Rain in Aleppo.

Immense quantities of locusts have appeared in Spain this year, devouring everything in their way; and a shower of flesh and blood is reported in the southern part of the United States.

Thursday, 15.—Many of the newspapers are publishing lies about me by the wholesale; should I attempt to enumerate them, I could write nothing else; suffice it to say, every falsehood wicked men can invent, assisted by their father the devil, is trumpeted to the world as sound doctrine, which proves the words of Jesus, "They have persecuted me, they will persecute you also."

Press Falsehoods.

I spent considerable part of the day with several of the Twelve Apostles.

Letter of Elder Orson Hyde to President Smith—Detailing Events while en Route to Jerusalem.

RATISBON ON THE DANUBE, July 17, 1841.

Dear Brother Josph, and all whom it may concern: With pleasure I take my pen to write to you at this time, hoping this communication may find you as it leaves me, in good health and enjoying a comfortable measure of the Holy Spirit.

On the twentieth of June last, I left London for Rotterdam in Holland, after writing a lengthy epistle to you, and also the copy of a letter addressed to the Rev. Dr. S. Hirschell, President Rabbi of the Hebrews in London; which I hope you have received ere this; the work of the Lord is steadily advancing in London under the efficient and zealous labors of our worthy brother, Elder Lorenzo Snow.

The fine steamer *Batavier* brought me safely over the billows of a tremendous rough sea in about thirty hours. Never did I suffer more from sea sickness, than during this short voyage; but it was soon over, and we landed safely in Rotterdam. I took my lodgings at the London Hotel, at two florins per diem, about three shillings and five pence sterling, or seventy-five cents. Here I called on the Hebrew Rabbi, and proposed certain questions to him; but as he did not understand a word of English, it was hard for me to enter into particulars with him; I asked, him, however, whether he expected his Messiah to come directly from heaven, or whether he expected Him to be born of a woman on earth? He replied that he expected Him to be born of a woman of the seed and lineage of David. At what period do you look for this event? Answer. "We have been looking a long time, and are now living in constant expectation of His coming." Do you believe in the restitution of your nation to the land of your fathers, called the land of *promise*? "We hope it will be so," was the reply. He then added, "We believe that many Jews will return to Jerusalem and rebuild the city—rear a temple to the name of the Most High, and restore our ancient worship; Jerusalem shall be the capital of our nation—the centre of our union and the standard and ensign of our national existence. But we do not believe that all the Jews will go there, for the place is not large enough to contain them. They are now gathering there," continued he, "almost continually." I told him I had written an address to the Hebrews, and was about procuring its publication in his own language (Dutch), and when completed I would leave him a copy. He thanked me for this token of respect, and I bade him adieu. I soon obtained the publication of five hundred copies of the address, and left one at the house of the Rabbi—he being absent from home, I did not see him.

After remaining here about one week, I took the coach for Amsterdam, distance seven hours or about thirty English miles. Rotterdam is a fine town of about eighty thousand inhabitants. The cleanliness of its streets, the antique order of its architecture, the extreme height of its buildings, the numerous shade trees with which it is beautified, and the great number of canals, through almost every part of the town, filled with ships of various sizes from different parts of the world; all these, with many other things not mentioned, contributed to give this place a peculiarity resembled no where else in the course of my travels, except in Amsterdam. Most of the business men here speak a little English—some speak it very well.

In ascending the waters of the Rhine from the sea to Rotterdam, the numerous windmills which I beheld in constant operation, led me to think, almost, that all Europe came here for their grinding. But I ascertained that they were grinding for distilleries, where the floods of gin are made, which not only deluge our beloved country, with fatal consequences, but many others.   Gin is one of the principal articles of exportation from this country.

In going to Amsterdam, I passed through a very beautiful town called "The Hague," the residence of the King of Holland. I saw his palace, which was guarded by soldiers both horse and foot. For grandeur it bore here a faint resemblance to Buckingham Palace, in London. But the beautiful parks and picturesque scenery in and about the Hague, I have never seen equalled in any country.

I remained in Amsterdam only one night and a part of two days. I called on the President Rabbi here, but he was gone from home. I left at his house a large number of the addresses for himself and his people, and took coach for Arnhem on the Rhine. Took boat the same evening for Mainz. Traveling by coach and steam is rather cheaper in this country than in the United States. We were three days in going up the river to Mainz.

Holland and the lower part of Prussia are very low, flat countries. The French and German languages are spoken all along the Rhine; but little or no English. The Rhine is about like the Ohio for size, near its mouth where it empties into the Mississippi. Its waters resemble the Mississippi waters, dark and muddy. The scenery and landscapes along this river have been endowed with art and nature's choicest gifts.

I have been made acquainted with Europe in America, by books, to a certain extent; yet now my eyes behold! It is impossible for a written description of a stranger's beauty to leave the same impression upon the mind, as is made by an ocular view of the lovely object. This is the difference between reading of and seeing the countries of Europe. From Mainz I came to Frankfort on the Maine by railroad—distance seven hours. From Frankfort I came to this place—distance about thirty hours, where Napoleon gained a celebrated victory over the Prussians and Austrians. The very ground on which I now write this letter was covered by about sixty thousand slain in that battle. It is called the battle of Ackeynaeal.

It was my intention to have gone directly down the Danube to Constantinople, but having neglected to get my passport vised by the Austrian Ambassador at Frankfort, I had to forward it to the Austrian Ambassador at Munich and procure his permission, signature and seal before I could enter the Austrian dominions. This detained me five days, during which time I conceived the idea of sitting down and learning the German language scientifically. I became acquainted with a lady here who speaks French and German to admiration, and she was very anxious to speak the English—she proposed giving me instruction in the German, if I would instruct her in English. I accepted her proposal. I have been engaged eight days in this task. I have read one book through and part of another, and translated and written considerable. I can speak and write considerable German already, and the lady tells me that I make astonishing progress. From the past experience I know that the keen edge of any work translated by a stranger, in whose heart the spirit of the matter does not dwell, is lost—the life and animation thereof die away into a cold monotony, and it becomes almost entirely another thing. This step is according to the best light I can get, and hope and trust that it is according to the mind of the Lord. The people will hardly believe but that I have spoken German before; but I tell them *nein* (no). The German is spoken in Prussia, Bavaria, and all the states of Germany, Austria, the south of Russia, and in fine, more or less all over Europe. It appears to me, therefore, that some person of some little experience ought to know this language so as to translate himself, without being dependent on strangers. If I am wrong in my movement pray that the Spirit of the Lord may direct me aright. If I am right, pray that heaven may speedily give me this language.

It is very sickly in Constantinople and Syria and Alexandria at present. I would rather, therefore, wait until cool weather before I go there. I might have written most of this letter in German, but as you would more readily understand it in English, I have written it in English.

With pleasure I leave the historical part of my letter to touch a softer note, and give vent to the feelings of my heart. I hope and trust that the cause which you so fearlessly advocate, is rolling forth in America, with that firm and steady motion which characterizes the work of Jehovah. The enemies which we are forced to encounter are numerous, strong, shrewd and cunning. Their leader transfuses into them his own spirit, and brings them into close alliance with the numerous hosts of precious immortals who have been earlier taken captives by the haughty tyrant, and sacrificed upon the altar of iniquity, transgression and sin. May it please our Father in heaven to throw around thee his protecting arms, to place beneath thee almighty strength ever buoy thy head above the raging waves of tribulation, through which the chart of destiny has evidently marked thy course. I am happy in the enjoyment of the distinguished consideration with which heaven's favor alone has endowed me, of bearing with you some humble part in laying the foundation of the glorious kingdom of Messiah, which is destined in its onward course to break in pieces and destroy all others, and stand for ever. The friendship and good will which are breathed towards me through all your letters, are received as the legacy which noble minds and generous hearts are ever anxious to bequeath. They soften the hard and rugged path in which heaven has directed my course. They are buoyancy in depression— joy in sorrow; and when the dark clouds of despondency are gathering thick around the mental horizon, like kind angels from the fountain of mercy, they dispel the gloom, dry the tear of sorrow, and pour humanity's healing balm into my grieved and sorrowful heart. Be assured, therefore, Brother Joseph, that effusions from the altar of a grateful heart, are smoking to heaven daily in thy behalf; and not only in thine, but in behalf of all Zion's suffering sons and daughters. Though now far separated from you, and also from her, who, with me, has suffered the chilling blasts of adversity, yet hope lingers in this bosom, brightened almost into certainty by the implicit confidence reposed in the virtue of that call which was born on the gentle breeze of the Spirit of God, through the dark shades of midnight gloom, till it found a mansion in my anxious and inquiring heart, that my feet shall once more press the American soil; and under the shade of her streaming banner, embrace again the friends I love.

I never knew that I was in reality an American, until I walked out one fine morning in Rotterdam along the wharf where many ships lay in the waters of the Rhine. Suddenly my eye caught a broad pendant floating in a gentle breeze over the stern of a fine ship at mizzen half mast; and when I saw the wide spread eagle perched on her banner with the stripes and stars under which our fathers were led to conquest and victory, my heart leaped into my mouth, a flood of tears burst from my eyes, and before reflection could mature a sentence, my mouth involuntarily gave birth to these words, "I am an American." To see the flag of one's country in a strange land, and floating upon strange waters, produces feelings which none can know except those who experience them. I can now say that I am an American. While at home the warmth and fire of the American spirit lay in silent slumber in my bosom; but the winds of foreign climes have fanned it into a flame.

I have seen some of the finest specimens of painting and sculpture of both ancient and modern times. The vast varieties of curiosities, also, from every country on the globe, together with every novelty that genius could invent or imagination conceive, which I have been compelled to witness in the course of my travels, would be too heavy a tax upon my time to describe, and upon your patience to read. I have witnessed the wealth and splendor of many of the towns in Europe—have gazed with admiration upon the widely-extended plains, her lofty mountains, her mouldering castles, and her extensive vineyards: for at this season nature is clad in her bridal robes, and smiles under the benign jurisprudence of her Author. I have also listened to the blandishments, gazed upon the pride and fashion of a world grown old in luxury and refinement, viewed the pageantry of kings, queens, lords, and nobles; and am now where military honor, and princely dignity, must bow at the shrine of clearical superiority. In fine, my mind has become cloyed with novelty, pomp, and show; and turns with disgust from the glare of fashion to commune with itself in retired meditation.

Were it consistent with the will of Deity, and consonant with the convictions of my own bosom, most gladly would I retreat from the oppressing heat of public life, and seek repose in the cool and refreshing shades of domestic endearments, and bask in the affections of my own little family circle. But the will of God be done! Can the Messiah's kingdom but be advanced through my toil, privation, and excessive labors, and at last sanctify my work through the effusion of my blood! I yield, O Lord! I yield to thy righteous mandate! Imploring help from thee in the hour of trial, and strength in the day of weakness to faithfully endure until my immortal spirit shall be driven from its earthly mansion to find a refuge in the bosom of its God.

If the friends in America shall be edified in reading this letter from Brother Hyde, I hope they will remember one thing; and that is this, that he hopes he has a wife and two children living there; but the distance is so great between him and them, that his arm is not long enough to administer to their wants. I have said enough. Lord, bless my wife and children, and the hand that ministers good to them, in the name of Jesus Christ. Amen. Adieu for the present.

Good rest on all the Saints throughout the world.

ORSON HYDE.

A violent and destructive hurricane swept over portions of France, Germany, and Switzerland.

Sunday, 18.—This day was observed as a day of fasting and prayer by the Saints in Nauvoo, that they might mourn with them that mourn, "and weep with them that weep," on account of the death of Honorable Sidney H Little of the Senate, who was killed by jumping from a wagon last Sunday, while his horse was unmanageable. Mr. Little was a patriot, statesman, and lawyer.

Death of Senator Little.

Meeting was held in the grove, west of the Temple; Elders Sidney Rigdon, John Taylor, and Geo. A. Smith preached.

Monday, 19.—Council of the Twelve, viz.—Brigham Young, Heber C. Kimball, John Taylor, Orson Pratt, and George A. Smith met at Elder Young's house, conversing with Lyman E. Johnson, who formerly belonged to the quorum. President Rigdon and myself were with them part of the time.

Sunday, 25.—Attended meeting in the grove. Elders Orson Pratt and George A. Smith preached in the forenoon. In the afternoon Elder Sidney Rigdon preached a general funeral sermon, designed to comfort and instruct the Saints, especially those who had been called to mourn the loss of relatives and friends. I followed him, illustrating the subject of the resurrection by some familiar figures.

General Funeral Sermon.

Elder George A. Smith married Bathsheba W. Bigler. Don Carlos Smith performed the ceremony, which was the last official act of his life, he being very feeble at the time.

Brother William Yokum had his leg amputated by Dr. John F. Weld, who operated free of charge; he was wounded in the massacre at Haun's Mill, October 30th, 1838, and had lain on his back ever since; and now it was found the only chance to save his life was to have his leg cut off. He was also shot through the head at the same massacre.

Wednesday, 28.—The Jewish quarter of Smyrna was burned. Three thousand houses and eight synagogues were destroyed.

Sunday, August 1.—All the Quorum of the Twelve Apostles who were expected here this season, with the exception of Elders Willard Richards and Wilford Woodruff, have arrived. We have listened to the accounts which they give of their success, and the prosperity of the work of the Lord in Great Britain with pleasure. They certainly have been the instruments in the hands of God of accomplishing much, and must have the satisfaction of knowing that they have done their duty. Perhaps no men ever undertook such an important mission under such peculiarly distressing and unpropitious circumstances. Most of them when they left this place, nearly two years ago, were worn down with sickness and disease, or were taken sick on the road. Several of their families were also afflicted and needed their aid and support. But knowing that they had been called by the God of Heaven to preach the Gospel to other nations, they conferred not with flesh and blood, but obedient to the heavenly mandate, without purse or scrip, they commenced a journey of five thousand miles entirely dependent on the providence of that God who had called them to such a holy calling. While journeying to the sea board they were brought into many trying circumstances; after a short recovery from severe sickness, they would be taken with a relapse, and have to stop among strangers, without money and without friends. Their lives were several times despaired of, and they have taken each other by the hand, expecting it would be the last time they should behold one another in the flesh. However, notwithstanding their afflictions and trials, the Lord always interposed in their behalf, and did not suffer them to sink

The Prophet's Account of the Mission of the Twelve.

in the arms of death. Some way or other was made for their escape—friends rose up when they most needed them, and relieved their necessities; and thus they were enabled to pursue their journey and rejoice in the Holy One of Israel. They, truly, "went forth weeping, bearing precious seed," but have "returned with rejoicing, bearing their sheaves with them."

The minds of thousands are already prepared to hear of the sacking of cities—the marching and countermarching of armies—the burning of towns and villages—the flight of citizens—the rising of the Indians—the commotion in Illinois—the distress in Iowa—the consternation and flight of the Missourians, the exploits of mighty chieftains, &c.—on account of the fooleries and lies which have been trumpeted forth from the press in the United States.

Thursday, 5.—Letters from London, state that there are a number—more or less—baptized every week.

There was a general election of members of Parliament last month. Serious riots occurred in different parts of the kingdom between the Whigs and Tories.

Letter of William Smith to President Smith—Land Transactions.

CHESTER COUNTY, PENNSYLVANIA,
August 5th, 1841.

BROTHER JOSEPH:—I expect to leave here for the Jersey country next week. Doctor Galland left for Nauvoo last week. In the Hotchkiss business, Hyrum requested me to do all I could. Brother James Ivins has received orders on you from Doctor Galland to the amount of twenty-five hundred dollars. The property that he has given these orders for, is well worth the money. I expect Mr. Hotchkiss in new Jersey in a few days to receive this property, which is Cook's Mills Tavern stand, attached to six acres of ground with all the appurtenances. Some of the Jersey people think it worth three thousand dollars. Now the question is, shall I let Mr. Hotchkiss have this property for less than twenty-five hundred, since that is the price you will have to pay at Nauvoo. Why I ask this question is—I have understood that Hotchkiss has said that he would not allow over twenty-two hundred dollars. I got hold of another small piece of land, worth five hundred; and if Hotchkiss will take all at a fair price, I shall be enabled to settle the amount of three thousand dollars soon. Please write me an answer to the above question. The cause in these eastern lands is flourishing, and we want more laborers; fifty doors opened for preaching where there is but one laborer. I wish you would send us help.

Yours in the bonds of the covenant,

WILLIAM SMITH.

CHAPTER XXIII.

THE DEATH OF DON CARLOS SMITH—HIS LIFE AND LABORS—
SPECIAL CONFERENCE AT NAUVOO.

Saturday, August 7.—My youngest brother, Don Carlos Smith, died at his residence in Nauvoo this morning, at twenty minutes past two o'clock, in the 26th year of his age. He was born 25th March, 1816, was one of the first to receive my testimony, and was ordained to the Priesthood when only 14 years of age. The evening after the plates of the Book of Mormon were shown to the eight witnesses, a meeting was held, when all the witnesses, as also Don Carlos bore testimony to the truth of the latter-day dispensation. He accompanied father to visit grandfather, Asael Smith, and relatives in St. Lawrence county, New York, in August, 1830. During that mission he convinced Solomon Humphrey, a licentiate of the Baptist order, of the truth of the work. He was one of the 24 Elders who laid the corner stones of the Kirtland Temple. In the fall of 1833, he entered the office of Oliver Cowdery to learn the art of printing. On the 30th July, 1835, he married Agnes Coolbrith, in Kirtland, Ohio. On the 15th January, 1836, he was ordained President of the High Priests' quorum. He took a mission with Wilber Denton in the spring and summer of 1836, in Pennsylvania and New York. On the commencement of the publication of the *Elders' Journal* in Kirtland, he took the control of the establishment until the office was destroyed by fire in December, 1837, when, in consequence of persecution, he moved his family to

The Death of Don Carlos Smith.

New Portage.   Early in the spring of 1838 he took a mission through the states of Virginia, Pennsylvania and Ohio, and raised means to assist his father; and immediately after his return he started to Missouri with his family, in company with father and family, and purchased a farm in Daviess county.   On the 26th September he started on a mission to the states of Tennessee and Kentucky, to collect means to buy out the claims and property of the mobbers in Daviess county, Missouri.   During his absence, his wife and two little children were driven by the mob from his habitation, and she was compelled to carry her children three miles, through snow three inches deep, and wade through Grand river, which was waist deep, during the inclement weather.   He returned about the 25th of December, after a very tedious mission, having traveled 1,500 miles, 650 of which were on foot.

I extract the following from his journal—

On the 30th of September, 1838, in company with George A. Smith, Lorenzo D. Barnes, and Harrison Sagers, I went on board the *Kansas* (which had one wheel broken); the Missouri river was very low, and full of snags and sand bars.   General Samuel Lucas and Moses Wilson, of Jackson county, Colonel Thompson, from Platt Purchase, and many others of the active mobbers were on board, as also General David R. Atchison.   On touching at De Witt, on 1st October, for wood, we found about seventy of the brethren, with their families, surrounded by an armed mob of upwards of two hundred.   The women and children there were much frightened, expecting it was a boat loaded with mobbers. We would have stopped and assisted them, but being unarmed, we thought it best to fulfill our mission.   From this onward the "Mormons" were the only subject of conversation, and nothing was heard but the most bitter imprecations against them.   General Wilson related many of his deeds of noble daring in the Jackson mob, one of which was the following: "I went, in company with forty others, to the house of Hiram Page, a Mormon, in Jackson county.   We got logs and broke in every door and window at the same instant; and pointing our rifles at the family, we told them, we would be d—d if we didn't shoot every one of them, if Page didn't come out.   At that, a tall woman made her appearance, with a child in her arms.   I told the boys she was too d—d tall. In a moment the boys stripped her, and found it was Page.   I told them to give him a d—d good one. We gave him sixty or seventy blows with hickory withes which we had prepard. Then after pulling the roof off the house, we went to the next d—d Mormon's house, and whipped him in like manner. We continued until we whipped ten or fifteen of the d—d Mormons, and demolished their houses that night. If the Carroll boys would do that way they might conquer; but it is no use to think of driving them without four or five to one. I wish I could stay, I would help drive the d—d Mormons to hell, Old Joe, and all the rest." At this I looked the General sternly in the face, and told him, that he was neither a republican nor a gentleman, but a savage, without a single principle of honor, or humanity. "If," said I, "the 'Mormons' have broken the law, let it be strictly executed against them; but such anti-republican, and unconstitutional acts as these, related by you, are beneath the brutes." We were upon the hurricane deck, and a large company present were listening to the conversation. While I was speaking, Wilson placed his hand upon his pistol, which was belted under the skirt of his coat; but Cousin George stood by his side, watching every move of his hand, and would have knocked him into the river instantly, had he attempted to draw a deadly weapon. But General Atchison saved him the trouble, by saying, "I'll be d—d to hell if Smith ain't right." At this, Wilson left the company crest-fallen. In the course of the conversation, Wilson said that the best plan was to rush into the Mormon settlements, murder the men, make slaves of the children, take possession of the property, and use the women as they pleased.

A gentleman, present from Baltimore, Maryland, said he never was among such a pack of d—d savages before: he had passed through Far West, and saw nothing among the "Mormons" but good order. Then drawing his pistols, he discharged them, and re-loading, said, "If God spares my life till I get out of Upper Missouri, I will never be found associating with such devils again."

Shortly after this we were invited to preach on board, Elder Barnes and I preached. The rest of the way we were treated more civilly; but being deck passengers, and having very little money, we suffered much for food.

We continued our journey together through every species of hardship and fatigue, until the 11th of October, when Elders Barnes and Harrison Sagers left us at Paducah, after our giving them all the money we had, they starting up the Ohio river, and we to visit the churches in west Tennessee and Kentucky. Soon after this, Julian Moses gave us a five-franc piece, and bade us farewell.

We soon found that the mob spirit was in Kentucky, as well as in Missouri; we preached in a small branch of the Church in Calloway county, and stayed at the house of Sister Selah Parker, which was surrounded in the night by about twenty armed men, led by John McCartney, a Campbellite priest, who had sworn to kill the first "Mormon" Elder who should dare to preach in that place.   The family were very much terrified.   After trying the doors, the mobbers finally went away. We visited a number of small branches in Tennessee; the brethren generally arranged to be on hand with their money, or lands for exchange in the spring.   Brother Samuel West gave us twenty-eight dollars to help defray our traveling expenses.   We also received acts of kindness from others, which will never be forgotten.

About this time our minds were seized with an awful foreboding — horror seemed to have laid his grasp upon us—we lay awake night after night for we could not sleep.   Our forebodings increased, and we felt sure that all was not right; yet we continued preaching until the Lord showed us that the Saints would be driven from Missouri.   We then started home, and, on arriving at Wyatt's Mills, we were told that if we preached there it would cost us our lives.   We had given out an appointment at the house of Mrs. Foster, a wealthy widow.   She also advised us to give it up; but, as she had no fears for herself, her property or family, we concluded to fill our appointment.   The hour of meeting came, and many attended.   George A. preached about an hour; during which time Captain Fitch came in at the head of twelve other mobbers, who had large hickory clubs, and they sat down with their hats on. When George A. took his seat, I arose and addressed them for an hour and a half, during which time, I told them that I was a patriot—that I was free—that I loved my country—that I loved liberty—that I despised both mobs and mobbers—that no gentleman, or Christian at heart would ever be guilty of such things, or countenance them.   Whereupon the mob pulled off their hats, laid down their clubs, and listened with almost breathless attention.

After meeting Mr. Fitch came to us and said that he was ashamed of his conduct, and would never do the like again; that he had been misinformed about us by some religious bigots, and begged of us to forgive him, which we did.

We continued our journey to Columbus, Hickman county, Kentucky, and put up with Captain Robinson, formerly an officer in the army, who treated us very kindly, assuring us that we were welcome to stay at his house until a boat should come, if it were three months.   We stayed nine days, during which a company of thirteen hundred Cherokee Indians were ferried over the river.

We went on board the steamer *Louisville*, and had to pay all our money for a deck passage.   About ninety miles from St. Louis our boat got aground, where it lay three days.   We had nothing to eat but a little parched corn.   We then went on board of a little boat, *The Return*, which landed us in St. Louis the next morning.   Here we found Elder Orson Pratt, and learned that Joseph was a prisoner with many others, and that David Patten was killed, and of the sufferings of the Saints, which filled our hearts with sorrow.

The next morning we started on foot for home; at Huntsville, about 200 miles, we stopped at the house of George Lyman to rest.   George A.'s feet had now become very sore from walking.

We had not been long in Huntsville before the mob made a rally to use us up, as they said, with the rest of the Smiths: and, at the earnest request of our friends, we thought best to push on, and started about ten at night.   The wind was in our faces, the ground slippery, and the night very dark; nevertheless we proceeded on our journey. Traveling twenty-two miles, we came to the Chariton river, which we found frozen over, but the ice too weak to bear us, and the boat on the west side of the river.   We went to the next ferry, but finding there was no boat, and knowing that in the next neighborhood a man's brains were beaten out for being a "Mormon," we returned to the first ferry, and tried by hallowing to raise the ferryman on the opposite side of the river, but were not able to awake him.   We were almost benumbed with the cold, and to warm ourselves we commenced scuffling and jumping: we then beat our feet upon the logs and stumps, in order to start a circulation of blood; but at last George A. became so cold and sleepy, that he could not stand it any longer, and lay down.   I told him he was freezing to death; I rolled him on the ground, pounded and thumped him; I then cut a stick and said I would thrash him.   At this he got up, and undertook to thrash me: this stirred his blood a little, but he soon lay down again.   By this time the ferryman came over, and set us across the river, where we warmed ourselves a little, and pursued our journey until about breakfast time, when we stopped at the house of a man, who we afterwards learned was a leader of the mob at Haun's Mill massacre.   The next morning we started without breakfast.   Our route lay through a wild prairie, where there was but very little track, and only one house in forty miles   The northwest wind blew fiercely in our faces, and the ground was so slippery that we could scarcely keep our feet, and when the night came on, to add to our perplexity, we lost our way: soon after which, I became so cold that it was with great difficulty I could keep from freezing.   We also became extremely thirsty; however, we found a remedy for this by cutting through ice three inches thick with a penknife.   While we were drinking, we heard a cowbell; this caused our hearts to leap for joy, and we arose and steered our course towards the sound.   We soon entered Tenny's Grove, which sheltered us from the wind, and we felt more comfortable.   In a short time we came to the house of Whitford G. Wilson, where we were made welcome and kindly entertained. We lay down to rest about two o'clock in the morning, after having traveled one hundred and ten miles in two days and two nights.   After breakfast I set out for Far West, leaving George A. sick, with our hospitable friends.   When I arrived on the evening of December 25th, I was fortunate enough to find my family alive, and in tolerable health, which was more than I could have expected, considering the scenes of persecution through which they had passed.

Don Carlos visited us several times while we were in Liberty jail, and brought our wives to see us, and some money and articles to relieve our necessities. He took charge of father's family in his flight from Missouri, and saw them removed to Quincy, Illinois.

The Visits of Don Carlos to Liberty Prison.

In June, 1839, he commenced making preparations for printing the *Times and Seasons*. The press and type had been resurrected by Elias Smith, Hyrum Clark, and others, from its grave in Dawson's yard, Far West, where it was buried for safety the night that General Lucas surrounded the city with the mob militia. The form for a number of the *Elders' Journal* was buried with the ink on it. The types were considerably injured by the damp; it was therefore necessary to get them into use as soon as possible, and in order to do this, Don Carlos was under the necessity of cleaning out a cellar through which a spring was constanly flowing, as the only place where he could put up the press. Ebenezer Robinson and wife being sick, threw the entire burden on him.

His Ministrations to the Sick.

As a great number of brethren lay sick in the town, on Tuesday, 23rd July, 1839, I told Don Carlos and George A. Smith to go and visit all the sick, exercise mighty faith, and administer to them in the name of Jesus Christ, commanding the destroyer to depart, and the people to arise and walk; and not leave a single person on the bed between my house and Ebenezer Robinson's, two miles distant; they administered to over sixty persons, many of whom thought they would never sit up again; but they were healed, arose from their beds, and gave glory to God; some of them assisted in visiting and administering to others who were sick.

Working in the damp cellar, and administering to the sick impaired his health so that the first number of the *Times and Seasons* was not issued until November. He edited thirty-one numbers.

He was elected major in the Hancock county militia, and on the death of Seymour Brunson, was made lieutenant-colonel.

He was elected on 1st February, 1841, a member of the City Council of Nauvoo, and took the necessary oath on 3rd February, and on the fourth he was elected brigadier-general of the second cohort of the Nauvoo Legion.

He was six feet four inches high, was very straight and well made, had light hair, and was very strong and active. His usual weight when in health was 200 pounds. He was universally beloved by the Saints. Personal Appearance of Don Carlos Smith.

He left three daughters, namely, Agnes C., Sophronia C., and Josephine D.

President John Smith was unanimously acknowledged as the president of the stake in Iowa, David Pettigrew, M. C. Nickerson, counselors. Elias Smith was sustained as Bishop, and Joseph B. Noble and Joseph Mecham as his counselors. The Iowa Stake of Zion.

A conference of the Church was held at Zarahemla, and the branches in Iowa, so far as represented, consisted of 750 members.

Shocks of an earthquake felt at several places in Spain.

Sunday, 8.—A water-spout destroyed twenty houses of Portpatrick, Scotland.

The funeral of Brother Don Carlos was attended by a vast concourse of friends and relatives; he was buried with military honors.

The Zarahemla conference appointed George W. Gee, Church Recorder, and was addressed by Elders John Taylor and George A. Smith, on building the Temple, and on temperance.

Monday, 9.—The steamboat *Erie* was burned on Lake Erie, thirty miles from Buffalo, and eight from the shore, two hundred persons on board, of whom one hundred and seventy-five perished.

Tuesday, *10*—I spent the day in council with Brigham Young, Heber C. Kimball, John Taylor, Orson Pratt, and George A. Smith, and appointed a special conference for the 16th instant. I directed them to send missionaries to New Orleans; Charleston, South Carolina; Salem, Massachusetts; Baltimore, Maryland; and Washington, District of Columbia. I also requested the Twelve to take the burthen of the business of the Church in Nauvoo, and especially as pertaining to the selling of Church lands.

New Mission Movement Planned.

The department of English literature and mathematics, of the University of the City of Nauvoo, is in operation under the tuition of Professor Orson Pratt.

General Orders, Nauvoo Legion.

HEADQUARTERS, NAUVOO LEGION,
CITY OF NAUVOO, Aug. 10, 1841.

It becomes our painful duty to officially notify the troops of our command of the untimely decease of that noble chief, Brigadier-General Don Carlos Smith—he fell, but not in battle—he perished, but not by the weapons of war—at his burial you paid him honor, but he is gathered to his fathers to receive greater honor.

In consequence of this afflicting dispensation of Divine Providence, the commissioned officers of the staff and line will wear crape on the left arm for thirty days. The commissioned officers of the second cohort will convene at General Smith's office, on Saturday, the 4th day of September, at 10 o'clock a. m:, for the purpose of electing a brigadier-general, at which time and place the court of appeals will sit.

The legion will assemble at the usual place of rendezvous, in the city of Nauvoo, on Saturday, the 11th day of September, at 10 o'clock a.m., for the purpose of general parade. The militia officers of the county of

Hancock, Illinois; and the county of Lee, Iowa, are respectfully invited to attend. The adjutants of regiments will form their respective regiments at 9 o'clock and at 10 o'clock; the adjutant of the Legion will form the line by regiments, and not by companies as heretofore. A special court-martial will convene at the usual place, on Saturday, the 28th day of August, at 10 o'clock a. m., for the transaction of business.

JOSEPH SMITH, Lieutenant General.

A shower of meteoric stones fell at Iwan in Hungary.

Letters from various parts of England and Scotland show that numbers are daily added to the Church; while shipwrecks, floods, houses and work- Depression of the Times. shops falling, great and destructive fires, sudden deaths, banks breaking, men's hearts failing them for fear, shop-keepers and manufacturers failing, because no man buyeth their merchandise, many accidents on the railways, etc., betoken the coming of the Son of Man.

Thursday, 12.—A considerable number of the Sac and Fox Indians have been for several days encamped in the neighborhood of Montrose. The ferryman Visit of the Sac and Fox Indians to Nauvoo. brought over a great number on the ferryboat and two flat boats for the purpose of visiting me. The military band and a detachment of Invincibles [part of the Legion] were on shore ready to receive and escort them to the grove, but they refused to come on shore until I went down. I accordingly went down, and met Keokuk, Kis-ku-kosh, Appenoose, and about one hundred chiefs and braves of those tribes, with their families. At the landing, I was introduced by Brother Hyrum to them; and after salutations, I conducted them to the meeting grounds in the grove, and instructed them in many things which the Lord had revealed unto me concerning their fathers, and the promises that were made concerning them in the Book of Mormon. I advised them to cease killing each other and warring with other tribes; also to keep peace with the whites; all of which was interpreted to them.

Keokuk replied that he had a Book of Mormon at his

wigwam which I had given him some years before. "I believe," said he, "you are a great and good man; I look rough, but I also am a son of the Great Spirit. I have heard your advice—we intend to quit fighting, and follow the good talk you have given us."

After the conversation they were feasted on the green with good food, dainties, and melons by the brethren; and they entertained the spectators with a specimen of their dancing.

Saturday, 14.—Sir J. M. Brunel, the engineer, with fifty ladies and gentlemen, made the first passage under the river Thames, England.

Sunday, 15.—My infant son, Don Carlos, died, aged 14 months, 2 days.

Conference met in Zarahemla, and was addressed by Elders Brigham Young and George Miller on building the Temple in Nauvoo.

Monday, 16.—Elder Willard Richards arrived at Nauvoo this morning.

Ebenezer Robinson succeeded Brother Don Carlos as editor of the *Times and Seasons*, with Elder Robert B. Thompson assistant editor.

Minutes of a Special Conference at Nauvoo—Important Action in Relation to the Twelve.

At a special conference of the Church of Jesus Christ of Latter-day Saints, held in the city of Nauvoo, August 16, 1841, Elder Brigham Young was unanimously appointed to preside over the conference, and Elias Smith and Lorenzo D. Barnes were appointed clerks.

Singing by the choir; conference opened by prayer, by the president.

The object of the conference was then presented by the president, who stated that President Joseph Smith (who was then absent on account of the death of his child) had called a special conference to transact certain items of business necessary to be done previous to the October conference—such as to select men of experience to send forth into the vineyard, take measures to assist emigrants who may arrive at the places of gathering, and prevent impositions being practiced upon them by unprincipled speculators. The speaker hoped that no one would view him and his brethren as aspiring, because they had come forward to take part in the proceedings before the conference; he could assure the brethren that nothing could be further from his wishes, and those of his quorum, than to interfere with Church affairs in Zion and her stakes. He had been in the vineyard so long, he had become attached to foreign missions, and nothing could induce him to retire therefrom and attend to the affairs of the Church at home but a sense of duty, the requirements of heaven, or the revelations of God; to which he would always submit, be the consequence what it might; and the brethren of his quorum responded, Amen.

A list of names of Elders and cities were read by the president, and a few were selected by nomination, and designated as follows: Voted that Elders Henry G. Sherwood go to New Orleans; Abraham O. Smoot to Charleston, South Carolina; Erastus Snow and Benjamin Winchester to Salem, Massachusetts; John Murdock to Baltimore, Maryland; and Samuel James to Washington, D. C.

On motion of Vinson Knight, seconded by Samuel Bent, resolved: that the quorum of the Twelve select the individuals to go and preach in such places as they may judge expedient, and present the same to the conference, with a view of expediting the business of the day.

The situation of the poor of Nauvoo City was then presented by Bishops Knight and Miller, and a collection taken for their benefit.

After singing, conference adjournd until 2 o'clock p. m.

All of the Twelve present at the conference went and visited President Joseph Smith to comfort him in his affliction.

Conference assembled at 2 p. m., and was addressed by Elders Lorenzo D. Barnes and Henry G. Sherwood, concerning the spread of the Gospel and the building up of the kingdom of God in these last days.

President Joseph Smith now arriving, proceeded to state to the conference at considerable length, the object of their present meeting, and, in addition to what President Young had stated in the morning, said that the time had come when the Twelve should be called upon to stand in their place next to the First Presidency, and attend to the settling of emigrants and the business of the Church at the stakes, and assist to bear off the kingdom victoriously to the nations, and as they had been faithful, and had borne the burden in the heat of the day, that it was right that they should have an opportunity of providing something for themselves and families, and at the same time relieve him, so that he might attend to the business of translating.

Moved, seconded and carried, that the conference approve of the instructions of President Smith in relation to the Twelve, and that they proceed accordingly to attend to the duties of their office.

Moved, seconded and carried unanimously, that every individual who shall hereafter be found trying to influence any emigrants belonging to the Church, either to buy of them (except provisions) or sell to them (except the Church agents), shall be immediately tried for fellowship, and dealt with as offenders, and unless they repent shall be cut off from the Church.

President Rigdon then made some appropriate remarks on speculation.

Moved, that the conference accept the doings of the Twelve, in designating certain individuals to certain cities, &c.; when President Smith remarked that the conference had already sanctioned the doings of the Twelve; and it belonged to their office to transact such business, with the approbation of the First Presidency; and he would then state what cities should now be built up—viz., Nauvoo, Zarahemla, Warren, Nashville, and Ramus.

Resolved: That this conference adjourn to the general conference in October next.

Closed with prayer by President Young.

BRIGHAM YOUNG, President.

ELIAS SMITH,
LORENZO BARNES,
            Clerks.

CHAPTER XXIV.

HOTCHKISS LAND PURCHASE TROUBLES—DEATH'S HARVEST, OLIVER GRANGER, ROBERT B. THOMPSON—IMPORTANT ACTION RELATING TO THE TWELVE—THE MISSION IN FOX ISLAND.

Thursday, August 19, 1841.—Elders Young, Kimball and Richards went to Warsaw, and examined the town plat of Warren which is situated about a mile south of the village of Warsaw, and made some arrangements with the proprietors for building up the place.

The Founding of Warren.

The plat designed for the city of Warren is the school section, No. 16, and opposite the first permanent and good landing place on the Mississippi River below the falls; which is about two miles below the Warsaw landing, which is filling up with sand bars.

The brethren returned about eleven p. m., quite exhausted.

Sunday, 22.—I preached at the stand, on wars and desolations that await the nations.

Wednesday, 25.—I received the following letter:

Letter of Horace R. Hotchkiss to Joseph Smith—Land Affairs in Nauvoo.

FAIR HAVEN, 24th July, 1841.

Rev. Joseph Smith:

DEAR SIR:—I have this moment received a letter from Dr. Galland, dated yesterday, at New York, in which he states his intention of leaving for the west.

It certainly was my expectation that I should again see him before his departure, and be able to make some arrangement with him respecting the interest due to myself, Mr. Tuttle and Mr. Gillet. In this I am disappointed, and considering that a proposition for effecting this object emanated from your brother Hyrum and the doctor, [Isaac Galland] to which no allusion has since been made by them or anybody else, I and Mr. Tuttle think that we have much reason to be dissatisfied at this silence and apparent neglect.

Now, all the transactions relating to Nauvoo have by me and my friends been entered into in the most perfect good faith, and will continue to be conducted on the most honorable principles.

Permit me to ask whether this is a proper return for the confidence we have bestowed, and for the indulgence we have extended?

If you have not already requested your brother Hyrum to call on me when he arrives east, will you write him immediately, and say that it is my urgent wish?

Relative to the Ivins note the Doctor has written me, and referred to Mr. William Smith at New Egypt, on whom I shall call next week.

Your obedient servant,
HORACE R. HOTCHKISS.

I wrote the following answer:

Letter of the Prophet to Horace R. Hotchkiss—Nauvoo Land Transactions.

NAUVOO, August 25, 1841.

To Horace R. Hotchkiss, Esq., New Haven, Connecticut:

DEAR SIR:—Yours of the 24th ultimo came to hand this day, the contents of which I duly appreciate. I presume you are well aware of the difficulties that occurred before, and at the execution of the writings in regard to the land transaction between us, touching the annual payment of interest: if you have forgotten, I will here remind you, you verbally agreed on our refusal and hesitancy to execute the notes for the payment of the land, that you would not exact the payment of the interest that would accrue on them under five years, and that you would not coerce the payment even then; to all this you pledged your honor; and upon an after arrangement you verbally agreed to take land in some one of the Atlantic States, that would yield six per cent interest (to you) both for the principal and interest, and in view of that matter, I delegated my brother Hyrum and Dr. Isaac Galland to go east and negotiate for lands with our friends, and pay you off for the whole purchase that we made of you; but upon an interview with you, they learned that you were unwilling to enter into an arrangement according to the powers that I had delegated to them; that you would not receive any of the principal at all, but the interest alone, which we never considered ourselves in honor or in justice bound to pay under the expiration of five years. I presume you are no stranger to the part of the city plat we bought of you being a deathly sickly hole, and that we have not been able in consequence to realize any valuable consideration from it, although we have been keeping up appearances, and holding out inducements to encourage immigration, that we scarcely think justifiable in consequence of the mortality that almost invariably awaits those who come from far distant parts (and that with a view to enable us to meet our engagements), and now to be goaded by you, for a breach of good faith, and neglect and dishonorable conduct, seems to me to be almost beyond endurance.

You are aware that we came from Missouri destitute of everything but physical force, had nothing but our energies and perseverance to rely upon to meet the payment of the extortionate sum that you exacted for the land we had of you. Have you no feelings of commiseration? Or is it your design to crush us with a ponderous load before we are able to walk? Or can you better dispose of the property than we are doing for your interest? If so, to the alternative.

I therefore propose, in order to avoid the perplexity and annoyance that has hitherto attended the transaction, that you come and take the premises, and make the best you can of it, or stand off and give us an opportunity that we may manage the concern, and enable ourselves by the management thereof to meet our engagements, as was originally contemplated.

We have taken a city plat at Warsaw (at the head of navigation for vessels of heavy tonnage) on the most advantageous terms: the proprietors waiting upon us for the payment of the plat, until we can realize the money from the sales, leaving to ourselves a large and liberal net profit. We have been making every exertion, and used all the means at our command to lay a foundation that will now begin to enable us to meet our pecuniary engagements, and no doubt in our minds to the entire satisfaction of all those concerned, if they will but exercise a small degree of patience, and stay a resort to coercive measures which would kill us in the germ, even before we can (by reason of the season) begin to bud and blossom in order to bring forth a plentiful yield of fruit.

I am, with considerations of high respect,

Your obedient servant,

JOSEPH SMITH.

The Hotchkiss purchase, to which the foregoing letters
<small>Location and Character of the Hotchkiss Lands.</small> relate includes all the land lying north of the White purchase to the river and thence on the river south, including the best steamboat landing, but is the most sickly part of Nauvoo.

Elder Oliver Granger died at Kirtland, Lake county, Ohio, aged forty-nine years. He was the son of Pierce and Clarissa Granger, born in the town of Phelps, Ontario county, New York, 7th February, 1794; received <small>Death of Oliver Granger.</small> a common school education, was two years a member of the Methodist Church and was a licensed exhorter. On the 8th September, 1813, he married Lydia Dibble; in the year 1827, he in a great measure lost his sight by cold and exposure; he was sheriff of Ontario county, and colonel of the militia. He received the Gospel on reading the Book of Mormon, which he providentially obtained, and was baptized at Sodus, Wayne county, and ordained an Elder by Brigham and Joseph Young, they being the first Elders he saw, and immediately devoted his time to preaching and warning the people.

In the year 1833 he moved to Kirtland, and then took a mission to the east with Elder Samuel Newcomb; returned and was ordained a High Priest; took another mission in the spring of 1836 to New York with John P. Greene; and after his return built up a branch at Huntsburg, Geauga county, Ohio; also a branch at Perry, Richfield county, where he baptized Bradley Wilson and his seven sons and their wives. When the Church left Kirtland he was appointed to settle the Church business.

In June, 1838, he went to Far West, and returned in August of same year; in October he again started, taking his family; he went seventy miles into Missouri, and was driven back by the mob; in the spring of 1839 he went to Nauvoo; in 1840 removed to Kirtland with his family, where he remained until his death.

He was a man of good business qualifications, but had been for many years nearly blind. His funeral was attended by a vast concourse of people from the neighboring towns, although there were but few Saints in the country.

Character.

Thursday, 26.

An Epistle of the Twelve Apostles to the Saints Scattered Abroad Among the Nations, Greeting.

NAUVOO, August 26, 1841.

BELOVED BRETHREN:—You will perceive by the minutes of a conference, held in this city, on the 16th instant, that we have returned from a mission which was required of us by the Lord, and have now been called upon to assist in building up the stakes of Zion, and of planting the Saints upon the lot of their inheritance; and feeling as we do a humble reliance upon divine aid at all times, in our unremitting desire to be useful to our fellow men, and especially to the household of faith, that they may be prepared for the great things which God is about to reveal, and which speedily await this generation, we feel anxious to improve the earliest opportunity to make known unto you the mind of the Spirit concerning those things which require your more immediate attention.

It will be discovered, in the minutes before referred to, that we have already begun to select such individuals as have been with the Church and have had the opportunity of becoming acquainted with the principles thereof to some extent; and to designate certain towns and cities where they will locate themselves and build up churches, inasmuch as the people are willing to receive them. These generally will not take their departure from this to their several stations, until after the October conference, previous to which they will have the opportunity of receiving particular instructions in relation to their mission. and of becoming more perfectly acquainted with those principles which are necessary to be acted upon in order that they may become highly useful in helping to roll forth the kingdom of God in these last days.

All those Elders and Priests who are now in the vineyard, will communicate with us immediately, and inform us of their situations, designs, and all things relating to their ministry, and improve the earliest opportunity of repairing hither, where they will have the privilege of instruction from the First Presidency, and thereby understanding principle and doctrine, not to be learned elsewhere, and which is necessary for them to know, that they may become wise stewards in their Master's house.

We are engaged in a great work, and but little comparatively can be known of the magnitude thereof, of the revelations of heaven, and the order of the kingdom by the Saints, while they are scattered to the four winds; and this being well understood by the ancient prophets and apostles, was the reason why they so often spoke of the gathering in the last days, and as this is the place where the Elders are to receive instruction concerning their ministry, so as to become successful ministers of the dispensation of the fulness of times, so also this is the place where the brethren may receive such instructions as are necessary to constitute them a righteous and holy people, prepared for the reception of the Lord Jesus; therefore, we say to all Saints who desire to do the will of heaven, Arise, and tarry not, but come up hither to the places of gathering as speedily as possible, for the time is rapidly approaching when the Saints will have occasion to regret that they have so long neglected to assemble themselves together and stand in holy places, awaiting those tremendous events which are so rapidly approaching the nations of the earth.

It will be recollected that in a recent communication from the First Presidency, all places of gathering are discontinued, excepting Hancock county, Illinois, and Zarahemla, in Lee county, Iowa territory, opposite Nauvoo, and we would suggest to those coming up the Mississippi particularly, and all others who are disposed, to look at Warsaw, a beautifully located village about twenty miles below Nauvoo, consisting of about five hundred inhabitants, a steam flour and lumber mill; one mile below is a section already surveyed, on which the town of Warren is to be built, and every facility is now offered to the brethren, for the immediate erection of houses, the location being very desirable at the lowest point of the DesMoines rapids.

As we have been called upon to act as agents for the Church, it may be expected that some one or more of our quorum may be found at Nauvoo, Zarahemla, and Warren, ready to render every assistance in our power, towards the location of immigrants; and that we shall occasionally visit the other places of gathering, as necessity requires.

We recommend to the brethren in England to emigrate in the fall or winter; by so doing they will be likely to spare themselves much affliction in becoming accustomed to this climate.

Further communications may be expected from the Twelve.

BRIGHAM YOUNG,
HEBER C. KIMBALL.
ORSON PRATT,
WILLARD RICHARDS,
JOHN TAYLOR,
GEO. A. SMITH.

Friday, *27.*—Elder Robert Blashel Thompson died at his residence in Nauvoo, in the 30th year of his age, in the full hope of a glorious resurrec- Death of Robert B. tion. He was associate editor of the *Times* Thompson. *and Seasons*, colonel in the Nauvoo Legion, and had done much writing for myself and the Church.

The following synopsis of his life is from the pen of his widow:

Biography of Robert Blashel Thompson.

Robert Blashel Thompson was born October 1st, 1811, in Great Driffield, Yorkshire, England, was educated at Dunnington, in the same county. He united with the Methodists at an early age and preached what he believed to be the Gospel in connection with that sect for a number of years. Emigrated to Upper Canada in 1834. Embraced the Gospel there; being baptized and confirmed by Elder Parley P. Pratt in May, 1836. Was ordained an Elder by Elder John Taylor, at a conference held in Upper Canada, July 22nd, 1836. Removed to Kirtland in May, 1837, where he married Mercy Rachel Fielding, June 4th, 1837, and being appointed to take a mission to Upper Canada, he returned the same month, and commenced preaching in Churchville and the villages adjacent, baptized a considerable number, continued his labors there until he was called upon to remove to Missouri.

He arrived at Kirtland in March, and started from thence in company with Hyrum Smith and family, arrived in Far West June 3rd, where his daughter, Mary Jane, was born on the 14th of June. He remained there until November, when he, with many of the brethren had to flee into the wilderness to escape the fury of the mob, who swore they would kill every man who had been engaged in the Crooked River battle.

He stood near to Brother Patten when he [Patten] fell. With the rest of the brethren he suffered much from exposure and lack of food. He arrived at Quincy, I believe, in December, where he engaged as clerk in the court house, and remained there until the liberation of Joseph and Hyrum from prison; when the Saints settled in Commerce, he removed there, and was engaged as a scribe to Brother Joseph; he was also Church clerk.

When the Nauvoo Legion was formed, he received the office of colonel and also aid-de-camp. In May, 1841, he became associated with Don Carlos Smith in the editing of the *Times and Seasons*. On the 16th of August he was seized with the same disease of which Don Carlos had died on the 7th. The attachment between them was so strong, it seemed as though they could not long be separated. He died on the 27th, leaving one child; was interred in the burying ground on the 29th. By his special request no military procession was formed at his funeral.

Saturday, *28.*—At a conference held at Attica, New York, six branches, ten Elders, seven Priests, five Teachers, two Deacons and one hundred and forty-six members were represented.

Tuesday, *21.*

Minutes of a Council Meeting of the Twelve Apostles at the House of Brigham Young, Nauvoo.

At a council of the Quorum of the Twelve Apostles at the house of President Brigham Young, Nauvoo, August 31, 1841, for the purpose of taking into consideration the situation of the Church, it was resolved unanimously, that as we [the Twelve] have been called upon by the voice of the conference to attend to the business of the Church, assist the Trustee in Trust in his arduous duties, attend to the settling of immigrants, &c.; we sensibly feel the great responsibility that is resting upon us, and will do all in our power to carry out the wishes of the Church, and prove ourselves worthy of the trust imposed in us by the brethren.

Resolved unanimously, that, so far as may be practicable, we will attend to the counseling and locating of immigrants in person, and at present we will appoint no agents for that purpose out of our own body.

Voted, that Elder Willard Richards be requested to locate himself for a season at Warsaw, or vicinity, for the purpose of selling lots on the town plat of Warren, counseling the brethren, and attending to such other business as may be necessary relating to the Church. The foregoing vote was taken after hearing a favorable report from Elders Young, Kimball, and Richards, of the quorum, for building the town called Warren, they having visited the location, accompanied by Mr. Mark Aldrich and other proprietors of the plat.

Resolved, unanimously, that we deeply feel for our beloved President Joseph Smith, and his father's family, on account of the great losses they have sustained in property by the unparalleled persecutions in Missouri, as well as the other many persecutions they have sustained since the rise of the Church, which has brought them to their present destitute situation. Therefore, voted unanimously, that we for ourselves, and the Church we represent, approve of the proceedings of President Smith, so far as he has gone, in making over certain properties to his wife, children, and friends for their support, and that he continue to deed and make over certain portions of Church property which now exist, or which may be obtained by exchange, as in his wisdom he shall judge expedient, till his own, and his father's household, shall have an inheritance secured to them in our midst, agreeably to the vote of the general conference of the Church held at Commerce in October, 1839.

Resolved: that on account of the peculiar situation of the Church hitherto, it has been expedient and necessary, that the deeds, bonds, and properties of the Church should be, and have been taken and holden by committees of the Church, and private individuals; but that we now have a trustee-in-trust, viz., President Joseph Smith, appointed according to the laws of the land. Therefore, voted unanimously, that we advise the trustee-in-trust to gather up all deeds, bonds, and properties belonging to the Church, and which are now held either by committees or individuals, and take the same in his own name as trustee-in-trust for the Church of Jesus Christ of Latter-day Saints, as soon as such arrangements can be made consistently with his various and multiplied cares and business; and that we individually and collectively will use all diligence to render him every assistance possible to accomplish this desirable object.

Voted, that Elder Lorenzo D. Barnes proceed on his mission to England without delay.

Voted, that Elder Harrison Sagers proceed immediately on his mission to Jamaica, West Indies; and Elder Joseph Ball to South America, according to their appointment on the 16th, and that they accompany each other to New Orleans.

It was proposed, that Elder Simeon Carter go on a mission to Germany; but the vote being taken, it was decided that his mission be suspended for the present.

After much deliberation on the situation of the Church at home and abroad, temporarily and spiritually, and in view of the poverty and distress of many who had been robbed of all by unrelenting mobbers, and of others who have sacrificed all they possessed to assist those who had thus been robbed, and others who had borne the burden in the heat of the day; it was voted unanimously, that President Smith, as trustee-in-trust, be requested and instructed by this conference in behalf of the Church, to extend relief to such indigent suffering brethren, either by land or goods, as the properties of the Church will admit, and his wisdom shall judge expedient; so that no one shall be denied the privilege of remaining in our midst and enjoying the necessaries of life, who has been faithful in his duties to God and the Church.

                                        BRIGHAM YOUNG, President.
                                        WILLARD RICHARDS, Clerk.

Wednesday, Sept. 1.—The *New York Sun* contains an account of some singular phenomena; viz., a shower of flesh and blood, a pillar of smoke, and a shower of manna.

Thursday, 2.—The town of Cartago, on the isthmus of Darien, containing 10,000 inhabitants, destroyed by an earthquake.

Saturday, 4.—Colonel Charles C. Rich was elected brigadier-general of the second cohort, to fill the vacancy of General Don Carlos Smith, deceased, and Lieutenant-Colonel Titus Billings was elected colonel in the place of Colonel Rich, promoted, and Major John Scott was elected lieutenant-colonel in his place, and Captain Hosea Stout was elected major in his place.

Changes of Officers in the Legion.

The City Council elected Brigham Young councilor in place of Don Carlos Smith, deceased; and John Taylor and Heber C. Kimball were elected regents of the University, in place of Don Carlos Smith and Robert B. Thompson, deceased.

Changes Among the Civil Officers of Nauvoo.

Orson Pratt was elected professor of mathematics in the University of the City of Nauvoo, and the degree of master of arts conferred on him by the chancellor and board of regents.

A committee was instructed to purchase two blocks for a burying ground; and the city recorder was instructed to procure a seal for the corporation.

Elder Orson Spencer arrived in the city.

Sunday, 5.—I preached to a large congregation at the stand, on the science and practice of medicine, desiring to persuade the Saints to trust in God when sick, and not in an arm of flesh, and live by faith and not by medicine, or poison; and when they were sick, and had called for the Elders to pray for them, and they were not healed, to use herbs and mild food.

The Prophet on Medicine.

Tuesday, 7.—Another shower of flesh and blood is reported in the Boston papers to have fallen in Kensington. "There had been a drizzling rain during a great part of the day, until about 4 o'clock in the afternoon, when the rain stopped and the dark clouds began gradually to assume a brassy hue, until the whole heavens above seemed a sea of fire. The sky continued to grow more bright until about a quarter past five, when almost instantly it became of burnished red, and in a few moments it rained moderately a thick liquid of the appearance of blood, clothing fields and roads for two miles in circumference in a blood-stained garment. The bloody rain continued for about ten minutes, when it suddenly cleared away, and the atmosphere became so intensely cold that overcoats were needed."

A Shower of "Flesh."

Elder Willard Richards went to Warsaw, and located himself, for the purpose of counseling the Saints, and settling the town of Warren, and the day following made sale of three city lots.

The war between England and China continues. The English have fitted out a new expedition to proceed against China with the utmost rigor, and his celestial majesty on the other hand has issued orders for the raising of a "grand army," and the extermination of the English.

British-Chinese War.

Wednesday, 8.—Wars and rumors of wars, earthquakes, tempests, pestilence, and great fires, connected with every kind of wickedness, distress and destruction of property are heard in almost every land and nation.

Sunday, 11.

Extracts from Legion Minutes.

The Legion was out for general parade, in conformity with a special act of the court martial, and was reviewed by Lieutenant-General Joseph Smith, who delivered a military speech to the troops in his usual energetic style. The official returns of the Legion show the aggregate to be 1,490 men.

HOSEA STOUT, Clerk.

Monday, 13.—Brother Edward Hunter, Sen,* of Chester county, Pennsylvania, visited Nauvoo, and invested $4,500 in town lots and farming land; paid me $2,000 in cash, and made arrangements to pay the balance in two months.

The Coming of Edward Hunter to Nauvoo.

Received an invitation from Brigadier-General Ezekiel W. Swazey, and Colonel Amos B. Fuller, of the militia of Lee county, Iowa, to attend the military parade tomorrow, at Montrose, as visitor. Generals Hyrum Smith and John C. Bennett received a similar invitation.

Tuesday, 14.—Went over to Montrose, accompanied by Brothers Edward Hunter and William A. Gheen. I was very courteously received by General Swazey, the officers and militia.

Mr. D. W. Kilbourn attempted to get up an ill feeling by reading the following proclamation at noon, during the recess of exercise, to a considerable number of persons collected round his store, which I insert verbatim—

Bitterness of D. W. Kilbourn.

---

* Edward Hunter was the second son and seventh child of Edward and Hannah Hunter. He was born in Newtown Township, Delaware county, Pennsylvania. June 22, 1793. His paternal ancestors were from the north of England, and on his mother's side he was of Welsh extraction. John Hunter, his great-grandfather, passed over to Ire and some time in the seventeenth century and served as a lieutenant of cavalry under William of Orange at the battle of the Boyne, where he was wounded. He afterwards came to America and settled in Delaware county, Pennsylvania, about twelve miles from Philadelphia. Edward Hunter, Esq., the Bishop's father, was justice of the peace in Delaware county for forty years. On his mother's side three generations back was Robert Owen of North Wales, a man of wealth and character, a firm sympathizer with Cromwell and the Protectorate, who on the restoration of Charles the Second, refused to take the oath of allegiance, and was imprisoned for five years. After his release he emigrated to America and purchased property near the "City of Brotherly Love." Like the founder of that city, Robert Owen was a Quaker. His son George sat in the state legislature and held various positions of public trust   (Whitney).

Edward Hunter finally settled in Chester county, Pennsylvania, where he purchased an extensive farm, and married Ann Standley, daugher of Jacob and Martha Standley. Here Mormonism found him in 1839, through the preaching of some of the Elders laboring in that vicinity, and Mr. Hunter extended to them the hospitality of his home. En route from Washington to Nauvoo, in the winter of 1839-40, the Prophet Joseph visited him, and for several days preached in the vicinity of the Hunter homestead. Other prominent Elders of the Church also visited the Hunter home, among them the Prophet's brother, Hyrum. Finally on the 8th of

Citizens of Iowa:—The laws of Iowa do not require you to muster under, or be *reviewed* by *Joe Smith* or *General Bennett*, and should they have the impudence to attempt it, it is hoped that every person having a proper respect for himself, will at once leave the ranks.

This, however, had no effect whatever on the people.

Myself and brother were not in military uniform, but were treated with every respect that visiting officers of our rank could be, through the entire day. At the dismissal of the military, I went to Mr. Kilbourn's store, and desired to have some conversation with him, but was peremptorily ordered out of doors. This conduct greatly disgusted his few friends, who upbraided Kilbourn with his ungentlemanly conduct, and accompanied me to the ferry, where I left them, showing me every manifestation of friendship.

Tuesday, 21.—The ship *Tyrean* sailed from Liverpool to New Orleans, with 204 Saints, bound for Nauvoo.

Her British Majesty's war steamer *Madagascar*, totally destroyed by fire in the Chinese seas, and fifty-seven lives lost.

Wednesday, 22.—The High Council of Nauvoo adopted the following preamble and resolution—

High Council Resolution.

Whereas this High Council in times past, had of necessity, and by the advice and instruction of the First Presidency, to transact business of a temporal nature for the Church, and thereby involve itself with debts and other temporal burdens which, under other circumstances would not have devolved upon it; and as the proper authorities to which such temporalities belong are now organized and acting in their proper places; therefore, be it

Resolved, that this High Council is prepared to transfer all debts and temporal business; and that all business of a temporal nature, be, and the same is in readiness to be transferred to the proper authorities.

Alpheus Cutler stated [to the council] that he was going to the pineries the ensuing winter, and nominated Elias Higbee, counselor *pro tem.*

October, 1841, Edward Hunter was baptized by Elder Orson Hyde, then on his way to Jerusalem. This brings the biography of the future Bishop of the Church up to the time of his first appearance in Nauvoo, on the 13th of September, 1841, and henceforth the events of his life will be closely interwoven in the history of the Church.

A company of the brethren started for the pinery, some
five or six hundred miles north, on the river, Lumber for
the Temple.
for the purpose of procuring lumber for the
Temple and Nauvoo House.

The Jews in Smyrna are suffering great persecutions on
account of their religion—"one was thrown into prison
because a cat was missing"—say the journals.

Saturday 25.—Hyrum Smith, son of Hyrum and Jeru-
sha Smith, died, aged seven years, four months, and
twenty-eight days.

A conference was held at Vinal Haven, Fox Island;
eight Elders, one Priest, two Teachers, one Deacon, and
one hundred and forty members were represented, and the
work is progressing.

I extract the following from Elder Wilford Woodruff's
journal—

The Work on Fox Island.

We left Manitou Island, Lake Michigan, at 4 o'clock p. m., on the
steamer *Chesapeake*, which contained 300 passengers, six of whom were
members of the Church; a large quantity of freight and coal, eighty
cords of wood, eighty mules, besides pigs, chickens, geese, ducks, &c.

We continued our journey towards Chicago without any interruption,
until half-past eleven p. m., when we were overtaken by a tremendous
storm of wind and rain; it blew a hurricane, and the lake became as
rough as it could be by the force of wind, and such a scene as quickly
followed I never before witnessed in my travels, either by land or sea.
The captain, officers, hands, and most of the passengers expected to go
to the bottom of the lake. To have judged from outward appearances
I should think there were twenty chances of being lost to one of being
saved, yet I did not once expect to be lost, for I believed the Lord
would by some means save me and my wife and child, who were with
me, from a watery grave.

We were some forty miles from land when the gale struck us, and I
was awakened from a sound sleep by the cry, "We are all lost." The
first thought that entered my mind was, "No, we shall not be lost."

I immediately leaped out of my berth and went on to the upper deck.
I saw we were in imminent danger of being wrecked; the bow of the
boat was heavily laden, and frequently engulfed by the heavy waves
that washed over her; there were judged to be fifty tons of water at a

time on her bow; at one time her bow ran under water, and some thought she would never rise; the water set the mules and all the live stock afloat; washed away the partition; and the mules, pigs, chickens, ducks, and geese, were all hurled in one mass down into the steerage cabin, mixed pell mell with sixty Irish passengers, men, women, and children; at that moment the roaring of the wind, the rush of the waters, the peals of thunder, the flashes of lightning, the braying of asses, the squealing of pigs, the quacking of ducks, geese and chickens, the praying, swearing and screaming of men, women and children, created a confusion of sounds which rent the air, and sent a gloomy thrill through the heart.

We immediately went to work, and helped all the passengers out of the water, and from among the beasts, upon the deck, so their lives were preserved, while all the fowls, pigs, and part of the mules were drowned or killed; many tons of water rushed through the boat, until the water stood nearly to the boilers; it drove the firemen from their places.

About this time when the boat was laboring against wind and tide one of the wheel chains broke, and the boat rolled over on to one side. I again heard the cry that "all was lost," but about thirty of us caught hold of the two detached pieces of chain, and held them together until the engineer mended them with wire.

It took three strong men to manage the wheel; while the boat lay upon her side, it washed away a part of the state rooms; orders were given to clear the boat of everything that was movable; all the wood was fastened with stanchions, on the side that was down, the stanchions were knocked out by the passengers, and forty cords of wood tumbled into the sea at one surge; this caused the boat to right up, and we expected every moment our state room would be washed away. I left it three times with my wife and child, and stepped upon the main deck, expecting to see it washed away; and to add to the horror of the situation, we were wrapped in darkness, as all the lanterns were dashed to pieces.

The men at the wheel labored hard for five hours to turn the boat round, before they accomplished it, so that they could run before the storm. At length daylight appeared, and with it a cessation of the storm in a measure. We returned to Manitou Island at 4 o'clock, being twenty-fours hours out, mostly in the storm.

Thursday, 30.—The following is a copy of a statement of expenses consequent upon the arrest of Joseph Smith, upon demand from Governor Boggs, and sent to the deputy sheriff of Adams county, he having officiated June, 1841.

NAUVOO, September 30, 1841.

The Deputy Sheriff of Adams County:

The following is a statement of my expenses, costs, and liabilities, consequent upon my arrest and trial while in your custody, to-wit—

To amount of fees in Esquires Ralston, Warren, and Co.	$250.00
To Esquires Little, Williams, Walker, and Browning	100.00
To seven days for self, horse, and carriage, at $5.00	35.00
To money expended during that time, consequent upon the arrest	60.00
To twelve witnesses, to-wit: Elias Higbee, John P. Greene, Amasa Lyman, Darwin Chase, Francis Higbee, Chauncy Higbee, Reynolds Cahoon, George W. Robinson, J. Younger, L. Woodworth, Vinson Knight, and Robert B. Thompson, four days each; their time, carriages, horses and expenses, at $5.00 each day	240.00
	$685.00

DEAR SIR:—You will please take such measures as to put me in possession of the above amount, which is justly due me as above stated; to say nothing of false imprisonment and other expenses.   This would have been presented earlier, but for the sickness and death of Robert B. Thompson, my clerk.

Receive my respects, &c.,

JOSEPH SMITH.

Per JOHN S. FULLMER.

Friday, October 1.—Among the interesting relics of antiquity which have been brought to light in these days, is the following sentence from the *Courier des Etats Unis:*

Sentence Rendered by Pontius Pilate, Acting Governor of Lower Galilee, Stating that Jesus of Nazareth shall Suffer Death on the Cross.

In the year seventeen of the Emperor Tiberius Cæsar, and the 25th day of March, the city of the Holy Jerusalem, Anna and Caiaphas being priests, sacrificators of the people of God, Pontius Pilate, governor of Lower Galilee, sitting on the presidential chair of the Prætory, condemns Jesus of Nazareth to die on the cross between two thieves—the great and notorious evidence of the people saying—1. Jesus is a seducer.   2. He is seditious.   3. He is an enemy of the law.   4. He calls himself falsely the Son of God.   5. He calls himself falsely the King of Israel.   6. He entered into the temple, followed by a multitude bearing palm branches in their hands. Order the first centurion, Quills Cornelius, to lead him to the place of execution.   Forbid to any person whomsoever, either poor or rich, to oppose the death of Jesus.

The witnesses who signed the condemnation of Jesus are, viz.—1. Daniel Robani. 2. Raphel Robani. 3. Capet, a citizen.   Jesus shall go out of the city of Jerusalem by the gate of Struenus.

The above sentence is engraved on a copper plate; on one side are written these words—"A similar plate is sent to each tribe." It was found in an antique vase of white marble, while excavating in the ancient city of Aquilla, in the kingdom of Naples, in the year 1820, and was discovered by the Commissaries of Arts attached to the French armies. At the expedition of Naples, it was found enclosed in a box of ebony, in the Sacristy of the Chartrem. The vase in the Chapel of Caserta.   The French translation was made by the members of the Commission of Arts.   The original is in the Hebrew language.   The Chartrem requested earnestly that the plate should not be taken away from them.   The request was granted as a reward for the sacrifice they had made for the army.   M. Denon, one of the Savans, caused a plate to be made of the same model, on which he had engraved the above sentence. At the sale of his collection of antiquities, &c., it was bought by Lord Howard for 2,890 francs.   Its intrinsic value and interest are much greater.

A few years ago, there was found at Catskill, in New York, a shekel of Israel, of the time of our Savior.   On one side was the representation of a palm leaf, on the other a picture of the temple, with the words underneath, "Holy Jerusalem," in the Hebrew tongue.

Relics like these, properly authenticated, have about them an inexpressible sacredness.*

* To the sentiment here expressed by the Prophet, no one will withhold his assent, but he will need to emphasize the phrase "properly authenticated," because it is unquestionably the case that many alleged early Christian documents of the character of the above are spurious: and whether the above alleged formal sentence was really rendered by Pontius Pilate or not, may not be determined. As remarked by nearly all authorities upon this subject, it is probable that Pilate made an official report to Tiberius of both the condemnation and punishment of Jesus Christ. Rev. J. R. Beard, D.D., member of the Historico-Theological Society of Leipzig, and author of the article "Pilate," in Kitto's Biblical Literature, says: "The voice of antiquity intimates that Pilate did make such a report; the words of Justin Martyr are: [second century] 'That these things were so done you may know from the 'Acts' made in the time of Pontius Pilate.'   A similar passage is found a little

further on in the same work [i. e. Justin's apology].   Now when it is considered that Justin's Apology was a set defense of Christianity, in the shape of an appeal to the heathen world through the persons of its highest functionaries, it must seem very unlikely that the words would have been used had no such document existed; and nearly as improbable that these 'Acts' [of Pilate] would have been referred to had they not been genuine." Dr. Lardner, who has, perhaps, more fully discussed the subject than any other writer upon it, decides that, "It must be allowed by all that Pontius Pilate composed some memoirs concerning our Savior, and sent them to the emperor." (See Lardner, Vol. vi, p. 610.)   And yet this very author says that the Acts of Pontius Pilate, "and his letter to Tiberius which we now have, are not genuine, but manifestly spurious."

In Smith's Dictionary of the Bible, it is stated that "We learn from Justin Martyr, Tertullian, Eusebius and others, that Pilate made an official report to Tiberius of our Lord's trial and condemnation, and in a homily ascribed to, though marked as spurious by his Benedictine editors, certain 'acts' or 'comments' of Pilate, are spoken of as well known documents in common circulation." (Article Pilate.) Then the author of this article on Pilate—Rev. Henry Wright Phillott, student of Christ Church, Oxford, adds: "That he, (Pilate) made such a report is highly probable, and it may have been in existence in Chrysostom's time; but the 'Acts of Pilate,' (Acta Pilati,) now extant in Greek, and two Latin epistles from him to the emperor, are certainly spurious;" and it is further said, "The number of extant 'Acta Pilati,' in various forms, is so large as to show that very early the demand created a supply of documents manifestly spurious, and we have no reason for looking on any one of those that remain as more authentic than the others."

Whether or not the above document in the text, purported to be Pilate's formal sentence of death upon Jesus is among the early Christian documents that are spurious, I am not able to determine by any works at my command, and the modification in the sentence of the Prophet above, which states, that "relics like these, *properly authenticated*, have about them an inexpressible sacredness," would rather indicate the existence of doubt in his own mind as to the absolute certainty of the above document being genuine; and I by no means consider that he commits himself to the genuineness of the document by publishing it in the annals of the Church.   Such documents are only inexpressibly sacred if the authentication is beyond question; and he does not here discuss that question.

CHAPTER XXV.

THE GENERAL CONFERENCE OF THE CHURCH AT NAUVOO—
DOCTRINAL SERMON BY THE PROPHET—BAPTISM FOR
THE DEAD—ANGELS AND MINISTERING SPIRITS—EPISTLE
OF THE TWELVE REVIEWING STATUS OF THE CHURCH.

GEORGE M. HINCKLE, who robbed my house in Far West while I was in prison, passing down the river with a flat boat, I commenced suit against him before the District Court, now sitting at Burlington, Iowa. I sent Elias Smith, and Geo. W. Gee *Suit Against Geo. M. Hinckle.*
to attend to the suit; but Hinckle gave security, and got it put off till spring.

Day stormy and cold, a few assembled, but conference did not organize.

I received a letter from Benjamin Winchester, requesting to be excused from accompanying Elder Erastus Snow on his mission to Salem, Massachusetts, on account of ill health and pecuniary embarrassments, and expressing his conviction that Elder John E. Page had means enough to accompany Elder Orson Hyde to Jerusalem.

Saturday, October 2, 1841.

Minutes of the General Conference of the Church Held at Nauvoo.

Conference met in the Grove. The Presidency being absent laying the corner stone of the Nauvoo House, the meeting was called to order by President Brigham Young; the several quorums were arranged and seated in order.

President Brigham Young opened conference by prayer.

The conference then made choice of President Joseph Smith to preside, and Elias Smith and Gustavus Hills, Clerks. Meeting adjourned until 2 p. m.

Prayer by Orson Pratt.

2 p. m., President Joseph Smith opened the meeting.   Choir sung the 18th hymn.

The President then read a letter from Elder Orson Hyde, dated Ratisbon, July 17, 1841, giving an account of his journey and success in his mission, which was listened to with intense interest; and the conference by vote, expressed their approbation of the style and spirit of said letter.   The President then made remarks on the inclemency of the weather, and the uncomfortable situation of the Saints with regard to a place of worship, and a place of public entertainment.

The conference was then called upon by the President, to elect a general Church clerk, in place of Robert B. Thompson, deceased. James Sloan was nominated and elected.

Elder Lyman Wight nominated Bishop George Miller to preside over the High Priests' quorum in place of Don Carlos Smith, deceased. He was duly elected.

President Brigham Young then presented the business commenced at the late special conference of the 16th of August with regard to the appointment of suitable and faithful men to the several important stations of labor in this and other countries.

Elder Lyman Wight addressed the conference on the importance of order, uniformity of instruction, and unanimity of effort to spread the work of the kingdom.

President Joseph Smith made some corrections of doctrine, quoting I Cor. xii:28, showing the principle of order and unity in the offices of the Priesthood.

The Patriarch Hyrum Smith made remarks disapproving of the course pursued by some Elders in counteracting the efforts of the presidency to gather the Saints, and in enticing them to stop in places not appointed for the gathering, particularly referring to the conduct of Elder Almon W. Babbitt of Kirtland.

Elders Lyman Wight, and Henry W. Miller testified that they had traveled in places where Elder Babbitt had been, on his return from his visit to Nauvoo, [he had] taught doctrine contrary to the revelations of God, and detrimental to the interests of the Church.

Moved and carried that Elder Almon W. Babbitt be disfellowshiped until he shall make satisfaction.

Choir sang Hymn 124.   Prayer by Elder George A. Smith.

Conference adjourned until tomorrow at nine o'clock.

Sunday, 3.

Conference assembled in Nauvoo according to adjournment; prayer by Elder Heber C. Kimball.

President Joseph Smith, by request of the Twelve Apostles, gave instructions on the doctrine of baptism for the dead, which were listened to with intense interest by the large assembly. He presented baptism for the dead as the only way that men can appear as saviors on Mount Zion.

The proclamation of the first principles of the Gospel was a means of salvation to men individually; and it was the truth, not men, that saved them; but men, by actively engaging in rites of salvation substitutionally became instrumental in bringing multitudes of their kindred into the kingdom of God.

He explained the difference between an angel and a ministering spirit; the one a resurrected or translated body, with its spirit ministering to embodied spirits—the other a disembodied spirit, visiting and ministering to disembodied spirits. Jesus Christ became a ministering spirit (while His body was lying in the sepulchre) to the spirits in prison, to fulfill an important part of His mission, without which He could not have perfected His work, or entered into His rest. After His resurrection He appeared as an angel to His disciples.

Translated bodies cannot enter into rest until they have undergone a change equivalent to death. Translated bodies are designed for future missions.

The angel that appeared to John on the Isle of Patmos was a translated or resurrected body [i. e. personage], Jesus Christ went in body after His resurrection, to minister to resurrected bodies. There has been a chain of authority and power from Adam down to the present time.

The best way to obtain truth and wisdom is not to ask it from books, but to go to God in prayer, and obtain divine teaching. It is no more incredible that God should *save* the dead, than that he should *raise* the dead.

There is never a time when the spirit is too old to approach God. All are within the reach of pardoning mercy, who have not committed the unpardonable sin, which hath no forgiveness, neither in this world, nor in the world to come. There is a way to release the spirits of the dead; that is by the power and authority of the Priesthood—by binding and loosing on earth. This doctrine appears glorious, inasmuch as it exhibits the greatness of divine compassion and benevolence in the extent of the plan of human salvation.

This glorious truth is well calculated to enlarge the understanding, and to sustain the soul under troubles, difficulties and distresses. For illustration, suppose the case of two men, brothers, equally intelligent, learned, virtuous and lovely, walking in uprightness and in all good conscience, so far as they have been able to discern duty from the muddy stream of tradition, or from the blotted page of the book of nature.

One dies and is buried, having never heard the Gospel of reconciliation; to the other the message of salvation is sent, he hears and embraces it, and is made the heir of eternal life. Shall the one become the partaker of glory and the other be consigned to hopeless perdition? Is there no chance for his escape? Sectarianism answers "none." Such an idea is worse than atheism. The truth shall break down and dash in pieces all such bigoted Pharisaism; the sects shall be sifted, the honest in heart brought out, and their priests left in the midst of their corruption.

Many objections are urged against the Latter-day Saints for not admitting the validity of sectarian baptism, and for withholding fellowship from sectarian churches. Yet to do otherwise would be like putting new wine into old bottles, and putting old wine into new bottles. What! new revelations in the old churches? New revelations would knock out the bottom of their bottomless pit. New wine into old bottles! The bottles burst and the wine runs out! What! Sadducees in the new church! Old wine in new leathern bottles will leak through the pores and escape. So the Sadducee saints mock at authority, kick out of the traces, and run to the mountains of perdition, leaving the long echo of their braying behind them.

He then referred to the [lack of] charity of the sects, in denouncing all who disagree with them in opinion, and in joining in persecuting the Saints, who believe that even such may be saved, in this world and in the world to come (murderers and apostates excepted).

This doctrine presents in a clear light the wisdom and mercy of God in preparing an ordinance for the salvation of the dead, being baptized by proxy, their names recorded in heaven and they judged according to the deeds done in the body. This doctrine was the burden of the scriptures. Those Saints who neglect it in behalf of their deceased relatives, do it at the peril of their own salvation. The dispensation of the fullness of times will bring to light the things that have been revealed in all former dispensations; also other things that have not been before revealed. He shall send Elijah, the Prophet, &c., and restore all things in Christ.

President Joseph Smith then announced: "There shall be no more baptisms for the dead, until the ordinance can be attended to in the Lord's House; and the Church shall not hold another General Conference, until they can meet in said house. *For thus saith the Lord!*"

Prayer by President Hyrum Smith.

Adjourned for one hour.

Afternoon conference opened by the choir singing hymn 105, and prayer by Elder Lyman Wight.

President Brigham Young addressed the Elders at some length, on the importance of teaching abroad the first principles of the Gospel, leaving the mysteries of the kingdom to be taught among the Saints, also on the propriety of many of the Elders remaining at home, and working on the Lord's House; and that their labors will be as acceptable to the Lord as their going abroad, and more profitable for the Church. That those who go abroad must take a recommend from the proper authorities, without which they will not be fellowshiped; and that those who go, and those who remain make consecrations more abundantly than heretofore.

Elder Lyman Wight followed with remarks of a similar purport; resigning his mission of gathering means for the Temple and Nauvoo House.

The conference appointed Elias Higbee, John Taylor, and Elias Smith, to petition Congress for redress of wrongs sustained in Missouri; and Elder John Taylor to present the petition.

Closed by the choir singing hymn 125, and prayer by President John Smith.

Conference assembled on the morning of Monday, the 4th.

Prayer by Elder George A. Smith.

President Joseph Smith made a lengthy exposition of the condition of the temporal affairs of the Church, the agency of which had been committed to him at a general conference in Quincy—explaining the manner that he had discharged the duties involved in the agency, and the conditions of the lands and other property of the Church.

On motion, resolved: that Elder Reuben McBride be invested with power of attorney to settle the business at Kirtland, left in an uncertain condition by Elder Oliver Grange, deceased.

Prayer by Elder Lyman Wight.

Adjourned for one hour.

Afternoon conference opened. Prayer by President John Smith.

Elder Lyman Wight spoke at some length on the subject introduced in the former part of the day, and on the old debts and obligations that are frequently brought up from Kirtland and Missouri; one of which, in the form of a $50 note, he held in his hand, and proclaimed it as his text.

On motion, voted unanimously, that the trustee-in-trust be instructed not to appropriate Church property to liquidate old claims that may be brought forward from Kirtland and Missouri.

President Hyrum Smith presented to the notice of the conference some embarrassment growing out of his signing as security, a certain obligation in Kirtland in favor of Mr. Eaton.

Voted, that Church property here shall not be appropriated to liquidate said claim.

President Brigham Young made some appropriate and weighty remarks on the importance of more liberal consecrations and more energetic efforts to forward the work of building the Temple and Nauvoo House; and after purchasing Elder Wight's text, by paying him fifty cents, tore it in pieces and gave it to the winds, saying, "Go ye and do likewise, with all old claims against the Church."

Choir sang hymn 104, and President Hyrum Smith closed by prayer.

Tuesday, 5th. Conference opened by the choir singing hymn 274, and prayer by Elder Orson Pratt.

Elder Orson Pratt, by request of President Joseph Smith, read a letter from Smith Tuttle, Esq., one of the proprietors of the Hotchkiss purchase, in reference to some misunderstanding in the adjustment of their claims, and conciliatory of any hard feelings growing out of such misunderstanding.

President Brigham Young spoke on the contents of the letter, and expressed his earnest desire that the business might be speedily adjusted, and a proper title obtained by the Church.

Elders Lyman Wight and Hyrum Smith followed with appropriate remarks.

On motion, voted, That President Joseph Smith write to Mr. Hotchkiss on the subject.

On motion by President Joseph Smith, voted, that the Twelve write an epistle to the Saints abroad, to use their influence and exertions to secure by exchange, purchase, donation, &c., a title to the Hotchkiss purchase.

President Brigham Young presented an appeal from the decision of the Elders' quorum on a charge made against Elder John A. Hicks by Dimick B. Huntington for a breach of the ordinances of the city, for falsehood and schismatical conversation. After hearing the testimony in the case it was voted that Elder John A. Hicks be cut off from the Church.

Closed by the choir singing hymn 275; prayer by President Brigham Young.

Adjourned for one hour.

Afternoon conference opened by the choir singing hymn 104, and prayer by Elder Orson Pratt, who then read the minutes of a special conference held in Nauvoo, August 16, 1841.

President Joseph Smith made remarks explanatory of the importance of the resolutions and votes passed at that time.

On motion, voted, that this conference sanction the doings of said special conference.

President Brigham Young proposed to the congregation, that those who would take laborers on the Lord's House to board, while thus laboring, should manifest their willingness by rising and giving their names. About sixty persons arose.

Conference closed by the choir singing hymn 284, and prayer by President Brigham Young.

Conference adjourned *sine die.*

Although the conference commenced under discouraging circumstances owing to the inclemency of the weather, yet a vast number of the brethren and visitors from abroad were present, and on Saturday and Sunday, the weather having become favorable, the congregation was immense. The greatest unanimity prevailed; business was conducted with the most perfect harmony and good feelings, and the assembly dispersed with new confidence in the great work of the last days.

JOSEPH SMITH, President.

ELIAS SMITH,
GUSTAVUS HILLS,
          Clerks.

An earthquake at Constantinople, occasioning extensive destruction of property.

Elder Joseph Beebee writes from New York that he has been preaching in that city, and has baptized twenty-nine.

Wednesday, 6.—Elder Woodruff arrived in Nauvoo.

Elders Kimball, Richards, and Woodruff laid hands on President Young, who was very sick, and he recovered.

Thursday, 7.

Minutes of a Meeting of the Council of the Twelve.

Elders Brigham Young, Heber C. Kimball, Orson Pratt, Lyman Wight, John Taylor, Wilford Woodruff, and Willard Richards, of the quorum of the Twelve Apostles, assembled in council at the house of Elder John Taylor. Voted, that

Elder John D. Lee go on a mission to Jackson and Rutherford counties, Tennessee.

Elder David Evans, to Augusta, Iowa Territory.

Elder Elisha H. Groves, to Iowa county, Wisconsin.

Elder Hiram Clark, to Pike, Brown, and Adams counties, Illinois.

Elder Joseph Ball, to South America.

Elder Harrison Sagers, to Jamaica.

Elder William Bosley, to Utica, New York.

Elder Amasa Lyman, to New York City.

Elder Arza Adams to Kingston, Canada.

Elder Lyman Stoddard, to go with Elisha H. Groves to Wisconsin.

Elder Phinehas H. Young, to Cincinnati, Ohio.

Elder Abraham Palmer, to Chicago, Illinois.

Elder George W. Gee, to Pittsburg, Pennsylvania.

Elder James Blakesley, to Nauvoo, Illinois.

Elder John D. Parker, to New Orleans, Louisiana.

Voted, that Phinehas H. Young be ordained to a High Priest and recommended accordingly.

That Daniel Garns be nominated for president of the Elders' quorum.

That a conference be held at Father Morley's, at Lima, on Saturday and Sunday, the 23rd and 24th instant.

That a committee of three, namely, Brigham Young, Willard Richards, and John Taylor be a committee to draft an address to the eastern churches, as directed by the general conference.

Adjourned to Bishop Miller's tomorrow evening at 6 o'clock.

BRIGHAM YOUNG, President.

WILLARD RICHARDS, Clerk.

Saturday, 9.

Copy of a Letter to Smith Tuttle, Esq.—The Hotchkiss Land Troubles.

DEAR SIR:—Your kind letter of September was received during our conference, which is just over, containing a full and particular explanation of everything which gave rise to some feelings of disappointment in relation to our business transactions; and I will assure you it has allayed on our part every prejudice. It breathes the spirit of kindness and truth. I will assure you that we exceedingly regret that there has been any ground for hardness and disappointment. But as far as I am concerned, I must plead innocent, and you will consider me so, when you come to know all the facts. I have done all that I could on my part. I will still do all that I can. I will not leave one stone unturned.

Now the facts are these: I sent my brother Hyrum, and Doctor Galland with means in their hands—say not money—but with power to obtain either property or money which was necessary to enable them to fulfill the contract I made with Mr. Hotchkiss. My brother Hyrum was under the necessity of returning to this place on account of his ill health, leaving the business in the hands of Dr. Galland, with the fullest expectation that he would make over the property or money to Mr. Hotchkiss, and make everything square so far as the interest is concerned, if not the principal. He was instructed to pay the interest that had accrued, and should accrue up to the fall of 1842, so as to be in advance of our indebtedness.

I had also made arrangements with the eastern churches, and had it in my power to deed over lands for the whole debt, and had expected that an arrangement of that kind would have been entered into.

I am well assured that Dr. Galland did not look for any means whatever, to pay the interest at any rate, if not the principal; and, why he has not done according to my instructions, God only knows. I do not feel to charge him with having done wrong, until I can investigate the matter, and ascertain to a certainty where the fault lies. It may be through sickness or disaster, this strange neglect has happened. I would to God the thing had not happened.

When I read Mr. Hotchkiss' letter, I learned that he was dissatisfied. I thought that he meant to oppress me, and felt accordingly mortified and sorrowful in the midst of affliction, to think that he should distrust me for a moment that I would not do all that was within my power.

But upon having an explanation of the whole matter, my feelings are changed, and I think that you all have had cause for complaining. But you will in the magnanimity of your good feelings, certainly not blame me when you find that I have discharged an honorable duty on my part.

I regret exceedingly that I did not know some time since what I now know, that I might have made another effort before it got so late. Cold weather is now rolling in upon us. I have been confined here this season by sickness, and various other things that were beyond my control; such as having been demanded by the governor of Missouri, of the governor of this state, and he did not have moral courage enough to resist the demand, although it was founded in injustice and cruelty. I accordingly was taken prisoner, and they put me to some ten or eleven hundred dollars' expense and trouble, such as lawyer's fees, witnesses, &c., &c., before I could be redeemed from under the difficulty. But I am now clear of them once more.

And now in contemplating the face of the whole subject, I find that I am under the necessity of asking a little further indulgence—say, till next spring, so that I may be enabled to recover myself, and then, if God spares my life, and gives me power to do so, I will come in person to your country, and will never cease my labors until the whole matter is completely adjusted to the full satisfaction of all of you. The subject of your debt was fairly presented before our general conference held on the first of this month, consisting of ten thousand people for their decision on the wisest and best course in relation to meeting your demands.

The Twelve, as they are denominated in the *Times and Seasons* were ordered by the conference to make arrangements in the Eastern branches of the Church, ordering them to go to you and turn over their property as you and they might agree, and take up our obligations and bring them here, and receive property here for them; and I have been ordered by the conference to write this letter to you, informing you of the measures which are about to be taken to make all things right.

I would inform you that Dr. Galland has not returned to the western country as yet. He has a considerable amount of money in his hands, which was to have been paid to you, as we intended. He is on his way, for aught we know, and is retarded in his journey by some misfortune or other. He may return, however, as yet, and give a just and honorable account of himself. We hope this may be the case. I am sorrowful on account of your disappointments. It is a great disappointment to me, as well as to yourselves.

As to the growth of our place, it is very rapid, and it would be more so, were it not for sickness and death. There have been many deaths, which leaves a melancholy reflection, but we cannot help it. When God speaks from the heavens to call us hence, we must submit to His mandates.

And as for your sincerity and friendship, gentlemen, we have not the most distant doubt of it. We will not have any. We know it is for your interest to do us good, and for our welfare and happiness to be punctual in fulfillment of all our vows, and we think for the future you will have no cause for complaint. We intend to struggle with all our misfortunes in life, and shoulder them up handsomely, like men.

We ask nothing, therefore, but what ought to be required between man and man, and by those principles which bind man to man, by kindred blood, in bearing our own part in everything which duty calls us to do, as not inferior to any of the human race; and we will be treated as such, although we differ with some in matters of opinion in things (viz., religious matters), for which we only feel ourselves amenable to the Eternal God. And may God forbid that pride, ambition, a want of humanity, in any degree of importance, should have any unjust dominion in our bosoms.

We are the sons of Adam. We are the free born sons of America, and having been trampled upon, and our rights taken from us—even our constitutional rights, by a good many who boast themselves of being valiant in freedom's cause, while their hearts possess not a spark of its benign and enlightening influence—will afford a sufficient excuse, we hope, for any harsh remarks that may have been dropped by us, when we thought there was an assumption of superiority designed to gall our feelings.

We are very sensitive as a people—we confess it: but we want to be pardoned for our sins, if any we have committed. With regard to the

time when the first payment of interest should be called for, it appears
we misunderstood each other, but suffice it to say, that it shall not prevent our making arrangements concerning the whole matter. It is
still, however, my firm conviction that my understanding concerning
the interest was correct.

I remain, gentlemen, with sentiments of respect, yours, &c.,

JOSEPH SMITH.

Monday, 10.—The Twelve met for the purpose of counsel, and spent most of the day in visiting the sick.

Elder Erastus Snow writes from Northbridge, Massachusetts. He had been laboring in Salem and vicinity
four weeks, organized a branch of thirty members, and
the prospects are flattering.

Tuesday, 12.

*An Epistle of the Twelve Apostles, to the Brethren Scattered Abroad on
the Continent of America, Greeting:*

BELOVED BRETHREN:—It seemeth good to us to write unto you at
this time concerning the great things of the kingdom of our God, and
more especially as we have been called upon by the late general conference so to do, that the work may not be hindered, but that all may understand their privilege and duty in this day of glorious events, so that
by exercising themselves therein, they may attain unto those blessings
which God has in store for His people in the last days.

We have abundant occasion, and we rejoice exceedingly at the privilege we have had of beholding so many thousands of our brethren and
sisters as were assembled at the late conference; and for the perfect
harmony and good feeling which prevailed throughout all their deliberations; for the great amount of valuable instructions by President
Joseph Smith and others; and for the disposition which we have seen
manifested, by all who were present, to carry into effect all those noble
plans and principles which were derived from heaven, and have been
handed down to earth to carry forward the great and glorious work
which is already commenced, and which must be consummated to secure
the salvation of Israel.

While the minutes of the general conference are before you, which
will be read with interest by every lover of Zion, we shall recapitulate
some items, and detail more particularly to the understanding of those
who had not the privilege of being present on that interesting occasion,

the past, present and future situation and prospects of the Church, and the stakes, and those things which immediately concern their best interests.

A short time since, and the Saints were fleeing from their enemies. Whippings, imprisonments, tortures, and death stared them in the face, and they were compelled to seek an asylum in a land of strangers. They sought, they found it within the peaceful bosom of Illinois—a state whose citizens are inspired with a love of liberty, whose souls are endowed with those noble principles of charity and benevolence which ever bid the stranger welcome, and minister to his wants; in this state, whose soil is vieing with its citizens in all that is good and lovely, the Saints have found a resting place where, freed from tyranny and mobs, they are beginning to realize the fulfillment of the ancient prophets—"They shall build houses and inhabit them, plant vineyards and eat the fruit thereof, having none to molest or make afraid."

In this city, the Church has succeeded in securing several extensive plats of land, which have been laid out in city lots, a part of which have been sold, a part has been distributed to the widow and orphan, and a part remains for sale. These lots are for the inheritance of the Saints, a resting place for the Church, a habitation for the God of Jacob; for here He has commanded a house to be built unto His name where He may manifest Himself unto His people as in former times, when He caused the ark, the tabernacle, and the temple to be reared, and the cloud, and the fire to rest down thereon; and not that the temple be built only, but that it be completed quickly, and that no more general conference be held, till it shall be held therein; and that the Nauvoo House be finished for the accommodation of the brethren from afar, and the stranger who shall come up hither to inquire after the work of the Lord, and worship in His temple.

Scores of brethren in this city have offered to board one and two laborers each, till the temple is completed, many have volunteered to labor continually, and the brethren generally are giving one-tenth part of their time, or one-tenth part or their income, according to circumstances; while those sisters who can do nothing more, are knitting socks and mittens, and preparing garments for the laborers, so that they may be made as comfortable as possible during the coming winter. In view of these things we would invite our brethren for many miles distant around us, to send in their teams for drawing stone, lumber, and materials for the building; and at the same time load their wagons with all kinds of grain and meat, provisions, and clothing, and hay, and provender in abundance, that the laborer faint not, and the teams be made strong; also that journeymen stonecutters, &c., come, bringing their tools with them, and enlist in the glorious enterprise.

Most of the plats in this city before referred to, as well as several farms and large lots of land in this, and adjoining counties are paid for, and secured to the Church by good and sufficient titles; while the town plat for the town of Warren, near Warsaw, is secured on such conditions that the brethren can be accommodated with lots on very reasonable terms; but the large plat in Nauvoo, purchased of Messrs. Hotchkiss, Tuttle & Co., of New Haven, Connecticut, remains unpaid for, and the time has now arrived, when it is very desirable on the part of the Church, as well as on the part of the gentlemen of whom it was purchased, that payment should be made, and a warrantee title secured: to accomplish which we have been called upon by the united voice of the general conference to address the churches in the eastern states, to advise with the brethren in those regions, and devise ways and means whereby this debt may be liquidated, Hotchkiss & Co. satisfied, the plat secured to the Church, and the brethren in the East at the same time transfer their real estate from the place where it now is, to this city or region of country, according to their desire.

The contract for the "Hotchkiss purchase" in Nauvoo, consisting of upwards of five hundred acres, was entered into on or about the 9th of August, 1839, for the specified sum of fifty-three thousand five hundred dollars, and security was given to Messrs. Horace R. Hotchkiss, Smith Tuttle and John Gillet, for the amount of the same, in two notes of equal amount, one payable in ten years, and the other in twenty years from the date thereof; signed by Messrs. Hyrum Smith, Joseph Smith and Sidney Rigdon. In August last interest to the amount of six thousand dollars or upwards had accumulated on said notes, which it has not been in the power of the Church to pay up to the present time. The nature of this purchase and the situation of the Church is such, that it is necessary that the notes should be taken up, the interest stopped, and a warrantee title secured immediately; a correspondence is now in progress with Messrs. Hotchkiss and Co., to effect this thing, and bring forward a final settlement.

But, say you, what can we do to accomplish this great and desirable object? Let the brethren in the eastern states who have lands which they wish to dispose of, so that they may remove hither, and secure to themselves an inheritance among the Saints either in the cities or farms in the vicinity, and are willing to have their lands in the East made over to Messrs. Hotchkiss and Co. towards the payment of the foregoing notes, communicate with us immediately, at this place, stating to us the extent and value of their property.

Then, as soon as we shall have received communications concerning property, sufficient to cancel the obligations, and the necessary preliminaries are understood with Messrs. Hotchkiss and Co., we will dispatch an agent to New Haven to complete the negotiation, transfer your property, take up the notes and secure a deed; and those whose property is thus transferred can have the value thereof here in city lots or lands in the vicinity; and thus your property will prove to you as good as money, inasmuch as you desire to emigrate; and you will no longer be obliged to tarry afar off because that money is so scarce you cannot sell and get your pay. If there are those among you to whom God has given in abundance, and they desire to appropriate some portion thereof for the benefit of His people, for the redemption of Zion, for a blessing to the widows of those who have been slain for the word of God,—and been buried in a well,—for a sustenance to their fatherless children, and provide for them a habitation, they cannot do it more effectually than by devoting a portion of their sustenance toward liquidating this claim.

To those brethren who live so far distant that they cannot send in their loaded teams, and yet desire to assist in building the Lord's house, we would say, gather yourselves together and bring of your substance, your silver, and gold, and apparel, and of your superabundance cast into the treasury of the Lord, and see if He will not pour you out a blessing till there is not room enough to receive it.

Brethren, the blessings of the kingdom are for you, for the body of Christ, for all the members, and God will help those who will help themselves, and bless those who will bless each other, and do as they would be done unto. The gold and the silver is the Lord's; all the treasures of the earth, the flocks and the herds of the fields, and the cattle on the thousand hills are His; if He were hungry, would He crave thy food, or thirsty, would He ask thy drink? Nay! He would only ask that which was His own, He would feast on His own flocks and quench His thirst at His own springs. This God is the God of the Saints, He is your God and He has made you stewards of all that has been committed to you, and will require His own with usury, and will you not be faithful in a little, that you may be made rulers over many cities? Yes, you will, we know you will.

The journeyings, and gatherings and buildings of the Saints are nothing new, and as they are expecting, looking and praying for the completion of the dispensation of the fullness of times, they must also expect that their progress will be onward, or they will be of no avail, for what is not of faith is sin, and can you believe that God will hear your prayers and bring you on your journey, gather you and build your houses, and you not put forth your hand or make one exertion to help yourselves? No. Therefore, inasmuch as the Saints believe that Father Abraham journed to a distant land at the command of the Highest, where himself and household, (whose household we are if we keep the commandments) might enjoy the fruits of their labors unmolested, and worship the God of heaven according to the dictates of their own conscience and His law; that his seed afterwards gathered to Canaan, the land of promise; that the people of God were commanded to build a house where the Son of Man might have a place to lay his head, and the disciples be endowed with power from on high, and were with one accord in one place; they must also believe that this dispensation comprehends all the great works of all former dispensations; and that the children must gather as did the fathers, must build a house where they may be endowed, and be found together worshiping and doing as their fathers did when Jehovah spake, and the angels of heaven ministered unto them; and if these things are not in this generation, then we have not arrived at the dispensation of the fullness of times as we anticipate, and our faith and prayers are vain.

Is it possible that we labor in vain and toil for nought, and that we shall be disappointed at the last? No! We know assuredly that the set time to favor Zion has come, and her sons and daughters shall rejoice in her glory. The time has come when the great Jehovah would have a resting place on earth, a habitation for His chosen where His law shall be revealed, and His servants be endowed from on high, to bring together the honest in heart from the four winds; where the Saints may enter the baptismal font for their dead relatives, so that they may be judged according to men in the flesh, and live according to God in the spirit, and come forth in the celestial kingdom; a place over which the heavenly messengers may watch and trouble the waters as in days of old, so that when the sick are put therein, they shall be made whole: a place wherein all the ordinances shall be made manifest, and the Saints shall unite in the songs of Zion, even praise, thanksgiving and hallelujahs to God and the Lamb, that He has wrought out their deliverance, and bound Satan fast in chains.

What then shall we do? Let us all arise, and with one united and mighty exertion, by the strength of Israel's God, oppose the powers of darkness, and every being and principle that may rise up against us and complete the work already commenced. Let us not for a moment lend an ear to evil and designing men who would subvert the truth and blacken the character of the servant of the Most High God, by publishing abroad that the Prophet is enriching himself on the spoils of the brethren.

When Brother Joseph stated to the general conference the amount and situation of the property of the Church, of which he is Trustee-in-Trust by the united voice of the Church, he also stated the amount of his own possessions on earth; and what do you think it was? We will tell you: his old Charley (a horse) given him in Kirtland, two pet deer, two old turkeys and four young ones, the old cow given him by a brother in Missouri, his old Major, (a dog) his wife, children and a little household furniture; and this is the amount of the great possessions of that man whom God has called to lead His people in these last days, this is the sum total of the great estates, the splendid mansions and noble living of him who has spent a life of toil and suffering, of privation and hardships, of imprisonments and chains, of dungeons and vexatious lawsuits, and every kind of contumely and contempt ungodly men could heap upon him, and last of all report him as rolling in wealth and luxury which he had plundered from the spoils of those for whose good he had thus toiled and suffered. Who would be willing to suffer what he has suffered, and labor near twenty years, as he has done, for the wealth he is in possession of?

Brethren, in view of all these things, let us be up and doing. Let those in the eastern states use all diligence in communicating to us their ability to assist in the Hotchkiss payment, being assured that no exertion they can make will equal what has already been made for them and the Church generally; and let all the Saints come up to the places of gathering, and with their mites and their abundance as God has given them in trust, help to build up the old waste places which have been thrown down for many generations, knowing that when they are completed they will belong unto the people of the Most High God, even the meek, the honest in heart, they shall possess all things, in the due time of the Lord. Be not covetous, but deal in righteousness, for what the Saints shall not possess by purchase and in righteousness they shall not possess, for no unrighteous thing can enter into the kingdom; therefore beloved brethren, deal gently, love mercy, walk humbly before God, and whatever your hands find to do, do it with your might, keeping all the commandments, and then, whether in life or in death, all things will be yours, whether they be temples or lands, houses or vineyards, baptisms or endowments, revelations or healings, all things will be yours, for you will be Christ's and Christ is God's.

BRIGHAM YOUNG,
HEBER C. KIMBALL,
ORSON PRATT,
LYMAN WIGHT,
JOHN TAYLOR,
WILFORD WOODRUFF,
GEORGE A. SMITH,
WILLARD RICHARDS.

Nauvoo, October 12, 1841.

CHAPTER XXVI.

AFFAIRS IN KIRTLAND AND NAUVOO—EPISTLE OF THE TWELVE
TO THE SAINTS IN THE BRITISH ISLANDS—ORSON HYDE'S
PRAYER ON THE MOUNT OF OLIVES, DEDICATING THE HOLY
LAND PREPARATORY TO THE RETURN OF THE TRIBES OF
ISRAEL.

Wednesday, October 20, 1841.—The following extract of
a letter from Elder Hyde, dated Jaffa, October 20, 1841,
on his way to Jerusalem.

Extract from Orson Hyde's Letter.

On my passage from Beyrut to this place (Jaffa) night before last,
at one o'clock, as I was meditating on the deck of the vessel, as she was
beating down against a sultry wind, a very bright glittering sword appeared in the heavens, about six feet in length, with a beautiful hilt, as
plain and complete as any cut you ever saw; and what is still more remarkable, an arm with a perfect hand stretched itself out, and took hold
of the hilt of the sword. The appearance really made my hair rise, and
the flesh, as it were, crawl on my bones. The Arabs made a wonderful
outcry at the sight. Allah! Allah! Allah! [O Lord, O Lord, O Lord]
was their exclamation all over the vessel. I mention this because you
know there is a commandment of God for me, which says, "Unto you
it shall be given to know the signs of the times, and the sign of the
coming of the Son of Man."

Yours in Christ,
ORSON HYDE.

Saturday, 23.—I attended the city council.

Minutes of Conference held at Lima.

Lima [Adams county, Illinois] conference convened pursuant to previous appointment. Elders Brigham Young, John Taylor, and Willard

Richards, of the Twelve Apostles, were in attendance. Elder Brigham Young was unanimously chosen president, and James C. Snow, clerk of the conference.

President Young then made some preliminary remarks, setting forth and explaining the object of the meeting; followed by President Isaac Morley. Elder James C. Snow then represented the branch of the Church at Lima, consisting of 424 members, including 9 High Priests, 32 Elders, 4 Priests, 5 Teachers, and 4 Deacons, mostly in good standing.

President Young, Elders Taylor and Richards, then made some very appropriate remarks, showing and proving the absolute necessity of finishing and completing the House of the Lord now building in Nauvoo, in preference to anything else that can be done, either by mental or physical exertion, in spreading light, knowledge, and intelligence among the nations of the earth.

Conference adjourned till tomorrow, ten o'clock.

In the evening President Morley met with his counselors together with President Young, Elders Taylor, and Richards, and brethren of the Lima branch, for the purpose of entering into certain resolutions necessary, in order to become more active in forwarding the work on the House of the Lord.

After much deliberation, it was moved and seconded, that all those who are willing to consecrate one tenth of their time and property to the building of the temple at Nauvoo, under the superintendence of President Morley and counselors, to signify it by the uplifted hands; when the motion was carried unanimously.

Sunday morning, at ten o'clock conference met pursuant to adjournment.

Elder John Taylor delivered an address, upon the object of Christ's mission into this world, the resurrection and redemption of the Saints, and pointed out very clearly the course to be pursued in order to become the sons of God, through the ordinances of the gospel, that the Saints may, at last, be exalted at the right hand of God, to dwell with Him eternally in the heavens.

After an intermission of one hour, the sacrament was administered by President Young and Elder Richards. The minutes of the conference were then read and accepted.

President Young made some very just remarks on the priesthood, authority, and calling.

Conference adjourned *sine die.*

Benediction by President Morley.

BRIGHAM YOUNG, President,
JAMES C. SNOW, Clerk.

Extract of a Letter from Parley P. Pratt—Emigration of Saints, and Status of the Work in England.

MANCHESTER, ENGLAND.

On the 20th of September, the ship *Tyrean* sailed from Liverpool for New Orleans, under a charter of the Latter-day Saints; she had upwards of two hundred Saints on board, with Elder Joseph Fielding at their head. By chartering [the vessel] we saved the company [of Saints] at least 500 or 600 dollars. The splendid new ship *Chaos*, 1,200 tons burthen, will sail on the 5th of November, under our charter. She will have from one to two hundred Saints on board, with Patriarch Peter Melling at their head.

The Saints in this country are generally rejoicing, and filled with the testimony of Jesus. Great zeal is manifested by the officers in general, of whom there are probably more than a thousand. We are increasing in numbers, and in gifts and blessings. New branches of the Church are rising in many places, and great additions made to the old ones. Manchester and vicinity has poured forth a stream of emigration for the last eighteen months, and still we numbered at our conference, two weeks ago, nearly sixteen hundred members, and between one and two hundred officers; all these within one hour's journey of Manchester.

There has been a general time of pruning; we have cut off upwards of one hundred members from this conference in a few months; this causes the young and tender branches to grow with double vigor.

Thursday, 28.

Copy of a Letter of Attorney from Joseph Smith, "Sole Trustee in Trust for the Church of Jesus Christ of Latter-day Saints," to Reuben McBride, of Kirtland, Ohio.

Know all men by these presents, that I, Joseph Smith, of Nauvoo, Hancock county, and State of Illinois, "sole trustee in trust for the Church of Jesus Christ of Latter-day Saints," have made, constituted and appointed, and by these presents do make, constitute, and appoint, Reuben McBride, of Kirtland, Lake county, and state of Ohio, my true and lawful attorney for me and in my name, and for my use as "sole trustee in trust for the Church of Jesus Christ of Latter-day Saints," to ask, demand, sue for, recover, and receive all such sum or sums of money, debts, goods, wares, and other demands which are or shall be due, owing, payable, or belonging to me, as trustee in trust as aforesaid, by any manner or means whatsoever; also, to dispose of in my name, to grant, bargain, sell, release, and confirm all or any part of my real estate as trustee in trust as aforesaid, in and about Kirtland, Lake county, and state of Ohio, and throughout any of the northern and eastern states, and to receive all such sum or sums of money accruing therefrom, for me and for my use as sole trustee in trust for the Church of Jesus Christ of Latter-day Saints, and to take up the power of attorney which I gave to Oliver Granger, and all the papers and obligations of every description specified therein, or in his possession by virtue thereof, and to settle the same in my name, for me and for my use as above described; and I, as trustee in trust as aforesaid, hereby give and grant unto the said Reuben McBride, my attorney, full power and authority in and about the premises, to have, use, and take all lawful ways and means in my name for the purposes aforesaid, and upon the receipt of any such debts, dues, or sums of money (as the case may be), acquittances, or other sufficient discharges, for me and in my name as aforesaid Trustee, to make and give, and generally to do all other acts and things in the law whatsoever needful and necessary to be done, in the before mentioned places, for me and in my name as aforesaid Trustee, to do, execute, and perform, as fully and to all intents and purposes, as I might or could do, if personally present. Hereby ratifying all and whatsoever my said attorney shall, in the place above specified, by virtue hereof.

In witness whereof I have hereunto set my hand and seal this 28th day of October, 1841.

JOSEPH SMITH, (L.S.)

Witness: John Taylor, John S. Fullmer.

Friday, 29.—Those of the Twelve Apostles who were in Nauvoo, met in council.

Saturday, 30.—I attended the city council, and spoke against the council remitting a fine assessed against John Eagle by a jury of twelve men, considering that the jury might be as sensible men as any of the city council, and I asked the council not to remit the fine.

Lyman Wight, Willard Richards, and Wilford Woodruff were elected councilors, and Hiram Kimball and George W. Harris, Aldermen.

In obedience to an order from the mayor, I called out two companies of the Nauvoo Legion, and removed a grog shop kept by Pulaski S. Cahoon, which had been declared a nuisance by the city council.

Sunday, 31.—I was in council with the brethren at brother Hyrum's office.

Attended a council with the Twelve Apostles. Benjamin Winchester being present, complained that he had been neglected and misrepresented by the Elders, and manifested a contentious spirit. I gave him a severe reproof, telling him of his folly and vanity, and showing him that the principles which he suffered to control him would lead him to destruction. I counseled him to change his course, govern his disposition, and quit his tale-bearing and slandering his brethren.

I instructed the council on many principles pertaining to the gathering of the nations, the wickedness and downfall of this generation, &c.

After having received the following minutes—"A conference was held at Kirtland, Ohio, Oct. 2, 1841. Almon W. Babbitt, president, and William W. Phelps, clerk. Resolved, that Thomas Burdick, Bishop of Kirtland, and his counselors, be constituted a company to establish a press in Kirtland, and publish a religious paper, entitled *The Olive Leaf*, and that the Saints adjacent be solicited to carry the above resolution into effect"—my brother Hyrum wrote to the brethren in Kirtland, of which the following is an extract—

Excerpt of Hyrum Smith's Letter to the Saints in Kirtland—Disapproving of Certain Plans for Building up Kirtland.

All the Saints that dwell in that land are commanded to come away, for this is "Thus saith the Lord;" therefore pay out no moneys, nor properties for houses, nor lands in that country, for if you do you will lose them, for the time shall come, that you shall not possess them in peace, but shall be scourged with a sore scourge; yet your children may possess them, but not until many years shall pass away; and as to the organization of that branch of the Church, it is not according to the Spirit and will of God; and as to the designs of the leading members of that branch relative to the printing press, and the ordaining of Elders, and sending out Elders to beg for the poor, are not according to the will of God; and in these things they shall not prosper, for they have neglected the House of the Lord, the baptismal font, in this place, wherein their dead may be redeemed, and the key of knowledge that unfolds the dispensation of the fullness of times may be turned, and the mysteries of God be unfolded, upon which their salvation, and the salvation of the world, and the redemption of their dead depends; for "thus saith the Lord," there shall not be a general assembly for a general conference assembled together until the House of the Lord and the baptismal font shall be finished; and if we are not diligent the Church shall be rejected, and their dead also, saith the Lord." Therefore, dear brethren, any proceedings of the Saints otherwise than to put forth their hands with their might to do this work, is not according to the will of God, and shall not prosper; therefore, tarry not in any place whatever, but come forth unto this place from all the world, until it is filled up, and polished, and sanctified according to my word, saith the Lord. Come ye forth from the ends of the earth, that I may hide you from mine indignation that shall scourge the wicked, and then I will send forth and build up Kirtland, and it shall be polished and refined according to my word; therefore your doings and your organizations and designs in printing, or any of your councils, are not of me, saith the Lord, even so. Amen.

HYRUM SMITH,
Patriarch for the whole Church.

Monday, November 1.—I attended the city council, spoke and acted on many local matters, and contended at great length against paying the owner of a city nuisance, damages sustained by the removal of that nuisance.*

* The circumstance of removing the nuisance here referred to, for which damages were demanded, is related in an editorial note in the *Times and Seasons* as follows: The "Mr. Kilbourn," referred to in the editorial, was a very bitter anti-Mormon, and became one of the Prophet's most deadly enemies.

THE NUISANCE.

"It is known to many of our patrons, that a certain young man very injudiciously, and contrary to the remonstrances of his friends, and in violation of the ordinances of this city, not long since erected a small building, near the Temple square avowedly for the purpose of transacting the business of a grocer. Said building was for a short time occupied for that purpose; but so heavy did the frown of public disapprobation rest upon it, that it was finally vacated, and stood some time, a lonely wreck of folly. In the meantime, the very sanctimonious and extremely unfortunate Mr. Kilbourn of Montrose, throw out to the public, ungentlemanly and slanderous imputations concerning the matter, saying that the Presidency of the Church abetted and approbated the concern, etc., and the building having become a monument for every fool to write upon and exhibit his folly, to the annoyance of the citizens, the city council very judiciously ordered the building removed as a nuisance. Some opposition to the execution of this order was exhibited, and the authorities called out a few of the military and demolished the building. The city authorities manifest a determination to carry out strictly the temper-

Sidney Rigdon resigned his seat in the city council, on account of ill health.

Tuesday, 2.—I executed letters today revoking the power of attorney given to Almon W. Babbitt.

Saturday, 6.—Wilford Woodruff took the oath as a councilor in the city council.

Sunday, 7.—Elder William O. Clark preached about two hours, reproving the Saints for a lack of sanctity, and a want of holy living, enjoining sanctity, solemnity, and temperance in the extreme, in the rigid sectarian style.

I reproved him as Pharisaical and hypocritical and not edifying the people; and showed the Saints what temperance, faith, virtue, charity, and truth were. I charged the Saints not to follow the example of the adversary in accusing the brethren, and said, "If you do not accuse each other, God will not accuse you. If you have no accuser you will enter heaven, and if you will follow the revelations and instructions which God gives you through me, I will take you into heaven as my back load. If you will not accuse me, I will not accuse you. If you will throw a cloak of charity over my sins, I will over yours—for charity covereth a multitude of sins. What many people call sin is not sin; I do many things to break down superstition, and I will break it down;" I referred to the curse of Ham for laughing at Noah, while in his wine, but doing no harm. Noah was a righteous man, and yet he drank wine and became intoxicated; the Lord did not forsake him in consequence thereof, for he retained all the power of his priesthood, and when he was accused by Canaan, he cursed him by the priesthood which he held, and the Lord had respect

Reproof of William O. Clark.

ance ordinances of the city, and in this we wish them 'God speed.' We suppose, however, that Kilbourn and his junto will bray worse than ever, and 'Mormonism' be adjudged by 'witch law.' 'Take the accused, bind him head and foot, and cast him into the pool; if he sinks and drowns he is innocent, if he floats take him out and hang him or burn him with fire.' We say, let the poor fools judge till they themselves are overtaken by judgment, and let them bray till they burst their wind chests." (*Times and Seasons*, Vol. III, pp. 559-560).

to his word, and the priesthood which he held, notwithstanding he was drunk, and the curse remains upon the
posterity of Canaan until the present day.

In the p. m., I attended a council of the Elders at my
council room, relative to some affairs in which my brother
William was interested.

Monday, 8.—At five o'clock p. m., I attended the
dedication of the baptismal font in the Lord's
House. President Brigham Young was
spokesman.

Dedication of
the Baptismal
Font.

The baptismal font is situated in the center of the basement room, under the main hall of the Temple; it is constructed of pine timber, and put together of staves tongued
and grooved, oval shaped, sixteen feet long east and
west, and twelve feet wide, seven feet high from the foundation, the basin four feet deep, the moulding of the cap
and base are formed of beautiful carved work in antique
style. The sides are finished with panel work. A flight
of stairs in the north and south sides lead up and down
into the basin, guarded by side railing.

The font stands upon twelve oxen, four on each side,
and two at each end, their heads, shoulders, and fore
legs projecting out from under the font; they are carved
out of pine plank, glued together, and copied after the
most beautiful five-year-old steer that could be found in
the country, and they are an excellent striking likeness of
the original; the horns were formed after the most perfect horn that could be procured.

The oxen and ornamental mouldings of the font were
carved by Elder Elijah Fordham, from the city of New
York, which occupied eight months of time. The font
was enclosed by a temporary frame building sided up with
split oak clapboards, with a roof of the same material,
and was so low that the timbers of the first story were
laid above it. The water was supplied from a well thirty
feet deep in the east end of the basement.

This font was built for the baptisms for the dead until

the Temple shall be finished, when a more durable one will supply its place.

I received a letter from N. K. Whitney, stating that he had purchased $5,000 worth of goods for me; and that he should visit Kirtland before his return home.

Up to this period a series of storms and earthquakes have desolated parts of the two Sicilies.

A second English edition of the Saints' hymn book has been issued by Elder Parley P. Pratt.

A great part of Vicksburg, Mississippi, has been consumed by fire.

Saturday, 13.—I attended the city council, and moved that the mayor and recorder of the city receive each one hundred dollars per annum for their services, which became a law.

I also presented a bill for "An ordinance concerning vagrants and disorderly persons," which passed into an ordinance as follows—

An Ordinance Concerning Vagrants and Disorderly Persons.

Be it ordained by the city council of the city of Nauvoo, that all vagrants, idle, or disorderly persons; persons found drunk in or about the streets; all suspicious persons; persons who have no fixed place of residence, or visible means of support, or cannot give a good account of themselves; persons guilty of profane and indecent language or behavior; persons guilty of using indecent, impertinent, or unbecoming language towards any city officer when in the discharge of his duty, or of menacing, threatening or otherwise obstructing said officer, shall on conviction thereof before the mayor or municipal court, be required to enter into security for good behavior for a reasonable time, and indemnify the corporation against any charge, and in case of refusal or inability to give security, they shall be confined to labor for a time not exceeding ninety days, or be fined in any sum not exceeding five hundred dollars, or be imprisoned not exceeding six months or all, [i.e. or both imprisonment and fine] at the discretion of said mayor or court.

I also presented a bill for "An ordinance in relation to appeals," which passed unanimously.

I also argued before the council the right of taxation, but

that the expense of the city did not require it at present.

Sunday, 14.—I preached to a large congregation at the Temple.

Nine of the Twelve Apostles met in council, to prepare an epistle to the Saints in Europe.

Monday, 15.

An Epistle of the Twelve Apostles to the Saints Scattered Abroad in England, Scotland, Ireland, Wales, the Isle of Man, and the Eastern Continent, Greeting:

BELOVED BRETHREN:—We rejoice and thank our Heavenly Father daily in your behalf, that we hear of your faithfulness and diligence in the great work unto which you have been called, by the Holy Spirit, through the voice of the servants of the Most High, who have been, and are now amongst you, for the purpose of instructing you in those principles which are calculated to prepare the children of men for the renovation of the earth, and the restitution of all things spoken by the Prophets.

Several months have passed away, since we bid adieu to our brethren and sisters on the islands of the sea, and passed over the great deep to our homes, our kindred, the bosom of the Church, and the stakes of Zion: but neither time nor distance can efface from our memories the many expressions of kindness which we have heard from your lips and experienced from your hands, which have so often ministered to our necessities, while we were wandering in your midst, like our Master, having no place to lay our heads, only as furnished by your liberality and benevolence; and it is a subject of no small consolation to us that we have this testimony of so many of you, that you are the disciples of the Lord Jesus;* and we give you our warmest thanks, and our blessing, that you have not only ministered unto us, but that you continue to minister to our brethren who are still laboring amongst you, for which an hundred fold shall be returned unto your bosoms.

After parting with the Saints in Liverpool, and sailing thirty days, much of the time against head winds, with rough seas, which produced much sea sickness among the brethren and sisters who accompanied us, we arrived in the city of New York, where we were received by the brethren with open hearts, and by whom we were entertained most cordially some days, till we were rested from the fatigues of the ship: we were then assisted on our journey, and taking different routes, and

---

* "Whoso receiveth you receiveth me, and the same will clothe you and give you money. And he who feeds you, or clothes you or gives you money, shall in no wise lose his reward: And he who doeth not these things is not my disciple; by this you may know my disciples." (Doc. & Cov., sec. lxxxiv.)

visiting many of the churches in different states, we have all safely arrived in this city.

In our travels in this land, we have discovered a growing interest among the people generally, in the great work of the Lord. Prejudice is giving way to intelligence; darkness to light; and multitudes are making the important discovery that error is abroad in the earth, and that the signs of the times proclaim some mighty revolution among the nations. The cry is from all quarters, send us Elders to instruct us in the principles of your religion, that we may know why it is that you are had in derision by the multitude, more than other professors are. Teach us of your principles and your doctrines, and if we find them true we will embrace them.

The Saints are growing in faith, and the intelligence of heaven is flowing into their understanding, for the Spirit of the Lord is with them, and the Holy Ghost is instructing them in things to come. The spirit of union is increasing, and they are exerting themselves to come up to the gathering of the faithful, to build up the waste places and establish the stakes of Zion.

Since our arrival in this place there has been one special and one general conference of the Church, and the Twelve have been called to tarry at home for a season, and stand in their lot next to the First Presidency, and assist in counseling the brethren, and in the settling of immigrants, &c.; and the first great object before us, and the Saints generally, is to help forward the completion of the Temple and the Nauvoo House— buildings which are now in progress according to the revelations, and which must be completed to secure the salvation of the Church in the last days; for God requires of His Saints to build Him a house wherein His servants may be instructed, and endowed with power from on high, to prepare them to go forth among the nations, and proclaim the fullness of the Gospel for the last time, and bind up the law, and seal up the testimony, leaving this generation without excuse, and the earth prepared for the judgments which will follow. In this house all the ordinances will be made manifest, and many things will be shown forth, which have been hid from generation to generation.

The set time to favor the stakes of Zion is at hand, and soon the kings and the queens, the princes and the nobles, the rich and the honorable of the earth will come up hither to visit the Temple of our God, and to inquire concerning His strange work; and as kings are to become nursing fathers, and queens nursing mothers in the habitations of the righteous, it is right to render honor to whom honor is due; and therefore expedient that such, as well as the Saints, should have a comfortable house for boarding and lodging when they come hither, and it is according to the revelations that such a house should be built.

The foundations of this house, and also of the Temple, are laid; and the walls of the basement stories of each nearly completed; and the finishing of the whole is depending on the exertions of the Saints. Every Saint on earth is equally interested in these things, and all are under equal obligations to do all in their power to complete the buildings by their faith, and by their prayers, with their thousands and their mites, their gold and their silver, their copper and their zinc, their goods and their labors, until the top stone is laid with shoutings, and the place is prepared to be filled with the glory of the Highest; and if there are those among you who have more than they need for the gathering, and for assisting the destitute who desire to gather with them, they cannot make a more acceptable offering unto the Lord, than by appropriating towards the building of His Temple.

He that believeth shall not make haste, but let all the Saints who desire to keep the commandments of heaven and work righteousness, come to the place of gathering as soon as circumstances will permit. It is by united efforts that great things are accomplished, and while the Saints are scattered to the four winds, they cannot be united in action, if they are in spirit; they cannot all build at one city, or lift at one stone of the great Temple, though their hearts may all desire the same thing. We would not press the subject of the gathering upon you, for we know your hearts, and your means; and so far as means fail, let patience have its perfect work in your souls, for in due time you shall be delivered, if you faint not.

We are not altogether ignorant of the increase of difficulty among the laboring classes in England since our departure through the stoppage of factories and similar occurrences, and we would counsel those who have, to impart unto those who have not, and cannot obtain; remembering that he who giveth unto the poor lendeth unto the Lord, and he shall receive in return four fold.

The idler shall not eat the bread of the laborer; neither must he starve who would [labor] but cannot find employment. Inasmuch as ye desire the fullness of the earth, let not the cries of the widow, the fatherless and the beggar ascend to heaven, or salute your ears in vain, but follow the example we have set before you, and give liberally of your abundance, even if it be but a penny, and it shall be returned unto you. Good measure pressed down and running over, shall the Lord return into your store house.

Cultivate the spirit of patience, long-suffering, forbearance and charity among yourselves, and ever be as unwilling to believe an evil report about a brother or a sister as if it were about yourself, and as you dislike to be accused, be slow to accuse the brethren, for the measure you mete shall be measured to you again, and the Judge condemneth no man who is not accused.

Keep all the commandments, nothing fearing, nothing doubting, for this is virtue, this is wisdom, and the wise, the virtuous and the meek shall inherit the earth and the fullness thereof. In all things follow the counsel which you shall receive from the president and council who are among you; and inasmuch as you uphold Elders Pratt, Richards and Snow by the prayer of faith, you shall receive right counsel.

Remember that those whom John saw on Mount Zion were such as had come up through great tribulation; and do not imagine that you can ever constitute a part of that number without sharing a part of their trials.   You must necessarily pass through perils and trials, and temptations and afflictions by sea and land in your journeyings hither, and if you cannot settle it in your hearts to endure unto the end as good soldiers, you may as well remain where you are to be destroyed, as to suffer all the privations and hardships you will be obliged to suffer before the walls of Zion shall be built, no more to be thrown down, and after all to turn away and be destroyed.

The ancient prophet has said, they shall wear out the Saints of the Most High. This has already been fulfilled to some extent, for many through the abundance of their persecutions have become exhausted, and laid their bodies down to rest, to rise no more till the morn of the first resurrection; and although the people of these states are at peace with us, yet there are those who would gladly wear out and destroy the weak in faith, through the influence of their foolish lies. When you arrive on our shores, and while sailing up our rivers, you need not be surprised if your ears are saluted by the false and filthy language of wicked and designing men who are ever ready to speak evil of the things they understand not, and who would gladly blast the character of the Prophet of the Most High God, and all connected with him, with their foul anathemas, beyond anything you ever thought of. We would not dishearten you, neither would we have you ignorant of the worst that awaits the righteous.

If the Saints are not prepared to rejoice and be glad when they hear the name of the Prophet and their own name cast out as evil, as gluttonous, wine-bibber, friend of publicans and sinners, Beelzebub, thief, robber and murderer, they are not prepared for the gathering.   The wheat and tares must grow together till the harvest; at the harvest the wheat is gathered together into the threshing floor, so with the Saints—the stakes are the threshing floor. Here they will be threshed with all sorts of difficulties, trials, afflictions and everything to mar their peace, which they can imagine, and thousands which they cannot imagine; but he that endures the threshing till all the chaff, superstition, folly and unbelief are pounded out of him, and does not suffer himself to be blown away as chaff by the foul blast of slander, but endures faithfully to the end, shall be saved. If you are prepared for all these things; if you choose rather to suffer afflictions with the people of God, than to enjoy the pleasures of sin for a little moment, come up hither; come direct to New Orleans, and up the Mississippi river, for the expense is so much less, and the convenience of water navigation is so much greater than it is by Montreal, New York or Philadelphia, that it is wisdom for the Saints to make New Orleans their general established port, and be sure to start at such times that they may arrive here during the cold months, for the change from the cold climate of England to this place in the hot season, is too great for the health of immigrants, till there is more faith in the Church.

In this region of country there are thousands and millions of acres of beautiful prairie unoccupied, which can be procured on reasonable terms, and we will hail the time with joy when these unoccupied lands shall be turned into fruitful fields, and the hands of those who are now idle for want of employment shall be engaged in the cultivation of the soil.

When the brethren arrive they will do well to call on some of the Twelve, inasmuch as they desire counsel, for by so doing they may escape the influence of designing men who have crept in unawares, and would willingly subvert the truth by conniving to their own advantage, if they have the opportunity.

The Church has commenced a new city twenty miles below this, and one mile below Warsaw, called Warren, where many city lots and farms in the vicinity can be had on reasonable terms; and it will be wisdom for many of the brethren to stop at that place, for the opportunity for erecting temporary buildings will be greater than at this place, also the chance for providing food will be superior to those who wish to labor for it.

Warsaw is at the foot of the Des Moines Rapids, and one of the best locations for mercantile purposes there is in this western country.

So far as the brethren have the means they will do well to come prepared with a variety of mechanical tools according to their professions, such as carpenters, joiners, cabinet-makers, hatters, coopers, masons, printers, binders, tanners, curriers, &c., and all sorts of manufactory and foundry implements convenient for transportation, so that when they arrive they may be prepared to establish themselves in business, and give employment to spinners, weavers, moulders, smelters and journeymen of every description; for all sorts of woollens, cottons, hardware, &c., will find a ready market in new countries, and a great field is now open to the capitalists in this vicinity, even though the capital be small, and we would urge the importance of the immediate establishment of all kinds of manufactories among us, as well for the best interests of the individuals concerned, as for the Church generally.

Cities cannot be built without houses, houses cannot be built without materials, or occupied without inhabitants, the inhabitants cannot exist without food and clothing; food and clothing cannot be had without planting, sowing, and manufacturing, so that Zion and her stores cannot be built without means, without industry, without manufacturing establishments unless the windows of heaven were opened, and cities and their appendages were rained down among us. But this we do not expect until the new Jerusalem descends, and that will be some time hence; therefore it is necessary and according to godliness and the plan of salvation in these last days, that the brethren should see to all these things, and clothe and adorn themselves with the labor of their own hands, build houses and inhabit them, plant vineyards and eat the fruit thereof.

Brethren, pray for us and the First Presidency, the leader of the people, even Joseph, that his life and health may be precious in the sight of heaven, till he has finished the work which he has commenced: and for the Elders of Israel, that every man may be faithful in his calling, the whole household of faith, and all subjects of prayer.

Brethren, farewell; may the blessings of heaven and earth be multiplied unto you in spirit and in body, in basket and in store, in the field and in the shop, on the land and on the sea, in the house and by the way, and in all situations and circumstances, until you shall stand on Mount Zion, and enter the celestial city; in the name of Jesus Christ. Amen.

> BRIGHAM YOUNG,
> HEBER C. KIMBALL.
> ORSON PRATT,
> WILLIAM SMITH,
> LYMAN WIGHT,
> WILFORD WOODRUFF,
> JOHN TAYLOR,
> GEO. A. SMITH.
> WILLARD RICHARDS,

Nauvoo, Hancock County, Illinois, Nov. 15, 1841.

The greater part of the city of St. John's, New Brunswick, and a large quantity of shipping, destroyed by fire.

Wednesday, 17.—Elders Brigham Young and Willard Richards went to La Harpe.

Thursday, 18.

Minutes of a Meeting at Ramus, Illinois—Alanson Brown, et al. Disfellowshiped.

Proceedings of a meeting of the Church of Jesus Christ of Latter-day

Saints, held at Ramus, November 18, 1841, opened by singing and prayer by Elder Brigham Young. The object of the meeting was then stated by the president, which was for the purpose of taking into consideration the cases of Alanson Brown, James B. T. Page and William H. Edwards, who stand indicted for larceny, &c.

After the evidence was brought forward, it was unanimously resolved, that said persons be expelled from the Church. Appropriate remarks for the occasion were then made by Elders Young, Richards, Savage, Gurley, and others.

A charge was then preferred against Thomas S. Edwards for assault and battery, with evidence that a warrant was issued for his apprehension, and against William W. Edwards for being accessory to the same. Unanimously resolved, that Thomas S. Edwards also be expelled from the Church; and that the proceedings of this meeting be published in the *Times and Seasons.*

JOEL H. JOHNSON, President.
JOSEPH E. JOHNSON, Church Recorder.

Saturday, 20.—Seven of the Twelve Apostles met in council at the house of President Young, on the subject of the *Times and Seasons;* they not being satisfied with the manner in which Gustavus Hills had conducted the editorial department since the death of Robert B. Thompson.

Sunday, 21.—My brother Hyrum and Elder John Taylor preached.

The Twelve met in council at President Young's, and at four o'clock, repaired to the baptismal font in the basement of the Temple. Elders Brigham Young,
Baptisms for the Dead. Heber C. Kimball and John Taylor baptized about forty persons for the dead. Elder Willard Richards, Wilford Woodruff and George A. Smith confirming. These were the first baptisms for the dead in the font.

Monday, 22.—The following letter from Elder Orson Hyde, is from the *Millennial Star:*

Elder Orson Hyde's Letter—His Prayer of Dedication on the Mount of Olives.

ALEXANDRIA, Nov. 22, 1841.

DEAR BROTHER PRATT:—A few minutes now offer for me to write, and I improve them in writing to you.

I have only time to say that I have seen Jerusalem precisely according to the vision which I had. I saw no one with me in the vision; and although Elder Page was appointed to accompany me there, yet I found myself there alone.

The Lord knows that I have had a hard time, and suffered much, but I have great reason to thank Him that I enjoy good health at present, and have a prospect before me of soon going to a civilized country, where I shall see no more turbans or camels. The heat is most oppressive, and has been all through Syria.

I have not time to tell you how many days I have been at sea, without food, or how many snails I have eaten; but if I had had plenty of them, I should have done very well. All this is contained in a former letter to you written from Jaffa.

I have been at Cairo, on the Nile, because I could not get a passage direct. Syria is in a dreadful state—a war of extermination is going on between the Druses and Catholics. At the time I was at Beyroot, a battle was fought in the mountains of Lebanon, near that place, and about 800 killed. Robberies, thefts and murders are daily being committed. It is no uncommon thing to find persons in the streets without heads. An English officer, in going from St. Jean D'Acre to Beyroot, found ten persons murdered in the street, and was himself taken prisoner, but was rescued by the timely interference of the pasha. The particulars of all these things are contained in a former letter.

An American traveler, by the name of Gager, who was a licensed minister of the Congregational or Presbyterian church, left Jerusalem in company with me. He was very unwell with the jaundice when we left, and at Damietta, we had to perform six days quarantine before we ascended the Nile. On our passage up, he was taken very ill with a fever, and became helpless. I waited and tended upon him as well as our circumstances would allow; and when we landed at Bulack, I got four men to take him to the American consuls at Cairo, on a litter; I also took all his baggage there, and assisted in putting him upon a good bed—employed a good faithful Arabian nurse, and the English doctor. After the physician had examined him, he told me that he was very low with a typhus fever, and that it would be doubtful whether he recovered. Under these circumstances I left him to obtain a passage to this place. After I had gone on board a boat, and was just about pushing off, a letter came from the doctor, stating that poor Mr. Gager died in about two hours after I left him. He told me before we arrived at Cairo that he was twenty-seven years of age, and his friends lived in Norwich, Connecticut, near New London, I think. There are many particulars concerning his death, which would be interesting to his friends, but I have no time to write them now.

On Sunday morning, October 24, a good while before day, I arose from sleep, and went out of the city as soon as the gates were opened, crossed the brook Kedron, and went upon the Mount of Olives, and there, in solemn silence, with pen, ink, and paper, just as I saw in the vision, offered up the following prayer to Him who lives forever and ever—

Prayer of Orson Hyde on the Mount of Olives.

"O Thou! who art from everlasting to everlasting, eternally and unchangeably the same, even the God who rules in the heavens above, and controls the destinies of men on the earth, wilt Thou not condescend, through thine infinite goodness and royal favor, to listen to the prayer of Thy servant which he this day offers up unto Thee in the name of Thy holy child Jesus, upon this land, where the Sun of Righteousness set in blood, and thine Anointed One expired.

"Be pleased, O Lord, to forgive all the follies, weaknesses, vanities, and sins of Thy servant, and strengthen him to resist all future temptations. Give him prudence and discernment that he may avoid the evil, and a heart to choose the good; give him fortitude to bear up under trying and adverse circumstances, and grace to endure all things for Thy name's sake, until the end shall come, when all the Saints shall rest in peace.

"Now, O Lord! Thy servant has been obedient to the heavenly vision which Thou gavest him in his native land; and under the shadow of Thine outstretched arm, he has safely arrived in this place to dedicate and consecrate this land unto Thee, for the gathering together of Judah's scattered remnants, according to the predictions of the holy Prophets —for the building up of Jerusalem again after it has been trodden down by the Gentiles so long, and for rearing a Temple in honor of Thy name. Everlasting thanks be ascribed unto Thee, O Father, Lord of heaven and earth, that Thou hast preserved Thy servant from the dangers of the seas, and from the plague and pestilence which have caused the land to mourn. The violence of man has also been restrained, and Thy providential care by night and by day has been exercised over Thine unworthy servant. Accept, therefore, O Lord, the tribute of a grateful heart for all past favors, and be pleased to continue Thy kindness and mercy towards a needy worm of the dust.

"O Thou, Who didst covenant with Abraham, Thy friend, and Who didst renew that covenant with Isaac, and confirm the same with Jacob with an oath, that Thou wouldst not only give them this land for an everlasting inheritance, but that Thou wouldst also remember their seed forever. Abraham, Isaac, and Jacob have long since closed their eyes in death, and made the grave their mansion.   Their children are scattered and dispersed abroad among the nations of the Gentiles like sheep that have no shepherd, and are still looking forward for the fulfillment of those promises which Thou didst make concerning them; and even this land, which once poured forth nature's richest bounty, and flowed, as it were, with milk and honey, has, to a certain extent, been smitten with barrenness and sterility since it drank from murderous hands the blood of Him who never sinned.

"Grant, therefore, O Lord, in the name of Thy well-beloved Son, Jesus Christ, to remove the barrenness and sterility of this land, and let springs of living water break forth to water its thirsty soil.   Let the vine and olive produce in their strength, and the fig-tree bloom and flourish.   Let the land become abundantly fruitful when possessed by its rightful heirs; let it again flow with plenty to feed the returning prodigals who come home with a spirit of grace and supplication; upon it let the clouds distil virtue and richness, and let the fields smile with plenty.   Let the flocks and the herds greatly increase and multiply upon the mountains and the hills; and let Thy great kindness conquer and subdue the unbelief of Thy people. Do Thou take from them their stony heart, and give them a heart of flesh; and may the Sun of Thy favor dispel the cold mists of darkness which have beclouded their atmosphere. Incline them to gather in upon this land according to Thy word.   Let them come like clouds and like doves to their windows.   Let the large ships of the nations bring them from the distant isles; and let kings become their nursing fathers, and queens with motherly fondness wipe the tear of sorrow from their eye.

"Thou, O Lord, did once move upon the heart of Cyrus to show favor unto Jerusalem and her children.   Do Thou now also be pleased to inspire the hearts of kings and the powers of the earth to look with a friendly eye towards this place, and with a desire to see Thy righteous purposes executed in relation thereto.   Let them know that it is Thy good pleasure to restore the kingdom unto Israel—raise up Jerusalem as its capital, and constitute her people a distinct nation and government, with David Thy servant, even a descendant from the loins of ancient David to be their king.

"Let that nation or that people who shall take an active part in behalf of Abraham's children, and in the raising up of Jerusalem, find favor in Thy sight. Let not their enemies prevail against them, neither let pestilence or famine overcome them, but let the glory of Israel overshadow them, and the power of the Highest protect them; while that nation or kingdom that will not serve Thee in this glorious work must perish, according to Thy word—'Yea, those nations shall be utterly wasted.'

"Though Thy servant is now far from his home, and from the land bedewed with his earliest tear, yet he remembers, O Lord, his friends who are there, and family, whom for Thy sake he has left. Though poverty and privation be our earthly lot, yet ah! do Thou richly endow us with an inheritance where moth and rust do not corrupt, and where thieves do not break through and steal.

"The hands that have fed, clothed, or shown favor unto the family of Thy servant in his absence, or that shall hereafter do so, let them not lose their reward, but let a special blessing rest upon them, and in Thy kingdom let them have an inheritance when Thou shalt come to be glorified in this society.

"Do Thou also look with favor upon all those through whose liberality I have been enabled to come to this land; and in the day when Thou shalt reward all people according to their works, let these also not be passed by or forgotten, but in time let them be in readiness to enjoy the glory of those mansions which Jesus has gone to prepare. Particularly do Thou bless the stranger in Philadelphia, whom I never saw, but who sent me gold, with a request that I should pray for him in Jerusalem. Now, O Lord, let blessings come upon him from an unexpected quarter, and let his basket be filled, and his storehouse abound with plenty, and let not the good things of the earth be his only portion, but let him be found among those to whom it shall be said, 'Thou hast been faithful over a few things, and I will make thee ruler over many.'

"O my Father in heaven! I now ask Thee in the name of Jesus to remember Zion, with all her Stakes, and with all her assemblies. She has been grievously afflicted and smitten; she has mourned; she has wept; her enemies have triumphed, and have said, 'Ah, where is thy God?' Her Priests and Prophets have groaned in chains and fetters within the gloomy walls of prisons, while many were slain, and now sleep in the arms of death. How long, O Lord, shall iniquity triumph, and sin go unpunished?

"Do Thou arise in the majesty of Thy strength, and make bare Thine arm in behalf of Thy people. Redress their wrongs, and turn their sorrow into joy. Pour the spirit of light and knowledge, grace and wisdom, into the hearts of her Prophets, and clothe her Priests with salvation. Let light and knowledge march forth through the empire of darkness, and may the honest in heart flow to their standard, and join in the march to go forth to meet the Bridegroom.

"Let a peculiar blessing rest upon the Presidency of Thy Church, for at them are the arrows of the enemy directed. Be Thou to them a sun and a shield, their strong tower and hiding place; and in the time of distress or danger be Thou near to deliver. Also the quorum of the Twelve, do Thou be pleased to stand by them for Thou knowest the obstacles which they have to encounter, the temptations to which they are exposed, and the privations which they must suffer. Give us, [the Twelve] therefore, strength according to our day, and help us to bear a faithful testimony of Jesus and His Gospel, to finish with fidelity and honor the work which Thou hast given us to do, and then give us a place in Thy glorious kingdom. And let this blessing rest upon every faithful officer and member in Thy Church. And all the glory and honor will we ascribe unto God and the Lamb forever and ever. Amen."

On the top of Mount Olives I erected a pile of stones as a witness according to ancient custom. On what was anciently called Mount Zion, [Moriah?] where the Temple stood, I erected another, and used the rod according to the prediction upon my head.

I have found many Jews who listened with intense interest. The idea of the Jews being restored to Palestine is gaining ground in Europe almost every day. Jerusalem is strongly fortified with many cannon upon its walls. The wall is ten feet thick on the sides that would be most exposed, and four or five feet where the descent from the wall is almost perpendicular. The number of inhabitants within the walls is about twenty thousand. About seven thousand of this number are Jews, the balance being mostly Turks and Armenians. Many of the Jews who are old go to this place to die, and many are coming from Europe into this eastern world. The great wheel is unquestionably in motion, and the word of the Almighty has declared that it shall roll.

I have not time to write particulars now, but suffice it to say that my mission has been quite as prosperous as I could expect.

I am now about to go on board a fine ship for Trieste, and from thence I intend to proceed to Regensburg and there publish our faith in the German language. There are those who are ready and willing to assist me.

I send you this letter by Captain Withers, an English gentleman, who goes direct to England, on board the Oriental steamer. He has come with me from Jerusalem. If I had money sufficient I should be almost tempted to take passage on board of her to England, but this I cannot do.

On receipt of this, I wish you to write to me immediately, and direct to Regensburg, on the Danube, Bayern, or Bavaria. If you know anything of my family tell me.

My best respects to yourself and your family, to Brothers Adams and Snow, and to all the Saints in England.

May grace, mercy and peace, from God our Father, and from the Lord Jesus Christ, rest upon you all from this time, henceforth and for ever. Amen.

                              Your brother in Christ,
                                      ORSON HYDE.

CHAPTER XXVII.

OFFICIAL DENUNCIATION OF THIEVES AT NAUVOO—THE MORAL
   LAW OF THE CHURCH—ABANDONMENT OF RAMUS AS A
   STAKE OF ZION—BAPTISM FOR THE DEAD, AN EPISTLE.

Wednesday, 24.—Elder Joseph Fielding, who sailed from Liverpool, on the *Tyrean*, with 204 Saints, arrived at Warsaw with his company; and Elders Willard Richards and John Taylor went to meet them and to give such counsel as their situation required.

Friday, 26.

Affidavit of Hyrum Smith—Denouncing Theft.

Whereas it hath been intimated to me by persons of credibility that there are persons in the surrounding country, who profess to be members of the Church of Jesus Christ of Latter-day Saints, who have been using their influence and endeavors to instil into the minds of good and worthy citizens in the state of Illinois, and the adjoining states, that the First Presidency, and others in authority and high standing in said Church, do sanction and approbate the members of said Church in stealing property from those persons who do not belong to said Church, and thereby to induce persons to aid and abet them in the act of stealing, and other evil practices; I therefore, hereby disavow any sanction or approbation by me, of the crime of theft, or any other evil practice, in any person or persons whatever, whereby either the lives or property of our fellow men may be unlawfully taken or molested; neither are such things sanctioned or approbated by the First Presidency, or any other person in authority or good standing in said Church, but such acts are altogether in violation of the rules, order, and regulations of the Church, contrary to the teachings given in said Church, and the laws of both God and man. I caution the unwary, who belong to the aforesaid Church, and all other persons, against being duped or led into any act or scheme which may endanger their character, lives, or property, or bring reproach upon the Church; and I certify that I hold my person and property ready to support the laws of the land, in the detection of any person or persons who may commit any breach of the same.   To which I subscribe my name, and testify, this 26th day of November, 1841.

HYRUM SMITH.

Sworn to and subscribed before me this 26th day of November, 1841.
EBENEZER ROBINSON, J.P.

I attended city council and presented a bill for "an Ordinance in relation to Hawkers, Pedlars, Public Shows, and Exhibitions, in order to prevent any immoral or obscene exhibition," which passed the council by unanimous vote.

Sunday, 28.—I spent the day in the council with the Twelve Apostles at the house of President Young, conversing with them upon a variety of subjects.   Brother Joseph Fielding was present, having been absent four years on a mission to England.   I told the brethren that the Book of Mormon was the most correct of any book on earth, and the keystone of our religion, and a man would get nearer to God by abiding by its precepts, than by any other book.

The Prophet's Estimate of the Book of Mormon.

Monday, 29.—I gave the following affidavit, and published it in the *Times and Seasons.*

The Prophet's Denunciation of Thieves.

CITY OF NAUVOO, ILLINOIS, November 29, A.D. 1841.

TO THE PUBLIC.

The occurrence of recent events makes it criminal for me to remain longer silent.   The tongue of the vile yet speaks, and sends forth the poison of asps, the ears of the spoiler yet hear, and he puts forth his hands to iniquity.   It has been proclaimed upon the house top and in the secret chamber, in the public walks and private circle, throughout the length and breadth of this vast continent, that stealing by the Latter-day Saints has received my approval; nay, that I have taught the doctrine, encouraged them in plunder, and led on the van—than which nothing is more foreign from my heart.   I disfellowship the perpetrators of all such abominations—they are devils and not Saints, totally unfit for the society of Christians or men.   It is true that some professing to be Latter-day Saints have taught such vile heresies, but all are not Israel that are of Israel; and I wish it to be distinctly understood in all coming time, that the Church, over which I have the honor of presiding, will ever set its brows like brass, and its face like steel, against all such abominable acts of villainy and crime; and to this end I append my affidavit of disavowal, taken this day before General Bennet, that there may be no mistake hereafter as to my real sentiments, or those of the leaders of the Church, in relation to this important matter.

STATE OF ILLINOIS, HANCOCK COUNTY.

Before me, John C. Bennett, Mayor of the City of Nauvoo, personally came Joseph Smith, President of the Church of Jesus Christ of Latter-day Saints (commonly called the Mormon Church), who being duly sworn according to law, deposeth and saith, that he has never directly or indirectly encouraged the purloining of property, or taught the doctrine of stealing, or any other evil practice, and that all such vile and unlawful acts will ever receive his unreserved and unqualified disapproval, and the most vigorous opposition of the Church over which he presides; and further this deponent saith not.

JOSEPH SMITH,
President of the Church of Jesus Christ
of Latter-day Saints.

Sworn to and subscribed before me, at my office, in the city of Nauvoo, this 29th day of November, A.D. 1841.

JOHN C. BENNETT,
L. S.   Mayor of the City of Nauvoo.

Now it is to be hoped that none will hereafter be so reckless as to state that I, or the Church to which I belong, approve of thieving—but that all the friends of law and order will join in ferreting out thieves wherever and whenever they may be found, and assist in bringing them to that condign punishment which such infamous crimes so richly merit.

JOSEPH SMITH,
President of the Church of Jesus Christ
of Latter-day Saints.

A conference was held in New York City, Elder John E. Page presiding; in which were represented New York City, 17 Elders, 2 Priests, 1 Teacher, 2 Deacons, 179 members. Five branches were rep-

Conference in New York.

resented, including 5 Elders, 6 Priests, 3 Teachers, 3 Deacons, 149 members. 3 Elders, 2 Priests, 1 Teacher, were ordained. There were present at the conference, 1 Apostle, 6 High Priests, 16 Elders, 3 Priests, 2 Teach ers, 2 Deacons.

Tuesday, 30.—Attended a council of the Twelve Apostles at President Brigham Young's home. President Brigham Young, Heber C. Kimball, Willard Richards, Orson Pratt, Lyman Wight, John Taylor, and Wilford Woodruff were present.

It was voted that Ebenezer Robinson be solicited to give up the department of printing the *Times and Seasons* to Elder Willard Richards.

Voted, that if Brother Robinson does not comply with this solicitation, Elder Richards be instructed to pro cure a press and type, and publish a paper for the Church.

Moved by Elder Young, and seconded by Elder Woodruff, that Lyman Wight and John Taylor present these resolutions to Brother Robinson.

Wednesday, December 1.—In view of the proceedings of the meeting of the Church at Ramus, on the 18th November, when certain individuals were cut off from the Church for stealing, the Twelve issued the following epistle:

Warning of the Twelve Apostles Against Thieves.

We are glad that the perpetrators of the above crime have been caught in their iniquitous practices; and we are only sorry that anybody should be found who would bail them out of prison, for such individuals, if the charges are true, ought to be made an example of, and not be suffered to run at large.

We have been informed that some of them have been talking of moving into this place, but we would here inform them that persons whose conduct has exposed them to the just censure of an indignant public, can have no fellowship amongst us, as we cannot, and will not countenance rogues, thieves, and scoundrels knowingly; and, we hereby warn them that the law will be as rigorously enforced against them in this place as in any other, as we consider such characters a curse to society, whose pestilential breath withers the morals, and blasts the fame and reputation of any people among whom they may sojourn. There is no person that is, and ought to be despised more than the thief, by any respectable community; yet more especially ought such persons to be abhorred who have taken upon them the name of Christ, and thus with the pretext of religion, and garb of sanctity, cloak their nefarious practices.

We have been told that some individual or individuals have, under false pretenses, been wishing to palm their wicked and devilish principles upon the authorities of the Church, stating that it was part and parcel of the Gospel which God had revealed, and that it is one of the mysteries which the initiated only are acquainted with. We know not how to express our abhorrence at such an idea, and can only say that it is engendered in hell, founded in falsehood, and is the offspring of the devil; and it is at variance with every principle of righteousness and truth, and will damn all that are connected with it, for all mysteries are only such to the ignorant, and vanish as soon as men have sufficient intelligence to comprehend them; and there are no mysteries connected with godliness and our holy religion, but what are pure, innocent, virtuous, just, and righteous. If this [the foregoing practice of thieving] is a mystery, it is the "mystery of iniquity." We are at a loss to know who could be vile enough to propagate such base and unfounded statements, and we would say to the Church, beware of such men! Set them down as the worst of scoundrels, and reject their foul insinuations with the indignation and disgust that such unhallowed and vile insinuations deserve; for such men are either avowed apostates, or on the eve of apostasy, or have only taken the name of religion to cloak their hypocrisy; we fear the latter, in some instances is the case, and that Mississippi scoundrels* palm themselves upon us to cover their guilt. We fur-

---

* This has reference to the blacklegs that infested the upper Mississippi region, and who plied their trade in disposing of counterfeit money and stolen goods along the river. The character of the old inhabitants in Northern Illinois at this time, (1840-44), Governor Ford describes in his "History of Illinois" as follows: "Then, again, the northern part of the State was not destitute of its organized bands of rogues, engaged in murders, robberies, horse-stealing, and in making and passing counterfeit money. These rogues were scattered all over the north; but the most of them were located in the counties of Ogle, Winnebago, Lee, and De-Kalb. In the county of Ogle, they were so numerous, strong, and well-organized, that they could not be convicted for their crimes. By getting some of their numbers on the juries, by producing hosts of witnesses to sustain their defense by perjured evidence, and by changing the venue from one county to another, and by continuances from term to term, and by the inability of witnesses to attend from time to time at a distant and foreign county, they most generally managed to be acquitted."

ther call upon the Church to bring all such characters before the authorities, that they may be tried, and dealt with according to the law of God, and delivered up unto the laws of the land.

It is scarcely possible that any virtuous man could be made to believe any such statements, however ignorant; yet lest through false pretenses the innocent might be drawn into a snare, we would quote the following from the Book of Doctrine and Covenants, section 42, paragraph 84, 85, "And if any man or woman shall rob, he or she shall be delivered up unto the law of the land. And if he or she shall steal, he or she shall be delivered up unto the law of the land." Again, section 42, paragraph 20,* "Thou shalt not steal, and he that stealeth and will not repent shall be cast out." The broad law of God is, "Thou shalt not steal," and thieves, together with "liars and whoremongers," will eventually be found without the city, with dogs and sorcerers. We need only say that if we find such characters engaged in their nefarious practices, whether in or out of the Church, we shall take them up, and deal with them according to the law of God and man; and we wish the Church to inform us of such delinquents, or the sin will lie at their own door.

As there are gangs of robbers up and down this river, from whom we have suffered much, having had many horses, cattle and other property stolen, we purpose instituting a police for the protection of our property, and the rigorous enforcement of the laws of our country; and should any, who call themselves Latter-day Saints, be found in their midst, they will be cut off from the Church, and handed over to the law of the land.

We hope that what we have written may suffice, and take this opportunity of expressing our decided and unqualified disapprobation of anything like theft in all its bearings, as being calculated to destroy the peace of society, to injure the Church of Jesus Christ, to wound the character of the people of God, and to stamp with eternal infamy all

---

* The above references are published to correspond in current editions of the Doctrine and Covenants. The revelation quoted was given as a law to the Church, February 9, 1831. It was given in the presence of twelve Elders, at Kirtland, in fulfillment of the promise that the Lord made to the Church while yet located in New York, in a revelation commanding them to move from the eastern countries to the Ohio; "And there," said the Lord, "I will give unto you my law, and there you shall be endowed with power from on high." (Doctrine and Covenants, section 38: 32.) As introductory to the revelation the Prophet said under date of February 9: "According to the promise heretofore made, the Lord gave the following revelation embracing the Law of the Church;" and indeed, it is appropriately so called, for it embraces well nigh every moral law of the Gospel, and is a most valuable chapter of divine instructions to the Church.

who follow such diabolical practices; to blast their character on earth, and to consign them to eternal perdition.

> BRIGHAM YOUNG,
> HEBER C. KIMBALL,
> PARLEY P. PRATT,
> ORSON HYDE,
> WILLIAM SMITH,
> ORSON PRATT,
> JOHN E. PAGE,
> WILLARD RICHARDS,
> LYMAN WIGHT,
> WILFORD WOODRUFF,
> JOHN TAYLOR,
> GEORGE A. SMITH.

Nauvoo, Illinois, December 1, 1841.*

*About this time there were gangs of robbers operating up and down the Mississippi River, from which the Saints suffered, as many of their horses and cattle were stolen, but more serious injury arose from the fact that the acts of these robbers were attributed to the Saints themselves, and did much to prejudice the minds of the public against them. Governor Ford in his "History of Illinois," from 1814 to 1847 in referring to these charges against the Saints, and speaking of events taking place about this time in Nauvoo, said: "It was a fact also, that some larcenies and robberies had been committed, and that Mormons had been convicted of the crimes, and that other larcenies had been committed by persons unknown, but suspected to be Mormons. Justice, however, requires me here to say, that upon such investigation as I then could make, the charge of promiscuous stealing appeared to be exaggerated." (History of Illinois, Ford, p. 329.)

The practice of charging these robberies upon members of the Church continued through the next three or four years. Speaking of the time somewhat later than the period with which our annals above deal, the Governor said: "On my late visit to Hancock county, I was informed by some of their violent enemies, that the larcenies of the Mormons had become unusually numerous and insufferable. They indeed admitted that but little had been done in this way in their immediate vicinity. But they insisted that sixteen horses had been stolen by the Mormons in one night, near Lima in the county of Adams. At the close of the expedition, I called at this same town of Lima, and upon inquiry was told that no horses had been stolen in that neighborhood, but that sixteen horses had been stolen in one night in Hancock county. This last informant being told of the Hancock story, again changed the venue to another distant settlement in the northern edge of Adams." (History of Illinois, p. 331.)

And thus sensational reports of "Mormon stealings" were made the shuttle-cock between the battle-doors of various neighborhoods.

In addition to the very emphatic utterances of the Prophet Joseph, his brother Hyrum, and the Twelve, the *Times and Seasons* editorially said:

"THIEVES.

"We are highly pleased to see the very energetic measures taken by our citizens to suppress thieving. It has been a source of grief unto us that there were any in our midst who would wilfully take property from any person which did not belong

Thursday, 2.—I received the following revelation to Nancy Marinda Hyde—

Revelation.

Verily thus saith the Lord unto you my servant Joseph, that inasmuch as you have called upon me to know my will concerning my handmaid Nancy Marinda Hyde—behold it is my will that she should have a better place prepared for her, than that in which she now lives, in order that her life may be spared unto her; therefore go and say unto my servant, Ebenezer Robinson, and to my handmaid his wife—Let them open their doors and take her and her children into their house and take care of them faithfully and kindly until my servant Orson Hyde returns from his mission, or until some other provision can be made for her welfare and safety. Let them do these things and spare not, and I the Lord will bless them and heal them if they do it not grudgingly, saith the Lord God; and she shall be a blessing unto them; and let my handmaid Nancy Marinda Hyde hearken to the counsel of my servant Joseph in all things whatsoever he shall teach unto her, and it shall be a blessing upon her and upon her children after her, unto her justification, saith the Lord.

Saturday, 4.—I attended the city council, and spoke in defense of the marshal, in his not serving a warrant, when his life would have been endangered.

A conference was held at Ramus on the 4th and 5th of December, 1841, over which the Patriarch of the Church, Hyrum Smith, presided; Joseph Johnson acted as clerk; Brigham Young, Heber C. Kimball, Willard Richards and John Taylor, of the

Conference at Ramus.

to them, knowing that if any person, who does, or ever did belong to this Church, should steal, the whole Church would have to bear the stigma, and the sound goes abroad that the Mormons are a set of thieves and robbers, a charge which we unequivocally deny, and pronounce a falsehood of the basest kind. That there are some amongst us base enough to commit such acts we do not pretend to deny, but whether they are all members of this Church or not, we do not know; but some who are have been caught in their iniquity, and one was among the missing after a warrant was out for him; circumstantial proof is so strong against him, that his guilt is established without a doubt. We have heard that some of those characters have said that such things are sanctioned by the authorities of the Church, this is the most base of all lies: and we would here warn all well disposed persons, to be aware of such characters, and if any such thing is ever intimated to them, to heed it not, unless it be to report such persons to the proper authorities so that they can be brought to condign punishment; for know assuredly that if you listen to them, they will prove an adder in your path, and eventually lead you down to destruction."—*Times and Seasons*, p. 615.

quorum of the Twelve Apostles were present. It was unanimously resolved by the conference that the organization of the Church at Ramus as a Stake be discontinued and that John Lawson be presiding Elder over the branch at Ramus, and Joseph Johnson, clerk; and that William Wightman, the Bishop, transfer all the Church property in Ramus to the sole Trustee in Trust, Joseph Smith, President of the whole Church.

Sunday, 5. I commenced to proof read the Book of Mormon, previous to its being stereotyped; read sixty pages.

Prophet Proof
Reads Book of
Mormon.

In the evening Brother Wilford Woodruff and wife visited me. We conversed about the Missouri troubles, and the death of David W. Patten; also his last request.*

Tuesday, 7.—The following is a copy of a letter to Lawyers Bushnell and Browning of Quincy:

Letter of the Prophet to Esquires Browning and Bushnell—Payment of Notes.

Esquires Browning and Bushnell:

GENTLEMEN:—Your letter of the 23rd ultimo, concerning two notes placed in your hands by Messrs. Halsted, Haines and Co., against myself and thirty-one others, for collection, was duly received. In reply, I must inform you, that I am not in possession of means, belonging to me individually to liquidate those notes at present; the reason is apparent to every one; I need not relate to you the persecution I have suffered, and the loss and confiscation of all my effects at various times as a reason of my inability; you know it all, and so do the gentlemen whose notes you hold for collection. But I wish you to say to them that if they will give me my time (and no more than I must necessarily have), they shall have their pay in some way or other. I have the means at command in the East, which, with a sufficient indulgence, will enable me to pay them every whit, but unless this is granted me, it will be impossible for me to do so. All I ask of those gentlemen and this generation is that they should not tie up my hands, nor thwart me in my operations. If this is granted me, I pledge my word, yea, my sacred honor, that all that can in fairness be demanded at my hands, either now or at any time shall ultimately be adjusted to the satisfaction of all concerned. This is all that I can say at this time, or do,

* See Vol. III., p. 171.

hoping that you will communicate to Messrs. Holsted, Haines and Co. the contents, or at all events the purport of this letter, together with my sincere regard for their welfare, and as regards you, gentlemen,

I remain very respectfully,

Your obedient servant,

JOSEPH SMITH.

Wednesday, 8.—The Twelve who attended the Ramus conference on the 4th instant returned with nearly a thousand dollars worth of property, consisting of horses, wagons, provisions, clothing, etc., for the Temple, which had been donated by the Saints at Ramus.

Friday 10.—I wrote to Horace R. Hotchkiss, Esq.

The Prophet's Letter to Mr. Hotchkiss—Commerce Lands.

DEAR SIR:—Your letters, dated October, 11th and November 9th, 1841, have both been received, and that of the 9th of November is now before me. I am glad that you are pleased with the proceedings of our last conference relative to "Mr. Hotchkiss purchase," concerning which there had been some unpleasant feeling which had originated partly from a misunderstanding between us, and partly through the inefficiency, neglect or sickness of Dr. Galland. I wrote a letter to your friend and partner, Esquire Tuttle, some time since, which no doubt you have seen before now, and with which I hope you are also satisfied. I have handed your request to the editor of the *Times and Seasons*, who will forward you the desired papers. I am glad that James Ivins settled with you the $2,500 note, but sorry that you suffered yourself to lose in the sale of the land you had of him. As regards the Cook's Mill Tavern stand, and the one hundred and thirty-seven acres of pine land, which you propose to allow the Church three thousand dollars for, I have to say in reply, that I have consulted, not only my own feelings as sole Trustee in Trust for the Church; but also the feelings of those of the Church whose opinions I can always rely upon in such matters, and the conclusion is that thirty-two hundred dollars is the least the property ought to be sold for. You can, therefore, have it for three thousand two hundred, which is considerably less than it cost the Church; we are willing to make a partial sacrifice in the property, but under the circumstances, think that you can afford to give us two hundred dollars more than you proposed. The health of our place is at this time pretty good, and we hope it may continue to improve, with the improvements of the city.

I remain very respectfully yours, &c.,

JOSEPH SMITH.

Saturday, 11.—Late this evening, while sitting in council with the Twelve in my new store on Water street, I directed Brigham Young, President of the Twelve Apostles, to go immediately and instruct the building committee in their duty, and forbid them receiving any more property for the building of the Temple, until they received it from the Trustee in Trust, and if the committee did not give heed to the instruction, and attend to their duty, to put them in the way so to do.

Elder Willard Richards has left Warsaw for Nauvoo, it being considered unnecessary for him to tarry there any longer.

Since I have been engaged in laying the foundation of the Church of Jesus Christ of Latter-day Saints, I have been prevented in various ways from continuing my journal and history in a manner satisfactory to myself or in justice to the cause. Long imprisonments, vexatious and long-continued law-suits, the treachery of some of my clerks, the death of others, and the poverty of myself and brethren from continued plunder and driving, have prevented my handing down to posterity a connected memorandum of events desirable to all lovers of truth; yet I have continued to keep up a journal in the best manner my circumstances would allow, and dictate for my history from time to time, as I have had opportunity so that the labors and suffering of the first Elders and Saints of this last kingdom might not wholly be lost to the world.

The Prophet's Difficulties in Writing the Annals of the Church.

Sunday, 12.—I preached in the morning at Snyder's Hotel.

In the evening, the Twelve met in council at Brother Heber C. Kimball's.

Monday, 13.—I appointed Willard Richards recorder for the Temple, and my private Secretary and general Clerk, and he commenced his labors in my new office in the brick store.

Some time in the fall of 1839, Daniel S. Witter, of the

steam mill at Warsaw, solicited the First Presidency of the Church to make a settlement on the school section No. 16, one mile south of Warsaw, and the solicitations were continued by Dan- *Anti Mormonism at Warsaw.* iel S. Witter, Mark Aldrich and others, from time to time, till the spring or summer of 1841, when articles of agreement were entered into between Calvin A. Warren, Esq., Witter, Aldrich and others, owners of the school section and the First Presidency, giving the Saints the privilege of settling on the school section, which had been surveyed and laid out in town lots, and called *Warren*, on certain conditions, and Willard Richards went to Warsaw on the 8th of September, and spent several weeks to prepare for the reception of immigrants. In the meantime the inhabitants of Warsaw attempted to form an anti-Mormon society, and were much enraged because Esquire Davis (who had spoken favorably of the Saints) was appointed clerk of the county by Judge Stephen A. Douglas.

In November two hundred and four Saints arrived at Warsaw, from England, led by Joseph Fielding, and were visited on the 24th of November by Elders Willard Richards, and John Taylor of the Twelve, and counseled to tarry at Warsaw according to the instruction of the First Presidency.

December 13.—Isaac Decker, presiding Elder at Warsaw, stated to the Presidency of Nauvoo, that Mr. Witter had raised one dollar per barrel on flour, and sold the sweepings of his mill to the Saints at $2.25 per hundred; and that Witter and Aldrich had for- *Further Trouble at Warsaw.* bidden the brethren the privilege of getting the old wood on the school section, which they had full liberty to get; that the price of wood on the wharf had fallen twenty-five cents per cord since the arrival of the Saints; that the citizens had raised their rent, &c.; and the First Presidency decided that the Saints should remove from

Warsaw to Nauvoo immediately; and that the proceedings at Warsaw be published in the *Times and Seasons*.

This morning President Young delivered the message I gave him on Saturday evening to Reynolds Cahoon and Elias Higbee, the Temple Committe, in presence of Elders Kimball, Woodruff, and Richards.

Elder Richards by letter instructed the Saints at Warsaw to remove to Nauvoo.

BAPTISM FOR THE DEAD.

An Epistle of the Twelve Apostles to the Saints of the Last Days.

The building of the Temple of the Lord in the city of Nauvoo, is occupying the first place in the exertions and prayers of many of the Saints at the present time, knowing, as they do, that if this building is not completed speedily, "we shall be rejected as a Church with our dead;" for the Lord our God hath spoken it.

But while many are thus engaged in laboring and watching and praying for this all important object, there are many, very many more, who do not thus come up to their privilege and their duty in this thing, and in many instances we are confident that their neglect arises from a want of proper understanding of the principles upon which this building is founded, and by which it must be completed.

The children of Israel were commanded to build a house in the land of promise; and so are the Saints of the last days, as you will see in the Revelation given to Joseph the Seer, January 19, 1841, wherein those ordinances may be revealed which have been hid for ages, even their anointings and washings, and baptisms for the dead; wherein they may meet in solemn assemblies for their memorials, sacrifices, and oracles in their most holy places; and wherein they may receive conversations and statutes, and judgments, for the beginning of the revelations and foundations of Zion, and the glory and honor and adornment of all her municipals through the medium which God has ordained.

In the same revelation the command is to "all the Saints from afar," as well as those already gathered to this place: to arise with one consent and build the Temple; to prepare a place where the Most High may manifest Himself to His people. No one is excepted who hath aught in his possession, for what have ye that ye have not received? And I will require mine own with usury, saith the Lord; so that those who live thousands of miles from this place, come under the same law, and are entitled to the same blessings and privileges as those who have already gathered. But some may say, how can this be, I am not there, therefore I cannot meet in the Temple, cannot be baptized in the font? The command of heaven is to you, to all, gather; and when you arrive here, if it is found that you have previously sent of your gold, or your silver, or your substance, the tithing and consecrations which are required of you for this building, you will find your names, tithings and consecrations written in the Book of the Law of the Lord, to be kept in the Temple, as a witness in your favor, showing that you are a proprietor in that building, and are entitled to your share of the privileges thereunto belonging.

One of those privileges which is particularly attracting the notice of the Saints at the present moment, is baptism for the dead, in the font which is so far completed as to be dedicated, and several have already attended to this ordinance by which the sick have been made whole, and the prisoner set free; but while we have been called to administer this ordinance, we have been led to inquire into the propriety of baptizing those who have not been obedient, and assisted to build the place for baptism; and it seems to us unreasonable to expect that the Great Jehovah will approbate such administration; for if the Church must be brought under condemnation, and rejected with her dead, if she fail to build the house and its appurtenances, why should not individuals of the Church, who thus neglect, come under the same condemnation? For if they are to be rejected, they may as well be rejected without baptism as with it; for their baptism can be of no avail before God, and the time to baptize them may be appropriated to building the walls of the house, and this is according to the understanding which we have received from him who is our spokesman.

Let it not be supposed that the sick and the destitute are to be denied the blessings of the Lord's house; God forbid; His eye is ever over them for good. He that hath not, and cannot obtain, but saith in his heart, if I had, I would give freely, is accepted as freely as he that gives of his abundance. The Temple is to be built by tithing and consecration, and every one is at liberty to consecrate all they find in their hearts so to do; but the tithings required, is one-tenth of all any one possessed at the commencement of the building, and one-tenth part of all his increase from that time until the completion of the same, whether it be money, or whatever he may be blessed with.

Many in this place are laboring every tenth day for the house, and this is the tithing of their income, for they have nothing else; others would labor the same, but they are sick, therefore excusable; when they get well, let them begin; while there are others who appear to think their own business of more importance than the Lord's. Of such we would ask, who gave you your time, health, strength, and put you into business? And will you not begin quickly to return with usury that which you have received? Our God will not wait always.

We would remind some two or three hundred Elders, who offered to go on missions, some six months, others one year, and some two years, and had their missions assigned them at the general conference to labor on the Temple, that most of their names are still with us, and we wish them to call and take their names away, and give them up to the building committee.

Brethren, you have as great an interest at stake in this thing as we have, but as our Master, even the Master-builder of the Temple, whose throne is on high, has seen fit to constitute us stewards in some parts of His household; we feel it important for us to see to it that our Master is not defrauded, and especially by those who have pledged their word, their time, their talents, to His services; and we hope this gentle hint will suffice, that we may not be compelled to publish the names of those referred to.

Probably some may think they could have gone on a mission, but cannot labor, as they have no means of boarding themselves, but let such remember that several score of brethren and sisters in this city, offered at the general conference, to board one or more laborers on the Temple till the same should be completed, and but few of those as yet have had the opportunity of boarding any one. To all such we would say, you are not forgotten, we have your names also, and we expect soon to send someone to your table, therefore put your houses in order and never be ready to refuse the first offer of a guest.

Large stores of provisions will be required to complete the work, and now is the time for securing it, while meat is plenty and can be had for one half the value that it can at other seasons of the year, and the weather is cool and suitable for packing. Let the brethren for two hundred miles around drive their fat cattle and hogs to this place, where they may be preserved, and there will be a supply till another favorable season rolls around, or till the end of the labor.

Now is the time to secure food, now is the time that the trustee is ready to receive your droves. Not the maimed, the lean, the halt, and the blind, and such that you cannot use; it is for the Lord, and He wants no such offering; but if you want His blessing, give Him the best, give Him as good as He has given you. Beds and bedding, socks, mittens, shoes, clothing of every description, and store goods are needed for the comfort of the laborers this winter; journeymen, stone cutters, quarrymen, teams and teamsters for drawing stone and all kinds of provision for men and beast, are needed in abundance.

There are individuals who have given nothing as yet, either as tithing or consecration, thinking that they shall be able to do a great deal some time hence if they continue their present income to their own use, but this is a mistaken idea. Suppose that all should act upon this principle, no one would do ought at present, consequently the building must cease, and this generation remain without a house, and the Church be rejected; then suppose the next generation labor upon the same principle, and the same in all succeeding generations, the Son of God would never have a place on earth to lay His head.

Let every individual remember that their tithings and consecrations are required from what they have, and not what they expect to have some time hence, and are wanted for immediate use. All money and other property designed for tithing and consecrations to the building of the Temple must hereafter be presented to the Trustee in Trust, President Joseph Smith, and entered at the recorder's office, in the book before referred to; and all receipts now holden by individuals, which they have received of the building committee for property delivered to them, must also be forwarded to the recorder's office for entry, to secure the appropriation of said property according to the original design.

The Elders everywhere will instruct the brethren both in public and in private, in the principles and doctrines set forth in this Epistle, so that every individual in the Church may have a perfect understanding of his duty and privileges.

> BRIGHAM YOUNG,
> HEBER C. KIMBALL,
> ORSON PRATT,
> WILLIAM SMITH,
> LYMAN WIGHT.
> WILFORD WOODRUFF
> JOHN TAYLOR,
> GEO. A. SMITH,
> WILLARD RICHARDS.

Nauvoo, Illinois, December 13, 1841.

CHAPTER XXVIII.

KIRTLAND *vs*. NAUVOO—POLITICAL ATTITUDE OF THE PEOPLE OF NAUVOO DECLARED — PUBLICATIONS MORMON AND ANTI-MORMON FOR 1841—CLOSE OF THE YEAR.

Tuesday, December 14, 1841.—I commenced opening, unpacking, and assorting a lot of dry goods in the second story of my new store, situate on the northwest corner of block 155.* The joiners and masons are yet at work in the lower part of the building.

Wednesday, 15.—In reply to inquiries concerning Almon W. Babbitt, and the printing press at Kirtland, contained in a letter written at Kirtland, November 16, 1841, by Lester Brooks and Zebedee Coltrin, acting presidents, and Thomas Burdick, Bishop and council, to President Joseph Smith and Brigham Young, it was decided as follows:

Decision in the Case of Almon W. Babbitt and Kirtland.

It remains for Almon W. Babbitt to offer satisfaction, if he wishes so to do, according to the minutes of the conference. You are doubtless all well aware that all the stakes, except those in Hancock county, Illinois, and Lee county, Iowa, were discontinued some time since by the First Presidency, as published in the *Times and Seasons*; but as it appears that there are many in Kirtland who desire to remain there, and build up that place, and as you have made great exertions according to your letter, to establish a printing press, and take care of the poor, &c., since that period, you may as well continue operations according to your designs, and go on with your printing, and do what you can in righteousness to build up Kirtland, but do not suffer yourselves to harbor the idea that Kirtland will rise on the ruins of Nauvoo. It is the privilege of brethren emigrating from any quarter to come to this place, and it is not right to attempt to persuade those who desire it, to stop short.

The foregoing is an extract from my letter in reply.

* On the corner of Granger and Water streets, in the southwest part of the city.

The Twelve Apostles were in council at Elder Kimball's.

Tuesday, 16.—William Wightman of Ramus, delivered to President Joseph Smith, sole trustee-in-trust, the deed to the unsold and bonded lots of land in the town of Ramus, bearing date December 8, 1841; also the plat of the "first addition to Ramus," and the notes which have been received of individuals who have purchased lots, and the bonds of William Miller, September 21, 1840, and of Ute Perkins, November 26, 1840, and of William J. Perkins, November 7, 1840, and of John F. Charles, November 16, 1841, for lots of land adjoining Ramus, and which may hereafter be added to the town plats (a part of the land included in William Miller's bond is included in the first addition to Ramus, and the notes were transferred to the sole trustee-in-trust, for the benefit of the whole Church, by a vote of the Ramus conference, December 4 and 5, 1841), after applying sufficient of said property to liquidate the claims of those from whom the town was purchased, and also paying two notes given by William Wightman for money borrowed to pay for the above property, viz., to Lyman Prentice $11.45, and James Cummins $50.00, and some other small demands against said Wightman which have been contracted for the benefit of the Church in Ramus.

Saturday, 18.—I attended the city council, and stated circumstances which I had heard concerning mobocracy, from a person late from Macombe, and requested an ordinance passed, so that persons ordering any person to leave their peaceful homes could be dealt with rigorously; also presented the following—

Expressions of Gratitude to James Gordon Bennett and the New York Herald.

Resolved by the city council of the city of Nauvoo, that the high-minded and honorable editor of the *New York Weekly Herald*, James Gordon Bennett, Esq., is deserving of the lasting gratitude of this community, for his very liberal and unprejudiced course towards us as a people, in giving us a fair hearing in his paper, thus enabling us to reach the ears of a portion of the community, who, otherwise would ever have remained ignorant of our principles and practices.

Resolved, That we recommend our fellow citizens to subscribe for the *New York Weekly Herald*, and thus be found patronizing true merit, industry, and enterprise.

Sunday, 19.—The Twelve were in council at Elder Brigham Young's—morning.

Meeting at my house in the evening.

The subjoined minutes are from Elder Wilford Woodruff's journal—

Minutes of a Meeting of the Twelve in the House of the Prophet.

Elder Heber C. Kimball preached at the house of President Joseph Smith, on the parable in the 18th chapter of Jeremiah, of the clay in the hands of the potter, that when it marred in the hands of the potter it was cut off the wheel and then thrown back again into the mill, to go into the next batch, and was a vessel of dishonor; but all clay that formed well in the hands of the potter, and was pliable, was a vessel of honor; and thus it was with the human family, and ever will be: all that are pliable in the hands of God and are obedient to His commands, are vessels of honor, and God will receive them.

President Joseph arose and said—"Brother Kimball has given you a true explanation of the parable," and then read the parable of the vine and its branches, and explained it, and said, "if we keep the commandments of God, we should bring forth fruit and be the friends of God, and know what our Lord did.

"Some people say I am a fallen Prophet, because I do not bring forth more of the word of the Lord. Why do I not do it? Are we able to receive it? No! not one in this room. He then chastened the congregation for their wickedness and unbelief, 'for whom the Lord loveth he chasteneth, and scourgeth every son and daughter whom he receiveth,' and if we do not receive chastisements then we are 'bastards and not sons."

On the subject of revelation, he said, a man would command his son to dig potatoes and saddle his horse, but before he had done either he would tell him to do something else. This is all considered right; but as soon as the Lord gives a commandment and revokes that decree and commands something else, then the Prophet is considered fallen. Because we will not receive chastisement at the hand of the Prophet and

Apostles, the Lord chastiseth us with sickness and death.   Let not any man publish his own righteousness, for others can see that for him; sooner let him confess his sins, and then he will be forgiven, and he will bring forth more fruit.   When a corrupt man is chastised he gets angry and will not endure it.   The reason we do not have the secrets of the Lord revealed unto us, is because we do not keep them but reveal them; we do not keep our own secrets, but reveal our difficulties to the world, even to our enemies, then how would we keep the secrets of the Lord?   I can keep a secret till Doomsday.   What greater love hath any man than that he lay down his life for his friend; then why not fight for our friend until we die?

Elder Brigham Young said—one thing lay with weight on his mind; that is, that we should be prepared to keep each commandment as it came from the Lord by the mouth of the Prophet, and as the Lord had commanded us to build a temple, we should do it speedily.

Monday, 20.—I communicated to the *Times and Seasons*, as follows—

The Prophet on the Attitude of the Saints in Politics.

To my Friends in Illinois—The Gubernatorial Convention of the state of Illinois has nominated Colonel Adam W. Snyder* for Governor, and Colonel John Moore for Lieutenant-Governor, of the state of Illinois, election to take place in August next.

Colonel Moore, like Judge Douglas and Esquire Warren, was an intimate friend of General Bennett long before that gentleman became a member of our community; and General Bennett informs us that no men were

* Governor Ford, in his "History of Illinois," gives the following biographical information about Adam W. Snyder, and as I can find nothing concerning him elsewhere, I quote Ford:—

"In December, 1841, a State Democratic convention assembled at Springfield, and nominated Adam W. Snyder as the Democratic candidate for governor, to be elected in August, 1842.   Mr. Snyder was a native of Pennsylvania, and a distant relative of Gov. Snyder of that State.   In his early youth, he learned the trade of a fuller and woolcarder.   He came to Illinois when he was about eighteen years old; settled in the French village of Cahokia: followed his trade for several years: studied law; removed to the county seat, where he commenced his profession, in which he was successful in getting practice.   In 1830 he was elected to the State Senate, and was afterwards elected to Congress, from his district; and was again elected to the State Senate in 1840.   Mr. Snyder was a very showy, plausible and agreeable man in conversation, and was gifted with a popular eloquence, which was considerably effective.   He was a member of the Senate when the Mormon charters were passed, and had taken an active part in furthering their passage."   In fact Mr. Snyder was chairman of the Judiciary committee, to which the charters were referred, and he reported them to the Senate with a recommendation that they pass.

more efficient in assisting him to procure our great chartered privileges, than were Colonel Snyder, and Colonel Moore. They are sterling men, and friends of equal rights, opposed to the oppressor's grasp, and the tyrant's rod. With such men at the head of our State, government will have nothing to fear. In the next canvass, we shall be influenced by no party consideration, and no Carthagenian coalescence or collusion with our people will be suffered to effect, or operate against General Bennett, or any other of our tried friends, already semi-officially in the field; so the partizans in this county, who expect to divide the friends of humanity and equal rights, will find themselves mistaken—we care not a fig for Whig or Democrat; they are both alike to us, but we shall go for our friends, our tried friends, and the cause of human liberty, which is the cause of God. We are aware that "divide and conquer" is the watchword with many, but with us it cannot be done—we love liberty too well—we have suffered too much to be easily duped—we have no catspaws amongst us. We voted for General Harrison because we loved him—he was a gallant officer and a tried statesman; but this is no reason why we should always be governored by his friends. He is now dead, and all of his friends are not ours. We claim the privilege of freemen, and shall act accordingly. Douglas is a master spirit, and his friends are our friends—we are willing to cast our banners in the air, and fight by his side in the cause of humanity and equal rights—the cause of liberty and the law. Snyder and Moore are his friends—they are ours. These men are free from the prejudices and superstitions of the age, and such men we love, and such men will ever receive our support, be their political predilections what they may. Snyder and Moore are known to be our friends; their friendship is vouched for by those whom we have tried. We will never be justly charged with the sin of ingratitude—they have served us, and we will serve them.*

JOSEPH SMITH.
Lieutenant-General of the Nauvoo Legion.

* For some time there had been an agitation going on in respect of the Saints and their relationship to the politics of the State; and political capital was sought to be made by manifestations of friendliness or of hostility towards them. Although, in the main, the people of Nauvoo had sustained the Whig candidates, both locally and nationally, in the preceding election, including the Whig candidate for Congress, Mr. John J. Stuart, yet there were outbreaks against them both among the Whig politicians and in the Whig press of Illinois. "The Whig newspapers," writes Governor Ford, in his "History of Illinois," "teemed with accounts of the wonders and enormities of Nauvoo, and of the awful wickedness of a party which could consent to receive the support of such miscreants. Governor Duncan, [nominated in opposition to Snyder] who was really a brave, honest man, and who had nothing to do with getting the Mormon charters passed through the legislature, took the stump on this subject in good earnest, and expected to be elected governor almost on this question alone." (History of Illinois, Ford, p. 269.)

Tuesday, 21.—I received from Edward Hunter a letter on business, to which I wrote the following reply—

The Prophet's Letter to Edward Hunter—Business Affairs at Nauvoo.

NAUVOO, Dec. 21, 1841.

Mr. Edward Hunter,

BELOVED BROTHER:—Yours of the 27th of October came to hand at a late date, but I am now able to say to you that the power of attorney is executed and sent up to the clerk's office for the seal of the state, and

The position of the Saints in their relation to the political parties in the state of Illinois is tersely set forth by the late President John Taylor in his review of affairs at Nauvoo, leading up to the martyrdom of the Prophet; which document was prepared at the request of the Historians of the Church, and filed in the archives of the Church as the testimony of an eye witness and participant in those events. The document, under the title of "The Martyrdom of Joseph Smith," was published by permission of the author in Tyler's "History of the Mormon Battalion." Of the political situation at Nauvoo—which was forming at the period to which the political announcement of the text above belongs—President Taylor says:

"There were always two parties, the Whigs and Democrats, and we could not vote for one without offending the other; and it not unfrequently happened that candidates for office would place the issue of their election upon opposition to the 'Mormons,' in order to gain political influence from religious prejudice, in which case the 'Mormons' were compelled, in self-defense, to vote against them, which resulted almost invariably against our opponents. This made them angry; and although it was of their own making, and the 'Mormons' could not be expected to do otherwise, yet they raged on account of their discomfiture, and sought to wreak their fury on the 'Mormons.' As an instance of the above, when Joseph Duncan was candidate for the office of governor of Illinois, [in the campaign to which the document in the body of the text above relates] he pledged himself to his party that, if he could be elected, he would exterminate or drive the 'Mormons' from the State. The consequence was that Governor Ford was elected." (History of the Mormon Battalion, Introduction, pp. 12 and 13.)

It cannot in truth be claimed that any favor shown by the Democratic party, as such, to the Mormon people was the cause of the announcement of the above independent attitude in politics. For while Judge Douglas, a leading Democrat, had recently rendered a decision favorable to the Prophet, liberating him from the clutches of Missouri, it should be remembered that the Judge had but pronounced upon the course of the officers of the states of Missouri and Illinois and found that course at variance with the law, and there was no alternative but to set the Prophet free. But it was the law that vindicated Joseph Smith, not the favor of Judge Douglas. And then, if a Democratic Judge had decided a case in favor of the Prophet, it should be remembered that it was the act, and I might say the unwarranted, the illegal act, of a Democrat, Governor Carlin, which had put the life and liberty of the Prophet in jeopardy by issuing an illegal requisition for his arrest and deliverance to Missouri. This to show that it was not any favor that had been shown by the Democratic party, as such, that prompted the assumption of an independent attitude in politics by the Prophet; but that for weal or woe, the attitude was taken as a measure of self-defense, and for the protection of the people in whose interest it was announced.

will be forwarded direct from them; it is now on the way most probably.

Your letter did not arrive till after Mr. Potter returned with the goods, which I received in safety; and Brother Potter has started on a mission to the inhabitants of Jamaica, one of the West India isles.

I will accept the goods as you propose, on your debt, so far as it goes, and answer the remainder on the payments which you mention, as they become due.

I have purchased ninety acres of timber land in the vicinity of Nauvoo, a little up the river, and have made proposals to McFall, but as yet, am waiting for him to receive answers from his correspondent in the east.   I shall be able to purchase all the wood land you will want, in a little time.

As respects steam engines and mills, my opinion is, we cannot have too many of them. This place has suffered exceedingly from the want of such mills in our midst, and neither one nor two can do the business of this place another season. We have no good grain or board mill in this place; and most of our flour and lumber has to be brought twenty miles; which subjects us to great inconvenience.

The city is rapidly advancing, many new buildings have been erected since you left us, and many more would have arisen, if brick and lumber could have been obtained.   There is scarcely any limits which can be imagined to the mills and machinery and manufacturing of all kinds which might be put into profitable operation in this city, and even if others should raise a mill before you get here, it need be no discouragement either to you or Brother Buckwalter, for it will be difficult for the mills to keep pace with the growth of the place, and you will do well to bring the engine.   If you can persuade any of the brethren who are manufacturers of woollens or cottons to come on and establish their business, do so.

I have not ascertained definitely as yet how far the goods will go towards liquidating Dr. Foster's note, or finishing your house; but this I can say, I will make the most of it, and benefit you every possible way.

Your message is delivered to Mrs. Smith, and she will be glad to have returns on her letter of attorney, as speedily as circumstances will permit, according to the understanding thereof.

I am happy to hear of your welfare, and the health of your family; and also to inform you that the health of Nauvoo has much improved since last summer, and considering the very mild state of the weather most of the time, it is excellent.

Myself and family are in health, and our enemies are at peace with us, as much as can be expected in this generation.   Should anything new occur, which may be for our advantage, you will please write, and I will do the same.   I remain, yours in the Gospel of Christ,

JOSEPH SMITH.

P.S.—You will endeavor to have the money on your letter of attorney from Mrs. Smith, ready to furnish a fresh supply of goods early in the spring.   J. S.

Wednesday, 22.

NAUVOO, December 22, 1841.

Revelation to John Snyder and Amos B. Fuller.

The word of the Lord came unto Joseph the Seer, verily thus saith the Lord, let my servant John Snyder take a mission to the eastern continent, unto all the conferences now sitting in that region; and let him carry a package of epistles, that shall be written by my servants the Twelve making known unto them their duties concerning the building of my houses which I have appointed unto you, saith the Lord, that they may bring their gold and their silver, and their precious stones, and the box-tree, and the fir-tree, and all fine wood to beautify the place of my sanctuary, saith the Lord; and let him return speedily with all means which shall be put into his hands, even so. Amen.

Elder Amos B. Fuller, of Zarahemla, stated to me that he had settled all his debts, made all necessary provision for his family, and desired to know the will of God concerning him.

Revelation.

"Verily thus saith the Lord unto my servants the Twelve, let them appoint unto my servant A. B. Fuller a mission to preach my Gospel unto the children of men, as it shall be manifested unto them by my Holy Spirit. Amen."

This day I commenced receiving the first supply of groceries at the new store. Thirteen wagons arrived from Warsaw, loaded with sugar, molasses, glass, salt, tea, coffee, &c., purchased in St. Louis. The original stock purchased in New Orleans having been detained at St. Louis by one Holbrook, innkeeper, under false pretenses.

This evening I commenced giving instructions to the scribe concerning writing the

Work on Proclamation to Kings of the Earth.

proclamation to the kings of the earth, mentioned in the revelation given January 19, 1841.

Friday, 24.—This evening I had a consultation with President Young and Bishop Whitney about establishing an agency in England for the cheap and expeditious conveyance of the Saints to Nauvoo. and for our convenience in merchandise; and I said, "in the name of the Lord we will prosper, if we will go forward in this thing."

Immigration Agency in England.

Elder Truman Gillett, Jun., returned from a short mission to Van Buren county, Iowa, where he baptized fourteen, bringing $20 as a donation to the building of the Temple, from Samuel Moore.

Saturday, 25.—Being Christmas, Brigham Young, Heber C. Kimball, Orson Pratt, Wilford Woodruff, John Taylor, and their wives, and Willard Richards spent the evening at Hiram Kimball's; and after supper, Mr. Kimball gave each of the Twelve Apostles a fractional lot of land lying on the west side of his second addition to Nauvoo.

Xmas at Nauvoo, 1841.

Alpheus Gifford, a member of the Church since 1831, and a faithful Elder in the Church [it was he who baptized Heber C. Kimball] died at his home some five miles above Nauvoo.*

Conference Minutes—New York and Maine.

At a conference held in Batavia, Genessee county, New York, 11 branches, comprising 15 Elders, 7 Priests, 7 Teachers, 4 Deacons, and 207 members were represented.

A conference met in the Universalist Church, in Hope, Waldo

---

* Alpheus Gifford was born in Adams township, Berkshire county, Massachusetts, August 28, 1793. At the age of eighteen, having scarcely sufficient learning to enable him to read the Bible, he commenced preaching the Gospel, not for hire, but for the salvation of souls.

In 1817, he married Anna Nash, who bore him seven sons and three daughters. In the spring of 1831, hearing of the doctrines taught by Joseph Smith, he made diligent inquiry, and found they were scriptural, and was baptized and ordained a county, Maine, when Fox Islands, with five Elders, 1 Priest, 2 Teachers, 1 Deacon, and 100 members, also the Main Land, with 6 Elders, 2 Priests, 3 Teachers, 1 Deacon, and 68 members were represented; Otis Shaw, president, and Calvin C. Pendleton, clerk.

Sunday, 26.—The public meeting of the Saints was at my house this evening, and after Patriarch Hyrum Smith and Elder Brigham Young had spoken on the principles of faith, and the gifts of the Spirit, I read the 13th chapter of First Corinthians, also a part of the 14th chapter, and remarked that the gift of tongues was necessary in the Church; but that if Satan could not speak in tongues, he could not tempt a Dutchman, or any other nation, but the English, for he can tempt the Englishman, for he has tempted me, and I am an Englishman; but the gift of tongues by the power of the Holy Ghost in the Church, is for the benefit of the servants of God to preach to unbelievers, as on the day of Pentecost.   When devout men from every nation

Purpose of the Gift of Tongues.

priest; he brought home five Books of Mormon which he distributed among his friends; he was then living in Tioga county, Pennsylvania. Soon after he went to Kirtland, Ohio, to see the Prophet Joseph Smith and the brethren, when he was ordained an Elder; he was accompanied by his brother Levi, Elial Strong, Eleazar Miller, Enos Curtis and Abraham Brown, who were baptized. On returning to Pennsylvania he preached and baptized many, among whom was Heber C. Kimball. The gifts of the Gospel were enjoyed by many; signs following those that believed, devils were cast out; the sick were healed; many prophesied; some spake with new tongues; while others interpreted the same. Mr. Calvin Gilmour, with whom Brother Gifford had previously been associated in preaching, heard him speak in tongues and interpret. Gilmour declared he understood the languages and that they were interpreted correctly, but that he would rather be damned than believe in Mormonism.

In June, 1832, Brother Gifford started for Missouri; traveled to Cincinnatti and wintered there with a few Saints, who had been baptized by Lyman Wight. He arrived in Jackson county, Mo., in March, 1833, where he preached much. He was driven with the Saints in the fall of that year. He removed to Clay county, and subsequently went to Kirtland, Ohio, and attended the dedication of the Temple and received the ordinances there administered. He returned to Missouri, and removed with the Saints to Far West, Caldwell county. In the winter of 1839 he was driven from Missouri. He located in the Morley settlement near Lima, Illinois, and subsequently removed five miles above Nauvoo, where he died December 25, 1841. (The above is taken from a sketch of his father's life by Samuel K. Gifford, furnished the Church Historian in November, 1861, and filed in the History of the Church under date of December, 1841.)

shall assemble to hear the things of God, let the Elders preach to them in their own mother tongue, whether it is German, French, Spanish or "Irish," or any other, and let those interpret who understand the language spoken, in their own mother tongue, and this is what the Apostle meant in First Corinthians xiv: 27.*

Monday, 27.—I was in council with Brothers Brigham Young, Heber C. Kimball, Willard Richards and John Taylor, at my office, instructing them in the principles of the kingdom, and what the Twelve should do in relation to the mission of John Snyder, and the European conferences, so as to forward the gathering of means for building the Temple and Nauvoo House; that Brigham might go with John Snyder on his mission if he chose, but the object of the mission could be accomplished without.

Instructions to the Twelve.

Tuesday, 28.—I baptized Sidney Rigdon in the font, for and in behalf of his parents; also baptized Reynolds Cahoon and others.

Thursday and Friday, December 30th and 31st—Calvin A. Warren, Esq., Mark Aldrich and Daniel S. Witter, visited me at my office, and after much explanation and conversation concerning Warren and Warsaw, in which Esquire Warren manifested the kindest and most confidential feelings and Aldrich and Witter expressed their entire approbation of past proceedings of the Presidency, they all agreed that if I did not succeed in the next attempt to establish and build up Warren, that they would fully excuse me from all censure, and would feel satisfied that I had done all that could reasonably be required of any man in a like case, be the consequence what it might to themselves; and Esquire Warren frankly acknowledged that his temporal salvation depended on the success of the enterprise, and

Warren and Warsaw Affairs.

"* If any man speak in an unknown tongue, let it be by two, at the most by three, and that by course, and let one interpret. But if there be no interpreter, let him keep silence in the Church; and let him speak to himself and to God."

made liberal proposals for the benefit of the brethren, to help forward the undertaking. The party retired manifesting the best of feeling, and expressing the most perfect satisfaction with their visit, with me and all concerned.

Thursday evening at the office, while conversing with Calvin A. Warren, Esq., about the proceedings at Warsaw, I prophesied in the name of the Lord, that the first thing toward building up Warsaw was to break it down, to break down them that are there, that it never would be built up till it was broken down, and after that keep them entirely in the dark concerning our movements; and it is best to let Sharp* publish what he pleases and go to the devil, and the more lies he prints the sooner he will get through; not buy him out or hinder him; and after they have been in the dark long enough, let a certain set of men go there who will do as I tell them, a certain kind of men, some of those capitalists from the Eastern States, say from Pennsylvania; wise men who will take the lead of business, and go ahead of those that are there before they know what we are about, and the place will prosper, and not till then.

A Prophecy
Respecting
Warsaw.

The following list shows some of the books, pamphlets, letters, &c., published for and against the Latter-day Saints in 1841.

Mormon Literature, (pro et con) 1841.

"A Proclamation to the Saints Scattered Abroad:" January 15, by Joseph Smith, Sidney Rigdon, Hyrum Smith.

Twenty-three numbers of the "Times and Seasons," published at Nauvoo.

Twelve numbers of the "Millennial Star," published in England by Parley P. Pratt.

First European edition of the Book of Mormon, published in England, 21st January, by Elders Brigham Young, and Willard Richards.

---

* This reference is to Thomas Sharp, editor of the Warsaw *Signal*, a bitter anti-Mormon, and described by the late President John Taylor, as "a violent and un-principled man, who shrank not from any enormity."

A third edition of the "Voice of Warning" was published in Manchester, England, by Parley P. Pratt.

"A Letter to Queen Victoria of England, Touching the Signs of the Times, and the Political Destiny of the World:" in pamphlet form, by Parley P. Pratt, Manchester, England.

Five hundred copies of "An Address to the Hebrews," in the Dutch language, by Orson Hyde. Published in Rotterdam, Holland, in July; being the first pamphlet pertaining to the Church of Jesus Christ of Latter-day Saints, written in a foreign language.

A pamphlet containing 116 pages, 8vo., by Orson Hyde, containing "A Synopsis of the Faith of the Church of Jesus Christ of Latter-day Saints:" addressed to the German nation in their own language.

A Small Collection of Hymns, by Christopher Merkley.

"Evidences in Proof of the Book of Mormon:" a work of 256 pages, 32 mo. Published at Batavia, New York, by Charles Thompson.

A lengthy "Address to the Citizens of Salem, Massachusetts, and Vicinity," by Erastus Snow, and Benjamin Winchester, October.

"Gospel Reflector," a monthly periodical, by Benjamin Winchester, published in Philadelphia.

"Proclamation and Warning to the Inhabitants of America," by Charles Thompson.

The editor of the "Times and Seasons" noticed the following "From the 'Upper Mississippian,' a series of letters, entitled 'Nauvoo Mormon Religion,' &c., the writer no doubt intended to give a fair statement, and in the main did so; but respecting our faith (on some points), the Book of Mormon, &c., he is wide of the mark."

An article published in the "North Staffordshire Mercury," showing the difference between the Baptists and Latter-day Saints. Hanley, February, 16, signed "A Baptist." Replied to by Parley P. Pratt, who showed the difference between the Baptists and Former-day Saints.

A severe article against the Latter-day Saints, which filled several columns of fine print, was published in "Edinburgh Intelligencer" of April 7th, taken from the "Athenæum" on the subject of the "Book of Mormon and the Latter-day Saints." Replied to by Parley P. Pratt. May.

Mr. J. B. Rollo, of Edinburgh, Scotland, published a pamphlet entitled "Mormonism Exposed." Replied to by Parley P. Pratt, July 10.

The "Preston Chronicle" of April 24, published a long article against the Latter-day Saints, which was replied to by Parley P. Pratt, in the "Millennial Star," July 10.

A bitter article was published in the "Cheltenham Free Press" of

August 23rd, headed "Latter-day Saints' Swindle," replied to by Parley P. Pratt in the "Star" of October.

"A Few Plain Facts, Showing the Folly, Wickedness and Imposition of the Rev. Timothy R. Matthews." By George J. Adams, Bedford, England.

The St. Louis, Missouri, "Atlas" published a favorable article entitled, "The Latter-day Saints."

The "Juliet Courier" published a favorable account of the late trial of Joseph Smith. Monmouth, June.

The "Philadelphia Saturday Courier" and the "Public Ledger" on July 10, published several articles anathematizing the Latter-day Saints.

A slanderous pamphlet entitled "Mormonism Unmasked," by A. Gardner, of Rochdale, England.

"The Mormons—Arrest of Joe Smith" was the heading of an article published in the "New York Herald of Commerce," and copied in many of the Eastern papers.

"The Christian Messenger and Reformer" published an account of the Latter-day Saints, collected from the book of Edward D. Howe, of Painsville, Ohio.

Thomas Sharp, editor of the "Warsaw Signal," devoted his entire time to slandering, to lying against and misrepresenting the Latter-day Saints.

CHAPTER XXIX.

THE OPENING OF THE YEAR 1842—WHEREABOUTS OF THE
  TWELVE APOSTLES—CORRESPONDENCE OF ELDER HYDE
  FROM TRIESTE—REPORT OF HIGH COUNCIL ON AFFAIRS
  IN NAUVOO—EVENTS AND CONDITIONS IN BRITISH MIS-
  SION.

Saturday, January 1, 1842.—I again have the pleasure
to report the location of the Twelve Apostles. Brigham
Young, Heber C. Kimball, Orson Pratt,
John Taylor, Wilford Woodruff and Willard
Richards are in Nauvoo. George A. Smith, in
Zarahemla, Ohio. Orson Hyde in quarantine at Trieste,
Italy. Parley P. Pratt in Liverpool. Lyman Wight in
Ohio. William Smith in New Jersey. John E. Page
somewhere in the Eastern States.

*Sundry La-
bors of the
Prophet.*

I commenced placing goods on the shelves of my new
store, assisted by Bishop Newel K. Whitney and others;
and in the evening attended city council.

Five hundred and twelve Saints were reported at the
Glasgow Conference of this date.

Several of the Twelve spent the day at Sylvester B.
Stoddard's and in the city council, which lasted from 6
p.m. until midnight, on the trial of Gustavus Hills.

Sunday, 2.—Meeting at my house, day and evening;
Brother Hyrum and Elder Woodruff preached.

Tuesday, 4.—I wrote Dr. John M. Bernhisel, of New
York, on business.

Joseph Duncan, candidate for Governor of Illinois,
made an inflammatory speech against the Saints at Ed-
wardsville, a mass of falsehoods.

Wednesday, 5.—William Wightman signed over and delivered the town plat of Ramus to me, as sole Trustee in Trust for the Church of Jesus Christ of Latter-day Saints.

My new store was opened for business this day for the first time, it was filled with customers, and I was almost continually behind the counter, as clerk, waiting on my friends.

I dictated a letter to Edward Hunter, West Nant-meal, Pennsylvania, as follows:

The Prophet's Letter to Edward Hunter—Reports Opening of the New Store.

NAUVOO, January 5, 1842.

Mr. Edward Hunter.

BELOVED BROTHER:—I am happy that it is my privilege to say to you that the large new building which I had commenced when you were here is now completed, and the doors are opened this day for the sale of goods for the first time. The foundation of the building is somewhat spacious (as you will doubtless recollect) for a country store.

The principal part of the building below, which is ten feet high, is devoted exclusively to shelves and drawers, except one door opening back into the space, on the left of which are the cellar and chamber stairs, and on the right the counting room; from the space at the top of the chamber stairs opens a door into the large front room of the same size with the one below, the walls lined with counters, covered with reserved goods.

In front of the stairs opens the door to my private office, or where I keep the sacred writings, with a window to the south, overlooking the river below, and the opposite shore for a great distance, which, together with the passage of boats in the season thereof, constitutes a peculiarly interesting situation, in prospect, and no less interesting from its retirement from the bustle and confusion of the neighborhood and city, and altogether is a place the Lord is pleased to bless.

The painting of the store has been executed by Edward Martin, one of our English brethren; and the counters, drawers, and pillars present a very respectable representation of oak, mahogany and marble for a backwoods establishment.

The Lord has blessed our exertions in a wonderful manner, and although some individuals have succeeded in detaining goods to a considerable amount for the time being, yet we have been enabled to secure goods in the building sufficient to fill all the shelves as soon as they were completed, and have some in reserve, both in loft and cellar.

Our assortment is tolerably good—very good, considering the different purchases made by different individuals at different times, and under circumstances which controlled their choice to some extent; but I rejoice that we have been enabled to do as well as we have, for the hearts of many of the poor brethren and sisters will be made glad with those comforts which are now within their reach.

The store has been filled to overflowing, and I have stood behind the counter all day, dealing out goods as steady as any clerk you ever saw, to oblige those who were compelled to go without their usual Christmas and New Year's dinners, for the want of a little sugar, molasses, raisins, &c., &c; and to please myself also, for I love to wait upon the Saints, and be a servant to all, hoping that I may be exalted in the due time of the Lord.

With sentiments of high consideration, I remain your brother in Christ.

JOSEPH SMITH.

Thursday, 6.—The new year has been ushered in and continued thus far under the most favorable auspices, and

Rejoicing of the Prophet.

the Saints seem to be influenced by a kind and indulgent Providence in their dispositions and [blessed with] means to rear the Temple of the Most High God, anxiously looking forth to the completion thereof as an event of the greatest importance to the Church and the world, making the Saints in Zion to rejoice, and the hypocrite and sinner to tremble. Truly this is a day long to be remembered by the Saints of the last days,—a day in which the God of heaven has begun to restore the ancient order of His kingdom unto His servants and His people,—a day in which all things are concurring to bring about the completion of the fullness of the Gospel, a fullness of the dispensation of dispensations, even the fullness of times; a day in which God has begun to make manifest and set in order in His Church those things which have been, and those things which the ancient prophets and wise men desired to see but died without beholding them; a day in which those things begin to be made manifest, which have been hid from before the foundation of the world, and which Jeho-

vah has promised should be made known in His own due
time unto His servants, to prepare the earth for the return
of His glory, even a celestial glory, and a kingdom of Priests
and kings to God and the Lamb, forever, on Mount Zion,
and with him the hundred and forty and four thousand
whom John the Revelator saw, all of which is to come to
pass in the restitution of all things.

Conference held at Zarahemla, at which that stake was
discontinued; a branch was organized in place thereof,
and John Smith appointed president.

Wednesday, 12.—The ship *Tremont* sailed from Liverpool for New Orleans with the Saints, about this time.

The following notice was published in the *Times and
Seasons*:

Tithings and Consecrations for the Temple of the Lord.

From this time the Recorder's Office will be opened on the Saturday
of each week for the reception of the tithings and consecrations of the
brethren. and closed on every other day of the week. This regulation
is necessary, to give the Trustee and Recorder time to arrange the Book
of Mormon, translation of the Bible, Hymn Book, and Doctrine and
Covenants for the press, all of which the brethren are anxious to see in
their most perfect form, consequently the Saints should be particular to
bring their offerings on the day specified, until further notice, but not
relax their exertions to carry on the work.

The Elders will please give the above notice in all public meetings,
until the plan is understood.

WILLARD RICHARDS,
Recorder for the Temple.

NAUVOO, January 12, 1842.

I rode south about seven miles to my wood land, accompanied by Brother John Sanders and Peter Maughan,*

* Peter Maughan was born May 7, 1811, at Breckenridge, in the parish of Parley,
county of Cumberland, England. He married Miss Ruth Harrison in 1829. He was
baptized into the Church by Elder Isaac Russell in 1838, and emigrated to Nauvoo
with his family of six children, now motherless, his wife having died in 1841. He
came on ths ship *Rochester*, in company with Brigham Young and several other
members of the quorum of the Twelve on their return home. He was a man of keen
intelligence and commanding personal influence.

and found a vein of coal about eighteen inches thick, apparently of good quality for the western country.

Elder Benjamin Winchester was suspended by the quorum of the Twelve until he made satisfaction for disobedience to the First Presidency.

Thursday, 13.—My clerk, Willard Richards, commenced boarding with me.

The British forces having evacuated Cabul,* they were attacked in the Pass, a few miles from the city, and after three days' fighting; they were nearly all slaughtered.

Saturday, 15.—I commenced reading the Book of Mormon, at page 54, American stereotype edition
Book of Mormon Corrections. (the previous pages having been corrected), for the purpose of correcting the stereotype plates of some errors which escaped notice in the first edition.

Attended city council, and was appointed on committee of ways and means and municipal laws.

Sunday, 16.—I preached at my house, morning and evening, illustrating the nature of sin, and showing that it is not right to sin that grace may abound.

Monday, 17.—Transacted a variety of business in the city. Myself and Brother Willard Richards dined with Sister Agnes M. Smith.†

In the evening I attended a council of the Twelve at my office; present, Elders Young, Kimball, Orson Pratt,
Meeting with the Twelve. Taylor, Woodruff, George A. Smith and Richards—appointed Elder Amos B. Fuller a mission to Chicago, according to the revelation of the 22nd of December, and Elder Henry Jacobs to accompany him. The council were unanimously opposed to Robin-

---

* Cabul is the capital of Afghanistan, situated on the river Kabul. It is noted as a commercial and strategic center, and the event named in the text above is an incident in what is usually called the first Afghan War. While the British were compelled to evacuate the place, as stated in the text, they re-took it in September following.

† Widow of the late Don Carlos Smith, the Prophet's brother.

son's publishing the Book of Mormon and other books.

Tuesday, 18.—This day revoked my power of attorney given to Dr. Isaac Galland to transact business for the Church.

After transacting a variety of business, sleeping an hour from bodily infirmities, I read for correction in the Book of Mormon, and debated in the evening with the mayor [John C. Bennett] concerning the Lamanites and Negroes.

For an extract of a letter from Elder Orson Hyde, "Trieste, January 1 and 18, 1842," see *Millennial Star*, vol. II, pages 166-169.*

HIGHLY INTERESTING FROM JERUSALEM.

We have lately received two lengthy and highly interesting communications from Elder Orson Hyde, dated at Trieste, January 1st, and 18th, containing a sketch of his voyages and travels in the East, his visit to Jerusalem, a description of ancient Zion, the pool of Siloam, and many other places famous in holy writ, with several illustrations of the manners and customs of the East, as applicable to Scripture texts, and several conversations held between himself and some of the Jews, missionaries, etc., in Jerusalem, together with a masterly description of a terrible tempest and thunder storm at sea, with a variety of miscellaneous reflections and remarks, all written in an easy, elegant, and masterly style, partaking of the eloquent and sublime, and breathing a tone of that deep feeling, tenderness, and affection so characteristic of his mission and the spirit of his holy and sacred office.

Elder Hyde has by the grace of God been the first proclaimer of the fullness of the Gospel both on the continent of Europe and in far off Asia, among the nations of the East.   In Germany, Turkey (Constantinople), Egypt, and Jerusalem. He has reared as it were the ensign of the latter-day glory, and sounded the trump of truth, calling upon the people of those regions to awake from their thousand years' slumber, and to make ready for their returning Lord.

* The article from the *Star* here referred to is inserted *in extenso*, and that for the reason that so many letters of Elder Hyde's concerning his journey to Jerusalem have already appeared in this volume, that this one seems necessary to the completion of the history of that mission, which must be regarded as an important movement on the part of the Church at this period.

In his travels he has suffered much, and has been exposed to toils and dangers, to hunger, pestilence and war. He has been in perils by land and sea, in perils among robbers, in perils among heathens, Turks, Arabs, and Egyptians; but out of all these things the Lord hath delivered him, and hath restored him in safety to the shores of Europe, where he is tarrying for a little season, for the purpose of publishing the Truth in the German language, having already published it in French and English in the various countries of the East, and we humbly trust that his labors will be a lasting blessing to Jew and Gentile.

We publish the following extract of his communication, and we shall soon issue the whole from the press in pamphlet form. It will, no doubt, meet with a ready sale; and we purpose devoting the profits to his benefit, to assist him in his mission.

Excerpts from Elder Hyde's Letters.

"Summoning up, therefore, what little address I had, I procured a *valet d'place*, or lackey, and proceeded to the house of Mr. Simons, a very respectable Jew, who with some of his family had lately been converted and joined the English Church. I entered their dwelling. They had just sat down to enjoy a dish of coffee, but immediately arose from the table to meet me. I spoke to them in German and asked them if they spoke English. They immediately replied 'Yes,' which was a very agreeable sound to my ear. They asked me in German if I spoke English; I replied, 'Ya, mein Herr.' I then introduced myself to them, and with a little apology it passed off as well as though I had been introduced by the pasha. With that glow of warmth and familiarity which is a peculiar trait in the German character, they would have me sit down and take a dish with them; and as I began to relate some things relative to my mission, the smiles of joy which sat upon their countenances bespoke hearts not altogether indifferent. There were two ministers of the Church of England there. One was confined to his bed by sickness, and the other, a German, and a Jew by birth, soon came in. After an introduction, I took the liberty to lay open to him some of our principles, and gave him a copy of the communication to the Jews in Constantinople to read. After he had it, he said that my motives were undoubtedly very good. but questioned the propriety of my undertaking from the fact that I claimed God had sent me. If, indeed, I had gone to Jerusalem under the direction of some missionary board or society, and left God out of the question altogether, I should have been received as a celestial messenger. How truly did our Savior speak, when He said, 'I am come in my Father's name, and ye receive me not; but if another were to come in his own name, him ye would receive.' I replied, however, that so far as I could know my own heart, my motives were most certainly good; yet, said I, no better than the cause which has brought me here. But he, like all others who worship a God 'without body or parts,' said that miracles, visions, and prophecy had ceased.

"The course which the popular clergy pursue at this time in relation to the Divine economy looks to me as though they would say, 'O Lord, we will worship Thee with all our hearts, serve Thee with all our souls, and be very pious and holy; we will even gather Israel, convert the heathen, and bring in the millennium, if Thou wilt only let us alone that we may do it in our own way, and according to our own will; but if Thou speakest from heaven to interfere with our plan, or cause any to see visions or dreams, or prophesy, whereby we are disturbed or interrupted in our worship, we will exert all our strength and skill to deny what Thou sayest, and charge it home upon the devil or some wild, fanatic spirit, as being its author.'

"That which was looked upon by the ancient saints as among the greatest favors and blessings, viz., revelation from God and communion with Him by dreams and by visions, is now looked upon by the religious world as the height of presumption and folly. The ancient saints considered their condition most deplorable when Jehovah would not speak to them; but the most orthodox religionists of this age deem it quite heterodox to even admit the probability that He ever will speak again. O my soul! language fails to paint the absurdity and abomination of such heaven-opposing and truth-excluding dogmas; and were it possible for those bright seraphs that surround the throne above, and bask in the sunbeams of immortality, to weep over the inconsistency and irrationality of mortals, the earth must be bedewed with celestial tears. My humble advice to all such is, that they repent and cast far from them these wicked traditions, and be baptized into the new and everlasting covenant, lest the Lord speak to them in His wrath, and vex them in His sore displeasure.

"After some considerable conversation upon the priesthood and the renewal of the covenant, I called upon him [i. e. the aforesaid German-Jew church of England minister] to be baptized for the remission of his sins, that he might receive the gift of the Holy Ghost. 'What' said he, 'I be baptized?' 'Yes,' said I, 'you be baptized.' 'Why,' saith he, 'I have been baptized already.' I replied something after the following: 'You have probably been sprinkled, but that has no more to do with baptism than any other ordinance of man's device; and even if you had been immersed, you would not have bettered your condition, for your priesthood is without power. If, indeed, the Catholic church has power to give you an ordination, and by that ordination confer the priesthood upon you, they certainly had power to nullify that act, and take the priesthood from you; and this power they exercised when you dissented from their communion, by excluding you from their church.   But, if the Catholic church possessed not the priesthood, of course your claims to it are as groundless as the airy phantoms of heathen mythology. So, view the question on which side you may, there is no possible chance of admitting the validity of your claims to it.   Be it known, therefore, that ordinances performed under the administration of such a priesthood, though they may even be correct in form, will be found destitute of the seal of that authority by which heaven will recognize His [own] in the day when every man's work shall be tried.   Though a priesthood may be clothed with the wealth and honors of a great and powerful nation and command the respect and veneration of multitudes whose eyes are blinded by the thick veil of popular opinion, and whose powers of reflection and deep thought are confused and lost in the general cry of 'Great is Diana of the Ephesians,' yet all this does not impart to it the Divine sanction, or animate it with the spirit of life and power from the bosom of the living God; and there is a period in future time when, in the smoking ruins of Babel's pride and glory, it must fall and retire to the shades of forgetfulness, to the grief and mortification of its unfortunate votaries.'

"In consequence of his great volubility, I was under the disagreeable necessity of tuning my voice to a pretty high key, and of spacing short between words, determining that neither his greatness or learning should shield him from the shafts of a faithful testimony.   But there is more hope of those Jews receiving the fullness of the gospel, whose minds have never been poisoned by the bane of modern sectarianism, which closes the mouth of Deity and shuts up in heaven all the angels, visions, and prophesyings.   Mrs. Whiting told me that there had been four Jewish people in Jerusalem converted and baptized by the English minister, and four only; and that a part of the ground for an English church had been purchased there.   It was by political power and influence that the Jewish nation was broken down, and her subjects dispersed abroad; and I will here hazard the opinion, that by political power and influence they will be gathered and built up; and further, that England is destined in the wisdom and economy of heaven to stretch forth the arm of political power, and advance in the front ranks of this glorious enterprise.   The Lord once raised up a Cyrus to restore the Jews, but that was not evidence that He owned the religion of the Persians.   This opinion I submit, however, to your superior wisdom to correct if you shall find it wrong.

"There is an increasing anxiety in Europe for the restoration of that people [the Jews]; and this anxiety is not confined to the pale of any religious community, but it has found its way to the courts of kings. Special ambassadors have been sent, and consuls and consular agents have been appointed. The rigorous policy which has hitherto characterized the course of other nations towards them now begins to be softened by the oil of friendship, and modified by the balm of humanity. The sufferings and privations under which they have groaned for so many centuries have at length touched the main-springs of Gentile power and sympathy; and may the God of their fathers, Abraham, Isaac, and Jacob, fan the flame by celestial breezes, until Israel's banner, sanctified by a Savior's blood, shall float on the walls of old Jerusalem, and the mountains and valleys of Judea reverberate with their songs of praise and thanksgiving to the Lamb that was slain.

"The imperial consul of Austria, at Galatz, near the mouth of the Danube, to whom I had a letter of introduction from his cousin in Vienna, told me that in consequence of so many of their Jewish subjects being inclined, of late, to remove to Syria and Palestine, his government had established a general consul at Beyroot for their protection. There are many Jews who care nothing about Jerusalem, and have no regard for God. Their money is the god they worship, yet there are many of the most pious and devout among them who look towards Jerusalem as the tender and affectionate mother looks upon the home where she left her lovely little babe."

Wednesday, 19.—I wrote Dr. Galland as follows:

The Prophet's Letter to Isaac Galland—On Settlement of Accounts.

DEAR SIR:—By your reply of the 18th instant to my note of the 17th, I am led to conclude that you received my communication in a manner altogether unintended by me, and that there may be no misunderstanding between us, and that you may be satisfied that I did not intend, and that I do not now intend anything, only upon the principles of the strictest integrity and uprightness before God, and to do as I would be done unto, I will state I have become embarrassed in my operations to a certain extent, and partly from a presentation of notes, which you, as my agent, had given for lands purchased in the eastern states, they having been sent to me. I have been obliged to cash them, and having no returns from you to meet those demands, or even the trifling expenses of your outfit, it has placed me in rather an unpleasant situation, and having a considerable amount of your scrip on hand, enough, as I suppose, to counterbalance the debts due you, and leave a balance in my favor, to some extent, even if it were small; and as I was pressed for funds, from the causes above mentioned, as well as others, I had hoped it would be convenient for you to lend me some assistance at the present time, and this was the reason why I sent a messenger to you as I did.

And now, sir, that we may have no misunderstanding in this matter, I think we had better have a settlement, and if I am owing you, I will pay you as soon as I can, and if you owe me, I shall only expect the same in return, for it is an old and trite maxim, that short reckonings make long friends. With this view of the matter, I would request you to call as soon as you possibly can make it convenient, and compare accounts, so that all things may be understood most perfectly between us in future time, and that all occasion for unpleasant feelings, if any such there be, may be entirely obliterated.

I remain, sir, most respectfully yours, &c.,

JOSEPH SMITH.

Read in the Book of Mormon, and in the evening visited Bishop Miller's wife, who was very sick, and the Bishop absent, collecting the funds for building the Temple and Nauvoo House.

Thursday, 20.—I attended a special conference of the Church at 10 o'clock a. m., concerning Dr. Galland. The conference voted to sanction the revocation of Dr. Galland's agency, dated the 18th of January, as published in the *Times and Seasons*, and also instructed the trustee-in-trust to proceed with Dr. Galland's affairs in relation to the Church, as he shall judge most expedient.

Isaac Galland Affair.

Six o'clock evening, attended a special council in the upper room of the new store.

George Washington Gee died today.*

* George W. Gee was the first son of Solomon and Sarah W. Gee, born in Rome, Ashtabula county, Ohio, August 13, 1815. Was baptized at Kirtland, Geauga county, Ohio, February 17, 1833. Married Mary Jane Smith in Kirtland, February 5, 1838, by whom he had two sons named Elias S. and George W. Went to Caldwell county, Missouri, 1838. Was driven out by a mob in the spring of 1839. Went to Nauvoo, and was ordained an Elder in the Church of Jesus Christ of Latter-day Saints, at the first conference held at Nauvoo, in October, 1839. Removed to Ambrosa, Lee county, Iowa, where he was appointed postmaster and deputy county surveyor; he surveyed the city plats of Nashville and Zarahemla, under the direction of President Joseph Smith. Was sent by the fall conference in 1841, to Pittsburg, Pennsylvania, where he died, January 20, 1842, while in discharge of his duties, having won the affections of all the Saints with whom he had become acquainted, by his integrity and perseverance. His opportunity for schooling had been limited, but by his own exertion he attained to an excellent education, and collected quite a respectable library.

Friday, 21.—I read the Book of Mormon, transacted a variety of business in the store and city, and spent the evening in the office with Elders Taylor and Richards, interpreting dreams, &c.

The presidents of the different quorums met with the High Council at Brother Hyrum's office, to receive instructions, according to appointment of the council on the 18th.

President Joseph Young stated the reasons why the quorum of Seventies had granted licenses; that he applied to President Joseph Smith for permission, on the solicitations of the quorums; that their reasons for so doing were because licenses could not be obtained from the Church clerk. President Joseph Butterfield testified to the same, and the council was satisfied with the testimony. The council was then addressed by President Hyrum Smith on the Word of Wisdom.

Seventies'
Quorum Af-
fairs

Saturday, 22.—I was very busy in appraising tithing property, and in the evening revised the rules of the city council, attended council, and spoke on their adoption, and was elected mayor, *pro tem.* of the city of Nauvoo.

Sunday, 23.—Spent the day mostly at the office, and on the presentation of charges by Elder William Draper, Jun., silenced Elder Daniel Wood, of Pleasant Vale, for preaching that the Church ought to unsheath the sword, and Elder A. Litz for preaching that the authorities of the Church were done away, &c., and cited him to appear before the High Council of Nauvoo for trial.

Monday, 24.—Reckoned with William and Wilson Law in the counting room, and examined the lots on which they are about to build a steam, grain, and sawmill.

Tuesday, 25.—Signed deeds for lots, to Law; transacted a variety of business in the city and office. In the evening debated with John C. Bennett and others to show that the Indians have greater cause to complain of the treatment of the whites, than the negroes, or sons of Cain.

General Orders. All the public arms will be required to be in the best possible condition, at the general inspection and parade, on the 7th of May proximo, and no deficiency whatever will be countenanced, overlooked, or suffered to pass without fine, on that occasion. All persons, therefore, holding said arms, will take notice, and govern themselves accordingly; and in order that the general inspection may pass off in a truly military style, alike honorable to the Legion, and creditable to the citizen soldiers, the brigadiers are required to attend the battalion parades within their respective commands, and inspect said arms in *propria personæ*, prior to the general parade. Persons disregarding these general orders, whether officers or privates, will find themselves in the *vocative*. The invincibles (Captain Hunter's company of light infantry), will be detailed for fatigue duty, on escorts and special service, and will take post by assignment, and receive their orders direct from the major general, through his herald and armor bearer. His Excellency the Governor of Illinois, the circuit judge of the judicial circuit, and the members of the bar, the officers of Hancock county, Colonel Williams and Colonel Deming, with their respective field and staff officers of the Illinois militia, and General Swazey and Colonel Fuller, with their respective field and staff officers, and Captain Davis and Avery's companies of cavalry of Iowa militia, are respectfully invited to attend and participate in the general parade on the 7th May.

JOSEPH SMITH, Lieutenant General.

Wednesday, 26.—Rode out to borrow money, to refund for money borrowed of John Benbow, as outfit for Dr. Galland in his agency. Transacted a variety of business, explained scripture to Elder Orson Spencer in my office, read in the Book of Mormon in the evening. Wrote a long letter to Edward Hunter, West Nantmeal, on temporal business.

The Church is in a prosperous condition, and the Saints are exerting themselves to build the Temple. The health of the city is good.

Upwards of twenty-three vessels wrecked on different parts of the British coast.

Thursday, 27.—Attended to baptism in general; in the afternoon, in council with the recorder, and gave some particular instructions concerning the order of the kingdom, and the management of business; placed the carpet given by Carlos Granger on the floor of my office; and spent the evening in general council in the upper room.

In the course of the day, Brigam Young, and James Ivins returned, and gave a favorable report from Dr. Galland, with his letter of attorney, letters and papers which he had received of me and the Church.

Friday, 28.—While I was at my office, Emma and Sister Whitney came in and spent an hour.

I received the following revelation to the Twelve concerning the *Times and Seasons*, given January 28, 1842—

Revelation.

Verily thus saith the Lord unto you, my servant Joseph, go and say unto the Twelve, that it is my will to have them take in hand the editorial department of the *Times and Seasons*, according to that manifestation which shall be given unto them by the power of my Holy Spirit in the midst of their counsel, saith the Lord. Amen.

I also decided that Elder John Snyder should go out on a mission, and if necessary some one go with him and raise up a church, and get means to go to England, and carry the epistle required in the revelation of December 22nd; and instructed the Twelve, Brigham Young, Heber C. Kimball, Wilford Woodruff and Willard Richards being present, to call Elder Snyder into their council and instruct him in these things, and if he will not do these things he shall be cut off from the Church, and be damned.

Elias Higbee, of the temple committee, came into my office, and I said unto him: The Lord is not well pleased with you; and you must straighten up your loins and do better, and your family also; for you have not been as diligent as you ought to have been, and as spring is approaching, you must arise and shake yourself, and be active, and make your children industrious, and help build the Temple.

Elder Snyder had appeared very backward about fulfilling the revelation concerning him, and felt that he
could not do it unless the Twelve would furnish him
means, when he was more able to furnish his own means,
as all the Elders were obliged to do when they went on
missions, or go without.

The High Council heard and accepted the report of their
committee of the 18th instant, as follows—

Report of High Council Committee.

The High Council of the Church of Jesus Christ to the Saints of
    Nauvoo, greeting—

DEAR BRETHREN:—As watchmen upon the walls of Zion, we feel it
to be our duty to stir up your minds, by way of remembrance, of things
which we conceive to be of the utmost importance to the Saints.

While we rejoice at the health and prosperity of the Saints, and the
good feeling which seems to prevail among them generally, and their
willingness to aid in the building of the "House of the Lord," we are
grieved at the conduct of some, who seem to have forgotten the purpose for which they have gathered.

Instead of promoting union,they have appeared to be engaged in sowing strifes and animosities among their brethren, spreading evil reports,
brother going to law with brother for trivial causes, which we consider
a great evil, and altogether unjustifiable, except in extreme cases, and
then not before the world.

We feel to advise taking the word of God for our guide, and exhort
you not to forget that you have come up as saviors upon Mount Zion,
consequently to seek each other's good—to become one, inasmuch as the
Lord has said, "Except ye become one, ye are not mine."

Let us always remember the admonition of the Apostle—"Dare any of
you, having a matter against another,go to law before the unjust,and not
before the Saints? Do ye not know the Saints shall judge the world? and
if the world shall be judged by you, are ye unworthy to judge the small-
est matters? Know ye not that we shall judge angels? how much more
things that pertain to this life? If, then, ye have judgments of things
pertaining to this life, set them to judge who are least esteemed in the
Church. I speak to your shame. Is it so, that there is not a wise
man among you? no, not one that shall be able to judge between his
brethren. But brother goeth to law with brother, and that before the
unbelievers. Now therefore there is utterly a fault among you, because ye go to law one with another. Why do ye not rather take wrong?

why do ye not rather suffer yourselves to be defrauded? Nay, ye do wrong, and defraud, and that your brethren. Know ye not that the unrighteous shall not inherit the kingdom of God? Be not deceived; neither fornicators, nor idolaters, nor adulterers, nor effeminate, nor abusers of themselves with mankind, nor thieves, nor covetous, nor drunkards, nor revilers, nor extortioners, shall inherit the kingdom of God" (I Cor. 6:1-10). Who, observing these things, would go to law distressing his brother, thereby giving rise to hardness, evil speaking, strifes and animosities among those who have covenanted to keep the commandments of God—who have taken upon them the name of Saints, and if Saints are to judge angels, and also to judge the world—why then are they not competent to judge in temporal matters, especially in trivial cases, taking the law of the Lord for their guide, brotherly kindness, charity, &c., as well as the law of the land? Brethren, these are evils which ought not to exist among us. We hope the time will speedily arrive when these things will be done away, and everyone stand in the office of his calling, as a faithful servant of God, building each other up, bearing each other's infirmities, and so fulfill the law of Christ.

William Marks, President; Samuel Bent, Lewis D. Wilson, David Fullmer, Thomas Grover, Newel Knight, Leonard Soby, James Allred, Elias Higbee, George W. Harris, Aaron Johnson, William Huntington, Sen., Daniel Carrier, Austin Cowles, Charles C. Rich, Counselors.

Attest: Hosea Stout, Clerk.

Sir Robert Sale [commander of the British forces in Afghanistan] received a letter from Sha-Shoojah, requiring him to evacuate Jellalabad, with which he refused to comply.

Saturday, 29.—I was much engaged with the tithings; in the afternoon in my office, counseling various individuals: and in the evening in council with Brothers Young, Kimball, Richards and others, showing forth the Kingdom and the order thereof concerning many things, and the will of God concerning His servants.

Letter of G. Walker to Elder Brigham Young et al.—Affairs in England since Departure of the Apostles.

MANCHESTER, ENGLAND, Jan. 29, 1842.

To President Young, Elders Kimball and Richards.

BELOVED BRETHREN—Soon after your departure, a clergyman of the church of England called upon my employer, to request that he might have an interview with me, as he had a wish to propound certain questions to me; upon his request being complied with, we retired to a private room, when he produced a long list of questions, written down, opposite to which he wrote my answers. The rise of the Church, Priesthood, doctrines offices, sacraments, &c., were the principal queries he advanced. When he demurred to any of our principles I was proceeding to explain, he cut my discourse short by saying he would not hold any controversy, his object being only to obtain information. After the disposal of his queries, he wished to be informed where he could obtain the whole of the publications of the Latter-day Saints, as he wished to be in possession of them; I informed him at 47 Oxford street, Manchester, and he promised to send for them.

Soon after the visit of this reverend gentleman, I had reason to suspect that undermining operations were in progress against me, I therefore tendered my resignation to the directors, but they would not accept it; and very soon after a public accountant was employed by them to investigate their accounts for several years back, and I was happy to be able to answer satisfactorily every question that was asked of me respecting them.

After this another minister sent a lengthy article extracted from an American paper, purporting to be the production of a Mr. Anthon, with a request that I would "read, mark, learn, and inwardly digest" the same. I replied to the statements of Mr. Anthon, and after disposing of them paragraph for paragraph, I told him that I was obliged by his favoring me with it, inasmuch as it satisfied my mind, and was confirmatory of the prediction of Isaiah being fulfilled, seeing that Mr. Anthon admitted that "the words of the book were delivered to the learned," &c. I then proceeded to contrast the church of England with churches established by the Apostles; but he has not acknowledged the receipt of my letter as yet. The clergy are building ten new churches in this town and neighborhood, and are employing additional curates to go round to the houses of their parishoners, to coerce or intimidate them into an attendance upon their services in fulfillment of the words of Paul, In the last days perilous times will come, &c., that they would have a form of godliness, but deny the power, and would creep into houses to lead captive silly women," &c. (See II Timothy, 1st chapter, 1st to 8th verses.) These curates make repeated visits, generally when the heads of families are from home, and take special care to enquire where the family are employed, and what place of worship they attend, &c., and leave tracts for the family to read.

One of the Rev. Hugh Stowell's curates has paid several visits to my house, but always in my absence, although he was requested to call

when I was at home, and informed of the time when he might meet
with me.

The following discourse took place in our own neighborhood:
Curate: What religion may you be, my good woman? I am a church-
woman, sir. What church do you usually attend? I never attend any,
sir.

After reprimanding the woman for pretending to be one of his flock,
while she absented herself from the fold, he went to the house of a poor
woman who had lately joined the Saints. I am a minister of the
Church of Jesus Christ in England, and have called to inquire what
school you send your children to, and what religion you profess? The
woman replied she was a "Latter-day Saint." "Oh! delusion, delusion!" he rejoined, and began to rail against the Saints, whereupon she
handed him the Bible, and requested him to read the place where she
casually opened to, namely the third chapter of Micah, and to preach a
discourse from that part of the Bible; but he retreated from before her
and has not troubled her since.

The Lord Bishop of Chester and the Protestant clergymen, have hired
a person of the name of Brindley to go about lecturing against the
Saints, and have commenced a monthly periodical in which the foul
slanders heaped upon the Saints in America and elsewhere are retailed
out to satisfy the malice of the enemies of truth. The *Manchester
Courier* has had several articles against our society and principles, and
the old Spaulding romance has been resuscitated for the occasion. The
Rev. Charles Burton, Doctor of Laws, minister of "All Saints," has
been several times to see me lately, and upon one occasion invited me to
his house, where I went and discussed our principles for several hours,
until he was glad to withdraw from the contest; I found him ignorant
in a great measure of what the Bible contains respecting the latter-days.
He admitted that the Saints would reign on earth.

The great work of the Lord is still progressing in spite of all the opposition of lying priests and their auxiliaries of the newspaper press. I
baptized Elizabeth Smith, who resided with us when you were in England, and she purposes coming out to America along with us.

There is very great distress among the operatives and the poor generally, and great excitement respecting the agitation of the repeal of the
corn laws. Great fires have frequently occurred at the commencement
of this year; a large carrier's warehouse was consumed by fire, about
from £200,000 to £300,000 ($1,000,000 to $1,500,000) worth of cotton
and grain, &c., destroyed. It was the Union Company's carrying ware
house, Piccadilly. There is great depression in almost every branch of
manufactures, and great perplexity; and I am daily more and more convinced that the time is not far distant when Babylon the great will be

fallen and become a desolation, and the kings and the merchants of the earth will weep and mourn over her, and she will be cast down, even as a great mill-stone cast into the sea, and will be found no more at all.

I opened a place for preaching at Blakesley, about six week's ago; and there were three baptized and confirmed there last week. I was with Elder John Brotherton at Middleton on Sunday last, where he and Elder Hardman had obtained a room to preach to the Chartists.* We have also a place opened at Disbury and Heaton.

About three weeks ago there was a letter inserted in the *Manchester Courier*, by a writer who signs himself R P., calling upon the clergymen of the church of England, and the respectable inhabitants, and the most respectable and intelligent of the police, to attend our meetings at the Carpenters' Hall, as they had fondly hoped that the system would have fallen to the ground by the weight of its own absurdity; but they found that there was method and consistency in the apparent madness of these deluded people, and that experience had taught them that such expectations were vain: as they had observed that there was considerable consistency displayed, and method attending our arrangements, there being an emigration office established in this town, &c. The writer suspected there was a genuine American trick being practiced by the interested parties at the head of the system, to decoy the ignorant and unwary to perish in the swamps of New Orleans, and that they were draining the country of their best artists; and it was high time some steps were taken to put a stop to such practices.

We have since discovered that the writer is no other than Robert

---

* "Chartism" and the "Chartists," may be said to have come into existence early in the reign of Queen Victoria, in consequence of the formal declarations of the leaders of the Liberal party in parliament not to proceed further in the reforms to which it was generally understood they were pledged. "Quietly studied now," says Justin McCarthy (1878) "the people's charter does not seem a very formidable document. There is so little smell of gun-powder about it. Its 'points' as they were called were six:" Manhood suffrage; annual parliaments; vote by ballot; abolition of the "property qualification" for members of parliament; payment of the members of parliament; and the division of the country into equal electoral districts. "There's your charter," said Daniel O'Connel, to the secretary of the Workingmen's Association—"There's your charter, agitate for it, and never be content with anything less." It was this circumstance that gave to the movement and to its supporters the name "chartism" and "chartists." "Nothing," to again quote McCarthy, "can be more unjust than to represent the leaders and promoters of the movement as mere factions and self-seeking demagogues. Some of them were impassioned young poets drawn from the class whom Kingsley has described in 'Alton Locke;' some were men of education; many were earnest and devoted fanatics; and so far as we can judge, all, or nearly all, were sincere." *History of Our Own Times*, Vol. I. Chapter V. This to show that the preaching of the Elders of the Church to the "Chartists," was no effort to unite Church work with any wild and disorderly political movement in England.

Philips, Esq., an extensive manufacturer and merchant, brother to Mark Philips, Esq., another great manufacturer and member of parliament for the Borough of Manchester. The editor of the *Courier* has been playing upon the same string for several weeks since, and feels satisfied that from the exposure he has given the whole system, it must inevitably die away. He was therefore satisfied with having done his duty, and could safely leave them to the management of the proper parties, and recommend the police to do their duty. It appears that the gallant officer at the head of the police (Sir Charles Shaw), has too much discretion and good sense to be set on like a dog to worry out a society of Christians, because the editor of the Puseyite Oracle pointed the finger of scorn at them, because they dared to worship God according to the dictates of their own consciences. I should have liked very well for the police to have been there on Sunday last, for three persons had to be put out by the brethren for disturbing the meeting in the sacrament services.

I remain, beloved brethren, your brother and fellow laborer,

G. WALKER.

P. S.—I omitted to say that the writer in the paper alluded to, informed the public that he was endeavoring to obtain information respecting the movements of the people. He had previously sent a person to Elder Pratt to get him to state something in writing respecting emigration, and after the publication of the letter before referred to, he again sent to Elder Pratt for additional information in writing. I happened to be at Elder Pratt's when he made the second application, and I told Elder Pratt that he was the individual who had published the letter in the *Courier*. Elder Pratt sent him another letter containing the required information; and also stated that he had no objection to submit to him, or to the government of this country, or any of its departments, the religious principles of our society, our place of emigration, and indeed the whole of our movements in this and other countries, for the strictest investigation.

The manufacturers are evidently beginning to be jealous of the mechanics and workmen emigrating with people having so systematic an organization as the Latter-day Saints display in their arrangements in this town.

I remain yours, &c.   G. W.

CHAPTER XXX.

EMIGRATION OF THE SAINTS FROM ENGLAND TO NAUVOO—THE
BOOK OF ABRAHAM.

Sunday, January 30, 1842.—I preached at my house morning and evening, concerning the different spirits, their operations, designs, &c.

Monday, 31.—Assisted in appraising the tithings of Saturday with Emma. Received many calls. Read in the Book of Mormon. After dinner visited Brother Chase who was very sick, and in the evening was in council with Brigham Young, Heber C. Kimball, Orson Pratt, Wilford Woodruff, and Willard Richards concerning Brother Snyder and the printing office; spent the evening very cheerfully, and retired about ten o'clock.

Tuesday, February 1.—Two large stones, for door sills, for the Nauvoo House, were landed.

The following article is from the *Millennial Star* of this date:

EMIGRATION.

In the midst of the general distress which prevails in this country on account of the want of employment, the high price of provisions, the oppression, priestcraft, and iniquity of the land, it is pleasing to the household of faith to contemplate a country reserved by the Almighty as a sure asylum for the poor and oppressed,—a country every way adapted to their wants and conditions—and still more pleasing to think that thousands of the Saints have already made their escape from this country, and all its abuses and distress, and that they have found a home, where, by persevering industry, they may enjoy all the blessings of liberty, peace and plenty.

It is not yet two years since the Saints in England, in obedience to the command of their heavenly Father, commenced a general plan of emigration to the land of Zion.

They were few in number, generally poor, and had every opposition to encounter, both from a want of means and from the enemies of truth, who circulated every falsehood calculated to hinder or discourage them. Newspapers and tracts were put in circulation, sermons and public speeches were delivered in abundance, to warn the people that Nauvoo was a barren waste on the sea shore—that it was a wild and uninhabited swamp—that it was full of savages, wild beasts and serpents—that all the English Saints who should go there would be immediately sold for slaves by the leaders of the Church—that there was nothing to eat, no water, and no way possible to obtain a living; that all who went there would have their money taken from them, and themselves imprisoned, &c. But notwithstanding all these things, thousands have emigrated from this country, and now find themselves comfortably situated, and in the enjoyment of the comforts of life, and in the midst of society where God is worshiped in the spirit of truth and union, and where nearly all are agreed in religious principles. They all find plenty of employment and good wages, while the expense of living is about one-eighth of what it costs in this country. For instance —beef and pork costs about one penny per pound, flour from 2s to 3s for forty pounds, and Indian meal about one shilling for sixty pounds; butter from 4d to 6d per pound, while milch cows are to be had in plenty for about £3 per head, and other things in proportion. Millions on millions of acres of land lie before them unoccupied, with a soil as rich as Eden, and a surface as smooth, clear, and ready for the plough as the park scenery of England.

Instead of a lonely swamp or dense forest filled with savages, wild beasts and serpents, large cities and villages are springing up in their midst, with schools, colleges, and temples. The mingled noise of mechanism, the bustle of trade, the song of devotion, are heard in the distance, while thousands of flocks and herds are seen grazing peacefully on the plains, and the fields and gardens smile with plenty, and the wild red men of the forest are only seen as they come on a friendly visit to the Saints and to learn the way of the Lord.

Several large ships have been chartered by the Saints during the present fall and winter, and have been filled with emigrants, who have gone forth with songs of joy; and some of them have already arrived safely in the promised land, while others are, doubtless, still tossing upon the ocean.

The expense of passage and provisions to New Orleans has, at no time this season, exceeded £4, and it is generally as low as three pounds fifteen shillings. This is remarkable when we reflect that each passenger has provisions and water provided in plenty for ten weeks. But it is obtained at this low price by a union of effort among the Saints, and by the faithful and persevering exertions of their agents. For instance they purchase provisions by the quantity, and duty free, and the moment they bid farewell to their native shores they hoist the *Flag of Liberty*—the Ensign of Zion—the stars and stripes of the American Union; and under its protection they completely and practically nullify the bread tax. They eat free bread, free tea, free sugar, free everything, and thus accomplish a journey of five thousand miles on the same money that is would cost to feed them for the same length of time in England.

Who that has a heart to feel, or a soul to rejoice, will not be glad at so glorious a plan of deliverance? Who will not hail the messengers of the Latter-day Saints as the friends of humanity—the benefactors of mankind.

> Thousands have gone, and millions more must go,
> The Gentiles as a stream to Zion flow.

Yes, friends, this glorious work has but just commenced; and we now call upon the Saints to come forward with united effort, with persevering exertion, and with union of action, and help yourselves and one another to emigrate to the Land of Promise.

In this way we shall not only bring about the deliverance of tens of thousands, who must otherwise suffer in this country, but we shall add to the strength of Zion, and help to rear her cities and temples—"to make her wilderness like Eden, and her desert like the garden of the Lord," while the young men and the middle aged will serve to increase her legions—to strengthen her bulwarks—that the enemies of law and order who have sought her destruction, may stand afar off and tremble, and her banner become terrible to the wicked.

Ye children of Zion, once more we say, in the name of Israel's God, arise, break off your shackles, loose yourselves from the bands of your neck, and go forth to inherit the earth, and to build up waste places of many generations.

All who would go before September next, should go in the early part of March, as it is as late as is advisable to venture by way of New Orleans, on account of the extreme heat of summer; and to go by New York or Quebec, will be double the expense. Experience has taught us that an emigrant can go from Liverpool to New Orleans, and from thence 1,500 miles up the river to Nauvoo for something like £5 per head, including all provisions and expenses; while by way of New York or Quebec it will cost from ten to thirteen pounds; and besides there is another consideration, and that is, goods will cost but a trifle for freight up the Mississippi on a steamer, while the expense would be immense the other way.

Therefore the Saints will please take notice, that after the 10th of March next, emigration had better entirely cease, till about the 20th of

September following. If thousands should wish to go between this time and the 10th of March, they have only to furnish us with their names and about £4 per head (children under fourteen years half price), and we will provide them passage and provisions, for the voyage, and return the overplus, if any, at Liverpool.

We would again urge upon emigrants the important fact that if they make known to us their intentions, and send their money and names some weeks beforehand, it will be a great convenience, and save confusion, trouble and expense. All applications should be addressed to Messrs. Pratt and Fielding, 36 Chapel street, Liverpool, or to the *Star* office, 47 Oxford street, Manchester.

We do not wish to confine the benefit of our emigration plan to the Saints, but are willing to grant all industrious, honest, and well-disposed persons who may apply to us the same information and assistance as emigrants to the western states, there being abundant room for more than a hundred millions of inhabitants.

Wednesday, 2.—Sister Laura Phelps, wife of Morris Phelps, died, aged 36 years. She was driven from Jackson county in 1833, was in the persecution of Missouri, in 1838, and went from Iowa to Missouri to assist in liberating her husband, Death of Laura Phelps. and was left in the prison yard when he made his escape, willing to suffer all the abuses a savage horde could inflict upon her to set her companion free from the grasp of his murderous enemies. Her rest is glorious.

I spent the day in council with Dr. Isaac Galland and Calvin A. Warren, Esq.

Thursday, 3.—In council with Calvin A. Warren, Esq., concerning a settlement with the estate of Oliver Granger, and delivered him the necessary papers.

Elder Woodruff took the superintendence of the printing office, and Elder Taylor the editorial department of the *Times and Seasons*; and he commenced by taking an inventory of the establishment this day.

Friday, 4.—Instructed that an invoice of Dr. Galland's scrip be made.

Closed a contract with Ebenezer Robinson for the printing office on the corner of Bain and Water streets, also

the paper fixtures, bookbindery, and stereotype foundry,
Debates in by proxy, namely, Willard Richards, cost
Nauvoo. between 7,000 and 8,000 dollars. In the
evening attended a debate. At this time debates were
held weekly, and entered into by men of the first talents
in the city, young and old, for the purpose of eliciting
truth, acquiring knowledge, and improving in public
speaking.

Saturday, 5.—Elder Daniel Wood, who had been silenced by Presidents Smith and Young, on a complaint for
Vindication teaching false doctrine, came before the High
of Daniel Council at Nauvoo, and proved that he had
Wood. not taught false doctrine, but had been complained of by those who had prejudice and hardness
against him, and was restored to his former standing in
the Church.

This being Tithing Day, upwards of $1,000 worth of
property was received.

The ship *Hope* sailed from Liverpool for New Orleans
with 270 Saints.

Sunday, 6.—Elders Brigham Young and Heber C. Kimball went to La Harpe to hold a two-days meeting.

From this time I was engaged in counseling the brethren and attending to the common vocations of life and my
calling, reading the Book of Mormon, &c.

Thursday, 10.—I was sick and kept my bed.

The war continues to rage between England and
China.

Friday, 11.—I was convalescent, and walked twice to
the store.

Saturday, 12.—An ordinance regulating weights and
measures was passed, also an ordinance regulating auctions, by the city council which I attended. During the
sitting of the council the subject of our chartered rights
was discussed.

In the afternoon, plead in an action of slander before
the mayor, in behalf of the city against Lyman O. Little-

field, and obtained judgment of $500 bonds to keep the peace.

Sunday, *13*—In council with the mayor, Brother Hyrum and Elder Willard Richards, and visited Samuel Bennett (who was sick) in company with William Law and wife.

Monday, *14*.—Spent the day at my office, transacting a variety of business, and continued to do the same from day to day till the 17th.

Thursday, *17*.—I attended a special session of the city council, when an ordinance was passed authorizing and regulating marriages in the city of Nauvoo.

Letter of Alfred Cordon to Joseph Smith—Reporting Affairs in England.

HANLEY, STAFFORD COUNTY, ENGLAND, February 17, 1842.

PRESIDENT JOSEPH SMITH:—The work in which we are engaged rolls on in this lands and in spite of all its enemies, moves onward in majesty and power; there are many who devote all their time and talent in endeavoring to overthrow it; but I discover that they can "do nothing against the truth but for the truth." Many tracts have been published against us, containing all manner of lies, but in the end good will be the result. "He that knoweth God, heareth us." Some of the tools of Satan are doing more in spreading the truth than we are able to do; one in particular, a Mr. Brindley, is publishing a periodical showing the "errors and blasphemies" of "Mormonism;" and in order to do this, he publishes many of the revelations of God given to us, and through this means, the testimony is visiting the mansions of the high and mighty ones—the "reverends, right reverends" and all the noble champions of sectarians receive them as a precious morsel; and they are read with much interest; whereas, if we had sent them, they would have been spurned from their dwellings, and would not have been considered worth reading.

The state of this country is very awful, and is, according to prospects, on the eve of a mighty revolution; all confidence is gone between master and man, and men are afraid of each other; peace is fast removing from this land; in the course of the last few days, in many parts of this isle, they have been burning the effigy of the great men of this nation—poverty, distress and starvation abound on every hand. The groans, and tears and wretchedness of the thousands of people are enough to rend the hearts of demons; many of the Saints are suffering much through hunger and nakedness; many with large families can scarcely get bread and water enough to hold the spirit in the tabernacle; many, very many, are out of employment, and cannot get work to do,and others that do work hard fourteen or fifteen hours per day, can scarcely earn enough to enable them to live upon the earth. Surely there is need of deliverance in Zion, and I am ready to exclaim, thanks be to Thy name, O Lord, for remembering Thy covenants! and that the "set time to favor Zion has come," and that He has chosen the west for a refuge for His people.

Wishing you all success, I remain, yours in the new and everlasting covenant.

ALFRED CORDON.

Friday, 18.—I attended an adjourned city council, and spoke at considerable length in committee of the whole on the great privileges of the Nauvoo Charter, and especially on the registry of deeds for Nauvoo, and prophesied in the name of the Lord God, that Judge Douglas and no other judge of the Circuit Court will ever set aside a law of the city council, establishing a registry of deeds in the city of Nauvoo.

Confidence in the Nauvoo Charter.

Saturday, 19.—I was engaged in the Recorder's Office (in the first story of the Brick Store), on the tithings, and in council in my office with Elders Brigham Young, Heber C. Kimball and others.

A severe shock of an earthquake threw down all the parapets, bastions, and guard houses constructed by Sir Robert Sale, and demolished a third part of the town of Jellalabad, India.

Sunday, 20.—I attended the meeting on the hill. About this time the ship *John Cummins* sailed from Liverpool for New Orleans with Saints. The *Tremont* sailed on the 12th of January with 143 passengers, mostly Saints. The expenses of passage from Liverpool to New Orleans averages from £3, 15s to £4, including provisions.

Monday, 21.—I was visiting in the city in the morning, and transacting a variety of business at the office in the afternoon and evening.

Announcement of the Trustee in Trust for the Church Respecting Work on the Temple.

To the Brethren in Nauvoo City: Greeting—It is highly important for the forwarding of the Temple, that an equal distribution of labor should be made in relation to time; as a superabundance of hands one week, and none the next, tends to retard the progress of the work: therefore every brother is requested to be particular to labor on the day set apart for the same, in his ward; and to remember that he that sows sparingly, shall also reap sparingly, so that if the brethren want a plentiful harvest, they will do well to be at the place of labor in good season in the morning, bringing all necessary tools, according to their occupation, and those who have teams bring them also, unless otherwise advised by the Temple Committee. Should any one be detained from his labor by unavoidable circumstances on the day appointed, let him labor the next day, or the first day possible.

N.B —The captains of the respective wards are particularly requested to be at the place of labor on their respective days, and keep an accurate account of each man's work, and be ready to exhibit a list of the same when called for.

The heart of the Trustee is daily made to rejoice in the good feelings of the brethren, made manifest in their exertion to carry forward the work of the Lord, and rear His Temple; and it is hoped that neither planting, sowing, or reaping will hereafter be made to interfere with the regulations hinted at above.

Joseph Smith, Trustee in Trust.

An Additional Word from the Twelve.

Recorder's Office, Febr. 21, 1842.

We would also say to all the churches, that inasmuch as they want the blessings of God and angels, as also of the Church of Jesus Christ, and wish to see it spread and prosper through the world, and Zion built up and truth and righteousness prevail,—let all the different branches of the Church of Jesus Christ of Latter-day Saints in all the world, call meetings in their respective places and tithe themselves and send up to this place to the Trustee in Trust, so that his hands may be loosed, and the Temple go on, and other works be done, such as the new translation of the Bible, and the record of Father Abraham published to the world.

Beloved brethren, we as the messengers of the Lord feel to call upon you to help roll on the mighty work, it is our duty so to do, and it is your reasonable service—and the Lord will bless you in so doing.

We subscribe ourselves your humble servants, and standard bearers to the world.   BRIGHAM YOUNG, President,
          WILLARD RICHARDS, Clerk of the Twelve.

Tuesday, 22.—Attended to a variety of business as usual.

Wednesday, 23.—Settled with and paid Brother Chase, and assisted in the counting room in settling with Ebenezer Robinson, visiting the printing office, and gave Reuben Hedlock instruction concerning the cut for the altar and gods in the Records of Abraham, as designed for the *Times and Seasons*.

Thursday, 24.—Engaged in council with the brethren, attended to business at the general office. In the afternoon explained the records of Abraham to the recorder. Sisters Marinda, Mary, and others present to hear the explanations.

Letter of the Prophet's to an Unknown Brother on Tithing.

NAUVOO, Feb. 24, 1842.

BELOVED BROTHER—Yours of the 24th ult. is received, in relation to certain tithings of your neighborhood being transferred to your account, which you hold against the Church to the amount of $305, including $150 of your own.

There are no receipts issued for property received on tithing; but an entry is made in the Book of the Law of the Lord, and parties living at a distance notified of the same.

If the parties named will pay you the sum specified in your letter, and you will endorse the same, i. e. $305, on the obligation you hold against the Church, and give me notice accordingly, with a schedule of individuals' names and payments, the same shall be entered to their credit on tithing.   Yours, &c.
          JOSEPH SMITH,
          WILLARD RICHARDS, Scribe.

Friday, 25.—Engaged in counseling and general business.

Saturday, 26.—At the recorder's office engaged in the tithing, and at the court at the office of the Patriarch.

Sunday, 27.—Engaged in counseling the Saints.

Monday, 28.—I offered a settlement to Father Snow by

Jenkins' notes, which he declined, choosing to take land in Ramus;paid Brother Robert Pierce $2,700, the balance due him for a farm Dr. Galland bought of Brother Pierce in Brandywine Township, Chester county, Pennsylvania, for $5,000, namely a deed for lot 2, block 94, $1,100, and lot 1, block 95, $800, and lot 4, block 78, $806, the remainder having been previously paid. The bond was cancelled and given up, and Brother Pierce expressed his satisfaction of the whole, in the *Times and Seasons*, as follows—

Note of Robert Pierce—Expressing Satisfaction at Financial Settlement.

NAUVOO, Feb. 28, 1842.

President Joseph Smith.

DEAR SIR—I feel anxious to express my feelings concerning the business transactions between the Church and myself; as it is well known to many, that Dr. Galland, as agent for the Church, purchased my farm while I was living in Brandywine Township, Chester county, Pennsylvania, and many supposed, or pretended to suppose, I would get nothing in return; but I wish to say to all my old friends and enemies in Pennsylvania,through the medium of the *Times and Seasons*, that I have received my pay in full from the Church of Jesus Christ of Latter-day Saints, through yourself, sir, as their trustee in trust, according to the original contract; and that from my acquaintance with yourself, and those brethren who are assisting you in the great and increasing business of the Church, I have the fullest confidence in all the transactions of the Church,and I request those papers in Philadelphia,who published concerning my sale and loss, with such bitter lamentations, to publish this also.

I am, sir, your brother and well-wisher,

ROBERT PIERCE.

Thursday, March 1, 1842.—During the forenoon I was at my office and the printing office, correcting the first plate or cut of the records of Father Abraham, prepared by Reuben Hedlock, for the *Times and Seasons*, and in council in my office, in the afternoon; and in the evening with the Twelve and their wives at Elder Woodruff's, at which time I explained many important principles in relation to progressive improvement in the scale of intelligent existence.

I commenced publishing my translations of the Book of Abraham in the *Times and Seasons* as follows—

FAC-SIMILE FROM THE BOOK OF ABRAHAM—NO. 1.

EXPLANATION OF THE ABOVE CUT.

Fig. 1.   The angel of the Lord.

Fig. 2.   Abraham fastened upon an altar.

Fig. 3.   The idolatrous priest of Elkenah attempting to offer up Abraham as a sacrifice.

Fig 4.   The altar for sacrifice, by the idolatrous priests, standing before the gods of Elkenah, Libnah, Mahmackrah, Korash, and Pharaoh.

Fig. 5.   The idolatrous god of Elkenah.

Fig. 6.   The idolatrous god of Libnah.

Fig. 7.   The idolatrous god of Mahmackrah.

Fig. 8.   The idolatrous god of Korash.

Fig 9.   The idolatrous god of Pharaoh.

Fig. 10.   Abraham in Egypt.

Fig. 11.   Designed to represent the pillars of Heaven, as understood by the Egyptians.

Fig. 12.   Raukeeyang, signifying expanse, or the firmament over our heads; but in this case in relation to this subject, the Egyptians meant it to signify Shauman, to be high, or the heavens; answering to the Hebrew word, Shaumahyeem.

EXPLANATION OF THE ABOVE CUT.

Fig. 1. Kolob, signifying the first creation, nearest to the celestial, or the residence of God. First in government, the last pertaining to the measurement of time. The measurement, according to celestial time; which celestial time signifies one day to a cubit. One day in Kolob is equal to a thousand years, according to the measurement of this earth, which is called by the Egyptians Jah-oh-eh.

Fig 2. Stands next to Kolob, called by the Egyptians Oliblish, which is the next grand governing creation near to the celestial, or the place where God resides; holding the key of power also, pertaining to other planets; as revealed from God to Abraham, as he offered sacrifice upon an altar which he had built unto the Lord.

Fig. 3. Is made to represent God, sitting upon His throne clothed with power and authority, with a crown of eternal light upon His head; representing, also, the grand key words of the Holy Priesthood, as reavealed to Adam in the Garden of Eden, as also to Seth, Noah, Melchisedek, Abraham, and all to whom the Priesthood was revealed.

Fig. 4. Answers to the Hebrew word Raukeeyang, signifying expanse or the firmament of the heavens; also a numerical figure in Egyptian, signifying one thousand; answering to the measuring of the time of Oliblish, which is equal with Kolob in its revolution and in its measuring of time.

Fig. 5. Is called in Egyptian Enish-go-on-dosh; this is one of the governing planets also, and is said by the Egyptians to be the Sun, and to borrow its light from Kolob, through the medium of Kae-e-vanrash, which is the grand Key, or in other words, the governing power, which governs fifteen other fixed planets or stars, as also Floeese or the Moon, the Earth and the Sun, in their annual revolutions. This planet received its power through the medium of Kli-flos-is-es, or Hah-ko-kau-beam, the stars represented by numbers 22, and 23, receiving light from the revolutions of Kolob.

Fig. 6.   Represents the earth in four quarters.

Fig. 7.   Represents God sitting upon His throne, revealing through the heavens the grand Key Words of the Priesthood; as also the sign of the Holy Ghost unto Abraham, in the form of a dove.

Fig. 8.   Contains writing that cannot be revealed unto the world; but is to be had in the Holy Temple of God.

Fig. 9.   Ought not to be revealed at the present time.

Fig. 10.   Also.

Fig. 11.   Also.—If the world can find out these numbers, so let it be.   Amen.

Figures 12, 13, 14, 15, 16, 17, 18, 19, and 20, will be given in the own due time of the Lord.

The above translation is given as far as we have any right to give at the present time.

EXPLANATION OF CUT NO. 3.

Fig. 1.   Abraham sitting upon Pharaoh's throne, by the politeness of the king, with a crown upon his head, representing the Priesthood, as emblematical of the grand Presidency in Heaven, with the sceptre of justice and judgment in his hand.

Fig. 2.   King Pharaoh, whose name is given in the characters above his head.

Fig. 3.   Signifies Abraham in Egypt; referring to Abraham, as given in the ninth number of the Times and Seasons.   (Also as given in the first fac-simile of this book.)

Fig. 4.   Prince of Pharaoh, King of Egypt, as written above the hand.

Fig. 5.   Shulem, one of the king's principal waiters, as represented by the characters above his hand.

Fig. 6.   Olimlah, a slave belonging to the prince.

Abraham is reasoning upon the principles of astronomy, in the king's court.

THE BOOK OF ABRAHAM.*

TRANSLATED FROM THE PAPYRUS, BY JOSEPH SMITH.†

A Translation of some Ancient Records that have fallen into our hands, from the Catacombs of Egypt, purporting to be the writings of Abraham, while he was in Egypt, called the Book of Abraham, written by his own hand upon papyrus.

In the land of the Chaldeans, at the residence of my father, I Abraham, saw that it was needful for me to obtain another place of residence, and finding there was greater happiness, and peace and rest for me, I sought for the blessings of the fathers, and the right whereunto I should be ordained to administer the same; having been myself a follower of righteousness, desiring also to be one who possessed great knowledge, and to be a greater follower of righteousness, and to possess a greater knowledge, and to be a father of many nations, a prince of peace; and desiring to receive instructions and to keep the commandments of God, I became a rightful heir, a High Priest, holding the right belonging to the fathers; it was conferred upon me from the fathers; it came down from the fathers, from the beginning of time, yea, even from the beginning, or before the foundations of the earth, to the present time, even the right of the first born, or the first man, who is Adam, our first Father, through the fathers, unto me.

2. I sought for mine appointment unto the Priesthood according to the appointment of God unto the fathers, concerning the seed. My

* For an account of how the Prophet came into possession of the Book of Abraham see this History Vol. II, pp. 235, 6, 8; also 236, and more especially pp. 349—50, and *note* p. 350.

† The Book of Abraham was first published in the *Times and Seasons* in two numbers, Vol. III, Nos. 9 and 10, March 1 and March 15, 1842, respectively. In this form it was copied into the Prophet's history with the several historical items which occurred between the dates of the publication of the two parts, and in this form is found in the *Millennial Star*, Vol. XIX, pp. 100-103 and 164-168; but it is now thought proper to publish the Book of Abraham entire without dividing it into two articles, as in the above named periodicals.

It is important to note also that the Book of Abaham was published in the *Times and Seasons* when the Prophet was responsible editor of the periodical (he announces his editorial responsibility in No. 9 of Vol. III, p. 710). Attention is called to this fact, in passing, because it is contended on the part of some, that the doctrine of the plurality of divine personages, as now understood by the Church, was not a doctrine taught by Joseph Smith; whereas it is a doctrine of the Book of Abraham, as will be seen by reference to it, published by him in a periodical of which he was the responsible editor; and, moreover, the Book of Abraham was often referred to by the Prophet in approving terms.

fathers having turned from their righteousness, and from the holy commandments which the Lord their God had given unto them, unto the worshiping of the gods of the heathen, utterly refused to hearken to my voice; for their hearts were set to do evil, and were wholly turned to the god of Elkenah, and the god of Libnah, and the god of Mahmackrah, and the god of Korash, and the god of Pharaoh, king of Egypt, therefore they turned their hearts to the sacrifice of the heathen in offering up their children unto their dumb idols, and hearkened not unto my voice, but endeavored to take away my life by the hand of the priest of Elkenah—the priest of Elkenah was also the priest of Pharaoh.

3. Now at this time it was the custom of the priest of Pharaoh, the king of Egypt, to offer up upon the altar which was built in the land of Chaldea, for the offering unto these strange gods, men, women and children. And it came to pass that the priest made an offering unto the god of Pharaoh, and also unto the god of Shagreel, even after the manner of the Egyptians. Now the god of Shagreel was the Sun. Even the thank-offering of a child did the priest of Pharaoh offer upon this altar, which stood by the hill called Potiphar's hill, at the head of the plain of Olishem. Now, this priest had offered upon the altar three virgins at one time, who were the daughters of Onitah, one of the royal descent, directly from the loins of Ham. These virgins were offered up because of their virtue; they would not bow down to worship gods of wood, or of stone, therefore they were killed upon this altar, and it was done after the manner of the Egyptians.

4. And it came to pass that the priests laid violence upon me, that they might slay me also, as they did those virgins, upon this altar; and that you may have a knowledge of this altar, I will refer you to the representation at the commencement of this record. It was made after the form of a bedstead, such as was had among the Chaldeans, and it stood before the gods of Elkenah, Libna, Mahmackrah, Korash, and also a god like unto that of Pharaoh, king of Egypt. That you may have an understanding of these gods, I have given you the fashion of them in the figures at the beginning, which manner of the figures is called by the Chaldeans Rahleenos, which signifies hieroglyphics.

5. And as they lifted up their hands upon me, that they might offer me up and take away my life, behold I lifted up my voice unto the Lord my God; and the Lord hearkened and heard, and he filled me with a vision of the Almighty, and the angel of his presence stood by me, and immediately unloosed my bands, and his voice was unto me, Abraham! Abraham! behold my name is JEHOVAH, and I have heard thee, and have come down to deliver thee, and to take thee away from thy father's house, and from all thy kinsfolk, into a strange land that thou knowest

not of, and this because they have turned their hearts away from me, to worship the god of Elkenah, and the god of Libnah, and the god of Mahmackrah, and the god of Korash, and the god of Pharaoh, king of Egypt; therefore I have come down to visit them, and to destroy him who hath lifted up his hand against thee, Abraham my son, to take away thy life. Behold I will lead thee by my hand, and I will take thee to put upon thee my name, even the Priesthood of thy father; and my power shall be over thee; as it was with Noah so shall it be with thee, but through thy ministry my name shall be known in the earth for ever, for I am thy God.

6. Behold Potiphar's Hill was in the land of Ur, of Chaldea; and the Lord broke down the altar of Elkenah, and of the gods of the land, and utterly destroyed them, and smote the priest that he died; and there was great mourning in Chaldea, and also in the court of Pharaoh, which Pharaoh signifies king by royal blood. Now this king of Egypt was a descendant from the loins of Ham, and was a partaker of the blood of the Canaanites by birth. From this descent sprang all the Egyptians, and thus the blood of the Canaanites was preserved in the land.

7. The land of Egypt being first discovered by a woman, who was the daughter of Ham, and the daughter of Egyptus, which, in the Chaldean, signifies Egypt, which signifies, that which is forbidden. When this woman discovered the land it was under water, who afterwards settled her sons in it: and thus from Ham, sprang that race which preserved the curse in the land. Now the first government of Egypt was established by Pharaoh, the eldest son of Egyptus, the daughter of Ham, and it was after the manner of the government of Ham, which was patriarchal. Pharaoh being a righteous man, established his kingdom and judged his people wisely and justly all his days, seeking earnestly to imitate that order established by the fathers in the first generations, in the days of the first partriarchal reign, even in the reign of Adam, and also of Noah, his father, who blessed him with the blessings of the earth, and with the blessings of wisdom, but cursed him as pertaining to the Priesthood.

8. Now Pharaoh being of that lineage by which he could not have the right of Priesthood, notwithstanding the Pharaohs would fain claim it from Noah, through Ham, therefore my father was led away by their idolatry; but I shall endeavor hereafter to delineate the chronology, running back from myself to the beginning of the creation, for the records have come into my hands which I hold unto this present time.

9. Now, after the priest of Elkenah was smitten, that he died, there came a fulfillment of those things which were said unto me concerning the land of Chaldea, that there should be a famine in the land. Accordingly a famine prevailed throughout all the land of Chaldea, and my

father was sorely tormented because of the famine, and he repented of the evil which he had determined against me, to take away my life. But the records of the fathers, even the patriarchs, concerning the right of Priesthood, the Lord my God preserved in mine own hands, therefore a knowledge of the beginning of the creation, and also of the planets, and of the stars, as they were made known unto the fathers, have I kept even unto this day, and I shall endeavor to write some of these things upon this record, for the benefit of my posterity that shall come after me.

10. Now, the Lord God caused the famine to wax sore in the land of Ur, insomuch that Haran, my brother died, but Terah, my father, yet lived in the land of Ur of the Chaldees. And it came to pass that I, Abraham, took Sarai to wife, and Nehor, my brother, took Milcah to wife, who were the daughters of Haran. Now the Lord said unto me, Abraham, get thee out of thy country, and from thy kindred and from thy father's house unto a land that I will show thee. Therefore I left the land of Ur, of the Chaldees, to go into the land of Canaan; and I took Lot, my brother's son, and his wife, and Sarai, my wife, and also my father followed after me, unto the land which we denominated Haran. And the famine abated; and my father tarried in Haran and dwelt there, as there were many flocks in Haran; and my father turned again unto his idolatry, therefore he continued in Haran.

11. But I, Abraham, and Lot, my brother's son, prayed unto the Lord, and the Lord appeared unto me, and said unto me, arise, and take Lot with thee, for I have purposed to take thee away out of Haran, and to make of thee a minister, to bear my name in a strange land which I will give unto thy seed after thee for an everlasting possession, when they hearken to my voice, for I am the Lord thy God; I dwell in heaven, the earth is my footstool; I stretch my hand over the sea, and it obeys my voice; I cause the wind and the fire to be my chariot; I say to the mountains depart hence, and behold they are taken away by a whirlwind, in an instant, suddenly. My name is Jehovah, and I know the end from the beginning, therefore, my hand shall be over thee, and I will make of thee a great nation, and I will bless thee above measure; and make thy name great among all nations, and thou shalt be a blessing unto thy seed after thee, that in their hands they shall bear this ministry and Priesthood unto all nations: and I will bless them through thy name; for as many as receive this Gospel shall be called after thy name, and shall be accounted thy seed, and shall rise up and bless thee, as their father, and I will bless them that bless thee, and curse them that curse thee, and in thee (that is, in thy Priesthood), and in thy seed (that is thy Priesthood), for I give unto thee a promise that this right shall continue in thee, and in thy seed after thee (that is to say, the

literal seed, or the seed of the body) shall all the families of the earth be blessed, even with the blessings of the Gospel, which are the blessings of salvation, even of life eternal.

12. Now, after the Lord had withdrawn from speaking to me, and withdrawn his face from me, I said in my heart, thy servant has sought thee earnestly, now I have found thee. Thou didst send thine angel to deliver me from the gods of Elkenah, and I will do well to hearken unto thy voice, therefore let thy servant rise up and depart in peace. So I, Abraham, departed as the Lord had said unto me, and Lot with me, and I, Abraham, was sixty and two years old when I departed out of Haran. And I took Sarai, whom I took to wife when I was in Ur in Chaldea, and Lot, my brother's son, and all our substance that we had gathered, and the souls that we had won in Haran, and came forth in the way to the land of Canaan, and dwelt in tents, as we came on our way: therefore, eternity was our covering, and our rock, and our salvation, as we journeyed from Haran by the way of Jershon, to come to the land of Canaan.

13. Now I, Abraham, built an altar in the land of Jershon, and made an offering unto the Lord, and prayed that the famine might be turned away from my father's house, that they might not perish; and then we passed from Jershon through the land, unto the place of Sechem. It was situated in the plains of Moreh, and we had already come into the borders of the land of the Canaanites, and I offered sacrifice there in the plains of Moreh, and called on the Lord devoutly, because we had already come into the land of this idolatrous nation.

14. And the Lord appeared unto me in answer to my prayers, and said unto me, unto thy seed will I give this land. And I, Abraham, arose from the place of the altar which I had built unto the Lord, and removed from thence unto a mountain on the east of Bethel, and pitched my tent there; Bethel on the west, and Hai on the east; and there I built another altar unto the Lord, and called again upon the name of the Lord.

15. And I, Abraham, journeyed, going on still towards the south; and there was a continuation of a famine in the land, and I, Abraham, concluded to go down into Egypt, to sojourn there, for the famine became very grievous. And it came to pass when I was come near to enter into Egypt, the Lord said unto me, behold Sarai, thy wife, is a very fair woman to look upon, therefore it shall come to pass, when the Egyptians shall see her they will say, she is his wife; and they will kill you, but they will save her alive: therefore, see that ye do on this wise, let her say unto the Egyptians she is thy sister, and thy soul shall live. And it came to pass that I, Abraham, told Sarai, my wife, all that the Lord had said unto me; therefore, say unto them, I pray thee, thou art

my sister, that it may be well with me for thy sake, and my soul shall live because of thee.

16. And I, Abraham, had the Urim and Thummim, which the Lord my God had given unto me, in Ur of the Chaldees; and I saw the stars, that they were very great, and that one of them was nearest unto the throne of God: and there were many great ones which were near unto it; and the Lord said unto me, these are the governing ones; and the name of the great one is Kolob, because it is near unto me; for I am the Lord thy God. I have set this one to govern all those which belong to the same order as that upon which thou standest. And the Lord said unto me, by the Urim and Thummim, that Kolob was after the manner of the Lord, according to its times and seasons in the revolutions thereof, that one revolution was a day unto the Lord, after His manner of reckoning, it being one thousand years according to the time appointed unto that whereon thou standest; this is the reckoning of the Lord's time, according to the reckoning of Kolob.

17. And the Lord said unto me, the planet which is the lesser light, lesser than that which is to rule the day, even the night, is above, or greater than that upon which thou standest in point of reckoning, for it moveth in order more slow; this is in order, because it standeth above the earth upon which thou standest, therefore the reckoning of its time is not so many as to its number of days, and of months and of years. And the Lord said unto me, Now Abraham, these two facts exist, behold thine eyes see it; it is given unto thee to know the times of reckoning, and the set time, yea, the set time of the earth upon which thou standest, and the set time of the greater light, which is set to rule the day, and the set time of the lesser light, which is set to rule the night.

18. Now the set time of the lesser light, is a longer time as to its reckoning than the reckoning of the time of the earth upon which thou standest; and where these two facts exist, there shall be another fact above them; that is, there shall be another planet whose reckoning of time shall be longer still; and thus there shall be the reckoning of the time of one planet above another, until thou come nigh unto Kolob, which Kolob is after the reckoning of the Lord's time; which Kolob is set nigh unto the throne of God, to govern all those planets which belong to the same order as that upon which thou standest. And it is given unto thee to know the set time of all the stars, that are set to give light, until thou come near unto the throne of God.

19. Thus I, Abraham, talked with the Lord face to face, as one man talketh with another; and He told me of the works which His hands had made; and He said unto me, My son, my son, (and His hand was stretched out,) behold, I will show you all these. And He put His hand upon mine eyes, and I saw those things which His hands had made,

which were many; and they multiplied before mine eyes, and I could not see the end thereof; and He said unto me this is Shinehah which is the sun. And He said unto me, Kokob, which is star. And He said unto me, Olea, which is the moon. And He said unto me, Kokaubeam, which signifies stars, or all the great lights which were in the firmament of heaven. And it was in the night time when the Lord spake these words unto me: I will multiply thee and thy seed after thee, like unto these; and if thou canst count the number of sands so shall be the number of thy seeds.

20. And the Lord said unto me, Abraham, I show these things unto thee, before ye go into Egypt, that ye may declare all these words. If two things exist, and there be one above the other, there shall be greater things above them; therefore Kolob is the greatest of all the Kokaubeam that thou hast seen, because it is nearest unto me; now if there be two things, one above the other, and the moon be above the earth, then it may be that a planet, or a star may exist above it, (and there is nothing that the Lord thy God shall take in His heart to do, but what He will do it;) howbeit that He made the greater star; as, also, if there be two spirits, and one shall be more intelligent than the other, yet these two spirits, notwithstanding one is more intelligent than the other, have no beginning, they existed before; they shall have no end, they shall exist after, for they are gnolaum or eternal.

21. And the Lord said unto me, these two facts do exist, that there are two spirits, one being more intelligent than the other, there shall be another more intelligent than they: I am the Lord thy God, I am more intelligent than they all. The Lord thy God sent His angel to deliver thee from the hands of the priest of Elkenah. I dwell in the midst of them all; I, now, therefore, have come down unto thee, to deliver unto thee the works which my hands have made, wherein my wisdom excelleth them all, for I rule in the heavens above, and in the earth beneath, in all wisdom and prudence, over all the intelligences thine eyes have seen from the beginning; I came down in the beginning in the midst of all the intelligences thou hast seen.

22. Now the Lord had shown unto me, Abraham, the intelligences that were organized before the world was; and among all these there were many of the noble and great ones, and God saw these souls that they were good, and He stood in the midst of them, and He said, These I will make my rulers; for He stood among those that were spirits, and he saw that they were good; and He said unto me, Abraham, thou art one of them, thou wast chosen before thou wast born. And there stood one among them that was like unto God, and he said unto those who were with Him, We will go down, for there is space there, and we will take of these materials, and we will make an earth whereon these may

dwell; and we will prove them herewith, to see if they will do all things whatsoever the Lord their God shall command them; and they who keep their first estate, shall be added upon; and they who keep not their first estate shall not have glory in the same kingdom with those who keep their first estate; and they who keep their second estate, shall have glory added upon their heads for ever and ever.

23. And the Lord said: Whom shall I send? And one answered like unto the Son of Man: Here am I, send me. And another answered and said: Here am I, send me. And the Lord said: I will send the first. And the second was angry, and kept not his first estate, and at that day many followed after him. And then the Lord said: Let us go down; and they went down at the beginning, and they (that is, the Gods), organized and formed the heavens and the earth. And the earth, after it was formed, was empty and desolate; because they had not formed anything but the earth; and darkness reigned upon the face of the deep, and the Spirit of the Gods was brooding upon the face of the waters.

24. And they (the Gods), said: Let there be light, and there was light. And they, the Gods, comprehended the light for it was bright; and they divided the light, or caused it to be divided from the darkness, and the Gods called the light day, and the darkness they called night. And it came to pass that from the evening until morning they called night; and from the morning until the evening they called day; and this was the first, or the beginning of that which they called day and night.

25. And the Gods also said: Let there be an expanse in the midst of the waters and it shall divide the waters from the waters. And the Gods ordered the expanse, so that it divided the waters which were under the expanse, from the waters which were above the expanse, and it was so, even as they ordered. And the Gods called the expanse heaven. And it came to pass that it was from evening until morning that they called night; and it came to pass that it was from morning until evening that they called day; and this was the second time that they called night and day.

26. And the Gods ordered, saying: Let the waters under the heaven be gathered together unto one place, and let the earth come up dry, and it was so, as they ordered; and the Gods pronounced the dry land earth. and the gathering together of the waters, pronounced they great waters; and the Gods saw that they were obeyed. And the Gods said: Let us prepare the earth to bring forth grass; the herb yielding seed; the fruit tree yielding fruit after his kind, whose seed in itself yieldeth its own likeness upon the earth; and it was so, even as they ordered. And the Gods organized the earth to bring forth grass from its own seed, and the herb to bring forth herb from its own seed, yielding seed

after his kind, and the earth to bring forth the tree from its own
seed, yielding fruit, whose seed could only bring forth the same, in
itself after his kind; and the Gods saw that they were obeyed. And it
came to pass that they numbered the days: from the evening until
the morning they called night. And it came to pass from the morning
until the evening they called day; and it was the third time.

27. And the Gods organized the lights in the expanse of the heavens,
and caused them to divide the day from the night; and organized them
to be for signs, and for seasons, and for days, and for years and organized them to be for lights in the expanse of the heaven, to give light
upon the earth; and it was so. And the Gods organized the two great
lights, the greater light to rule the day, and the lesser light to rule the
night, with the lesser light they set the stars, also; and the Gods set
them in the expanse of the heavens, to give light upon the earth, and
to rule over the day and over the night, and to cause to divide the light
from the darkness. And the Gods watched those things which they had
ordered, until they obeyed. And it came to pass that it was from evening until morning that it was night; and it came to pass that it was
from morning until evening that it was day; and it was the fourth time.

28. And the Gods said, Let us prepare the waters to bring forth
abundantly the moving creatures that have life; and the fowl that they
may fly above the earth, in the open expanse of heaven. And the Gods
prepared the waters that they might bring forth great whales, and
every living creature that moveth, which the waters were to bring forth
abundantly after their kind; and every winged fowl after their kind;
and the Gods saw that they would be obeyed, and that their plan was
good. And the Gods said, We will bless them and cause them to be
fruitful and multiply, and fill the waters in the seas, or great waters;
and cause the fowl to multiply in the earth. And it came to pass
that it was from evening until morning that they called night; and
it came to pass that it was from morning until evening that they
called day; and it was the fifth time.

29. And the Gods prepared the earth to bring forth the living
creature after his kind, cattle, and creeping things, and beasts of the
earth after their kind; and it was so as they had said. And the
Gods organized the earth to bring forth the beasts after their kind,
and cattle after their kind, and everything that creepeth upon the
earth after its kind; and the Gods saw they would obey. And the
Gods took counsel among themselves, and said: Let us go down,
and form man in our image, after our likeness, and we will give
them dominion over the fish of the sea, and over the fowl of the air,
and over the cattle, and over all the earth, and over every creeping
thing, that creepeth upon the earth. So the Gods went down

to organize man in their own image, in the image of the Gods, to form they him male and female, to form they them; and the Gods said We will bless them.   And the Gods said, We will cause them to be fruitful, and multiply and replenish the earth, and subdue it, and to have dominion over the fish of the sea, and over the fowl of the air, and over every living thing that moveth upon the earth.   And the Gods said, Behold, we will give them every herb bearing seed that shall come upon the face of all the earth, and every tree which shall have fruit upon it, yea the fruit of the tree, yielding seed to them we will give it, it shall be for their meat; and to every beast of the earth, and to every fowl of the air, and to everything that creepeth upon the earth, behold we will give them life, and also we will give to them every green herb for meat, and all these things shall be thus organized.   And the Gods said, We will do everything that we have said, and organize them; and behold, they shall be very obedient.   And it came to pass that it was from evening until morning that they called night; and it came to pass that it was from morning until evening that they called day, and they numbered the sixth time.

30.   And thus we will finish the heavens and the earth, and all the hosts of them.   And the Gods said among themselves, On the seventh time, we will end our work, which we have counseled; and we will rest on the seventh time from all our work which we have counseled. And the Gods concluded upon the seventh time, because that on the seventh time they would rest from all their works, which they, the Gods, counseled among themselves to form, and sanctified it.   And thus were their decisions, at the time that they counseled among themselves to form the heavens and the earth.   And the Gods came down and formed these, the generations of the heavens and of the earth, when they were formed, in the day that the Gods formed the earth and the heavens, according to all that which they had said, concerning every plant of the field, before it was in the earth, and every herb of the field, before it grew; for the Gods had not caused it to rain upon the earth, when they counseled to do them; and had not formed a man to till the ground; but there went up a mist from the earth, and watered the whole face of the ground.   And the Gods formed man from the dust of the ground, and took his spirit, that is the man's spirit, and put it into him, and breathed into his nostrils the breath of life, and man became a living soul.

31.   And the Gods planted a garden, eastward in Eden, and there they put the man, whose spirit they had put into the body, which they had formed.   And out of the ground made the Gods to grow every tree that is pleasant to the sight, and good for food; the tree of life also, in the midst of the garden, and the tree of knowledge of good

and evil. There was a river running out of Eden, to water the garden, and from thence it was parted and became into four heads. And the Gods took the man and put him in the garden of Eden, to dress it and to keep it; and the Gods commanded the man, saying: Of every tree of the garden thou mayest freely eat, but of the tree of knowledge of good and evil, thou shalt not eat of it; for in the time that thou eatest thereof, thou shalt surely die. Now I, Abraham, saw that it was after the Lord's time, which was after the time of Kolob; for as yet, the Gods had not appointed unto Adam his reckoning.

32. And the Gods said, Let us make an helpmeet for the man, for it is not good that the man should be alone, therefore we will form an helpmeet for him. And the Gods caused a deep sleep to fall upon Adam; and he slept, and they took one of his ribs, and closed up the flesh in the stead thereof, and of the rib which the Gods had taken from man, formed they a woman, and brought her unto the man. And Adam said this was bone of my bones, and flesh of my flesh, now she shall be called woman, because she was taken out of man; therefore shall a man leave his father and his mother and shall cleve unto his wife, and they shall be one flesh. And they were both naked, the man and his wife, and were not ashamed. And out of the ground the Gods formed every beast of the field, and every fowl of the air, and brought them unto Adam to see what he would call them, and whatsoever Adam called every living creature, that should be the name thereof. And Adam gave names to all cattle, to the fowl of the air, to every beast of the field; and for Adam, there was found an helpmeet for him.

CHAPTER XXXI.

THE WENTWORTH LETTER.*

March 1, 1842.—At the request of Mr. John Wentworth, Editor and Proprietor of the *Chicago Democrat*, I have written the following sketch of the rise, progress, persecution, and faith of the Latter-day Saints, of which I have the honor, under God, of being the founder. Mr. Wentworth says that he wishes to furnish Mr. Bastow, a friend of his, who is writing the history of New Hampshire, with this document. As Mr. Bastow has

* The "Wentworth Letter" is one of the choicest documents in our Church literature; as also it is the earliest published document by the Prophet making any pretension to consecutive narrative of those events in which the great latter-day work had its origin. It was published in number 9 of Volume III of the "Times and Seasons," March 1st, 1842; while the publication of that more pretentious History of the Church under the title "History of Joseph Smith," of which these volumes are but a reproduction, was not commenced until number 10, Volume III, of the "Times and Seasons," March 15th, 1842. Introducing this "History of Joseph Smith" in the "Times and Seasons" (Vol. III, p. 726) is the following note referring to the Wentworth Letter and the more pretentious "History."

"In the last number I gave a brief history of the rise and progress of the Church, I now enter more particularly into that history, and extract from my journal."

Referring again to this Wentworth Letter, I may say that for combining conciseness of statement with comprehensiveness of treatment of the subject with which it deals, it has few equals among historical documents, and certainly none that excel it in our Church literature. In it one has in a few pages (less than six of these pages) a remarkably full history of the leading events in the Church, and an epitome of her doctrines, from the beginning (the birth of the Prophet, 1805) up to the date of publication, March, 1842, a period of thirty-six years. The epitome of the doctrines of the Church, since called "The Articles of Faith," and published by millions, has been carried to all the nations of the earth and tribes of men where the gospel has been preached. These Articles of Faith were not produced by the labored efforts and harmonized contentions of scholastics, but were struck off by one inspired mind at a single effort to make a declaration of that which is most assuredly believed by the Church, for one making earnest inquiry about the truth. The combined directness, perspicuity, simplicity and comprehensiveness of this statement of the principles of our religion may be relied upon as strong evidence of a divine inspiration resting upon the Prophet, Joseph Smith.

taken the proper steps to obtain correct information, all that I shall ask at his hands, is, that he publish the account entire, ungarnished, and without misrepresentation.

I was born in the town of Sharon, Windsor County, Vermont, on the 23rd of December, A.D. 1805. When ten years old, my parents removed to Palmyra, New York, where we resided about four years, and from thence we removed to the town of Manchester. My father was a farmer and taught me the art of husbandry. When about fourteen years of age, I began to reflect upon the importance of being prepared for a future state, and upon inquiring [about] the plan of salvation, I found that there was a great clash in religious sentiment; if I went to one society they referred me to one plan, and another to another; each one pointing to his own particular creed as the *summum bonum* of perfection. Considering that all could not be right, and that God could not be the author of so much confusion, I determined to investigate the subject more fully, believing that if God had a Church it would not be split up into factions, and that if He taught one society to worship one way, and administer in one set of ordinances, He would not teach another, principles which were diametrically opposed.

Believing the word of God, I had confidence in the declaration of James—"If any of you lack wisdom, let him ask of God, that giveth to all men liberally, and upbraideth not; and it shall be given him." I retired to a secret place in a grove, and began to call upon the Lord; while fervently engaged in supplication, my mind was taken away from the objects with which I was surrounded, and I was enwrapped in a heavenly vision, and saw two glorious personages, who exactly resembled each other in features and likeness, surrounded with a brilliant light which eclipsed the sun at noon day. They told me that all religious denominations were believing in incorrect doctrines, and that none of them was acknowledged of God as His Church and kingdom: and I was expressly commanded "to go not after them," at the same time receiving a promise that the fullness of the Gospel should at some future time be made known unto me.

On the evening on the 21st of September, A.D. 1823, while I was praying unto God, and endeavoring to exercise faith in the precious promises of Scripture, on a sudden a light like that of day, only of a far purer and more glorious appearance and brightness, burst into the room, indeed the first sight was as though the house was filled with consuming fire; the appearance produced a shock that affected the whole body; in a moment a personage stood before me surrounded with a glory yet greater than that with which I was already surrounded. This messenger proclaimed himself to be an angel of God, sent to bring the joyful tidings that the covenant which God made with ancient Israel was at hand to be fulfilled, that the preparatory work for the second coming of the Messiah was speedily to commence; that the time was at hand for the Gospel in all its fullness to be preached in power, unto all nations that a people might be prepared for the Millennial reign. I was informed that I was chosen to be an instrument in the hands of God to bring about some of His purposes in this glorious dispensation.

I was also informed concerning the aboriginal inhabitants of this country and shown who they were, and from whence they came; a brief sketch of their origin, progress, civilization, laws, governments, of their righteousness and iniquity, and the blessings of God being finally withdrawn from them as a people, was made known unto me; I was also told where were deposited some plates on which were engraven an abridgment of the records of the ancient Prophets that had existed on this continent. The angel appeared to me three times the same night and unfolded the same things. After having received many visits from the angels of God unfolding the majesty and glory of the events that should transpire in the last days, on the morning of the 22nd of September, A.D. 1827, the angel of the Lord delivered the records into my hands.

These records were engraven on plates which had the appearance of gold, each plate was six inches wide and eight inches long, and not quite so thick as common tin. They were filled with engravings, in Egyptian characters, and bound together in a volume as the leaves of a book, with three rings running through the whole. The volume was something near six inches in thickness, a part of which was sealed. The characters on the unsealed part were small, and beautifully engraved. The whole book exhibited many marks of antiquity in its construction, and much skill in the art of engraving. With the records was found a curious instrument, which the ancients called "Urim and Thummim," which consisted of two transparent stones set in the rim of a bow fastened to a breast plate. Through the medium of the Urim and Thummim I translated the record by the gift and power of God.

In this important and interesting book the history of ancient America is unfolded, from its first settlement by a colony that came from the Tower of Babel, at the confusion of languages to the beginning of the fifth century of the Christian Era. We are informed by these records that America in ancient times has been inhabited by two distinct races of people. The first were called Jaredites, and came directly from the Tower of Babel. The second race came directly from the city of Jerusalem, about six hundred years before Christ. They were principally Israelites, of the descendants of Joseph. The Jaredites were destroyed about the time that the Israelites came from Jerusalem, who succeeded them in the inheritance of the country. The principal nation of the second race fell in battle towards the close of the fourth century. The remnant are the Indians that now inhabit this country. This book also tells us that our Savior made His appearance upon this continent after His resurrection; that He planted the Gospel here in all its fulness, and richness, and power, and blessing; that they had Apostles, Prophets, Pastors, Teachers, and Evangelists; the same order, the same priest-hood, the same ordinances, gifts, powers, and blessings, as were en-joyed on the eastern continent, that the people were cut off in conse-quence of their transgressions, that the last of their prophets who ex-isted among them was commanded to write an abridgment of their prophecies, history,&c, and to hide it up in the earth, and that it should come forth and be united with the Bible for the accomplishment of the purposes of God in the last days. For a more particular account I would refer to the Book of Mormon, which can be purchased at Nauvoo, or from any of our Traveling Elders.

As soon as the news of this discovery was made known, false reports, misrepresentation and slander flew, as on the wings of the wind, in every direction; the house was frequently beset by mobs and evil designing persons. Several times I was shot at, and very narrowly es-caped, and every device was made use of to get the plates away from me; but the power and blessing of God attended me, and several began to believe my testimony.

On the 6th of April, 1830, the "Church of Jesus Christ of Latter-day Saints" was first organized in the town of Fayette, Seneca county, state of New York. Some few were called and ordained by the Spirit of revelation and prophecy, and began to preach as the Spirit gave them utterance, and though weak, yet were they strengthened by the power of God, and many were brought to repentance, were immersed in the water, and were filled with the Holy Ghost by the laying on of hands. They saw visions and prophesied, devils were cast out, and the sick healed by the laying on of hands. From that time the work rolled forth with astonishing rapidity, and churches were soon formed in the states of New York, Pennsylvania Ohio, Indiana, Illinois, and Missouri; in the last named state a considerable settlement was formed in Jackson county: numbers joined the Church and we were increasing rapidly; we made large purchases of land, our farms teemed with plenty, and peace and happiness were enjoyed in our domestic circle, and through-out our neighborhood; but as we could not associate with our neighbors (who were, many of them, of the basest of men, and had fled from the face of civilized society, to the frontier country to escape the hand of justice,) in their midnight revels, their Sabbath breaking, horse racing and gambling; they commenced at first to ridicule, then to persecute, and finally an organized mob assembled and burned our houses, tarred and feathered and whipped many of our brethren, and finally, contrary to law, justice and humanity, drove them from their habitations; who, houseless and homeless, had to wander on the bleak prairies till the children left the tracks of their blood on the prairie. This took place in the month of November, and they had no other covering but the canopy of heaven, in this inclement season of the year; this proceeding was winked at by the government, and although we had warantee deeds for our land, and had violated no law, we could obtain no redress.

There were many sick, who were thus inhumanly driven from their houses, and had to endure all this abuse and to seek homes where they could be found. The result was, that a great many of them being deprived of the comforts of life, and the necessary attendances, died; many children were left orphans, wives, widows and husbands, widowers; our farms were taken possession of by the mob, many thousands of cattle, sheep, horses and hogs were taken, and our household goods, store goods, and printing press and type were broken, taken, or otherwise destroyed.

Many of our brethren removed to Clay county, where they continued until 1836, three years; there was no violence offered, but there were threatenings of violence. But in the summer of 1836 these threatenings began to assume a more serious form, from threats, public meetings were called, resolutions were passed, vengeance and destruction were threatened, and affairs again assumed a fearful attitude, Jackson county was a sufficient precedent, and as the authorities in that county did not interfere they boasted that they would not in this; which on application to the authorities we found to be too true, and after much privation and loss of property, we were again driven from our homes.

We next settled in Caldwell and Daviess counties, where we made large and extensive settlements, thinking to free ourselves from the power of oppression, by settling in new counties, with very few inhabitants in them; but here we were not allowed to live in peace, but in 1838 we were again attacked by mobs, an exterminating order was issued by Governor Boggs, and under the sanction of law, an organized banditti ranged through the country, robbed us of our cattle, sheep, hogs, &c., many of our people were murdered in cold blood, the chastity of our women was violated, and we were forced to sign away our property at the point of the sword; and after enduring every indignity that could be heaped upon us by an inhuman, ungodly band of marauders, from twelve to fifteen thousand souls, men women, and children were driven from their own firesides, and from lands to which they had warantee deeds, houseless, friendless, and homeless (in the depths of winter) to wander as exiles on the earth, or to seek an asylum in a more genial clime, and among a less barbarous people.   Many sickened and died in consequence of the cold and hardships they had to endure; many wives were left widows, and children, orphans, and destitute.   It would take more time than is allotted me here to describe the injustice, the wrongs, the murders the bloodshed. the theft, misery and woe that have been caused by the barbarous, inhuman, and lawless proceedings of the state of Missouri,

In the situation before alluded to, we arrived in the state of Illinois in 1839, where we found a hospitable people and a friendly home: a people who were willing to be governed by the principles of law and humanity.   We have commenced to build a city called "Nauvoo," in Hancock county.   We number from six to eight thousand here, besides vast numbers in the county around, and in almost every county of the state.   We have a city charter granted us, and charter for a Legion, the troops of which now number 1,500.   We have also a charter for a University, for an Agricultural and Manufacturing Society, have our own laws and administrators, and possess all the privileges that other free and enlightened citizens enjoy.

Persecution has not stopped the progress of truth, but has only added fuel to the flame, it has spread with increasing rapidity.   Proud of the cause which they have espoused, and conscious of our innocence, and of the truth of their system, amidst calumny and reproach, have the Elders of this Church gone forth, and planted the Gospel in almost every state in the Union; it has penetrated our cities, it has spread over our villages, and has caused thousands of our intelligent, noble, and patriotic citizens to obey its divine mandates, and be governed by its sacred truths.   It has also spread into England, Ireland, Scotland, and Wales, where, in the year 1840, a few of our missionaries were sent, and over five thousand joined the Standard of Truth; there are numbers now joining in every land.

Our missionaries are going forth to different nations, and in Germany, Palestine, New Holland, Australia, the East Indies, and other places, the Standard of Truth has been erected; no unhallowed hand can stop the work from progressing; persecutions may rage, mobs may combine, armies may assemble, calumny may defame, but the truth of God will go forth boldly, nobly, and independent,till it has penetrated every continent, visited every clime, swept every country, and sounded in every ear, till the purposes of God shall be accomplished, and the Great Jehovah shall say the work is done.

We believe in God the eternal Father, and in His Son Jesus Christ, and in the Holy Ghost.

We believe that men will be punished for their own sins, and not for Adam's transgression.

We believe that through the atonement of Christ all mankind may be saved by obedience to the laws and ordinances of the Gospel.

We believe that the first principle and ordinances of the Gospel are: (1) Faith in the Lord Jesus Christ; (2) Repentance; (3) Baptism by immersion for the remission of sins; (4) Laying on of hands for the gift of the Holy Ghost.

We believe that a man must be called of God by prophecy and by the laying on hands, by those who are in authority, to preach the Gospel and administer in the ordinances thereof.

We believe in the same organization that existed in the primitive Church, viz: apostles, prophets, pastors, teachers, evangelists, etc.

We believe in the gift of tongues, prophecy, revelation, visions, healing, interpretation of tongues, etc.

We believe the Bible to be the word of God, as far as it is translated correctly; we also believe the Book of Mormon to be the word of God.

We believe all that God has revealed: all that He does now reveal, and we believe that He will yet reveal many great and important things pertaining to the kingdom of God.

We believe in the literal gathering of Israel and in the restoration of the Ten Tribes; that Zion will be built upon this [the American] continent; that Christ will reign personally upon the earth; and that the earth will be renewed and receive its paradisiacal glory.

We claim the privilege of worshiping Almighty God according to the dictates of our own conscience, and allow all men the same privilege, let them worship how, where, or what they may.

We believe in being subject to kings, presidents, rulers and magistrates, in obeying honoring, and sustaining the law.

We believe in being honest, true, chaste, benevolent, virtuous, and in doing good to *all men;* indeed we may say that we follow the admonition of Paul, "We believe all thing, we hope all things, we have endured many things, and hope to be able to endure all things. If there is anything virtuous, lovely, or of good report, or praiseworthy, we seek after these things.

Respectfully, &c.,

JOSEPH SMITH.

CHAPTER XXXII.

THE BENNETT-DYER CORRESPONDENCE—THE PROPHET'S DIS-
COURSE ON THE SUBJECT OF THE RESURRECTION, AND THE
SALVATION OF CHILDREN—EPISTLE OF THE TWELVE TO
THE SAINTS IN ENGLAND CONCERNING THEIR EMIGRATION
TO AMERICA.

Wednesday, March 2.—I read the proof of the *Times and Seasons*, as editor for the first time, No. 9, Vol. III, in which is the commencement of the Book of Abraham;*

Tax Contro-
versy.

paid taxes to Mr. Bagby, in the general business office, for county and state purposes, but refused to pay the taxes in the city and town of Commerce, as the demand was illegal, there being no such place known in law, the city and town of Commerce having been included in the city plat of Nauvoo, but continued by our enemies on the tax list for the purpose of getting more money from the Saints; I commenced a settlement with Gilbert Granger on the estate [Kirtland] of his father, Oliver Granger; and continued in my office till nine in the evening, having received a visit from General Dudley of Connecticut.

Thursday, 3.—I attended council in the general business office (over the store) at nine o'clock a. m.

In the afternoon, continued the settlement with Gilbert Granger, but finally failed to effect anything, except to

Attempted
Settlement
with Hilbert
Granger.

get Newel's note.† Granger refused to give up the papers to me, which he had received of his father, the same being Church property, although I presented him deeds, mort-

---

* No. 9 of the *Times and Seasons* was evidently not published on time, since it is supposed to have been published on March the first, and here is an account of the proofs being read on the second of March.

† This refers doubtless to Bishop Newel K. Whitney.

gages and paper to the amount of some thousands against his father, more than he had against the Church.

I also wrote Hiram Barney, Esq., of New York, in reply to his letter of the 24th of January, offering him one hundred dollars per acre, for his twenty acres of land in this city, lying somewhere between the Hotchkiss purchase on the north, and Galland's purchase on the south, or to take an agency to sell the same.

Friday, 4.—At my office exhibiting the Book of Abraham in the original to Brother Reuben Hedlock, so that he might take the size of the several plates or cuts, and prepare the blocks for the *Times and Seasons;* and also gave instruction concerning the arrangement of the writing on the large cut,* illustrating the principles of astronomy, with other general business.

Book of Abraham Fac-similes.

Attended city council, and moved "that when property is sold at sheriff's, marshal's or constable's sale under ordinance of this city, the persons having their property sold shall have the privilege of redeeming the same, by paying the principal and fifteen per cent on principal, with cost and charges, within thirty days after sale."

Saturday, 5.—Attended the city council, and spoke at considerable length on the powers and privileges of our city charter; among other business of importance, the office of registrar of deeds was established in the city of Nauvoo, and I was chosen registrar by the city council.

Sunday, 6.—I preached at Elder Orson Spencer's near the Temple.

Monday, 7.—At the general business office. Peter Melling, the Patriarch from England, brought to the office cash $13.47½, and clothing $65 from Parley P. Pratt and Amos Fielding, of England; I transacted much general business and wrote the mayor as follows:

---

* This refers to Fac-simile No. 2, p. 521, which was published in the *Times and Seasons* in double page size.

Letter of the Prophet to John C. Bennett—on Bennett's Correspondence Anent Slavery.

EDITOR'S OFFICE, NAUVOO, ILLINOIS, March 7, 1842.

General Bennett:

RESPECTED BROTHER:—I have just been perusing your correspondence with Doctor Dyer, on the subject of American slavery, and the students of the Quincy Mission Institute, and it makes my blood boil within me to reflect upon the injustice, cruelty, and oppression of the rulers of the people. When will these things cease to be, and the Constitution and the laws again bear rule? I fear for my beloved country —mob violence, injustice and cruelty appear to be the darling attributes of Missouri, and no man taketh it to heart! *O tempora! O mores!* What think you should be done?

Your friend,

JOSEPH SMITH.

Correspondence between Dr. C. V. Dyer and General J. C. Bennett.

CHICAGO, January 3, 1842.

DEAR SIR:—I am not sure that I am not indebted to you for your last letter, not having answered it, as I remember. But as I have been very sick during the long interval of my silence, you will readily excuse any apparent neglect on my part. I thank you for your paper sent me, the *Times and Seasons*, and have got much information from it, and since that, from other sources, in relation to the outrages committed upon the Latter-day Saints by the authorities as well as the people of the state of Missouri; and my blood boiled with indignation to see the whole Christian world—and the whole political world, too, look tamely on, and never raise a warning voice— a voice of expostulation, nor even giving the facts in the case! O what outrages will not be allowed or winked at by those in authority, and the people generally, if they happen to be inflicted upon those who bear an

---

* The correspondence between Dr. Dyer, Chicago, and Dr. John C. Bennett, referred to in the Prophet's letter above, is thought to be of sufficient importance to be inserted in the body of the History, though heretofore, when the history of the Prophet has been published, it has been omitted. The case of the three men from the Quincy Mission Institute being imprisoned for twelve years in the Missouri penitentiary "for no crime at all, or only as such as God would regard as a virtue" —"for barely teaching a fellow being," as Dr. Dyer naively put it, "how to go to a place where he may learn the sciences, have his own wages, aye, and his own person. This case was one in which the three men had violated some local law of the state of Missouri against encouraging slaves to leave their masters for the purpose of going into free states as the national fugitive slave law was not then in existence, and was not enacted until 1850.

unpopular name, espouse an unpopular cause, and are poor and obscure! It seems as if we had again fallen upon the middle ages, when the privileged classes could pour out their sympathies by the hour, and the very circumstantial and minute details of the loss of the life, or any other serious evil that befel one of their own number; but they could write [of] or hear without emotion, and even with satisfaction and joy, the history of the massacre of a thousand defenseless women and children, if they belonged to the common sort of people. Just read, for example, Madame de Sevigne's account in a letter to her daughter, dated "Aux Rochers," 30 Oct., 1675, in the second volume of De Toquerville's Democracy in America. What, my dear sir, do you think of the treatment which the subject of American slavery receives at the hands of the American press—amongst the people generally, and especially in the halls of Congress? What think you of the sentencing of three men from the Quincy Mission Institute in this state, a short time since, to twelve years confinement in the penitentiary of Missouri, for no crime at all, or only such as God would regard as a virtue? Please look into this matter, and see if you cannot join with the benevolent and fearless, and call the attention of the nation or the state, to these outrages of Missouri, I send you a paper, and mark one of the pieces for your perusal. Read it. I do not know whether you have examined the whole subject of American slavery; but if you have not, I beseech you to do so, and let me hear from you. Is it not sin? Yes. Then is it not right to repent of it? Yes. When? God allows not a moment. Is not repentance and abandonment of sin safe, so long as God commands, and stands ready to look after the consequences? Certainly so. Well, can any court, either state or national, rob me of liberty for twelve years (even against their own state laws), for acting precisely in accordance with the letter and spirit of the Constitution of the United States, and the precepts of Jesus Christ? Is it to be submitted to tamely, that three men shall be immured in a dungeon for twelve years, torn from their families and friends, and from society and usefulness, for barely teaching a fellow being how to go to a place where he may learn the sciences—have his own wages, aye, and his own person? Let me hear from you. Have we not a right to sympathize with each other?

I am, very sincerely, your friend and obedient servant,

CHARLES V. DYER.

Gen. John C. Bennett.
Nauvoo, Hancock county, Illinois.

NAUVOO, ILL., January 20th, A. D. 1842.

DEAR SIR:—Yours of the 3rd inst., accompanied by the *Genius of Liberty*, containing the address of Alvin Stewart, Esq., is before me, and I seize upon this, the first, opportunity to reply. You refer me to Madame de Sevigne's letter to her daughter, dated "Aux Rochers," 30th Oct., A. D. 1675, in the second volume of De Toquerville's Democracy in America; and ask me to examine the subject of American slavery. I have done so: I gave it a full and fair investigation years ago—I swore in my youth that my hands should never be bound nor my feet fettered, nor my tongue palsied—I am the friend of liberty, "Universal liberty," both civil and religious. I ever detested servile bondage. I wish to see the shackles fall from the feet of the oppressed, and the chains of slavery broken. I hate the oppressor's grasp, and the tyrant's rod; against them I set my brows like brass, and my face like steel; and my arm is nerved for the conflict. Let the sons of thunder speak, achieve victories before the cannon's mouth, and beard the lion in his den; till then the cry of the oppressed will not be heard; till then the wicked will not cease to trouble, nor the weary bondman be at rest. Great God, has it come to this—that the free citizens of the sovereign state of Illinois can be taken and immured within the walls of a Missouri penitentiary for twelve long years, for such a crime as God would regard as a virtue! simply for pointing bondsmen to a state of liberty and law! and no man take it to heart? Never, no never, no never! Let the friends of freedom arise and utter their voice, like the voice of ten thousand thunders—let them take every constitutional means to procure a redress of grievances—let there be a concerted effort, and the victory is ours. Let the broad banners of freedom be unfurled, and soon the prison doors will be opened, the captive set at liberty, and the oppressed go free. Missouri will then remember the unoffending Mormons in the days of their captivity and bondage—when murder and rapine were her darling attribute,—why, my heart is filled with indignation, and my blood boils within me, when I contemplate the vast injustice and cruelty which Missouri has meted out to that great philanthropist and devout Christian, General Joseph Smith, and his honest and faithful adherents—the Latter-day Saints, or Mormons; but the time has passed, and God will avenge their wrongs in His own good time. Dr. Dyer, put your hand upon your heart, and remember Zion. Just investigate the wrongs which our people have suffered in their unprecedented privations, the confiscation of their property, and the murder of their friends—the persecutions of the Waldenses in former ages were not to be compared to it, and history affords not a parallel. Now let us make a strong, concerted, and vigorous effort, for Universal Liberty, to every soul of man—civil, religious and political. With high considerations of respect and esteem, suffer me to subscribe myself,

Yours respectfully,

Charles V. Dyer, M. D.   JOHN C. BENNETT.

P. S.   Gen. Smith informs me that there are white slaves in Missouri* (Mormons) in as abject servitude as the blacks, and we have, as yet, no means of redress!   God grant that the day of righteous retribution may not be procrastinated.

J. C. B.

Letter of John C. Bennett to Joseph Smith—Anent the Dyer-Bennett Correspondence.†

MAYOR'S OFFICE, CITY OF NAUVOO, ILLINOIS,
March 8, A. D., 1842.

Esteemed Friend:

Yours of the 7th inst. has been received, and I proceed to reply, without undue emotion or perturbation.   You ask, "When will these things cease to be, and the Constitution and the laws again bear rule?" I reply—once that noble bird of Jove, our grand national emblem, soared aloft, bearing in her proud beak the words "Liberty and Law," and that man that had the temerity to ruffle her feathers, was made to feel the power of her talons; but a wily archer came, and with his venomed arrow dipped in Upas' richest sap, shot the flowing label from the eagle's bill—it fell inverted, and the bird was sick, and is—the label soon was trampled in the dust—the eagle bound and caged.   The picture is now before you in bold relief.   What think you should be done? The master spirits of the age must rise and break the cage, restore the label, unbind the bird, and let her tower unfettered in the air—then will the nation have repose, and the present minions of power hide their faces in the dust.   Many of Missouri's noble sons detest her acts of cruelty and crime, and gladly would they wipe them from the escutcheon of her fame, and will; yes they will lend a helping hand—and all must help, for the time is at hand—and if man, rebellious, cowardly, faltering man, will not do the work, the thunderings of Sinai will wind up the scene—the blood of the murdered Mormons cries aloud for help, and the restoration of the inheritances of the Saints; and God has

---

* The "slaves" here referred to are explained in an editorial note in the *Times and Seasons* in which the above correspondence appears (Vol. III, No. 10) to mean children of Mormon parentage still in Missouri—"the children of murdered parents; others of Mormon parents now in this city"—Nauvoo.   The charge of their being "slaves" is far-fetched and was made only because of the severe stress of feeling experienced by the Saints when contemplating things that related to Missouri, and some allowance must be made for the bombast, bragadocio and hypocrisy of John C. Bennett.

† Because of its bearing upon the character of John C. Bennett, as also to complete this Dyer-Bennett correspondence, the letter of John C. Bennett to the Prophet in answer to the note of the latter, introducing this whole correspondence, the following communication is inserted.

heard the cry—and the moral battle must be fought, and the victory won, he who answers by fire will cause sword and flame to do their office, and again make the Constitution and the laws paramount to every other consideration—and I swear by the Lord God of Israel, that the sword shall not depart from my thigh, nor the buckler from my arm, until the trust is consummated, and the hydra-headed, fiery dragon slain. This done the proud southron will no longer boast of ill-gotten gain, or wash his hands in the blood of the innocent, or immure the freemen of the prairie State within Missouri's sullied, poisoned, deathly prison walls. Let us always take refuge under the broad folds of the Constitution and the laws, and fear no danger, for the day of vengeance will assuredly come when the Omnipotent hand of the Great God will effect the restitution of the trophies of the brigand victories of Missouri, and again place the Saints on high.

Yours respectfully,
JOHN C. BENNETT.

General Joseph Smith.

Tuesday, 8.—Recommenced translating from the Records of Abraham for the tenth number of the *Times and Seasons,* and was engaged at my office day and evening.

Wednesday, 9.—Examining copy for the *Times and Seasons,* presented by Messrs. Taylor and Bennett, and a variety of other business in my office, in the morning; in the afternoon continued the translation of the Book of Abraham, called at Bishop Knight's and Mr. Davis', with the recorder, and continued translating and revising, and reading letters in the evening, Sister Emma being present in the office.

I also wrote Edward Hunter, as follows—

Letter of the Prophet to Edward Hunter—Business Transactions.

DEAR SIR:—I yesterday had the pleasure of receiving your letter of February 10. Am much pleased that you have effected a sale, and are so soon to be with us, &c.

I have purchased the lands you desired, and will use my influence to have the improvements made which you wish. Brother Weiler received your letter and says he will do what he can to have all done.

The eight hundred dollars for the Temple and Nauvoo House, I wish you to bring in goods, for which I will give you stock and credit as soon as received.

I wish you to invest as much money as you possibly can in goods, to bring here, and I will purchase them of you when you come, if we can agree on terms; or you can have my new brick store to rent. I wish the business kept up by some one in the building, as it is a very fine house, and cost me a handsome amount to build it. Some eight or ten thousand dollars worth of goods would be an advantage to this place; therefore, if you or some of the brethren, would bring them on, I have no doubt but that I can arrange for them in some way to your or their advantage.

As to money matters here, the State Bank is down, and we cannot tell you what bank would be safe a month hence. I would say that gold and silver is the only safe money a man can keep these times, you can sell specie here for more premium than you have to give; therefore there would be no loss and it would be safe. The bank you deposit in might fail before you had time to draw out again.

I am now very busily engaged in translating, and therefore cannot give as much time to public matters as I could wish, but will nevertheless do what I can to forward your affairs. I will send you a memorandum of such goods as will suit this market.

Yours affectionately,
JOSEPH SMITH.

Thursday, *10*.—Gave instructions concerning a deed to Stephen Markham, Shadrack Roundy, and Hiram Clark, and letter of attorney from Miss Smith to Edward Hunter, and did a great variety of business; rode out; and in the evening attended trial at Brother Hyrum's office, the City of Nauvoo *versus* Amos Davis, for indecent and abusive language about me while at Mr. Davis' the day previous. The charges were clearly substantiated by the testimony of Dr. Foster, Mr. and Mrs. Hibbard, and others. Mr. Davis was found guilty by the jury, and by the municipal court, bound over to keep the peace six months, under $100 bond; after which I retired to the printing office with Emma, and supped with the Twelve and their wives, who were spending the evening with Sister Hyde.

Friday, *11*.

Extract from the Legion Minutes.

The Nauvoo Legion was on parade, commanded by Lieutenant-General Joseph Smith in person. Several of the Twelve Apostles rode in the general staff as Chaplains. The line was formed at ten o'clock, a. m., and soon the Legion marched from their usual place of parade, below the Temple, to Water-street, in front of General Smith's house, where the troops were inspected, and after a recess marched west on the bank of the river, and taking a circuitous route, resumed their usual post on the parade ground, and closed the day in good order and with good feelings, and to the full satisfaction of the Commander-in-Chief.

Extract of High Council Minutes.

In the evening President Smith attended the trial of Elder Francis Gladden Bishop, at his (the president's) house. Elder Bishop appeared before the High Council of Nauvoo on complaint of having received, written, and published or taught certain "revelations" and doctrines not consistent with the Doctrine and Covenants of the Church. Mr. Bishop refusing to present the written "revelation" the Mayor, (John C. Bennett) issued his warrant and brought them before the council, when parts of the same were read by Mr. Bishop himself to council, the whole mass of which appeared to be the extreme of folly, nonsense, absurdity, falsehood and bombastic egotism—so much so as to keep the Saints laughing, when not overcome by sorrow and shame. President Joseph explained the nature of the case and gave a very clear elucidation of the tendency of such prophets and prophesyings, and gave Mr. Bishop over to the buffetings of Satan until he shall learn wisdom. After a few appropriate observations from Patriarch Hyrum and some of the council, the council voted unanimously that Francis Gladden Bishop be removed from the fellowship of the Church; President Joseph having previously committed the "revelation" above referred to, to the flames.

Saturday, 12.—I presided over a court-martial of the officers of the Nauvoo Legion at my own house, for the purpose of deciding upon the rank and station of the several officers, and the more perfect organization of the Legion.

Sunday, 13.—I was with my family.

Monday, 14.—Transacted a great variety of business at the office.

Tuesday, 15.—I officiated as grand chaplain at the installation of the Nauvoo Lodge of Free Masons, at the Grove near the Temple. Grand Master Jonas, of Columbus, being present, a large number of people assembled on the occasion. The day was exceedingly fine; all things were done in order, and universal satisfaction was manifested. In the evening I received the first degree in Free Masonry in the Nauvoo Lodge, assembled in my general business office.

Some time previous to this [March 15th] Sister Elizabeth Morgan died at London without medical aid, after calling for the Elders, &c., which created much excitement, and a coroner's inquest was called by Mr. Baker, who brought in a verdict of "natural death."

The Prophet Becomes Editor of the Times and Seasons.

This paper commences my editorial career: I alone stand responsible for it, and shall do for all papers [i.e. Nos. of the *Times and Seasons*,] having my signature henceforward. I am not responsible for the publication or arrangement of the former paper; the matter did not come under my supervision.

JOSEPH SMITH.

We extract the following from the New York *Tribune:*

Honor Among Thieves.

"The paymaster of the Missouri Militia, called out to put down the Mormons some two years since, was supplied with money some time since, and started for Western Missouri, but has not yet arrived there. It is feared he has taken the Saline slope."

We are not surprised that persons who could wantonly, barbarously, and without shadow of law, drive fifteen thousand men, women and children from their homes, should have among them a man who was so lost to every sense of justice, as to run away with the wages for this infamous deed; it is not very difficult for men who can blow out the brains of children; who can shoot down and hew to pieces our ancient veterans who fought in defense of our country, and delivered it from the oppressor's grasp; who could deliberately and in cold blood, murder men and rob them of their boots, watches, &c., and whilst their victims were yet weltering in their blood, and grappling with death, proceed to rob the widows' houses. Men who can deliberately do this, and steal nearly all the horses, cattle, sheep, hogs, and property of a whole community, and drive them from their homes *en masse*, in an inclement season of the year, will not find many qualms of conscience in stealing the pay of his brother thieves, and taking the "Saline slope." The very idea of Government paying these men for their bloody deeds, must cause the sons of liberty to blush, and to hang their harps upon the willow, and make the blood of every patriot run chill.

The proceedings of that state have been so barbarous and inhuman that our indignation is aroused when we reflect upon the scene. We are here reminded of one of the patriotic deeds of the government of that state, who after they had robbed us of everything we had in the world, and taken from us many hundred thousand dollars' worth of property, had their sympathies so far touched (*alias* their good name) that they voted two thousand dollars to the relief of the "*suffering Mormons*," and choosing two or three of her noblest sons, to carry their heavenly boon, these angels of salvation came in the plentitude of their mercy and in the dignity of their office to Far West. To do what? To feed its hungry and clothe its naked with the $2,000? Verily nay! but to go into Daviess county and steal the Mormons' hogs (which they were prohibited themselves from obtaining under penalty of death) to distribute among the destitute, and to sell where they could obtain the money. These hogs thus obtained were shot down in their blood and not otherwise bled; they were filthy to a degree. These, the Mormons' own hogs, and a few goods, the sweepings of an old store in Liberty, were what these patriotic and noble-minded men gave to the "poor Mormons," and then circulated to the world how sympathetic, benevolent, kind and merciful the Legislature of the State of Missouri was, in giving two thousand dollars to the "suffering Mormons." Surely "the tender mercies of the wicked are cruel."

Wednesday, March 16.—I was with the Masonic Lodge and rose to the sublime degree.

Thursday, 17.—The High Council withdrew the hand of fellowship from Elder Oliver Olney for setting himself up as a prophet, and took his license.

I assisted in commencing the organization of "The Female Relief Society of Nauvoo" in the Lodge Room.
Sister Emma Smith, President, and Sister Elizabeth Ann Whitney and Sarah M. Cleveland, Counselors. I gave much instruction, read in the New Testament, and Book of Doctrine and Covenants, concerning the Elect Lady, and showed that the elect meant to be elected to a certain work, &c., and

Origin of the
Female Relief
Society.

that the revelation was then fulfilled by Sister Emma's
election to the Presidency of the Society, she having
previously been ordained to expound the Scriptures.
Emma was blessed, and her counselors were ordained by
Elder John Taylor.

Friday, 18 and Saturday 19. — At home and at my
office engaged in business, temporal and spiritual.

Sunday, 20. — I preached to a large assembly in the
grove, near the Temple on the west.   The body of a deceased child of Mr. Windsor P. Lyon being before the
assembly, changed my design in the order of my remarks.

[The following is a brief synopsis of the Prophet's remarks, by Elder
Wilford Woodruff:]

The Prophet's Sermon on Life and Death; the Resurrection and the Salvation of Children.

President Smith read the 14th chapter of Revelation, and said—We
have again the warning voice sounded in our midst, which shows the
uncertainty of human life; and in my leisure moments I have meditated
upon the subject, and asked the question, why it is that infants, innocent children, are taken away from us, especially those that seem to be
the most intelligent and interesting. The strongest reasons that present
themselves to my mind are these: This world is a very wicked world;
and it is a proverb that the "world grows weaker and wiser;" if that is
the case, the world grows more wicked and corrupt.   In the earlier
ages of the world a righteous man, and a man of God and of intelligence,
had a better chance to do good, to be believed and received than at the
present day: but in these days such a man is much opposed and persecuted by most of the inhabitants of the earth, and he has much sorrow
to pass through here.   The Lord takes many away, even in infancy,
that they may escape the envy of man, and the sorrows and evils of this
present world; they were too pure, too lovely, to live on earth; therefore, if rightly considered, instead of mourning we have reason to rejoice as they are delivered from evil, and we shall soon have them
again.

What chance is there for infidelity when we are parting with our
friends almost daily? None at all. The infidel will grasp at every straw
for help until death stares him in the face, and then his infidelity takes
its flight, for the realities of the eternal world are resting upon him in
mighty power; and when every earthly support and prop fails him, he

then sensibly feels the eternal truths of the immortality of the soul. We should take warning and not wait for the death-bed to repent, as we see the infant taken away by death, so may the youth and middle aged, as well as the infant be suddenly called into eternity. Let this, then, prove as a warning to all not to procrastinate repentance, or wait till a death-bed, for it is the will of God that man should repent and serve Him in health, and in the strength and power of his mind, in order to secure His blessing, and not wait until he is called to die.

The doctrine of baptizing children, or sprinkling them, or they must welter in hell, is a doctrine not true, not supported in Holy Writ, and is not consistent with the character of God. All children are redeemed by the blood of Jesus Christ,and the moment that children leave this world, they are taken to the bosom of Abraham. The only difference between the old and young dying is, one lives longer in heaven and eternal light and glory than the other, and is freed a little sooner from this miserable, wicked world. Notwithstanding all this glory, we for a moment lose sight of it, and mourn the loss, but we do not mourn as those without hope.

My intention was to have spoken on the subject of baptism, but having a case of death before us, I thought proper to refer to that subject. I will now, however say a few words upon baptism, as I intended.

God has made certain decrees which are fixed and immovable; for instance,—God set the sun, the moon, and the stars in the heavens, and gave them their laws, conditions and bounds, which they cannot pass, except by His commandments; they all move in perfect harmony in their sphere and order, and are as lights, wonders and signs unto us. The sea also has its bounds which it cannot pass. God has set many signs on the earth, as well as in the heavens; for instance, the oak of the forest, the fruit of the tree, the herb of the field—all bear a sign that seed hath been planted there; for it is a decree of the Lord that every tree, plant, and herb bearing seed should bring forth of its kind, and cannot come forth after any other law or principle. Upon the same principle do I contend that baptism is a sign ordained of God, for the believer in Christ to take upon himself in order to enter into the kingdom of God, "for except ye are born of water and of the Spirit ye cannot enter into the kingdom of God," said the Savior. It is a sign and a commandment which God has set for man to enter into His kingdom. Those who seek to enter in any other way will seek in vain; for God will not receive them,neither will the angels acknowledge their works as accepted, for they have not obeyed the ordinances,nor attended to the signs which God ordained for the salvation of man,to prepare him for, and give him a title to, a celestial glory; and God had decreed that all who will not obey His voice shall not escape the damnation of hell. What is the damnation of hell? To go with that society who have not obeyed His commands.

Baptism is a sign to God, to angels, and to heaven that we do the will of God, and there is no other way beneath the heavens whereby God hath ordained for man to come to Him to be saved, and enter into the kingdom of God, except faith in Jesus Christ, repentance, and baptism for the remission of sins, and any other course is in vain; then you have the promise of the gift of the Holy Ghost.

What is the sign of the healing of the sick? The laying on of hands is the sign or way marked out by James, and the custom of the ancient Saints as ordered by the Lord, and we cannot obtain the blessing by pursuing any other course except the way marked out by the Lord. What if we should attempt to get the gift of the Holy Ghost through any other means except the signs or way which God hath appointed—would we obtain it? Certainly not; all other means would fail. The Lord says do so and so, and I will bless you.

There are certain key words and signs belonging to the Priesthood which must be observed in order to obtain the blessing. The sign of Peter was to repent and be baptized for the remission of sins, with the promise of the gift of the Holy Ghost; and in no other way is the gift of the Holy Ghost obtained.

There is a difference between the Holy Ghost and the gift of the Holy Ghost. Cornelius received the Holy Ghost before he was baptized, which was the convincing power of God unto him of the truth of the Gospel, but he could not receive the gift of the Holy Ghost until after he was baptized. Had he not taken this sign or ordinance upon him, the Holy Ghost which convinced him of the truth of God, would have left him. Until he obeyed these ordinances and received the gift of the Holy Ghost, by the laying on of hands, according to the order of God, he could not have healed the sick or commanded an evil spirit to come out of a man, and it obey him; for the spirits might say unto him, as they did to the sons of Sceva: "Paul we know and Jesus we know, but who are ye?" It mattereth not whether we live long or short on the earth after we come to a knowledge of these principles and obey them unto the end. I know that all men will be damned if they do not come in the way which He hath opened, and this is the way marked out by the word of the Lord.

As concerning the resurrection, I will merely say that all men will come from the grave as they lie down, whether old or young; there will not be "added unto their stature one cubit," neither taken from it; all will be raised by the power of God, having spirit in their bodies, and not blood. Children will be enthroned in the presence of God and the

Lamb with bodies of the same stature* that they had on earth, having been redeemed by the blood of the Lamb; they will there enjoy the fullness of that light, glory and intelligence, which is prepared in the celestial kingdom. "Blessed are the dead who die in the Lord, for they rest from their labors and their works do follow them."

The speaker, before closing, called upon the assembly before him to humble themselves in faith before God, and in mighty prayer and fast-

* It must be remembered that the above report of the Prophet's remarks, as also the report of the King Follett sermon (preached in April, 1844, and which will appear in Volume V of this history), where the same matter of infants being enthroned in power while remaining of the same stature as when on earth, and at the time of their death, is mentioned—were reported in long hand and from memory, so that they are very likely to contain inaccuracies and convey wrong impressions. This matter of children after the resurrection remaining of the same stature as at their death is well known to be such an error. The writer of this note distinctly remembers to have heard the late President Wilford Woodruff, who reported the above sermon, say, that the Prophet corrected the impression that had been made by his King Follett sermon, that children and infants would remain fixed in the stature of their infancy and childhood in and after the resurrection. President Woodruff very emphatically said on the occasion of the subject being agitated about 1888-9, that the prophet taught subsequently to his King Follett sermon that children while resurrected in the stature at which they died would develope to the full stature of men and women after the resurrection; and that the contrary impression created by the report of the Prophet's King Follett sermon was due to a misunderstanding of his remarks and erroneous reporting. In addition to this personal recollection of the writer as to the testimony of the late President Wilford Woodruff, the following testimony of Elder Joseph Horne and his wife, M. Isabella Horne, on the same subject is important. The statements here copied were delivered in the presence of President Angus M. Cannon, of the Salt Lake Stake of Zion, and Elder Arthur Winter, at the residence of Brother Horne, in Salt Lake City, on November 19, 1896, and were reported stenographically by Arthur Winter, the Church official reporter.

Sister M. Isabella Horne said:

"In conversation with the Prophet Joseph Smith once in Nauvoo, the subject of children in the resurrection was broached. I believe it was in Sister Leonora Cannon Taylor's house. She had just lost one of her children, and I had also lost one previously. The Prophet wanted to comfort us, and he told us that we should receive those children in the morning of the resurrection just as we laid them down, in purity and innocence, and we should nourish and care for them as their mothers. He said that children would be raised in the resurrection just as they were laid down, and that they would obtain all the intelligence necessary to occupy thrones, principalities and powers. The idea that I got from what he said was that the children would grow and develop in the Millennium, and that the mothers would have the pleasure of training and caring for them, which they had been deprived of in this life.

"This was sometime after the King Follett funeral, at which I was present."

Brother Joseph Horne said:

"I heard the Prophet Joseph Smith say that mothers should receive their children just as they laid them down, and that they would have the privilege of doing for them what they could not do here, the Prophet remarked: "How would you know them if you did not receive them as you laid them down?" I also got the idea that

ing to call upon the name of the Lord, until the elements were purified over our heads, and the earth sanctified under our feet, that the inhabitants of this city may escape the power of disease and pestilence, and the destroyer that rideth upon the face of the earth, and that the Holy Spirit of God may rest upon this vast multitude.

At the close of the meeting, President Smith said he should attend to the ordinance of baptism in the river, near his house, at two o'clock, and at the appointed hour, the bank of the Mississippi was lined with a multitude of people, and President Joseph Smith went into the river and baptized eighty persons for the remission of their sins, and what added joy to the scene was, that the first person baptized was M. L. D. Wasson, a nephew of Mrs. Emma Smith—the first of her kindred that has embraced the fullness of the Gospel.

At the close of this interesting scene, the administrator lifted up his hands towards heaven, and implored the blessing of God to rest upon the people; and truly the Spirit of God did rest upon the multitude, to the joy and consolation of our hearts.

After baptism, the congregation again repaired to the grove, near the Temple, to attend to the ordinance of confirmation, and, notwithstanding President Smith had spoken in the open air to the people, and stood in the water and baptized about eighty persons, about fifty of those baptized received their confirmation under his hands in the after part of the day.

While this was progressing, great numbers were being baptized in the font.

children would grow and develop after the resurrection, and that the mothers would care for them and train them."

We hereby certify that the foregoing is a full, true and correct account of the statements made by Joseph and M. Isabella Horne on the subject mentioned.

ANGUS M. CANNON.

ARTHUR WINTER.

We have read the foregoing, and certify that it is correct.

JOSEPH HORNE.

M. ISABELLA HORNE.

In the Improvement Era for June, 1904, President Joseph F. Smith in an editorial on the Resurrection said:

"The body will come forth as it is laid to rest, for there is no growth or development in the grave. As it is laid down, so will it arise, and changes to perfection will come by the law of restitution. But the spirit will continue to expand and develop, and the body, after the resurrection will develop to the full stature of man."

This may be accepted as the doctrine of the Church in respect to the resurrection of children and their future development to the full stature of men and women; and it is alike conformable to that which will be regarded as both reasonable and desirable.

After this, I baptized a large number in the font myself.

An Epistle of the Twelve to the Church of Jesus Christ of Latter-day Saints in its Various Branches and Conferences in Europe. Greeting:

BELOVED BRETHREN.—We feel it our privilege and a duty we owe to the great and glorious cause in which we have enlisted, to communicate to you at this time, some principles which if carried into effect, will facilitate the gathering of the Saints, and tend to ameliorate the condition of those who are struggling with poverty and distress, in this day when the usual means of support seem to be cut short to the laboring classes, through the depression that everywhere prevails in the general business mart of the civilized world. Our situation is such in these last days, and our salvation spiritually is so connected with our salvation temporally, that if one fail, the other necessarily must be seriously affected, if not wholly destroyed. God has made us social beings; He has endowed us with capacities for enjoying each other's society, and it is our duty to bring those powers and privileges into exercise, so far as we can, and for this it is our duty to strive by all lawful and expedient measures within our reach.

While we remain in this state of existence, we need food and raiment, habitations and society, and without these our enjoyments must be greatly limited, and the real object of our existence diminished, if not wholly destroyed. Though the Saints should possess all the common gifts of the Spirit of God, and yet remain destitute of those comforts so much needed for the sustenance of their bodies, they would be comparatively miserable; but when they arrive at that state of perfection, and are clothed upon with the more special gifts and power of increasing the widow's oil and meal, or if receiving their food from the ravens, like Elijah, they will not need to bestow so much attention on every trifle of the passing moments, as they now do; and until that period arrives they will recollect that to be in the exercise of the fullness of spiritual blessings they must be watchful and careful to provide things honest in the sight of all men for the sustenance and comfort of all these frail, perishable bodies. That we may be instruments in the hands of God of thus promoting your present and future temporal and spiritual welfare, we write you at the present time.

Many of you are desirous of emigrating to this country, and many have not the means to accomplish their wishes, and if we can assist you by our prayers and our counsels to accomplish the desires of your hearts in this thing, so far we will rejoice and be satisfied. You not only wish to emigrate to this section of the earth, but you desire also to have some laudable means of comfortable subsistence after you arrive here, and this also is important. How then, shall these things be accomplished and your souls be satisfied? We answer, by united understanding and concert of action.

You all, or most of you, have trades or different kinds of business, with which you have been long familiarized, and in which you would like to continue for the purpose of procuring a subsistence; and a great proportion of your occupation is such that no employment can be had in this city or vicinity; for instance: there are no cotton manufactories established here, and many of you know no other business. You want to come here, and when here, want to continue your labors in your accustomed branches of business; but you have no means to get here, and when here there are no factories, and yet factories are needed here, and there would be a ready market for all the fabrics which could be manufactured.

Now comes the concert of action; if the Church will arise unitedly; if the brethren will individually feel that the great work of the Lord is depending on themselves as instruments to assist in carrying it forward; and will unite all their means, faith and energy, in one grand mass, all that you desire can speedily be accomplished. A short time only will elapse before you yourselves will be astonished at the result, and you will feel that your desires are more than realized.

While the Saints are united, no power on the earth, or under the earth can prevail against them; but while each one acts for himself, many, very many, are in danger of being overthrown. God has promised all things to those who love Him and keep His commandments; then why be afraid that one should get a little more than another, or that one should gain, for a little moment, what another might lose; when Jesus has promised that the faithful shall be one with Him, as He is one with the Father, and shall possess all things in the due time of the Lord; not by stealth, not by force, not by the sword, but by the gift of the Father, through faithfulness to His commands; and the more they shall suffer, while they work in righteousness on the earth, the greater will be their reward, the more glorious their kingdom, the more extended their power, when they shall arrive in the celestial paradise.

Knowing and feeling these things as we do, and having respect unto the recompense of reward to be revealed hereafter, regardless of all necessary privation and labor to accomplish what our Master has given us to do, and desiring not to possess the kingdom alone, but that all the honest in heart should be united with us in the great and glorious work of building up Zion and her stakes, we will call upon you, dear brethren, to unite with us, all with one accord, to do what? To do the very things you desire should be done; to convey you to the place where you are, and then put you in possession of all the means you may need for your support; so that you may enjoy the fullness of the blessings belonging to the sons and daughters of Zion's King.

Had we means we would not ask your aid; we would gladly send the ships of Tarshish to bear you across the great waters, we would bring you to our homes, to our firesides; we would provide you habitations, lands and food, when you arrive among us. Our hearts are large enough to do all this, and a great deal more; but we have not the means; we have to labor for our own subsistence, as well as attend to those things which are laid upon us of the Lord, and which concern the whole Church as much as ourselves.

It is not the will of heaven that any one should be put in possession of all things without striving for them.   Where much is given, much is required; and he who has but one talent, must be as diligent in the use thereof as he that has ten, or he will lose his talent and his blessing; and it becometh him who hath but one, five or ten, to use them in the most economical manner possible, or he will not have enough to bring him hither; and that he who hath five pounds may have enough and to spare to him who hath but one, or in other words to help the brethren to accomplish with a little what otherwise would require much more than they can command, is the object of this Epistle.

Had we the means we would send vessels of our own, laden with flour, meats, fruits, and all sea stores nesessary for the comfort of the brethren on the water, so that they would have nothing more to do than go on shipboard, and land at New Orleans; from thence we would take them on our steamers, and bring them to this place, for this is the best place for the Saints to stop at for the present.

There may be other places where individuals might have the prospect of adding at once, more rapidly to their pecuniary interest, than they could here; but we can only say, it is the will of the Lord that the Saints build Nauvoo, and settle therein or in the vicinity; and we know assuredly that those who give heed to every word that proceedeth out of the mouth of the Lord, will be richer eventually—and not far distant —than those who may seem to prosper more by following their own inclinations.

Brethren, we wish not to control you or your means; it is not for our peace or interest; nay, rather, it is a source of labor, trouble and anxiety to have ought to do with the pecuniary business of the Church, which we would gladly avoid, could we do it, and do our duty—could we do it, and the things desired be accomplished, and we stand guiltless where God hath placed us—and for this reason we desire to make such arrangements as will most tend to leave the business in your own hands, or in the hands of those whom you shall select; men of your own acquaintance, in whom you can repose confidence that they will execute

their trust in righteousness. And that our plans may be understood by
you, and carried into execution, we have sent unto you our beloved
brother, Elder John Snyder, the bearer of this Epistle, and other Epistles also, previously written by us to you; and we beseech you, brethren, to receive him as a servant of the Most High, authorized according
to the order of the kingdom of heaven, and assist him by all lawful
means in your power, to execute the mission entrusted to him: for great
events depend upon his success; but to none will they be greater than
to yourselves.

Our authority for thus sending Brother Snyder to you, is found in the
"Book of the Law of the Lord," page 36, as follows—

"Nauvoo, December 22, 1841. The word of the Lord came unto
Joseph the Seer; verily thus saith the Lord—Let my servant John Snyder take a mission to the Eastern continent, unto all the conferences
now sitting in that region, and let him carry a package of epistles that
shall be written by my servants the Twelve, making known unto the
Saints their duties concerning the building of my houses, which I have
appointed unto you, saith the Lord, that they may bring their gold, and
their silver, and their precious stones, and the box tree, and the fir
tree, and all fine wood to beautify the place of my sanctuary, saith the
Lord, and let him return speedily, with all means which shall be put
into his hands: even so. Amen.

In this revelation, the brethren will discover their duty in relation to
the building of the Temple of the Lord in Nauvoo, and the Nauvoo
House; and we call upon them with united cry to give heed unto the
things written, and help to build the houses which God has commanded,
so that Brother Snyder may speedily return with means to strengthen
the hands of the laborers, and adorn and beautify the Tabernacle of Jehovah.

Brethren, while you are thus preparing to send up your offerings to
this place, if you will act in concert with our well beloved brother, Elder
Parley P. Pratt, and the regularly constituted authorities of the Church
in England; and collect as great an amount of cotton, linen, and wool-
len goods, silks, cutlery, and hardware, &c., even all the varieties of
goods which might be useful in this country, and which can be obtained
by the brethren in this time of monied scarcity, and forward the same
to us by Brother Snyder, or your own agent, in company with him, or
otherwise, and at other times, we will pay you for those goods, in lands,
in or out of the city, in houses, cattle, and such kind of property as you
may need; and with those goods we will purchase lands, &c., flour,
meat, and all things necessary for a sea voyage, which can be had
cheaper here than in England, and charter ships, and forward the same
to England, or such places as emigration may require, and bring back

in return a ship load of emigrants, at a cheaper rate than they can now emigrate; while, at the same time, those who remain can continue to collect and forward merchandize as before, which will give us the means of continuing our purchases here, of keeping ships passing and repassing, and of building manufacturing establishments ready for the brethren when they arrive in our midst.

While the great depression of the moneyed institutions continues as it now is, the people are compelled to resort to all laudable measures to effect those exchanges of property which are necessary to accomplish their designs in removing from one place to another, and from one kingdom to another; and by a faithful execution of the plans proposed above, much, very much, may be effected in emigration without the aid of cash, or with very little, at the most; and goods may be obtained to advantage for houses and lands which the brethren may have to dispose of, and in payment of debts due them, when it would be impossible for them to sell for cash at any price, or get their pay for debts due them even at a great discount, and thus thousands and tens of thousands may be made to rejoice in this land of plenty, while, were it not for a concert of action, they might remain where they are for years, or never have the opportunity of appearing among us on this side the great waters, until the morning of the first resurrection.

But, brethren, we want to see you here. We long to see all here who want to be here, and none others, for we desire the increase of those who love God and work righteousness, that Zion's cords may be lengthened, and her stakes strengthened; though the country is free to all who will abide her laws, and we have no disposition to cast out any from our midst who will submit thereto.

For many particulars in relation to the times and course of emigration, and many other important items connected with the general and particular interest of the Church, we would refer you to our former epistles, as to enter into a particular and minute detail of all items referred to in this epistle, would be impossible. Brother Snyder will enter into the subject more minutely, and with the assistance of the presidency among you, will unfold the same, so that no one need misunderstand.

The brethren need not suppose that this thing is of our own imagination, simply; or that the result thereof, if fully carried into execution, will be of doubtful character. We have been guided by the Spirit of the Lord in our deliberations concerning the matter; and have been instructed by the Prophet of the Most High, even Joseph, the Seer and Revelator, for the Church, whose instructions to us are as the voice of the Lord, and whose admonitions we ever regard as true and faithful, and worthy the confidence of all who profess the Gospel of Jesus Christ.

We have been with him in prosperity and adversity, in sickness and health, in public and private, in all situations where men may reasonably associate with each other, and know that his words are true, his teachings sacred, his character unsullied among men of truth, and that he is what the Church acknowledge him to be, a man of God, and the spokesman of the Most High unto His people; and we bear this testimony unto the world, calling on all the honest in heart to uphold him by their faith and prayers, that he may live long, enjoy much, and accomplish great things for the kingdom which he has been the honored instrument of establishing on the earth in these last days, even that he may lead a great multitude into the celestial kingdom.

That the Saints may enjoy the teachings of the Prophet; those teachings which can be had only at this place, so that they may go on from knowledge to knowledge even to perfection, they want to come up hither; and that the plans before suggested may by facilitated, let some individuals with capital come immediately and build factories—individuals who have the means, understand the business, and are capable of superintending the concerns thereof.

There is every natural advantage at this place for facilitating such an order of things; water, wood, and coal in abundance, and it only wants the hand of the laborer to bring them forth in form suited to their several uses; and, while the gold and the silver are secreted by the hands of unprincipled speculators, let us go forward and accomplish without gold or silver, that which might be more easily and expeditiously done with it.

Let the brethren ever remember the admonitions we have so often given, that Zion is not to be built up without labor, fatigue, and trial of the faith of many; that when John saw the great company on Mount Zion, he saw those who had come up through great tribulation; he also saw those who had endured great tribulation after they had arrived, and before the kingdom was completed.

The Saints of this day are of the number John saw, and those—and those only who are willing to endure tribulation, as good soldiers, without murmuring—will eventually find their names enrolled in the Lamb's Book of Life, and obtain an inheritance in the holy city.

To all those who are desirous of sharing in the poverty and sufferings incident to new countries and the children of the kingdom, we would say, come up hither, and help us to bear the burden, and you shall share the riches, glory and honors of the kingdom. And those who are not willing to suffer afflictions, losses, crosses, and disappointments with the people of God, may as well stay away and be destroyed, as to come here and perish, for perish they must who cannot abide a celestial law, and endure to the end in all meekness, patience, and faithfulness.

Inasmuch as Elder Levi Richards has asked for counsel, we would recommend him to return to Nauvoo, as soon as circumstances shall permit.

Praying that you may be blessed with wisdom, intelligence, and perseverance, in every good word and work, so that you may accomplish your desires, and help to roll on the great work in which you have enlisted, we subscribe ourselves your brethren and fellow laborers in the kingdom of patience.   Amen.

BRIGHAM YOUNG, President.
HEBER C. KIMBALL,
WILLIAM SMITH,
ORSON PRATT,
JOHN E. PAGE,
LYMAN WIGHT,
WILFORD WOODRUFF,
JOHN TAYLOR,
GEO. A. SMITH,
WILLARD RICHARDS, Clerk.

City of Nauvoo, Hancock County, Illinois, March 20, 1842.

CHAPTER XXXIII.

A MASON'S ESTIMATE OF NAUVOO AND THE PROPHET—ORGAN-
    IZATION OF THE FEMALE RELIEF SOCIETY—"TRY THE
    SPIRITS"—THE PROPHET'S EDITORIAL.

Monday, March 21, 1842.—I commenced a settlement
with William Marks, who had loaned money and property to the Church at various times.

Tuesday, 22.—I was at the general business office
through the day, and at home in the evening.

The following is from the *Advocate*, printed at Columbus, the residence of Grand Master [i. e. grand master
mason] Jonas:

NAUVOO AND THE MORMONS.

MR. EDITOR.—Having recently had occasion to visit the city of
Nauvoo, I cannot permit the opportunity to pass without expressing
the agreeable disappointment that awaited me there. I had supposed,
from what I had previously heard, that I should witness an impoverished, ignorant and bigotted population, completely priest-ridden, and
tyrannized over by Joseph Smith, the great prophet of these people.

On the contrary, to my surprise, I saw a people apparently happy,
prosperous and intelligent. Every man appeared to be employed in
some business or occupation. I saw no idleness, no intemperance, no
noise, no riot—all appeared to be contented, with no desire to trouble
themselves with anything except their own affairs. With the religion
of these people I have nothing to do; if they can be satisfied with the
doctrines of their new revelation, they have a right to be so. The Constitution of the country guarantees to them the right of worshiping God
according to the dictates of their own conscience, and if that can be so
easily satisfied, why should we who differ from them complain?

But I protest against the slanders and persecutions that are continually heaped upon these people. I could see no disposition on their part
to be otherwise than a peaceable and law-abiding people, and all they
ask of the country is to permit them to live under the protection of the

laws, and to be made amenable for their violations.   They may have among them bad and desperate characters, and what community has not?   But I am satisfied the Mormon people. as a body, will never be the aggressors or violators of the law.

While at Nauvoo I had a fine opportunity of seeing the people in a body.   There was a Masonic celebration, and the Grand Master of the state was present for the purpose of publicly installing the officers of a new lodge.   An immense number of persons assembled on the occasion, variously estimated from five to ten thousand persons, and never in my life did I wittness a better-dressed or a more orderly and well-behaved assemblage: not a drunken or disorderly person to be seen, and the display of taste and beauty among the females could not well be surpassed anywhere.

During my stay of three days, I became well acquainted with their principal men, and more particularly with their Prophet, the celebrated "Old Joe Smith."   I found them hospitable, polite, well-informed and liberal.   With Joseph Smith, the hospitality of whose house I kindly received, I was well pleased; of course on the subject of religion, we widely differed, but he appeared to be quite as willing to permit me to enjoy my right of opinion, as I think we all ought to be to let the Mormons enjoy theirs; but instead of the ignorant and tyrannical upstart, judge my surprise at finding him a sensible, intelligent, companionable and gentlemanly man.   In frequent conversations with him he gave me every information that I desired, and appeared to be only pleased at being able to do so.   He appears to be much respected by all the people about him, and has their entire confidence.   He is a fine looking man about thirty-six years of age, and has an interesting family.

The incorporated limits of Nauvoo contains, it is said, about seven thousand persons; the buildings are generally small and much scattered.   The Temple and Nauvoo House, now building, will probably, in beauty of design, extent and durability, excel any public building in the state, and will both be enclosed before winter.

From all I saw and heard, I am led to believe that, before many years, the city of Nauvoo will be the largest and most beautiful city of the west, provided the Mormons are unmolested in the peaceable enjoyment of their rights and privileges, and why they should be troubled while acting as good citizens, I cannot imagine; and I hope and trust that the people of Illinois have no disposition to disturb unoffending people who have no disposition but to live peaceably under the laws of the country, and to worship God under their own vine and fig tree.—An Observer, Adams County.

Extract from a Letter from Elder E. P. Maginn, Salem, Massachusetts.

I am on a visit to assist Elder Erastus Snow in his successful and extended field of labor in this branch. Sixty-five have been obedient to the faith of the Gospel, and hundreds of others almost persuaded. In Boston near forty have obeyed through the faithful labors of Elder Freeman Nickerson. I have been absent from Peterborough two weeks; have preached three or four times in Boston, Salem, Marblehead, Chelsea, &c., and purpose returning to Peterborough next Sunday, where I have been laboring with good success, thirty-six have obeyed since last fall; at New Salem, Massachusetts, thirty-five to forty have obeyed since August last; Leverett, eighteen or twenty; Gilsum, New Hampshire, twenty to thirty. I have preached from one to three times every day, and cannot fill one in twenty of the calls for preaching; there is the greatest excitement in this country that I ever beheld during my travels since I left Nauvoo—a period of near three years, in which I have traveled through eighteen states and British provinces.

Wednesday, 23.—In council with Heber C. Kimball, Willard Richards and others at my office.

Thursday, 24.—I attended by request, the Female Relief Society, whose object is the relief of the poor, the destitute, the widow and the orphan, and for the exercise of all benevolent purposes. Its organization was completed this day. Mrs. Emma Smith takes the presidential chair; Mrs. Elizabeth Ann Whitney and Sarah M. Cleveland are her counselors; Miss Elvira Cole is treasurer, and our well-known and talented poetess, Miss Eliza R. Snow, secretary. There was a very numerous attendance at the organization of the society, and also at the subsequent meetings, of some of our most intelligent, humane, philanthropic and respectable ladies; and we are well assured from a knowledge of those pure principles of benevolence that flow spontaneously from their humane and philanthropic bosoms, that with the resources they will have at command, they will fly to the relief of the stranger; they will pour in oil and wine to the wounded heart of the distressed; they will dry up the tears of the orphan and make the widow's heart to rejoice.

Our women have always been signalized for their acts of benevolence and kindness; but the cruel usage that they

Organization of the Relief Society.

received from the barbarians of Missouri, has hitherto
prevented their extending the hand of charity in a conspicuous manner; yet in the midst of their
persecution, when the bread has been torn
from their helpless offspring by their cruel
oppressors, they have always been ready to open their
doors to the weary traveler, to divide their scant pittance
with the hungry, and from their robbed and impoverished
wardrobes, to divide with the more needy and destitute;
and now that they are living upon a more genial soil, and
among a less barbarous people, and possess facilities that
they have not heretofore enjoyed, we feel convinced that
with their concentrated efforts, the condition of the
suffering poor, of the stranger and the fatherless will
be ameliorated.

Character of the Mormon Women.

We had the privilege of being present at their organization, and were much pleased with their *modus operandi*,
and the good order that prevailed. They are strictly par-
liamentary in their proceedings.

An earthquake at Falmouth this morning.

Friday, 25.—Attending to a variety of business; counseling, &c.

Saturday, 26.—Elder John Snyder received his final
instructions from the President, and received his blessing
from Elder Brigham Young, with the laying on
of the hands of President Joseph Smith, John
E. Page and Willard Richards, and started
for England this day.

Mission of John Snyder.

Sunday, 27.—After speaking to the Saints for some
time on the subject of baptism for the dead, I baptized
one hundred and seven individuals.

[The following brief extract is from Elder Woodruff's journal.]

Synopsis of the Prophet's Sermon on Baptism for the Dead.

This was an interesting day. A large assembly met in the grove near
the Temple. Brother Amasa Lyman addressed the people in a very in-

teresting manner. He was followed by Joseph, the Seer, who made some highly edifying and instructive remarks concerning baptism for the dead. He said the Bible supported the doctrine, quoting 1 Cor., xv: 29: "Else what shall they do which are baptized for the dead, if the dead rise not at all, why are they then baptized for the dead?" If there is one word of the Lord that supports the doctrine of baptism for the dead, it is enough to establish it as a true doctrine. Again; if we can, by the authority of the Priesthood of the Son of God, baptize a man in the name of the Father, of the Son, and of the Holy Ghost, for the remission of sins, it is just as much our privilege to act as an agent, and be baptized for the remission of sins for and in behalf of our dead kindred, who have not heard the Gospel, or the fullness of it.

After meeting closed, the congregation again assembled upon the banks of the river, and Joseph, the Seer, went into the river, and baptized all that came unto him.

I also witnessed the landing of 170 English brethren from the steamer *Ariel*, under the presidency of Elder Lyman Wight; also about $3,000 worth of goods for the Temple and Nauvoo House.

Monday, 28.—I was at the office. Received Parley P. Pratt's donations from England, and attended to a variety of business; as also on the 29th and 30th.

The following extract is from a letter received from Elder Lorenzo D. Barnes—

BRISTOL, March 28, 1842.

Letter of Lorenzo D. Barnes to Parley P. Pratt—Reporting Labors.
Elder Pratt.

MUCH ESTEEMED BROTHER:—I am happy to be able to state to you that I arrived here in safety and in health on Saturday, the 26th instant, after making a tour through a number of churches on my way from Cheltenham, which place I left in the evening of the 14th; visited the church at Lea; in the neighborhood of which I preached twice. I then went to Garway, where I preached five times to overflowing congregations; from thence visited Abergavenny, and preached three times. The work appears to be upon the onward march in all these places. Many are inquiring after truth and embracing it. The brethren and friends appeared very anxious for me to tarry longer, but being desirous to commence my labors in this city, I took my leave on Saturday, the 26th, and came *via* Newport, by the packet to this city, and preached

three times yesterday.   There appears to be a good feeling manifested
here at present.   In the evening our hall was quite full, and the people
listened very attentively; persons of respectable appearance were present.   We intend getting a large hall, and putting out bills shortly. Enclosed is an order for ten shillings, it being a donation for the building
of the Temple at Nauvoo, mostly from the branch of the Church at
Frogmarsh.

Yours in the bonds of the new covenant,

LORENZO D. BARNES.

Wednesday, 30.—I met with the Female Relief Society,
and gave them some instructions, of which the following
brief sketch was reported by Miss Eliza R. Snow—

Synopsis of the Prophet's Remarks to the Female Relief Society.

President Joseph Smith arose.   Spoke of the organization of the
Female Relief Society; said he was deeply interested, that it might be
built up to the Most High in an acceptable manner; that its rules must
be observed; that none should be received into it but those who were
worthy; proposed a close examination of every candidate; that the
society was growing too fast. It should grow up by degrees, should commence with a few individuals, thus have a select society of the virtuous,
and those who would walk circumspectly; commended them for their
zeal, but said sometimes their zeal was not according to knowledge.
One principal object of the institution was to purge out iniquity; said
they must be extremely careful in all their examinations, or the consequences would be serious.

All difficulties which might and would cross our way must be sur-
mounted. Though the soul be tried, the heart faint, and the hands hang
down, we must not retrace our steps; there must be decision of character,
aside from sympathy. When instructed, we must obey that voice, observe the laws of the kingdom of God, that the blessing of heaven may
rest down upon us.   All must act in concert, or nothing can be done,
and should move according to the ancient Priesthood; hence the Saints
should be a select people, separate from all the evils of the world—
choice, virtuous, and holy.   The Lord was going to make of the Church
of Jesus Christ a kingdom of Priests, a holy people, a chosen generation, as in Enoch's day, having all the gifts as illustrated to the Church
in Paul's epistles and teachings to the churches in his day—that it is the
privilege of each member to live long and enjoy health.   He then
blessed the Saints.

Monday, 31.—In council at my office with Elders

Brigham Young, John Taylor, Willard Richards,&c.; and wrote an epistle to the Female Relief Society, and spoke to the society in the afternoon.

Friday, April 1, 1842.—I was engaged in the general business office.

"Try the Spirits"—The Prophet's Editorial in the Times and Seasons.

Recent occurrences that have transpired amongst us render it an imperative duty devolving upon me to say something in relation to the spirits by which men are actuated.

It is evident from the Apostles' writings, that many false spirits existed in their day, and had "gone forth into the world," and that it needed intelligence which God alone could impart to detect false spirits, and to prove what spirits were of God. The world in general have been grossly ignorant in regard to this one thing, and why should they be otherwise—"for no man knows the things of God, but by the Spirit of God."

The Egyptians were not able to discover the difference between the miracles of Moses and those of the magicians until they came to be tested together; and if Moses had not appeared in their midst, they would unquestionably have thought that the miracles of the magicians were performed through the mighty power of God, for they were great miracles that were performed by them—a supernatural agency was developed, and great power manifested.

The witch of Endor is a no less singular personage; clothed with a powerful agency she raised the Prophet Samuel from his grave, and he appeared before the astonished king, and revealed unto him his future destiny. Who is to tell whether this woman is of God, and a righteous woman—or whether the power she possessed was of the devil, and she a witch as represented by the Bible? It is easy for us to say now, but if we had lived in her day, which of us could have unravelled the mystery?

It would have been equally as difficult for us to tell by what spirit the Apostles prophesied, or by what power the Apostles spoke and worked miracles. Who could have told whether the power of Simon, the sorcerer, was of God or of the devil?

There always did, in every age, seem to be a lack of intelligence pertaining to this subject. Spirits of all kinds have been manifested, in every age, and almost amongst all people. If we go among the pagans, they have their spirits; the Mohammedans, the Jews, the Christians, the Indians—all have their spirits, all have a supernatural agency, and all contend that their spirits are of God. Who shall solve the mystery? "Try the spirits," says John, but who is to do it? The learned, the eloquent, the philosopher, the sage, the divine—all are ignorant. The heathens will boast of their gods, and of the great things that have been unfolded by their oracles. The Mussulman will boast of his Koran, and of the divine communications that his progenitors have received. The Jews have had numerous instances, both ancient and modern, among them of men who have professed to be inspired, and sent to bring about great events, and the Christian world has not been slow in making up the number.

"Try the spirits," but what by? Are we to try them by the creeds of men? What preposterous folly—what sheer ignorance—what madness! Try the motions and actions of an eternal being (for I contend that all spirits are such) by a thing that was conceived in ignorance, and brought forth in folly—a cobweb of yesterday! Angels would hide their faces, and devils would be ashamed and insulted, and would say, "Paul we know, and Jesus we know, but who are ye?" Let each man of society make a creed and try evil spirits by it, and the devil would shake his sides; it is all that he would ask—all that he would desire. Yet many of them do this, and hence "many spirits are abroad in the world."

One great evil is, that men are ignorant of the nature of spirits; their power, laws, government, intelligence, &c., and imagine that when there is anything like power, revelation, or vision manifested, that it must be of God. Hence the Methodists, Presbyterians, and others frequently possess a spirit that will cause them to lie down, and during its operation, animation is frequently entirely suspended; they consider it to be the power of God, and a glorious manifestation from God—a manifestation of what? Is there any intelligence communicated? Are the curtains of heaven withdrawn, or the purposes of God developed? Have they seen and conversed with an angel—or have the glories of futurity burst upon their view? No! but their body has been inanimate, the operation of their spirit suspended, and all the intelligence that can be obtained from them when they arise, is a shout of "glory," or "hallelujah," or some incoherent expression; but they have had "the power."

The Shaker will whirl around on his heel, impelled by a supernatural agency or spirit, and think that he is governed by the Spirit of God; and the Jumper will jump and enter into all kinds of extravagances. A Primitive Methodist will shout under the influence of that spirit, until he will rend the heavens with his cries; while the Quakers (or Friends) moved as they think, by the Spirit of God, will sit still and say nothing. Is God the author of all this? If not of all of it, which does He recognize? Surely, such a heterogeneous mass of confusion never can enter into the kingdom of heaven.

Every one of these professes to be competent to try his neighbor's spirit, but no one can try his own, and what is the reason? Because they have not a key to unlock, no rule wherewith to measure, and no criterion whereby they can test it. Could any one tell the length, breadth or height of a building without a rule? test the quality of metals without a criterion, or point out the movements of the planetary systems, without a knowledge of astronomy? Certainly not; and if such ignorance as this is manifested about a spirit of this kind, who can describe an angel of light? If Satan should appear as one in glory, who can tell his color, his signs, his appearance, his glory?—or what is the manner of his manifestation? Who can detect the spirit of the French prophets with their revelations and their visions, and power of manifestations? Or who can point out the spirit of the Irvingites, with their apostles and prophets, and visions and tongues, and interpretations, &c., &c. Or who can drag into daylight and develop the hidden mysteries of the false spirits that so frequently are made manifest among the Latter-day Saints? We answer that no man can do this without the Priesthood, and having a knowledge of the laws by which spirits are governed; for as "no man knows the things of God, but by the Spirit of God," so no man knows the spirit of the devil, and his power and influence, but by possessing intelligence which is more than human, and having unfolded through the medium of the Priesthood the mysterious operations of his devices; without knowing the angelic form, the sanctified look and gesture, and the zeal that is frequently manifested by him for the glory of God, together with the prophetic spirit, the gracious influence, the godly appearance, and the holy garb, which are so characteristic of his proceedings and his mysterious windings.

A man must have the discerning of spirits before he can drag into daylight this hellish influence and unfold it unto the world in all its soul-destroying, diabolical, and horrid colors; for nothing is a greater injury to the children of men than to be under the influence of a false spirit when they think they have the Spirit of God. Thousands have felt the influence of its terrible power and baneful effects. Long pilgrimages have been undertaken, penances endured, and pain, misery and ruin have followed in their train; nations have been convulsed, kingdoms overthrown, provinces laid waste, and blood, carnage and desolation are habiliaments in which it has been clothed.

The Turks, the Hindoos, the Jews, the Christians, the Indian; in fact all nations have been deceived, imposed upon and injured through the mischievous effects of false spirits.

As we have noticed before, the great difficulty lies in the ignorance of the nature of spirits, of the laws by which they are governed, and the signs by which they may be known; if it requires the Spirit of God

to know the things of God; and the spirit of the devil can only be unmasked through that medium, then it follows as a natural consequence
that unless some person or persons have a communication, or revelation
from God, unfolding to them the operation of the spirit, they must eternally
remain ignorant of these principles; for I contend that if one man cannot understand these things but by the Spirit of God, ten thousand men
cannot; it is alike out of the reach of the wisdom of the learned, the
tongue of the eloquent, the power of the mighty. And we shall at last
have to come to this conclusion, whatever we may think of revelation,
that without it we can neither know nor understand anything of God,
or the devil; and however unwilling the world may be to acknowledge
this principle, it is evident from the multifarious creeds and notions
concerning this matter that they understand nothing of this principle,
and it is equally as plain that without a divine communication they
must remain in ignorance. The world always mistook false prophets for
true ones, and those that were sent of God, they considered to be false
prophets, and hence they killed, stoned, punished and imprisoned the
true prophets, and these had to hide themselves "in deserts and dens,
and caves of the earth," and though the most honorable men of the
earth, they banished them from their society as vagabonds, whilst they
cherished, honored and supported knaves, vagabonds, hypocrites,
impostors, and the basest of men.

A man must have the discerning of spirits, as we before stated, to
understand these things, and how is he to obtain this gift if there are
no gifts of the Spirit? And how can these gifts be obtained without
revelation? "Christ ascended into heaven, and gave gifts to men; and He
gave some Apostles, and some Prophets, and some Evangelists, and
some Pastors and Teachers. And how were Apostles, Prophets,
Pastors, Teachers and Evangelists chosen? By prophecy (revelation) and by laying on of hands:—by a divine communication,
and a divinely appointed ordinance—through the medium of the Priesthood, organized according to the order of God, by divine appointment.
The Apostles in ancient times held the keys of this Priesthood—of the
mysteries of the kingdom of God, and consequently were enabled to
unlock and unravel all things pertaining to the government of the
Church, the welfare of society, the future destiny of men, and the
agency, power and influence of spirits; for they could control them at
pleasure, bid them depart in the name of Jesus, and detect their mischievous and mysterious operations when trying to palm themselves
upon the Church in a religious garb, and militate against the interest of
the Church and spread of truth. We read that they "cast out devils in
the name of Jesus," and when a woman possessing the spirit of divina-
tion, cried before Paul and Silas, "these are the servants of the Most
High God that show unto us the way of salvation," they detected the

spirit. And although she spake favorably of them, Paul commanded the spirit to come out of her, and saved themselves from the opprobrium that might have been heaped upon their heads, through an alliance with her, in the development of her wicked principles, which they certainly would have been charged with, if they had not rebuked the evil spirit.

A power similar to this existed through the medium of the Priesthood in different ages. Moses could detect the magician's power, and show that he [himself] was God's servant—he knew when he was upon the mountain (through revelation) that Israel was engaged in idolatry; he could develop the sin of Korah, Dathan and Abiram, detect witches and wizards in their proceedings, and point out the true prophets of the Lord. Joshua knew how to detect the man who had stolen the wedge of gold and the Babylonish garment. Michaiah could point out the false spirit by which the four hundred prophets were governed; and if his advice had been taken, many lives would have been spared, (II Chronicles xviii) Elijah, Elisha, Isaiah, Jeremiah, Ezekiel, and many other prophets possessed this power. Our Savior, the Apostles. and even the members of the Church were endowed with this gift, for, says Paul, (I Corinthians xii), "To one is given the gift of tongues, to another the interpretation of tongues, to another the working of miracles, to another prophecy, to another the discerning of spirits." All these proceeded from the same Spirit of God, and were the gifts of God. The Ephesian church were enabled by this principle, "to try those that said they were apostles, and were not, and found them liars," (Revelation ii: 2.)

In tracing the thing to the foundation, and looking at it philosophically, we shall find a very material difference between the body and the spirit; the body is supposed to be organized matter, and the spirit, by many, is thought to be immaterial, without substance. With this latter statement we should beg leave to differ, and state that spirit is a substance; that it is material, but that it is more pure, elastic and refined matter than the body; that it existed before the body, can exist in the body; and will exist separate from the body, when the body will be mouldering in the dust; and will in the resurrection, be again united with it.

Without attempting to describe this mysterious connection, and the laws that govern the body and the spirit of man, their relationship to each other, and the design of God in relation to the human body and spirit, I would just remark, that the spirits of men are eternal, that they are governed by the same Priesthood that Abraham, Melchisedek, and the Apostles were: that they are organized according to that Priesthood which is everlasting, "without beginning of days or end of years,"— that they all move in their respective spheres, and are governed by the law of God; that when they appear upon the earth they are in a probationary state, and are preparing, if righteous, for a future and greater glory; that the spirits of good men cannot interfere with the wicked beyond their prescribed bounds, for "Michael, the Archangel, dared not bring a railing accusation against the devil, but said, "The Lord rebuke thee, Satan."

It would seem also, that wicked spirits have their bounds, limits, and laws by which they are governed or controlled, and know their future destiny; hence, those that were in the maniac said to our Savior, "Art thou come to torment us before the time," and when Satan presented himself before the Lord, among the sons of God, he said that he came "from going to and fro in the earth, and from wandering up and down in it;" and he is emphatically called the prince of the power of the air; and, it is very evident that they possess a power that none but those who have the Priesthood can control, as we have before adverted to, in the case of the sons of Sceva.

Having said so much upon general principles, without referring to the peculiar situation, power, and influence of the magicians of Egypt, the wizards and witches of the Jews, the oracles of the heathen, their necromancers, soothsayers, and astrologers, the maniacs or those possessed of devils in the Apostles' days, we will notice, and try to detect (so far as we have the Scriptures for our aid) some few instances of the development of false spirits in more modern times, and in this our day.

The "French Prophets" were possessed of a spirit that deceived; they existed in Vivaris and Dauphany, in great numbers in the year 1688; there were many boys and girls from seven to twenty-five; they had strange fits, as in tremblings and faintings, which made them stretch out their legs and arms, as in a swoon; they remained awhile in trances, and coming out of them, uttered all that came in their mouths [see Buck's Theological Dictionary].

Now God never had any prophets that acted in this way; there was nothing indecorous in the proceeding of the Lord's prophets in any age; neither had the apostles, nor prophets in the apostles's day anything of this kind. Paul says, "Ye may all prophesy, one by one; and if anything be revealed to another let the first hold his peace, for the spirit of the prophets is subject to the prophets;" but here we find that the prophets are subject to the spirit, and falling down, have twitchings, tumblings, and faintings through the influence of that spirit, being entirely under its control. Paul says, "Let everything be done decently and in order," but here we find the greatest disorder and indecency in the conduct of both men and women, as above described. The same rule would apply to the fallings, twitchings, swoonings, shaking, and trances of many of our modern revivalists.

Johanna Southcott professed to be a prophetess, and wrote a book of prophecies in 1804, she became the founder of a people that are still extant.   She was to bring forth, in a place appointed, a son, that was to be the Messiah, which thing has failed.   Independent of this, however, where do we read of a woman that was the founder of a church, in the word of God?   Paul told the women in his day, "To keep silence in the church, and that if they wished to know anything to ask their husbands at home;" he would not suffer a woman "to rule, or to usurp authority in the church;" but here we find a woman the founder of a church, the revelator and guide, the Alpha and Omega, contrary to all acknowledged rule, principle, and order.

Jemimah Wilkinson was another prophetess that figured largely in America, in the last century.   She stated that she was taken sick and died, and that her soul went to heaven, where it still continues.   Soon after, her body was reanimated with the spirit and power of Christ, upon which she set up as a public teacher, and declared that she had an immediate revelation.   Now the Scriptures positively assert that "Christ is the first fruit, afterwards those that are Christ's at His coming, then cometh the end."   But Jemimah, according to her testimony, died, and rose again before the time mentioned in the Scriptures.   The idea of her soul being in heaven while her body was [living] on earth, is also preposterous.   When God breathed into man's nostrils, he became a living soul, before that he did not live, and when that was taken away his body died; and so did our Savior when the spirit left the body, nor did His body live until His spirit returned in the power of His resurrection.   But Mrs. Wilkinson's soul [life] was in heaven, and her body without the soul [or life] on earth, living [without the soul, or] without life!

The Irvingites, are a people that have counterfeited the truth, perhaps the nearest of any of our modern sectarians.   They commenced about ten years ago in the city of London, in England; they have churches formed in various parts of England and Scotland, and some few in Upper Canada.   Mr. Irving, their founder, was a learned and talented minister of the Church of Scotland, he was a great logician, and a powerful orator, but withal wild and enthusiastic in his views.   Moving in the higher circles, and possessing talent and zeal, placed him in a situation to become a conspicuous character, and to raise up a society similar to that which is called after his name.

The Irvingites have apostles, prophets, pastors, teachers, evangelists, and angels.   They profess to have the gift of tongues, and the interpretation of tongues, and, in some few instances, to have the gift of healing.

The first prophetic spirit that was manifested was in some Misses

Campbell that Mr. Irving met with, while on a journey in Scotland; they had [what is termed among their sect] "utterances," which were evidently of a supernatural agency.   Mr. Irving, falling into the common error of considering all supernatural manifestations to be of God, took them to London with him, and introduced them into his church.

They were there honored as the prophetesses of God, and when they spoke, Mr. Irving or any of his ministers had to keep silence.   They were peculiarly wrought upon before the congregation, and had strange utterances, uttered with an unnatural, shrill voice, and with thrilling intonations they frequently made use of a few broken, unconnected sentences, that were ambiguous, incoherent, and incomprehensible; at other times they were more clearly understood.   They would frequently cry out, "There is iniquity!   There is iniquity!"   And Mr. Irving has been led, under the influence of this charge, to fall down upon his knees before the public congregation, and to confess his sin, not knowing whether he had sinned, nor wherein, nor whether the thing referred to him, or somebody else.   During these operations, the bodies of the persons speaking were powerfully wrought upon, their countenances were distorted, they had frequent twitchings in their hands, and the whole system was powerfully convulsed at intervals; they sometimes, however, (it is supposed) spoke in correct tongues, and had true interpretations.

Under the influence of this spirit the church was organized by these women; apostles, prophets, &c. were soon called, and a systematic order of things introduced, as above mentioned.   A Mr. Baxter (afterwards one of their principal prophets) upon going into one of their meetings, says, "I saw a power manifested, and thought that was the power of God, and asked that it might fall upon me, and it did so, and I began to prophesy."   Eight or nine years ago they had about sixty preachers going through the streets of London, testifying that London was to be the place where the "two witnesses" spoken of by John, were to prophesy; that (they) "the church and the spirit were the witnesses, and that at the end of three years and a half there was to be an earthquake and great destruction, and our Savior was to come.   Their apostles were collected together at the appointed time watching the event, but Jesus did not come, and the prophecy was then ambiguously explained away.   They frequently had signs given them by the spirit to prove to them that what was manifested to them should take place. Mr. Baxter related an impression that he had concerning a child.   It was manifested to him that he should visit the child, and lay hands upon it, and that it should be healed; and to prove to him that this was of God, he should meet his brother in a certain place, who should speak unto him certain words.   His brother addressed him precisely in the way and manner that the manifestation designated. The sign took place, but when he laid his hands upon the child it did not recover. I cannot vouch for the authority of the last statement, as Mr. Baxter at that time had left the Irvingites, but it is in accordance with many of their proceedings, and the thing never has been attempted to be denied.

It may be asked, where is there anything in all this that is wrong?

1st. The church was organized by women, and "God placed in the Church (first apostles, secondarily prophets), and not first women; but Mr. Irving placed in his church first women (secondarily apostles, and the church was founded and organized by them. A woman has no right to found or organize a church—God never sent them to do it.

2nd. Those women would speak in the midst of a meeting, and rebuke Mr. Irving or any of the church. Now the Scripture positively says, "Thou shalt not rebuke an Elder, but entreat him as a father:" not only this, but they frequently accused the brethren, thus placing themselves in the seat of Satan, who is emphatically called "the accuser of the brethren."

3rd. Mr. Baxter received the spirit on asking for it, without attending to the ordinances, and began to prophesy, whereas the scriptural way of attaining the gift of the Holy Ghost is by baptism, and by laying on of hands.

4th. As we have stated in regard to others, the spirit of the prophets is subject to the prophets; but those prophets were subject to the spirits, the spirits controlling their bodies at pleasure.

But it may be asked how Mr. Baxter could get a sign from a second person? To this we would answer, that Mr. Baxter's brother was under the influence of the same spirit as himself, and being subject to that spirit he could be easily made to speak to Mr. Baxter whatever the spirit should dictate; but there was not power in the spirit to heal the child.

Again it may be asked, how it was that they could speak in tongues if they were of the devil! We would answer that they could be made to speak in another tongue, as well as their own, as they were under the control of that spirit, and the devil can tempt the Hottentot, the Turk, the Jew, or any other nation; and if these men were under the influence of his spirt, they of course could speak Hebrew, Latin, Greek, Italian, Dutch, or any other language that the devil knew.

Some will say, "try the spirits" by the word. "Every spirit that confesseth that Jesus Christ is come in the flesh is of God, and every spirit that confesseth not that Jesus Christ is come in the flesh is not of God." John 4:2, 3. One of the Irvingites once quoted this passage whilst under the influence of a spirit, and then said, "I confess that Jesus Christ is come in the flesh." And yet these prophecies failed, their Messiah did not come; and the great things spoken of by them have fallen to the ground. What is the matter here? Did not the Apostle speak the truth? Certainly he did—but he spoke to a people who were under the penalty of death, the moment they embraced Christianity; and no one without a knowledge of the fact would confess it, and expose themselves to death, and this was consequently given as a criterion to the church or churches to which John wrote. But the devil on a certain occasion cried out, "I know thee, who thou art, the Holy One of God!" Here was a frank acknowledgment under other circumstances that "Jesus had come in the flesh." On another occasion the devil said, "Paul we know, and Jesus we know"—of course, "come in the flesh." No man nor set of men without the regular constituted authorities, the Priesthood and discerning of spirits, can tell true from false spirits. This power they possessed in the Apostles' day, but it has departed from the world for ages.

The Church of Jesus Christ of Latter-day Saints has also had its false spirits; and as it is made up of all those different sects professing every variety of opinion, and having been under the influence of so many kinds of spirits, it is not to be wondered at if there should be found among us false spirits.

Soon after the Gospel was established in Kirtland, and during the absence of the authorities of the Church, many false spirits were introduced, many strange visions were seen, and wild, enthusiastic notions were entertained; men ran out of doors under the influence of this spirit, and some of them got upon the stumps of trees and shouted, and all kinds of extravagances were entered into by them; one man pursued a ball that he said he saw flying in the air, until he came to a precipice, when he jumped into the top of a tree, which saved his life; and many ridiculous things were entered into, calculated to bring disgrace upon the Church of God, to cause the Spirit of God to be withdrawn, and to uproot and destroy those glorious principles which had been developed for the salvation of the human family. But when the authorities returned, the spirit was made manifest, those members that were exercised with it were tried for their fellowship, and those that would not repent and forsake it were cut off.

At a subsequent period a Shaker spirit was on the point of being introduced, and at another time the Methodist and Presbyterian falling down power, but the spirit was rebuked and put down, and those who would not submit to rule and good order were disfellowshiped. We have also had brethren and sisters who have had the gift of tongues falsely; they would speak in a muttering unnatural voice, and their bodies be distorted like the Irvingites before alluded to; whereas, there is nothing unnatural in the Spirit of God. A circumstance of this kind took place in Upper Canada, but was rebuked by the presiding Elder; another, a woman near the same place, professed to have the discerning of spirits, and began to *accuse* another sister of things that she was not guilty of, which she said she knew was so by the spirit, but was afterwards proven to be false; she placed herself in the capacity of the "*accuser* of the brethren," and no person through the discerning of spirits can bring a charge against another, they must be proven guilty by positive evidence, or they stand clear.

There have also been ministering angels in the Church which were of Satan appearing as an angel of light. A sister in the state of New York had a vision, who said it was told her that if she would go to a certain place in the woods, an angel would appear to her. She went at the appointed time, and saw a glorious personage descending, arrayed in white, with sandy colored hair; he commenced and told her to fear God, and said that her husband was called to do great things, but that he must not go more than one hundred miles from home, or he would not return; whereas God had called him to go to the ends of the earth, and he has since been more than one thousand miles from home, and is yet alive. Many true things were spoken by this personage, and many things that were false. How, it may be asked, was this known to be a bad angel? By the color of his hair; that is one of the signs that he can be known by, and by his contradicting a former revelation.

We have also had brethren and sisters who have written revelations, and who have started forward to lead this Church. Such was a young boy in Kirtland, Isaac Russel, of Missouri, and Gladden Bishop, and Oliver Olney of Nauvoo. The boy is now living with his parents who have submitted to the laws of the Church. Mr. Russell stayed in Far West, from whence he was to go to the Rocky Mountains, led by three Nephites; but the Nephites never came, and his friends forsook him, all but some of the blood relations, who have since been nearly destroyed by the mob. Mr. Bishop was tried by the High Council, his papers examined, condemned and burned, and he cut off the Church. He acknowledged the justice of the decision, and said "that he now saw his error, for if he had been governed by the revelations given before, he might have known that no man was to write revelations for the Church, but Joseph Smith," and begged to be prayed for, and forgiven by the brethren. Mr. Olney has also been tried by the High Council and disfellowshiped, because he would not have his writings tested by the word of God; evidently proving that he loves darkness rather than light, because his deeds are evil.

CHAPTER XXXIV.

SPECIAL CONFERENCE OF THE CHURCH AT NAUVOO — THE
PROPHET'S REPROOF OF THE WICKED—EPISTLE OF THE
TWELVE TO THE SAINTS IN KIRTLAND—STATUS OF THE
CHURCH.

Saturday, April 2.—I paid Hugh Rhodes $1,150 for a
farm.

The fourth regiment of the second cohort of the Nauvoo
Legion, consisting of four companies, was organized,
Jonathan Dunham was elected colonel, James Brown, lieu-
tenant-colonel, and Jesse P. Harmon, major of the same.

Monday, 4.—Transacted business at my house with
Josiah Butterfield, concerning the Lawrence estates; and
closed a settlement with William Marks in the counting
room, and paid him off, principal and interest to the last
farthing, for all that myself or the Church had had of him.

Tuesday, 5.—Settled with Brother Niswanger.

Wednesday, 6.—The first day of the thirteenth year of
the rise of the Church of Jesus Christ of Latter-day Saints. A special conference had been
appointed at the city of Nauvoo, but it was
so wet and cold, that it was not prudent for me
to go out, as my health was not good, and I spent the day
with my family. Brother Hyrum and Elders Brigham
Young, Heber C. Kimball, and Willard Richards called
on me in the morning, and I gave them instructions how
to organize and adjourn the conference. Before they left,
Brother Hyrum and the Twelve present bore testimony

The Thir-
teenth Anni-
versary of the
Organization
of the Church.

that they had never heard me teach any principles but those of the strictest virtue, either in public or private.

CONFERENCE MINUTES.

Special Conference of the Church of Jesus Christ of Latter-day Saints. City of Nauvoo, April 6, 1842.

The day being wet, the First Presidency did not attend, and Elder Page addressed those present upon the subject of the charges against him, and said he would be happy to have an opportunity of laying his statement before the conference at a convenient time. President William Law, General Bennett, president *pro tem*, and President Hyrum Smith all spoke upon the subject of military affairs, showing the necessity of a well organized and efficient force; that as we were bound to serve our country, if required, in common with all good citizens, we ought not to be behind any of our neighbors in point of good order, neat uniforms and equipments, and a well organized and thoroughly disciplined legion.

Thursday, April 7. Conference met. President Joseph Smith had the several quorums put in order and seated. He then made some very appropriate remarks concerning the duties of the Church, the necessity of unity of purpose in regard to the building of the houses, and the blessings connected with doing the will of God, and the inconsistency, folly, and danger of murmuring against the dispensations of Jehovah.

He said that the principal object of the meeting was, to bring the case of Elder Page before them; and that another object was, to choose young men and ordain them, and send them out to preach, that they may have an opportunity of proving themselves, and of enduring the tarring and feathering, and such things as those of us who have gone before them have had to endure.

Elder Page, having arrived, was called upon, and addressed the congregation in relation to the non-performance of his mission to Jerusalem. He said that when he started with Elder Hyde, joy filled their hearts, and they were aware of the responsibility of their mission. Elder Hyde's vision was that he should be in Jerusalem alone, Elder Page considered Elder Hyde to be his father and guide in the mission, and felt it his duty to submit to Elder Hyde's opinion in all things; no Elders ever were more in concert on a mission than they were while together. They made a covenant in Quincy to stand by each other while on the mission; and if they were insulted or imposed upon they would stand by each other, even unto death, and not separate unless to go a few miles to preach a sermon, that all moneys should go into one purse, and it did so.

Elder Hyde, in Indiana, first said he would go to visit Brother Knight, and that Elder Page should stay and preach; he assented, and went and returned to Indianapolis.   Elder Page had a mare given him on account of both.   Elder Hyde then took the mare, went on, left his luggage with Elder Page; while away he sold the mare for $40, and received $60 more as a donation from the man to whom he had sold the mare; he returned, they preached at Dayton and received a handsome contribution.   Elder Page preached sixteen miles off, and raised a branch.   Elder Hyde went to Cincinnati, revised the "Missouri Persecutions," got 2,000 copies printed, paid for them, and took part of them with him, and left a large box full, and about 150 loose copies with Elder Page.   Elder Hyde started for Philadelphia, purposing to visit churches on the way; he left Elder Page $23.31.   Elder Page returned to Dayton and Milton, and sold books, with the intention of following Elder Hyde as soon as practicable; but he stayed a day or two too long, and the river closed by the frost, from one to two weeks earlier than usual.   Elder Hyde told him that it was possible they might be from one to two years before they would leave America, as it would take upwards of $1,000 each to take them to Jerusalem and back, that it would be slow gleaning in England, and assigned this as a reason for not immediately following Elder Hyde, thinking that he would be sure of seeing him in the spring.   Elder Page accused himself of not using better economy in proceeding on his journey.

There came out a piece in the paper, stating the displeasure of the Lord respecting Elder Hyde and Elder Page, he sat down and wrote a piece to put in the paper, acknowledging the justice of the charge, but wisdom prevented its being published; preached about Washington, &c., gathered funds for the mission in Westchester and in Philadelphia.

Elder Hyde raised funds on behalf of the mission, by applauding Elder Page's talents, wisdom, &c., but they were disappointed in him when they saw him; he raised funds for the mission, the most liberal was in Philadelphia.   He intended to sail on the 25th of July, but the brethren said that if he would remain two weeks, they would raise funds for him; they found that it would take longer, and he decided to stay a month, he then received a command through a letter from President Hyrum Smith to an official character in Philadelphia, requesting him to return; he wrote to ascertain the reason but did not get an answer, he was then called in by President Joseph Smith and Elder Brigham Young.

Elder Hyde would often renew the covenant between them to never part with each other in that mission. Elder Page had no blame to attach to Elder Hyde; he supposed he had done right, but if he had been in his place, he would have tarried for him until the spring.   The reports of his having apostatized, &c., returned even from this place to New York.   Many reproved him for leaving Cincinnati for Dayton.

President Joseph Smith then arose and stated that it was wrong to make the covenant referred to by him; that it created a lack of confidence for two men to covenant to reveal all acts of secrecy or otherwise, to each other, and Elder Page showed a little grannyism.   He said that no two men, when they agreed to go together ought to separate, that the Prophets of old would not, and quoted the circumstance of Elijah and Elisha, 2 Kings ii., when about to go to Gilgal, also when about to go to Jericho, and to Jordan, that Elisha could not get clear of Elijah, that he clung to his garment until he was taken to heaven; and that Elder Page should have stuck by Elder Hyde, and he might have gone to Jerusalem, that there is nothing very bad in it, but by the experience let us profit; again the Lord made use of Elder Page as a scape goat to procure funds for Elder Hyde.   When Elder Hyde returns, we will reconsider the matter, and perhaps send them back to Jerusalem; we will fellowship Elder Page until Elder Hyde comes, and we will then weld them together and make them one.   A vote was then put and carried that we hold Elder Page in full fellowship.

Voted that Elder Page be sent to Pittsburgh.

Sung a hymn—adjourned for one hour and a half, at one o'clock.

Met agreeable to adjournment—choir sung a hymn—prayer by Elder H. C. Kimball.

Elder Lyman Wight called to know if there were any present of the rough and weak things, who wished to be ordained, and go and preach, who have not been before ordained. Elder Lyman Wight then addressed those who intended to be ordained, on the subject of their duty and requirements to go and preach.

President Hyrum Smith spoke concerning the Elders who went forth to preach from Kirtland, and were afterwards called in for the washing and anointing at the dedication of the House, and those who go now will be called in also, when this Temple is about to be dedicated, and will then be endowed to go forth with mighty power, having the same anointing, that all may go forth and have the same power, the first, second, and so on, of the Seventies, and all those formerly ordained. This will be an important and beneficial mission, and not many years until those now sent will be called in again.   He then spoke in contradiction of a report in circulation about Elders Heber C. Kimball, Brigham Young, himself, and others of the Twelve, alleging that a sister had been shut in a room for several days, and that they had endeavored to induce her to believe in having two wives. Also cautioned the sisters against going to the steamboats.

President Joseph Smith spoke upon the subject of the stories respecting Elders Kimball and others, showing the folly and inconsistency of spending any time in conversing about such stories, or hearkening to them, for there is no person that is acquainted with our principles who would believe such lies, except Sharp, the editor of the *Warsaw Signal.*

Baptisms for the dead, and for the healing of the body must be in the font, those coming into the Church, and those re-baptized may be baptized in the river. A box should be prepared for the use of the font, that the clerk may be paid, and a book procured by the moneys to be put therein, by those baptized, the remainder to go to the use of the Temple.

Sung a hymn.

Ordinations to take place tomorrow morning. Baptisms in the font also.

There were 275 ordained to the office of Elder, under the hands of the Twelve, during the Conference.

Friday 8. Conference assembled. Sung a hymn. Prayer by Elder Heber C. Kimball.

Elder Page then addressed the assembly upon several subjects; made many interesting remarks concerning being called to the ministry, labor in the vineyard, &c. Spoke of his own travels and the fruits of his labors as an encouragement to the young Elders who were going into the vineyard.

President Joseph Smith said the baptisms would be attended to, also the ordinations.

Sung a hymn.

Elder John Taylor preached a sermon while the ordinations and baptisms were going on, on the subject of infidelity, showing that the arguments used against the Bible were rationally, scientifically, and philosophically false.

The stand was occupied in the afternoon by Elder Amasa M. Lyman, who was followed by Elder William Smith; then the Conference closed by the benediction of President Joseph Smith.

JAMES SLOAN, Clerk.

Saturday, 9.—In the morning I attended the funeral of Brother Ephraim Marks, and in the evening attended city council.

[The following brief synopsis of President Smith's remarks is from Elder Wilford Woodruff's journal:]

Remarks of the Prophet at the Funeral of Ephraim Marks.

The Saints in Nauvoo assembled at the house of President Marks, at an early hour in the morning, to pay their last respects to the body of Ephraim Marks, son of President William Marks, who died on the evening of the 7th. A large procession formed and walked to the Grove, where a numerous congregation had assembled. President Joseph Smith spoke upon the occasion with much feeling and interest. Among his remarks he said, "It is a very solemn and awful time. I never felt more solemn; it calls to mind the death of my oldest brother, Alvin, who died in New York, and my youngest brother, Don Carlos Smith, who died in Nauvoo. It has been hard for me to live on earth and see these young men upon whom we have leaned for support and comfort taken from us in the midst of their youth. Yes, it has been hard to be reconciled to these things. I have sometimes thought that I should have felt more reconciled to have been called away myself if it had been the will of God; yet I know we ought to be still and know it is of God, and be reconciled to His will; all is right. It will be but a short time before we shall all in like manner be called: it may be the case with me as well as you. Some have supposed that Brother Joseph could not die; but this is a mistake: it is true there have been times when I have had the promise of my life to accomplish such and such things, but, having now accomplished those things, I have not at present any lease of my life, I am as liable to die as other men.

I can say in my heart, that I have not done anything against Ephraim Marks that I am sorry for, and I would ask any of his companions if they have done anything against him that they are sorry for, or that they would not like to meet and answer for at the bar of God, if so, let it prove as a warning to all to deal justly before God, and with all mankind, then we shall be clear in the day of judgment.

When we lose a near and dear friend, upon whom we have set our hearts, it should be a caution unto us not to set our affections too firmly upon others, knowing that they may in like manner be taken from us. Our affections should be placed upon God and His work, more intensely than upon our fellow beings.

Sunday, April 10.—I preached in the Grove, and pronounced a curse upon all adulterers, and fornicators, and unvirtuous persons, and those who have made use of my name to carry on their iniquitous designs.

[The following brief synopsis of the Prophet's remarks is from the journal of Elder Wilford Woodruff:]

Synopsis of Remarks of the Prophet—Reproof of all Wickedness.

Joseph the Seer arose in the power of God; reproved and rebuked wickedness before the people, in the name of the Lord God. He wished to say a few words to suit the condition of the general mass, and then said: I shall speak with authority of the Priesthood in the name of the Lord God, which shall prove a savor of life unto life, or of death unto death. Notwithstanding this congregation profess to be Saints, yet I stand in the midst of all [kinds of] characters and classes of men. If you wish to go where God is, you must be like God, or possess the principles which God possesses, for if we are not drawing towards God in principle, we are going from Him and drawing towards the devil. Yes, I am standing in the midst of all kinds of people.

Search your hearts, and see if you are like God. I have searched mine, and feel to repent of all my sins.

We have thieves among us, adulterers, liars, hypocrites. If God should speak from heaven, he would command you not to steal, not to commit adultery, not to covet, nor deceive, but be faithful over a few things. As far as we degenerate from God, we descend to the devil and lose knowledge, and without knowledge we cannot be saved, and while our hearts are filled with evil, and we are studying evil, there is no room in our hearts for good, or studying good. Is not God good? Then you be good; if He is faithful, then you be faithful. Add to your faith virtue, to virtue knowledge, and seek for every good thing.

The Church must be cleansed, and I proclaim against all iniquity. A man is saved no faster than he gets knowledge, for if he does not get knowledge, he will be brought into captivity by some evil power in the other world, as evil spirits will have more knowledge, and consequently more power than many men who are on the earth. Hence it needs revelation to assist us, and give us knowledge of the things of God.

What is the reason that the Priests of the day do not get revelation? They ask only to consume it upon their lust. Their hearts are corrupt, and they cloak their iniquity by saying there are no more revelations. But if any revelations are given of God, they are universally opposed by the priests and Christendom at large; for they reveal their wickedness and abominations.

Many other remarks of interest were made.

Monday, 11.—I was at the lodge and at home. The following is from the *West Messenger.*

A METEOR FALLS.

Mr. Horace Palmer who was on his way from Dunkirk to Westfield, about three o'clock this morning, states that when about three miles from Dunkirk, he was suddenly surrounded by a painful vivid light proceeding from a quantity of jelly-like substance, which fell on and about him, producing a sulphurous smell, a difficulty of breathing and a severe sensation of heat. As soon as he could so far recover from his astonishment as to look up, he saw the body of a terrific meteor passing above him, and appearing to be about a mile high. Its size appeared to be three or four feet in diameter, and nearly a mile in length. Its dimensions soon varied, becoming at first broader, and then diminishing to one fourth less than its former size, when it apparently separated in pieces, and fell to the earth; and immediately after he heard the explosion, which he says was tremendous.

When Mr. Palmer arrived at Westfield, his face had the appearance of being severely scorched, and his eyes were much affected, and he did not recover for two or three days. Mr. Palmer is reputed to be a man of integrity and temperate habits; and his story, though marvelous, is generally believed.

The meteor was seen by several other people, who speak of luminous bodies being detached from it. Its progress was attended by a noise similar to that of a train of cars on a railroad.

A man who saw it from Salem represents it to have been of dimensions much larger than described by Mr. Palmer. The report of the explosion was heard also at Buffalo.

Tuesday, 12.—I attended the meeting of the lodge. The Twelve, namely Brigham Young, Heber C. Kimball,

Council Meeting with the Twelve. Orson Pratt, William Smith, Wilford Woodruff, John Taylor, John E. Page, and Willard Richards, clerk, assembled in the lodge room at four o'clock p. m., and appointed John Taylor, Brigham Young and Heber C. Kimball a committee to make arrangements for the payments due from President Smith as Trustee in Trust, to Mr. Wilkie, and voted that Randolph Alexander go on a mission south to preach the Gospel. Also voted that the Twelve unite their influence to persuade the brethren to consecrate all the old notes, deeds, and obligations which they hold against each other to the building of the Temple in Nauvoo, and that Willard Richards write an epistle in the name of the Twelve on that subject, and publish it in the *Times and Seasons*, which he did as follows:

An Epistle of the Twelve to the Saints in America, Greeting.

BELOVED BRETHREN: We have whereof to congratulate you at the present time, as we have the opportunity from day to day to witness the progress of the building of the Temple of the Lord in this city, and which is and must be accomplished by the united exertions of the labors of the brethren who reside here, and the tithings and contributions of those who are scattered abroad in the different states.

In this glorious object the hearts of all the faithful are united, the hands of the laborer are made strong continually, and the purse strings of the more opulent are unloosed from time to time, to supply those things which are necessary for upraising the stones of this noble edifice; and it may truly be said that the blessing of the Lord is upon His people; we have peace without and love within the borders of our beautiful city; beautiful, indeed, for situation is Nauvoo; the crown of the great valley of the Mississippi, the joy of every honest heart.

Although all things are more prosperous concerning the Temple than at any former period, yet the Saints must not suppose that all is done, or that they can relax their exertions and the work go on. It is a great work that God has required of His people, and it will require long and unwearied diligence to accomplish it; and redoubled diligence will be necessary with all, to get the building enclosed before another winter, so that the joiner can be employed during the cold weather; and we would again call upon all the Saints abroad to unite in making their deposits in banks known to be good and safe, and forward their certificate to the Trustee in Trust, as speedily as possible; when trusty men are not coming immediately to this place who can bring your offerings. All will want the privileges and blessings of the sanctuary, when it is completed; and all can have their wishes; but they can obtain them only by faithfulness and diligence in striving to build.

We praise our God for the liberality that has hitherto been manifested; many have given more than was required of them, many have given their all, but they have done it cheerfully; they have done it voluntarily; and they shall have a great reward; for the blessings of heaven and earth shall be multiplied unto such; even the blessings of that Priesthood which hath neither beginning of days nor end of life.

While there are those who of their abundance have built unto themselves fine houses, and who ride in fine carriages and on horseback, and regale themselves with the good things of the land, and at the same time they have left the Lord's house untouched, or, if touched at all, have touched it so lightly as scarce to leave the print of their little finger: their reward will be according to their deeds, and unless they speedily repent, and come up with their abundance to the help of the Lord, they will find in the end that they have no part nor lot in this matter; their gold and silver will become cankered, their garments moth eaten, and they will perish in their own slothfulness and idolatry, leaving none to mourn their absence.

But, brethren, the Temple will be built. There are hundreds and thousands who stand ready to sacrifice the last farthing they possess on the earth rather than have the building of the Lord's house delayed, and while this spirit prevails no power beneath the heavens can hinder its progress: but we desire you all to help with the ability which God has given you; that you may all share the blessings which will distil from heaven to earth through this consecrated channel.

This is not all. It will be in vain for us to build a place where the Son of Man may lay his head, and leave the cries of the widow and the fatherless, unheard by us, ascending up to the orphan's God and widow's Friend. It is in vain, we cry Lord, Lord. and do not the things our Lord hath commanded; to visit the widow, the fatherless, the sick, the lame, the blind, the destitute, and minister to their necessities; and it is but reasonable that such cases should be found among a people who have but recently escaped the fury of a relentless mob on the one hand, and gathered from the half-starved population of the scattered nations on the other.

Neither is this all. It is not sufficient that the poor be fed and clothed, the sick ministered unto, the Temple built—no, when all this is accomplished, there must be a year of Jubilee: there must be a day of rejoicing· there must be a time of release to Zion's sons, or our offerings, our exertions, our hopes, and our prayers will be in vain, and God will not accept of the doings of His people.

On these days of darkness which overspread our horizon; when the wolf was howling for his prey around the streets of Kirtland; when the burglar was committing his midnight and midday depredations in Jackson county; when the heartless politician was thrusting his envious darts in Clay county—and when the savage war whoop, echoed and reechoed through Far West, and Zion's noblest sons were chained in dungeons, and her defenseless daughters driven by a horde of savages, from their once peaceful homes, to seek a shelter in a far distant land— many of the brethren stepped forward to their rescue, and not only expended all they possessed for the relief of suffering innocence, but gave their notes and bonds to "obtain more means, with which to help those who could not escape the overwhelming surge of banishment from all that they possessed on earth."

Death, wounds, and sickness, from the mob, and the cold and shelterless situation of the brethren, followed in quick succession; and all the means which could possibly be obtained from each other, in addition to the noble charities of the citizens of Illinois, were brought into requisition to sustain a remnant of the Saints, who now mostly inhabit this place.

To accomplish this, the President and Bishops loaned money and such things as could be obtained, and gave their obligations in good faith for the payment of the same; and many of the brethren signed with them at different times and in different places, to strengthen their hands and help them carry out their designs; fully expecting, that, at some future day, they would be enabled to liquidate all such claims, to the satisfaction of all parties.

Many of these claims have already been settled; many have been given up as cancelled by those who held them, and many yet remain unsettled. The Saints have had many difficulties to encounter since they arrived at this place. In a new country, destitute of houses, food, clothing, and nearly all the necessaries of life, which were rent from them by an unfeeling mob—having to encounter disease and difficulties unnumbered, it is not surprising that the Church has not been able to liquidate all such claims, or that many individuals should yet remain involved, from the foregoing circumstances; and while things remain as they are, and men remain subject to the temptations of evil as they now are, the day of release, and year of jubilee cannot be; and we write you especially at this time, brethren, for the purpose of making a final settlement of all such claims, of brother against brother; of the brethren against the Presidency and Bishops, &c.; claims which have originated out of the difficulties and calamities the Church has had to encounter, and which are of long standing, so that when the Temple is completed, there will be nothing from this source to produce jars, and discords, strifes and animosities, so as to prevent the blessings of heaven descending upon us as a people.

To accomplish this most desirable object, we call on all the brethren who hold such claims, to bring them forward for a final settlement; and also those brethren who have individual claims against each other, of long standing, and the property of the debtor has been wrested from him by violence, or he has been unfortunate, and languished on a bed of sickness till his means are exhausted; and all claims whatsoever between brother and brother, where there is no reasonable prospect of a just and equitable settlement possible, that they also by some means, either by giving up their obligations, or destroying them, see that all such old affairs be adjusted, so that it shall not give occasion for difficulties to arise hereafter. Yes, brethren, bring all such old accounts, notes, bonds, etc., and make a consecration of them to the building of the Temple, and if anything can be obtained on them, it will be obtained; and if nothing can be obtained, when the Temple is completed, we will make a burnt-offering of them, even a peace-offering, which shall bind the brethren together in the bonds of eternal peace, and love and union; and joy and salvation shall flow forth into your souls, and you shall rejoice and say it is good that we have harkened unto counsel, and set our brethren free, for God hath blessed us.

How can we prosper while the Church, while the Presidency, while the Bishops, while those who have sacrificed everything but life, in this thing, for our salvation, are thus encumbered? It cannot be. Arise, then, brethren, set them free, and set each other free, and we will all be free together, we will be free indeed.

Let nothing in this epistle be so construed as to destroy the validity of contracts, or give any one license not to pay his debts. The commandment is to pay every man his dues, and no man can get to heaven who justly owes his brother or his neighbor, who has or can get the means and will not pay it; it is dishonest, and no dishonest man can enter where God is.

We remain, your brethren in the Gospel of Peace,

BRIGHAM YOUNG, President,
HEBER C. KIMBALL,
ORSON PRATT,
WILLIAM SMITH,
JOHN E. PAGE,
LYMAN WIGHT,
WILFORD WOODRUFF,
JOHN TAYLOR,
GEO. A. SMITH,
WILLARD RICHARDS, Clerk.

Military Appointments.

James Arlington Bennett, of Arlington House, Long Island, is hereby appointed Inspector-General of the Nauvoo-Legion, with the rank and title of Major-General; his place to be supplied when absent, by the Major-General of the Legion.

JOSEPH SMITH, Lieutenant-General.

City of Nauvoo, Illinois, April 12th, A. D. 1842.

CHAPTER XXXV.

THE GENERAL BANKRUPT LAW—THE DOCTRINE OF BAPTISM
FOR THE DEAD—THE PROPHET'S ADDRESS TO THE FEMALE
RELIEF SOCIETY—THE KEYS OF THE PRIESTHOOD AND THE
NAUVOO TEMPLE.

Wednesday, April 13.—I introduced Messrs. Backenstos, Stiles, and Robinson into the Lodge Room in the morning, and Samuel H. Smith, William Smith, and Vinson Knight in the evening.

About 150 Saints, from England landed in Nauvoo from the steamer *Louisa*, and about 60 from the *Amaranth*.

Thursday, 14.—Calvin A. Warren, Esq., lawyer, from Quincy, arrived, and commenced an investigation of the principles of general insolvency in my behalf according to the statutes; for the United States Congress had previously instituted a general bankrupt law, by which any individual who was owing to a certain amount more than he was able to pay, could make out a schedule of his property, and of debts due from himself, and by a specified process, pass the same in the hands of a commissioner, government agent, or "assignee," who could make a dividend of all his effects, and pay his creditors whatever percentage his property amounted to, and then the individual was at liberty to start anew in the world, and was not subject to liquidate any claims which were held against him previous to his insolvency, although his property might not have paid but the least percentage, or none at all.

The justice or injustice of such a principle in law, I leave for them who made it, the United States. Suffice it to say, the law was as good for the Saints as for the Gentiles, and whether I would or not, I was forced into the measure by having been rob- bed, mobbed, plundered, and wasted of all my *The Prophet Forced into Bankruptcy.* property, time after time, in various places, by the very ones who made the law, namely, the people of the United State, thereby having been obliged to contract heavy debts to prevent the utter destruction of myself, family and friends, and by those who were justly and legally owing me, taking the advantage of the same act of bankruptcy, so that I could not collect my just dues, thus leaving me no alternative but to become subject again to stripping, wasting, and destitution, by vexatious writs, and law suits, and imprisonments, or take that course to extricate myself, which the law had pointed out.

Friday, 15.—Editorial from the *Times and Seasons:*

BAPTISM FOR THE DEAD.

The great designs of God in relation to the salvation of the human family, are very little understood by the professedly wise and intelligent generation in which we live. Various and conflicting are the opinions of men concerning the plan of salvation, the requisitions of the Almighty, the necessary preparations for heaven, the state and condition of departed spirits, and the happiness or misery that is consequent upon the practice of righteousness and iniquity according to their several notions of virtue and vice.

The Mussulman condemns the heathen, the Jew, and the Christian, and the whole world of mankind that reject his Koran, as infidels, and consigns the whole of them to perdition. The Jew believes that the whole world that rejects his faith and are not circumcised, are Gentile dogs, and will be damned. The heathen is equally as tenacious about his principles, and the Christian consigns all to perdition who cannot bow to his creed, and submit to his *ipse dixit.*

But while one portion of the human race is judging and condemning the other without mercy, the Great Parent of the universe looks upon the whole of the human family with a fatherly care and paternal regard; He views them as His offspring, and without any of those contracted feelings that influence the children of men, causes ''His sun to rise on the evil and on the good, and sendeth rain on the just and on the unjust.'' He holds the reins of judgment in His hands; He is a wise Lawgiver, and will judge all men, not according to the narrow, contracted notions of men, but, "according to the deeds done in the body whether they be good or evil," or whether these deeds were done in England, America, Spain, Turkey, or India.   He will judge them, "not according to what they have not, but according to what they have," those who have lived without law, will be judged without law, and those who have a law, will by judged by that law. We need not doubt the wisdom and intelligence of the Great Jehovah; He will award judgment or mercy to all nations according to their several deserts, their means of obtaining intelligence, the laws by which they are governed, the facilities afforded them of obtaining correct information, and His inscrutable designs in relation to the human family; and when the designs of God shall be made manifest, and the curtain of futurity be withdrawn, we shall all of us eventually have to confess that the Judge of all the earth has done right.

The situation of the Christian nations after death, is a subject that has called forth all the wisdom and talent of the philosopher and the divine, and it is an opinion which is generally received, that the destiny of man is irretrievably fixed at his death, and that he is made either eternally happy, or eternally miserable; that if a man dies without a knowledge of God, he must be eternally damned, without any mitigation of his punishment, alleviation of his pain, or the most latent hope of a deliverance while endless ages shall roll along. However orthodox this principle may be, we shall find that it is at variance with the testimony of Holy Writ, for our Savior says, that all manner of sin and blasphemy shall be forgiven men wherewith they shall blaspheme; but the blasphemy against the Holy Ghost shall not be forgiven, neither in this world, nor in the world to come, evidently showing that there are sins which may be forgiven in the world to come, although the sin of blasphemy [against the Holy Ghost] cannot be forgiven.   Peter, also, in speaking concerning our Savior, says, that "He went and preached unto the spirits in prison, which sometimes were disobedient, when once the long suffering of God waited in the days of Noah," (I Peter iii: 19, 20). Here then we have an account of our Savior preaching to the spirits in prison, to spirits that had been imprisoned from the days of Noah; and what did He preach to them? That they were to stay there? Certainly not!   Let His own declaration testify.   "He hath sent me to heal the broken hearted, to preach deliverance to the captives, and recovering of sight to the blind, to set at liberty them that are bruised."   (Luke iv: 18. Isaiah has it—"To bring out the prisoners from the prison, and them that sit in darkness from the prison house." (Isaiah xlii: 7. It is very evident from this that He not only went to preach to them, but to deliver, or bring them out of the prison house. Isaiah, in testifying concerning the calamities that will overtake the inhabitants of the earth, says, "The earth shall reel to and fro like a drunkard, and shall be removed like a cottage; and the transgression thereof shall be heavy upon it; and it shall fall and not rise again. And it shall come to pass in that day, that the Lord shall punish the host of the high ones that are on high, and the kings of the earth upon the earth. And they shall be gathered together, as prisoners are gathered in the pit, and shall be shut up in the prison, and after many days shall they be visited." Thus we find that God will deal with all the human family equally, and that as the antediluvians had their day of visitation, so will those characters referred to by Isaiah, have their time of visitation and deliverance, after having been many days in prison.

The great Jehovah contemplated the whole of the events connected with the earth, pertaining to the plan of salvation, before it rolled into existence, or ever "the morning stars sang together" for joy; the past, the present, and the future were and are, with Him, one eternal "now;" He knew of the fall of Adam, the iniquities of the antediluvians, of the depth of iniquity that would be connected with the human family, their weakness and strength, their power and glory, apostasies, their crimes, their righteousness and iniquity; He comprehended the fall of man, and his redemption; He knew the plan of salvation and pointed it out; He was acquainted with the situation of all nations and with their destiny; He ordered all things according to the council of His own will; He knows the situation of both the living and the dead, and has made ample provision for their redemption, according to their several circumstances, and the laws of the kingdom of God, whether in this world, or in the world to come.

The idea that some men form of the justice, judgment, and mercy of God, is too foolish for an intelligent man to think of: for instance, it is common for many of our orthodox preachers to suppose that if a man is not what they call converted, if he dies in that state he must remain eternally in hell without any hope. Infinite years in torment must he spend, and never, never, never have an end; and yet this eternal misery is made frequently to rest upon the merest casualty. The breaking of a shoe-string, the tearing of a coat of those officiating, or the peculiar location in which a person lives, may be the means, indirectly of his damnation, or the cause of his not being saved. I will suppose a case which is not extraordinary: Two men, who have been equally wicked, who have neglected religion, are both of them taken sick at the same time; one of them has the good fortune to be visited by a praying man, and he gets converted a few minutes before he dies; the other sends for three different praying men, a tailor, a shoemaker, and a tinman; the tinman has a handle to solder to a can, the tailor has a button-

hole to work on some coat that he needed in a hurry, and the shoemaker has a patch to put on somebody's boot; they none of them can
go in time, the man dies, and goes to hell: one of these is exalted to
Abraham's bosom, he sits down in the presence of God and enjoys eternal, uninterrupted happiness, while the other, equally as good as he,
sinks to eternal damnation, irretrievable misery and hopeless despair,
because a man had a boot to mend, the button-hole of a coat to work, or
a handle to solder on to a saucepan.

The plans of Jehovah are not so unjust, the statements of holy writ
so visionary, nor the plan of salvation for the human family so incom-
patible with common sense; at such proceedings God would frown with
indignance, angels would hide their heads in shame, and every virtuous, intelligent man would recoil.

If human laws award to each man his deserts, and punish all delinquents according to their several crimes, surely the Lord will not be
more cruel than man, for He is a wise legislator, and His laws are more
equitable, His enactments more just, and His decisions more perfect
than those of man; and as man judges his fellow man by law, and pun-
ishes him according to the penalty of the law, so does God of heaven
judge "according to the deeds done in the body." To say that the
heathens would be damned because they did not believe the Gospel
would be preposterous, and to say that the Jews would all be damned
that do not believe in Jesus would be equally absurd; for "how can
they believe on him of whom they have not heard, and how can they
hear without a preacher, and how can he preach except he be sent;"
consequently neither Jew nor heathen can be culpable for rejecting the
conflicting opinions of sectarianism, nor for rejecting any testimony but
that which is sent of God, for as the preacher cannot preach except he
be sent, so the hearer cannot believe without he hear a "sent" preacher,
and cannot be condemned for what he has not heard, and being without
law, will have to be judged without law.

When speaking about the blessings pertaining to the Gospel, and the
consequences connected with disobedience to the requirements, we are
frequently asked the question, what has become of our fathers? Will
they all be damned for not obeying the Gospel, when they never heard
it? Certainly not. But they will possess the same privilege that we here
enjoy, through the medium of the everlasting priesthood, which not only
administers on earth, but also in heaven, and the wise dispensations of
the great Jehovah; hence those characters referred to by Isaiah will be
visited by the Priesthood, and come out of their prison upon the same
principle as those who were disobedient in the days of Noah were
visited by our Savior [who possessed the everlasting Melchisedek
Priesthood] and had the Gospel preached to them, by Him in prison;

and in order that they might fulfill all the requisitions of God, living friends were baptized for their dead friends, and thus fulfilled the requirement of God, which says, "Except a man be born of water and of the Spirit, he cannot enter into the kingdom of God," they were baptized of course, not for themselves, but for their dead.

Chrysostum says that the Marchionites practiced baptism for their dead. "After a catechumen was dead, they had a living man under the bed of the deceased; then coming to the dead man, they asked him whether he would receive baptism, and he making no answer, the other answered for him, and said that he would be baptized in his stead; and so they baptized the living for the dead." The church of course at that time was degenerate, and the particular form might be incorrect, but the thing is sufficiently plain in the Scriptures. hence Paul, in speaking of the doctrine, says, "Else what shall they do which are baptized for the dead, if the dead rise not at all? Why are they then baptized for the dead?" (1 Cor. xv: 29). Hence it was that so great a responsibility rested upon the generation in which our Savior lived, for, says he, "That upon you may come all the righteous blood shed upon the earth, from the blood of righteous Abel unto the blood of Zacharias, son of Barachias, whom ye slew between the temple and the altar. Verily I say unto you, all these things shall come upon this generation." (Matthew xxiii: 35, 36). Hence as they possessed greater privileges than any other generation, not only pertaining to themselve, but to their dead, their sin was greater, as they not only neglected their own salvation but that of their progenitors, and hence their blood was required at their hands.

And now as the great purposes of God are hastening to their accomplishment, and the things spoken of in the Prophets are fulfilling, as the kingdom of God is establised on the earth, and the ancient order of things restored, the Lord has manifested to us this day and privilege, and we are commanded to be baptized for our dead, thus fulfilling the words of Obadiah, when speaking of the glory of the latter-day: "And saviors shall come upon Mount Zion to judge the remnant of Esau, and the kingdom shall be the Lord's." A view of these things reconciles the Scriptures of truth, justifies the ways of God to man, places the human family upon an equal footing, and harmonizes with every principle of righteousness, justice and truth. We will conclude with the words of Peter: "For the time past of our life may suffice us to have wrought the will of the Gentiles." "For, for this cause was the Gospel preached also to them that are dead, that they might be judged according to men in the flesh, but live according to God in the spirit."

I continued busily engaged in making out a list of

debtors and an invoice of my property to be passed into the hands of the assignee, until—

Saturday evening the 16th.—On this day the first number of *The Wasp*, a miscellaneous weekly newspaper was first published at my office, William Smith, editor, devoted to the arts, sciences, literature, agriculture, manufacture, trade, commerce, and the general news of the day, on a small sheet, at $1.50 per annum.

Sunday, 17.—Spent the day with my family at home.

Monday, 18.—In consequence of the utter annihilation of our property by mob violence in the state of Missouri, and the immense expenses which we were compelled to incur, to defend ourselves from the cruel persecutions of that state, we were reduced to the necessity of availing ourselves of the privileges of the general bankrupt law; therefore I went to Carthage with my brothers Hyrum and Samuel H. Smith, and severally testified to our list of insolvency before the clerk of the county commissioners' court. Sidney Rigdon and many more brethren were at Carthage the same day on business. My clerk, Dr. Richards, went with us.

Causes of the Prophet's Insolvency.

About this time a disturbance broke out in Rhode Island by a part of the inhabitants, wishing to change their Constitution, and make it like those of other states in the Union, which created much confusion and angry feeling in that state, and excitement in other states.

Tuesday, 19.—Rode out and examined some land near the northern limits of the city, &c.

Wednesday, 20.—Assisted in surveying some land in section 25, which I sold to William Cross.

Thursday, 21.—Friday and Saturday was engaged in temporal and spiritual affairs at home, the office, &c.

Friday, 22.—

James Arlington Bennett Honored.

Honorary Degree. Ordered by the chancellor and regents of the University of the City of Nauvoo, that the honorary degree of L. L.

D. be, and the same hereby is, conferred on General James Arlington Bennett, of Arlington House, New York.

Passed April 22, 1842.

JOHN C. BENNETT, Chancellor,

WILLIAM LAW, Registrar.

Sunday, 24.—Preached on the hill near the Temple, concerning the building of the Temple, and reproved the merchants and the rich who would not assist in building it.

Monday, 25, Tuesday, 26 and Wednesday, 27.—I was engaged in reading, meditation, &c., mostly with my family.

Thursday, 28.—

"*Repast Militaire.*"

General Joseph Smith and lady, present their compliments to the officers (and their respective ladies) of the consolidated General Staff of the Nauvoo Legion, that is to say, his personal staff, Major-General Bennett's staff, including the band, Brigadier-General Law's staff, and Brigadier-General Rich's staff, and respectfully solicit their company at a *Repast Militaire,* at his quarters on the 7th day of May *proximo,* at one o'clock p. m.

General Bennett has been ordered to issue a programme of the operations and field exercises of the day, which will appear in ample form, and due season.

April 28, A. D. 1842.

HEADQUARTERS, NAUVOO LEGION,

CITY OF NAUVOO, ILLINOIS, April 28, 1842.

General Orders—

The Lieutenant-General directs that a *programme militaire* issue from the office of his commanding general for the 7th of May *proximo,* which I now proceed to consummate.

1st. The Adjutants will form the lines of their respective regiments, and the Colonels of the line assume command at nine o'clock, a. m.

2nd. The Adjutant-General will form the line of the Legion, and the Brigadier-Generals assume the command of their respective cohorts at half-past nine o'clock a. m.

3rd. The Major-General will assume the command of the Legion at ten o'clock a. m.

4th. At a quarter past ten o'clock a. m., the Lieutenant-General will be escorted to the field at the review station.

5th. General review and inspection will follow, accompanied by such evolutions and exercises as the time will admit of.

6th. At half-past twelve o'clock p. m. the forces will be dismissed until a quarter before two o'clock p. m.

7th. At two o'clock p. m. the Major-General will resume the command and perform such military movements and field exercises as the Lieutenant-General may direct.

8th. At three o'clock p. m. the cohorts will separate and form the line of battle, the Brigadiers assume their respective commands and General Law's command will make a descent upon that of General Rich's in order of sham battle.

9th. At half-past three o'clock p. m. the cohorts will resume their positions in the line of the Legion, and a sham battle will be fought between the mounted riflemen under the immediate command of Lieutenant General Smith and the Invincibles under the immediate command of Major-General Bennett.

10th. At half-past four o'clock p. m. the forces will be dismissed for the day.

11. Every officer, musician and private will be required to be at their respective posts at the hours specified throughout the day, under the most severe penalties of the law.

JOHN C. BENNETT.
Major-General.

At two o'clock I met the members of the "Female Relief Society," and after presiding at the admission of many new members, gave a lecture on the Priesthood, showing how the sisters would come in possession of the privileges, blessings and gifts of the Priesthood, and that the signs should follow them, such as healing the sick, casting out devils, &c., and that they might attain unto these blessings by a virtuous life, and conversation, and diligence in keeping all the commandments; a synopsis of which was reported by Miss Eliza R. Snow, as follows:

The Rights and Privileges of Women in the Church.

Remarks of the Prophet to the Relief Society.

President Smith arose and called the attention of the meeting to the 12th chapter 1st Corinthians—"Now concerning spiritual gifts, I would not have you ignorant." Said that the passage in the third verse, which reads, "No man can say that Jesus is the Lord, but by the Holy Ghost,' should be translated "no man can *know* that Jesus is the Lord, but by the Holy Ghost." He continued to read the chapter, and give instructions respecting the different offices, and the necessity of every individual acting in the sphere allotted him or her, and filling the several offices to which they are appointed. He spoke of the disposition of many men to consider the lower offices in the Church dishonorable, and to look with jealous eyes upon the standing of others who are called to preside over them; that it was the folly and nonsense of the human heart for a person to be aspiring to other stations than those to which they are appointed of God for them to occupy; that it was better for individuals to magnify their respective callings, and wait patiently till God shall say to them, "Come up higher."

He said the reason of these remarks being made was, that some little foolish things were circulating in the society, against some sisters not doing right in laying hands on the sick. Said that if the people had common sympathies they would rejoice that the sick could be healed; that the time had not been before that these things could be in their proper order; that the Church is not fully organized, in its proper order, and cannot be, until the Temple is completed, where places will be provided for the administration of the ordinances of the Priesthood.

President Smith continued the subject, by quoting the commission given to the ancient Apostles in Mark, 16th chapter, 15th, 16th, 17th, 18th verses, "Go ye into all the world, and preach the Gospel to every creature. He that believeth and is baptized shall be saved; but he that believed not shall be damned. And these signs shall follow them that believe: In my name shall they cast out devils; they shall speak with new tongues; they shall take up serpents; and if they drink any deadly thing, it shall not hurt them; they shall lay hands on the sick, and they shall recover."

No matter who believeth, these signs, such as healing the sick, casting out devils, &c., should follow all that believe, whether male or female. He asked the Society if they could not see by this sweeping promise, that wherein they are ordained, it is the privilege of those set apart to administer in that authority, which is conferred on them; and if the sisters should have faith to heal the sick, let all hold their tongues, and let everything roll on.

He said, if God has appointed him, and chosen him as an instrument to lead the Church, why not let him lead it through? Why stand in the way when he is appointed to do a thing? Who knows the mind of God? Does He not reveal things differently from what we expect? He remarked that he was continually rising, although he had everything bearing him down, standing in his way, and opposing; notwithstanding all this opposition, he always comes out right in the end.

Respecting females administering for the healing of the sick, he further remarked, there could be no devil in it, if God gave His sanction by healing; that there could be no more sin in any female laying hands on and praying for the sick, than in wetting the face with water; it is no sin for anybody to administer that has faith, or if the sick have faith to be healed by their administration.

He reproved those that were disposed to find fault with the management of the concerns of the Church, saying God had called him to lead the Church, and he would lead it right; those that undertake to interfere will be ashamed when their own folly is made manifest; that he calculates to organize the Church in its proper order as soon as the Temple is completed.

President Smith continued by speaking of the difficulties he had to surmount ever since the commencement of the work, in consequence of aspiring men. "Great big Elders," as he called them, who had caused him much trouble; to whom he had taught the things of the kingdom in private councils, they would then go forth into the world and proclaim the things he had taught them, as their own revelations; said the same aspiring disposition will be in this Society, and must be guarded against; that every person should stand, and act in the place appointed, and thus sanctify the Society and get it pure. He said he had been trampled under foot by aspiring Elders, for all were infected with that spirit; for instance, John E. Page and others had been aspiring; they could not be exalted, but must run away as though the care and authority of the Church were vested with them. He said he had a subtle devil to deal with, and could only curb him by being humble.

As he had this opportunity, he was going to instruct the ladies of this Society, and point out the way for them to conduct themselves, that they might act according to the will of God; that he did not know that he should have many opportunities of teaching them, as they were going to be left to themselves; they would not long have him to instruct them; that the Church would not have his instructions long, and the world would not be troubled with him a great while, and would not have his teachings [in person].

He spoke of delivering the keys of the Priesthood to the Church, and said that the faithful members of the Relief Society should receive them in connection with their husbands, that the Saints whose integrity has been tried and proved faithful, might know how to ask the Lord and receive an answer; for according to his prayers, God had appointed him elsewhere.

He exhorted the sisters always to concentrate their faith and prayers for, and place confidence in their husbands, whom God has appointed for them to honor, and in those faithful men whom God has placed at the head of the Church to lead His people; that we should arm and sustain them with our prayers; for the keys of the kingdom are about to be given to them, that they may be able to detect everything false; as well as to all the Elders who shall prove their integrity in due season.

He said if one member becomes corrupt, and you know it, you must immediately put it away, or it will either injure or destroy the whole body. The sympathies of the heads of the Church have induced them to bear a long time with those who were corrupt until they are obliged to cut them off, lest all become contaminated; you must put down iniquity, and by your good examples, stimulate the Elders to good works; if you do right, there is no danger of your going too fast.

He said he did not care how fast we run in the path of virtue; resist evil, and there is no danger; God, men, and angels will not condemn those that resist everything that is evil, and devils cannot; as well might the devil seek to dethrone Jehovah, as overthrow an innocent soul that resists everything which is evil.

This is a charitable Society, and according to your natures; it is natural for females to have feelings of charity and benevolence. You are now placed in a situation in which you can act according to those sympathies which God has planted in your bosoms.

If you live up to these principles, how great and glorious will be your reward in the celestial kingdom! If you live up to your privileges, the angels cannot be restrained from being your associates. Females, if they are pure and innocent, can come in the presence of God; for what is more pleasing to God than innocence; you must be innocent, or you cannot come up before God: if we would come before God, we must keep ourselves pure, as He is pure.

The devil has great power to deceive; he will so transform things as to make one gape at those who are doing the will of God. You need not be teazing your husbands because of their deeds, but let the weight of your innocence, kindness and affection be felt, which is more mighty than a millstone hung about the neck; not war, not jangle, not contradiction, or dispute, but meekness, love, purity—these are the things that should magnify you in the eyes of all good men. Achan [see Joshua vii.] must be brought to light, iniquity must be purged out from the midst of the Saints; then the veil will be rent, and the blessings of heaven will flow down—they will roll down like the Mississippi river.

If this Society listen to the counsel of the Almighty, through the heads of the Church, they shall have power to command queens in their midst.

I now deliver it as a prophecy, if the inhabitants of this state, with the people of the surrounding country, will turn unto the Lord with all their hearts, ten years will not roll round before the kings and queens of the earth will come unto Zion, and pay their respects to the leaders of this people; they shall come with their millions, and shall contribute of their abundance for the relief of the poor, and the building up and beautifying of Zion.

After this instruction, you will be responsible for your own sins; it is a desirable honor that you should so walk before our heavenly Father as to save yourselves; we are all responsible to God for the manner we improve the light and wisdom given by our Lord to enable us to save ourselves.

President Smith continued reading from the above-mentioned chapter, and to give instructions respecting the order of God, as established in the Church, saying everyone should aspire only to magnify his own office and calling.

He then commenced reading the 13th chapter—"Though I speak with the tongues of men and angels, and have no charity, I am become as sounding brass, or a tinkling cymbal;" and said, don't be limited in your views with regard to your neighbor's virtue, but beware of self-righteousness, and be limited in the estimate of your own virtues, and not think yourselves more righteous than others; you must enlarge your souls towards each other, if you would do like Jesus, and carry your fellow-creatures to Abraham's bosom. He said he had manifested long-suffering, forbearance and patience towards the Church, and also to his enemies; and we must bear with each other's failings, as an indulgent parent bears with the foibles of his children.

President Smith then read the 2nd verse—"Though I have the gift of prophecy, and understand all mysteries, and all knowledge; and though I have all faith, so that I could remove mountains, and have not charity, I am nothing." He then said, though a man should become mighty, do great things, overturn mountains, perform mighty works, and should then turn from his high station to do evil, to eat and drink with the drunken, all his former deeds would not save him, but he would go to destruction! As you increase in innocence and virtue, as you increase in goodness, let your hearts expand, let them be enlarged towards others; you must be long-suffering, and bear with the faults and errors of mankind.

How precious are the souls of men! The female part of the community are apt to be contracted in their views. You must not be contracted, but you must be liberal in your feelings. Let this Society teach women how to behave towards their husbands, to treat them with mildness and affection. When a man is borne down with trouble, when he is perplexed with care and difficulty, if he can meet a smile instead of an argument or a murmur—if he can meet with mildness, it will calm down his soul and soothe his feelings; when the mind is going to despair, it needs a solace of affection and kindness.

You will receive instructions through the order of the Priesthood which God has established, through the medium of those appointed to lead, guide and direct the affairs of the Church in this last dispensation; and I now turn the key in your behalf in the name of the Lord, and this Society shall rejoice, and knowledge and intelligence shall flow down from this time henceforth; this is the beginning of better days to the poor and needy, who shall be made to rejoice and pour forth blessings on your heads.

When you go home, never give a cross or unkind word to your husbands, but let kindness, charity and love crown your works henceforward; don't envy the finery and fleeting show of sinners, for they are in a miserable situation; but as far as you can, have mercy on them, for in a short time God will destroy them, if they will not repent and turn unto him.

Let your labors be mostly confined to those around you, in the circle of your own acquaintance, as far as knowledge is concerned, it may extend to all the world; but your administering should be confined to the circle of your immediate acquaintance, and more especially to the members of the Relief Society. Those ordained to preside over and lead you, are authorized to appoint the different officers, as the circumstances shall require.

If you have a matter to reveal, let it be in your own tongue; do not indulge too much in the exercise of the gift of tongues, or the devil will take advantage of the innocent and unwary. You may speak in tongues for your own comfort, but I lay this down for a rule, that if anything is taught by the gift of tongues, it is not to be received for doctrine.

President Smith then gave instruction respecting the propriety of females administering to the sick by the prayer of faith, the laying on hands, or the anointing with oil; and said it was according to revelation that the sick should be nursed with herbs and mild food, and not by the hand of an enemy. Who are better qualified to administer than our faithful and zealous sisters, whose hearts are full of faith, tenderness, sympathy and compassion. No one. Said he was never placed in similar circumstances before, and never had given the same instruction; and closed his instructions by expressing his heart-felt satisfaction in improving this opportunity.

The Spirit of the Lord was poured out in a very powerful manner, never to be forgotten by those present on this interesting occasion.

Friday, 29.—A conspiracy against the peace of my household was made manifest, and it gave me some trouble

to counteract the design of certain base individuals, and
restore peace.   The Lord makes manifest to me many
things, which it is not wisdom for me to make public,
until others can witness the proof of them.

Saturday, 30.—I received a visit from Judge James
Adams, of Springfield, and spent most of the day with
him and my family.   Signed deeds to James and Charles
Ivins, and many others.

Sunday, May 1, 1842.—I preached in the grove, on the
keys of the kingdom, charity, &c.   The keys are certain
signs and words by which false spirits and personages
may be detected from true, which cannot be revealed to
the Elders till the Temple is completed.   The rich can
only get them in the Temple, the poor may get them on
the mountain top as did Moses.   The rich cannot be saved
without charity, giving to feed the poor when and how
God requires, as well as building.   There are signs in
heaven, earth and hell; the Elders must know them all,
to be endowed with power, to finish their work and prevent
imposition.   The devil knows many signs, but does not
know the sign of the Son of Man, or Jesus.   No one can
truly say he knows God until he has handled something,
and this can only be in the holiest of holies.

Monday, 2.—The following Editorial appeared in the
Times and Seasons:

THE TEMPLE.

This noble edifice is progressing with great rapidity; strenuous exertions are being made on every hand to facilitate its erection, and materials of all kinds are in a great state of forwardness, and by next fall
we expect to see the building enclosed; if not the top stone raised with
"shouting of grace—grace unto it."   There have been frequently, during the winter, as many as one hundred hands quarrying rock, while at
the same time multitudes of others have been engaged in hauling, and
in other kinds of labor.

A company was formed last fall to go up to the pine country to purchase mills, and prepare and saw lumber for the Temple and the Nauvoo House, and the reports from them are very favorable: another com-

pany has started, this last week, to take their place and to relieve those that are already there: on their return they are to bring a very large raft of lumber, for the use of the above-named houses.

While the busy multitudes have thus been engaged in their several vocations performing their daily labor, and working one-tenth of their time, others have not been less forward in bringing in their tithings and consecrations for the same great object. Never since the foundation of this Church was laid, have we seen manifested a greater willingness to comply with the requisitions of Jehovah, a more ardent desire to do the will of God, more strenuous exertions used, or greater sacrifices made than there have been since the Lord said, "Let the Temple be built by the tithing of my people." It seemed as though the spirit of enterprise, philanthropy and obedience rested simultaneously upon old and young, and brethren and sisters, boys and girls, and even strangers, who were not in the Church, united with an unprecedented liberality in the accomplishment of this great work; nor could the widow, in many instances, be prevented, out of her scanty pittance from throwing in her two mites.

We feel at this time to tender to all, old and young, both in the Church and out of it, our unfeigned thanks for their unprecedented liberality, kindness, diligence, and obedience which they have so opportunely manifested on the present occasion. Not that we are personally or individually benefitted in a pecuniary point of view, but when the brethren, as in this instance, show a unity of purpose and design, and all put their shoulder to the wheel, our care, labor, toil and anxiety is materially diminished, our yoke is made easy and our burden is light.

The cause of God is one common cause, in which the Saints are alike all interested; we are all members of the one common body, and all partake of the same spirit, and are baptized into one baptism and possess alike the same glorious hope. The advancement of the cause of God and the building up of Zion is as much one man's business as another's. The only difference is, that one is called to fulfill one duty, and another another duty; "but if one member suffers, all the members suffer with it, and if one member is honored all the rest rejoice with it, and the eye cannot say to the ear, I have no need of thee, nor the head to the foot, I have no need of thee;" party feelings, separate interests, exclusive designs should be lost sight of in the one common cause, in the interest of the whole.

The building up of Zion is a cause that has interested the people of God in every age; it is a theme upon which prophets, priests and kings have dwelt with peculiar delight; they have looked forward with joyful anticipation to the day in which we live; and fired with heavenly and joyful anticipations they have sung and written and prophesied of this our day; but they died without the sight; we are the favored people that God has made choice of to bring about the Latter-day glory; it is left for us to see, participate in and help to roll forward the Latter-day glory, "the dispensation of the fullness of times, when God will gather together all things that are in heaven, and all things that are upon the earth, "even in one," when the Saints of God will be gathered in one from every nation, and kindred,and people, and tongue, when the Jews will be gathered together into one, the wicked will also be gathered together to be destroyed, as spoken of by the prophets; the Spirit of God will also dwell with His people, and be withdrawn from the rest of the nations, and all things whether in heaven or on earth will be in one, even in Christ. The heavenly Priesthood will unite with the earthly, to bring about those great purposes; and whilst we are thus united in the one common cause, to roll forth the kingdom of God, the heavenly Priesthood are not idle spectators, the Spirit of God will be showered down from above, and it will dwell in our midst. The blessings of the Most High will rest upon our tabernacles, and our name will be handed down to future ages; our children will rise up and call us blessed; and generations yet unborn will dwell with peculiar delight upon the scenes that we have passed through, the privations that we have endured; the untiring zeal that we have manifested; the all but insurmountable difficulties that we have overcome in laying the foundation of a work that brought about the glory and blessing which they will realize; a work that God and angels have contemplated with delight for generations past; that fired the souls of the ancient patriarchs and prophets; a work that is destined to bring about the destruction of the powers of darkness, the renovation of the earth, the glory of God, and the salvation of the human family.

END OF VOLUME IV.

INDEX TO VOLUME IV.

A

Abraham, Book of—520 and note; preparation of cuts, 519, 543.

Adams, James—friendship for the Prophet, 20 and note.

Address, by First Presidency to Saints scattered abroad, 184 *et seq.*

Affidavits, on suffering of Saints in Missouri, 49-53, also 56-73 and note, 60; of Hyrum Smith denouncing thieves, 460-61.

Allred, James—statement of on kidnapping, 156-7.

Alvord, T., affidavit of, 57.

Apostles, The Twelve — farewell addresses of, 1-2; Apostles engaged in selecting hymns, 3; trials of en route for England, 15; meeting of at Cleveland, 19-20; granted permission to publish certain books in England, 161-2; whereabouts of, January 1, 1841, 256; minutes of meeting of in England, 324; ditto, 325-26; council of at Manchester, 332-335; epistle of to the Church in the British Isles, 344-348; departure of from England, 352; arrival of at New York, 360-61; return of to Nauvoo, 390; to share in labor of the Prophet, 400 and 403-404; epistle of to Saints scattered abroad, 409-10; council meeting of, 412; minutes of council meeting of, 429-30; epistles of to brethren in America, 433-38; case of Benjamin Winchester before, 443; epistle of, to Saints in England, 448-53; warning against thieves, 463-66 and notes; epistle of on baptism for the dead, 472-5; minutes of a meeting of, 478-79; gift of Hiram Kimball to,

484; whereabouts of, January 1, 1842, 490; epistle of to Saints in Europe, 558 *et seq.;* meeting of with the Prophet in Masonic lodge, 589; epistles of to Saints in America, 590 *et seq.*

Australia — report of work in, 343.

B

Babbitt, Elder Almon W. — preaches in Indiana, 17; permitted to build up Kirtland, 476.

Bagley, Mr.—tax difficulty with the Prophet, 542.

Barlow, Israel—assists Brigham Young on Journey, 9.

Barnes, Lorenzo D.—report of to Elder Parley P. Pratt, 569.

Baptists—difference between and former day Saints, 350-51.

Baptisms—in Temple font, 558; for the dead, 568-9; for the dead, editorial in *Times and Seasons* on, 595 *et seq.;* first mentioned, 231.

Benbow, Elder John — liberality of, 188; receives testimony, 150; is baptized, 151.

Bennett, Caleb — conference at House of, 6.

Bennett, James Arlington—honored, 600.

Bennett, James Gordon — editor New York *Herald*, course of approved, 477.

Bennett, John C. — first letters of to the Prophet, 169-72; biography, 169; elected mayor Nauvoo, 287; inaugural address of, 288-92.

Bennett, Samuel — sent on mission, 161; credentials of, 164.

Bishop, Gladden—disfellowshiped by High Council, 550.

Books—list of for and against the Latter-day Saints, 253-6.

Book of Mormon—first English edition of, 274-286; Nauvoo edition, proofs of read by Prophet, 494; ditto, 500-501; corrections of, 494; Prophet's estimate of, 461.

Boyce, Benjamin—kidnapping of, 154-6; 180.

British Mission — history of, 313-321.

Brown, Alanson—kidnapping of, 154-56; 180.

Browning, O. H.—lawyer, counsel for the Prophet at Monmouth trial, 367 et seq.

Brunson, Col. Seymour—death of, 179.

Burke, John M.—affidavit of, 56.

C

Cahoon, William F.—affidavit of, 52.

Calhoun, John C.—Prophet's interview with, 80.

Carpenter's Hall — Manchester, England, leased by the Saints, 141.

Carlin, Governor of Illinois — issues order for arrest of Prophet, 198-9.

Carter, Samuel—affidavit of, 49; Prophet's instructions to, 153.

Casper, Thomas D.—Affidavit of, 63.

Church, the—admonished by the Prophet, 5; anniversary of organization of, celebrated, 326-31; thirteenth anniversary of, 582.

Clark, Hiram—starts on mission to England, 7.

Clark, Joseph—affidavit of, 63.

Clark, Timothy B.—affidavit of, 58.

Clark, William O.—reproved by the Prophet, 445.

Clayton, William — preaches in Staffordshire; appointed clerk, Iowa High Council, 382.

Cock Pit, Preston, England — preaching of Twelve in, 114.

Cole, Owen—Affidavit of, 64.

Commerce, Illinois, (afterwards Nauvoo)—appointed a stake of Zion, 12; boundary lines to be changed, 39; name of changed to Nauvoo, 21; merged into Nauvoo plat, 322.

Committee, Senate Judiciary — case of the Missouri Saints before, 81-88; adverse report of, 90-92; of Nauvoo citizens resolutions by, 157-9.

Conferences—minutes of at Commerce, 12; minutes of general, at Nauvoo, 105 et seq.; at Gadfield Elm, England, 131; ditto, 134 et seq.; minutes at Stanley Hall, 138; of Church in England at Manchester, 146 et seq.; general at Nauvoo, minutes of, 204-7; general in England, minutes of, 214-18; at Walnut Grove, Illinois, 387; London, minutes of, 298; at Philadelphia, 331; general of the Church at Nauvoo, minutes of, 336-343; in New York City, 344; minutes of London, 360; at Kirtland, 361; at Attica, New York, 412; at Nauvoo, minutes of, general, 423-29; at Lima, minutes of, 439-40; New York, 462; minutes of special at Nauvoo, 583 et seq.

Conner, Henry — converted, 184.

Council, High at Commerce, (Nauvoo) — names of councilors, 12; Advice of to Saints west of Kirtland, 45 and note; authorizes publication of hymn book, 49; appoints committee to collect testimony on case before courts, 49; votes among for poor, 75, 76; votes to return consecrations to the people, 88; memorial of Joseph Smith before, 136-138, 141, 143; Elijah Fordham before, 180; minutes, 187-8; minutes of, 219-20; account of inspecting temporal concerns, 417; report of to the Saints, 504-5; trial of Gladden Bishop before, 550.

Council, High at Iowa—appointed for Stake in Iowa, 16; minutes of, 16; order of speaking in, 16 and note; organization of completed, 21; action of on Missouri debts, 42, 54; minutes of, 94; changes in, 352.

Council, of the Twelve—see Apostles.

Council, special—Liverpool, England, 296-7; at Nauvoo, 402.

Curtis, Simon P.—affidavit of, 67.

Curtis, Elder Theodore — before the Court of Sessions, Gloucester, England, 380.

D

Davis, Amos — abuse of the Prophet, 549.

Davis, Matthew S. — reports Prophet's Washington discourse, 78.

Decker, Brother — assists Elders Young and Kimball en route for England, 11.

Discourse—the Prophet's at Nauvoo, 358-360.

Dispatch, England weekly newspaper — article against the Saints, 236.

Donaldson, Elder Wm. — goes to East India, 168.

Draper, Father — assists Elders Young and Kimball et al, en route for England, 14.

Duel, Osmon M.—assists Elders Young and Kimball on mission, 9-10.

Duel, Sister O. M. — cares for Elders Young and Kimball, 10.

Duncan, Joseph — politician, speech against the Saints, 490, also note 480.

E

Election and Reprobation, Elders Brigham Young and Willard Richards, 256.

Emigration — arrangements of for English Saints, 510-13.

England—arrival of Apostles in, 76; labors of Elders in, 76; emigration agency in, 484.

Epistles—see *Letters.*

F

Female Relief Society—organization of, 552; ditto, 567-8; remarks of the Prophet to, 570; 602-7.

Fielding, Joseph — preaches in England, 7.

Font—baptismal of Temple described, 446.

Fordham, Elijah—healed by the Prophet, 4 and note; before High Council at Nauvoo, 180.

Foster, Dr. Robert D.—attends on Sidney Rigdon, 19-21; on trial for slandering, 239-250; fails to keep Prophet's journal, 89.

Foutz, Jacob—affidavit of, 68.

Freedom, Adams County, Illinois —Stake organized at, 233.

Fulmer, David—prefers charges, 219.

G

Galland, Isaac—letter of Prophet to; his power of attorney for the Prophet cancelled, 495-500.

Gates, Gibson—affidavit of, 71.

Gee, George Washington—death of and biography, 500 and note.

Geneva, Morgan County, Illinois —stake organized at, 236.

Gifford, Alpheus—biography of, 109-110 and note; death of, 484.

Granger, Gilbert — difficulty in settlement of father's estate, 542.

Granger, Elder Oliver—to provide funds for publication, 18; death of, 408-9.

Green, A.—affidavit of, 65.

Greene, John P.—affidavit of, 65.

Groves, Elisha H.—affidavit of, 68.

H

Harris, George W.—sent on special mission, 161; credentials of, 164.

Haight, Isaac—entertains Elders, 39; assists Elder Brigham Young et al. on journey, 44.

Hawk, William—affidavit of, 58.

Hayes, Elder Ezra—license taken from, 14.

Hedlock, Elder Reuben — starts on mission for England, 10; prepares cuts for book of Abraham, 543.

Higbee, Judge Elias—appointed to go to Washington, 13; attends Prophet to Washington, 19; letters of concerning case of Saints before United States Senate, 81, 88, 94, 95; course at Washington approved, 96 *et seq.*; presides at mass meeting,

Nauvoo, 157-60; writes petition to committee, 237; reproved by the Prophet, 503.

Higbee, Francis M. — elected colonel of legion, 353.

Hinckle, George M. — suit of Prophet against, 423.

Hotchkiss land purchase, 405-408.

Hotchkiss, Horace R. — letter to Prophet, 505-8.

Hunter, Edward—visits Nauvoo, biography of, 416-17 and note.

Hyde, Marinda — revelation to, 467.

Hyde, Elder Orson—his allusion to his fall, 2; restored, 12; appointed on Mission to Jerusalem, 106; credentials of, 112-113; departure of from Nauvoo for Jerusalem, 114; at conference in Philadelphia, 224; ditto, New York, 237; reproved, 274; his arrival in Palestine and dedication of the land for the return of Jews, 454-59; incidents enroute from Palestine to Europe, 496-99.

J

Jews—memorial of to Protestant Powers of Europe and America, 167 and note; circular of to Israelites of Europe and America, 173-5.

Johnson, Lyman E. — at Nauvoo, 389.

Johnston, Jesse W.—affidavit of, 64.

Jonas, Grand Master Mason—on Nauvoo and the Mormons, 565 et seq.

K

Keokuk, Indian chief—visits the Prophet, 401.

Kilbourn, D. W., anti-Mormon — attempts disturbance in Iowa, 416-17; ditto, 444 and note.

Kimball, Heber C. — departs on mission to England, 9 and note; morphine given to, 15-16; reports of from England, 182 et seq.; dreams of, 203; arrives at Nauvoo from England, 381.

Kiskukosh, Indian chief — visits the Prophet, 401-2.

Knight, Bishop Vinson — appointed Bishop of lower ward, Commerce, 12.

L

Lathrop, Asahel A.—affidavit of, 65-67.

Latter-day Saints—difference between and Baptists, 348, 350.

Law, William—en route for Nauvoo, 20, and note; appointed member First Presidency, 284-6.

Legion, Nauvoo — character of, 269; minutes of organization of, 295; general review of, 236; officers of, 253; general orders to, 354; defended by the Prophet, 355-6; general orders to, 362; minutes of, 382; general orders, 400; minutes of, 415; general order to, 502; extract from minutes of, 549; fourth regiment of second cohort of, 582; Repast Militaire of, 601; general orders to, 601.

Letters — James Mulholland to Isaac Russell, 5-6; Joseph Smith to Isaac Galland, 8-9; Parley P. Pratt to Prophet, 22; the Prophet to Hyrum Smith, 29; the Prophet et al. to High Council, Nauvoo, 43-44; Hyrum Smith to Parley P. Pratt; Hyrum Smith to the Prophet et al., 52; Charles Adams to Joseph Smith, 53; Orson Pratt to his wife, 54; John B. Webber to the Prophet, 55; Matthew S. Davis on Prophet's sermon; Elias Higbee to the Prophet reporting progress in Saints' appeal to United States Senate, 81; ditto, 83; ditto, 85; ditto, 88; John Taylor, to the Prophet, 96; R. B. Thompson to Elias Higbee, 96; Horace R. Hotchkiss to Sidney Rigdon et al., 98; Elias Higbee to the Prophet, 98; Horace R. Hotchkiss to Joseph Smith, 100; Sidney Rigdon to the Prophet, 102; Hon. Richard W. Young to Elias Higbee, 111; Heber C. Kimball to the Saints in the United States, 114 et seq.; Brigham Young to the Prophet, 119;

Robert Johnson to Senator Young, 121; Senator Young to Judge Elias Higbee, 121; Wilford Woodruff to Don Carlos Smith, 122; Elders Hyde and Page to the Prophet, 123; Brigham Young to the Prophet, 125; the Prophet to Elders Hyde and Page, 128; Willard Richards to the *Star*, 130; Heber C. Kimball et al. to Bishop at Nauvoo, 132; William W. Phelps to the Prophet, 141, 142; Hyde and Page to Joseph Smith, 142; Elder Woodruff to the *Star*, 150 *et seq.*; William Barratt to Saints in England, 161; Prophet to William W. Phelps, 162 *et seq.*; Prophet to Oliver Granger, 164-7; John C. Bennett to Joseph Smith et al., 168; ditto, 169; ditto, 172; Prophet to Horace R. Hotchkiss, 170-1; Wilford Woodruff to the *Star*, 176; the Prophet to John C. Bennett, 177-8; John C. Bennett to Messrs. Smith and Rigdon, 179; Samuel Bent and George W. Harris to Presidency of Church, 199; John E. Page to the Presidency, 201; Orson Hyde to Saints in Nauvoo, 202; Heber C. Kimball et al. to Robinson et al., 220-224; Joseph and Hyrum Smith to the Saints in Kirtland, 225; the Prophet to the Twelve, 226; Heber C. Kimball et al. to *Times and Seasons*, 234; a staunch Wesleyan to the *Manx Liberal*, 234-6; Brigham Young to Presidency, 237; John C. Bennett to *Times and Seasons*, 248-9; Brigham Young to the Prophet, 251-2; Parley P. Pratt to Sidney Rigdon, 266; Joseph Smith to County Recorder, 287; Levi Richards to the *Star*, 296; Brigham Young to the *Star*, 308-9; Wilford Woodruff to Don Carlos Smith, 323-4; George A. Smith to the *Star*, 343; the Prophet to the *Times and Seasons*, 356-58; R. B. Thompson to *Times and Seasons*, 369-70; Orson Hyde to Joseph Smith, 372-4; Orson Hyde to Rabbi Hirschel, 374-8; extract from a letter to the *Juliet Courier*, 380-1; Orson Hyde to President Smith, 384-88; William Smith, to the Prophet, 391; Horace R. Hotchkiss to Joseph Smith, 405; the Prophet to Hotchkiss, 406-7; Joseph Smith to Smith Tuttle, Esq., 430-33; extract from Orson Hyde, 439; Parley P. Pratt, extract, of, 441; Joseph Smith to Reuben McBride, 441; Hyrum Smith to Saints in Kirtland, 443; Orson Hyde to Parley P. Pratt, 454-9; the Prophet to Esq. Browning et al., 468; ditto to Mr. Hotchkiss, 469; Joseph Smith to Edward Hunter, 481-3; Joseph Smith to Edward Hunter, 491; Orson Hyde to the *Star*, 495-99; Joseph Smith to Isaac Galland, 499; G. Walker to Brigham Young et al., 505-509; Alfred Cordon to Joseph Smith, 515-16; Joseph Smith to the Church, 517; from the Twelve to all the churches, 517-18; Joseph Smith on tithing, 518; Robert Pierce to Joseph Smith, 519; Joseph Smith to John Wentworth, 535 *et seq.*; Joseph Smith to John C. Bennett, 544; Dr. C. V. Dyer to John C. Bennett, 544; John C. Bennett to Dr. C. V. Dyer, 545; John C. Bennett to Joseph Smith, 547; Joseph Smith to Edward Hunter, 548; the Twelve to the Saints in Europe, 558 *et seq.*; extract from Elder E. P. Maginn, 566; Lorenzo D. Barlow to Parley P. Pratt, 569.

Legion, Nauvoo, organization of, 353.

Liberty — religious in Nauvoo, 306.

Lima, Adams Co., Illinois—Stake organized at, 233.

Literature of Latter-day Saints, 487.

Little, Sidney H., Senator—death of, 389.

Littlefield, Lyman O. — action against for slander, 514.

Litz, Elder A. — suspended from preaching, 501.

Lowry, John—affidavit of, 56.

M

Maginn, Ezekiel—affidavit of, 64.

Marks, Ephraim — funeral of, 586-587.

Marks, William—appointed President of Stake at Commerce, 12; President of Stake at Nauvoo, 323; financial settlement of Prophet with, 582.

Maughan, Peter—493 and note.

Melling, Peter—ordained a patriarch, first in England, 120 and note; reports to the Prophet at Nauvoo, 543.

Memorials—of Saints to Senate and House of Representatives, 24 et seq.; to Joseph Smith and High Council at Nauvoo, 136; answer to foregoing, 138, 141 and note, 144, 145; to Governor Carlin of Illinois on kidnapping, 159-60.

Millennial Star — Latter-day Saints, 119; prospectus of, 122, 133 and note.

Missouri — action of Legislature on Mormon difficulties, 299 and note.

Modisett, Dr.—gives morphine to Heber C. Kimball, 15; aids Elders Young and Kimball on journey, 17.

Monmouth, Warren Co., Illinois—the Prophet's trial at, 365 et seq.

Moon, Elder John — arrival of with Saints in America, 162.

Morgan, Elizabeth — death of, 551.

Mormon, Prophet's estimate of, Book of, 461; correction of, 494.

Mormon Literature—Pro et con, 487-489.

Mormons—Nauvoo and the, 565.

Mulholland, James — Prophet's Secretary, writes Isaac Russell, appointed clerk for land contracts. 16; salary of, 17; death of, 88-9 and note.

N

Nashville, city of — meetings at, 182 and note.

Nauvoo—Agricultural and Manufacturing Association incorporated, 303.

Nauvoo—burying ground for, 353.

Nauvoo, City of—made Post Office at, 121; charters of, 239-249; first election in, 287; City Council organized, 288; officers of, 292, 308; divided into wards, 305; concentration at, 362.

Nauvoo — House Association incorporated, 301.

Nauvoo Legion, organized, 353.

News—the prospectus of, 112.

Noble, Joseph Bates — healed by the Prophet, 4 and note.

O

Olney, Elder Oliver — license taken from, 552.

Owen, Ephraim — confession of accepted, 12.

Owen, Jedediah—affidavit of, 56.

P

Page, John E. — one of the Twelve. Address on the Book of Mormon, 2; appointed on mission to Palestine, 109; reproved, 274; disregards advice, 372; presides at New York conference, 462-3.

Partridge, Bishop Edward—appointed Bishop upper ward, Commerce, 12; instructs Saints on removal from the West, 39; death of 132.

Perry, Asahel—received into fellowship, 14.

Petition—Elias Higbee, Robert B. Thompson to Congress, 237; presented to the House, 250-51.

Pettigrew, David — affidavit of, 71-73.

Phelps. Laura, wife of Morris—death of, 513.

Phelps, Wm. W., confession of errors, 141; Prophet's letter to, 162.

Pierce, Robert — business settlement of with the Prophet, 519.

Powell, James — affidavit of, 61.

Pratt, Orson—one of the Twelve, addresses Saints at Nauvoo, 4; starts on mission for England, 7; opens mission in Edinburg, 120; publishes Remarkable Visions, 224; success in Edinburg, 251; elected Professor of Mathematics, Nauvoo University, 414.

Pratt, Elder Parley P., one of the Twelve—preaches at Nauvoo, 4; ditto, 6; starts on mission for England, 7; errors in writings of, 7; letter to the Prophet, 22; his artcile on eternal duration of matter, 54, 55 and notes; appointed editor of the *Millennial Star*, 133; returns to America for family, 177; returns to England, 224.

Presidency, First of Church—report of, 212-14; proclamation of to the Church scattered abroad, 267-73; report of at General Conference, 336-339.

Priesthood—article on prepared by the Prophet, 207-212; lesser organized in Nauvoo, 312.

Proclamation—preparation of to Kings, 383.

Q

Quincy, Illinois—a Stake organized at, 233.

R

Ramus, Illinois — minutes of a meeting at, 453; conferences at, 467; deeds to certain lands of, transferred to the Prophet, 477.

Redfield, Harlow — suspended from office, 12; restored, 16.

Resurrection in general and of children, 553 *et seq.;* and note.

Revelations—to Joseph Smith at Nauvoo, January 19, 1841, 274, *et seq.;* to William Allred *et al.*, 311; to the Saints in Iowa, 311; to Brigham Young in Nauvoo, July 9, 1841, 382; concerning Nancy Marinda Hyde, 467; to John Snyder *et al.*, 483; to the Twelve, 483; respecting the *Times and Seasons*, 503.

Rich, Charles C. — elected Brigadier General, 414.

Richards, Levi—affidavit of, 70-71.

Richards, Elder Willard, one of the Twelve — visits Staffordshire, 7; son of dies, 48; on Election and Reprobation, 256-66; assists in indexing Book of Mormon, 274, 286; writes history of British mission, 313-321; appointed private secretary to the Prophet and Temple Recorder, 470.

Rigdon, Elder Sidney, counselor to Joseph Smith — address of to Twelve, 2, 3, appointed to accompany Prophet to Washington, 13; starts with Prophet to Washington, 19; sickness of, left at Columbus, Ohio, 21; in Washington, 48; in Philadephia, 76; speech of at laying corner stone of Nauvoo Temple, 327-29; baptized for in behalf of his parents, 486.

Riggs, Burr—affidavit of, 67.

Roberts, Sidney — excommunicated, 237.

Robinson, Ebenezer—publisher of *Times and Seasons*, 23; co-partnership with Don Carlos Smith dissolved, 239; editor *Times and Seasons*, 402.

Rockwell, Orrin P. — starts with Prophet for Washington, 19.

Rogers, D. W. — his hymn-book discarded, 14.

Root, Henry—affidavit of, 62.

Russell, Isaac — reproved, 5, 6 and note.

S

Saints, Latter-day — sickness among at Nauvoo, 3; healing of the, 3, 4 and notes; admonished to set houses in order, 4-5; petition of to Congress, 24-38.

Sharp, Thomas — editor *Warsaw Signal*, anti-Mormon, the Prophet on, 487 and note.

Sherwood, Henry G. — healed by the Prophet, 4 and note.

Shoemaker, David—affidavit of, 69.

Sloan, James—statement of, 69.

Smith, Don Carlos, brother of the Prophet—President of the High Priests at Commerce, 12; publisher *Times and Seasons*, 23; dissolves partnership with Robinson, 239; death of, 393; career of, 393-399.

Smith, Elias—appointed Bishop, 154; ordained a Bishop, 161.

Smith, Emma, wife of the Prophet—appointed to compile hymn-
book, 17; assists husband in labors, 510; appointed President
of Female Relief Society, 552.

Smith, George Albert—one of the
Twelve, starts on mission for
England, 10; preaches at Richmond, New York, 75; begins
out-door preaching in England,
182 et seq.; injures his health
at, 236; arrives at Nauvoo
from England, 383; marriage
of, 389.

Smith, Humphery—affidavit of,
62.

Smith, Hyrum, brother of the
Prophet—appointed on committee to establish Nauvoo, 39;
testimony of to Book of Mormon, 46 and note; is appointed
Patriarch to the Church, 229
and note and 282; appointed
Prophet and Revelator, 286.

Smith, John—affidavit of, 59, 62.

Smith, Joseph, the Prophet—literary methods of, 1; heals the
sick at Commerce, Nauvoo, 3-5
and notes; ditto, 7; preaches on
the "other Comforter," 10 and
note; ditto "Judgments," 11;
attends general conference,
Commerce, 11-12 et seq.; appointed to represent cause of
the Saints at Washington, 13;
starts for Washington, 19; adventure of, by the way, 23; arrives at Washington, 24; meets
President Van Buren, 39 et
seq.; preaches at Philadelphia,
47; in New Jersey, 49; comment on Missouri affidavits,
73-4; returns to Washington,
77; description of by a Con-
gressman, 78 et seq.; interview
with Martin Van Buren, 80;
ditto, John C. Calhoun, 80; returns to Nauvoo, 88-9; reflection of on actions of Congress,
145; plans charter of Nauvoo,
249; made sole Trustee-in-trust,
of the Church, 287; elected
member of the Nauvoo City
Council, 287; introduces several bills in City Council, 293
et seq.; appointed Lieutenant-
General of Nauvoo Legion, 309;

assists in laying corner stone
Nauvoo Temple, 329-331; arrest of by officers from Missouri, 364 et seq.; visited by
Indians at Nauvoo, 401; views
on use of medicine, 414; his experience at Monmouth trial,
419-20; views on relics of antiquity, 420-21 and note; reproves
sanctimoniousness, 445; denunciation of thieves, 461-2;
his estimate of the Book of
Mormon, 461; proof-reads Book
of Mormon, 468; difficulties in
keeping daily journal, 470; pro-
claims political attitude of the
Saints, 479-80 and notes; his
views on the gift of tongues,
485; reflections on opening of
the year, 1842, 492; debates
race question, 501; purpose of
debates in Nauvoo, 514; views
on privileges of Nauvoo charter, 516; settlement of with
Robert Pierce, 519; settlement
of taxes with Mr. Bagley, 542;
becomes editor of Times and
Seasons, 551; sermon on "Life,
Death, and Resurrection," 553
et seq. and note, 556; remarks
of at funeral of Edward Marks,
587; reproof of unvirtuous persons by, 587-88; insolvency of,
594; cause of Prophet's insolvency, 600; remarks respecting
signs and key words received
in the Temple, 608.

Smith, Joseph, Sen. — death of,
189; biography of, 189 et seq.;
funeral services of, 191-97;
benediction of, on Hyrum
Smith, 229 and note.

Smith, Samuel—affidavit of, 60.

Smith, William, brother of the
Prophet — allowed to retain
standing in quorum of the
Twelve, 12.

Snow, Erastus, labors of in
Salem, 433.

Snow, Lorenzo— sent to England,
161-2 and note; arrives at Manchester, 233; public discussion with Mr. Barker, 234.

Snyder, Elder John—appointed a
mission, 503-504; set apart and
instructed, 568.

Spirits, try the, 571-581.

Springfield, Illinois a Stake organized at, 236.

T

Taylor, Elder John, one of the Twelve Apostles — testimony of to Book of Mormon, 2; preaches at Kirtland, 21; sails for England, 46; arrives at Preston, England, 76; leaves Liverpool for Ireland, 170 and note; in the Isle of Man, 234-6 and note; discussion with Rev. Robert Hayes, 238; reports baptisms, 288; arrives at Nauvoo from England, 381; appointed editor *Times and Seasons*, 513.

Temple, Nauvoo — corner stones of laid, 327-331; announcement of Trustee-in-trust respecting, 517; word of the Twelve respecting, 517; progress of building the, 608 *et seq.*

Thompson, Elder Robert B.—delivers discourse at the funeral of Joseph Smith, Sen., 191-197; writes petition to Congress, 237; Associate editor *Times and Seasons*, 353; death of and biography of, 411-412.

Times and Seasons—first number of, 23.

Tithing, arrangements for reception of, 493; record of, 518.

Tongues, purpose of gift of, 485.

Translated beings, 425.

Tribune, New York—criticism of on the course of Missouri, 551.

Trustee-in-trust — sole for the Church of Jesus Christ of Latter-day Saints, see Joseph Smith.

Turley, Elder Theodore — starts for England on mission, 10; imprisonment of, 127.

U

University of City of Nauvoo, 243, and 301.

V

Van Buren, President of the United States—Joseph Smith's interview with, 40, 80, 89 and note.

W

Walker, Cyrus—lawyer, counselor for the Prophet, at Monmouth trial, 367 *et seq.*

Walker, Oliver — before High Council, Nauvoo, 219-20.

Warren, city of, 405; consultation respecting, 486.

Wasp, The—first number, 600.

Wentworth, John — letter of Prophet to, 535 *et seq.*

Wells, Squire Daniel H.—biography, 154-55.

Whitney, Bishop Newel K. — appointed Bishop middle ward Commerce, 12.

Wight, Lyman—addresses conference, 13.

Wilber, Brother — assists Elder Young *et al.*, 11.

Williams, Frederick G.—affidavit of, 69; received in fellowship 110.

Witter, Daniel S. — course of respecting settlement at Warren, 470-1.

Wood, Elder Daniel—suspended from preaching, 501; vindication of, 514.

Woodruff, Elder Wilford, one of the Twelve—his account of miraculous healings at Commerce by the Prophet, 3-5 and notes; sent by the Prophet to heal the sick, 5; departure of for England, 46; arrives in England, 76; labors of in England, 182 *et seq.*; mission on Fox Islands, 418-19.

Women, The character of Mormon, 568.

World, The—commotions in, 125, 189, 252-3, and 383, 401, 415.

Y

Yokum, William, Haun's Mill victim, 389.

Young, Elder Brigham, one of the Twelve Apostles—remarks of at Nauvoo, 2; starts for England, 9; arrival of at Cleveland, Ohio, 20; rebukes storm, 23; preaches at Richmond, New York, 75; arrival in New York, 77; embarks with four others of the Twelve for England, 94; arrival of in England, 102;

farewell of the Saints to, 103; sustained as President of the Twelve, 115 and notes; also 146 and note; on Election and Reprobation, 256-66; assists in indexing Book of Mormon, 274 and 286; arrives at Nauvoo from England, 381; elected to Nauvoo Council, 414.

Young, John, Sen. — father of Brigham, dies, 14.

Young, Joseph, President of the Seventies, grants licenses, 501.

Young, Lorenzo, assists Young and Kimball enroute for England, 11.

Z

Zion, Stakes of, organized in Geneva; in Springfield, 236; Lima, 233; Quincy, 233; Mount Hope, 233; Freedom, 233.